Sherry

Microsoft Office 97 Professional 6 in 1, Second Edition

by Faithe Wempen, Peter Aitken, Jennifer Fulton, and Sue Plumley

que®

A Division of Macmillan Computer Publishing
201 West 103rd Street, Indianapolis, Indiana 46290 USA

A Division of Macmillan Computer Publishing

201 West 103rd Street, Indianapolis, Indiana 46290 USA

International Standard Book Number: 0-7897-1515-5

Library of Congress Catalog Card Number: 97-80837

00 99 98   8 7 6 5 4 3

Interpretation of the printing code: the rightmost double-digit number is the year of the book's first printing; the rightmost single-digit number is the number of the book's printing. For example, a printing code of 98-1 shows that this copy of the book was printed during the first printing of the book in 1998.

Screen reproductions in this book were created by means of the program Collage Complete from Inner Media, Inc., Hollis, NH.

Printed in the United States of America

Publisher
John Pierce

Executive Editor
Jim Minatel

Editorial Services Director
Carla Hall

Managing Editor
Thomas Hayes

Acquisitions Editor
Jane Brownlow

Development Editors
Rick Kughen
Henly Wolin

Technical Editor
Sherry Kinkoph

Project Editor
Gina Brown

Copy Editor
Tom Stevens

Book Designers
Kim Scott
Glenn Larsen

Cover Designer
Jay Corpus

Production Team
Erin Danielson
Jennifer Earhart
DiMonique Ford
Laura A. Knox
Heather Stephenson

Indexer
Tim Tate

Acknowledgments

Dedication:

To Margaret, who makes it possible.

Acknowledgments:

What a joy it is to work with the professionals at Que Corporation! Thanks to the entire team: Jane Brownlow, Rick Kughen, Gina Brown, Tom Stevens, and Sherry Kinkoph for a well-organized and executed job. Also thank you to Jay Corpus, who designed a great-looking cover, and to the dedicated and hard-working Macmillan Publishing layout, indexing, and proofreading staff, who do such a great job and so rarely get the acknowledgement they deserve. On the home front, thanks to Margaret for keeping me happy and keeping the dog hair vacuumed up, Jane for bagels on Saturday mornings, and Mom and Dad for starting it all.

Trademarks

Contents

Part 1: Windows

Part 3: Excel

Part 4: PowerPoint

Part 5: Outlook

Part 6: Access

xxiii

Appendix

Introduction

Need to learn Office 97 quickly? You've come to the right place.

With this book, you'll master Microsoft Windows 97 (or NT Workstation 4.0) plus the entire Microsoft Office suite: Word, Excel, PowerPoint, Access, and Outlook. With these products, you can create impressive business documents, presentations, and databases, and you can manage your address book and daily calendar.

Windows is a graphical user interface (GUI) that enables you to organize and run your software packages in a graphical operating system instead of using prompts and obscure commands (like you do with DOS). Windows comes with several useful applications, including a word processor (Write), a graphics painting program (Paint), and a communications program (HyperTerminal). It also features many accessories (such as a clock, a calendar, and a phone dialer) that will help organize and simplify your work. Windows 95 also includes Internet Explorer and other programs that integrate your computer with the Internet.

The five software packages in Microsoft Office are:

- **Word for Windows**   Arguably the best Windows-based word processing program on the market. Word has features that enable you to create a one-page memo, a newsletter with graphics, or even a 500-page report.
- **Excel**   A powerful yet easy-to-maneuver spreadsheet program. Excel can be used to generate impressive financial statements, charts and graphs, and databases, and to share the information with other software packages.
- **PowerPoint**   An easy-to-use presentation program that lets you create impressive slides and overheads or print-out presentations.
- **Outlook**   A daily planner, calendar, and to-do list that helps you get the most out of your day through careful schedule management.
- **Access**   A database program that's quickly becoming a leader in the industry because of its powerful capabilities and ease of use. Access is included only in the Professional edition of Office, not the standard version.

Using This Book

Microsoft Office 97 Professional 6 in 1 is designed to help you learn these six programs (Office's five programs plus Windows) quickly and easily. You don't have to spend any time figuring out what to learn. All the most important tasks are covered in this book. There's no need for long classes or thick manuals. Learn the skills you need in short, easy-to-follow lessons.

The book is organized into six parts—one for each of the six software packages, with approximately 20 lessons in each part. This book also includes four appendixes, which help you to seamlessly integrate the various programs in the Office 97 suite. These appendices also walk you through the installation process and the Office 97 Help system. Because each of these lessons takes 10 minutes or less to complete, you can quickly master the basic skills you need to navigate Windows; create documents, financial statements, or slide shows; or send and reply to e-mail messages.

If this is the first time you've ever used Windows 95 (or Windows NT) or a dependent product, begin with the Windows part of this book. What you learn in that part will help you navigate your way through the other software packages.

Conventions Used in This Book

Each of the short lessons in this book includes step-by-step instructions for performing specific tasks. The following icons (small graphic symbols) are included to help you quickly identify particular types of information:

 TIP These icons indicate ways you can save time when you're using any of the Microsoft Office products.

 TERM These icons point out definitions of words you'll need to know to understand how to use a software package.

 Caution icons help you avoid making mistakes.

CAUTION

In addition to the icons, the following conventions are also used:

What you type	Information you type appears in **bold type**.
Items you select	Items you select or keys you press appear in **bold type**.

We'd Like to Hear from You!

As part of our continuing effort to produce books of the highest possible quality, Que would like to hear your comments. To stay competitive, we really want you, as a computer book reader and user, to let us know what you like or dislike most about this book or other Que products.

You can mail comments, ideas, or suggestions for improving future editions to the address below, or send us a fax at (317) 581-4663. For the online inclined, the address of our Internet site is **http://www.mcp.com/que**.

In addition to exploring our Web site, please feel free to contact me personally to discuss your opinions of this book: I'm **rkughen@mcp.com** on the Internet.

Thanks in advance—your comments will help us to continue publishing the best books available on computer topics in today's market.

Rick Kughen
Development Editor
Que Corporation
201 West 103rd Street
Indianapolis, Indiana 46290
USA

Windows

Windows Basics for the Newcomer

In this lesson, you discover how Windows helps you use your computer, and you learn how to use a mouse. You also find out how Windows works differently when you have Microsoft Internet Explorer 4 installed.

What Is Windows?

Microsoft Windows is a program that sets up an environment for you to work in at your computer, based on colorful pictures (called *icons*) and menus, organized into boxed areas called *windows*. This friendly environment is called a *graphical user interface (GUI)*.

 Graphical User Interface A GUI (pronounced "GOO-ey") provides a picture-based way of interacting with your computer. Instead of typing commands at a prompt (DOS, for example), you select from menus and pictures to issue commands.

Windows helps you

- **Manage Files** With Windows, you can display lists of the files and folders on your computer. You can also move, copy, or delete those files and folders.
- **Run Applications** Windows provides icons and menus that you can click to run the applications you need to use.
- **Maintain Your System** Windows provides several utility programs that check your system for errors and improve its performance.

TERM   **Application**   A computer program that does something useful, such as enable you to compose a letter (Word) or create a spreadsheet (Excel).

In this book, you learn how to do the first two tasks: manage files and run programs. If you are interested in learning more about the Windows utility programs, such as Disk Compression, ScanDisk, and Disk Defragmenter, we suggest reading *Using Windows 95* or *The Complete Idiot's Guide to Windows 95*, both published by Que Corporation.

Using the Mouse

If you have never used a mouse before, you should read this section before going any further.

You can use the mouse to quickly select any object on-screen, such as an icon or a window. (You learn about working with windows in Lesson 3, "Shutting Down Windows.") The process involves two steps: pointing and clicking.

To *point* to an object (for example, an icon, window, or title bar), move the mouse across your desk or mouse pad until the on-screen mouse pointer touches the object. You might have to pick up the mouse and reposition it if you run out of room on your desk.

To *click*, point the mouse pointer at the object you want to select, and quickly press and release the left mouse button. When you click an object, you select it.

When you're pointing at an object, you also can click the right mouse button (*right-click*) to open a menu of actions that you can perform on the object (a shortcut menu). These shortcuts are mentioned throughout the book.

To *double-click* an item, point to the item and press and release the left mouse button twice in rapid succession. When you double-click an object, you activate it. For example, double-clicking the icon for Microsoft Word opens the program.

You can use the mouse to move an object (usually a window, dialog box, or icon) to a new position on-screen. You do this by *dragging* the object. To drag an object to a new location on-screen, point to the object, press and hold the left mouse button, move the mouse to a new location, and release the mouse button. The object moves with the mouse cursor. You also can *right-drag* (drag with the right mouse button) to see a menu when the icon reaches the drop point. This menu enables you to choose what you want to do with the icon (move it, copy it, or create a shortcut to it).

If you have a mouse with a wheel between the two buttons, you have an IntelliMouse. This is a special mouse designed for Windows and was packaged with some copies of Microsoft Office. It also comes with some new computers. The wheel has special uses in some programs; for example, in Word, you can scroll a few lines at a time in your document by turning the wheel. See the sections on the individual Office programs in this book for details about how the IntelliMouse works with each Office 97 program.

Determining Your Windows Version

Several versions of Windows are available that Office 97 can run on, and it may not be obvious which you have. Most of the procedures in this book apply to any of the versions; in the instances where the versions differ, it is pointed out. The versions are

- **Windows 95** This is the original. If you bought a new PC in 1996 or 1997, it probably came with Windows 95 pre-installed. You also can buy this version in stores as an upgrade to your old DOS/Windows 3.x system.

- **Windows NT 4.0 Workstation** This version of Windows is used mainly in corporations, for compatibility with a Windows NT file server. It looks and operates almost exactly the same as Windows 95.

- **Windows 95 or Windows NT with Internet Explorer 4's Desktop Updates** If you have any version of Windows 95 or Windows NT and install Internet Explorer 4 (and choose to install its desktop updates along with it), it changes how Windows 95 looks and operates. Appendix A, "Installing Microsoft Office 97," explains how to acquire and install Internet Explorer 4.0.

To determine whether you have Windows 95 or Windows NT, follow these steps:

1. Double-click the **My Computer** icon. A window opens.
2. Click the word **Help** near the top of the window. A menu appears.
3. Read the last line on that menu. Depending on the version you have, it will say About Windows 95 or About Windows NT (see Figure 1.1.)
4. Press the **Esc** key to close the menu.

This indicates whether you have
Windows 95 or Windows NT.

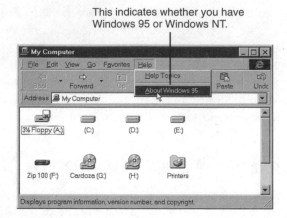

Figure 1.1   The bottom command on the Help menu indicates which version of the Windows operating system is installed on your computer.

In addition, you might have Microsoft Internet Explorer 4.0's desktop updates installed. Internet Explorer's desktop update includes several features that change the way the desktop looks and operates. However, each of these features can be turned off, so the absence of some or all of them does not necessarily mean that you do not have IE 4.0 installed.

Compare Figures 1.2 and 1.3 to determine your computer's configuration. Figure 1.2 shows a plain Windows 95 interface, and Figure 1.3 shows Windows 95 with all IE 4.0's desktop updates installed and activated.

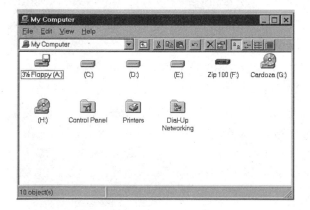

Figure 1.2   This is plain Windows 95.

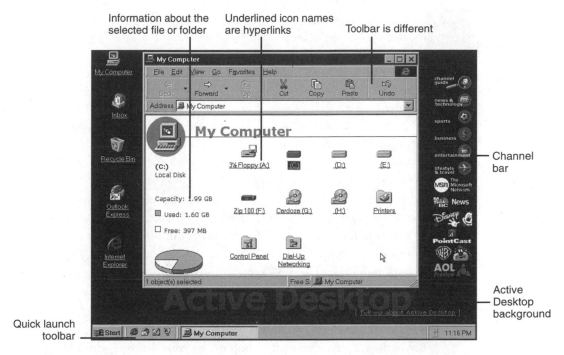

Figure 1.3 This is Windows 95 with all Internet Explorer 4.0's desktop updates activated.

What's Different with Internet Explorer 4.0 Installed?

When you install IE 4.0 and choose to also install the desktop updates, certain new features are enabled by default. Others can be enabled manually; you can pick and choose among the individual features as you want. In Lesson 9, "Drive, Folder, and File Management," you learn how to customize your system for any combination of regular (Classic) Windows 95 operations and IE 4.0 (Web) operations.

With IE 4.0's desktop updates, you can use the following special features:

- **Active Desktop** This special Windows wallpaper enables you to place active controls directly on the desktop that are updated through your Internet connection. You, for example, might have a stock ticker on your desktop that constantly displays the latest prices from the Internet.

TERM **Active Controls** Programs that interact automatically with Internet locations to bring the latest content directly to your desktop.

- **Channel Bar** The Channel bar is an Active Desktop control that comes with IE 4.0. When you subscribe to a channel (a type of active control), information on that subject is automatically downloaded to your computer whenever you are connected to the Internet. The Channel bar is one example of Active Desktop content; you can download additional Active Desktop components from Microsoft's Web site, as explained in Lesson 17, "Working with Channels and Active Content."

- **Web-Style Windows** In My Computer, the toolbar resembles the one in the IE 4 Web browser, complete with Forward and Back buttons. Each list of files and folders shows information about the currently selected file or folder in the top-left corner.

- **Single-Pane Displays** In My Computer, when you open a different drive or folder listing, it replaces the previous one in the same window. (By default in regular Windows 95, it opens a new window instead.)

- **Single-Click** You can set up Windows 95 with IE 4 to display the Windows desktop as well as the contents of your drives and folders as hyperlinks. That means you point at something to select it and click it to activate it. You never have to double-click.

- **Quick Launch Toolbar** When IE 4.0 is installed, you can have toolbars on the taskbar. The default toolbar is called Quick Launch. (You learn more about it in Lesson 5, "Using Menus, Toolbars, and Dialog Boxes.")

In this book, because not everyone may have IE 4.0 installed, the instructions and figures show mostly Classic style, with which everyone can follow along. Differences between Classic and Web-style operation are noted wherever appropriate. If you do not have Internet Explorer 4.0 installed, you may see subtle differences between your screen and what is shown here because using Classic style does not completely revert the computer to pre-IE 4.0 installation condition. The differences, however, are not important ones.

  TIP **Quick Switch to Classic** The figures in this book were done with IE 4.0's desktop updates installed and the interface set to Classic style. To quickly put your copy of Windows 95/IE 4.0 back to Classic style, so that you can more easily follow along, double-click the **My Computer** icon. Open the **View** menu and click **Folder Options**. Click **Classic Style**, and then click **OK**. (See Lesson 9 for more details about Classic versus Web style.)

In this lesson, you learned what Windows does, determined what version you have, and learned to use a mouse. In the next lesson, you are introduced to the Windows desktop.

Understanding the Windows Desktop

In this lesson, you learn the parts of the Windows desktop.

A Look at the Windows Interface

As you can see in Figure 2.1, the Windows interface is made up of several components. These components are used throughout Windows and Windows applications to make it easy for you to get your work done.

The components of the desktop include the following:

- **Icons**   Icons are pictures that represent programs (Microsoft Excel, or Word, for example), files (documents, spreadsheets, graphics), printer information (setup options, installed fonts), and computer information (hard and floppy disk drives). For example, in Figure 2.1, you see icons for My Computer, Recycle Bin, and others.
- **Desktop**   This is the background area on which everything else sits.
- **Mouse Pointer**   This is the on-screen pointer (usually an arrow) that you use to select items and choose commands. You move the pointer by moving the mouse across your desk or mouse pad. (You learned how to use a mouse in Lesson 1, "Windows Basics for the Newcomer.")
- **Start Button**   Click the Start button on the Windows 95 taskbar to display the Start menu, which contains a list of commands that enable you to get to work quickly and easily. The Start menu contains commands for launching programs, opening the most recently used files, changing settings, finding files or folders, accessing Help topics, running a program by entering a

specific command line, and shutting down Windows. (You learn more about the Start menu in Lesson 5, "Using Menus, Toolbars, and Dialog Boxes.")

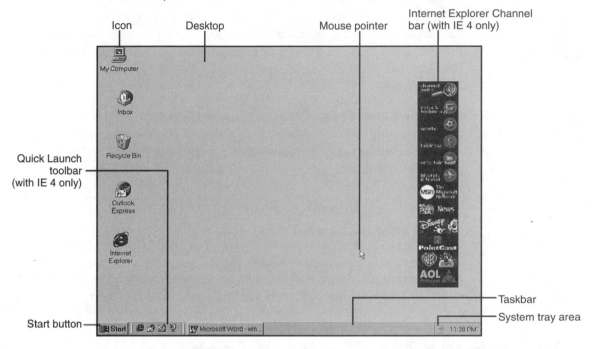

Figure 2.1 The Windows 95 desktop.

- **Taskbar** For each application that you open, a button appears on the taskbar. When you use more than one application at a time, you can see the names of all the open applications on the taskbar. At any time, you can click the appropriate button on the taskbar to work with an open application.

- **System Tray Area** At the bottom-right corner of the screen is a clock and some small icons. The clock (obviously) indicates what time it is; the icons are indicators for your system. In Figure 2.1, there is a pale gray volume control, which means this computer has a certain kind of sound card installed. (You may see a speaker icon instead of the volume control, depending on your sound card manufacturer.) You can double-click the clock to change the time, or double-click the volume control or speaker to set the sound volume. The controls appearing in the System tray depend on the programs installed on your computer. Your System tray is likely to be different than the one shown in Figure 2.1.

- **Quick Launch Toolbar**   If you have IE 4.0's desktop updates installed, you can place extra toolbars on the taskbar. The default one is Quick Launch, and the icons, from left to right, are Launch Internet Explorer Browser (see Lesson 16, "Using Internet Explorer"), Launch Mail, Show Desktop, and View Channels (see Lesson 17, "Working with Channels and Active Content").

- **Internet Explorer Channel Bar**   If you have IE 4.0's desktop updates installed, active controls appear on your desktop that let you quickly access Internet content. This Channel bar is one such control; it comes with IE 4.0. You can download other controls from the Microsoft Web site, as you'll learn in Lesson 17.

 TIP   **Don't Want the Channel Bar?**   If you don't want Channel bar to appear, you can turn it off easily, along with any other Internet objects. Right-click the desktop and point to **Active Desktop**. A submenu opens. Click **View as Web Page** to remove the checkmark beside that command. All Internet objects on the desktop are hidden. Repeat the same steps to bring them back.

Examining the Desktop Icons

When you first install Windows 95, certain icons appear on the desktop. (You can add other icons there later if you want.) The icons vary depending on what version of Windows 95 you are using, what kind of computer you have, whether you are on a network, and whether you have Internet Explorer 4 installed. When you double-click one of these icons, the associated program or folder opens. Here are some of the icons you might see:

- **My Computer**   The My Computer icon gives you access to a window in which you can browse through the contents of your computer or find out information about the disk drives, Control Panel, scheduled tasks, and printers that you have on your computer.

- **The Internet** or **Internet Explorer**   This icon opens Internet Explorer. The wording depends on the version of Internet Explorer installed on your computer.

- **Inbox**   This icon sets up Windows Messaging and opens Microsoft Exchange, a messaging program that your company may use for inter-office communications. You also can use Exchange to manage e-mail and work with faxes.

- **Outlook Express**   If you have IE 4 installed (with either a Standard or Full installation, as described in Appendix A, "Installing Microsoft Office 97"), you also have Outlook Express—a mail and news program— and an icon for it appears on your desktop. Outlook Express differs from Outlook 97 in that Outlook Express merely serves as an Internet mail and news reader. Outlook 97 serves as a full-featured Personal Information Manager (PIM) that enables you to manage your e-mail, contacts, calendar, journal, and notes, all from one application. (Part 5, "Outlook," of this book describes Outlook 97 in much greater detail.)

- **Network Neighborhood**   If your computer is on a network, you have an icon on the desktop called Network Neighborhood. Double-click the icon to browse through your network and see what it contains. This icon also provides information on mapped drives and interfaces. If your computer is not connected to a network (as the one in Figure 2.1 isn't), you will not see this icon.

- **Recycle Bin**   The Recycle Bin serves as your electronic trash can. You drag unwanted files, folders, or other icons to the Recycle Bin. To permanently delete the items, right-click the Recycle Bin icon and choose **Empty Recycle Bin**. (See Lesson 12, "Creating, Deleting, Renaming, and Finding Files and Folders," for more information.)

- **My Briefcase**   If you are using a laptop or if you chose to install My Briefcase, you have the My Briefcase icon on your desktop. You can use Briefcase to keep copies of your files updated at home on your main computer, or on the road on your portable computer.

- **Online Services**   If you bought a new PC with Windows 95 installed on it in 1997, you probably have an Online Services folder on your desktop. If you want to install an online service other than Microsoft Network (for example, America Online), double-click this folder and then double-click the appropriate icon inside it. Complete startup kits for Prodigy, America Online, CompuServe, The Microsoft Network, and AT&T WorldNet come with Windows 95. (You must pay to use any of these services, usually between $10 and $20 a month.)

- **Set Up the Microsoft Network** If you have this icon instead of an Online Services folder, you have an earlier version of Windows 95. You can double-click it to sign up for the Microsoft Network, which is Microsoft's own online service. (If you want America Online, CompuServe, or one of the other online services, you must get a startup disk from those companies.)

- **Welcome to Internet Explorer 4.0** If you have installed IE 4, you have this icon. Double-clicking it walks you through a setup process for registering your copy of IE 4 and setting up the channels you want to use.

If you don't have all these icons, don't worry; the icons available on the desktop vary depending on your Windows version and the hardware installed on your computer. At the minimum, every computer has My Computer and the Recycle Bin.

In this lesson, you learned about the Windows desktop. In the next lesson, you learn how to shut down Windows.

Shutting Down Windows

In this lesson, you learn the various ways you can shut down and restart Windows.

You can shut down Windows in one of three ways: You can shut down the computer, you can restart the computer, or you can restart the computer in MS-DOS mode. The following sections cover each of these methods.

Shutting Down the Computer

Most people shut down their computers when they are done working with them for the day, to save power. To shut down the computer, follow these steps:

1. Click the **Start** button. The Start menu appears.
2. Click **Shut Down** on the Start menu. The Shut Down Windows dialog box appears (see Figure 3.1), displaying a list of shut-down options. Your shut-down options may differ from the ones shown here, for example, if you are on a network or using a laptop.
3. Click the **Shut Down** option and then click **OK**. Depending on your computer type, the computer either shuts down automatically or you see a message telling you to turn off the power.
4. Turn off your computer if it is not already off.

 TIP **Shutting Down** If you close all open documents and applications and return to the Windows desktop, you can press **Alt+F4** to open the Shut Down Windows dialog box, shown in Figure 3.1.

Figure 3.1 The Shut Down Windows dialog box.

Because you can work with several documents and applications at one time, you may get carried away and forget to save a document before you shut down. Fear not; Windows protects you from losing your data. For example, if you're working on a Word document and try to shut down Windows without saving the document, the dialog box shown in Figure 3.2 appears, prompting you to save your changes. It is, however, always a good idea to save your Windows documents often to ensure that your documents are saved before choosing Shut Down from the Start menu. You also should be sure to close any open DOS applications before choosing Shut Down.

Figure 3.2 Word prompts you to save changes before shutting down.

Select **Yes** to save the changes; select **No** to discard any changes you made; select **Cancel** to cancel the shut-down command altogether.

Forget to Save? This message in Figure 3.2 is your only warning. If you accidentally respond No to saving changes, the changes you made in the Word document are lost.

CAUTION

Restarting the Computer

When you experience system problems (such as the mouse not responding or a program not operating), sometimes restarting the computer can fix them. To do so, follow these steps:

1. Click the **Start** button. The Start menu appears.

2. Choose **Shut Down** from the Start menu. The Shut Down Windows dialog box appears (Figure 3.1), displaying a list of shut-down options.

3. Click the **Restart** button and then click **OK**. Windows restarts your computer. If you're on a network, Windows asks you to log in again when it restarts.

Restarting the Computer Choosing the Restart option in the Shut Down Windows dialog box is different from pressing Ctrl+Alt+Delete. If you press Ctrl+Alt+Delete in Windows, the Close Program dialog box appears, in which you can end selected tasks or choose the Shut Down option.

Restarting the Computer in MS-DOS Mode

You can run most DOS programs from within Windows, but occasionally you may find a program that performs poorly from within Windows. In most cases, you can fine-tune its properties to run correctly, but you might find it simpler to restart the computer in MS-DOS mode and run the program from there. Because the Windows interface does not load when the computer is restarted in DOS mode, most potential conflicts with Windows are averted.

Follow these steps to restart in MS-DOS mode:

1. Click the **Start** button. The Start menu appears.

2. Choose **Shut Down** from the Start menu. The Shut Down Windows dialog box appears (Figure 3.1), displaying a list of shut-down options.

3. Choose the **Restart in MS-DOS Mode** option and click **OK**. Your computer is restarted, and the MS-DOS prompt appears on-screen.

4. Run the DOS program.

5. When you are finished with the DOS program, type **EXIT** at the MS-DOS prompt and press **Enter**. The computer restarts Windows.

Suspending on a Laptop

If you have a laptop computer, you are probably concerned about conserving battery life. On laptop computers, Windows 95 adds a Suspend command to the

Start menu, immediately above Shut Down. To use it, click the **Start** button and then click the **Suspend** command.

In Suspend mode, the computer conserves battery power by turning off the screen and stopping the disks from spinning. Everything remains in memory, so if you had a file open in Word, for example, that file would still be there when you came back. To come back to regular operation after standby mode, simply press a key or move the mouse.

CAUTION

Power in Suspend Mode   The laptop continues to use battery power even in Suspend mode, although it uses much less than it does when it is operational. Therefore it's a good idea to save your work before entering Suspend mode—in case the battery runs down completely before you unsuspend.

In this lesson, you learned how to shut down Windows. In the next lesson, you learn how to work with windows, the main building blocks of the Windows program.

Working with a Window

In this lesson, you learn how to open a window, use scroll bars, resize a window, move a window, and close a window.

What Is a Window?

A *window* is a rectangular area of the screen in which you view program folders, files, or icons. The window is made up of several components (see Figure 4.1) that are the same for all windows in Windows and Windows applications. Windows make it easy for you to manage your work. You learn to use these controls in the rest of this lesson.

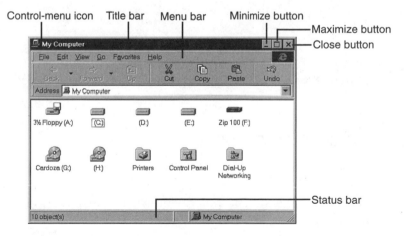

Figure 4.1 This figure shows a typical window.

CAUTION

Underlined Names?   If all the icons have underlined names on your desktop and in the My Computer window, the IE 4.0's Single-Click option is active. When this option is enabled, you point at an icon instead of clicking to select it, and you click it once instead of double-clicking to activate it. You can turn this off by choosing **View**, **Folder Options** and then clicking **Classic Style** and then **OK**. (See Lesson 9, "Drive, Folder, and File Management," for more customization options.)

If you have IE 4.0 installed, you can get extra information in the My Computer window (at the expense of a little bit of space) by activating the View as Web Page option. Open the **View** menu and choose **View as Web Page**. This makes the window appear a little differently; it adds a title and extra information about the window in its top-left corner, as shown in Figure 4.2. If you like this feature, see Lesson 9 to learn how to activate this feature for all windows.

Figure 4.2   IE 4.0 users can activate the View as Web Page feature if it is not already.

Opening Windows

To open a window from an icon, double-click the icon. For example, point at the My Computer icon on the desktop and double-click it. The My Computer icon opens up to the My Computer window, as shown in Figure 4.1 (or Figure 4.2, depending on your IE 4.0 settings).

TIP **Single-Click Option**   Don't forget, IE 4 users can choose the Single-Click option, whereby they can single-click instead of double-click to open a window. To use this setting, open the **View** menu and select the **Folder Options**, and then click the **Web Style** option button.

You also can use a shortcut menu to open a window. Just point to the icon and click the right mouse button, and a shortcut menu appears. Select **Open** on the shortcut menu, and the icon opens into a window.

Using Scroll Bars

Scroll bars appear along the bottom and right edges of a window when text, graphics, or icons in a window take up more space than the area shown. Using scroll bars, you can move up, down, left, or right in a window.

Figure 4.3 shows an example. Because this window's content is not fully visible in the window, scroll bars are present on the bottom and right sides of the window.

The following steps show you one way to use the scroll bars to view items outside the window:

1. To see an object that is down and to the right of the viewable area of the window, point at the down arrow located on the bottom of the vertical scroll bar.
2. Click the arrow, and the window's contents scroll up.
3. Click the scroll arrow on the right side of the horizontal scroll bar, and the window's contents move left.

By its size within the scroll bar, the scroll box indicates how much of a window is not visible. In Figure 4.3, the scroll box sizes indicate that you are seeing about one-quarter of the list vertically and about three-quarters of it horizontally.

If you know approximately where something is in a window (maybe two-thirds of the way down, for example), you might want to drag the scroll box. To drag a scroll box and move quickly to a distant area of the window (top or bottom, left or right), use this technique:

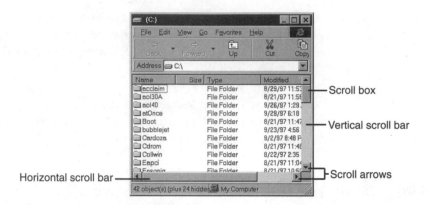

Horizontal scroll bar ⎯

Figure 4.3 Scroll bars appear when the window contains more content than can be shown.

1. Point to the scroll box in the scroll bar and hold down the left mouse button.
2. Drag the scroll box to the new location.
3. Release the mouse button.

Sometimes you might need to move slowly through a window. You can move through the contents of a window one window full at a time by clicking the scroll bar on either side of the scroll box. To scroll a few lines at a time (the slowest scrolling possible), click a scroll arrow button.

Sizing a Window with Maximize, Minimize, and Restore

You may want to increase the size of a window to see its full contents, or you may want to decrease a window's size (even down to button form on the taskbar) to make room for other windows. One way to resize a window is to use the Maximize, Minimize, and Restore buttons, in the top-right corner of the window. The following list defines the purpose of each of these buttons and commands:

- Click the **Maximize** button to enlarge the window to its maximum size. (If the window has already been maximized, the Restore button appears instead.)

- Click the **Minimize** button to reduce the window to a button on the taskbar.
- Click the **Restore** button to return a window to the size it was before it was maximized. (If the window is not maximized, the Maximize button appears instead.)

Figure 4.4 shows the My Computer window maximized to full-screen size.

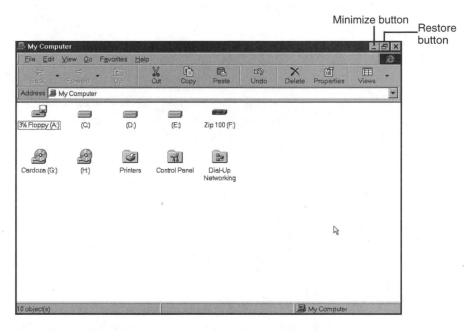

Figure 4.4 The My Computer window maximized to full-screen size.

Sizing a Window's Borders

At some point, you might need a window to be a particular size to suit your needs. If so, drag the window border to change the size of the window.

 TIP **Maximized, You Can't Resize** You can't resize a maximized window because by definition it is a certain size (full-screen). Restore the window with the Restore button first; then resize it.

To resize a window, follow these steps:

1. Place the mouse pointer on the portion of the border (vertical, horizontal, or corner) that you want to resize.

2. Press the mouse button and drag the border. A faint line appears, indicating where the border will be when you release the mouse button.

3. After the border is in the desired location, release the mouse button. The window is resized.

Moving a Window

When you start working with multiple windows, moving a window becomes as important as sizing one. For example, you may need to move one or more windows to make room for other work on your desktop.

You can move a window with the mouse or keyboard. To move a window follow these steps:

1. Point at the window's title bar with the mouse.

2. Press and hold down the left mouse button.

3. Drag the window to a new location.

4. Release the mouse button.

Closing a Window

When you're finished working with a window, you should close it. This can help speed up Windows, conserve memory, and keep your desktop from becoming cluttered.

To close a window with the mouse, do either of the following:

- Double-click the **Control-menu** icon (in the upper-left corner of the window), or

- Click the **Close** (x) button (in the upper-right corner of the window).

If you'd rather use the keyboard, select the window you want to close and press **Alt+F4**.

In this lesson, you learned how to control windows. In the next lesson, you learn about toolbars, menus, and dialog boxes.

Using Menus, Toolbars, and Dialog Boxes

In this lesson, you learn how to use menus, toolbars, and dialog boxes to issue commands in Windows.

Using Menus

A *menu* is a list of commands. You have already used menus in Windows if you have been following along with earlier lessons. The Start menu that appears when you click the Start button is a prime example. The Start menu displays a list of commands you can choose from (for example, Shut Down, as you learned in Lesson 3, "Shutting Down Windows").

Each window has its own menu bar, containing a list of menus you can open for that window. When you click a menu name, the menu opens, as shown in Figure 5.1. To choose a command from a menu, just click the command.

 TIP   **Grayed-Out Commands**   In Figure 5.1, notice that some commands appear in gray rather than black (or some alternate color, if you have a different color scheme). The grayed (or dimmed) commands are unavailable. The commands available to you are determined by their relevance to the actions you are performing at a given time. For example, in Figure 5.1, the Back command is not available because there is no other window to which to return.

 Different Menus?   Windows users without IE 4 installed have slightly different menus and commands, but they work the same way as described here.
CAUTION

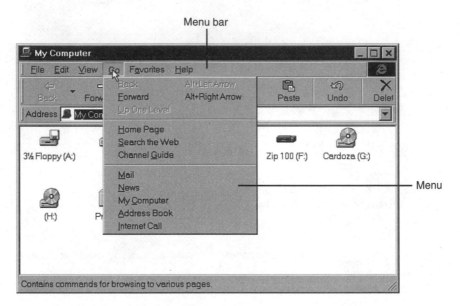

Figure 5.1 Clicking a menu name opens the menu.

Also notice that some commands have key combinations listed beside them (such as Alt+Right Arrow for the Forward command). These are keyboard shortcuts. You can press these keys instead of opening the menu and choosing the command.

Now look at the menu in Figure 5.2. Several menu commands should be noted here:

- Some commands have checkmarks beside them (like Status Bar in Figure 5.2). This indicates an on/off switch for that command. A checkmark means on.

- Some commands have a right-pointing triangle next to them. These commands open submenus when you point to them (for example, see the Arrange Icons command in Figure 5.2).

- Some commands have a black circle (called a bullet) next to them. Such commands come in groups, and you can select only one command from the group at a time. For example, in Figure 5.2, your display choices are Large Icons, Small Icons, List, and Details. One must always be chosen, and when you choose another, the original one becomes deselected.

- Some commands have ellipses (three dots) next to them. These commands open dialog boxes where you can enter more information. You learn about dialog boxes later in this lesson.

- All commands and menu names have an underlined letter. These are called the selection letters (or hot keys). To use these hot keys, press the Alt key in combination with the selection letter to open that menu or choose that command. Hot keys are a holdover from the earlier days of Windows, when not everyone's computer had a mouse. Hot key commands throughout this book are identified as follows: Choose Save or Alt+S.

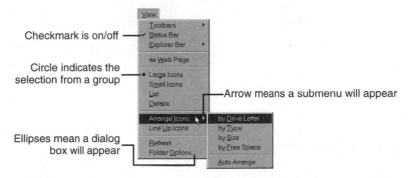

Figure 5.2 This menu showcases many types of menu controls.

Using Shortcut Menus

Shortcut menus are just like regular menus except they don't drop down from a menu bar. Instead, they appear when you right-click something. For example, when you right-click a folder icon in a window, you see a shortcut menu like the one in Figure 5.3. It lists all the most common actions you can take on that folder.

After a shortcut menu is open, click the command you want (with the left mouse button this time).

 TIP **Default Command** When you right-click something, one bold command always appears on the shortcut menu. (In Figure 5.3 it is the Open command.) This bold command is the command that is issued if you left-click (that is, click normally) on that object. If you ever wonder what would happen were you to click something, right-click it and see what action appears in bold.

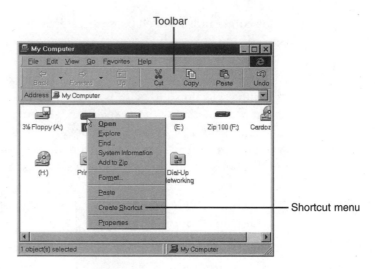

Figure 5.3 Right-click to open a shortcut menu.

Using Shortcut Keys

You saw in Figure 5.1 that some commands have shortcut keys next to them. You see this frequently in Office 97 applications; almost every important command in these applications has a shortcut key combination. Here are some common ones you might encounter:

Copy: Ctrl+C

Paste: Ctrl+V

Print: Ctrl+P

Cut: Ctrl+X

Undo: Ctrl+Z

Save: Ctrl+S

Using Toolbars

Most windows have toolbars in addition to menu bars, as shown in Figure 5.3. Toolbars contain buttons that you can click as shortcuts to issue menu commands. For example, instead of opening the Go menu and clicking Back, you can click the Back button on the toolbar.

If you do not have Internet Explorer 4 installed, your toolbar looks different. You do not have Back and Forward buttons, for example, and the icons on the toolbar are smaller. However, the buttons work the same way.

Changing the Way the Toolbar Appears

If you do not have the window maximized, you may not be able to see all the available toolbar buttons if you have IE 4's desktop updates installed (which use larger toolbar buttons by default). One solution is to maximize the window so that more toolbar buttons fit. Another is to change the toolbar to show only the button pictures so that more buttons fit across the window. To do this, follow these steps:

 IE 4 Users Only The following steps work only if you have IE 4 installed with Windows 95. If you don't have IE 4 installed, you already have the small toolbar buttons, so you should not need to change them.

CAUTION

1. In the window, open the **View** menu and point to **Toolbars**. A submenu appears.
2. Click **Text Labels** to remove the checkmark next to it. The toolbar buttons become smaller so that you can see them better, as shown in Figure 5.4.

Determining a Toolbar Button's Purpose

If you remove the text labels from the toolbar buttons, you might forget what the pictures stand for. Fortunately, you can remind yourself by pointing the mouse at the button. A ScreenTip appears with the button's name. For example, in Figure 5.4, a ScreenTip shows the Cut button's name. Move the mouse away from the button to make it disappear.

Using IE 4.0's Extra Toolbars

 If Internet Explorer 4.0's desktop update is installed, you can have extra toolbars in the taskbar area. By default, the Quick Launch toolbar appears there, as Lesson 2, "Understanding the Windows Desktop," pointed out. But you can turn it off, and/or turn other toolbars on, like this:

1. Right-click the taskbar. A shortcut menu appears.
2. On the shortcut menu, point to **Toolbars**. A list of available toolbars appears. Notice that a checkmark is already beside Quick Launch.

3. Do any of the following:

- To turn off the Quick Launch toolbar, click it to remove its checkmark.
- Click one of the other toolbar names to turn on that toolbar.

Experiment with the toolbars until you find the perfect settings for you. The available toolbars are

- **Quick Launch**   This one is on by default. Its buttons are Internet Explorer, Mail, Desktop, and View Channels.

 TIP   **Quick Launch Uses**   The most useful feature on the Quick Launch toolbar is the Desktop button. It displays your Windows 95 desktop so that you can access it without stopping to minimize any programs that may be running on top of it.

- **Address**   Adds an Internet Explorer-style Address box to the taskbar.
- **Links**   Adds a toolbar of links to common Web pages (the same as the one used in Internet Explorer).
- **Desktop**   Adds a toolbar consisting of the icons on your desktop so that you can access them even when your desktop is covered by some other application.

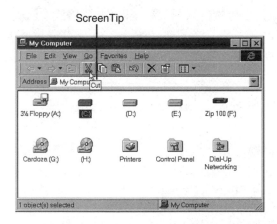

Figure 5.4   Now you can see all the toolbar buttons at once.

Toolbars Gobble Space on the Taskbar The more toolbars you activate, the less room is left on the taskbar for running programs to appear, so the more crowded the taskbar becomes when you have several programs running at once. For that reason, you should not activate all the toolbars unless you are really going to use them.

CAUTION

Using Dialog Boxes

Dialog boxes appear whenever you need to provide more information before Windows can issue a command. Dialog box controls are consistent in Windows and in the Office 97 applications, so if you learn them now, you will have a head start in working with Office.

Figure 5.5 shows some common dialog box controls you may encounter. The following list summarizes:

- **Option buttons** When you must choose one out of a group of options, these round buttons appear. They are like the round dots on the menu in Figure 5.2; you can select only one from the group at a time.
- **Text box** Click it to activate it and then type.
- **Increment buttons** Text boxes in which you enter a number often have increment buttons (sometimes called spin buttons) that you can use, if you prefer, instead of typing in the box. Click the up arrow to increase the number by one (from 1 to 2, for example). Click the down arrow button to decrease the number by one.
- **Check box** These are on/off switches, like the checkmarks on the menu you saw earlier in this lesson. Click to place or remove the checkmark.
- **Command button** Command buttons take you somewhere else. OK closes the dialog box and accepts your changes; Cancel closes it and rejects your changes. Use the Apply button to apply your changes and leave the box open. Command buttons with ellipses (...) open other dialog boxes; command buttons with >> on them expand the same dialog box to offer additional options.
- **List box** This is just a box with a list in it. If the list is too long to fit in the allotted space, it may have a scroll bar.
- **Drop-down list** Like a list box except the box is only one line tall. You have to click the down-pointing arrow to the right of the box to open it up and see the choices.

31

- **Tabs** Some dialog boxes have too many controls to fit in the box; in those cases, you click a tab to see the different sets of controls in the same dialog box.

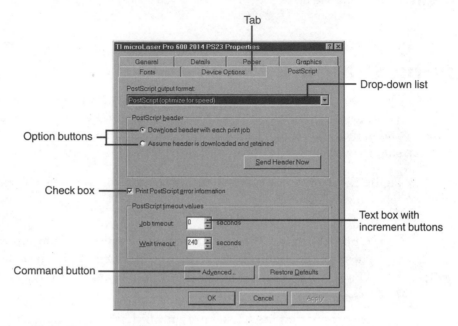

Figure 5.5 Common dialog box controls.

In this lesson, you learned how to use menus, dialog boxes, and toolbars. In the next lesson, you learn about the Windows Help system.

Using Windows Help

In this lesson, you learn how to get help, use Help's shortcut buttons, and use the What's This? feature.

Getting Help in Windows 95

Windows offers several ways to get instant on-screen help for menu commands or other tools. Online help is information that appears in its own window whenever you request it. The Help feature is organized like a reference book with three tabs: Contents, Index, and Find. The Contents and Index features show you step by step how to use commands and functions and how to perform operations in Windows applications and accessories. The Find feature enables you to search for specific words and phrases in a Help topic. Whether you use the keyboard or the mouse to access Help, help information is always at your fingertips. If you do not know or cannot remember how to perform some task, you can let the Windows Help system to tell you how.

 TIP **Consistent Help Systems** You should take the time now to master the Windows Help system because the Help systems in all Microsoft Office products are similar.

To get help on common tasks, follow these steps:

1. Click the **Start** button. The Start menu appears.
2. Choose **Help** from the Start menu. The Help Topics: Windows Help window appears, showing a list of Help topics.

3. Click the **Contents** tab to browse through the Help topics listed in the Help window; or click the **Index** tab to search for a specific Help topic; or click the **Find** tab to search for specific words or phrases in a Help topic.

TIP **Fast Help** You can press **F1** at any time to access the Help system from within a program.

Using the Contents Feature

You can get help with common tasks using Help's Contents feature. The Contents feature displays the top-level groups of information covered in Help, such as Introducing Windows and How To. When you open a major group, a list of main topics appears. As you can see in Figure 6.1, book icons represent both the major groups and the main topics within each group. Page icons (with a question mark) represent subtopics. You simply select a book to see a list of the subtopics.

Double-click a book icon to display a list of topics.

Double-click a page icon to display a Help window.

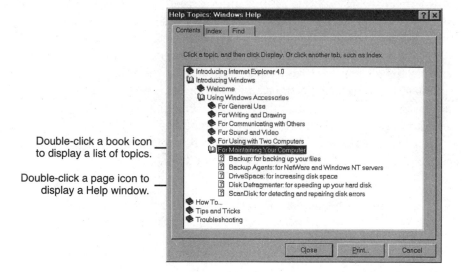

Figure 6.1 The Help Topics: Windows Help window.

Follow these steps to use Help's Contents feature.

1. Double-click the main group that contains the Help topic you want to open. A list of chapters in that group appears.

2. Double-click the chapter that contains the Help topic you want to open. A list of subtopics appears below the open chapter.

3. Double-click the subtopic you want to display. A window appears, displaying the Help information.

4. After you read the explanation, click the **Close** (X) button in the Help window's title bar to close the Help window.

If you want to print the list of Help topics in the Help Topics: Windows Help window (Figure 6.1), click the **Print** button at the bottom of the window. The Print dialog box appears. Click the **OK** button to print the list of Help topics and subtopics.

Using the Index Feature

Help's Index feature provides a list of Help topics arranged alphabetically in the Index list box. In Figure 6.2, for example, the Copying topic appears in the topic text box and is highlighted in the topic list.

In some cases, Windows displays more than one related topic in the topic list, and you can select the topic on which you need more information. The Index is especially useful when you cannot find a particular Help topic in Help Contents' list of topics.

To use the Help Index, follow these steps:

1. Click the **Index** tab in the Windows Help window. The Index options are displayed.

2. Type a topic in the text box. This enters the topic for which you want to search and scrolls to the first entry that matches the word you typed. That topic appears highlighted in the topic list. As an alternative to typing in the text box, you can scroll through the topic list and select the topic you want to view.

3. (Optional) Click a subtopic if necessary.

4. Click the **Display** button, and Windows displays the selected Help topic information in a Windows Help window.

5. When you are finished reading the Help information, click the **Close** (X) button to close the Windows Help window.

Figure 6.2   The Index tab in the Windows Help window.

Using the Find Feature

You can search for specific words and phrases in a Help topic instead of searching for a Help topic by category.

The first time you use the Find tab, you have to help Windows create a list that contains every word from your Help files. When this one-time list creation is finished, you can then search for words and phrases similar to existing words and phrases in a Help topic. The Find feature is especially useful when you cannot find a particular Help topic in Help Contents or in the list of topics found in the Index.

To build a word list (the first time only), follow these steps:

1. Click the **Find** tab in the Windows Help dialog box. The dialog box that appears gives an explanation of the Find feature and gives you these options: Minimize Database Size, Maximize Search Capabilities, and Customize Search Capabilities (see Figure 6.3.)

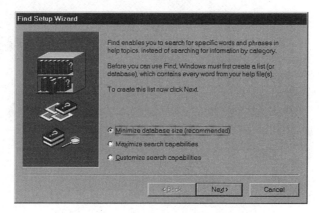

Figure 6.3 The first time you use Find, this dialog box prompts you to compile the list from which it needs to work.

2. Choose **Minimize Database Size** to create a short word list, choose **Maximize Search Capabilities** to create a long word list, or choose **Customize Search Capabilities** to create a shorter word list if you have limited disk space.

3. Click the **Next** button to continue.

4. Click the **Finish** button to create the word list.

After Windows creates the word list, the Find tab contains a text box, a word list, and a topic list.

To search for words or a phrase in a Help topic, follow these steps:

1. With the Find tab displayed, type the word you want to find in the first text box (1) at the top of the dialog box. This enters the word for which you want to search and scrolls to the first entry that matches the word you typed. The word appears highlighted in the word list (see Figure 6.4.)

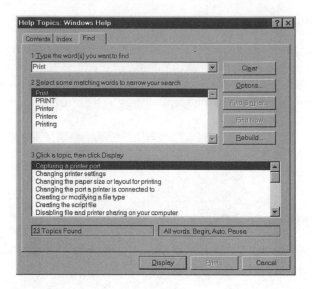

Figure 6.4 The Find tab helps you locate all Help topics that contain the word you specify.

2. (Optional) Click a word in the middle list (2) to narrow the search if necessary.

3. Click a topic in the topic list (3) and click the **Display** button. Windows displays the selected Help topic information in a Windows Help window.

4. When you are finished reading the Help information, click the **Close** (x) button to close the Windows Help window.

TIP **Topic List** Instead of typing something in the text box, you can scroll through the word list and select the word you want from the list. If you want to find words similar to the words in a Help topic, click the **Find Similar** button.

TIP **Accidents Happen** If you don't want to use the first list that Windows created, don't worry. You can rebuild that list to include more words or to exclude words. Click the **Rebuild** button and choose a word list option to re-create the word list.

Using the Windows Help Option

When you display any Windows Help option, a button bar appears at the top of the Help window; it remains visible as long as you're in Help. This button bar includes three buttons: Help Topics, Back, and Options. Click the **Help Topics** button to return to Help's table of contents. Click the **Back** button to close the current Windows Help window and return to the previous one. Click the **Options** button to display a menu with the following commands:

- **Annotate** Select this command if you want to add notes to the text in the Windows Help window. A dialog box appears, in which you can type and save your text. When you save the annotation, a green paper clip appears to the right of the Help topic to indicate that it has an annotation. Click the paper clip to view the annotation.

- **Copy** Select this command to copy Help text to the Clipboard.

- **Print Topic** Select this command to display the Print dialog box. Then click the **OK** button to print the topic using the current printer settings, or click the **Properties** button to change printer settings.

- **Font** Select this command to change the size of the font displayed in the Windows Help window. When you select this command, another menu appears from which you can select Small, Normal, or Large. A checkmark indicates the current size.

- **Keep Help on Top** Select this command if you want the Windows Help window to always be in the foreground of your screen. When you select this command, another menu appears, from which you can select Default, On Top, or Not On Top. A checkmark indicates the current selection.

- **Use System Colors** Select this command if you want Windows to use regular system colors for Help windows. When you select this command, a dialog box appears, informing you that you must restart Help for the color change to take effect. Choose **Yes** to close Help; choose **No** to return to the Windows Help window.

Help windows often display shortcut buttons as well. Using shortcut buttons, you can jump to the area of Windows to which the Help information refers. For example, suppose you're reading a Help topic that contains information on how to change the wallpaper on the desktop. You click the shortcut button (see Figure 6.5) to jump to the Control Panel's Properties for Display dialog box from within Help. There you can make the necessary changes and get on with your work.

To use a shortcut button, click it. You're immediately taken to that area of Windows.

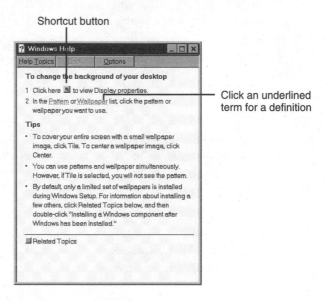

Shortcut button

Click an underlined term for a definition

Figure 6.5   The shortcut button in the Help window.

Using the What's This? Feature

The What's This? feature provides a handy way of getting more information about dialog box options. You activate this feature by selecting the question mark (?) icon that appears at the right end of the title bar in most Windows dialog boxes.

The following steps teach you how to use the What's This? feature to display a description of any option in a Windows dialog box.

1. Click the ? icon in the upper-right corner of a Windows dialog box. A large question mark appears next to the mouse pointer.

2. Click any option in the dialog box. Windows displays a box containing a short description of the item you selected.

3. When you are finished reading the Help information, click anywhere on the screen to close the Help box.

TIP   **Quick Description**   If you right-click an option in a dialog box, a shortcut menu appears displaying one menu command: What's This?. Click **What's This?** to view a description of the option.

In this lesson, you learned how to access the Windows Help system. In the next lesson, you learn how to work with Windows applications.

Working with Windows Applications

In this lesson, you learn how to start and exit Windows applications, open and save files, and move and copy information.

Starting Windows Applications

A Windows application is a program designed to take advantage of the graphical user interface (GUI) built into Windows. As you learned in Lesson 1, "Windows Basics for the Newcomer," a GUI provides a common interface between you and your programs that enables you to use the same procedures to execute commands in most compatible applications. That means that you can start (and exit) most Windows applications using the same procedures. If you are using a non-Windows (DOS) application through Windows, you need to consult that application's manual to learn how to start and exit.

To start a Windows-based application, follow these steps.

1. Click the **Start** button. The Start menu appears.
2. Point to **Programs** in the Start menu. The Programs menu appears.
3. Click the program folder that contains the program icon for the application you want to use. If, for example, you want to use WordPad, open the **Accessories** folder to access the WordPad program icon (see Figure 7.1).
4. Click the program icon for the application you want to start, and the application window appears.

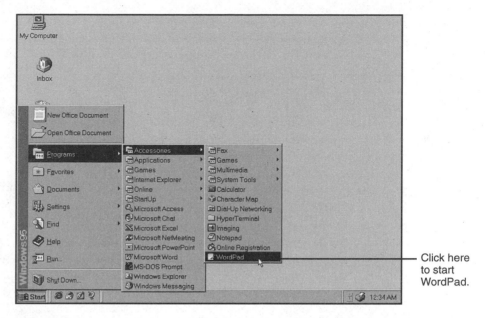

Figure 7.1 Work through the menus to find the program you want to run.

 TIP **The Run Command** Windows also offers a Run command on the Start menu. This command opens a dialog box where you can type the path to run a program. This is good for DOS-based programs that require parameters, because you can type them into the box along with the path to the program. If, for example, you need to type **MYGAME.EXE -VESA -SAVE** to run a game called MyGame, you could type that entire line there.

Placing a Shortcut on the Desktop

In Windows, icons can sit directly on the desktop (the background), and you can double-click them to run programs or open folders. If you use a program a lot, you may want to create a shortcut for it on the desktop. You can place shortcuts anywhere, not just on the desktop, but the desktop is one of the handiest places for one.

  TERM **Shortcut** A shortcut is a pointer to the original file. It can usually be distinguished from the original by a small black arrow in the bottom-left corner.

You may not have realized it, but all the programs on the Start menu are short-cuts. The actual programs are not really on the menu; the menu merely contains pointers to them. When you select a pointer, Windows retrieves the original program to which the pointer refers. Shortcuts work the same way, except they are standalone icons on the desktop.

An easy way to create a desktop shortcut is to copy one of the shortcuts on the Start menu. Follow these steps to create one for Microsoft Word. (If you don't have Word installed, use any other program instead.)

1. Right-click the **Start** button and choose **Open** from the shortcut menu that appears. A window appears showing the contents of the Start menu.

2. Double-click the **Programs** icon. The window changes to show all the folders and shortcuts on the Programs menu, as shown in Figure 7.2. (You may want to resize the window so that you can see more of its contents, as shown done in Figure 7.2, and then choose **View**, **Arrange Icons**, **By Name** to clean up the icon alignment.)

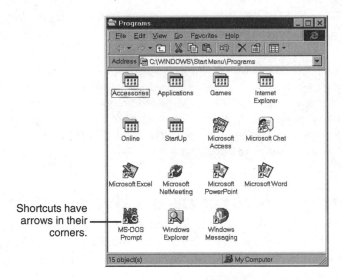

Figure 7.2   As you can see, the Programs menu is just a regular folder filled with folders and shortcuts.

TIP **Where is the Programs Folder, Really?** The Start menu and its Programs folder aren't just shadows; they're real folders on your hard disk. They're stored in a subfolder in the Windows folder called Start Menu. You can see for yourself when you learn to view drives and folders in Lesson 10, "Viewing Drives, Folders, and Files with Windows Explorer."

3. Hold down the **Ctrl** key and drag the Word icon to your desktop, creating a copy of it there.

4. Click the **Close** (x) button to close the window.

Now you have a shortcut on your desktop for Word, and you can start Word any time by double-clicking the shortcut. You no longer have to go through the Start menu.

Starting an Application When You Start Windows

Any applications that are in the Startup folder (on the Start menu) start automatically when you turn the computer on and Windows starts. To see which programs are already there, click the **Start** button, select **Programs**, and select **Startup**.

If you want to make a certain program start when Windows starts, you need to place a shortcut for it in the Startup folder. The easiest way to do this is to create a shortcut icon on the desktop for that program (see steps 1–3 in the previous section) and then, before closing the Programs window, drag the shortcut from the desktop into the Startup folder.

Starting an Application from a Document

If you want to start an application and open a specific document at the same time, you can double-click the document in any file folder (such as in Windows Explorer or My Computer). You learn how to display lists of files in these programs in Lesson 9, "Drive, Folder, and File Management." This opens the document in its native application for editing.

If you have recently worked on a document, it appears on the Documents list, and you can easily reopen it by following these steps:

1. Click the **Start** button. The Start menu appears.

2. Click **Documents**, and the Documents list appears, displaying the names of the 15 documents you've used most recently (see Figure 7.3).

3. Click the document you want. Windows opens the application in which the document was created and then opens the document.

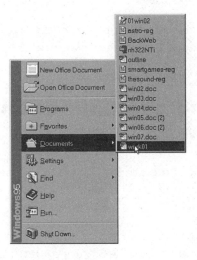

Figure 7.3 The Documents menu provides easy access to the documents you recently edited.

File Handling in Windows Applications

Most Windows applications have common commands that let you open, save, and close files. When you open a file in an application, it typically has its own window within the larger application window. Generally, you can work with that window using the same skills you learned in Lesson 4, "Working with a Window."

You learn about the specifics (as they pertain to Office 97) in each of the application-specific parts of this book, but the following sections provide an overview.

Creating a New Document

After you have a Windows application open, you want to start a new document or open an existing one. The term *document* is used generically for any file created by a Windows application.

Some programs start a new document automatically when you open them (for example, Word and Excel). If the program does not, open the **File** menu and click **New**. Some programs have a New toolbar button you can click if you prefer.

Saving a Document

When you're ready to save your work in a Windows application, open the **File** menu and click **Save**. Depending on the program, there may be a Save button on the toolbar that you can use instead. A dialog box appears prompting you for a filename. Enter one, and click the **Save** button in the dialog box.

 TIP   **Document Locations**   By default, all your Office 97 documents are saved to the My Documents folder (the same folder to which you see a shortcut on your desktop). To change the drive, select it from the **Save In** drop-down list. To change to a folder on that drive, double-click the folder. To go up to a higher-level folder, click the **Up One Level** button.

After a file has been saved once, your changes are saved automatically each time you use the Save command, without prompting you again for the filename. If you want to save under a different filename, use the **File**, **Save As** command instead. You also can use the Save As command to save your document into another format or to save it into another location.

 TIP   Choosing Save As is a good way to save your changes to a document without changing your original copy. Simply rename the changed document so that you can distinguish it from the original.

The dialog boxes for opening and saving files in Windows 95 are different from the ones in Windows 3.1. The Save As and Open dialog boxes take a bit of getting used to.

To change to a different drive, you must open the Save In or Look In list. (The name changes depending on whether you're saving or opening a file.) Figure 7.4 shows this list in the Open dialog box. From it, choose the drive on which you want to save the file.

Next, you must select the folder where you want to save the file (or open it from). When you select the drive, a list of the folders on that drive appears. Double-click the folder you want to select it.

Table 7.1 explains the buttons and other controls you see in the Save As and Open dialog boxes, as well as in other Windows dialog boxes you may encounter.

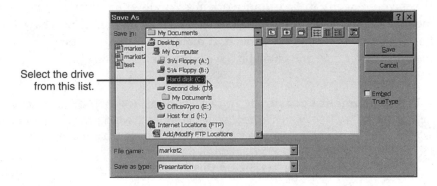

Figure 7.4 Use this list box to choose a different drive.

Table 7.1 Buttons for Changing Drives and Folders in Dialog Boxes

Control	Description
⬆	Moves to the folder above the one shown in the Save In box—that is, the folder in which the current one resides.
✳	Shows the C:\WINDOWS\FAVORITES folder, no matter which folder was previously displayed.
📁	Creates a new folder.
▦	Shows the folders and files in the currently displayed folder in a list.

Control	Description
	Shows details about each file and folder.
	Shows the properties of each file and folder.
	Opens a dialog box of settings you can change that affect the dialog box.
	(Only appears in the Open dialog box.) Switches to Preview view, in which you can see the first slide of a presentation before you open it.
	(Only appears in the Open dialog box.) Adds a shortcut for the currently displayed folder to the Favorites list.

Opening and Closing Documents

If you want to open an existing document, open the **File** menu and click **Open**. A dialog box appears prompting you to identify the file to open. (If you saved it in a folder other than the default one for that program, you may have to change the folder or drive.) Click the file, and then click the **Open** button in the dialog box, and the document opens.

To close a document, open the **File** menu and click **Close**. If you have made changes to the document since you last saved, you are prompted to save your changes. Click **Yes** or **No** to save or ignore your changes.

Exiting Windows Applications

Before you exit an application, be sure to save and close any documents on which you have worked in that application (using the **File, Save** command).

After you have saved and closed all document files, you can exit a Windows application by using any of the following four methods.

- To exit an application using its Control-menu icon (the icon in the upper-left corner of the application window), double-click the **Control-menu** icon.

- To exit an application using its Close button, click the **Close** button (the button with an X at the right end of the application's title bar).

- To exit an application using the menus, choose **File, Exit**.
- The quickest way to exit is to use the shortcut key. Press **Alt+F4**.

 TIP **Exit Quickly** You can close an application even if its window is minimized. Just right-click the application's button on the taskbar to display the shortcut menu. Then choose **Close** to close the application.

In this lesson, you learned how to start applications, manage files in an application, and exit applications. In the next lesson, you learn how to work with multiple windows.

Working with Multiple Windows

In this lesson, you learn how to arrange windows, move between windows in the same application, and move between applications.

In Windows, you can use more than one application at a time, and in each Windows application, you can work with multiple document windows. As you can imagine, opening multiple applications, each with its own windows can make your desktop pretty cluttered. That's why it's important that you know how to manipulate and switch between windows. The following sections explain how to do just that.

Arranging Windows

When you have multiple windows open, some windows are inevitably hidden by other windows, which makes the screen confusing. You can use the commands on the taskbar's shortcut menu (which you access by right-clicking the taskbar) to arrange windows.

Cascading Windows

A good way to get control of a confusing desktop is to right-click a blank area of the taskbar and choose the **Cascade Windows** command from the shortcut menu. When you choose this command, Windows lays all the open windows on top of each other so that the title bar of each is visible. (Figure 8.1 shows the resulting cascaded window arrangement.) To access any window that's not on top, click its title bar.

Each title bar is aligned in a cascading group

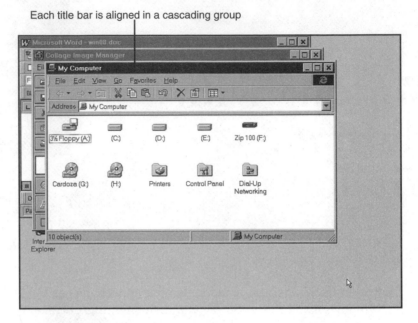

Figure 8.1 Cascaded windows.

Tiling Windows

If you need to see all your open windows at the same time, use the Tile command on the shortcut menu. When you choose this command, Windows resizes and moves each open window so that they appear side-by-side horizontally or vertically.

Right-click a blank area of the taskbar and choose the **Tile Windows Horizontally** command from the shortcut menu to create an arrangement similar to that shown in Figure 8.2. To arrange the windows in a vertically tiled arrangement (as shown in Figure 8.3), right-click a blank area of the taskbar and choose the **Tile Windows Vertically** command.

If you want to minimize all the windows at once, right-click a blank area of the taskbar and choose **Minimize All Windows**. The open windows disappear from the desktop, but the application buttons remain visible on the taskbar. You can maximize any of those windows by clicking its icon on the taskbar.

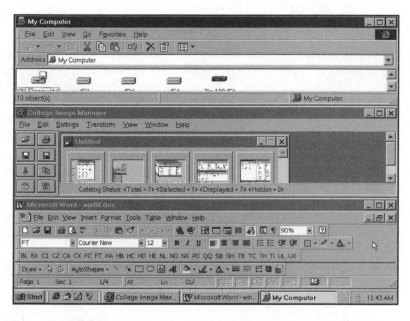

Figure 8.2 Horizontally tiled windows.

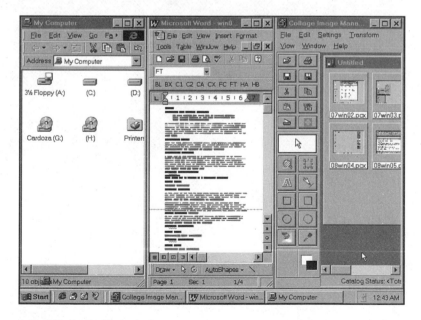

Figure 8.3 Vertically tiled windows.

Moving Between Applications

Windows enables you to have multiple applications open at the same time. This section tells you how to move between applications by using the taskbar.

The taskbar is a button bar that appears at the bottom of your screen by default. Each button on the taskbar represents an open window. The taskbar button of the currently active window appears depressed. For example, notice in Figures 8.2 and 8.3 that there are buttons on the taskbar for each open window, and that the window with the darkened (active) title bar is the same one with the depressed button.

To quickly switch between windows by using the taskbar, click the button for the window to which you want to switch. Windows immediately takes you to the window. Figure 8.4 shows two windows, both minimized, on the taskbar. One is for Word and the other is for the My Computer window.

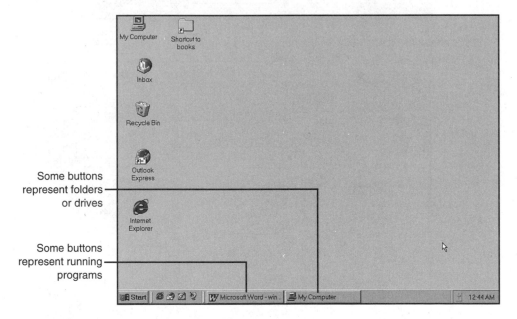

Some buttons represent folders or drives

Some buttons represent running programs

Figure 8.4 The taskbar buttons.

TIP **Bypass the Taskbar** Press and hold the **Alt** key and press and release the **Tab** key (continue to hold down **Alt**). A dialog box appears, displaying the icons and application names of all open applications. Each time you press Tab, a new (open) application becomes selected, and a border appears around the selected icon. When the application you want is selected, release the **Alt** key. Windows switches you to that application. If (while the dialog box is still on-screen) you decide you don't want to switch to that application, press **Esc** and release the **Alt** key.

Moving Between Windows in the Same Application

As stated earlier, in addition to working in multiple applications in Windows, you also can open multiple windows within an application. Moving to a new window means you are changing the window that is active. If you are using a mouse, you can move to a window by clicking any part of it. When you do, the title bar becomes highlighted, and you can work in the window. If the window you want isn't visible, open the application's Window menu and choose it from the list there. A checkmark appears next to the currently active document.

Figure 8.5 shows Microsoft Word with three open documents. One document, OUTLINE, is minimized, while the other two open documents are opened in Cascade view. Minimized windows within applications appear at the bottom of the application window, not in the taskbar.

Active Window The window currently in use. You can tell which window is active because its title bar is highlighted in a different color than the others. In Figure 8.5, the minimized window is the active one.

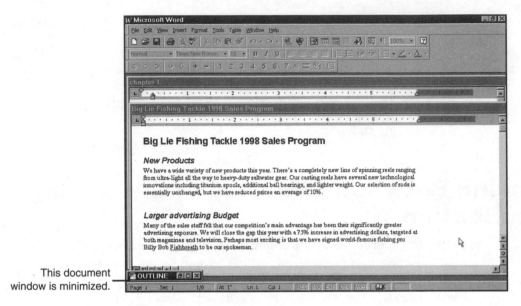

This document
window is minimized.

Figure 8.5 Three open documents in Microsoft Word.

In this lesson, you learned how to arrange windows, switch between open applications, and switch between windows in the same application. In the next lesson, you learn how to use Windows Explorer to view a disk's contents.

Drive, Folder, and File Management

In this lesson, you learn about drives, folders, and files, and find out what tools Windows provides for you to work with them.

Understanding Drives, Folders, and Files

Every computer has at least one drive. Most computers have two: a floppy drive (usually A:) and a hard drive (usually C:). The floppy drive is the one with the removable disk; the hard drive is the drive installed inside the computer.

Hard Disks Are Better   If you need to transport a file from one computer to another, you put the file on a floppy disk; otherwise, you should save everything to your hard disk because it is a faster, bigger, and less error-prone disk. Although, saving a spare copy of your important documents to a floppy disk is always a good idea.

CAUTION

When you open the My Computer window, you see icons for each of the drives on your system. In Figure 9.1, seven drives appear: A (a floppy drive), C, D, and E (hard drives), F (a ZIP drive, which is a type of removable hard disk), and G and H (CD-ROM drives). You probably will have fewer drives—perhaps only a floppy, a hard drive, and a CD-ROM drive.

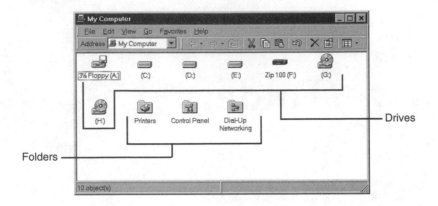

Figure 9.1 The My Computer window shows your system's drives at a glance.

If you double-click a drive icon (for example, C:), a list of the files and folders on that drive appears. Figure 9.2 shows the window that appears when you double-click the C drive (the computer's hard disk drive) in Figure 9.1. Though the contents of your C drive are undoubtedly different, this figure gives you a general idea of what appears when a drive icon is double-clicked.

  TIP

Single-Click Method If you are using IE 4's single-click feature, you can single-click instead of double-click the drive and folder icons in all instructions in this lesson. It doesn't hurt anything to double-click when this feature is on; it has the same effect as single-clicking. It's just not necessary.

In the case of a hard disk drive, a few files are stored directly on the "outer lobby" of the disk, but most are organized into folders. In Figure 9.2, for example, there are several folders, including My Documents, Program Files, and Windows. To see the content of a folder, double-click the folder.

Some folders contain subfolders within them. For example, if you double-click the Windows folder in Figure 9.2, you see not only a long list of files, but also quite a few subfolders. You can have as many levels of folders-within-folders as you want.

Folder

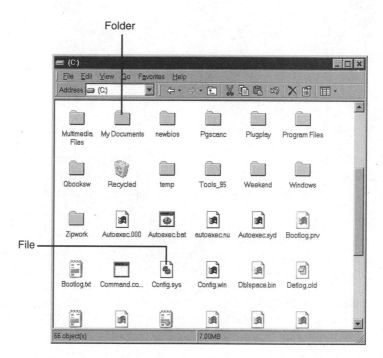

File

Figure 9.2 When you double-click a drive icon, you see its contents.

 TIP **Separate Windows** Depending on your Windows 95 setup, you may see a separate window each time you double-click a drive or folder in My Computer, or the same window may change its contents. If you are not happy with the method that your computer is currently using, follow the steps in "Customizing the File and Folder Display" later in this lesson.

 TIP **Reducing Window Clutter** To close the parent folder when opening a new folder, hold down the **Ctrl** key while double-clicking on the new folder being opened.

The My Computer window shows different icons for various files, depending on what type of file Windows recognizes them as being. For example:

📄 If Windows does not recognize the file type, it shows this generic icon.

⬜ If Windows recognizes this as a DOS-based program, you see this icon.

🖥 If the file is a DOS-based system startup file, you see this icon.

📃 Text files have this icon.

Most Windows-based applications have an icon picture embedded in them so that icon appears instead of a generic one. Though most Word documents you create are text files, for example, the Word icon is assigned to Word documents.

TIP **How Does Windows Know?** Windows displays the various icons depending on the file's extension. An extension is a three-character code (preceded by a period) at the end of the file's name that indicates the file type (for example, .doc and .xls). If you are curious about these extensions, you can activate their display in Windows on the View tab of the Folder Options dialog box, as explained later in this lesson.

My Computer Versus Windows Explorer

You just saw a demonstration of My Computer in the preceding section. My Computer is good for taking a quick look at a particular drive or folder, or getting access to a particular file.

The other file management tool that Windows 95 provides is Windows Explorer (shown in Figure 9.3). It provides a two-pane window for working with files, similar to the one you saw in the Help system in Lesson 6, "Using Windows Help." You will use it for the majority of the exercises in upcoming lessons because its two-pane design makes it easier to move and copy between folders and drives. To run Windows Explorer, click **Start**, point to **Programs**, and then click **Windows Explorer**.

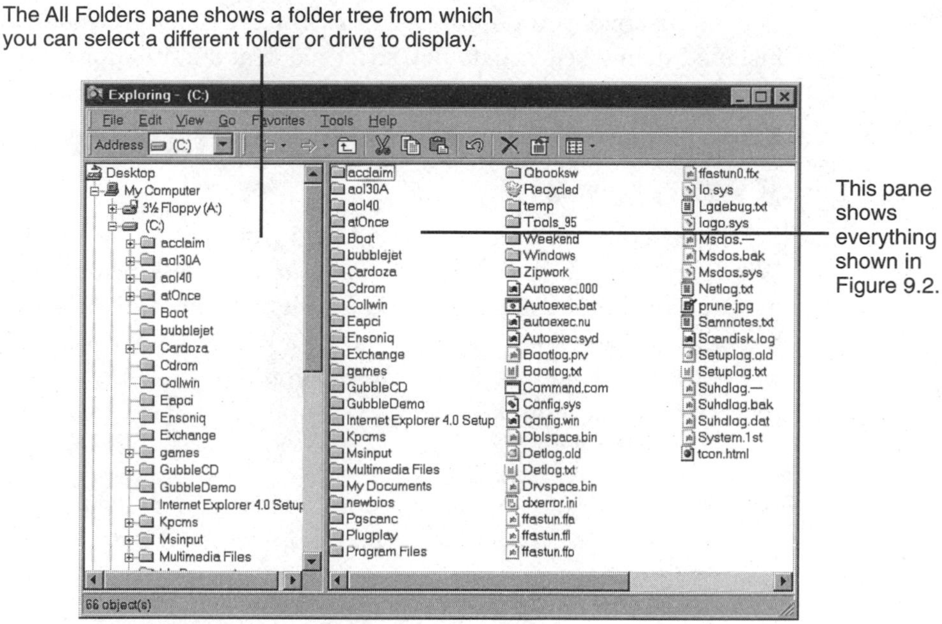

The All Folders pane shows a folder tree from which
you can select a different folder or drive to display.

This pane
shows
everything
shown in
Figure 9.2.

Figure 9.3 Windows Explorer's two-pane design shows you a folder tree and the
contents of the currently selected folder.

Customizing the File and Folder Display

You can alter the way Windows Explorer and My Computer display your files
and folders, to match your individual preferences.

CAUTION

Going Your Own Way? If you choose custom options in the following
steps, the instructions in upcoming lessons may not work exactly as described
on your computer. However, if you are experienced enough to have a preference about any of these settings, you may not need to follow closely the steps
in the upcoming lessons.

The dialog boxes you use for customization are different when you have IE 4.0 installed than when you do not, so let's look at the situations separately.

File-Handling Options with Internet Explorer 4.0

If you have Internet Explorer 4.0 installed, you can choose a Web style of Windows 95 operations. If you choose that, your desktop and your My Computer and Windows Explorer windows show all file and folder names as hyperlinks (underlined text), just like on a Web page. You can point to them, rather than clicking, to select them, and you can single-click them to activate them, rather than double-clicking. This option is not enabled by default, but you can activate it manually.

1. From the My Computer window, open the **View** menu and choose **Folder Options**. The Options dialog box appears (see Figure 9.4).

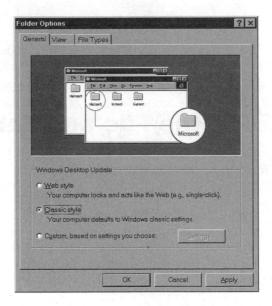

Figure 9.4 Here's where you customize Windows Explorer and My Computer.

2. Click one of the following option buttons. If you choose one of the first two, you can click **OK** afterward, and skip the remainder of the steps.

- **Classic Style** Choose this if you want Windows to work in the default way, the way described in this book. With the Classic style, you must single-click to select and double-click to activate an object. My Computer displays separate windows for each drive or folder that you open.

- **Web Style** Choose this if you want to try the Web style. With the Web style, you point to select and single-click to activate an object. My Computer uses a single window for each drive or folder, replacing the previous contents when you change drives or folders.

- **Custom, Based On Settings You Choose**. Choose this if you want your own custom combination of Classic and Web style. Then click **Settings** to open the **Custom Settings** dialog box (Figure 9.5).

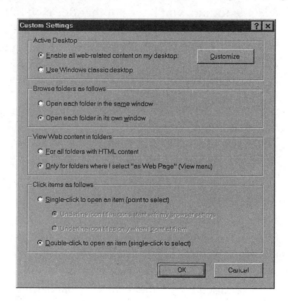

Figure 9.5 You can choose exactly how you want the program to behave in this dialog box.

3. From the Custom Settings dialog box, click your choice from each set of option buttons:

- **Active Desktop** You can enable all Web-related content (or click the **Customize** button to choose which features), or disable it all by choosing **Use Windows Classic Desktop**.

- **Browse Folders As Follows** You can choose to open each new folder in its own window (the default) or to have each subsequent folder you select replace the old one in the same window.

- **View Web Content In Folders** Choose For All Folders With HTML Content to always show Web content, or Only For Folders Where I Select "As Web Page" to control this feature yourself.

- **Click Items As Follows** To use the Web style method of point-and-click, choose **Single-Click to Open An Item**. Or, to use the Classic-style method, choose **Double-Click to Open An Item.** If you choose the former, you have another decision to make. If you choose **Underline Icon Titles Consistent With My Browser Settings**, icon titles are always underlined if they are set to be in IE 4. (This is the normal Web style way.) If you choose **Underline Icon Titles Only When I Point At Them**, the icon titles appear normal until you point at them, and then they are underlined.

4. Click **OK** when you are finished with the custom settings, and then **OK** again to close the Folder Options dialog box.

For other file-management options, click the **View** tab in the Folder Options dialog box (Figure 9.6) and choose from among the check boxes and option buttons there. These are mainly for advanced users who know exactly what they want. The most commonly-changed setting here is probably to deselect the **Hide File Extensions For Known File Types** check box so that you can see the file extensions for all files. (Experienced users often like to see these so that they know exactly what each file is for.) You might also choose to select **Show All Files** so that hidden files appear in your file listings.

Standard File-Handling Options

If you do not have IE 4 installed, you have fewer choices, but you still can adjust some settings. Follow these steps instead to change two of the most commonly-altered file-handling options:

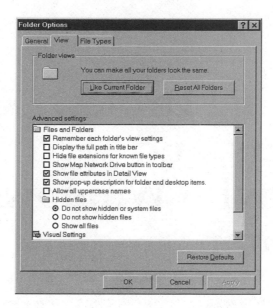

Figure 9.6   The View tab contains additional options for displaying files and folders.

1. From My Computer or Windows Explorer (both work the same), choose **View**, **Options**. The **Options** dialog box appears.

2. Click the **Folder** tab.

3. Click the option button for the My Computer behavior that you want: **Browse Windows Using A Separate Window For Each Folder** or **Browse Folders Using A Single Window That Changes As You Open Each Folder**.

4. Click the **View** tab.

5. If you want to see all files, click the **Show All Files** option button.

6. If you want to see file extensions click to remove the check box from the **Hide MS-DOS File Extensions For File Types That Are Registered** check box.

7. Click **OK**.

In this lesson, you learned about drives, files, and folders. You also learned the difference between My Computer and Windows Explorer, and how to customize the file-management settings. In the next lesson, you learn about viewing files and folders in Windows Explorer.

Viewing Drives, Folders, and Files with Windows Explorer

10

In this lesson, you learn how to use Windows Explorer to view a disk's contents.

Starting Windows Explorer

If you do not yet have Windows Explorer started (from the preceding chapter), follow these steps:

1. Open the Start menu and choose **Programs**.
2. From the Programs menu, choose **Windows Explorer**. The Windows Explorer window appears.

Using the Windows Explorer Window

Figure 10.1 shows the Windows Explorer window. The All Folders pane (the left side of the screen) shows all the folders on the selected drive (in this case, drive C).

The left side of the Windows Explorer window contains the folder list, a graphical representation of the folders and subfolders on your system. (The folder list on your screen contains different folders from those shown in Figure 10.1.) In Figure 10.1, you can see that drive C contains a folder named Windows, and the Windows folder has many subfolders, including one named All Users.

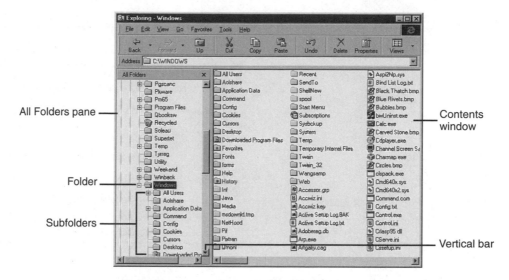

All Folders pane

Contents window

Folder

Subfolders

Vertical bar

Figure 10.1   The Windows Explorer window, displaying the contents of the C drive.

Folders and Subfolders   The folder that leads to all other folders (much like the trunk of a tree leads to all branches and leaves) is the main folder. In Figure 10.1, the main folder is C:. Any folder can have a subfolder. Subfolders are like file folders within file folders; they help you organize your files. In Figure 10.1, All Users is a subfolder of Windows.

The right side of the window contains a list of the files in the folder that's currently highlighted in the folder list. Notice that the folder icon next to the Windows folder (the highlighted folder) appears as an open folder. In this figure, the files and folders in the Windows (root directory) folder are listed in the right pane of the Windows Explorer window.

The status bar shows the number of objects in the window, the disk space those objects occupy, and the amount of remaining empty disk space.

Selecting Folders

When you select a folder using the All Folders list, its contents are displayed on the right side of the Explorer window. To select a folder with the mouse, click the folder you want. Table 10.1 shows the keys you can use to select a folder with the keyboard.

Table 10.1 Keys for Selecting a Folder

Key	Function
↑	Selects the folder above the selected one.
↓	Selects the folder below the selected one.
←	Closes the selected folder.
→	Opens the selected folder.
Home	Selects the first folder in the folder list.
End	Selects the last folder in the folder list.
First letter of folder name	Selects the first folder that begins with that letter. Press the letter again, if necessary, until you select the folder you want.

Opening and Closing Folders

In Figure 10.1, the All Folders list shows the subfolders of the Windows folder. You can close (decrease the detail of) the All Folders list so that subfolders do not appear, or you can open (increase the detail of) the list so that it shows all the folders. A plus sign (+) next to a folder indicates that there are subfolders to display; a minus sign (–) next to a folder indicates that the folder has been opened and can be closed.

To open or close a folder with the mouse, just double-click the folder icon. (Single-click if you are using Web style.) To open or close a folder with the keyboard, use the arrow keys to select the folder and press + (plus) to open it or – (minus) to close it.

TIP **It's Only for Show** Closing and opening affects this display only; it doesn't alter your folders or other contents in any way.

Changing Drives

You can change drives to see the folders and files contained on a different disk. To change drives with the mouse, click the drive icon on the All Folders list. You also can use the keyboard to change to a floppy drive. Press the first number for the drive type (for example, press **3** for a 3.5" floppy drive). Unfortunately, you can't type a drive letter to change to that drive. Windows Explorer interprets the typed letter as the first letter of a folder name to which you want to change.

Changing the Windows Explorer Display

The commands in Windows Explorer's View menu enable you to change how the All Folders pane and the file list pane display information. You can control the size of the windows, whether or not the toolbar and status bar are displayed, and how the files in the file list pane are displayed.

When you change the Windows Explorer display settings to suit your needs, Windows remembers those settings. They remain the same every time you start Windows (until you change them again).

Sizing the Windows

In Figure 10.1, both the All Folders pane and the list of files are shown. You can change the way each is shown by changing the amount of space allotted to each. You may want to see more files and less whitespace around the folders list. Follow these steps to change the way the space is divided between the panes:

1. A vertical dividing line is between the two panes. Point to the line, and the mouse pointer changes to a short vertical bar with two arrows.

2. Drag the line to where you want it. The display changes accordingly (see Figure 10.2).

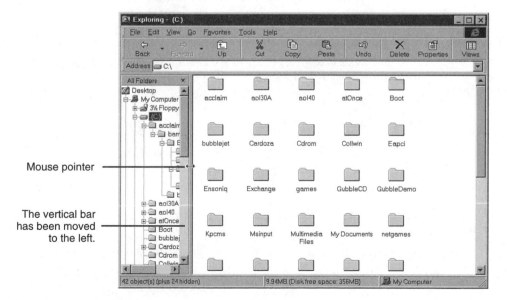

Figure 10.2 The changed window display.

Changing the File List Display

By default, Windows Explorer shows only the filenames and icons for each folder. However, you can change the display to include more information about each file if you want. The View menu provides you with four options you can use to customize the file list display: Large Icons, Small Icons, List, and Details.

The View, List command tells Windows to display only the icons and filenames for each folder (as shown in Figure 10.2). This is the default display. Choose **View, Details** to have Windows display the following information about each file:

- Size in bytes
- File type (to describe the file—such as Folder, Application, Help, and Settings)
- Last modification day and date
- Attributes (such as Archive, Read-Only, System, and Hidden)

You also can change the size of the icons that Windows displays in the file list pane. Choose **View, Large Icons** to display large icons with the filenames beneath the icons. Choose **View, Small Icons** to display small icons with the file names to the right of the icons.

TIP   **Small Icons Versus List**   Small Icons and List views both show small icons with the name to the right. The difference is how the files and folders are arranged. In List view, they're arranged in columns. In Small Icons view, they're arranged in rows.

Controlling the Order of the Display

As you can see in Figure 10.2, the files in the folder are listed in alphabetical order by filename. If you prefer, you can have Windows arrange the icons differently, by using one of the following methods:

- Choose **View, Arrange Icons, By Type** to arrange files alphabetically by their file type.
- Choose **View, Arrange Icons, By Size** to arrange files from smallest to largest.
- Choose **View, Arrange Icons, By Date** to arrange files alphabetically by date from newest to oldest.

Working with the Toolbar

The toolbar in Windows Explorer is much the same as one you saw in the My Computer window in earlier lessons. (Your toolbar will be different, remember, if you don't have IE 4 installed.) Table 10.2 explains what each toolbar button does. If you don't have a toolbar in your Windows Explorer window, choose **View, Toolbar** to turn it on.

Table 10.2 Windows Explorer Toolbar Buttons

Button	Name	Description
Address	Address	Displays the current folder name. Open the drop-down list to choose a different folder/drive.
	Back (IE 4 only)	Returns to the last folder displayed.
	Forward (IE 4 only)	If you have used Back, goes forward to the folder you were looking at before you clicked Back.
	Up One Level	Displays the folder up one level from the folder currently displayed in the Folder text box.
	Cut	Cuts the selected file or folder and places it on the Clipboard.
	Copy	Copies the selected file or folder to the Clipboard.
	Paste	Pastes the contents of the Clipboard to the location selected in the list.
	Undo	Undoes the last file or folder operation.
	Delete	Deletes the selected file or folder.
	Properties	Displays the properties of the selected file or folder.
	Views (IE 4 only)	Opens a drop-down list from which you can choose a different view (Large Icons, Small Icons, List, or Details). If you do not have IE 4 installed, you have four separate buttons for each of these views instead of the one button.

TIP   **Toolbar Text Labels**   The toolbar buttons shown in Table 10.2 are the small ones, without the text labels. As you learned in Lesson 5, "Using Menus, Toolbars, and Dialog Boxes," you can toggle the text labels on and off by choosing **View**, **Toolbars, Text Labels**.

Displaying the Status Bar

Initially, Windows displays the status bar at the bottom of the Windows Explorer window (see Figure 10.2). If you want to hide the status bar, open the **View** menu and select **Status Bar** (to deactivate it). To redisplay it, repeat the previous command sequence.

Closing Windows Explorer

If you're not going to use Windows Explorer again right away, you should close it instead of minimizing it to keep your system running efficiently with plenty of memory available. To close Windows Explorer, choose **File**, **Close**, click the **Close** (x) button, or double-click the **Control-menu** icon.

In this lesson, you learned how to use Windows Explorer to examine the contents of a disk. In the next lesson, you learn how to select, copy, and move files and folders.

Selecting, Copying, and Moving Files and Folders

In this lesson, you learn how to select multiple files and folders and how to copy and move them.

Selecting Multiple Files or Folders

To really speed up operations, you will want to select multiple files or folders and then execute commands that affect the entire group. You, for example, may want to select several files to copy to a floppy disk. Copying them all at once is much faster than copying each file individually. The following sections explain how you can select multiple files and folders.

Selecting Multiple Contiguous Files or Folders

It is easy to select multiple files or folders that are displayed *contiguously* in Windows Explorer's files list window or My Computer.

 TERM   **Contiguous Files**   When the files that you want to select are listed next to each other in Windows Explorer—without unwanted files between—they are *contiguous.*

Follow these steps to select contiguous files or folders:

1. Click the first file or folder that you want to select. When you click it, it becomes highlighted.

2. Hold down the **Shift** key and click the last file or folder that you want to select. All the items between (and including) the first and last selections are highlighted. (Figure 11.1 shows a selection of contiguous files.)

Selected contiguous files

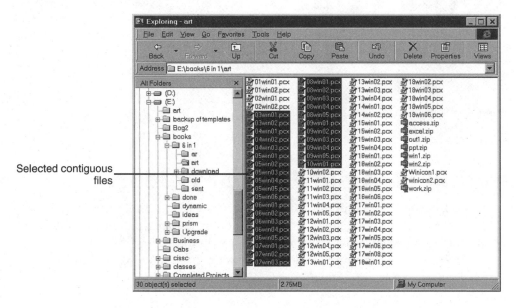

Figure 11.1 Selected contiguous files are highlighted.

  TIP **Web Style** If you are using IE 4's Web style of operation, you point instead of clicking in both steps 1 and 2 in the previously described procedure.

To deselect a contiguous group of files or folders, release the Shift key and point the mouse at a file or folder outside the selected items. You also can click anywhere in the window to deselect the files.

Selecting Noncontiguous Files or Folders

Often, the files or folders you want to select are *noncontiguous*, meaning that they are separated by several files that you do not want selected. To select such noncontiguous files or folders, you use the Ctrl key.

To select items with the mouse, hold down the **Ctrl** key and click the files or folders you want (or just point to them if you are using Web style). Each item you click, until you release the Ctrl key, becomes and remains highlighted. Figure 11.2 shows a selection of multiple noncontiguous files. To deselect an item, point to it again while the Ctrl key is still pressed. To deselect all items, release the Ctrl key and point to something else.

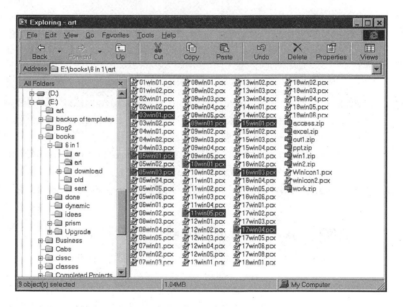

Figure 11.2 Selecting multiple noncontiguous files.

TIP **Narrowing the Selection** If you want to select or deselect files with related names, choose the **Tools**, **Find**, **Files or Folders** command. Enter the characters you want to find in the **Named** text box and choose (**C:**) from the **Look In** drop-down list. Then click **Find Now**. When Windows displays the files you want to select or deselect, choose **Edit**, **Select**, **All** from the menu bar of the Find dialog box to select all the files in the Search Results window. Then deselect any listed files that you don't want selected. (Lesson 12, "Creating, Deleting, Renaming, and Finding Files and Folders," explains in more detail how to use the Find command.)

Moving or Copying Files or Folders

To quickly move or copy files or folders through Windows Explorer or My Computer, you *drag and drop*—that is, you select the items you want from your source folder, drag them to the destination folder, and drop them there. You learn the details of using this technique later in this section.

 TIP **Move Versus Copy** When you move the file or folder, it no longer exists in its original location—only in the new location. When you copy a file or folder, the original file or folder remains in its original location, and a copy of the file or folder is placed in a second location.

Before you move or copy, make sure the source file or folder is visible so that you can highlight the file(s) you're going to drag. Also, make sure that the destination drive or folder is visible. In Figure 11.3, for example, the source folder, My Documents, has its contents displayed in the Contents window; the source file, the **Shopping** file, is visible in the Contents window; and the destination folder, the 3 1/2 Floppy (A:) drive, is visible in the All Folders window.

Copying Files and Folders

With the mouse, use this procedure to copy:

1. Select the files or folders to copy.
2. Press the **Ctrl** key and drag the files or folders to the destination drive or folder.
3. Release the mouse button and then the Ctrl key. The files or folders are copied to the new location.

If you are copying from one folder to another on the same drive, the Ctrl key is required; if you drag without it, Windows assumes you want to move rather than copy. However, if you are copying from one drive to another, you can safely omit the Ctrl key from step 2.

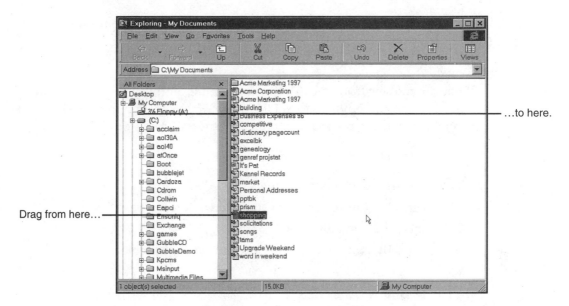

Drag from here...   ...to here.

Figure 11.3 The selected file can be moved or copied.

You also can copy with the menu commands:

1. Select the files or folders to copy.
2. Select **Edit**, **Copy** or click the **Copy** button on the toolbar.
3. Click the destination drive or folder to display its contents.
4. Select **Edit**, **Paste** or click the **Paste** button on the toolbar.

TIP   **The File Is Already There**   If you attempt to copy a file or folder to a location in which a file or folder with the exact same name exists, Windows lets you know with a message that says **This Folder Already Contains A File Called "filename". Would You Like To Replace The Existing File With This One?** Click **Yes** to replace the existing file, or click **No** to stop the copy operation.

Moving Files and Folders

With the mouse, follow these steps to complete a move:

1. Select the files or folders to move.

2. Hold down the **Shift** key and drag the files or folders to the destination drive or folder.

3. Release the mouse button.

If you are moving from one drive to another, the Shift key is required; otherwise, you end up copying instead. However, if you are moving from one folder to another on the same drive, you can omit the Shift key from step 2.

You also can use menus to move:

1. Select the files or folders to move.

2. Select **Edit, Cut** or click the **Cut** button on the toolbar.

3. Display the destination drive or folder.

4. Select **Edit, Paste** or click the **Paste** button on the toolbar.

 TIP **Wrong Move or Copy?**   If you move or copy the wrong files or folders, you can choose **Edit**, **Undo** in the Windows Explorer menu bar or click the **Undo** button on the Windows Explorer toolbar to undo the operation.

 TIP **Right-Drag**   Another way to move or copy is to drag with the right mouse button. When you *drop*, a shortcut menu appears from which you can choose to Move, Copy, Create Shortcut, or Cancel.

Using Send To

There are a few common locations that people copy files to, and Windows includes these on a special Send To menu. They include the floppy disks on your system, the desktop (as a shortcut), and the My Documents folder. You can copy a file or folder (or group of them) to one of the Send To locations by following these steps:

1. Right-click the selected files/folders. A shortcut menu appears.

2. Point to **Send To**. A submenu appears (see Figure 11.4).

 TIP **Extra Send To Commands**   The Send To menu shown in Figure 11.4 contains more commands than yours may contain; when you install certain programs (such as WinZip, for example), the programs install extra commands on your Send To menu.

3. Click the destination to copy to (for example, click My Documents to copy to the My Documents folder).

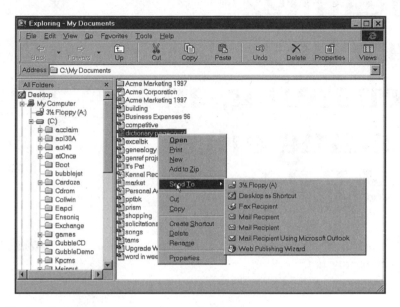

Figure 11.4   Right-click and then choose Send To.

In this lesson, you learned how to select multiple files and folders and how to copy and move files and folders. In the next lesson, you learn how to rename and find files and folders.

Creating, Deleting, Renaming, and Finding Files and Folders

In this lesson, you learn how to create and delete files and folders, how to find them on your system, and how to rename them.

Creating a File or Folder

Some files and folders are created automatically when you install a program. When you install Office 97, for example, the installation program creates a folder on your hard drive and places the Office 97 files in that folder. However, you also can create files and folders yourself.

You may want to create a folder for several reasons. Many application installation programs create a folder when you install the application on your computer. If one of your application installation programs does not, you will want to create a folder for that application.

A more common reason to create a folder is to store document files. You, for example, may want to create a subfolder within the My Documents folder in which to store documents that you create with Word so that they are separate from the documents created by other programs. Having a separate folder for Word documents makes it much easier to find and manipulate them. You can create a single folder to store data from more than one application, too; for example, if you have three clients, you might create a separate folder for data relating to each client.

TERM   **My Documents**   Microsoft Office automatically creates a folder called My Documents on your hard disk; by default, that's where it stores your files from Office programs. If you have more than one hard disk, My Documents is created on the same drive on which Windows is installed.

Creating a Folder with Windows Explorer

To create a folder using Windows Explorer, follow these steps:

1. Open the **Start** menu, choose **Programs**, and choose **Windows Explorer**. The Windows Explorer window appears.

2. Click the folder in the All Folders pane under which you want to create the new folder, to display its contents. (The folder you create is a subfolder of the folder you select.) If you don't want the new folder to be a subfolder of another folder, click the drive letter (for example, **C:**).

3. Right-click the Contents pane, and point to **New** on the shortcut menu that appears. A submenu appears (see Figure 12.1.) Your menu may be a little different from the one shown in Figure 12.1 if you do not have IE 4.0 installed.

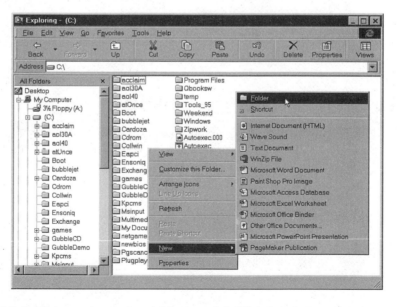

Figure 12.1 One way to create a folder is to right-click the place you want to create it and choose **New, Folder**.

4. Click **Folder** on the shortcut menu. A new folder appears in the Contents pane, temporarily called New Folder.

5. Type the new name using up to 255 characters (including spaces) in the text box that appears next to the new folder icon. The name you type replaces the words **New Folder** as you type.

CAUTION

Long Filenames   If you are renaming a folder that will be used on a computer running DOS/Windows 3.1, limit the name to eight characters. DOS/Win31 computers cannot read long filenames. If you have a filename with spaces or with more than eight characters, the DOS/Win3.1 user will see a truncated version—for example, Docume~1 instead of Documents.

6. Press **Enter**, and Windows renames the new folder.

Creating a Folder with My Computer

To create a folder with My Computer, follow these steps. (This works as an alternative method in Windows Explorer, too.)

1. In My Computer, display the contents of the drive or folder in which you want to create a folder.

2. Select **File**, **New**. Windows creates a new folder icon.

3. Type a new name for the folder and press **Enter**.

Deleting a File or Folder

Sometimes you need to delete a file or folder. You, for example, may have created a file or folder by mistake, or you may want to remove the files or folder for an application you no longer use, or you may need to make more room on your hard drive.

CAUTION

Better Safe than Sorry   Before you delete anything, it is a good idea to make a backup copy of any files or folders you might need later. See Lesson 11, "Selecting, Copying, and Moving Files and Folders," for directions on how to copy files and folders.

When you delete a file or folder, it doesn't go away immediately; instead it moves to the Recycle Bin, which is explained in the next section.

To delete a file or folder, follow these steps:

1. In the My Computer window or the Windows Explorer folders list, select the file or folder you want to delete. Be aware that when you delete a folder, Windows deletes all files in that folder.

2. Choose **File**, **Delete** or press the **Delete** key. The Confirm File (or Folder) Delete dialog box appears, indicating what will be deleted and asking you to confirm the deletion.

3. Look through the Confirm Folder Delete dialog box carefully to make certain you are deleting what you intended to delete.

4. Select **Yes** to delete the file(s) or folder(s) listed in the dialog box.

CAUTION

I Didn't Mean to Do That!   If you delete a folder or file by mistake, immediately choose **Edit**, **Undo Delete** to restore the deleted folder(s) and file(s).

Working with the Recycle Bin

The files you delete in Windows are stored temporarily in the Recycle Bin. You can retrieve files from the Recycle Bin if you decide you need them again, or you can purge the deleted files when you're sure you no longer need them. By purging deleted files, you make more room on your disk.

To retrieve files you've deleted, follow these steps:

1. Double-click the **Recycle Bin** icon on the desktop. The Recycle Bin window appears.

2. (Optional) You may want to select **View**, **Details** so that you can see more information about the files. This can help you determine which file you want to restore, if you are not sure. (Figure 12.2 shows the Recycle Bin in Details view.)

3. Click the file you want to retrieve. To select multiple files, hold down **Ctrl** and click each one.

4. Select **File**, **Restore**. Windows restores the files to their original locations.

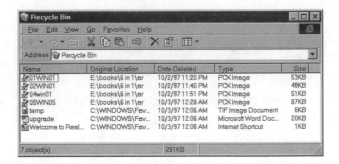

Figure 12.2 Use the Recycle Bin to delete files from your computer.

  TIP **Web Style** If you are following the preceding steps using IE 4's Web style, substitute point for click and click for double-click.

Follow these steps to purge deleted files in the Recycle Bin:

1. Select **File**, **Empty Recycle Bin**. A confirmation dialog box appears.

2. Choose **Yes** to delete all the files.

3. Click the **Close** button to close the Recycle Bin window.

You don't have to have the Recycle Bin folder open to empty it; just right-click its icon on the desktop and choose Empty Recycle Bin from the shortcut menu that appears.

 TIP **Purge Files Individually** To delete only one file from the Recycle Bin, select the file, open the **File** menu, choose **Delete**, and click **Yes**. Windows purges only that file.

Renaming Files or Folders

To rename a file, follow these steps:

1. In either the Windows Explorer or My Computer window, select the file or folder you want to rename.

2. Choose **File**, **Rename** or press **F2**. A box appears around the file or folder name, and the name is highlighted (see Figure 12.3).

3. Type the new name for the file or folder. As you type, the new name replaces the old name.

4. Press **Enter** when you finish typing.

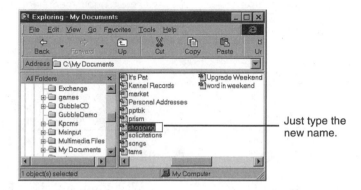

Just type the new name.

Figure 12.3 This file is ready to be renamed.

Don't Rename That One! Never rename program files. Some applications do not work if their files have been renamed, because their supporting files are looking for a particular filename to support.

CAUTION

Searching for a File

As you create more files, the capability to find a specific file becomes more critical. You can search for either a single file or a group of files with similar names by using the Tools, Find command. To search for a group of files, use the asterisk wild card (*) with a partial filename to narrow the search. You also can perform a partial name search without wild cards, search by last modification date, save complex searches, and do a full text search. (Table 12.1 shows some search examples and their potential results.)

Wild Cards When you're not sure of the filename you want to find, you can use the asterisk wild card (*) to replace multiple characters in the filename or the question mark wild card (?) to replace one character in the filename.

Table 12.1 Search Examples and Their Results

Characters Entered for Search	Sample Search Results
mem?.doc	mem1.doc, mem2.doc, memo.doc
mem1.doc	mem1.doc
mem*.doc	mem1.doc, mem2.doc, mem10.doc, memos.doc
c*.exe	calc.exe, calendar.exe
*.exe	calc.exe, calendar.exe, notepad.exe
c*.*	calc.exe, calendar.exe, class.doc

To search for a file, follow these steps:

1. Click the **Start** button, select **Find**, and select **Files or Folders**. The Find dialog box appears.

2. In the **Named** text box, enter the characters you want to find, using wild cards to identify unknown characters (see Figure 12.4).

3. If you want to search the entire drive, choose **C:** in the **Look In** text box (if it's not already there) and make sure the **Include Subfolders** check box is selected.

   If you want to search only the main folder, make sure the **Include Subfolders** check box is not selected.

   If you want to search a specific folder, click the **Browse** button and select a folder from the folders list.

4. If you want to search for a file according to its last modification date, select the **Date Modified** tab and select the date options you want.

5. If you want to search for a certain type of file, select the **Advanced** tab and choose a file type in the **Of Type** drop-down list box.

6. When you finish setting options, click the **Find Now** button to begin the search. The search results window appears under the Find dialog box, showing the files that were found (see Figure 12.5).

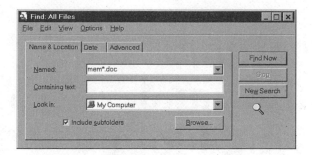

Figure 12.4 A completed Find dialog box.

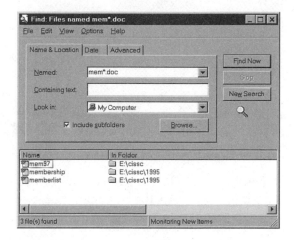

Figure 12.5 The search results appear below the Find settings.

In this lesson, you learned how to create, delete, rename, and find files and folders. In the next lesson, you learn how to format and copy floppy disks.

Formatting, Naming, and Copying Floppy Disks

In this lesson, you learn how to format and copy floppy disks and how to assign names to them.

Determining How Much Room Is on a Disk

In Windows Explorer, when you select a disk (hard or floppy) on the All Folders pane, the Status bar reports the amount of free space on the disk (see Figure 13.1.)

Look here for disk space information.

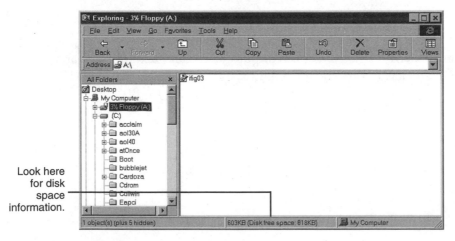

Figure 13.1 This floppy disk has one file on it, which takes up 603 KB. The disk has 818 KB free.

Formatting a Floppy Disk

Several years ago, most floppy disks you bought were unformatted and you had to format each one. These days, most disks are preformatted so that you do not usually have to format a new disk.

However, occasionally, you may want to reformat a disk, to refresh its formatting or to ensure that all its contents are wiped away (for security reasons). When you format a disk, all its contents are permanently erased.

Format Only Floppy Disks   You should never need to reformat your hard disk unless some horrible computer problem (such as a virus) causes your entire drive's contents to be lost, and you need to start over. In that rare case, **CAUTION**   you would issue the **Format** command from a boot disk at the DOS prompt. You would not format the hard disk as you do a floppy.

When you format a floppy disk, you can choose to make it bootable if you want. That means that system files are copied to the disk so that you can start your computer with it. You also can choose to copy the system files only (that is, make the disk bootable only, without actually reformatting it).

Making Disks Bootable   In practice, you rarely want to do this. Making a disk bootable uses some space on it, so the disk has less storage space available, and you only rarely need to use a disk's boot capability. When you **CAUTION**   installed Windows 95, you created an emergency boot disk, which serves in the event of a problem, and you do not usually use a floppy to start your computer unless you were experiencing system problems.

To format a disk (or reformat one that has already been formatted), follow these steps:

1. In My Computer or the Windows Explorer All Folders pane, right-click the icon for the floppy disk. A shortcut menu appears.

2. Click **Format** on the shortcut menu. A Format dialog box opens (see Figure 13.2.)

Figure 13.2 Choose your formatting options in this dialog box.

3. Choose the disk's capacity in the Capacity drop-down list. Unless you are using a very old disk, the capacity should be correct; almost all floppy disks are 3 1/2" and have a capacity of 1.44 MB these days.

 TIP **Determining Disk Capacity** If you are unsure of the capacity of a 3 1/2" disk, take it out of the drive and look at it. If it has two square holes (one covered by a black tab and one open), it is a 1.44 MB capacity disk. If it has only one hole (the one with the black tab), it is a 720 K capacity disk. (These are older, and are rarely seen anymore.)

4. Choose the format type:

- **Quick** Use this for a disk that has already been formatted.

- **Full** Use this for a new, unformatted disk or for a disk that you suspect of having errors.

- **Copy System Files Only** Use this for an existing disk that you do not want to reformat but only want to make bootable.

5. (Optional) Enter a label for the disk in the Label text box. This appears in Windows Explorer when you are working with the disk.

6. (Optional) If you want to make the disk bootable in addition to formatting it, select the **Copy System Files** check box.

7. Click **Start**. Windows formats the disk.

8. Wait until you see a Results window, and then click **Close**.

9. Format another disk, or click **Close** to close the Format window.

Labeling a Disk

If you want to label an already-formatted disk (or hard disk, for that matter), or change the existing label, follow these steps. (The label appears when you work with the disk in Windows Explorer and My Computer.)

1. Right-click the disk icon and choose **Properties**. The Properties dialog box opens.

2. On the General tab, type a name in the Label box (see Figure 13.3.)

3. Click **OK** to close the dialog box.

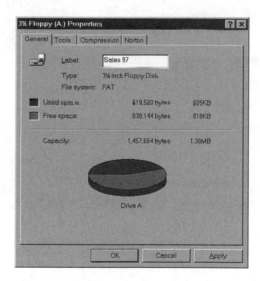

Figure 13.3   You can enter a new label or change an existing one.

Extra Tab?   Notice in Figure 13.3 there is an extra tab—Norton. It's there because a utility program called Norton Utilities is installed on the computer used to capture the figures for this section. If you don't have that program, you have only three tabs in the Properties dialog box.

Copying a Disk

If you have an important disk, you may want to make a copy of it. To do so, you must have another disk that is either blank or contains nothing that you want to save, because making the copy wipes the receiving disk's previous contents away.

Follow these steps to copy a disk:

1. Place the disk that you want to copy into your floppy drive.
2. Right-click the disk icon and choose **Copy Disk** from the shortcut menu that appears. The Copy Disk dialog box appears (Figure 13.4).

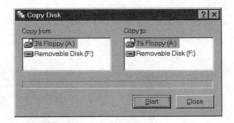

Figure 13.4 Here's where you copy a disk.

3. If you have more than one floppy disk drive in your system, you have a choice in the Copy From and Copy To lists. (In Figure 13.4, there are two choices.) Click the appropriate drive if needed, and then click **Start**.
4. Wait for Windows to read the disk that you want to copy.
5. When prompted, remove the original disk and insert the one onto which you want to place the copy. Then click **OK**.
6. Wait for the copy to be placed on the destination disk.
7. Click **Close** to close the Copy Disk dialog box.

In this lesson, you learned how to format, copy, and label disks. In the next lesson, you learn how to install and uninstall programs.

Installing and Uninstalling Programs

In this lesson, you learn how to add and remove Windows components and install and uninstall other applications.

Adding and Removing Windows Components

When you installed Windows, you chose either a standard or a custom installation. With a standard installation, the most common components were installed; with custom, you choose which components you want.

You can add and remove Windows components at any time; you don't have to rerun the setup program. If, for example, you did not install Character Map, you can install it later. Or, if you find that you never use a certain component, you can uninstall it to save room on your hard disk.

  TIP **IE 4 Web Style**   IE 4 users with Web style turned on should click instead of double-click the icons in the following steps.

Follow these steps to add or remove Windows components:

1. Open the My Computer window.
2. Double-click the **Control Panel** icon.
3. Double-click the **Add/Remove Programs** icon. The Add/Remove Programs Properties dialog box opens.

4. Click the **Windows Setup** tab. This shows you which Windows components are installed (see Figure 14.1.)

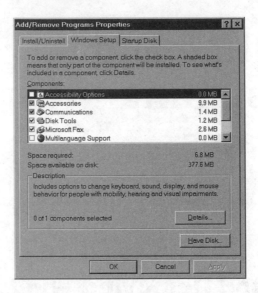

Figure 14.1 You can install or uninstall parts of Windows here.

5. Click the category of component you want to install or uninstall. For example, to install Character Map, click **Accessories**.

6. Click the **Details** button to display the individual components within that category.

7. Click to check the components you want to install. Or, if a component already has a checkmark next to it, click again to remove the checkmark and uninstall it.

8. When you have made all your selections in that category, click **OK**.

9. Repeat steps 5–7 as needed for other categories of components.

10. Click **OK** to install or remove the chosen components.

11. If prompted, insert your Windows CD-ROM in your CD drive and click **OK**.

12. Wait for the components to be installed. You see a progress bar showing the installation process. Then the dialog box closes.

Preparing to Install New Applications

If you are going to install a new application that you purchased separately from Windows, you need to read the instructions that came with the application. If the application includes installation instructions for Windows 95, follow those instructions instead of the steps here. Use the steps in the following section only if you do not have specific instructions for the program you are adding.

 TIP **Preparing Your Hard Disk** Before you install a new application, you may want to defragment your disk by running the Disk Defragmenter program. To run it, choose **Start**, **Programs**, **Accessories**, **System Tools**, **Disk Defragmenter**. Choose **Full Optimization**. This program reorganizes the files on your hard disk so that there is one large contiguous empty space rather than lots of small pockets of empty space. This ensures that the new program is installed in a single contiguous spot on your hard disk, improving its speed and performance.

Installing Software

To install new software, you can do any of the following:

- If you put the new software's CD in your drive and an installation program starts automatically, use that installation program, following the instructions on-screen.

- If you put the new software's CD in the drive and nothing happens, open **My Computer** and browse the CD's contents looking for a Setup or Install file. If you see one, double-click it (or single-click, in Web style) to start the installation program.

- If neither of the above works for you, follow the steps in the following procedure.

To install new software:

1. Open the **My Computer** window and double-click the **Control Panel** icon.

2. Double-click the **Add/Remove Programs** icon.

3. On the Install/Uninstall tab, click the **Install** button (see Figure 14.2). A dialog box appears telling you to insert the product's disk.

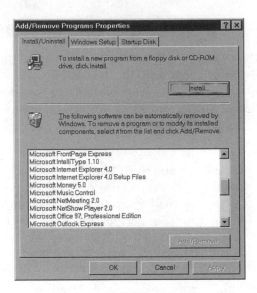

Figure 14.2 Click the Install button to have Windows search for and start the installation program.

4. Insert the first disk or the CD into the appropriate drive.

5. Click **Next**. Windows looks for the installation program, and reports when it has found it.

6. Click **Finish** to run the installation program, and follow the on-screen prompts for that program.

If Windows can't find your installation program, you can look for it yourself by using My Computer or Windows Explorer. When you locate the file that starts the Setup program, double-click it to start the installation.

Uninstalling Software

Uninstalling software can vary depending on how well the installation program communicated with Windows. As you can see in Figure 14.2, some programs place themselves on your Uninstall list when you install them. Microsoft Office 97, Professional Edition, for example, is on the list in Figure 14.2. To uninstall software on this list, click its name, click the **Add/Remove** button, and follow the prompts.

If you need to uninstall a Windows program that's not on this list, use My Computer or Windows Explorer to browse that program's folder on your hard disk, looking for an Uninstall program. You also can look on the Start menu in that program's submenu; sometimes an Uninstall is listed there that you can run.

Your last resort is to manually delete the program from your hard disk, but this is a poor solution because the program's information remains in your Windows Registry (a system file that tracks what programs and hardware are installed), cluttering it up with outdated data. In time, your Windows Registry file (which must load into memory each time you start Windows) can grow large and cumbersome, increasing the time needed for Windows to start. To delete a program manually, drag its folder into the **Recycle Bin** from Windows Explorer or My Computer. Make sure you have exhausted all other options before using this method.

CAUTION   **Registry Editing?**   You can edit the Windows Registry with a Registry editor program to remove the references to deleted programs, but this is dangerous! You can disable Windows if you delete the wrong thing. Leave Windows Registry editing to experts.

In this lesson, you learned to install and remove programs, including Windows components. In the next lesson, you learn about printing in Windows.

Printing in Windows

15

In this lesson, you learn to check printer installation, add a printer, and manage a print queue.

Checking the Printer Installation

When you installed Windows, Setup configured any printers connected to your computer and created the links to those printers automatically. Before you attempt to print, however, you need to make sure the settings are correct.

To check the print setup from Windows, go to the Printers folder by choosing **Start, Settings, Printers**. The Printers folder appears (see Figure 15.1). Figure 15.1 shows the window with IE 4 installed and the **View**, **As Web Page** option activated. Yours may not have this feature activated, and may look a little different. The basic functionality, however, is the same.

TIP   **No IE 4?**   If you have not installed Internet Explorer 4.0, your default printer also is not identified with a checkmark as shown in Figure 15.1. Select a printer icon and choose **File** to see if that printer is the default printer. You also may right-click any of the printer icons to see a shortcut menu from which you may designate a default printer.

The default printer has a checkmark.

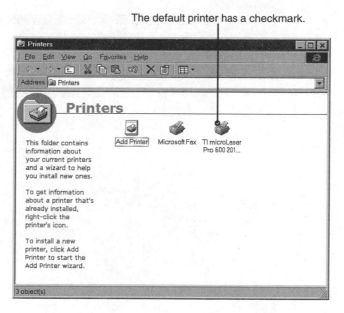

Figure 15.1 The Printers folder. You may have different printers.

 TIP **Easy Access to the Printers Folder** You can access the Printers folder from three other places in Windows: the My Computer window, the bottom of the All Folders list in Windows Explorer, and the Control Panel Printers icon.

From the Printers folder, you can open a Properties dialog box to check the settings for a particular printer. To do so, right-click the **Printer** icon in the Printers window to open its shortcut menu, and then choose **Properties** to display the Properties sheet. (Figure 15.2 shows the Properties sheet for the TI microLaser Pro 600 printer.)

You can choose from the following tabs in the Properties sheet to check the settings.

- The *General* options include the Printer Name, Comments, Separator Page, and Print Test Page.
- The *Details* tab displays the details about your installed printer. On it, you see the port connection to which your printer is attached (listed in the **Print To The Following Port** test box). This port is usually LPT1: (for parallel printers) or COM1: (for serial printers). You also can set your Timeout settings here.

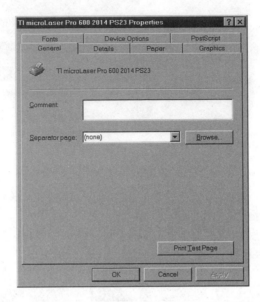

Figure 15.2   The Properties sheet for the TI microLaser Pro 600 printer.

 Printer Port   The connection on your computer to which your printer's cable is attached. If the port description indicates **Not Present**, Windows doesn't detect that port on your computer. Check your printer manual to see whether your printer uses the parallel or serial port.

- The *Paper* options enable you to enter information about the paper size and source and to set the orientation to either Portrait (in which the short side of the paper is the top of the page) or Landscape (in which the long side of the paper is at the top).

- The *Graphics* options enable you to enter information about resolution in dots per inch (dpi—the more dots the finer the resolution), dithering (none, coarse, fine, line art, error diffusion), and intensity (from darkest to lightest). If you have a PostScript printer, you do not see dithering or intensity options.

- The *Fonts* options list the installed printer fonts (if applicable) and enable you to install and remove printer fonts. On a PostScript printer, you can set up a font substitution table that uses the printer's PostScript fonts instead of TrueType (Windows fonts) whenever possible.

- The *Device* options enable you to change the printer memory settings and any other special settings for your printer. Check your printer manual if you are not sure of the amount of memory in your printer.

You may have other tabs too, depending on the printer model. PostScript printers, for example, have a PostScript tab.

After you have all the options set the way you want them, click the **OK** button in the Properties sheet to return to the Printers folder.

Setting a Default Printer

The default printer is the printer that the computer assumes you want to print with unless you select another printer. Windows automatically sets up a default printer when you install Windows. It has a checkmark on its icon, as you saw in Figure 15.1 (if Internet Explorer 4.0 is installed). To set up a default printer, follow these steps:

1. From the Printers folder, double-click the icon that represents the printer you want to set as the default. (Single-click for Web style.) The print queue window opens.

2. In the print queue window, choose the **Printer**, **Set as Default** command to specify the default printer.

3. Close the print queue window.

 TIP **Quick Method** Right-click a printer icon and choose **Set As Default** from the shortcut menu.

Checking Your Equipment

In addition to making sure Windows is ready for printing, you want to check your equipment. Be sure to double-check the following things:

- Is the cable between the computer and the printer securely attached on each end?
- Is the printer on?
- Is the printer ready for the computer's transmission with the Online light on?
- Is paper loaded in the printer?

Adding a Printer

The Add Printer Wizard in the Printers folder lets you add new printers to the list of installed printers available in the Printers folder. This wizard simplifies the process of adding a printer.

To add a new printer, follow these steps:

1. In the Printers window, double-click the **Add Printer** icon. (Single-click for Web style.) The Add Printer Wizard dialog box appears.

2. Click the **Next** button.

3. Select a printer from the **Manufacturers** list box. The wizard displays a list of printer models in the Models list box (see Figure 15.3.)

4. Select a printer model, and click **Next**.

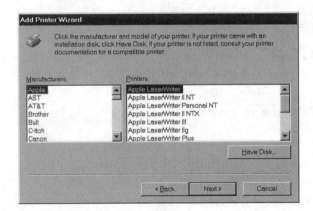

Figure 15.3 Choose the new printer's manufacturer on the left and model on the right.

5. Choose the port to which the printer is connected and click **Next**.

6. Enter a name to display for the printer in the Printer Name text box.

7. If you want this printer to be the default, click the **Yes** button; otherwise, leave No selected. Then click **Next**.

8. When asked whether you want to print a test page, click **Yes** or **No**, and then click **Finish**.

9. If prompted, insert the Windows 95 CD in your CD-ROM drive and click **OK**. Wait for the required files to be copied.

10. Close the Printers window.

TIP **Printer Drivers on Disk** If your printer doesn't appear on the list in steps 3 and 4, but it came with a disk containing drivers, put that disk in the floppy drive at step 4 and click the **Have Disk** button.

Printing from a Windows Application

To print from any Windows application, choose **File**, **Print**. A Print dialog box appears, asking you to specify a number of options. The options available depend on the application. When you click OK in this dialog box, the application hands off the font and file information to the Printers folder. This enables you to continue working in your application while your job is printing. The Printers folder acts as the middleman between your printer and the application from which you are printing.

Checking the Print Queue

When you print a document, the printer usually begins processing the job immediately. But what happens if the printer is working on another job that you (or someone else, if you're working on a network printer) sent? In this case, the Printers folder acts as a print queue and holds the job until the printer is ready for it.

TERM **Print Queue** A holding area for jobs waiting to be printed. If you were to list the contents of the queue, the jobs would appear in the order they were sent to the Printer.

Figure 15.4 shows a document in the print queue. As you can see, the print queue window displays the Document Name, Status, Owner, Progress (pages), and Started At (time and date). Notice also that the printer's status shows that it is printing. This indicates the document was just sent to the queue and is beginning to print.

To display the print queue, follow these steps:

1. Click the **Start** button and choose **Settings**. The Settings menu appears.
2. Choose **Printers**, and the Printers folder appears.
3. Double-click the printer icon for the printer to which you are printing. The print queue window appears with a list of queued documents. If no

103

documents are waiting to print, there won't be any jobs listed below the column headings.

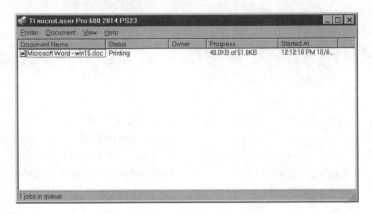

Figure 15.4 The print queue window.

 TIP **Display the Print Queue Quickly** You can check the print queue without opening the Printers folder. Simply double-click the printer icon that appears in the System Tray area (next to the clock in the bottom-right corner of the desktop). If no printer icon is there, no printers have any print jobs pending.

Controlling the Print Job

You can control print jobs after they're in the queue. This includes changing the order in which the jobs print, pausing and resuming the print job, and deleting a job before it prints.

Reordering Jobs in the Queue

To change the order of a job in the queue, drag the job entry to a new position in the list.

 First Come, First Served You can't reorder or place a job before the job that is currently printing.

CAUTION

Pausing and Resuming the Print Queue

You may want to pause the queue and then resume printing later. The paper in the printer, for example, may be misaligned. Pausing the print queue gives you time to correct the problem.

To pause the print queue, choose **Printer**, **Pause Printing** while in the print queue window. To resume printing, choose **Printer**, **Pause Printing** again.

Deleting a Print Job

Sometimes, you send a document to be printed and then change your mind. For example, you may think of other text to add to the document or realize you forgot to spell check your work. In such a case, deleting the print job is easy. Follow these steps:

1. Click the **Start** button and choose **Settings**. The Settings menu appears.
2. Choose **Printers**, and the Printers folder appears.
3. Double-click the printer icon for the printer to which you are printing. The print queue window appears.
4. Select the job you want to delete.
5. Choose **Document**, **Cancel Printing**.

 TIP **Clear the Queue!** To delete all the files in the print queue, choose **Printer**, **Purge Print Jobs** from the print queue menu bar or click the **Close** (X) button in the upper-right corner of the window.

In this lesson, you learned how to set up printers and control print jobs. In the next lesson, you learn how to set up an Internet connection and use Internet Explorer.

Using Internet Explorer

In this lesson, you set up an Internet connection and browse the Web with Internet Explorer 4.0.

Acquiring Internet Explorer 4.0

Windows 95 comes with Internet Explorer 3.0, which is a pretty good Web browser, but Internet Explorer 4.0 is even better. You can download it for free from Microsoft's Web site, as explained in Appendix A, "Installing Microsoft Office 97."

This lesson assumes that you are using Internet Explorer 4.0, because there's little reason not to upgrade to it. If you are using version 3.0, you will still be able to do most of the same things, but the procedures will be a little different in many cases.

Assembling Your Account Information

If you already have an account with an Internet service provider, you need to have some information handy. Make sure you have it ready before you set up your connection in Windows. If you don't have some of this information, contact your ISP (your Internet service provider—the company that provides your Internet service) and ask.

Username and password—for example, fwempen@provider.com.

Local phone number to dial—for example, 555-3948.

Domain Name Server (DNS) address—for example, 349.78.33.78.

Internet Protocol (IP) address—for example, 391.29.495.39.

Name of incoming mail server—for example, pop.provider.com.

Name of outgoing mail server—for example, smtp.provider.com.

Name of news server—for example, news.provider.com.

If you don't already have an account, the Internet Connection Wizard helps you set one up.

Running the Connection Wizard

The Connection Wizard creates a dial-up networking connection that dials your ISP and sends the correct settings that enable you to connect to the Internet. It also configures Outlook Express, the program that manages your e-mail and newsgroups, and Internet Explorer, the program that lets you browse the Web.

Follow these steps:

1. Choose **Start, Programs, Internet Explorer, Connection Wizard**. The Connection Wizard starts.

2. Click **Next** to begin.

3. Choose one of the three options presented:

   - **I Want to Choose an Internet Service Provider and Set Up a New Internet Account.** Choose this if you are starting from scratch, with no account.

   - **I Want to Set Up a New Connection on This Computer to My Existing Internet Account by Using My Phone Line or a Local Area Network (LAN).** Use this if you have an account but have not used it from this computer.

   - **I Already Have an Internet Connection Set Up on This Computer, and I Do Not Want to Change It.** Use this if you already have connected to your account with this computer.

4. Click **Next**.

Depending on which of these options you choose, the Wizard takes different paths at this point. If you choose the first option, it asks for the first three digits of your phone number and your area code, and dials a special number that downloads a list of service providers with a local access number in your area. (This is called the Microsoft Internet Referral Service.)

CAUTION

Not the Only Providers The companies shown by the Microsoft Internet Referral Service have paid a fee to be listed. There may be a good, economical service provider in your area that is not listed there. It may pay to shop around before selecting one of these providers.

If you choose the second option in step 3, you are prompted for information about how you plan to connect (phone line or LAN), and it walks you through creating the appropriate dial-up connection if needed. Just follow the prompts, entering any information for which it asks. When asked about Advanced settings, most people should answer No. Answer Yes only if your service provider has given you something you need to type in when you connect, or a specific IP or DNS address that you need to use every time. (Don't worry about what those are; just ask your service provider whether you need to use them. The Advanced options let you fill in this information.)

If you choose the third option in step 3, the Connection Wizard checks to make sure that the existing connection has all the right stuff, and then quickly ushers you out of the program.

Using the Internet Explorer 4.0 Browser

To use Internet Explorer to browse the Internet, you must have your Internet connection started. (In other words, your modem or LAN must be connecting you.) You can either start this connection before or after you start Internet Explorer. (With a LAN, you are probably always connected, so you don't need to worry about establishing the connection.)

To dial the connection first (assuming you are connecting with a modem), follow these steps:

1. Open **My Computer** and then **Dial-Up Networking**.
2. Double-click the icon for your dial-up connection to your service provider. A dialog box appears showing the ID/password, phone number, and modem to use (see Figure 16.1).
3. Enter any information that's missing (for example, your password), and click **Connect**.
4. Wait until the Connection dialog box disappears and a connection icon appears next to the clock on the taskbar, indicating the connection is active.

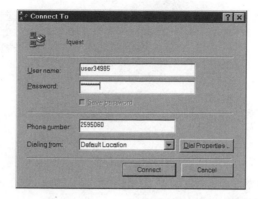

Figure 16.1 You can establish your connection first through dial-up networking.

5. Click the **Internet Explorer** icon on your desktop to open Internet Explorer. (The icon is called The Internet if you are using a version of IE prior to 4.0.)

To open Internet Explorer before establishing your Internet connection, follow these steps:

1. Click the **Internet Explorer** icon on your desktop (or the **The Internet** icon if you have that one instead). If you are not connected, a warning appears to that effect.

CAUTION

IE 4 Not Set Up to Dial? If you see a warning box that says Internet Explorer cannot open the Internet site, and a blank page loads in the browser, perhaps you do not have IE 4 configured to dial. In IE 4, choose **View**, **Internet Options**. Click the **Connection** tab, and make sure that the **Connect to the Internet Using a Modem** option button is selected.

2. Click **Connect** in the warning box. The Dial-Up Connection dialog box appears, as shown in Figure 16.2. It may start dialing automatically; if it doesn't, fill in any missing information, and then click **Connect**.

When the connection is made, Internet Explorer begins loading the Microsoft home page immediately.

Figure 16.2   The Dial-Up Connection dialog box dials your Internet access number and makes the connection.

Browsing with Hyperlinks

On most Web pages, one or more pictures or bits of underlined text are hyperlinks. This means you can click them to jump to other pages. For example, in Figure 16.3, on the Microsoft home page, almost everything you see is a hyperlink.

The mouse pointer turns into a hand when over a hyperlink.

Underlined text is usually a hyperlink.

Figure 16.3   Click hyperlinks to jump to related pages.

Going to a Specific Site

If, for example, someone gives you a Web address (a URL, or Uniform Resource Locator) to investigate, you can type it directly in the Address box located at the top of the screen. In Figure 16.3, for example, you would click the current address (**http://home.microsoft.com**) and type over it. Try **http://www.mcp.com** if you don't have another address handy.

Using Back and Forward

When you are on one page and then you click a hyperlink to move to another page, you are going forward. The Forward button is unavailable because the browser doesn't know where you might be going next. You can return to the last page you previously visited by clicking the **Back** button. When you click Back, the Forward button becomes available because it knows what comes next after the page you are now seeing; you can click **Forward** to return forward.

Notice that both the Back and Forward buttons have down-pointing arrows. Click one of these arrows to open a drop-down list of all the places you have been during this session, and click the one you want. Say, for example, you want to go back to the sixth-most-recent page you have visited. Open the Back drop-down list and choose the sixth page on the list to jump back there, as shown in Figure 16.4.

Returning Home

To return to the home page (the page you started with), click the **Home** button on the Internet Explorer toolbar.

Searching for Sites

If you are looking for information about a particular topic, click the **Search** button. A Search panel appears, as shown in Figure 16.5. Type what you are searching for (for example, Shetland Sheepdogs in Figure 16.5) and click the **Go Get It** button (or **Find**, or **Search**, or whatever the button under the text box is called).

The first time you do something in IE 4 that involves sending data to a site (for example, sending your search words to the search site, as you are doing now), you see a warning that you are sending information to the site. Just click **Yes** to continue.

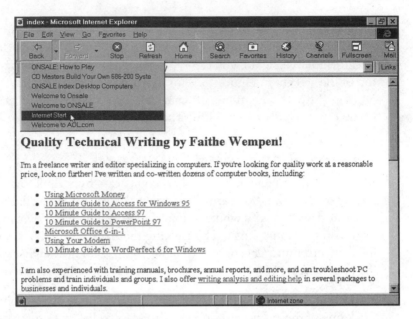

Figure 16.4 Use the Back (or Forward) drop-down list to scan and jump to previously visited pages.

TIP **Different Search Engines** Various companies on the Internet provide Web pages designed for searching other pages; these pages are called search engines. The reason the button name may be different in IE 4 (for example, Find, Search, or Go Get It) is that the Search feature uses a different search engine on different days, to be fair to all the search engine makers. Each search engine has slightly different controls. The one in Figure 16.5 is Lycos (a popular search engine), but you may see a different one. They all work basically the same way.

Internet Explorer shows your results, also in the Search panel. To see the results better, you may want to drag the divider between the browser window and the search panel to give the search panel more room. When you click a hyperlink to show results, the results appear in the Browser window, as shown in Figure 16.6.

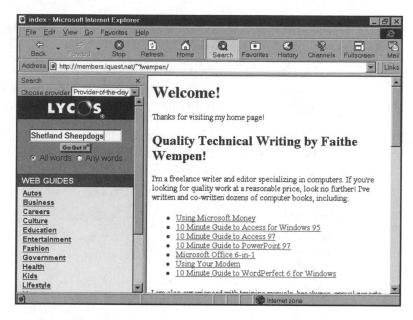

Figure 16.5 Type what you are looking for in the Search panel.

The browser shows the
page for the clicked-on link.

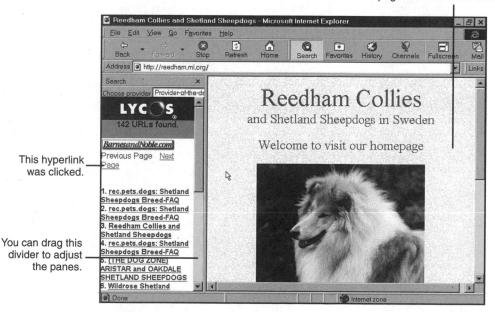

This hyperlink
was clicked.

You can drag this
divider to adjust
the panes.

Figure 16.6 The results of a search.

Accessing Your Computer Through Internet Explorer

If you need to check out a file on your computer while you're using Internet Explorer, just choose **Go**, **My Computer**. Your My Computer window appears in Internet Explorer. To return to Internet Explorer use, click **Back**.

In this lesson, you learned how to connect to the Internet and use Internet Explorer 4.0. In the next lesson, you learn about the Active Desktop and its channels provided by Internet Explorer 4.0.

Working with Channels and Active Content

In this lesson, you learn how to get information you want from the Internet Explorer 4.0/Windows 95 Active desktop.

If you have IE 4 installed, you can use Microsoft's newest Internet feature, the Channel bar, to browse graphical, ever-changing information from a variety of providers, ranging from Warner Brothers to NBC News. (If you don't have IE 4 installed, consider upgrading; see Appendix A, "Installing Microsoft Office 97.")

Using the Channel Bar

The desktop updates with IE 4 provide a Channel bar. You may have noticed it on your desktop as you completed the preceding lessons. Now it's time to explore those channels.

 TERM **Channel** A channel is like a Web site address except that it provides active (changing) content. When you subscribe to a channel, you enable that channel to broadcast new information to your desktop, where it is stored on your hard disk for later offline reading.

If you don't see the Channel bar on-screen, right-click the desktop and choose Properties. Click the **Web** tab, and click to place checkmarks next to **Internet Explorer Channel Bar** and **View My Active Desktop as a Web Page**. Then click **OK**.

Subscribing to Channels

Let's try it out by subscribing to the MSNBC News channel. Follow these steps:

1. Start your Internet connection if it's not already started. (Refer to Lesson 16, "Using Internet Explorer.")

2. Click the **MSNBC News** button on the Channel bar. After a brief animated introduction, a channel browser window opens, as shown in Figure 17.1. This is similar to Internet Explorer but contains a few additional controls.

TIP **First-Time Channel Users** If this is the first time you've used a channel, a dialog box appears asking whether you want more information about channels; if you see it, click **Yes** to see the demo or **No** to continue with these steps.

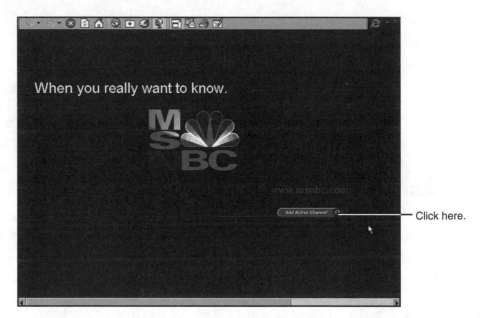

Click here.

Figure 17.1 The first time you visit a channel site, you see a welcome screen inviting you to subscribe.

3. Click the **Add Active Channel** button. The Modify Channel Usage dialog box appears, as shown in Figure 17.2.

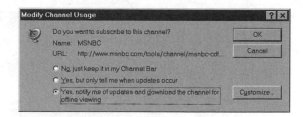

Figure 17.2   Choose how you want your subscription.

4. Click the **Yes, Notify Me of Updates** option button, and then click **OK**.

5. Wait for a different Welcome screen to appear, indicating that you are ready to browse the channel.

With some channels, you may need to make a few more selections the first time you visit the channel. Each channel handles subscription slightly different, but in all cases the prompts on the screen are self-explanatory. For example, after subscribing to the MSNBC News channel, you may see a screen of explanatory text, including a reminder that you must set your browser security settings to medium or lower to use the channel's News Browser feature. (Security settings are covered later in this lesson.)

CAUTION

Downloading Subscriptions   Even though you can begin working with channels almost immediately after subscribing, the actual subscription data may continue to download in the background for quite some time, especially the first time. Before disconnecting your Internet connection, make sure that no Downloading Subscriptions window is still open.

To find out what other channels are available besides those on the Channel bar, subscribe to the **Channel Guide** channel. New channels are added frequently.

Browsing a Channel

When you click a button on the Channel bar for a channel to which you have already subscribed, the channel appears in the channel viewer immediately, and you can browse it like a Web page.

The first time you browse a channel, you may need some special controls. If so, you see a dialog box, like the one in Figure 17.3, asking whether it is okay for them to be downloaded. Click **Yes**. To avoid this dialog box in the future for this channel, click the **"Always Trust"** check box in that dialog box.

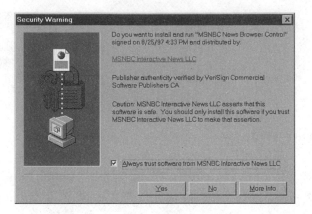

Figure 17.3 If tools are required that your computer does not have installed, you are asked whether you want to download them.

After all the needed controls are in place, the channel content appears, as in Figure 17.4. Figure 17.4 shows a page on the MSNBC News site to which you just subscribed. Just click links as you do in Internet Explorer.

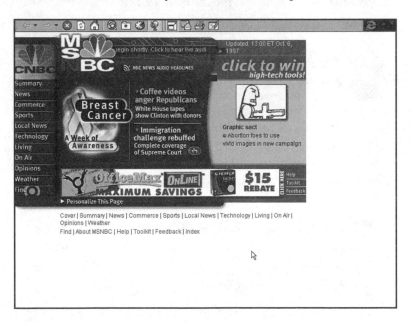

Figure 17.4 A channel is much like a regular Web page after you have subscribed.

TIP **Quick Channel Change** You can change channels quickly by moving the mouse all the way to the left. A channel listing pops up, and you can click a different channel from it.

When you are ready to close the Channel Browser, just click the **Close** (X) button in its top-right corner, the same as with any window.

Updating a Channel's Content

When you update a subscribed channel, you copy any new information needed to your hard disk. To do this, right-click the channel's button on the Channel bar and choose **Update Now**. The Downloading Subscriptions dialog box appears showing the progress made. You can continue using your Internet connection, but do not disconnect until the Downloading Subscriptions dialog box goes away indicating the channel has been updated.

You can start another channel updating before the first one has finished; it will be added to the queue. The Update Now command is not available on the channel's shortcut menu unless you have already subscribed to it.

You also can update all subscriptions at once. From Internet Explorer, choose **Favorites, Update All Subscriptions**.

TIP **Automatic Channel Updates** To set a channel to update automatically, view the Subscriptions window (choose **Favorites, Manage Subscriptions** from Internet Explorer) and then right-click that channel and choose **Proper-ties.** Click the **Schedule** tab. Click **Custom Schedule** and enter a time interval at which to do updates.

Managing Your Subscriptions

You may decide you want to change or delete some subscriptions. To do this from Internet Explorer, choose **Favorites, Manage Subscriptions**. The Manage Subscriptions dialog box opens (see Figure 17.5.)

To remove a channel, point to it to select it and then choose **File, Delete**. You also can change the way the channel behaves by right-clicking it and choosing **Properties**. Make changes to the channel's setting in its Properties dialog box and then click **OK**.

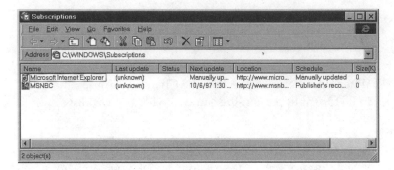

Figure 17.5 You can modify and delete subscriptions in this dialog box.

Removing Buttons from the Channel Bar

You may want to remove some of the buttons from the Channel bar to make room for the channels in which you are interested. The default buttons on the Channel bar are merely pointers to the sites where you can subscribe to certain popular channels. If, for example, you hate sports, you might want to remove the Sports button from your Channel bar.

To remove a button from the Channel bar, right-click it and choose **Delete**. At the warning message, click **Yes**.

Altering Security Settings

If you get a message while working with a channel that your security settings are preventing information from being displayed, you should change it in Internet Explorer. Follow these steps:

1. Close the channel browser window.
2. Double-click the **Internet Explorer** icon on the desktop.
3. Open the **View** menu and choose **Internet Options**.
4. Click the **Security** tab.
5. Make sure the Zone drop-down list is set to **Internet Zone**.
6. Click the **Medium** option button.
7. Click **OK**.

Working Offline

Some people like to work offline as much as possible to save on phone charges or online service fees. To work offline, open the **File** menu in Internet Explorer (or the Subscriptions window, or any of several other windows that have it) and select **Work Offline**. With Work Offline checked, Windows does not attempt to dial your Internet connection when you open a channel or a Web page. Instead, it loads the most recent information for that channel or page from your hard disk.

If you try to access a part of the channel that has not been downloaded to your computer, you see a dialog box giving you the choice of staying offline or connecting to retrieve that content.

Adding Active Desktop Controls

The Channel bar is only one of many Active Desktop controls you can use. To get and use others, follow these steps:

1. Right-click the desktop and choose **Properties**. The Display Properties dialog box opens.
2. Click the **Web** tab. The Items on the Active Desktop list show your current controls. By default, the Internet Explorer Channel bar is the only one.
3. Click **New**. A dialog box appears asking you whether you want to connect to the Microsoft Web site to install new Active Desktop items.
4. Click **Yes**. If you are not already connected to the Web, the Connection Manager connects you and Internet Explorer opens to show the Active Desktop Gallery site (see Figure 17.6).
5. Click a control that looks interesting (for example, MSN Investor Ticker). A description of it appears.
6. Click the **Add to my Desktop** button. A confirmation box appears.
7. Click **OK**. The control downloads to your PC.
8. Download more controls, or close Internet Explorer when you're finished. The new control appears on your desktop.
9. Right-click the desktop again and choose **Properties**, and click the **Web** tab again.
10. Place or remove checkmarks next to the controls that you want displayed on your desktop now. You don't have to have all controls displayed at all times. Then click **OK**.

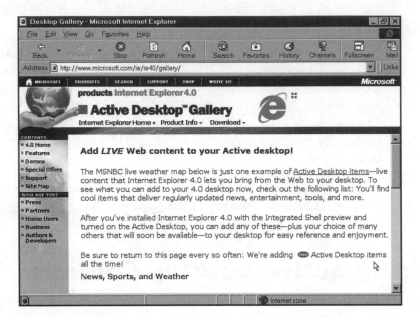

Figure 17.6 Microsoft provides extra controls for your Active Desktop.

In this lesson, you learned about subscriptions and Active Desktop controls.

Word

Getting Started with Word

In this lesson, you learn how to start and exit Word, identify the parts of the Word screen, and the basics of entering text.

Starting Word for Windows

You start Word from the Windows Start menu. Follow these steps:

1. Open the Start menu by clicking the **Start** button.
2. On the Start menu, click **Programs**.
3. On the next menu, click **Microsoft Word**.

Another way to start Word is to open the Start menu and click **New Office Document**. Or, if the Office Shortcut Bar is displayed along the right edge of your screen, click the **New Office Document** button. Either way, the New Office Document dialog box appears. In this dialog box, click the **General** tab (if necessary), and then double-click the **Blank Document** icon.

Can't Find Microsoft Word on the Menu? You must install Word (or Office) on your system before you can use it. Refer to Appendix A, "Installing Microsoft Office 97" for installation instructions.

Understanding the Word Screen

When you start Word, you see a blank document ready for you to enter text. Before you begin, however, you need to know about the various parts of the screen (see Figure 1.1). You'll use these screen elements, described in Table 1.1, as you work on your documents.

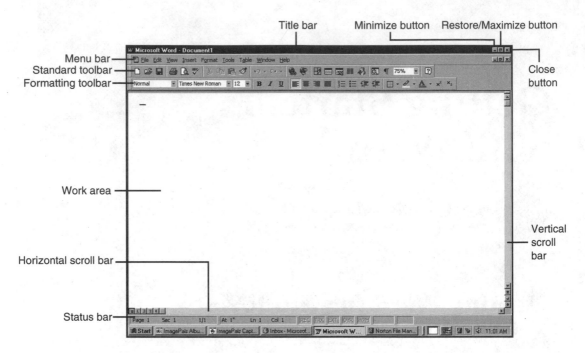

Figure 1.1 Word's opening screen is a blank document.

Table 1.1 Parts of the Word Screen

Screen Element	Function
Work area	Your document displays here for text entry and editing. Figure 1.1 shows a blank document.
Title bar	The program name, user name, and the name of the current document display here. At the right end of the title bar are buttons to minimize, restore, and close the program.
Menu bar	Menu headings on this bar let you access Word's menu commands.
Toolbars	The small pictures, or *buttons,* on the toolbars let you select commonly needed commands by clicking the mouse.
Status bar	Word displays information about the document and the state of the keyboard lock keys on the status bar.

Screen Element	Function
Scroll bars	Click the scroll bars to move around in your document.
Minimize button	Click this button to temporarily hide Word (to shrink it to an icon on the taskbar). You can then click the Microsoft Word button on the taskbar at the bottom of your screen to redisplay Word.
Close button	Click this button to close Word.
Restore/Maximize button	Click this button to enlarge Word to full-screen or to shrink Word to a partial-screen window.

Using Menus and Toolbars

As you use Word, you will issue commands to tell Word what actions you want done. You can carry out most Word commands using either the menus or the toolbars. The method you use depends on your personal preference.

To select a menu command:

1. Open a menu by clicking the menu title on the menu bar. You can also open a menu by holding down the **Alt** key and pressing the underlined letter in the menu title. For example, press **Alt+F** (hold down **Alt** and press **F**) to open the File menu.

2. With the menu open, click the desired command or press the underlined letter of the command name.

Throughout this book, a shorthand method of specifying menu commands is used. For example, click **File, Open,** means open the File menu and select the Open command.

CAUTION

Change Your Mind?   If you change your mind about a menu command, press the **Esc** key twice or click anywhere outside the menu to close the menu without making a selection.

Figure 1.2 shows the open File menu. Word uses several elements on its menus to provide you with additional information. Table 1.2 explains these elements.

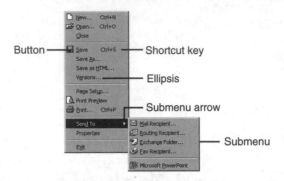

Figure 1.2 The File menu with the Send To submenu displayed.

Table 1.2 Parts of a Menu

Menu Element	Function
Button	If the menu command has a corresponding toolbar button, the button is displayed next to the menu command.
Ellipsis (...)	Indicates that the menu command leads to a dialog box.
Submenu arrow	Indicates that the menu command leads to another menu (called a submenu).
Shortcut key	Identifies the keys you can use to select the menu command using the keyboard.

You can use shortcut keys to select some commands without using the menus at all. Shortcuts keys are listed on the menu next to the corresponding command. In Figure 1.2, for example, you can see that the shortcut key for the Open command is Ctrl+O. This means that pressing Ctrl+O (press and hold the **Ctrl** key, press the **O** key, and then release both keys) has the same effect as clicking **File**, **Open**.

To use the toolbars, simply use your mouse to click the desired button. The buttons have pictures on them to help you identify each button's function. You can jog your memory by resting the mouse cursor on a button for a few seconds without clicking. Word will display a ScreenTip next to the button identifying its function.

CAUTION

What's This?   Press **Shift+F1** to activate What's This? help. Then click any element on the Word screen to view information about it.

Working in Dialog Boxes

Many of Word's commands result in a dialog box. Word uses dialog boxes to obtain additional information required to carry out a command. Each dialog box is different, but they all use the same basic elements.

In a dialog box, press the **Tab** key to move from item to item; press **Shift+Tab** to move backward. You can click an item or press **Alt** plus the underlined letter to select an item. When the dialog box selections are complete, press **Enter** or click the **OK** button to accept your entries and carry out the command. Click the **Cancel** button or press **Esc** to close the dialog box without carrying out the command.

Entering Text and Moving Around

Word displays a blinking vertical line in the work area. This is the *cursor* or *insertion point*, and it identifies the location in the document where text will be inserted and where certain editing actions will occur. To enter text, simply type it on the keyboard. You should not press Enter at the end of a line—Word will automatically wrap the text to a new line when you reach the right margin. Only press Enter when you want to start a new paragraph.

If you make a mistake, you can delete by:

- Pressing the **Backspace** key to erase characters to the left of the cursor.
- Pressing the **Delete** key to erase characters to the right of the cursor.

You can move the cursor around to add and edit text in different document locations. Table 1.3 describes the basic cursor movements.

Table 1.3 Moving the Cursor

To Move the Cursor...	Do This...
To any visible location	Click in the location
One character right or left	Press the right or left arrow key
One line up or down	Press the up or down arrow key
To the start or end of the line	Press the **Home** or **End** key
To the start or end of the document	Hold the **Ctrl** key and press **Home** or **End**

You'll learn more about moving around Word in Lesson 3, "Basic Editing Tasks."

Quitting the Program

When you are finished working with Word, you have several options for exiting the program. All these methods have the same result:

- Click **File**, **Exit**.
- Press **Alt+F4**.
- Click the **Close** (X) button at the right end of the title bar.

If you are saving the document for the first time, Word prompts you to save it before exiting. For now, you can just select **No**. You'll learn about saving documents in Lesson 4, "Saving and Opening Documents."

In this lesson, you learned how to start and exit Word, how to use menus and toolbars, and you learned about the basics of entering and editing text. The next lesson shows you how to create a new Word document.

Creating a New Document

In this lesson, you learn how to create a new Word document and about
the relationship between documents and templates. You also learn how to use wizards.

Understanding Document Templates

To work effectively with Word, you must understand that every Word document is based on a *template*. As the name suggests, a template is a model for a document.

 Document Template A model for a new document that may contain text and/or formatting.

Some templates contain no text, giving you a blank document with some basic formatting specifications in which you are responsible for entering all the text. Other templates contain text and/or detailed formatting specifications. For example, if you write a lot of business letters, you could use a template that contains the date, your return address, and a closing salutation. When you create a new document based on that template, all those elements will automatically be in the document—all you need to do is add the other parts. If a template contains formatting, all documents based on that template will have a uniform appearance (for example, the same font and margins).

Word comes with a variety of predefined templates that are ready for you to use. These templates cover a range of common document needs, such as fax forms, memos, business letters, and Web pages. You can also create your own templates. In this lesson, you will learn how to use Word's predefined templates. Lesson 15, "Page Numbers, Headers, and Footers," shows you how to create your own templates.

Starting a New Document

Many of the documents you create will be based on the Normal (Blank Document) template, which creates a blank document. As you learned in Lesson 1, "Getting Started with Word," when you start Word it automatically opens a blank document for you. If Word is already running, you can create a blank document by clicking the **New** button on the toolbar.

To start a document based on another non-blank template, follow these steps:

1. Click **File**, **New**. The New dialog box appears (see Figure 2.1).

2. The tabs along the top of the dialog box list the different template categories. Click the tab corresponding to the category of document you want to create.

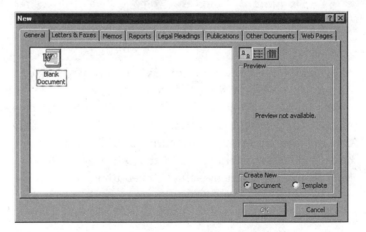

Figure 2.1 The New dialog box.

3. Click the icon that corresponds to the template you want. If a preview of the template's appearance is available, it will appear in the Preview area.

4. Click **OK**. Word creates the document and displays it, ready for editing.

When you create a document based on a template, the template's text and formatting will be displayed in the new document. There's nothing special about document text that came from a template—you can edit it just like any other text. You can also edit the actual templates, as you'll learn in Lesson 15.

 TIP **Word on the Web: Web Templates** Select the **Web Pages** tab in the New dialog box for templates that are useful for Web documents.

Some templates contain *placeholder* text that you must replace. For example, the résumé templates contain a dummy name and biography that you must delete and replace with your own information. The document might display text such as **[Click here and type your name]**. Simply follow the instructions displayed in brackets.

 No Templates? If you can't find any templates except Blank Document, they probably were not installed with Word. You can reinstall Word, choose the **Custom Setup** installation option, and specify which templates you want installed.

CAUTION

Using Wizards

Some of Word's templates are a special kind of template called a *wizard*. Whereas a standard template is a static combination of text and formatting, a wizard is an active tool that asks you questions about the document you want to create, and then uses your answers to create the new document. When you're starting a new document, you can recognize a wizard in the New dialog box by its title and the small "magic wand" in its icon.

Each wizard is unique, but they all follow the same basic procedures. Wizards have multiple steps; each step asks you for certain information about the document you want to create. Figure 2.2 shows an example; this is a step in the Fax Wizard.

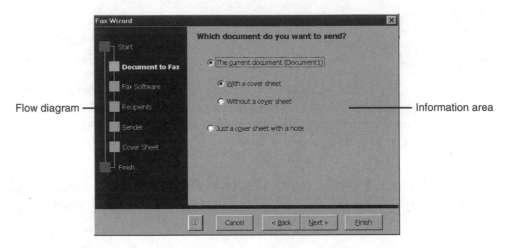

Flow diagram ——— | ——— Information area

Figure 2.2 The Fax Wizard dialog box.

Table 2.1 describes the different components of a wizard dialog box.

Table 2.1 The Parts of a Wizard Dialog Box

Wizard Component	*Function*
Title bar	Shows the name of the wizard that is running.
Flow diagram	Graphically represents the wizard steps, with the current step highlighted. Click any step to go directly to it.
Information area	Requests document information from you.
Cancel button	Cancels the wizard without creating a new document.
Back button	Moves to the previous wizard step.
Next Button	Moves to the next wizard step.
Finish button	Ends the wizard and creates the new document based on the information you have entered so far.
Help button	Click to display Help information about using the wizard.

To create a new document using a wizard, follow these steps:

1. Click **File**, **New** to open the New dialog box (refer to Figure 2.1).
2. Click the tab corresponding to the category of document you are creating. (Not all tabs contain wizards, however.)

3. Click the icon of the wizard you want to use and click **OK**.

4. In the wizard dialog box, enter the information Word needs, based on how you want the document created. Then click **Next**.

5. Repeat step 4 for each of the wizard steps. If needed, click **Back** one or more times to return to an earlier step to make changes in the information.

6. In the last wizard step, click **Finish** to close the wizard and create the new document.

 TIP **Know Your Templates** Spend some time becoming familiar with Word's various predefined templates; they can save you a lot of time.

In this lesson, you learned about document templates and how to create a new document. You also learned how to use wizards. The next lesson teaches you how to perform basic editing tasks in Word.

Basic Editing Tasks

In this lesson, you learn how to enter text, move around in a document, and perform other basic editing tasks.

Entering Text

When you start a new Word document based on the Normal template, you see a blank work area that contains only two items:

- **Blinking vertical line**   This is the cursor, or insertion point, which marks the location where text you type appears in the document and where certain editing actions occur.
- **Horizontal line**   This marks the end of the document.

In a new empty document, these two markers are at the same location. To enter text, simply type it using the keyboard. As you type, the text appears, and the insertion point moves to the right. If the line of text reaches the right edge of the screen, Word automatically starts a new line; this is called *word wrapping*. Do not press Enter unless you want to start a new paragraph. If you enter more lines than will fit on the screen, Word scrolls previously entered text upward to keep the cursor in view. Figure 3.1 shows word wrap and the end of document marker and cursor.

 TIP   **Leave It to Word Wrap**   Press Enter only when you want to start a new paragraph.

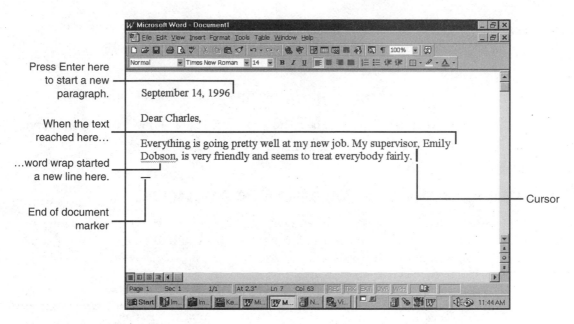

Figure 3.1 Using Enter and word wrap.

Paragraphs in Word

The idea of paragraphs is important in Word because certain types of formatting apply to individual paragraphs. In Word, you end one paragraph and start a new one by pressing **Enter**. Word inserts a new, blank line and positions the cursor at the beginning of it.

On your screen, the result may look the same as if word wrap had started the new line, but the difference is that Word has inserted a *paragraph mark*. These marks are normally invisible, but you can display them by clicking the **Show/Hide ¶** button on the Standard toolbar. Click the button again to hide the marks. This tool is very useful when you need to see exactly where the paragraphs begin and end in your document.

TIP **Other Marks?** When you display paragraph marks, Word also displays dots for spaces and arrows for tabs.

To combine two paragraphs into a single paragraph, follow these steps:

1. Move the cursor to the beginning of the first line of the second paragraph.
2. Press **Backspace** to delete the paragraph mark.

Moving Around in the Document

As you work on a document, you will often have to move the cursor to view or work on other parts of the text. Most of the time you'll use the keyboard to do that, as explained in Table 3.1.

Table 3.1 Moving the Cursor with the Keyboard

To Move...	Perform This Action...
Left or right one character	Press ← or →
Left or right one word	Press **Ctrl+←** or **Ctrl+→**
Up or down one line	Press ↑ or ↓
Up or down one paragraph	Press **Ctrl+↑** or **Ctrl+↓**
To the start or end of a line	Press **Home** or **End**
Up or down one screen	Press **Page Up** or **Page Down**
To the top or bottom of the current screen	Press **Ctrl+Page Up** or **Ctrl+Page Down**
To the start or end of the document	Press **Ctrl+Home** or **Ctrl+End**

You can also navigate with the mouse. If the desired cursor location is in view on the screen, simply click the location. If the desired location is not in view, you must scroll to bring it into view and then click the location. Table 3.2 describes how to scroll with the mouse.

Table 3.2 Scrolling with the Mouse

To Scroll...	Do This...
Up or down one line	Click the up or down arrow on the vertical scroll bar.
Up or down one screen	Click the vertical scroll bar between the box and the up or down arrow.
Up or down any amount	Drag the scroll box up or down.
Up or down one page	Click the Previous Page or Next Page button on the vertical scroll bar.

Note that scrolling with the mouse does not move the cursor; the cursor remains in its original location while the screen displays another part of the document. You must click the new location to move the cursor there.

TIP **Quick Go To** Press **Shift+F5** one or more times to move the cursor to locations in the document that you edited most recently.

Selecting Text

Many tasks you'll perform in Word require that you first select the text you want to modify. For example, to underline a sentence, you must select the sentence first and then click the **Underline** button. Selected text appears on the screen in reverse video, as shown in Figure 3.2, which has the phrase **Dear Ms. Kennedy:** selected.

You can select text with either the mouse or the keyboard. With the mouse, you can use the selection bar, an unmarked column in the left document margin. When the mouse pointer moves from the document to the selection bar, it changes from an I-beam to an arrow pointing up and to the right. Table 3.3 lists the methods you can use to select text.

TIP To select text quickly, place the insertion point where you want to start highlighting and then, holding down the Shift key, press the arrow key to extend the highlight in the direction you want to go. You can select one line at a time by pressing the down or up arrow keys as you press the Shift key. By holding down the Shift key and clicking with the mouse, you can select where you want the highlighting to extend.

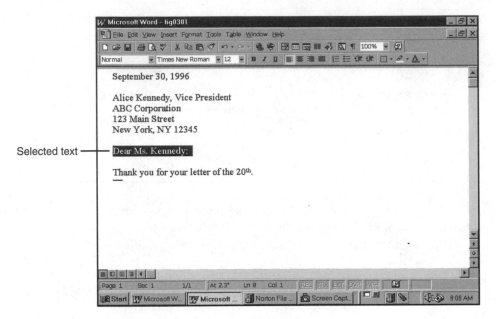

Selected text ——

Figure 3.2 Selected text appears in reverse video.

Table 3.3 Methods of Selecting Text

To Select Text...	*Perform This Action with the Mouse...*
Any amount	Point at the start of the text, press and hold the left mouse button, and drag the highlight over the text.
One word	Double-click anywhere on the word.
One sentence	Press and hold **Ctrl** and click anywhere in the sentence.
One line	Click the selection bar next to the line.
Multiple lines	Drag in the selection bar next to the lines.
One paragraph	Double-click the selection bar next to the paragraph.
Entire document	Press and hold **Ctrl** and click anywhere in the selection bar or press **Ctrl+A**.
Any amount	Move the insertion point to the start of the text, press and hold **Shift**, and move the insertion point to the end of the desired text using the movement keys described in Table 3.1.

To cancel a selection, click anywhere on the screen or use the keyboard to move the insertion point.

 TIP **Fast Select** Double-click a word to select it quickly. Hold **Ctrl** and double-click to select an entire sentence.

When you are selecting text by dragging with the mouse, Word's default is to automatically select entire words. If you need to select partial words you can turn this option off (or back on) as described here:

1. Click **Tools, Options** to open the Options dialog box.
2. Click the **Edit** tab.
3. Click the **When Selecting, Automatically Select Entire Word** check box to turn it on or off.
4. Click **OK**.

Deleting, Copying, and Pasting Text

You have already learned how to use the Delete and Backspace keys to delete single characters. In addition, you can delete larger amounts of text, and you can move or copy text from one document location to another.

To delete a block of text, first select the text. Then do one of these things:

- To delete the text, press **Delete** or **Backspace**.
- To delete the text and replace it with new text, type the new text.

To move or copy text, start by selecting the text. Then follow these steps:

 1. To copy the text, click **Edit, Copy**; or click the **Copy** button on the Standard toolbar; or press **Ctrl+C**.

 To move the text, click **Edit, Cut**; or click the **Cut** button on the Standard toolbar; or press **Ctrl+X**.

2. Move the cursor to the location where you want the text moved or copied.

 3. Click **Edit, Paste**; or click the **Paste** button on the Standard toolbar; or press **Ctrl+V**.

You also can use the mouse to move and copy text. This technique, called drag-and-drop, is most convenient for small amounts of text and when both the "from" and "to" locations are visible on-screen. Here's how you drag-and-drop:

1. Select the text.
2. Point at the text with the mouse. The mouse pointer changes from an I-beam to an arrow.
3. To copy the text, press and hold **Ctrl**. To move the text, do not press any key.
4. Drag to the new location. As you drag, a vertical dotted line indicates the text's new location.
5. Release the mouse button and, if you are copying, the Ctrl key.

CAUTION

Make a Mistake? You can recover from most editing actions (such as deleting text) by clicking **Edit**, **Undo** or by pressing **Ctrl+Z**.

In this lesson, you learned how to enter text, move around the document, and perform other basic editing tasks. In the next lesson, you'll learn how to save and retrieve documents.

Saving and Opening Documents

In this lesson, you learn how to name your document, save it to disk, and enter summary information. You also learn how to open a document you saved earlier.

Saving a New Document

When you create a new document in Word, it is stored temporarily in your computer's memory under the default name Document*n*, where *n* is a number that increases by 1 for each new unnamed document. Word only "remembers" the document until you quit the program or turn off the computer. To save a document permanently so that you can retrieve it later, you must assign a name and save it to disk. These steps show you how to do that.

1. Click **File**, **Save** or click the **Save** button on the Standard toolbar. The Save As dialog box appears (see Figure 4.1).

2. In the **File Name** text box, enter the name you want to assign to the document file. The name can be up to 256 characters long and should be descriptive of the document's contents.

3. If you want to save the document in a different folder or drive, click the **Save In** drop-down arrow and select a different folder and/or drive.

4. Click **Save**. The document is saved to disk, and the name you assigned appears in the title bar.

Save In list box

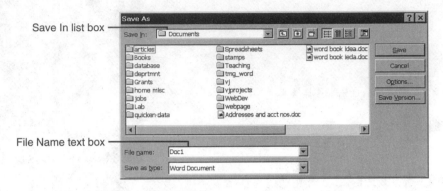

File Name text box

Figure 4.1 The Save As dialog box.

TIP **Word on the Web** Documents you make publicly available on your Web site must be saved in Hypertext Markup Language (HTML) format. Word provides a separate command for saving in this format: **File**, **Save as HTML**.

Saving a Document As You Work

After naming and saving a document, you still need to save it periodically as you work to minimize data loss in the event of a power failure or other system problem. After you name a document, you can easily save the current version:

- Click **File**, **Save**.
- Click the **Save** button on the Standard toolbar.
- Press **Ctrl+S**.

Word automatically saves the document with its current name, and no dialog boxes appear.

TIP **Don't Forget!** Save your document regularly as you work on it. If you don't, you may lose your work if there is a power outage or other problem.

Changing a Document's Name

After you name a document, you may need to change its name. For example, you might want to keep an old version of a document under its original name and then save a revised version under a new name. To change a document name, follow these steps:

1. Click **File**, **Save As**. The Save As dialog box appears, showing the current document name in the File Name text box.

2. In the **File Name** text box, change the filename to the new name.

3. (Optional) Select a different folder in the **Save In** list box to save the document in a different folder.

4. Click **Save**, and Word saves the document under the new name.

You can also change the format in which the file is saved by choosing a different format from the **Save As Type** drop-down list. You might do this, for example, if you need to give the file to a coworker who has a different version of Word or a different word processing program.

 TIP When you choose Word 6.0/95 format from the **Save As Type** drop-down list, Word actually saves the file in RTF (Rich Text Format). When the recipient of the file opens it, the file will open but it will appear to be in the RTF format rather than the native 6.0 or 95. If this bothers you, you can download the Microsoft Office Service Release 1 patch from the Microsoft Web site (**http://www.microsoft.com/office/office97/servicerelease/default.htm**), which includes a fix that makes Word 97 save Word 6.0/95 documents in their true format.

Using Document Properties

Every Word document has a set of properties that provide information about the document. Some properties contain summary information that you enter, while others contain information that is automatically generated by Word. To enter or view a document's properties, follow these steps:

1. Click **File**, **Properties** to open the Properties dialog box.

2. Click the **Summary** tab, and you'll see the options shown in Figure 4.2.

3. Enter or edit any summary information you want. These are the summary information properties you will use most often:

Title   Enter the title of the document. This is not the same as the document's filename.

Subject   Enter a phrase that describes the subject of the document.

Author   Word automatically fills this field with the username you entered when you installed the program. You can change it if necessary.

Manager   Enter your manager's name, if applicable.

Company   Your company name. This may be automatically entered for you based on your Windows installation.

Category   Enter a word or phrase that describes the type of document.

Keywords   Enter one or more words related to the document contents.

Comments   Enter any additional information you want saved with the document.

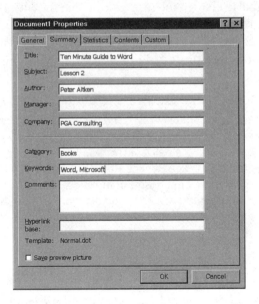

Figure 4.2   Entering document summary information.

4. Click **OK**. Word saves the document properties along with the document.

Word automatically generates useful statistics about each document, such as the number of words it contains and the date and time the document was created. To view a document's statistics, select the **File**, **Properties** command and click the **Statistics** tab.

TIP **Quick Word Count** To get a quick count of the words and other elements in your document, click **Tools**, **Word Count**.

Opening a Document

You can open any document created with Word for Windows to continue working on it. You also can open documents that were created with other programs, such as WordPerfect.

To open an existing file, click **File**, **Open** or click the **Open** button on the Standard toolbar. The Open dialog box appears (see Figure 4.3).

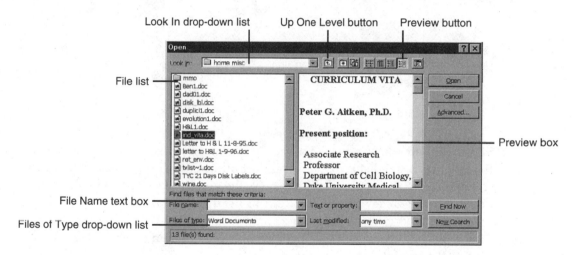

Figure 4.3 The Open dialog box.

The file list shows all the Word documents and folders in the current folder. Each document is represented by a small page icon that appears next to its name; folders have a file folder icon next to them. The Look In list box shows the name of the current folder. You can take the following actions in the Open dialog box:

- To open a file, click its name in the file list or type its name into the **File Name** list box; then press **Enter** or click the **Open** button. Or you can double-click the filename.

- To preview the contents of a file, click the filename, and then click the **Preview** button. Click the **Preview** button again to turn preview off.

- To look for files other than Word documents, click the **Files of Type** drop-down arrow and select the desired document type.

- To move up one folder, click the **Up One Level** button.

- To move down one level to a different folder, double-click the folder name in the file list.

- To move to another folder, click the **Look In** drop-down arrow and select the desired folder.

Folder   Windows uses folders to organize files on a disk. Before Windows 95, folders were called subdirectories.

Word on the Web   To open a Web document for editing in Word, select **HTML Document** from the **Files of Type** list. Then select the document and click Open.

To quickly open a document you recently worked on, you can use Word's Recently Used File List instead of the Open dialog box. To view this list, open the **File** menu. The list is displayed at the bottom of the menu just above the Exit command. To open a file on the list, press the number corresponding to the file, or click the filename with the mouse. This list displays the document files that you have saved most recently. If you have just installed Word, there will be no files displayed here, of course. If you have saved files and the list still doesn't display them, see the next paragraph.

You can control how many files appear on the Recently Used File List and whether the list appears at all. Click **Tools**, **Options** to open the Options dialog box. Click the **General** tab if necessary. Click the **Recently Used File List** check box to turn it on or off to control the display of the list. To change the number of files displayed in the list, enter a number in the **Entries** text box or click the up/down arrows to change the existing entry. Click **OK** when you're finished.

TIP   **Quick Open**   You can open a Word document (and start Word if it is not already running) by double-clicking the document name or icon in the Windows Explorer or My Computer window.

In this lesson, you learned how to name your document, save it to disk, and enter summary information. You also learned how to open a document you saved earlier. The next lesson shows you how to find and replace text.

Finding and Replacing Text

In this lesson, you learn how to find specific text in your document, and how to automatically replace it with new text.

Searching for Text

Word can search through your document to find occurrences of specific text. Word's default is to search the entire document; that's what it does unless you select some text before you issue the command. If you select text first, it searches only the selected text.

To search for specific text, select a block of text (if necessary). Then follow these steps:

1. Click **Edit**, **Find** or press **Ctrl+F**. The Find dialog box appears (see Figure 5.1).

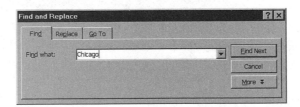

Figure 5.1   The Find tab in the Find and Replace dialog box.

2. In the **Find What** text box, enter the text for which you want to search . The text you enter is called the *search template*.

3. Click **Find Next**. Word looks through the document for text that matches the search template. If it finds matching text, it highlights it in the document and stops; the Find dialog box remains on-screen.

4. Click **Find Next** to continue the search for other instances of the search template. Or, press **Esc** to close the dialog box and return to the document. The found text remains selected.

When Word finishes searching the entire document, it displays one of two messages. It will inform you that the search template cannot be found, or it will let you know the search is complete.

TIP **Repeat Searches** When you open the Find dialog box, the previous search template (if there was one) will still be displayed in the **Find What** text box. This makes it easy to repeat the previous search.

TERM **Search Template** The search template is the model for the text you want to find.

Using Search Options

The default Find operation locates the search template you specify without regard to the case of letters or whether it's a whole word or part of a word. For example, if you enter the search template "the," Word will find "the," "THE," "mother," and so on. You can refine your search by using Word's search options. To do so, click the **More** button in the Find dialog box. The dialog box expands to offer additional options (see Figure 5.2).

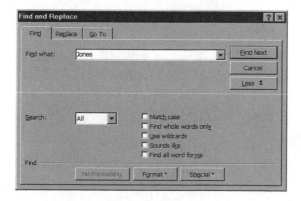

Figure 5.2 Setting options for the Find command.

You can choose from the following options:

- **Match Case**   Requires an exact match for uppercase and lowercase letters. By selecting this check box, "The" will match only "The" and not "the" or "THE."
- **Find Whole Words Only**   This will match whole words only. If you select this check box, "the" will match only "the"—not "mother," "these," and so on.
- **Use Wildcards**   Permits the use of the * and ? wildcards in the search template. The * wildcard stands in for any sequence of 0 or more unknown characters; the ? wildcard stands in for any single unknown character. Thus the template "th?n" would match "thin" and "then" but not "thrown" or "thn." And the template "th*n" would match "thin," "thn," "thrown," and so on.
- **Sounds Like**   Finds words that sound similar to the template. If you select this check box, for example, "their" will match "there."
- **Find All Word Forms**   Locates alternate forms of the search template. For example, "sit" will match not only "sit" but also "sat" and "sitting." This check box is not available if you select the Use Wildcards check box.

To control the extent of the search, click the **Search** drop-down arrow and select one of the following options:

- **All**   Searches the entire document.
- **Down**   Searches from the cursor to the end of the document.
- **Up**   Searches from the cursor to the start of the document.

TIP   After you have set the advanced search options, you may want to click the **Less** button to shrink the size of the Find and Replace dialog box before you begin the search. That way the dialog box takes up less room, and you are less likely to have to drag the dialog box out of the way to see the found text.

Can't Find It?   If you can't find text that you're sure is in the document, check the spelling of the search template and make sure unwanted search options are not enabled.

CAUTION

Finding and Replacing Text

Word's Replace command lets you search for instances of text and replace them with new text. This can be very helpful if, for example, you misspelled the same word multiple times in the same document. To replace text, follow these steps:

1. Click **Edit, Replace** or press **Ctrl+H**. The Replace dialog box appears (see Figure 5.3).

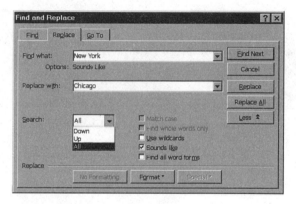

Figure 5.3 The Replace tab in the Find and Replace dialog box.

TIP   **Find or Replace**   You can access the Find dialog box from the Replace dialog box (and vice versa) by clicking the corresponding tab.

2. In the **Find What** text box, enter the text you want to replace.
3. In the **Replace With** text box, enter the replacement text.
4. (Optional) Click the **More** button and specify search options as explained in the previous section.
5. Click **Find Next** to locate and highlight the first instance of the target text.
6. For each occurrence Word finds, respond using one of these buttons:
   - Click **Replace** to replace the highlighted instance of the target text and then locate the next instance of it.
   - Click **Find Next** to leave the highlighted instance of the target text unchanged and to locate the next instance.

- Click **Replace All** to replace all instances of the target text in the entire document.

 TIP   **Deleting Text**   To delete the target text, follow the previous steps but leave the Replace With text box empty.

CAUTION   **Recovery!**   If you make a mistake replacing text, you can recover by clicking **Edit, Undo Replace**.

In this lesson, you learned how to search for and replace text in your document. In the next lesson, you will learn about Word's screen display options.

Screen Display Options

In this lesson, you learn how to control the Word screen display to suit your working style.

Document Display Options

Word offers several ways to display your document. Each of these views is designed to make certain editing tasks easier. The available views include:

- **Normal**   Best for general editing tasks.
- **Page Layout**   Ideal for working with formatting and page layout.
- **Online Layout**   Optimized for viewing on-screen.
- **Outline**   Designed for working with outlines.
- **Master Document**   Designed for managing large, multi-part projects.

The view you use has no effect on the contents of your document or on the way it will look when printed. They affect only the way the document appears on-screen.

Normal View

Normal view is suitable for most editing tasks; it is the view you will probably use most often. This is Word's default view. All special formatting is visible on-screen, including different font sizes, italic, boldface, and other enhancements. The screen display of your document is essentially identical to how the document will appear when printed. However, Word does not display certain aspects of the page layout, which makes it easier and quicker for you to edit. For example, you do not see headers and footers or multiple columns.

 To select Normal view, click **View**, **Normal** or click the **Normal View** button at the left end of the horizontal scroll bar. Figure 6.1 shows a document in Normal view.

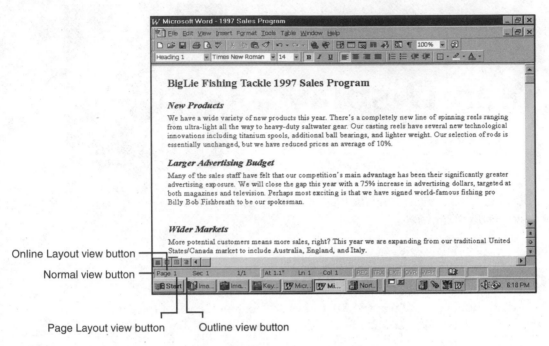

Online Layout view button

Normal view button

Page Layout view button   Outline view button

Figure 6.1 A document displayed in Normal view.

Page Layout View

Page Layout view displays your document exactly as it will print. Headers, footers, and all other details of the page layout appear on-screen. You can edit in Page Layout view; it's ideal for fine-tuning the details of page composition. Be aware, however, that the additional computer processing required makes display changes relatively slow in Page Layout view, particularly when you have a complex page layout.

TIP **Sneak Preview**   Use Page Layout view to see what your printed document will look like before you actually print. The Print Preview feature (File, Print Preview) is preferred for previewing entire pages.

Click **View**, **Page Layout** (or click the **Page Layout View** button) to switch to Page Layout view. Figure 6.2 shows a sample document in Page Layout view.

Header

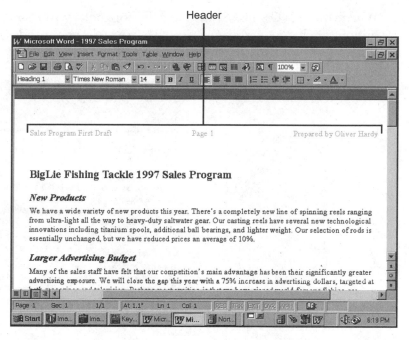

Figure 6.2 A document in Page Layout view displays the header.

Online Layout View

Online Layout view is optimal for reading and editing a document on-screen. Legibility is increased by using larger fonts; displaying shorter lines of text; hiding headers, footers, and similar elements; and basing the layout on the screen as opposed to the printed page. Also, the document map is displayed on the left side of the screen (the document map is covered later in this lesson). The screen display will not match the final printed appearance. Online Layout view is ideal for editing the document text, but is not suited for working with page layout or graphics.

TIP **Content Editing** Use Online Layout view when editing the document's contents, not the appearance.

 Click **View**, **Online Layout** (or click the **Online Layout View** button) to switch to Online Layout view.

157

When you're in Online Layout view, the horizontal scroll bar and its View buttons are hidden. You must use the **View** menu commands to switch to a different view. Figure 6.3 shows a document in Online Layout view.

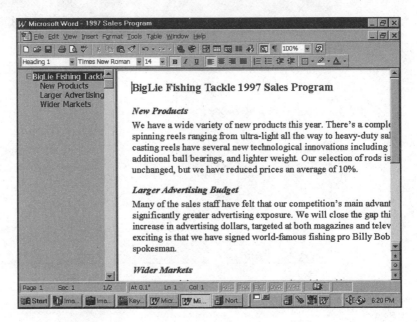

Figure 6.3 A document displayed in Online Layout view.

Outline View

Use Outline view to create outlines and to examine the structure of a document. Figure 6.4 shows a document in Outline view. In this view, you can choose to view only your document headings, thus hiding all subordinate text. You can quickly promote, demote, or move document headings along with subordinate text to a new location. For this view to be useful, you need to assign heading styles to the document headings, a technique you'll learn about in Lesson 12, "Making the Most of Styles."

 Click **View**, **Outline** to switch to Outline view, or click the **Outline View** button at the left end of the horizontal scroll bar.

Outline toolbar

Level 1 heading

Level 2 heading

Regular text

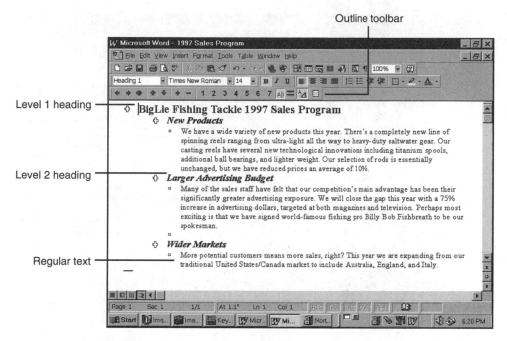

Figure 6.4   A document displayed in Outline view.

Draft Font View

Draft Font view is a display option you can apply in both Normal and Outline views. As you can see in Figure 6.5, Draft Font view uses a single generic font for all text; it indicates special formatting by underlining or boldface. Graphics display as empty boxes. Draft Font view provides the fastest editing and screen display, and it is particularly useful when editing the content of documents that contain a lot of fancy formatting and graphics. This view is ideal when you're concentrating on the contents of your document and not on its appearance.

Follow these steps to turn Draft Font view on or off:

1. Click **Tools**, **Options** to open the Options dialog box.
2. If necessary, click the **View** tab to display the View options.
3. Click the **Draft Font** check box to turn it on or off.
4. Click **OK**.

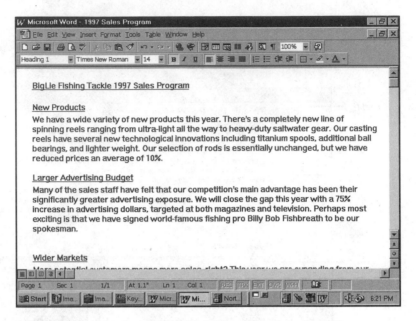

Figure 6.5 A document displayed in Draft Font view.

Full Screen View

Full Screen view provides the maximum amount of screen real estate to display your document contents. In Full Screen view, the title bar, menu, toolbars, status bar, and all other Word elements are hidden, and your document occupies the entire screen. You use Full Screen view in combination with other views. Thus you can use Full Screen view in Normal View, Page Layout View, and so on. You can enter and edit text in this view and select from the menus using the usual keyboard commands.

To turn on Full Screen view, click **View**, **Full Screen**. To turn off Full Screen view, select **View**, **Full Screen** again (using the keyboard) or click the **Close Full Screen** box that appears in the lower-right corner of the screen.

Zooming the Screen

The Zoom command lets you control the size of your document on-screen. You can enlarge it to facilitate reading small fonts, and you can decrease it to view an entire page at one time. Click **View**, **Zoom** to open the Zoom dialog box (see Figure 6.6).

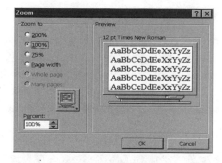

Figure 6.6 The Zoom dialog box.

The following options are available in the Zoom dialog box. As you make selections, the Preview area shows you what the selected zoom setting will look like.

- Select **200%**, **100%**, or **75%** to zoom to the indicated magnification. 200% is twice normal size, 75% is three-quarters normal size, and so on.
- Enter a custom magnification percentage of 10–200% in the **Percent** text box.
- Select **Page Width** to scale the display to fit the entire page width on-screen.
- Select **Whole Page** to scale the display to fit the entire page, vertically and horizontally, on-screen.
- Select **Many Pages** to display two or more pages at the same time. Click the **Monitor** button under the Many Pages option, and then drag to specify how many pages to display.

The Whole Page and Many Pages options are available only if you are viewing the document in Page Layout view.

TIP **Quick Zoom** You can quickly change the zoom setting by clicking the **Zoom** drop-down arrow on the Standard toolbar and selecting the desired zoom setting from the list.

Using the Document Map

The Document Map is a separate pane that displays your document's headings. You do not edit in the Document Map; rather, you use it to quickly move around your document. The Document Map is displayed automatically when you switch to Online Layout view. You can also display it in other views by clicking **View**, **Document Map**. Figure 6.7 shows a document with the map displayed.

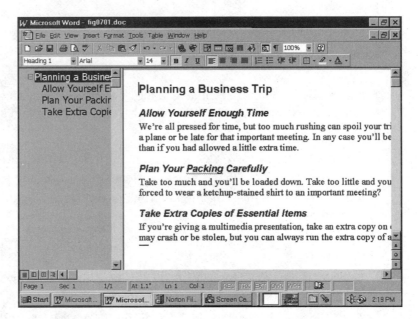

Figure 6.7   The Document Map is displayed to the left of the work area.

To use the Document Map, click the desired map heading. The main document window scrolls to that location in the document. You can control the width of the map display by dragging the border between the map and the document to the desired location. Dragging the border to the left edge of the screen has the same effect as turning the Document Map off.

Splitting the Screen

Word lets you split the work area into two panels, one above the other, so you can view different parts of one document at the same time. Each panel scrolls independently and has its own scroll bars. Figure 6.8 shows a document displayed on a split screen. Editing changes that you make in either panel affect the document. These steps walk you through splitting the screen:

1. Select **Window**, **Split** or press **Ctrl+Alt+S**. Word displays a horizontal split line across the middle of the work area.

2. To accept two equal size panes, click with the left mouse button or press **Enter**. To create different size panes, move the mouse until the split line is in the desired location, and then click or press **Enter**.

When working with a split screen, you move the editing cursor from one pane to the other by clicking with the mouse. To change the pane sizes, point at the split line and drag it to the new location. To remove the split and return to regular view, drag the split line to either the top or the bottom of the work area, or select **Windows**, **Remove Split**.

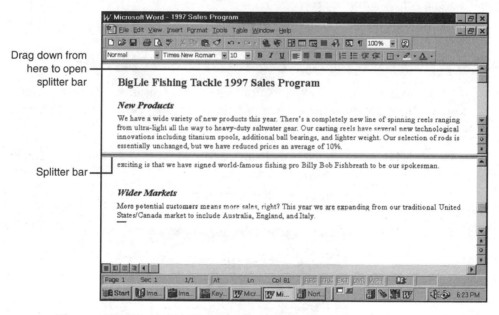

Drag down from here to open splitter bar

Splitter bar

Figure 6.8   Viewing a document in split screen view.

TIP   **Quick Split**   You can quickly split the screen by dragging the splitter bar, located just above the up arrow on the vertical toolbar (refer to Figure 6.8).

In this lesson, you learned how to control Word's screen display. In the next lesson, you'll learn how to print and fax your documents.

Printing, Mailing, and Faxing Your Document

In this lesson, you learn how to print your document, and how to send a document via e-mail or fax.

Printing Using the Default Settings

It's very simple to print using the default settings. This means to print a single copy of the entire document on the default Windows printer. This is all you have to do:

1. Click **File, Print** or click the **Print** button on the Standard toolbar. The Print dialog box appears (see Figure 7.1).

2. Click **OK**, and Word prints the document.

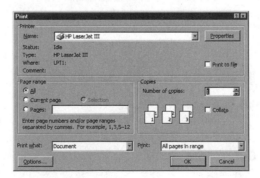

Figure 7.1   The Print dialog box.

TIP   **Another Way to Print**   You can also press **Ctrl+P** to print using the defaults without going to the Print dialog box.

Printer Not Working?   Refer to your Microsoft Windows and printer documentation for help. If you're using a network printer, see your network administrator.

CAUTION

Printing Multiple Copies

With the options in the Print dialog box, you can print more than one copy of a document, and you can specify that the copies be collated. To do either of those, follow these steps:

1. Click **File, Print** or click the **Print** button on the Standard toolbar. The Print dialog box appears.
2. In the **Number of Copies** box (refer to Figure 7.1), enter the desired number of copies. Or click the increment arrows to set the desired value.
3. Click the **Collate** check box to turn that feature on or off.
4. Click **OK**.

More Than One Printer?   If you have two or more printers installed, you can select the one to use by clicking the **Name** drop-down arrow at the top of the Print dialog box and selecting the desired printer from the list.

CAUTION

Printing Part of a Document

Most often you will want to print all of a document. You can, however, print just part of a document, ranging from a single sentence to a range of pages. Follow these steps to print a smaller portion:

1. To print a section of text, select the text. To print a single page, move the cursor to that page.
2. Click **File, Print** or click the **Print** button on the Standard toolbar. The Print dialog box appears.

165

3. In the Page Range area, specify what you want printed:

- Choose **Selection** to print the selected text.

- Choose **Current Page** to print the page containing the cursor.

- Choose **Pages** to print specified pages, and then enter the page numbers in the text box. For example, enter **1–3** to print pages 1 through 3, or enter **2,4** to print pages 2 and 4.

4. Click **OK**.

TIP **Printing Properties** To print a document's properties instead of its text, click the **Print What** drop-down arrow in the Print dialog box and select **Document Properties** from the list.

Changing Your Print Options

Word offers a number of printing options that you may need to use at times. You can print only the odd-numbered pages or the even-numbered pages. This option is useful to create two-sided output on a standard one-sided printer: print the odd-numbered pages, flip the printed pages over and place them back in the printer's paper tray, and then print the even-numbered pages. You select which pages to print by clicking the **Print** drop-down arrow in the Print dialog box and selecting **Odd Pages** or **Even Pages** from the list. Select **All Pages in Range** to return to printing all pages.

You can set other print options in the Print Options dialog box (shown in Figure 7.2). To display this dialog box, open the Print dialog box as described previously and click the **Options** button.

The following list outlines the options you will use most often.

- **Draft Output** Produces draft output that prints faster, but may lack some graphics and formatting (depending on your specific printer).

- **Reverse Print Order** Prints pages in last-to-first order. This setting produces collated output on printers that have face-up output.

- **Background Printing** Permits you to continue working on the document while printing is in progress. This setting uses additional memory and usually results in slower printing.

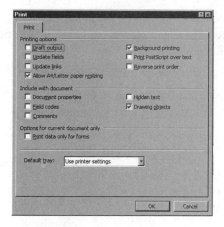

Figure 7.2 The Print Options dialog box.

- **Update Fields**   Updates the contents of all document fields before printing.
- **Document Properties**   Prints the document's properties in addition to its contents.
- **Comments**   Includes document comments in the printout.

After setting the desired printing options, click **OK** to return to the Print dialog box.

TIP   **Save Paper!**   Use Page Layout view or Print Preview to check the appearance of your document before you print it.

Faxing a Document

If your system is set up for fax, you can fax a document directly to one or more recipients without having to print a paper copy and feed it into a standard fax machine. This capability saves both time and paper. Follow these steps to fax the current document:

1. Click **File, Send To, Fax Recipient**. Word starts the Fax Wizard.

2. The Fax Wizard takes you through the steps of preparing the fax, choosing a cover page, and selecting recipients. For each step, enter the requested information and click **Next**.

3. After the final step, click **Finish**.

4. If you requested a cover sheet, Word displays it. You can make any additions or changes to the cover sheet at this time.

5. Click the **Send Fax Now** button to send the fax.

CAUTION

No Fax Option? If the Fax Recipient option is not available on your Send To submenu, it means that your system has not been set up for faxing.

TIP **Another Way to Fax** You can also fax a document by selecting Microsoft Fax (or the name of whatever fax program you use) as the destination printer in the Print dialog box and then printing in the usual fashion.

Mailing a Document

If you have Microsoft Messaging or another e-mail program installed on your system, you can send a document directly to a mail recipient. Here are the steps to take:

1. Click **File**, **Send To**, **Mail Recipient**.

2. Depending on the specifics of your system, Word may ask you to select a profile setting. Generally, the default setting is the one you should select.

3. Next you will see your usual New Message window. The appearance of this window will vary depending on the mail system you are using, but it will be the same mail form that you use for other e-mail messages. Figure 7.3 shows the New Message window used by Microsoft Outlook. The document will already be inserted in the message as an icon. Add text to the message if desired.

4. Fill in the **To** line of the message with the recipient's address.

5. When the message is complete, click the **Send** button.

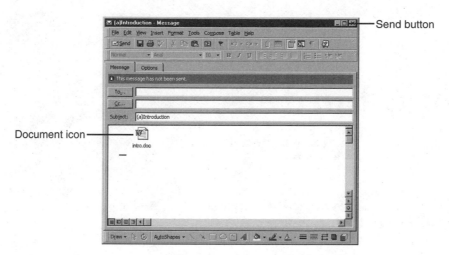

Document icon —

— Send button

Figure 7.3 A new message with the document inserted as an icon.

When the recipient receives your message, he or she will be able to double-click the document icon to open the document in Word for printing, editing, and so on.

In this lesson, you learned how to print your document and how to send it as a fax or as an e-mail message. The next lesson shows you how to use fonts, borders, and shading in your document.

Fonts, Borders, and Shading

In this lesson, you learn how to use different fonts in your document and how to apply borders and shading.

Font Terminology

Word offers you a huge assortment of fonts to use in your documents. Each font has a specific *typeface*, which determines the appearance of the characters. Typefaces are identified by names such as Arial, Courier, and Times New Roman. Each font also has a size, which is specified in *points*. There are 72 points in an inch, so a 36-point font would have its largest characters 1/2 inch tall. Most documents use font sizes in the 8- to 14-point range, but larger and smaller sizes are available for headings and other special needs.

Selecting a Font

You can change the font of text that already has been typed by first selecting the text. To specify the font for text you are about to type, move the cursor to the desired location. Then follow these steps to choose a font for the selected text or the text you're about to type:

1. Click **Format**, **Font** to open the Font dialog box shown in Figure 8.1.
2. The Font text box displays the name of the current font. Scroll through the **Font** list box and select a new font name.

Select the font name.

Select the font size.

Check out the font's appearance.

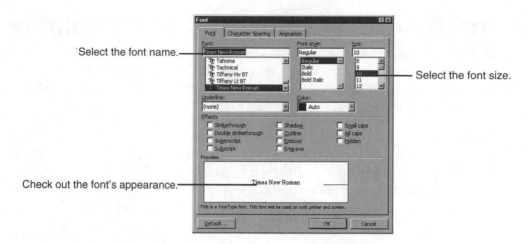

Figure 8.1 The Font dialog box.

3. The Size text box displays the current font size. Select a new size from the **Size** list box or type a number in the text box. The Preview box shows the appearance of the selected font.

4. Click **OK** to enter your settings.

TIP **Quick Select** If you want to change the font for a whole document, remember that you can select the entire document by pressing **Ctrl+A**.

You can quickly select a font name and size using the Formatting toolbar. The Font list box and the Font Size list box display the name and size of the current font. You can change the font by clicking the drop-down arrow of either list and making a selection. Note that in the Font list, the fonts you have used recently appear at the top.

TIP **Keyboard Happy?** From the keyboard, you can access the Font and Font Size lists on the toolbar by pressing **Ctrl+Shift+F** or **Ctrl+Shift+P** (respectively) followed by the down arrow key.

Using Boldface, Italics, and Underlining

You can apply bold, italics, or underlining to any of Word's fonts. You can also use two or three of these effects in combination. As you can with other formatting, you can apply these effects to existing text by first selecting the text, or you can apply them to text you are about to type.

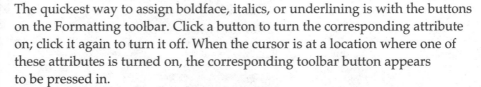

The quickest way to assign boldface, italics, or underlining is with the buttons on the Formatting toolbar. Click a button to turn the corresponding attribute on; click it again to turn it off. When the cursor is at a location where one of these attributes is turned on, the corresponding toolbar button appears to be pressed in.

You also can assign font attributes using the Font dialog box. (If you want to use underlining other than the default single underline, you must use this method.) Here's how to use the dialog box:

1. Click **Format**, **Font** to open the Font dialog box.

2. Under Font Style, select **Bold**, **Italic**, or **Bold Italic**. Select **Regular** to return to normal text.

3. Click the **Underline** drop-down arrow and select the desired underline style from the list; or select **None** to remove underlining.

4. Click **OK**.

TIP **A New Default** To change the default font used in documents based on the Normal template, open the Font dialog box, select the desired font and attributes, and click the **Default** button when asked to confirm, click **Yes**.

Applying Special Font Effects

Word has a number of special font effects that you can use. These include superscript and subscript, strikethrough, and several graphics effects (such as shadow and outline). You can also specify that text be hidden, which means it will not display on-screen or be printed.

To assign special font effects to selected text or text you are about to type, follow these steps:

1. Click **Format, Font** to open the Font dialog box.

2. In the Effects area, select the effects you want. To turn on an effect, click to place an X in the check box. To turn off an effect, click to remove the X from the check box. The Preview box shows you what the font will look like with the selected effects.

3. When you're satisfied with your settings, click **OK**.

Where's That Hidden Text? To locate hidden text, click **Tools**, **Options**, click the **View** tab, and then select the **Hidden Text** option. Word displays hidden text with a dotted underline. You also can display hidden text by clicking the **Show/Hide ¶** button on the Standard toolbar.

CAUTION

Displaying Borders

Word's Borders command lets you improve the appearance of your documents by displaying borders around selected text. Figure 8.2 shows examples of the use of borders (and it illustrates shading, covered in the section "Applying Shading" later in this lesson).

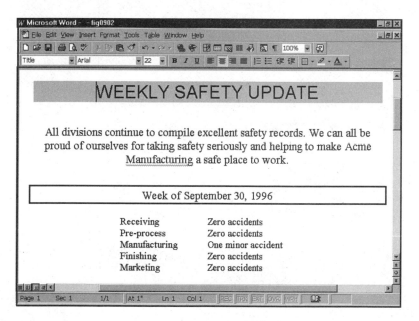

Figure 8.2 A document with borders and shading.

You can apply a border to selected text or to individual paragraphs. To put a border around text, select the text. For a paragraph, place the cursor anywhere in the paragraph. The quickest way to apply a border is to use the Border button on the Formatting toolbar. Click the **Border** drop-down arrow to view a palette of available border settings, and then click the desired border diagram. Click the **No Borders** diagram to remove borders.

If you need more control over the appearance of your borders, you must use the Borders and Shading dialog box (see Figure 8.3). To open this dialog box, click **Format**, **Borders and Shading**, and then click the **Borders** tab if necessary.

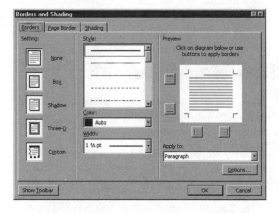

Figure 8.3   The Borders tab of the Borders and Shading dialog box.

The steps for creating a border are as follows:

1. Select the general appearance of the borders you want by clicking the corresponding icon in the Setting area (the Custom setting is explained later).

2. In the **Style** list, select the desired line style, color, and width.

3. In the Preview area, click the buttons or click directly on the page diagram to add or remove borders from the four sides of the text.

4. If you selected text before opening the dialog box, use the **Apply To** list to specify whether the border is to be displayed around the selected text or the current paragraph.

5. Click **OK**, and Word puts your settings into effect.

The normal border settings apply the same line style (solid, dotted, and so on) to all four sides of the border box. To create a custom border that combines different styles, use these steps:

1. Click the **Custom** icon.
2. In the **Style** list, select the line style, color, and width for one side of the border box.
3. In the Preview area, click the button or click directly on the page diagram to specify the side of the border box to which you want to apply the style you selected in step 2.
4. Repeat steps 2 and 3 to specify the style for the other three sides of the border box.
5. Select **OK**.

You can also place borders around entire pages in your document. To do so, click the **Page Border** tab of the Borders and Shading dialog box. This tab looks and operates just as the Borders tab does in terms of specifying the border's appearance. The only difference is specifying where the border will be applied, which is done with the options in the **Apply To** list. You have four choices:

- Whole Document
- This Section
- This Section - First Page Only
- This Section - All Except First Page

You'll learn how to divide a document into sections in Lesson 11, "Margins, Pages, and Sections."

CAUTION If you have two paragraphs in a row with the same indents and the same style (if you use styles), Word assumes that the paragraphs should be in a boxed border together. Say, for example, you have a box border around paragraphs 1 and 2. You will not see the top border on paragraph 2 or the bottom border on paragraph 1; they will appear to be together in a single box. If you don't want this, you must make one of the paragraphs a different style or add a blank line with a different style between the two paragraphs. You can make this line extremely small (with the **Format**, **Paragraph**, **Line Spacing** command) so that the blank line doesn't detract from your layout.

Applying Shading

You can use shading to display a background color under text (such as black text on a light gray background). Figure 8.2 shows an example of shading. You can apply shading to selected text or to individual paragraphs. Shading can be made up of a fill color, a pattern color, or a combination of both.

Here's how to apply shading:

1. Select the text to be shaded, or position the cursor anywhere in the paragraph to shade an entire paragraph.
2. Click **Format**, **Borders and Shading** to open the Borders and Shading dialog box. If necessary, click the **Shading** tab (see Figure 8.4).
3. To use a fill color, select it from the palette in the Fill area of the dialog box. To use only a pattern color, click the **None** button.
4. To use a pattern color, select its style and color from the lists in the Patterns section of the dialog box. To use only a fill color, select the **Clear** style. You can view the appearance of the selected settings in the Preview area of the dialog box.
5. If you selected text before opening the dialog box, use the **Apply To** list to specify whether the fill should apply to the selected text or the current paragraph.
6. Click **OK**.

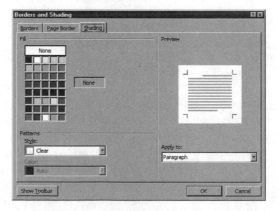

Figure 8.4   The Shading tab of the Borders and Shading dialog box.

TIP **Printing Color?** Of course, color shading will print in color only if you have a color printer. You need to perform test printouts of pages with shading because how Word displays shading on-screen is often quite different from the final printed results.

In this lesson, you learned how to use fonts, borders, and shading in your documents. In the next lesson, you learn how to control indentation and justification of text, and how to control line breaks.

Indents and Justification

In this lesson, you learn how to set the indentation and justification of text in your document, and how to control line breaks.

Indentation

The distance between your text and the left and right edges of the page is controlled by two things: the left and right page margins and the text indentation. Margins (which are covered in detail in Lesson 11, "Margins, Pages, and Sections") are usually changed only for entire documents or large sections of a document. For smaller sections of text, such as individual lines and paragraphs, you will use indentation.

Indentation   The distance between a paragraph's text and the margins for the entire document. For example, if the left margin is set at 1" and a particular paragraph has a 1" indentation, that paragraph starts 2" from the edge of the paper.

The easiest way to set indents is by using the Ruler and your mouse. To display the Ruler (or hide it), click **View**, **Ruler**. The numbers on the Ruler indicate the space from the left margin in inches. Figure 9.1 shows the Ruler and identifies the various elements you use to set indents. In addition, the sample text in the figure illustrates the various indent options.

Rapid Ruler   Quickly display the Ruler by positioning the mouse pointer at the top edge of the work area for a moment. When you finish using the Ruler, move the mouse pointer away, and the Ruler is automatically hidden again.

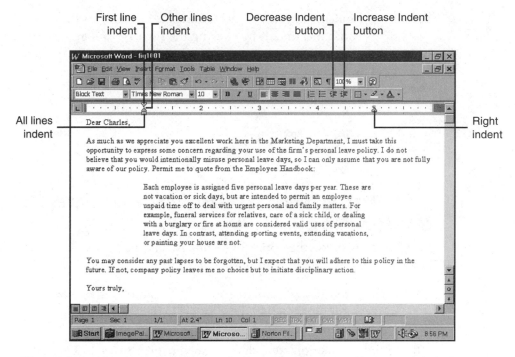

Figure 9.1 Use the Ruler to set text indentation. The second paragraph is indented one inch from both the right and left margins.

Indentation applies to individual paragraphs. To set indentation for one paragraph, position the cursor anywhere in the paragraph. For more than one paragraph, select those paragraphs. (Otherwise, the new indents will apply only to new paragraphs that you type from the insertion point forward.) Then drag the indent markers on the Ruler to the desired positions. As you drag, a dotted vertical line appears, stretching down through the document to show the new indent's location. Use these guidelines when setting paragraph indentation:

- To change the indent of the first line of a paragraph, drag the **First Line Indent** marker to the desired position.

- To change the indent of all lines of a paragraph except the first one, drag the **Other Lines Indent** marker to the desired position (this is called a *hanging indent*).

- To change the indent of all lines of a paragraph, drag the **All Lines Indent** marker to the desired position.

- To change the indent of the right edge of the paragraph, drag the **Right Indent** marker to the desired position.

179

You also can quickly increase or decrease the left indent for the current paragraph in 1/2-inch increments by clicking the **Increase Indent** or **Decrease Indent** buttons on the Formatting toolbar. And undoubtedly, the quickest way to indent the first line of a paragraph is to position the cursor at the start of the line and press **Tab**.

Hanging Indent   A paragraph in which the first line is indented less than all the other lines.

Setting Indents with the Paragraph Dialog Box

Word also gives you the option of setting indents using the Paragraph dialog box. These steps walk you through that process.

1. Click **Format**, **Paragraph** to open the Paragraph dialog box. Then click the **Indents and Spacing** tab if necessary to display the indents and spacing options (see Figure 9.2).

2. In the Indentation area, click the increment arrows for the **Left** and **Right** text boxes to increase or decrease the indentation settings. To set a first line or a hanging indent, select the indent type in the **Special** drop-down list and enter the indent amount in the **By** text box. The sample page in the dialog box illustrates how the current settings will appear.

3. Click **OK**, and Word applies the new settings to any selected paragraphs or to new text.

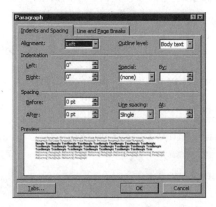

Figure 9.2 Setting indents in the Paragraph dialog box.

Setting Text Justification

Justification, sometimes called alignment, refers to the manner in which the left and right ends of lines of text are aligned. Word offers four justification options:

- Left justification aligns the left ends of lines.
- Right justification aligns the right ends of lines.
- Full justification aligns both the left and right ends of lines.
- Center justification centers lines between the left and right margins.

 TERM

Full Justification Both the left and right edges or paragraphs are aligned. This is accomplished by inserting extra space between words and letters in the text as needed.

Figure 9.3 illustrates the justification options. To change the justification for one or more paragraphs, first select the paragraphs to change. Then click one of the justification buttons on the Formatting toolbar. The toolbar button corresponding to the current paragraph's justification setting appears to be pressed in.

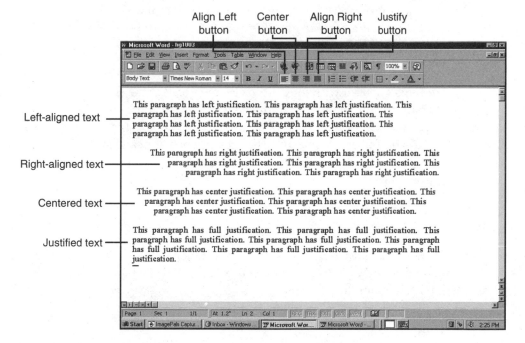

Figure 9.3 Click these buttons to set text justification.

If you prefer to use a dialog box to change justification, select the paragraphs and then use these steps:

1. Click **Format**, **Paragraph** to open the Paragraph dialog box, and click the **Indents and Spacing** tab if necessary.
2. Click the **Alignment** drop-down arrow and select the desired alignment from the list.
3. Select **OK**.

Controlling Line Breaks

The word wrap feature automatically breaks each line in a paragraph when it reaches the right margin. Word offers a couple of methods for controlling the way lines break. You can prevent a line break from occurring between two specific words to ensure that the words always remain together on the same line. These methods can be particularly useful when you modify indents and justification because this often changes where individual lines break.

Word's default is to break lines as needed at spaces or hyphens. To prevent a line break, you must insert a nonbreaking space or a nonbreaking hyphen instead. To insert a nonbreaking hyphen, press **Ctrl+Shift+-** (hyphen). To insert a nonbreaking space, press **Ctrl+Shift+Spacebar**.

You also can use an optional hyphen to specify where a word can be broken, if necessary. This is useful with long words that may fall at the end of the line; if word wrap moves the long word to the next line, there will be an unsightly gap at the end of the previous line. An optional hyphen remains hidden unless the word extends past the right margin. Then the hyphen appears, and only the part of the word after the hyphen wraps to the new line. To insert an optional hyphen, press **Ctrl+- (hyphen)**.

Finally, you can insert a line break without starting a new paragraph by pressing **Shift+Enter**.

In this lesson, you learned how to set the indentation and justification of text in your document, and how to control line breaks. The next lesson shows you how to work with tabs and line spacing.

Tabs and Line Spacing

In this lesson, you learn how to use and set tab stops, and how to change line spacing.

What Are Tabs?

Tabs provide a way for you to control the indentation and vertical alignment of text in your document. When you press the **Tab** key, Word inserts a tab in the document and moves the cursor (and any text to the right of it) to the next tab stop. By default, Word has tab stops at 0.5-inch intervals across the width of the page. You can modify the location of tab stops and control the way text aligns at a tab stop.

Types of Tab Stops

Word offers four types of tab stops, each of which aligns text differently:

- **Left-aligned**   The left edge of text aligns at the tab stop. Word's default tab stops are left-aligned.
- **Right-aligned**   The right edge of text aligns at the tab stop.
- **Center-aligned**   The text is centered at the tab stop.
- **Decimal-aligned**   The decimal point (period) is aligned at the tab stop. You use this type of tab for aligning columns of numbers.

Figure 10.1 illustrates the effects of the four tab alignment options and shows the four markers that appear on the Ruler to indicate the position of tab stops.

Left-aligned tab stop · Center-aligned tab stop · Right-aligned tab stop · Decimal-aligned tab stop

Click here until it shows the marker for the type of tab you want.

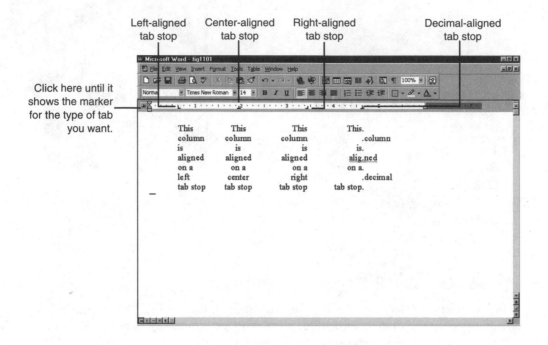

Figure 10.1 The four tab stop alignment options.

Changing the Default Tab Stops

Default tab stops affect all paragraphs for which you have not set custom tab stops (covered in the next section). You cannot delete the default tab stops, but you can change the spacing between them. The default tab stop spacing affects the entire document. Here are the steps to follow:

1. Click **Format**, **Tabs** to display the Tabs dialog box, shown in Figure 10.2.

2. In the **Default Tab Stops** box, click the increment arrows to increase or decrease the spacing between default tab stops.

3. Click **OK**.

TIP **Good-Bye Tab** To effectively "delete" the default tab stops, set the spacing between them to a value larger than the page width.

Figure 10.2 The Tabs dialog box.

Creating Custom Tab Stops

If the default tab stops are not suited to your needs, you can add custom tab stops. The number, spacing, and type of custom tab stops is totally up to you. Use these steps to set custom tab stops:

1. Select the paragraphs that will have custom tabs. If no text is selected, the new tabs will affect the paragraph containing the cursor and new text you type.

2. Click the tab symbol at the left end of the Ruler until it displays the marker for the type of tab you want to insert (refer to Figure 10.1).

3. Point at the approximate tab stop location on the Ruler, and press and hold the left mouse button. A dashed vertical line extends down through the document to show the tab stop position relative to your text.

4. Move the mouse left or right until the tab stop is at the desired location.

5. Release the mouse button.

TIP **No Ruler?** If your Ruler is not displayed, click **View**, **Ruler** or position the mouse pointer near the top edge of the work area for a few seconds.

When you add a custom tab stop, all the default tab stops to the left are temporarily inactivated. This ensures that the custom tab stop will take precedence. If custom tab stops have been defined for the current paragraph, the custom tabs are displayed on the Ruler; otherwise, the default tab stops are displayed.

185

Moving and Deleting Custom Tab Stops

Follow these steps to move a custom tab stop to a new position:

1. Point at the tab stop marker on the Ruler.

2. Press and hold the left mouse button.

3. Drag the tab stop to the new position.

4. Release the mouse button.

To delete a custom tab stop, follow the same steps, but in step 3, drag the tab stop marker off the Ruler. Then release the mouse button.

Changing Line Spacing

Line spacing controls the amount of vertical space between lines of text. Different spacing is appropriate for different kinds of documents. If you want to print your document on as few pages as possible, use single line spacing to position lines close together. In contrast, a document that will later be edited by hand should be printed with wide line spacing to provide space for the editor to write comments.

Word offers a variety of line spacing options. If you change line spacing, it affects the selected text; if there is no text selected, it affects the current paragraph and text you type at the insertion point.

Follow these steps to change line spacing:

1. Click **Format**, **Paragraph** to open the Paragraph dialog box. If necessary, click the **Indents and Spacing** tab (see Figure 10.3).

2. Click the **Line Spacing** drop-down arrow and select the desired spacing option from the list. The **Single**, **1.5 Lines**, and **Double** settings are self-explanatory. The other settings are:

- **Exactly**   Space between lines will be exactly the value—in points—that you enter in the **At** text box.
- **At Least**   Space between lines will be at least the value you enter in the **At** text box; Word will increase the spacing as needed if the line contains large characters.
- **Multiple**   Changes spacing by the factor you enter in the **At** text box. For example, enter **1.5** to increase spacing by one-and-a-half times, or enter **2** to double the line spacing.

Underline Missing?   If you set line spacing using the Exactly option at the same value as your font size, underline character formatting will display only for the last line of each paragraph. That's because the underline is cut off by the tops of the subsequent lines.

CAUTION

3. To add spacing before the first line or after the last line of the paragraph, enter the desired space (in points), or click the arrows in the **Before** and **After** text boxes.

4. Click **OK**.

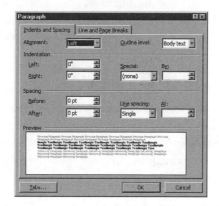

Figure 10.3   The Paragraph dialog box with the Indents and Spacing options displayed.

In this lesson, you learned how to use and set tab stops, and how to change line spacing. The next lesson shows you how to use margins, pages, and sections.

Margins, Pages, and Sections

In this lesson, you learn how to use document sections, how to set page margins, how to work with different paper sizes, and how to specify the source of paper used in printing.

Using Section Breaks

Word gives you the option of breaking your document into two or more *sections*, each of which can have its own page formatting. You need to use sections only when you want some aspect of page layout, such as page margins (covered later in this lesson) or columns, to apply to only part of the document. The default is for page layout settings such as these to apply to the entire document.

Word offers three types of section breaks. They have the same effect in terms of controlling page layout, but differ as to where the text that comes after the break is placed:

- **Next Page**   The new section begins at the top of the next page. This is useful for section breaks that coincide with major breaks in a document, such as a new chapter starting.

- **Continuous**   The new section begins on the same page as the preceding section. This is useful for a section that has a different number of columns from the preceding one but is still part of the same page. An example would be a newsletter: the title runs across the top of the page in one column, and then after a section break, the body of the newsletter appears below the title in three columns.

- **Odd Page or Even Page**   The new section begins on the next even- or odd-numbered page. This is useful when a section break coincides with a major break (like a chapter) in a document where each chapter must start on an odd page (or an even page).

In Normal view, Word marks the location of section breaks by displaying a double horizontal line with the label **Section Break** followed by the type of break. These markers do not appear in Page Layout view or in printouts.

To insert a section break, follow these steps:

1. Click **Insert**, **Break** to open the Break dialog box.
2. Select the desired type of section break (as described in the previous list).
3. Click **OK**.

A section break mark is just like any character in your document. To delete a section break, place the cursor right before it and press **Delete,** or place the cursor right after it and press **Backspace**. Each section break marker holds the settings for the text that comes before it, so when you delete a section break, text in the section before the break becomes part of the section that was after the break, and it assumes the page layout formatting of that section.

Inserting Manual Page Breaks

When text reaches the bottom margin of a page, Word automatically starts a new page and continues the text at the top of that page. However, you can manually insert page breaks to start a new page at any desired location. Here's how:

1. Click **Insert**, **Break** to open the Break dialog box.
2. Select **Page Break**.
3. Click **OK**.

 TIP **Quick Breaks** You can enter a page break by pressing **Ctrl+Enter**. To start a new line without starting a new paragraph, press **Shift+Enter**.

A page break appears in the document as a single horizontal line. Like section break markers, page break markers do not appear in Page Layout view or in printouts. To delete a page break, move the cursor to the line containing the break and press **Delete**.

Setting Page Margins

The page margins control the amount of whitespace between your text and the edges of the page. Each page has four margins: left, right, top, and bottom. When you change page margins, the new settings will affect the entire document or, if you have inserted one or more section breaks, the current section.

The easiest way to set page margins is with your mouse and the Ruler. You can work visually instead of thinking in terms of inches or centimeters. To display the Ruler, click **View**, **Ruler** or position the mouse pointer near the top edge of the work area.

You can use the Ruler to change margins only while working in Page Layout view (click **View**, **Page Layout**). In Page Layout view, Word displays both a horizontal ruler at the top of the page and a vertical ruler on the left edge of the page. This permits you to set both the left/right and the top/bottom margins using a Ruler.

On each ruler, the white bar shows the current margin settings, as shown in Figure 11.1. To change the left or right margin, point at the margin marker on the horizontal ruler, at the left or right end of the white bar; the mouse pointer will change to a two-headed arrow. Then drag the margin to the new position. For the top or bottom margin, follow the same procedure using the vertical ruler.

 Margins   The margins are the distances between the text and the edges of the page.

Note that the margin symbols—not the small triangular buttons—on the horizontal ruler are the vertical edges of the white margin bar. The small triangular buttons are the indent markers, which you learned about in Lesson 9, "Indents and Justification." If your mouse pointer has changed to a two-headed arrow, you know you have found the margin symbol.

 Changing Margins   Margins apply to the entire section, unlike indents (which apply to individual paragraphs). To change the margins for only a portion of a document, insert a section break as described previously in this lesson. You can then specify different margins for each section.

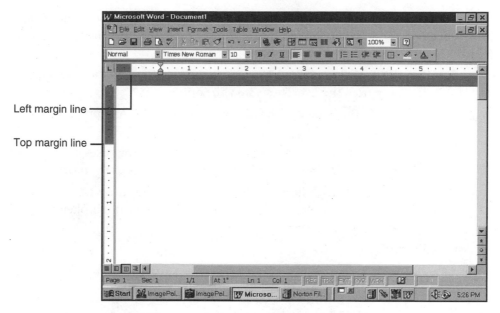

Left margin line

Top margin line

Figure 11.1 The Ruler displays a white bar showing the current margin settings.

Can't Change Margins? Be sure you're in Page Layout view or the rulers won't work for changing margins. (You can, however, drag the indent markers on the ruler in Normal view, as you learned in Lesson 9.)

CAUTION

You also can set the page margins using a dialog box. Use this method when you don't want to use the mouse or need to enter precise margin values. (You also don't have to switch to Page Layout view to do it.) It gives you more control over where in the document the new margins are applied. Here's how:

1. Click **File**, **Page Setup** to open the Page Setup dialog box.

2. If necessary, click the **Margins** tab to display the margins options shown in Figure 11.2.

3. In the **Top**, **Bottom**, **Left**, and **Right** text boxes, enter the desired margin size (in inches) or click the increment arrows to set the desired value. The Preview shows you the effects of your margin settings.

4. If your document will be bound and you want to leave an extra large margin on one side for the binding, enter the desired width in the **Gutter** text box. This extra space will be added to the left margin of every page or, if you select the **Mirror Margins** check box, it will be added to the left

margin of odd-numbered pages and the right margin of even-numbered pages (which is useful for binding a document that is printed on both sides of the paper).

5. Click the **Apply To** drop-down arrow and select where the new margins will apply from the list. These are your options:

- **Whole Document**   The new margin settings will apply to the entire document.

- **This Point Forward**   Word will insert a continuous section break at the cursor location and apply the new margins to the new section.

- **This Section**   Margins will be applied to the current document section. This option is not available if you have not broken your document into sections.

6. Click **OK**.

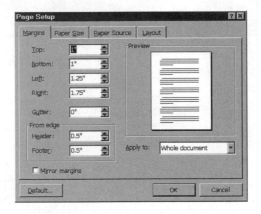

Figure 11.2   Setting margins in the Page Setup dialog box.

Controlling Paper Size and Orientation

Word's default is to format documents to fit on standard 8 1/2 × 11-inch letter size paper and to print in portrait orientation, which means the lines of text run parallel to the short edge of the paper. You can specify a different paper size, selecting from several standard paper and envelope sizes or defining a custom paper size. You can also print in landscape orientation, in which the lines of text are parallel to the long edge of the paper.

Follow these steps to specify paper size and orientation:

1. Click **File**, **Page Setup** to open the Page Setup dialog box.
2. If it isn't already on top, click the **Paper Size** tab (see Figure 11.3).
3. Click the **Paper Size** drop-down arrow and select a predefined paper size from the list. Or, enter a custom height and width in the text boxes provided.
4. Select **Portrait** or **Landscape** orientation.
5. Click the **Apply To** drop-down arrow and select the portion of the document to which the new paper setting is to apply:
   - **Whole Document** The new paper setting will be used for the entire document.
   - **This Point Forward** Word will insert a continuous section break at the cursor location and apply the new paper settings to the new section.
   - **This Section** Paper settings will be applied to the current document section. This option is not available if your document has not been broken into sections.
6. Select **OK**.

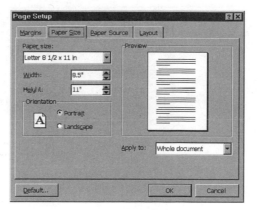

Figure 11.3 Setting paper size and orientation.

Specifying a Paper Source

Some documents require printing on different kinds of paper. For example, with a multipage business letter you may want to print the first page on company letterhead and the other pages on plain paper. Within the limitations of your printer, you can tell Word where it should get the paper for each section of the document. Most laser printers give you two choices: the regular paper tray or manual feed. Advanced printers will have more options, such as two or more paper trays and an envelope feeder.

Use these steps to specify the paper source:

1. Click **File**, **Page Setup** to open the Page Setup dialog box.
2. If it's not on top, click the **Paper Source** tab (see Figure 11.4).
3. In the **First Page** list box, specify the paper source for the first page. The choices available here will depend on your printer model.
4. In the **Other Pages** list box, specify the paper source for the second and subsequent pages.
5. Click the **Apply To** drop-down arrow and select which part of the document the paper source settings are to affect.
6. Select **OK**.

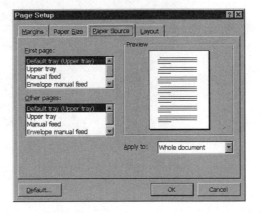

Figure 11.4   Specifying the paper source.

TIP If you print sheets of labels in your printer, and you find that the labels get jammed, try feeding the labels in manually. Set the Paper Source to **Manual Feed**, and your printer will stop and wait for you to feed each sheet into the printer. Be aware that when you manually feed in the sheet, you may need to orient it differently; for example, if you normally put labels face-up in the paper tray, you may have to feed them face-down into the manual feed slot on the printer.

In this lesson, you learned how to use document sections, how to set page margins, how to work with different paper sizes, and how to specify the source of paper used in printing. In the next lesson, you will learn how to use styles.

Making the
Most of Styles

In this lesson, you learn how to use styles in your documents.

Understanding Styles

Word's styles provide a great deal of power and flexibility when it comes to formatting your document. A *style* is a collection of formatting specifications that has been assigned a name and saved. For example, a given style could specify 14-point Arial font, 1-inch indent, double line spacing, and full justification. After you define a style, you can quickly apply it to any text in your document.

Applying a style is a lot faster than manually applying individual formatting elements, and it has the added advantage of assuring consistency. If you later modify a style definition, all the text in the document to which that style has been assigned will automatically change to reflect the new style formatting. Word has several predefined styles, and you can create your own.

 What Is a Style? A style is a named grouping of paragraph or character formatting that can be reused.

Word has two types of styles:

Paragraph styles apply to entire paragraphs and can include all aspects of formatting that affect a paragraph's appearance: font, line spacing, indents, tab stops, borders, and so on. Every paragraph has a style; the default paragraph style is called Normal.

Character styles apply to any section of text and can include any formatting that applies to individual characters: font name and size, underlining, boldface, and so on (in other words, any of the formats that you can assign by selecting Format, Font). There is no default character style.

When you apply a character style, the formatting is applied in addition to whatever formatting the text already possesses. For example, if you apply the bold character style to a sentence that is already formatted as italic, the sentence appears in both bold and italic. The uses of styles are covered in this lesson and the next one.

Assigning a Style to Text

To assign a paragraph style to multiple paragraphs, select the paragraphs. To assign a paragraph style to a single paragraph, place the cursor anywhere in the paragraph. To assign a character style, select the text you want the style to affect. Then follow these steps to apply the desired formatting:

1. Click the **Style** drop-down arrow on the Formatting toolbar to see a list of available styles, with each style name displayed in the style's font. Symbols in the list also indicate whether a style is a paragraph or character style, as well as its font size and justification (see Figure 12.1).

2. Select the desired style by clicking its name. The style is applied to the specified text.

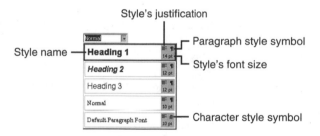

Figure 12.1 Select a style from the Style list on the Formatting toolbar.

TIP **Paragraph or Character Style?** In the Style list, paragraph styles are listed with the paragraph symbol next to them, and character styles are listed with an underlined letter "a" next to them.

To remove a character style from text, select the text and apply the character style **Default Paragraph Font**. This is not really a style; instead it specifies that the formatting defined in the current paragraph style should be used for the text.

Viewing Style Names

The Style list box displays the name of the style assigned to the text where the insertion point is located. If there is text selected or if the insertion point is in text that has a character style applied, the Style list box displays the character style name. Otherwise, it displays the paragraph style of the current paragraph.

Word can also display the name of the paragraph and character styles assigned to specific text in your document. Follow these steps to see how:

1. Press **Shift+F1** or click **Help, What's This?** to activate What's This Help. The mouse cursor displays a question mark.

2. Click the text of interest, and Word displays information about the text's assigned style in a balloon (see Figure 12.2).

3. Repeat step 2 as needed for other text.

4. Press **Esc** when you are done.

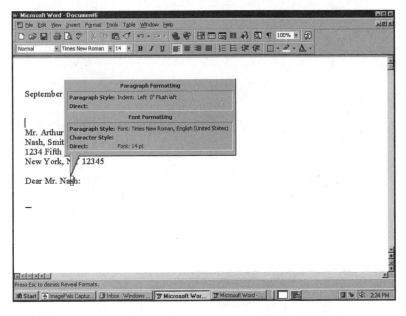

Figure 12.2 Displaying text's style information with What's This Help.

Creating a New Style

You are not limited to using Word's predefined styles. In fact, creating your own styles is an essential part of getting the most out of Word's style capabilities. One way to create a new style is "by example," as described in these steps:

1. Place the insertion point in a paragraph to which you want to apply the new style.

2. Format the paragraph as desired. In other words, apply the formatting you want included in the new style definition.

3. With the insertion point anywhere in the paragraph, click the **Style** list box or press **Ctrl+Shift+S** (both activate the Style list box).

4. Type a name for the new style and press **Enter**.

In step 4, make sure you do not enter the name of an existing style. If you do, that style's formatting will be applied to the paragraph, and the formatting changes you made will be lost. If this happens, you can recover the formatting by clicking **Edit**, **Undo**. Then repeat steps 3 and 4 and give the style a new and unique name.

CAUTION

You may not want to create your own styles for headings; using Word's default style names (Heading 1, Heading 2, and so on) has advantages. If, for example, you use Word's default styles for headings, you can switch to **Outline** view to see an outline of your document based on the headings. If you make up your own styles for the headings, you can't do that. Another benefit of using Word's predefined heading styles is that by default the heading styles are selected for Word's **Index and Table of Contents** tools.

You also can create a new style by making formatting entries in dialog boxes. You must use this method to create a character style; it is optional for paragraph styles. You can create a new style from scratch, or you can base it on an existing style. If you choose the latter method, the new style will have all the formatting of the base style plus any additions and changes you make while defining the style. Here are the required steps:

1. Click **Format**, **Style** to open the Style dialog box.

2. Click the **New** button. The New Style dialog box appears (see Figure 12.3).

Figure 12.3 The New Style dialog box.

3. Click the **Style Type** drop-down arrow and select **Character** or **Paragraph** from the list to indicate the type of style you're creating.

4. Click the **Name** text box and type the name for the new style.

5. If you want to base the new style on an existing style, click the **Based On** drop-down arrow and select the desired base style from the list.

6. If you want the new style to be part of the template that the current document is based on, select the **Add to Template** check box. If you do not select this check box, the new style will be available only in the current document.

7. (Optional) Select the **Automatically Update** check box if you want Word to add to the style definition all manual formatting changes you make to paragraphs with this style assigned. (This option is available only for paragraph styles.)

8. Click the **Format** button and select **Font** or **Border** to specify the font and/or border of the new style. As you make formatting changes, the Preview box displays an image of what the style will look like, and the Description area provides a description of the style elements.

9. For paragraph styles only, click the **Format** button and select **Paragraph** to set the style's indents and line spacing. Then select **Tabs** to set the new style's tab stops.

10. Click **OK** to return to the Style dialog box.

11. Click **Apply** to assign the new style to the current text or paragraph. Click **Close** to save the new style definition without assigning it to any text.

Modifying a Style

You can change the formatting associated with any paragraph or character style, whether it is a style you define or one of Word's predefined styles. When you do so, all text in the document that has the style assigned will be modified. Follow these steps to change a style throughout a document:

1. Click **Format**, **Style** to open the Style dialog box (see Figure 12.4).

2. Click the **List** drop-down arrow and select which styles should be displayed in the Styles list:

    - **All Styles**   All styles defined in the current document.
    - **Styles in Use**   Styles assigned to text in the current document.
    - **User Defined Styles**   All user-defined styles in the current document.

3. In the **Styles** list, click the name of the style you want to modify.

4. Click the **Modify** button. The Modify Style dialog box appears; it looks the same as the New Style dialog box (refer to Figure 12.3). Specify the style's new format specifications.

5. Click **OK** to return to the Style dialog box. Then click **Close**.

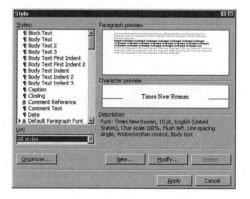

Figure 12.4   The Style dialog box.

TIP A quicker way to change a style is to apply the style to some text in your document and then change that text in your document, and then change that text to the way you want the style to be. Then click in the **Style** box on the **Formatting** toolbar so that the style name is highlighted, and press **Enter**. If you chose the **Update Automatically** check box in the New Style dialog box (refer to Figure 12.3), the style changes automatically; if you didn't, a dialog box asks whether you want to change the style or revert to the original formatting for that style.

In this lesson, you learned what styles are, how to apply styles to text, and how to create and modify styles. In the next lesson, you learn how to apply automatic formatting to text.

Applying Automatic Formatting

In this lesson, you learn how to use Word's automatic formatting capability.

What AutoFormatting Can Do

Automatic formatting is a feature that lets Word analyze the parts of a document, recognize certain elements (such as body text, headings, bulleted lists, and quotations), and then apply appropriate styles to the various text elements to create an attractively formatted document. (You learned about styles in Lesson 12, "Making the Most of Styles,") You can accept or reject the automatically applied format in part or in whole, and you can later make desired modifications to the document.

In addition to applying styles, automatic formatting removes extra returns between paragraphs; automatically formats Internet, network, and e-mail addresses as hyperlinks; applies bold or underline character formatting to text surrounded by asterisks (*) or underscores (_); replaces two hyphens (- -) with an em dash (—); and more.

TIP   **Word on the Web**   If you format Internet and e-mail addresses as hyperlinks, users will be able to access them over the Internet by clicking the link in the document.

Automatic formatting can be used in two ways: Word can format items as you type them, or you can create an unformatted document and then apply automatic formatting to the entire document.

Is automatic formatting right for you? The only way to find out is to try it yourself. Take a document that's typical of documents you usually work on, save it under a new name (so the original is not changed), and then experiment. You'll soon find out if you like automatic formatting—or if you prefer to format your documents manually.

 TIP   **Try It Out**   You should give automatic formatting a try. If you like the results, it can save you a lot of time.

Applying Formatting As You Type

Word can apply a variety of formatting to text as you type it. Some examples include:

- **Tables**   If you type a line of plus signs and hyphens (such as +--+--+) and then press **Enter**, Word creates a table with one column for each plus sign. Initially, the table will have one row, and the cursor will be positioned in the first cell.
- **Borders**   If you type three or more hyphens, underscores, or equal signs, Word will insert a thin, thick, or double border, respectively.
- **Bulleted Lists**   If you start a paragraph with an asterisk, a lowercase "o," or a hyphen, followed by a space or tab, Word automatically creates a bulleted list.

To set your preferences for which types of formatting are applied as you type, follow these steps:

1. Select **Format**, **AutoFormat** to display the AutoFormat dialog box.
2. Click the **Options** button to open the AutoCorrect dialog box.
3. If necessary, click the **AutoFormat As You Type** tab to see the options shown in Figure 13.1.
4. Select or deselect the check boxes as desired.
5. Click **OK**.

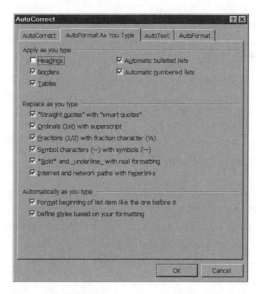

Figure 13.1 Setting the AutoFormat As You Type options.

Changing options in this dialog box does not affect text that has already been formatted. It affects only text that is typed after the options are changed.

What Does That Do? Remember, you can get Help information on any option by clicking the **AutoHelp** button (the question mark) in a dialog box's title bar and then clicking the option in question.

CAUTION

Applying AutoFormatting to Your Document

Here are the steps required to apply automatic formatting to the entire document after you've typed it:

1. Select **Format, AutoFormat** to open the AutoFormat dialog box.

2. Select **AutoFormat Now** to apply AutoFormatting without reviewing individual changes. Select **AutoFormat and Review Each Change** if you want to be able to accept or reject each format change.

3. (Optional) Open the drop-down list and select the type of document you are working on from the list. Your choices are General Document, Letter, and Email.

4. Click **OK**.

If you selected **AutoFormat Now** in step 2, Word analyzes your document and applies formatting based on the document contents. You cannot reverse individual formatting changes, but you can undo the entire AutoFormat effect by selecting **Edit**, **Undo AutoFormat**.

If you selected **AutoFormat and Review Each Change** in step 2, Word formats your document and displays the AutoFormat dialog box shown in Figure 13.2. You can scroll around in your document while this dialog box is displayed to view the changes that Word made. Then click one of the following command buttons to proceed:

- **Accept All**   Accepts all formatting changes.
- **Reject All**   Rejects all formatting changes.
- **Review Changes**   Lets you view each formatting change and accept or reject it (see the next paragraph).
- **Style Gallery**   Displays the Style Gallery, from which you can select an overall "look" for your document. After you select a style, you return to the AutoFormat dialog box.

Figure 13.2 The AutoFormat dialog box.

If you decide to review changes, the Review AutoFormat Changes dialog box appears (see Figure 13.3). You use the commands in this dialog box to examine the format changes one at a time, accepting or rejecting each one. Font changes are not reviewed, but all other formatting changes are. While you are working in this dialog box, Word displays the document with marks indicating the changes made. Table 13.1 lists the types of changes you can make and the marks Word displays in your document.

Table 13.1 Marks Displayed to Indicate AutoFormat Changes

Change Made	Mark Displayed
New style applied to the paragraph	Blue paragraph mark
Paragraph mark deleted	Red paragraph mark
Text or spaces deleted	Strikethrough
Characters added	Underline
Text or formatting changed	Vertical bar in left margin

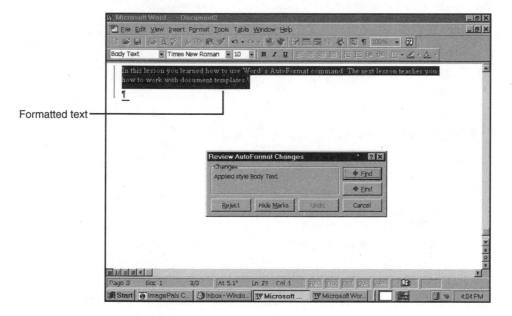

Figure 13.3 The Review AutoFormat Changes dialog box.

Word searches for the AutoFormatting changes that were made and highlights each one in the document. Use the command buttons in the dialog box to tell Word what to do with each AutoFormatting change:

← **Find** tells Word to locate and highlight the previous change.

→ **Find** tells Word to locate and highlight the next change.

Reject tells Word to undo the highlighted formatting change.

Hide Marks tells Word to hide the indicator marks in the document to make it easier to evaluate its appearance. Click **Show Marks** to redisplay the marks.

Undo tells Word to reinstate the previous rejected change.

Cancel returns you to the AutoFormat dialog box.

Note that you do not need to take any action to accept a change. If you do not explicitly reject a change, Word automatically accepts it.

CAUTION

Oops!   To be sure you can recover from unwanted AutoFormat changes, first save your document under a different name.

Setting AutoFormat Options

The AutoFormat feature has a number of settings that control which document elements it will modify. You can change these options to suit your preferences, as you'll learn in these steps:

1. Select **Format**, **AutoFormat** to open the AutoFormat dialog box.

2. Click the **Options** button to display the AutoFormat options (see Figure 13.4).

3. Select or deselect the various AutoFormat check boxes as desired. Use the What's This? Help as needed to get information on individual options. (Click the question mark in the dialog box's title bar, and then click the element you need help with.)

4. When you're finished making changes, click **OK**.

Changes you make to AutoFormat options will not affect a previously formatted document, but they will apply to future uses of the AutoFormat command.

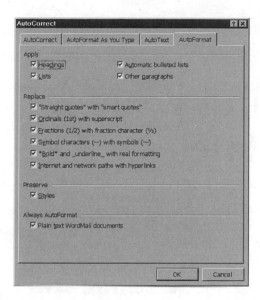

Figure 13.4 Setting AutoFormat options.

In this lesson, you learned how to use Word's AutoFormat command. The next lesson teaches you how to work with document templates.

Working with Templates

In this lesson, you learn how to create new document templates and how to modify existing templates.

Creating a New Template

You learned in Lesson 4, "Saving and Opening documents," that every Word document is based on a template, and that Word comes with a variety of pre-defined templates. You also can create your own templates or modify existing templates to suit your individual needs.

You can create a new template based on an existing template, and the new template will contain all the elements of the base template plus any text or formatting you add. To create a new template from scratch, base it on the Blank Document template. Here are the steps to follow:

1. Select **File**, **New** to open the New dialog box (see Figure 14.1).
2. Click the **Template** option button (in the lower-right corner).
3. If you want the new template based on an existing template, select that template icon in the dialog box. Otherwise, select the **Blank Document** icon on the General tab.
4. Click **OK**. A document-editing screen appears with a default name, such as TEMPLATE1.
5. Enter the boilerplate text and other items that you want to include in the new template, and then apply formatting to the text as desired. You should also create any styles that you want in the template.

 Boilerplate This is text that you want to appear in every document based on the new template.

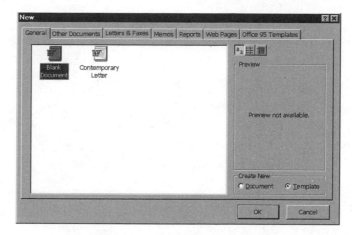

Figure 14.1 Creating a new template based on the Blank Document template.

6. Select **File, Save** or click the **Save** button on the Standard toolbar. The Save As dialog box appears.

7. If necessary, select the folder where you want the new template saved. For example, if it is a template for a letter, you would probably save it in the Letters & Faxes folder.

8. In the **File Name** text box, enter a descriptive name for the template, using up to 256 characters. Be sure to use a different name from the template you selected in step 3, or the new template will replace the original one.

9. Select **Save**. Word saves the template under the specified name. It is now available for use each time you start a new document.

CAUTION In step 7, you must save the template either in the Templates folder or in one of the subfolders beneath it. Each of these subfolders represents a tab in the New dialog box when you start a new template. If you save the template anywhere else, the New dialog box will not show it as a usable template.

Modifying an Existing Template

Suppose you create your own template, but then you find out that you need to change the boilerplate text slightly. You can retrieve any existing template from disk and modify it. Here's how:

1. Select **File, Open** to open the Open dialog box.
2. Navigate to the C:\Program Files\Microsoft Office\Templates folder.
3. Open the **Files of Type** drop-down list and choose **Document Templates**.
4. Select the template you want to modify.
5. Click **Open**. The template opens.
6. Make changes to the template as needed.

7. Select **File, Save** or click the **Save** button on the Standard toolbar, and Word saves the modified template to disk.

When you modify a template, changes you make are not reflected in documents that were created based on the template before it was changed. Only new documents will be affected.

TIP **Save the Old**   Instead of modifying a template, it's often better to create a new template based on it. This way the original template will still be available should you change your mind or want to use it again.

TIP **Recycle Old Templates?**   You can use old templates from earlier versions of Word (Word for Windows 95 and Word for Windows 6.0) to create new documents in Word 97. The templates must be placed in the Templates folder, however, so that you can acess them through Word 97.

Creating a Template from a Document

Sometimes you will find it useful to create a template based on an existing Word document. Here are the steps to follow:

1. Open the document on which you want to base the new template.
2. Use Word's editing commands to delete any document text and formatting that you do *not* want to include in the template.
3. Select **File, Save As** to open the Save As dialog box (see Figure 14.2).
4. Click the **Save As Type** drop-down arrow and choose **Document Template** from the list. The Save In box automatically changes to indicate the Templates folder.

5. If appropriate, double-click the name of the folder in which you want to save the template.
6. Type a descriptive name for the template in the **File Name** text box.
7. Click **Save**.

In step 5, it's important to select the proper template folder. When you select Document Template in step 4, Word automatically switches to the Templates folder. Templates saved in this folder will appear on the General tab in the New dialog box. Because Word organizes templates by category, you may want to place your new template in the appropriate folder because if you don't, you may have trouble finding it later. For example, if you create a template for a memo, save it in the Memos folder so that it will appear on the Memos tab in the New dialog box.

Figure 14.2 Saving a document template.

Updating a Document When the Template Changes

If you modify a template, only new documents based on that template will reflect the changes. Existing documents that were based on the old version of the template will not be affected. You can, however, import new styles from a modified template to an existing document. Here's how:

1. Open the document.
2. Select **Tools, Templates and Add-ins**.

3. Select the **Automatically Update Document Styles** check box.

4. Select **OK**.

With this check box selected, the document styles will automatically be updated to reflect the styles in its attached template each time the document is loaded. Other elements of a template, such as boilerplate text, will not be affected.

 TIP If you want the document to be updated with the latest template styles immediately, you can either close the document and reopen it, or you can attach a different template with the Tools, Templates and Add-Ins dialog box—and then reattach the original template by marking the **Automatically Update Document Styles** check box.

In this lesson, you learned how to create and modify document templates. The next lesson shows you how to use page numbers, headers, and footers in your documents.

Page Numbers, Headers, and Footers

In this lesson, you learn how to add page numbers, headers, and footers to your documents.

Adding Page Numbers

Many documents—particularly long ones—require that the pages be numbered. Word offers many choices as to the placement and appearance of page numbers. Page numbers are always part of a header or footer. You can place a page number by itself in a header or footer, as covered in this section. You also can include additional information in the header or footer, as covered later in this lesson.

To add page numbers to your document, follow these steps:

1. Select **Insert**, **Page Numbers**. The Page Numbers dialog box appears, as shown in Figure 15.1.

Figure 15.1 The Page Numbers dialog box.

2. Click the **Position** drop-down arrow and select the desired position on the page: **Top of Page (Header)** or **Bottom of Page (Footer)**.

3. Click the **Alignment** drop-down arrow and select **Left**, **Center**, or **Right**. You can also select **Inside** or **Outside** if you're printing two-sided pages and want the page numbers positioned near to (Inside) or away from (Outside) the binding.

4. The default number format consists of Arabic numerals (1, 2, 3, and so on). To select a different format (such as, i, ii, iii), click **Format** and select the desired format.

5. Click **OK**.

When you add a page number using this procedure, Word makes the page number part of the document's header or footer. The next section describes headers and footers.

TIP   **Can I Print Both Sides?**   Two-sided printing is an option on certain printers. Lesson 11, "Margins, Pages, and Sections," shows you how to set margins for two-sided printing.

CAUTION   **No Page Numbers Command?**   When you're in Online Layout view or Outline view, the **Page Numbers** option is not available on the **Insert** menu. In Normal view, you can add page numbers, but you cannot see them.

What Are Headers and Footers?

A *header* or *footer* is text that prints at the top (header) or bottom (footer) of every page of a document. Headers and footers can show the page number; they are also useful for displaying chapter titles, authors' names, and similar information. Word offers several header/footer options, including the following:

- The same header/footer on every page of the document.
- One header/footer on the first page of the document and a different header/footer on all other pages.

- One header/footer on odd-numbered pages and a different header/footer on even-numbered pages.
- If your document is divided into sections, you can have a different header/footer for each section.

Headers and Footers Text that is displayed at the top (header) or bottom (footer) of every page.

Adding or Editing a Header or Footer

To add a header or footer to your document, or to edit an existing header or footer, follow these steps:

1. If your document is divided into sections, move the cursor to any location in the section where you want the header or footer placed.
2. Select **View**, **Header and Footer**. Word switches to Page Layout view and displays the current page's header enclosed in a nonprinting dashed line (see Figure 15.2). Regular document text is dimmed, and the Header and Footer toolbar is displayed.

3. On the toolbar, click the **Switch Between Header and Footer** button to switch between the current page's header and footer as needed.
4. Enter the header or footer text and formatting using the normal Word editing techniques. Use the **Alignment** buttons on the Formatting toolbar to control the placement of items in the header/footer.
5. Use the other toolbar buttons, which are described in Table 15.1, to customize your header/footer.
6. When finished, click the **Close** button on the Header and Footer toolbar to return to the document.

TIP

Good-Bye, Header! To delete the contents of a header or footer, select all the text in the header or footer and press **Delete**.

Table 15.1 Header and Footer Toolbar Buttons

Button	Description
Insert AutoText ▾	Inserts an AutoText entry
[#]	Inserts a page number code
[page icon]	Inserts the total number of pages
[#]	Formats the page number
[date icon]	Inserts a date code
[clock icon]	Inserts a time code
[book icon]	Opens the Page Setup dialog box so that you can set margins (Lesson 11)
[icon]	Shows or hides document text
[icon]	Makes the header/footer the same as the previous one
[icon]	Switches between header and footer
[icon]	Shows the previous header or footer
[icon]	Shows the next header or footer
Close	Closes the Header and Footer toolbar and returns to the document

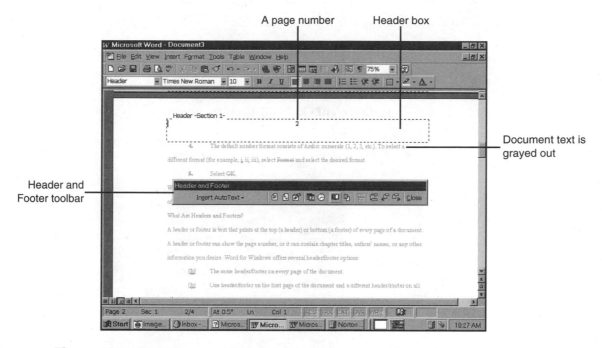

Figure 15.2 The Header and Footer toolbar.

Creating Different Headers and Footers for Different Pages

Word's default is to display the same header/footer on all the pages in a section or document. One way to have different headers/footers in different parts of the document is to break the document into two or more sections, as explained in Lesson 11. Then you can use the techniques described earlier in the lesson to add a different header/footer to each section.

In addition to using sections, you have the following options:

- One header/footer on the first page with a different header/footer on all other pages.
- One header/footer on odd-numbered pages with another header/footer on even-numbered pages.

To activate one or both of these options:

1. Select **View**, **Header and Footer**.
2. Click the **Page Setup** button on the Header and Footer toolbar. Word displays the Layout tab of the Page Setup dialog box (see Figure 15.3).
3. Select the **Different Odd and Even** check box and/or the **Different First Page** check box.
4. Click **OK** to close the Page Setup dialog box.

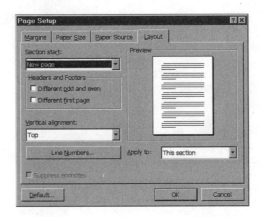

Figure 15.3 Setting header/footer options in the Page Setup dialog box.

After selecting one of these header/footer options, you use the techniques described earlier in this lesson (in the section "Adding or Editing a Header or Footer") to add and edit the header/footer text. For example, say you specified Different Odd and Even. If the cursor is on an even-numbered page and you select the View, Headers and Footers command, Word displays the header/ footer text that will display on even-numbered pages so that you can edit it. If you click the Show Next button on the Header/Footer toolbar, Word moves to the header/footer for odd-numbered pages.

In this lesson, you learned to add page numbers, headers, and footers to a document. In the next lesson, you will learn how to create numbered and bulleted lists.

Numbered and Bulleted Lists

In this lesson, you learn how to add numbered and bulleted lists to your documents.

Why Use Numbered and Bulleted Lists?

Numbered and bulleted lists are useful formatting tools for setting off lists of information in a document—you've seen plenty of both in this book! Word can automatically create both types of lists. Use bulleted lists for items that consist of related information that does not have to be listed in any particular order. Use numbered lists for items that must fall in a specific order. When you create a numbered or bulleted list, each paragraph is considered a separate list item and receives its own number or bullet.

Creating a Numbered or Bulleted List

You can create a list from existing text or create the list as you type. To create a numbered or bulleted list from existing text, follow these steps:

1. Select the paragraphs you want in the list.
2. Select **Format**, **Bullets and Numbering** to open the Bullets and Numbering dialog box.
3. Depending on the type of list you want, click the **Bulleted** tab or the **Numbered** tab. Figure 16.1 shows the Numbered tab options, and Figure 16.2 shows the Bulleted tab options.
4. Click the bullet or number style you want.
5. Click **OK**.

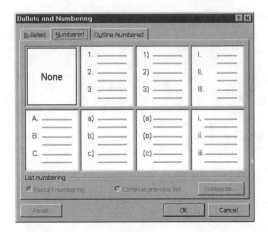

Figure 16.1 Numbered list style options in the Numbered tab.

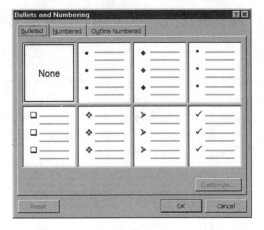

Figure 16.2 Bulleted list style options in the Bulleted tab.

Follow these steps to create a numbered or bulleted list as you type:

1. Move the insertion point to the location for the list, and then press **Enter**, if necessary, to start a new paragraph.

2. Select **Format, Bullets and Numbering** to open the Bullets and Numbering dialog box.

3. Depending on the type of list you want, click the **Bulleted** tab or the **Numbered** tab.

4. Click the bullet or number style you want.

5. Click **OK**.

6. Type the list elements, pressing **Enter** at the end of each paragraph. Word automatically places a bullet or number in front of each new paragraph.

7. At the end of the last paragraph, press **Enter** twice.

 TIP **Quick Lists** Quickly create a numbered or bulleted list in the default list style by clicking the **Numbering** or **Bullets** button on the Formatting toolbar before typing or after selecting the list text.

 TIP **Automatic Lists** If the corresponding AutoFormat options are on, Word automatically starts a numbered or bulleted list anytime you start a paragraph with a number and period or an asterisk followed by a space or tab. To turn these options on or off, select **Format**, **AutoFormat**, **Options** and click the **Lists** and the **Automatic Bulleted Lists** check boxes to turn them on or off.

Using Multilevel Lists

A multilevel list contains two or more levels of bullets or numbering within a single list. For example, a numbered list could contain a lettered list under each numbered item, or each level could be numbered separately, as in an outline. Here's how to create a multilevel list:

1. Select **Format**, **Bullets and Numbering** to open the Bullets and Numbering dialog box.

2. Click the **Outline Numbered** tab to display the multilevel options, as shown in Figure 16.3.

3. Click the list style you want. Avoid the ones that say "Heading 1" in gray; these options apply specific styles to different levels in the list, which you do not want to do.

4. Click **OK**.

5. Start typing the list, pressing **Enter** after each item.

6. (Optional) After pressing **Enter**, press **Tab** to demote the new item one level, or press **Shift+Tab** to promote the item. If you don't do either, the next item will be at the same level as the previous item.

7. After typing the last item and pressing **Enter**, click the **Numbering** button on the Formatting toolbar to end the list.

Figure 16.3 Use the Outline Numbered tab of the Bullets and Numbering dialog box to create a multilevel list.

You can convert regular text or a one-level numbered or bulleted list to a multilevel list. You also can change the style of an existing multilevel list. Here are the steps to follow:

1. Select all the paragraphs you want to include in the new list or whose format you want to modify.

2. Select **Format, Bullets and Numbering**, and then click the **Outline Numbered** tab.

3. Click the desired list style and click **OK**.

4. Move the insertion point to an item in the list whose level you want to change.

5. Click the **Decrease Indent** or the **Increase Indent** button on the Formatting toolbar to change the item's level.

6. Repeat steps 4 and 5 as needed to change other items.

Removing a Numbered or Bulleted List

Follow these steps to remove bullets or numbers from a list but keep the text and convert it to normal paragraphs:

1. Select the paragraphs from which you want the bullets or numbering removed. This can be the entire list or just part of it. The corresponding button (Bullets or Numbering) on the Formatting toolbar appears to be pressed in.

2. Click the **Bullets** or **Numbering** button to turn the formatting style off.

Changing the Format of a Numbered or Bulleted List

You also can change the format of an existing bulleted or numbered list, to change the bullet symbol or the numbering style. Here's how:

1. Select the paragraphs from which you want the bullets or numbering removed. (This can be the entire list or just part of it.)

2. Select **Format, Bullets and Numbering** to open the Bullets and Numbering dialog box.

3. For a bulleted list, click the **Bulleted** tab and select the desired style. Select **None** to remove bullets.

4. For a numbered list, click the **Numbered** tab and select the desired numbering style, or click **None** to remove numbering from the list.

5. Click **OK** to put your changes into effect.

Adding Items to Numbered and Bulleted Lists

You can add new items to a numbered or bulleted list using the steps here:

1. Move the insertion point to the location in the list where you want the new item.

2. Press **Enter** to start a new paragraph. Word automatically inserts a new bullet or number and renumbers the list items if necessary.

3. Type the new text.

 4. (Optional) If it's a multilevel list, click the **Decrease Indent** or the **Increase Indent** button on the Formatting toolbar to change the item's level.

5. Repeat these steps as many times as needed.

This lesson showed you how to create numbered and bulleted lists. The next lesson shows you how to add symbols and other special characters to your document.

Using Symbols and Special Characters

In this lesson, you learn how to use symbols and special characters.

What Are Symbols and Special Characters?

Symbols and *special characters* are not part of the standard character set and, therefore, will not be found on your keyboard. Accented letters (such as é), the Greek letter mu (μ), and the copyright symbol (©) are examples. Even though these characters are not on your keyboard, Word can still insert them in your documents.

Inserting a Symbol

To insert a symbol in your document, place the insertion point where you want the symbol, and then follow these steps:

1. Select **Insert**, **Symbol** to open the Symbol dialog box (see Figure 17.1). Click the **Symbols** tab if it is not already displayed.

2. Click the **Font** drop-down arrow and select the desired symbol set from the list. Those you will use most often include:

   - **Symbol**   Greek letters, mathematical symbols, arrows, trademark and copyright symbols, and more.
   - **Normal Text**   Letters with accents and other special marks, currency symbols, the paragraph symbol, and more.
   - **WingDings**   Icons for clocks, envelopes, telephones, and so on.

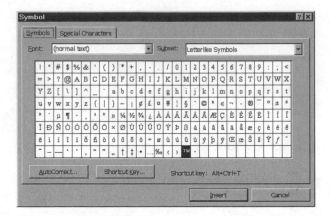

Figure 17.1 The Symbol dialog box.

3. Look through the grid of symbols for the one you want. To see an enlarged view of a symbol, click it.

4. To insert a selected symbol, click **Insert**. To insert any symbol (that's not selected), double-click the symbol.

5. Click **Close** to close the dialog box after you insert one or more symbols. (Or click the **Cancel** button to close the dialog box without inserting a symbol.)

Inserting a Special Character

The distinction between "special characters" and "symbols" is not a clear one. In fact, there is some overlap between the two. Symbols include letters with accents and other diacritical marks used in some languages, Greek letters, arrows, and mathematical symbols (such as ±). Special characters include the copyright symbol (©), the ellipsis (…), and typographic symbols such as em spaces (a wider than normal space). You'll see that Word provides many more symbols than it does special characters.

To insert a special character in your document, place the insertion point where you want the character, and then follow these steps:

1. Select **Insert**, **Symbol** to open the Symbol dialog box.

2. Click the **Special Characters** tab to display the list of available special characters (see Figure 17.2).

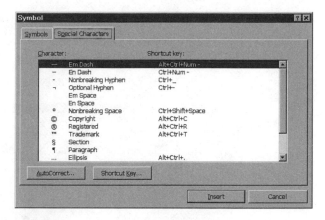

Figure 17.2 The Special Characters list.

3. Look through the list of special characters for the one you want.

4. To insert a selected character, double-click it, or select it and then click **Insert**.

5. Click the **Close** (X) button to close the dialog box after you insert a character. Or click the **Cancel** button to close the dialog box without inserting a character.

Assigning Shortcut Keys to Symbols

You may want to assign a shortcut key to any symbol you use frequently. Then you can insert it quickly by pressing that key combination. Most of the special characters already have shortcut keys assigned to them; these key assignments are listed on the Special Characters tab in the Symbol dialog box.

TIP **More Shortcuts** You also can use Word's AutoCorrect feature to quickly insert symbols and special characters. See Lesson 13, "Applying Automatic Formatting," for more information.

Follow these steps to assign a shortcut key to a symbol:

1. Select **Insert**, **Symbol** and click the **Symbols** tab (refer to Figure 17.1).

2. Click the desired symbol. (If necessary, first select the proper font from the **Font** list.)

229

3. If the selected symbol already has a shortcut key assigned to it, the key combination appears in the lower-right corner of the dialog box.

4. Click the **Shortcut Key** button to display the Customize Keyboard dialog box (see Figure 17.3).

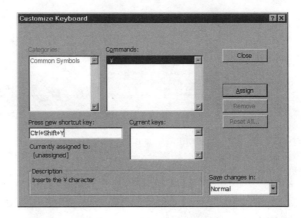

Figure 17.3 Assigning a shortcut key to a symbol.

5. Press **Alt+N** to move to the **Press New Shortcut Key** text box (or click in that box).

6. Press the shortcut key combination you want to assign. Its description appears in the Press New Shortcut Key text box. A list of permitted key combinations follows these steps.

7. If the specified key combination is unassigned, Word displays **[unassigned]** under the Press New Shortcut Key text box. If it has already been assigned, Word displays the name of the symbol, macro, or command to which the selected shortcut key is assigned.

8. If the shortcut key is unassigned, click **Assign** to assign it to the symbol. If it is already assigned, press **Backspace** to delete the shortcut key display and return to step 6 to try another key combination.

9. When you're done, click **Close** to return to the Symbol dialog box, and then click **Close** again to return to your document.

The shortcut keys are really key combinations. You can select from the following key combinations, where *key* is a letter key, number key, function key, or cursor movement key:

Shift+*key*   Alt+Shift+*key*

Ctrl+*key*   Ctrl+Shift+*key*

Alt+*key*   Ctrl+Shift+Alt+*key*

Alt+Ctrl+*key*

Understanding Special Characters

Some of the special characters that Word offers may seem unfamiliar to you, but they can be quite useful in certain documents. The following are brief descriptions of the less well-known ones:

- **En dash**   A dash that is longer than a hyphen (inserted with the key above the P key on your keyboard). The en dash is properly used in combinations of figures and capital letters, as in "Please refer to part 1–A."

- **Em dash**   Slightly longer than an en dash, the em dash has a variety of purposes, the most common of which is to mark a sudden change of thought. For example, "She said—and no one dared disagree—that the meeting was over."

- **En space**   A space slightly longer than the standard space. This space ( ) is an en space.

- **Em space**   A space slightly longer than the en space. This space ( ) is an em space.

- **Non-breaking space**   A space that will not be broken at the end of the line. The words separated by a non-breaking space always stay on the same line.

- **Non-breaking hyphen**   Similar to a non-breaking space. That is to say, two words separated by a non-breaking hyphen will always stay on the same line.

- **Optional hyphen**   A hyphen that will not be displayed unless the word it is in needs to be broken at the end of a line.

In this lesson, you learned how to use symbols and special characters in your Word documents. In the next lesson, you will learn how to proof your document.

Proofing Your Documents

This lesson shows you how to use Word's spelling and grammar checker, thesaurus, and Print Preview window to proof your document.

Using the Spelling Checker

Word's spelling checker lets you verify and correct the spelling of words in your document. Words are checked against a standard dictionary and unknown words are flagged. You can then ignore the word, correct it, or add it to the dictionary.

To check spelling in a portion of a document, select the text to check. Otherwise, Word will check the entire document starting at the location of the cursor. If you want to check starting at the beginning of the document, move the insertion point to the start of the document by pressing **Ctrl+Home**. Then follow these steps:

 1. Select **Tools**, **Spelling and Grammar**, or press **F7**, or click the **Spelling and Grammar** button on the Standard toolbar. The Spelling and Grammar dialog box appears (see Figure 18.1). If you want to check spelling only, deselect the **Check Grammar** check box. The remainder of these steps assume that you are only checking spelling. (If you tell Word to check grammar, it flags suspected grammar errors; how you deal with these is described later in this lesson.)

2. When Word locates a word in the document that is not in the dictionary, it displays the word and its surrounding text in the **Not in Dictionary** list box with the word highlighted in red. In Figure 18.1, for example, the word **checker** is highlighted. Suggested replacements for the word appear in the Suggestions list box (if Word has no suggestions, this box will be empty). For each word that Word stops on, take action in one of these ways:

- To correct the word manually, edit it in the **Not in Dictionary** list box and click **Change**.
- To use one of the suggested replacements, highlight the desired replacement word in the **Suggestions** list box and click **Change**.
- To replace all instances of the word in the document with either the manual corrections you made or the word selected in the Suggestions box, click **Change All**.
- To ignore this instance of the word, click **Ignore**.
- To ignore this and all other instances of the word in the document, click **Ignore All**.
- To add the word to the dictionary, click **Add**.

3. Repeat as needed. When the entire document has been checked, Word displays a message to that effect. (Or, you can click **Cancel** at any time to end spell checking early.)

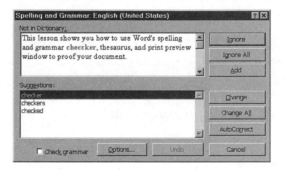

Figure 18.1 Checking spelling in the Spelling and Grammar dialog box.

 TIP **Use AutoCorrect** To add a misspelled word and its correction to the AutoCorrect list, select **AutoCorrect** in the Spelling and Grammar dialog box. Future misspellings will then be corrected automatically as you type them.

Checking Your Grammar

Word can check the grammar of the text in your document, flagging possible problems so that you can correct them if needed. Here are the steps required to run the grammar checker:

1. Select **Tools**, **Spelling and Grammar**, or press **F7**, or click the **Spelling and Grammar** button on the toolbar. The Spelling and Grammar dialog box appears (refer to Figure 18.1). Make sure the **Check Grammar** check box is selected.

2. When Word locates a word or phrase with a suspected grammatical error, it displays the word or phrase and its surrounding text in the dialog box with the word highlighted in green and a description of the suspected problem above the text. In Figure 18.2, for example, the word **wants** is highlighted and the problem **Subject-Verb Agreement** appears. Suggested fixes, if any, are listed in the Suggestions list box. For each potential mistake that Word stops on, take action in one of these ways:

   - To manually correct the error, edit the text and click **Change**.

   - To use one of the suggested replacements, select it in the **Suggestions** list box and click **Change**.

   - To ignore this instance of the problem, click **Ignore**.

   - To ignore this instance and all other instances of the problem in the document, click **Ignore All**.

3. Word will check spelling at the same time it is checking grammar. Deal with spelling errors as explained earlier in this lesson.

4. Repeat as needed. When the entire document has been checked, Word displays a message to that effect. (Or, you can click **Close** at any time to end grammar checking early.)

Don't Rely on Word Word's grammar checker is a useful tool, but don't rely on it to catch everything. It is no substitute for careful writing and editing.

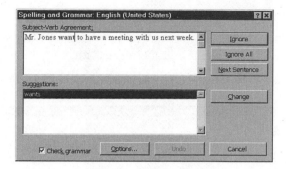

Figure 18.2 Checking grammar in the Spelling and Grammar dialog box.

Checking Spelling and Grammar As You Type

In addition to checking your document's spelling and grammar all at once, Word can check text as you type it. Words not found in the dictionary will be underlined with a wavy red line, and suspected grammatical errors will be marked with a wavy green line. You can deal with the errors immediately or whenever you choose. To turn automatic spell/grammar checking on or off:

1. Select **Tools, Options** to open the Options dialog box.
2. If necessary, click the **Spelling and Grammar** tab.
3. Select or deselect the **Check Spelling As You Type** and the **Check Grammar As You Type** check boxes.
4. Click **OK**.

To deal with a word that has been underlined by automatic spell checking or grammar checking, right-click the word. A pop-up menu appears, containing suggested replacements for the word (if any are found) as well as several commands. Figure 18.3 shows the pop-up menu that appears when you right-click a misspelled word.

For a spelling error, you have the following choices:

- To replace the word with one of the suggestions, click the replacement word.
- To ignore all occurrences of the word in the document, click **Ignore All**.

- To add the word to the dictionary, click **Add**.
- To add the misspelling to the AutoCorrect list, select **AutoCorrect**, and then select the proper replacement spelling.
- To start a regular spelling check, click **Spelling**.

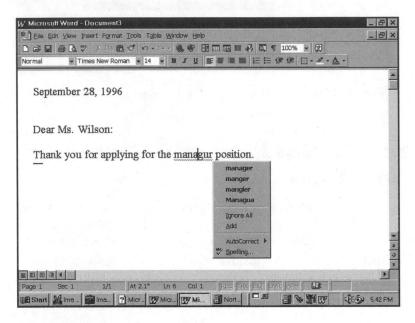

Figure 18.3 Correcting spelling as you type.

When you right-click a grammatical error, you are offered the following choices:

- Select a suggested replacement to insert it in the document.
- Select **Ignore Sentence** to ignore the possible error.
- Select **Grammar** to start a regular grammar check.

TIP **Hide Spelling/Grammar Marks** If your document contains words underlined by the automatic spelling or grammar checker and you want to hide the underlines, select **Tools**, **Options**, click the **Spelling and Grammar** tab, and select the **Hide Spelling Errors in This Document** check box or the **Hide Grammatical Errors in This Document** check box. Deselect these check boxes to redisplay the underlines.

Using the Thesaurus

A thesaurus provides you with synonyms and antonyms for words in your document. Using the thesaurus can help you avoid repetition in your writing (and improve your vocabulary).

 TERM **Synonyms and Antonyms** Words with the same and opposite meanings, respectively, as a given word.

To use the thesaurus:

1. Place the insertion point on the word of interest in your document.

2. Press **Shift+F7** or select **Tools, Thesaurus**. The Thesaurus dialog box opens (see Figure 18.4). This dialog box has several components:
   - The **Looked Up** list box displays the word of interest.
   - The **Meanings** list box lists alternate meanings for the word. If the word is not found, Word displays an **Alphabetical List** box instead; this list contains a list of words with spellings similar to the selected word.
   - If the thesaurus finds one or more meanings for the word, the dialog box displays the **Replace with Synonym** list showing synonyms for the currently highlighted meaning of the word. If meanings are not found, the dialog box displays a **Replace with Related Word** list.

3. While the Thesaurus dialog box is displayed, take one of these actions:
   - To find synonyms for the highlighted word in the Replace with Synonym list or the Replace with Related Words list (depending on which one is displayed), click **Look Up**.
   - To find synonyms for a word in the Meanings list, select the word and then click **Look Up**.
   - For some words, the thesaurus displays the term **Antonyms** in the Meanings list. To display antonyms for the selected word, highlight the term **Antonyms** and then click **Look Up**.

4. To replace the word in the document with the highlighted word in the Replace with Synonym list or the Replace with Related Word list, click **Replace**.

5. To close the thesaurus without making any changes to the document, click **Cancel**.

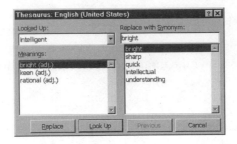

Figure 18.4   The Thesaurus dialog box.

TIP   **What Does It Mean?**   You can use the thesaurus like a dictionary to find the meaning of any word with which you are not familiar.

Using Print Preview

Word's Print Preview feature lets you view your document on the screen exactly as it will be printed. Although Page Layout view also displays your document in its final form, Print Preview offers some additional features that you may find useful. To use Print Preview, select **File**, **Print Preview** or click the **Print Preview** button on the Standard toolbar. The current page appears in the Preview window (see Figure 18.5).

These guidelines outline your available options in the Preview window:

- Press **Page Up** or **Page Down** or use the vertical scroll bar to view other pages.
- Click the **Multiple Pages** button and drag over the page icons to preview more than one page at once. Click the **One Page** button to preview a single page.
- Click the **Zoom Control** drop-down arrow and select a magnification to preview the document at different magnifications.
- Click the **View Ruler** button to display the Ruler. You can then use the Ruler to set page margins and indents as described in Lessons 9, "Indents and Justification," and 11, "Margins, Pages, and Sections."
- Click the **Magnifier** button and click in the document to enlarge that part of the document.

- Click the **Shrink to Fit** button to prevent a small amount of text from spilling onto the document's last page. Word will attempt to adjust formatting to reduce the page count by one.

- Click the **Print** button to print the document. Click again to return to the original view.

- Click **Close** or press **Esc** to end Print Preview display.

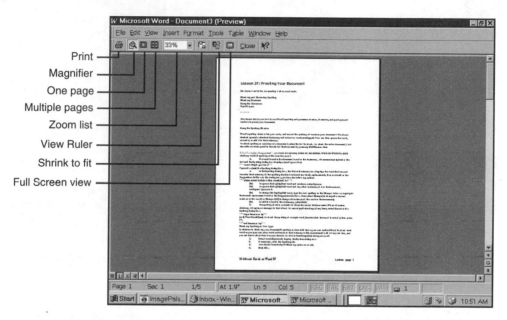

Figure 18.5   The Print Preview screen.

In this lesson, you learned how to use Word's proofing tools to check your document's spelling and grammar, and how to use the thesaurus and Print Preview. The next lesson shows you how to use tables.

Working with Tables

In this lesson, you learn how to add tables to your document, and how to edit and format tables.

What's a Table?

A *table* lets you organize information in a row and column format. Each entry in a table, called a *cell,* is independent of all other entries. You can have almost any number of rows and columns in a table. You also have a great deal of control over the size and formatting of each cell. A table cell can contain text, graphics, and just about anything that a Word document can contain. The one exception is that a table cannot contain another table.

 TIP **On the Table** Use tables for columns of numbers, lists, and anything else that requires a row and column arrangement.

Inserting a Table

To insert a new empty table at any location within your document, follow these steps:

1. Move the cursor to the document location where you want the table.
2. Select **Table, Insert Table**. The Insert Table dialog box appears (see Figure 19.1).
3. In the **Number of Columns** and **Number of Rows** text boxes, click the arrows or enter the number of rows and columns the table should have. (You can adjust these numbers later.)

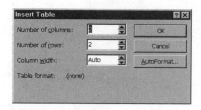

Figure 19.1 The Insert Table dialog box.

4. To apply one of Word's automatic table formats to the table, click the **AutoFormat** button, select the desired format, and click **OK**. (AutoFormat is covered in more detail later in this lesson.)

5. In the **Column Width** text box, select the desired width for each column (in inches). Select **Auto** in this box to have the page width evenly divided among the specified number of columns.

6. Select **OK**. Word creates a blank table with the cursor in the first cell.

 TIP **Quick Tables** To quickly insert a table, click the **Insert Table** button on the Standard toolbar and drag over the desired number of rows and columns.

Working in a Table

When the cursor is in a table cell, you can enter and edit text as you would in the rest of the document. Text entered in a cell automatically wraps to the next line within the column width. You can move the cursor to any cell by clicking it. You can also navigate in a table using the following special key combinations:

Press This...	To Move Here...
Tab	The next cell in a row
Shift+Tab	The previous cell in a row
Alt+Home	The first cell in the current row
Alt+Page Up	The top cell in the current column
Alt+End	The last cell in the current row
Alt+Page Down	The last cell in the current column

If the cursor is at the edge of a cell, you can also use the arrow keys to move between cells. To insert a Tab in a table cell, press **Ctrl+Tab**.

Editing and Formatting a Table

After you create a table and enter some information, you can edit its contents and format its appearance to suit your needs. The following sections explain common editing and formatting tasks you might want to perform.

Deleting and Inserting Cells, Rows, and Columns

You can clear individual cells in a table, erasing their contents and leaving the cells blank. To clear the contents of a cell, simply select the cell and press **Delete**.

TIP **Fast Select!** You can select the text in the cell or the entire cell itself. To select an entire cell, click in the left margin of the cell, between the text and the cell border. The mouse pointer changes to an arrow when it's in this area.

You can also remove entire rows and columns. When you do so, columns to the right or rows below move to fill in for the deleted row or column. To completely remove a row or column from the table, follow these steps:

1. Move the cursor to any cell in the row or column to be deleted.
2. Select **Table, Delete Cells**. The Delete Cells dialog box appears (see Figure 19.2).
3. Select **Delete Entire Row** or **Delete Entire Column**.
4. Click **OK**, and Word deletes the row or column.

Recovery Remember that you can undo table editing actions with the **Edit, Undo** command.

CAUTION

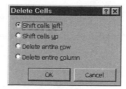

Figure 19.2   The Delete Cells dialog box.

Follow these steps to insert a single row or column into a table:

1. Move the cursor to a cell to the right of where you want the new column or below where you want the new row.

2. Select **Table, Insert Columns** to insert a new blank column to the left of the selected column. Select **Table, Insert Rows** to insert a new blank row above the selected row.

Changing Commands?   The commands on the Table menu change according to circumstances. For example, if you select a column in a table, the Insert Columns command is displayed, but the Insert Rows command is not.

CAUTION

Use these steps to insert more than one row or column into a table:

1. Select cells that span the number of rows or columns you want to insert. For example, to insert three new rows between rows 2 and 3, select cells in rows 3, 4, and 5 (in any column). To select several cells, drag across them or select one and then hold down Shift and use the arrow keys to extend the selections.

2. Select **Table, Select Row** (if inserting rows) or **Table, Select Column** (if inserting columns).

3. Select **Table, Insert Rows** or **Table, Insert Columns** as appropriate.

TIP   **Add a Row**   To insert a new row at the bottom of the table, move the cursor to the last cell in the table and press **Tab**.

To insert a new column at the right edge of the table, follow these steps:

1. Click just outside the table's right border.

2. Select **Table, Select Column**.

3. Select **Table, Insert Columns**.

Moving or Copying Columns and Rows

Here's how to copy or move an entire column or row from one location in a table to another:

1. Select the column or row by dragging over the cells, or by clicking in the column or row and selecting **Table**, **Select Row** or **Table**, **Select Column**.

2. To copy, press **Ctrl+C** or click the **Copy** button on the Standard toolbar. To move, press **Ctrl+X** or click the **Cut** button.

3. Move the cursor to the new location for the column or row. (It will be inserted above or to the left of the location of the cursor.)

4. Press **Ctrl+V** or click the **Paste** button on the Standard toolbar.

Changing Column Width

You can quickly change the width of a column with the mouse.

1. Point at the right border of the column whose width you want to change. The mouse pointer changes to a pair of thin vertical lines with arrowheads pointing left and right.

2. Drag the column border to the desired width.

CAUTION

When you drag a cell's border to change its width, if no cells are selected, the width changes for the entire table. However, if any cells are selected, the width changes for only the rows in which those cells lie. If you resize a column width and only one row changes, undo your changes (**Ctrl+Z**), click away from the table to deselect any selected cells, and try again.

You can also use a dialog box to change column widths. Follow these steps to learn how:

1. Move the cursor to any cell in the column you want to change.

2. Select **Table**, **Cell Height and Width**. The Cell Height and Width dialog box appears (see Figure 19.3). If necessary, click the **Column** tab to display the column options.

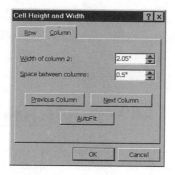

Figure 19.3 Changing column width.

3. In the **Width of Column** text box, enter the desired column width,,or click the up and down arrows to change the setting. Note that the label identifies which column you are working on by number. To automatically adjust the column width to fit the widest cell entry, click the **Autofit** button.

4. Change the value in the **Space Between Columns** text box to modify spacing between columns. Changing this setting increases or decreases the amount of space between the text in each cell and the cell's left and right borders.

5. Click **Next Column** or **Previous Column** to change the settings for other columns in the table.

6. Click **OK**. The table changes to reflect the new column settings.

Table Borders

Word's default is to place a single, thin border around each cell in a table. However, you can modify the borders or remove them altogether. The techniques for working with table borders are essentially the same as for adding borders to other text (see Lesson 8, "Fonts, Borders, and Shading"). Briefly, here are the steps involved.

1. Select the table cells whose borders you want to modify.

2. Select **Format**, **Borders and Shading** to display the Borders and Shading dialog box. Click the **Borders** tab if necessary.

3. Select the desired border settings, using the Preview box to see how your settings will appear.

4. Click **OK**.

In a table with no borders, you can display non-printing gridlines on-screen to make it easier to work with the table. Select **Table, Show Gridlines** to display gridlines. When you finish working with the table, select **Table, Hide Gridlines** to turn them off.

Automatic Table Formatting

Word provides a variety of predefined table formats. Using these formats makes it easy to apply attractive formatting to any table. These steps show you how to use a predefined table format:

1. Place the cursor anywhere in the table.

2. Select **Table, Table AutoFormat**. The Table AutoFormat dialog box appears (see Figure 19.4). This is the same dialog box you would see if you selected AutoFormat in the Insert Table dialog box when first creating a table (as covered earlier in this lesson).

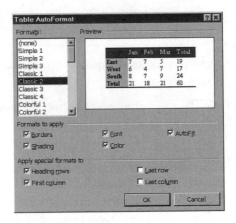

Figure 19.4   The Table AutoFormat dialog box.

3. The **Formats** list names the available table formats. As you scroll through the list, the Preview box shows the appearance of the highlighted format.

4. Select and deselect the formatting check boxes as needed until the Preview shows the table appearance you want.

5. When you're satisfied with what you see in the Preview area, click **OK**. Word applies the selected formatting to the table.

In this lesson, you learned how to add tables to your document, and how to edit and format tables. The next lesson shows you how to use columns in your documents.

Using Columns in Your Documents

In this lesson, you learn how to format your document text in two or more columns per page.

Why Use Columns?

Columns are commonly used in newsletters, brochures, and similar documents. The shorter lines of text provided by columns are easier to read, and they provide greater flexibility in formatting a document with graphics, tables, and so on. Word makes it easy to use columns in your documents. Figure 20.1 shows a document formatted with two columns.

The columns you create in Word are *newspaper* style columns, in which the text flows to the bottom of one column and then continues at the top of the next column on the page. For side-by-side paragraphs, such as you would need in a résumé or a script, use Word's Table feature, which is covered in Lesson 19, "Working with Tables."

When you define columns with text selected, the column definition will apply to the selected text. Word will insert section breaks before and after the selection. If you do not select text first, the column definitions will apply to the entire document unless you divided the document into two or more sections, in which case the columns will apply only to the current section. See Lesson 11, "Margins, Pages, and Sections," for more information about document sections.

Line between columns

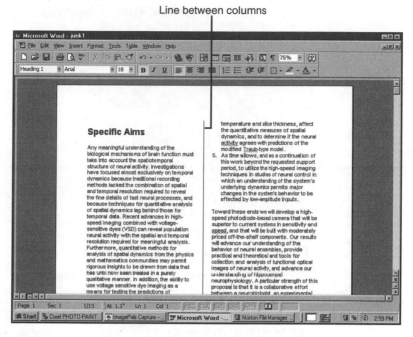

Figure 20.1 A document formatted with two columns.

Creating Columns

Word has four predefined column layouts:

- Two equal width columns
- Three equal width columns
- Two unequal width columns with the wider column on the left
- Two unequal width columns with the wider column on the right

You can apply any of these column formats to an entire document, to one section of a document, to selected text, or from the insertion point onward. Follow these steps to learn how:

1. If you want only a part of the document in columns, select the text you want in columns, or move the insertion point to the location where you want columns to begin. Word will insert section breaks before and/or after the text, as appropriate.

2. Select **Format**, **Columns** to open the Columns dialog box (see Figure 20.2).

249

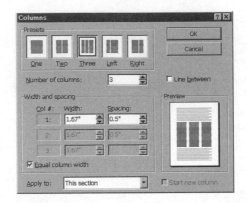

Figure 20.2 The Columns dialog box.

3. Under Presets, click the column format you want.

4. Click the **Apply To** drop-down arrow and specify the extent to which the columns should apply. The following options are available:

- **Whole Document**   This is available only if the document has not been broken into sections.

- **This Section**   Available only if you have broken the document into sections.

- **This Point Forward**   Word will insert a section break at the current cursor location and apply the new column setting to the latter of the two sections.

5. Select the **Line Between** check box to display a vertical line between columns (like in a newspaper).

6. Click **OK**.

Quick Columns   To display selected text, the current section, or the entire document in one to four equal-width columns, click the **Columns** button on the Standard toolbar and then drag over the desired number of columns.

No Columns?   Columns display on-screen only in Page Layout view. In Normal view, Word displays only a single column at a time (although your multiple columns will look fine when printed, even from Normal view). To switch to Page Layout view, select **View**, **Page Layout**.

Modifying Columns

You can modify existing columns, change the number of columns, change column widths, and change the spacing between columns. Here's how:

1. Move the cursor to the columns you want to modify.
2. Select **Format**, **Columns** to open the Columns dialog box (refer to Figure 20.2). The options in the dialog box will reflect the current settings for the columns you selected.
3. To apply a different predefined column format, click the desired format in the Presets area of the dialog box.
4. To change the width or spacing of a specific column, enter the desired width and spacing values (or click the arrows) in the column's **Width** and **Spacing** text boxes. The Preview box shows you what the settings will look like.
5. When you're satisfied with what you see in the Preview area, click **OK**.

Creating Column Breaks

As you are working with the columns, you may want to make a column break (and begin flowing into the next column) before the bottom of the page. To do so, position your insertion point where you want the break and then press **Ctrl+Shift+Enter**. In Page Layout view, you see that the text starts in the next column; in Normal view, you see a horizontal line that says Column Break.

To remove a column break, select the break and press **Delete**, or position the insertion point immediately after the column break and press **Backspace**.

Turning Columns Off

To convert multiple column text back to normal text (which is really just one column), follow these steps:

1. Select the text that you want to change from multiple columns to a single column.
2. Select **Format**, **Columns** to open the Columns dialog box (refer to Figure 20.2).

3. Under Presets, select the **One** option.

4. Click **OK**.

TIP   **A Quicker Way**   To quickly convert text in columns back to normal single-column text, select the text, click the **Columns** button on the Standard toolbar, and drag to select a single column.

This lesson showed you how to arrange text in columns. The next lesson shows you how to work with graphics in your document.

Adding Graphics to Your Document

In this lesson, you learn how to add graphics to your documents and how to create your own drawings.

Adding a Graphic Image

A *graphic image* is a picture that is stored on disk in a graphics file. Word can utilize graphics files created by a variety of applications, including PC Paintbrush, Windows' own Paint program, Lotus 1-2-3, Micrografx Designer, and AutoCAD. Additionally, your Word installation includes a library of clip art images that you can use in your documents. Figure 21.1 shows a document with a graphic image.

To add a graphic image (other than Word clip art) to a Word document, follow these steps:

1. Move the insertion point to the location for the graphic.

2. Select **Insert**, **Picture**, **From File**. The Insert Picture dialog box appears (see Figure 21.2).

3. If necessary, click the **Look In** drop-down arrow to specify the folder where the graphic file is located.

4. The large box in the center of the dialog box normally lists all graphics files in the specified directory. To have the list restricted to certain types of graphics files, click the **Files of Type** drop-down arrow and select the desired file type from the list.

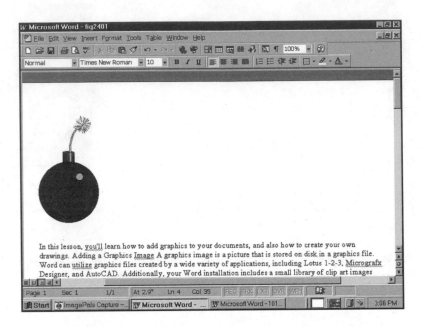

Figure 21.1   A document with a graphic.

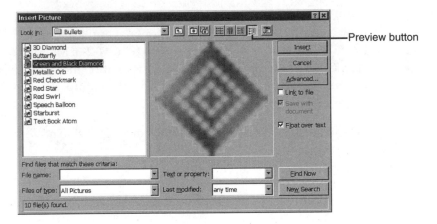

Preview button

Figure 21.2   The Insert Picture dialog box.

5. Type the name of the file to insert in the **File Name** text box, or select the filename from the list.

6. To preview the picture in the Preview box, click the **Preview** button.

7. Choose from the following options:

- Select **Link to File** if you want the graphic in your document updated if the graphics file on disk changes.

- If you selected **Link to File**, you can select **Save with Document** to save a copy of the picture with the document. Although this increases the document's file size, it makes it possible for the picture to be displayed even if the original file is no longer available.

- Select **Float over Text** to enable the picture to be displayed "behind" or "over" text and other objects (otherwise the image will be displayed inline with text).

8. Click **OK**, and Word inserts the graphic into your document.

Adding Clip Art

Clip art is a special category of pictures that consists of generally small, simple images that you use to add visual appeal and interest to your documents. Word comes with an extensive gallery of clip art that you can use freely. Here's how to add a clip art image to a document:

1. Move the cursor to the document location where you want the image.

2. Select **Insert**, **Picture**, **Clip Art** to open the Microsoft Clip Gallery dialog box (see Figure 21.3).

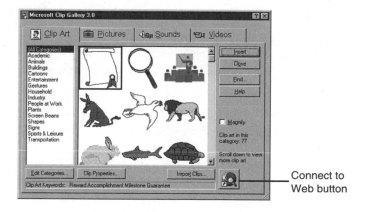

Figure 21.3 Selecting clip art from the Microsoft Clip Gallery.

3. In the list on the left, select the desired category of images. Or, select **(All Categories)** to view all clip art images.

4. Scroll through the image list until you find the image you want. Then click it to select it.

5. Click **Insert** to add the image to your document.

 TIP **Word on the Web** If you have Internet access, you can click the **Connect to Web** button in the Microsoft Clip Gallery dialog box to connect to Microsoft's Web site to access additional clip art images.

Displaying Graphics

The screen display of graphics images can slow down screen scrolling. If you're working on the document text in Page Layout or Online Layout view and don't need to see the images, you can speed up screen display by displaying empty rectangles called *placeholders* in place of the images (images are automatically hidden in Normal and Outline view). In addition, if you selected the Link to File option when inserting the graphic file, Word inserts a field code in the document. The screen will display this code instead of the picture when field codes are displayed.

 TERM **Field Code** A code in a document that tells Word to display a certain item, such as a graphic.

Here's how to control the display of graphics:

1. Select **Tools**, **Options** to open the Options dialog box.

2. If necessary, click the **View** tab to display the View options.

3. In the Show section, select or deselect the **Picture Placeholders** and **Field Codes** check boxes as desired.

4. Click **OK**.

The screen display of placeholders or field codes does not affect printing; the actual graphics are always printed in the document.

TIP **Speed It Up!** When working on a document that contains a lot of graphics, you can speed up screen display and scrolling by displaying placeholders for the graphics.

Cropping and Resizing a Graphic

Before you can work with a graphic in your document, you must select it. There are two ways to do this:

- Click the graphic.
- Using the keyboard, position the insertion point immediately to the left of the graphic, and then press **Shift+→**.

A selected graphic is surrounded by eight small white squares called *sizing handles*. Figure 21.4 shows sizing handles around a selected clip art image.

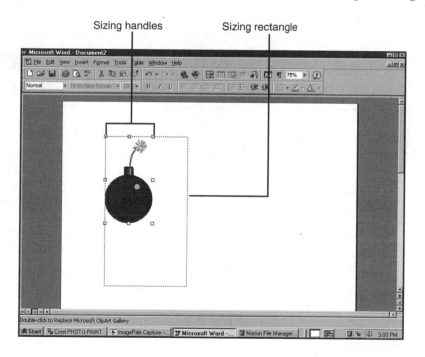

Figure 21.4 Resizing a selected graphic.

You can resize a graphic in your document to display the entire picture at a different size. You can also *crop* a graphic to hide portions of the picture that you don't want to display. To resize or crop a graphic, follow these steps:

1. Select the graphic.

2. Point at one of the resizing handles. The mouse pointer changes to a double-headed arrow.

3. Do either or both of the following, depending on how you want to modify the image:

   - To resize the graphic, press the left mouse button and drag the handle until the outline of the graphic reaches the desired size. You can either enlarge or shrink the graphic.

   - To crop the graphic, press and hold **Shift**, and then press the left mouse button and drag a handle toward the center of the graphic.

4. Release the mouse button.

Deleting, Moving, and Copying Graphics

To delete a graphic, select it and press **Delete**. To move or copy a graphic to a new location, follow these steps:

1. Select the graphic.

2. To copy the graphic, press **Ctrl+C**, or select **Edit**, **Copy**, or click the **Copy** button on the Standard toolbar. To move the graphic, press **Ctrl+X**, or select **Edit**, **Cut**, or click the **Cut** button on the Standard toolbar.

3. Move the cursor to the new location for the graphic.

4. Press **Ctrl+V**, or select **Edit**, **Paste**, or click the **Paste** button on the Standard toolbar.

TIP **Drag That Image** If the image and its destination are both in view, you can move it by dragging it to the new location. To copy instead of moving, hold down **Ctrl** while dragging.

Drawing in Your Document

In addition to adding existing graphics to a document, Word lets you create your own drawings. The drawing tools that are available let even the complete non-artist create simple drawings. To draw, you must display the Drawing toolbar. Select **View**, **Toolbars**, **Drawing**. Figure 21.5 shows the Drawing toolbar and identifies some of the buttons on it.

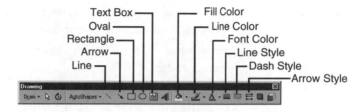

Figure 21.5 The Drawing toolbar.

The process of drawing consists of the following general actions:

- Adding drawing objects to the document. The available objects include lines, arrows, shapes, and text. Most of Word's drawing objects are called *AutoShapes*.

- Moving drawing objects to new locations and changing their size and proportions.

- Modifying drawing objects. For example, you might change the thickness of a line, the color of text, or the type of arrowhead on an arrow.

The Drawing toolbar displays buttons for the most commonly needed drawing objects: lines, arrows, 3-D shapes, and so on. (You access the less common drawing objects via menus or dialog boxes associated with the Drawing toolbar.) The following list explains the most frequently used drawing procedures.

- To draw an object, click its button on the Drawing toolbar. Or, click the **AutoShapes** button and select the shape from the list. Then draw in the document to insert the object. Hold down **Shift** while drawing to draw an object with a 1:1 aspect ratio (for example, to draw a square or circle instead of a rectangle or ellipse).

- To select an object you have already drawn, click it. The object will display small rectangles called *resizing handles*. Hold down **Shift** and click to select more than one object. Press **Delete** to delete the selected object(s).

- To move a selected object, point at it (but not at a handle) and drag to the new location.

- To change a selected object's size or shape, point at one of its resizing handles and drag to the desired size/shape.

- To change the color of an object's line, click the **Line Color** button on the Drawing toolbar and select the desired color.

- To change the interior color of a solid object, click the **Fill Color** button and select the desired color.

- To change the thickness or style of the lines used for an object, select the object and click the **Line Style** or **Dash Style** button.

- To add a text label, click the **Text Box** button, drag in the document to add the text box, and then type the text. Click outside the text box when you're done.

Word's drawing capabilities go much further than what is described here. You should experiment on your own to discover their full capabilities.

In this lesson, you learned how to add graphics and drawings to your documents. The next lesson teaches you how to work with multiple documents.

Working with Multiple Documents

This lesson shows you how to simultaneously edit multiple documents in Word.

Multiple Documents?

Being able to work on one document at a time is often all you need, but in some situations the capability to work on multiple documents at once can be very useful. For example, you can refer to one document while working on another, and you can copy and move text between documents. Word lets you have as many documents as you need open simultaneously.

Starting or Opening a Second Document

While you're working on one document, you can start a new document or open another existing document at any time. Use one of the following methods:

- To create a new document based on the Normal template, click the **New** button on the Standard toolbar.

- To create a document based on another template or one of Word's wizards, select **File, New**.

TIP **Opening Multiple Documents at Once**   In the Open dialog box, you can select multiple documents by holding **Shift** and clicking the document names. Then click **Open** to open all the selected documents.

- To open an existing document, select **File, Open** or click the **Open** button on the Standard toolbar.

A new window opens and displays the document you created or opened. Both the newly created and the original documents are in memory and can be edited, printed, and so on. You can continue opening additional documents until all the files you need to work with are open.

Switching Between Documents

When you have multiple documents open at one time, only one of them can be *active* at a given moment. The active document is displayed on-screen (although inactive documents may be displayed as well). The title bar of the active document is displayed in a darker color, and if documents are overlapping each other, the active one will be on top. The important thing you need to remember is that the active document is the only one affected by editing commands.

To switch between open documents, follow these steps:

1. Open the **Window** menu. At the bottom is a list of all open documents with a checkmark next to the name of the currently active document (see Figure 22.1).

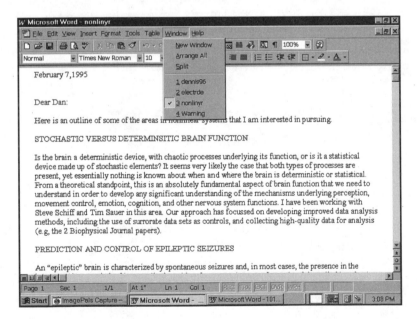

Figure 22.1   The Window menu lists open documents and indicates the currently active document.

2. Select the name of the document you want to make active. (You can click the document name or press the corresponding number key.) The selected document becomes active and appears on-screen.

3. (Optional) To cycle to the next open document, press **Ctrl+F6**.

Controlling Multiple Document View

Word gives you a great deal of flexibility in displaying multiple documents. You can have the active document occupy the entire screen, with other open documents temporarily hidden. You can also have several documents displayed at the same time, each in its own window. A document window can be in one of three states:

- **Maximized** The window occupies the entire work area, and no other open documents are visible. When the active document is maximized, its title appears in Word's title bar at the top of the screen. Figure 22.2 shows a maximized document.

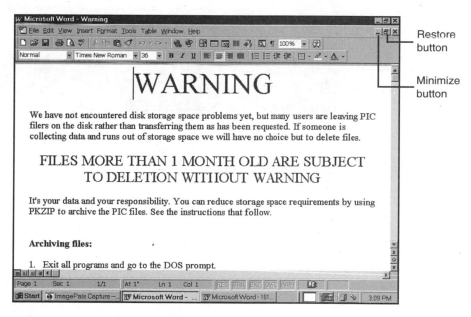

Figure 22.2 A maximized document window.

- **Minimized** The window is reduced to a small icon displayed at the bottom of the Word screen. The document title is displayed on the icon.

- **Restored** The document window assumes an intermediate size, and the document title is displayed in the title bar of its own window instead of Word's title bar. Figure 22.3 shows both a restored and a minimized document.

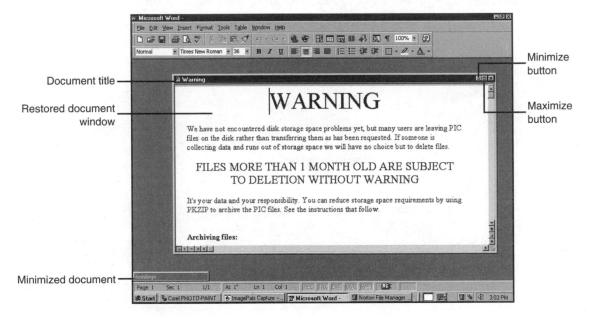

Figure 22.3 Restored and minimized document windows.

You can control the display of multiple documents in the following ways:

- To restore or minimize a maximized window, click its **Restore** or **Minimize** button.

- To maximize or minimize a restored window, click its **Maximize** or **Minimize** button.

- To display a minimized window, click its icon. Then either click its **Restore** or **Maximize** button or select from the pop-up menu that appears.

When a document is in the restored state, you can control the size and position of its window. To move the window, click its title bar and drag it to the new position. To change window size, point at a border or corner of the window (the mouse pointer changes to a two-headed arrow), and then click and drag the window to the desired size.

Viewing All Open Documents

Word has a command that displays all your open documents. Select **Window**, **Arrange All** to tile all document windows. When you tile your documents, every open document is displayed in a small window, and none of the windows overlap. If you have more than a few documents open, these windows will be quite small and won't be very useful for editing. They are useful, however, for seeing exactly which documents you have open and finding the one you need to work in at the moment. Figure 22.4 shows the result of the Window, Arrange All command with four documents open.

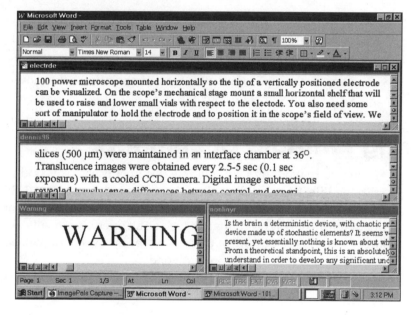

Figure 22.4 The Arrange All command displays all open documents, each in its own window.

Moving and Copying Text Between Documents

When you have more than one document open, you can move and copy text and graphics between documents. Follow these procedures to learn how:

1. Make the source document active, and then select the text and/or graphic you want to move or copy.

2. Press **Ctrl+X**, or select **Edit**, **Cut**, or click the **Cut** button on the Standard toolbar if you want to move the text. Press **Ctrl+C**, or select **Edit**, **Copy**, or click the **Copy** button on the Standard toolbar to copy the text.

3. Make the destination document active. Move the insertion point to the location for the text.

4. Press **Ctrl+V**, or select **Edit**, **Paste**, or click the **Paste** button on the Standard toolbar.

If both documents are visible, you can copy or move text from one to the other with drag-and-drop, as described here:

1. Select the text to be copied or moved.

2. Point at the selected text. To move the text, press and hold the left mouse button. To copy the text, press **Ctrl** and the left mouse button.

3. Drag to the new location for the text and release the mouse button (and the Ctrl key, if you were copying).

Saving Multiple Documents

When you're working with multiple documents, you save individual documents with the **File**, **Save** and **File**, **Save As** commands you learned about in Lesson 4, "Saving and Opening Documents." These commands save the only active document. There is no command to save all open documents in one step. If you attempt to close a document that has not been saved, you will be prompted to save it. If you try to quit Word with one or more documents unsaved, you will be prompted one-by-one to save each document.

TIP **No Save All** The Save All command that was available in earlier versions of Word is not present in Word 97.

Closing a Document

You can close an open document when you finish working with it. These steps teach you how to close a document:

1. Make the document active.

2. Select **File**, **Close** or click the **Close** button at the right end of the document's title bar. (Be sure not to click the Close button in Word's main title bar.)

3. If the document contains unsaved changes, Word prompts you to save the document. Click **Yes** to save the file, or click **No**. Either way, Word closes the document.

This lesson showed you how to simultaneously edit multiple documents in Word. In the next lesson, you'll use Word to create HTML (Internet) documents.

Creating Web Pages with Word

23

In this lesson, you learn how to prepare documents in Word to be published on the Internet.

What is the Internet?

The *Internet* is a vast interconnected network of computers all over the world. Most of the connected computers make information available to the public, and many of them provide Internet access to individuals and businesses.

You can get connected to the Internet through your company's LAN (local access network) or through an account that you sign up for with a service provider or online service. While you are connected to the Internet, you can use a Web browser program that runs on your PC to request various Web pages from all over the world to be displayed on your computer screen. These Web pages contain every imaginable kind of useful information, from the latest sports scores, to home remedies, to company research. The most popular Web browsers are Netscape Communicator (which you can download for free from **http://www.netscape.com**) and Microsoft Internet Explorer (which comes free with Microsoft Office products, including Word).

Hyperlinks You can jump from page to page with *hyperlinks*, which are hot links to other addresses (addresses are Uniform Resource Locators, or URLs). The links are called hot because you can click one to make your Web browser open that URL. Hyperlinks can point to other Web pages in your personal Web site or to pages at any site anywhere in the world.

To make your own Web documents available to everyone else on the Internet (or an intra-company intranet), you need to create and save the documents in HTML (Hyptertext Markup Language) format and then copy (upload) them to a computer that's connected to the Internet. This could be your company's server or your local service provider's computer.

Saving a Word Document in HTML Format

If you already have a Word document that you would like to make available on the Internet, you must save it in HTML format. This converts all its formatting into codes that a Web browser program can interpret.

Follow these steps to save a Word document in HTML format:

1. Open the document and make any last-minute edits.
2. Select **File**, **Save As HTML**. The Save As HTML dialog box opens. It works exactly like the regular Save As dialog box, except the default file type is HTML.
3. Change the file location and filename if needed. For now, just save the HTML document to your hard disk (the default My Documents folder is fine).
4. Click **Save**.
5. If you see a dialog box asking you whether you want to check the Web for a new version of the Web authoring tools, click **Yes** or **No**, depending on whether you have time to go through that process. If you choose Yes, your Web browser opens, jumps to the Microsoft Web site, and leads you through an update if it is available.

CAUTION

Formatting Losses HTML format is a lot simpler than Word format, so when you save in HTML format, you lose some of Word's formatting. The formatting lost includes embossed, shadowed, engraved, all caps, small caps, double strikethrough, and outlined text effects. You also lose comments, animated text, drop caps, drawings (bitmap images are saved separately), highlighting, revision marks, page numbering, special margins, borders around paragraphs and pages, headers and footers, footnotes and endnotes, and multiple columns.

Creating a New Web Page from Scratch

New Web content can be created in two ways: You can start with a blank page
or you can use the Web Page Wizard. In this section, you learn about creating a
Web page from scratch. Using the Web Wizard is covered later in this lesson.

Follow these steps to create a plain blank Web page into which you can enter
your Web page content and begin to enter headings and body text on it.

1. Choose **File, New**. In the New dialog box that appears, click the **Web
   Pages** tab.

2. Double-click the **Blank Web Page** icon. This starts a new document based
   on that template. It looks just like any other document, except that there
   are some different toolbar buttons. (Point to a toolbar button to find out
   what it does.)

3. If you see a dialog box asking you whether you want to check the Web for
   a new version of the Web authoring tools, click **Yes** or **No**, depending on
   whether you have time to go through that process. If you choose Yes, your
   Web browser opens, jumps to the Microsoft Web site, and leads you
   through an update if it is available.

 TIP **Online Layout** Notice that you are now in Online Layout view. Word
switches you to this view whenever you're working with a Web page.

4. To enter a heading for the Web page, open the **Style** drop-down list and
   choose **Heading 1** (or whichever heading size you prefer). Heading sizes
   range from 1 to 6, with Heading 1 being the largest.

5. Type the major heading for the page—for example, Welcome to Bob's
   Hardware.

6. Continuing entering the rest of your Web page text, using the styles
   provided in the Style drop-down list. Save your work when you are
   finished.

 TIP **Line Spacing** With the styles provided, there is a blank line between each
paragraph. If you want two lines together without a break, press **Shift+Enter**.
Just like in a regular Word document, **Shift+Enter** creates a line break without
starting a new paragraph.

Entering a Page Title

For each HTML document you create, you will want a title. The title appears in the title bar of the Web browser when your reader views your document. The title is different from the filename, which is used in the URL, or address, for the Web page. To create a page title, follow these steps:

1. Choose **File, Properties**. A different Document Properties dialog box appears than the one you have worked with before (see Figure 23.1.)

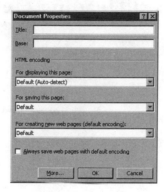

Figure 23.1 Web page documents have a different set of properties than normal documents.

TIP **Where Did My Properties Go?** The regular properties for the document haven't vanished completely; you can access the regular Properties dialog box by clicking the **More** button shown in Figure 23.1.

2. In the Title box, type the title for the page. This title will appear in the title bar of the Web browser window.

3. Click **OK** to close the dialog box.

Creating a Page with the Web Page Wizard

The Web Page Wizard helps you create professional-looking pages with not much more effort than it takes to create a Web page from scratch. You can choose from a variety of layouts, and start with preplaced sample text. Follow these steps:

1. Choose **File, New**, and click the **Web Pages** tab in the New dialog box.

2. Double-click the **Web Page Wizard** icon. A Web Page Wizard dialog box opens, along with a sample Web page in the background, as shown in Figure 23.2.

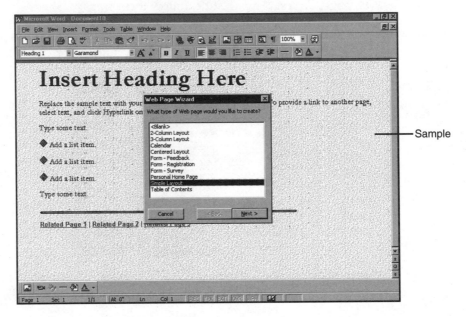

Figure 23.2   First, the wizard asks you what type of page you want to create.

3. Choose the layout you want. For this exercise, choose **Simple Layout** if it is not already selected. Then click **Next**.

4. The dialog box now asks what visual style you want to use and lists several styles from which you may choose. Click a style name, and then wait a moment. The page behind the dialog box changes to show that style. Check out each of the styles, and when you find the one you like best, click **Finish**. For the example shown in Figure 23.3, the Festive style was used.

Figure 23.3 shows the basic Web page you have just created using the Web Page Wizard. It contains the needed HTML styles on the Style list, a nice background, and some interesting fonts and bullets. All you have to do is fill in your own details by replacing the sample text and creating hyperlinks in place of the cold (unusable) links currently on the page. Don't forget to save your document frequently as you work.

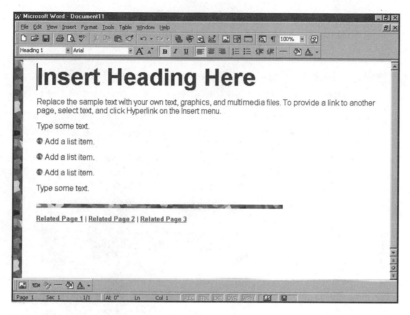

Figure 23.3 The Web Page Wizard leaves you with a nicely formatted, generic page to customize.

Creating Hyperlinks

You can create hyperlinks—links to other Web documents—in your Word document by typing the URLs. Word recognizes them and converts them to hyperlinks automatically. The same goes for e-mail addresses. You could, for example, put a note at the bottom of your document "E-mail johndoe@server.net for more information." This will appear as a clickable link when viewed with a Web browser. Clicking the mail link opens the user's mail client from which a message can be sent.

The sample pages you create with the Web Page Wizard have pre-underlined links at the bottom, as shown in Figure 23.3, but they are "cold," because they don't have a real hyperlink assigned to them. You can make them "hot," or make any other text or graphic into a hyperlink.

Confirm that you have the correct spelling of the URL for which you want to create a hyperlink, and save your work if you haven't done so already. Then follow these steps:

1. If you are working with one of the pages created with the Web Page Wizard, change the wording of the future link as needed. You might, for example, change Related Page 1 to Ordering Information.

2. Select the text that will be the hyperlink (for example, your new Ordering Information text), so that the entire word or phrase is highlighted.

3. Click the **Create Hyperlink** button on the Standard toolbar. (It looks like a globe with a piece of chain in front of it). The Insert Hyperlink dialog box opens.

4. Type the URL into the Link to File or URL text box (see Figure 23.4.)

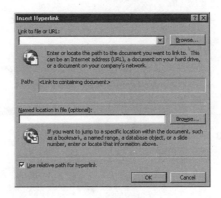

Figure 23.4   Insert the URL from the Clipboard into the text box.

5. Click **OK**. The dialog box closes, and the text you selected appears underlined, indicating that it is now a hyperlink.

6. Repeat the process to create hyperlinks for any other words on the page for which you want to point the reader to more information.

Previewing Your Page

If you have not done it yet, save your file (**File, Save**). The Save dialog box opens. Notice that the file type is already set to HTML. Enter the name to save under and click **Save**.

To see how your document will look in a Web browser, Choose **File, Web Page Preview**. The page opens in your default Web browser (probably Internet Explorer). When you are finished looking, close your Web browser and return to Word.

Transferring Your Pages to a Server

After you finish your pages, you need to transfer them to a server that is accessible to the Internet.

Determining the Save Location

Before you can publish your pages to the Internet, you need to contact your service provider and find out where on their server you need to put your pages. (If you are using an online service such as America Online, information is available in the online help about the service.) Your service provider, for example, might give you a path like this:

```
ftp.servername.com/pub/web/homepage/members/yourname
```

 File Transfer Protocol FTP is a protocol, or method, for transferring files from one computer to another over a network such as the Internet.

This is the physical location on the server where you send your files via FTP (File Transfer Protocol). This is *not* the address you will give to other people who want to access your page, however. This address represents the storage location for your Web files. The Web address to your page will likely be much simpler, like this:

```
http://www.servername.com/~yourname
```

These are examples for demonstration purposes. Consult your Internet service provider for the addresses you should use.

Publishing Your Work with the Web Publishing Wizard

Your Microsoft Office 97 CD comes with a program called Web Publishing Wizard that can transfer both HTML files and graphic files to a server. It's located in the ValuPack/WebPost folder on the Office 97 CD. You can install it from there, or you can download a more recent (better) version from Microsoft's Web site.

If you want to install the version on the CD, here's how:

1. Use **Windows Explorer** to open the contents of the **Microsoft Office 97 CD**, and navigate to the **ValuePack** folder.
2. Double-click the **WebPost** folder.
3. Double-click the **WEBPOST.EXE** file to run the installation program.
4. Follow the on-screen prompts to install.
5. Restart your computer before you attempt to use the Web Publishing Wizard.

To download and install the new version, do this:

1. Start your Internet connection if it is not already running, and open **Internet Explorer**.
2. Go to the following site:

   http://www.microsoft.com/windows/software/webpost/
3. Follow the downloading instructions and download the file to a temporary folder on your computer. (C:\Windows\Temp will do.)
4. Navigate to the new file on your hard disk using Windows Explorer and double-click it to install the program.
5. Follow the on-screen prompts to install.
6. Restart your computer before you attempt to use the Web Publishing Wizard.

To start the Web Publishing Wizard, open the **Start** menu and point to **Programs**, then **Accessories**, then **Internet Tools**, and then click **Web Publishing Wizard**. Specific steps for this are not provided here because the steps are different depending on which version of the wizard you are using. But the dialog boxes that appear are very clear in their instructions. You can transfer pages either to an Internet server or to your company's intranet server; if you are doing the latter, see your network administrator for instructions.

 TIP **Do It All at Once**   You will be uploading either a single file or a single folder at a time. That means you will have to run the wizard many times if you have many files to upload. The shortcut, of course, is to create a separate folder on your hard disk and put all the files into it that you want to upload. Then just run the wizard once and upload that one folder.

In this lesson, you learned how to create, save, and publish Web documents.

Excel

Starting and
Exiting Excel

*In this lesson, you learn how to start and end a typical
Excel work session.*

Starting Excel

After you installed Excel (as covered in Appendix A, "Installing Microsoft Office
97," of this book), the installation program returned you to the desktop. To start
Excel from there, follow these steps:

1. Click the **Start** button, and the Start menu appears.
2. Choose **Programs**, and the Programs menu appears.
3. Choose the **Microsoft Excel** program item to start the program.

The Excel opening screen appears (see Figure 1.1), displaying a blank *workbook*
labeled Book1. Excel is now ready for you to begin creating your workbook.

Workbook An Excel file is called a *workbook*. Each workbook consists of
three worksheets (although you can add or remove worksheets as needed).
Each worksheet consists of columns and rows that intersect to form boxes
called *cells* into which you enter text. The tabs at the bottom of the workbook
(labeled Sheet1, Sheet2, and so on) let you flip through the worksheets by
clicking them with the mouse.

What's the Office Assistant? When you first start Excel, you're greeted
by an animated icon called the Office Assistant. He's there to offer help, and
he'll pop up from time to time whenever you encounter new features. You'll find
information about the Office Assistant in Appendix B, "Using the Office 97 Help
System." For now, close the Assistant by clicking **Start Using Microsoft Excel**.

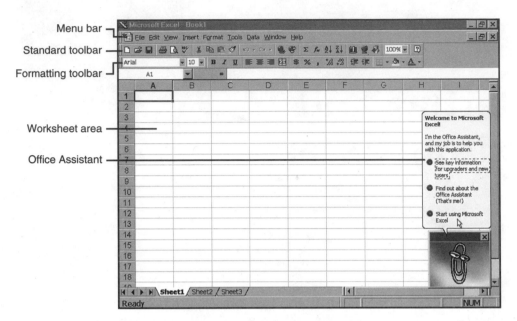

Menu bar
Standard toolbar
Formatting toolbar

Worksheet area

Office Assistant

Figure 1.1 Excel's opening screen displays a blank workbook named Book1.

You can also start Excel by opening an existing workbook. (You can do this only after you've created and saved a workbook, as you'll learn to do in upcoming lessons.) To start Excel and have Excel automatically open a workbook for you, follow these steps:

1. Click the **Start** button, and the Start menu appears.

2. Click **Open Office Document**. Excel displays the Open Office Document dialog box, displaying the contents of the My Documents folder.

3. Because you typically save your workbooks to the My Documents folder, they should be displayed at this point. However, if you don't see your workbook file listed, change to the folder that contains the workbook you want to open.

4. Click the workbook's filename to select it. Then click **Open** to open it and start Excel.

If you installed the Office Shortcut Bar, you can also start Excel by clicking the **Excel** button on the Shortcut Bar.

A Look at the Excel Screen

You will perform most operations in Excel using commands available through the menu bar at the top of the screen, and the Standard and Formatting toolbars just below the menu bar. In the next two lessons, you'll learn about the operations you can perform using the menu bar and the Standard toolbar.

Exiting Excel

To exit Excel and return to the Windows desktop, perform either of these two steps:

- Open the **File** menu and select **Exit**.

  or

- Click the **Close** (x) button in the Excel window.

If you changed the workbook in any way without saving the file, Excel displays a prompt asking if you want to save the file before exiting. Select the desired option. See Lesson 6, "Creating and Saving Workbook Files," for help in saving your workbook.

In this lesson, you learned how to start and exit Excel. In the next lesson, you'll learn about the Excel workbook window.

Examining the
Excel Window

*In this lesson, you learn the basics of moving around in
the Excel window and in the workbook window.*

Parts of the Excel Window

As you can see in Figure 2.1, the Excel window contains many common Windows elements, including a menu bar (from which you can select commands), a Status bar (which displays the status of the current activity), and toolbars (which contain buttons and drop-down lists that provide quick access to common commands and features).

Missing Status Bar?   To display the Status bar if it is not visible, open the **Tools** menu, select **Options**, and click the **View** tab. In the Show area, select **Status Bar** and click **OK**.

CAUTION

In addition, the window contains some elements that are unique to Excel, including:

Formula bar   When you enter information into a *cell*, anything you type appears in the Formula bar. The cell's location also appears in the Formula bar.

TERM

Cell   Each page in a workbook is a separate worksheet, and each worksheet contains a grid consisting of alphabetized columns and numbered rows. Where a row and column intersect, they form a box called a *cell*. Each cell has an *address* that consists of the column letter and row number (A1, B3, C4, and so on). You enter data and formulas in the cells to create your worksheets. You'll learn more about cells in Lesson 4, "Entering Different Kinds of Data," and Lesson 5, "Editing Entries."

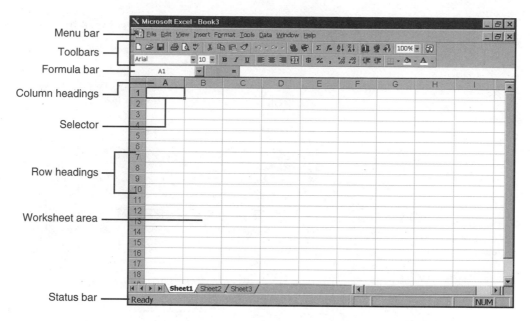

Figure 2.1 Elements of the Excel window.

Workbook window Each Excel file is a workbook that consists of one or more worksheets. You can open several files (workbooks) at a time, each in its own window.

Column headings The letters across the top of the worksheet, which identify the columns in the worksheet.

Row headings The numbers down the side of the worksheet, which identify the rows in the worksheet.

Selector The outline that indicates the active cell (the one in which you are working).

Moving from Worksheet to Worksheet

By default, each workbook starts off with three worksheets. You can add worksheets to or delete worksheets from the workbook as needed. Because each workbook consists of one or more worksheets, you need a way of moving from worksheet to worksheet easily. Use one of the following methods:

- Press **Ctrl+PgDn** to move to the next worksheet or **Ctrl+PgUp** to move to a previous one.

or

- Click the tab of the worksheet you want to go to (see Figure 2.2). If the tab is not shown, use the tab scroll buttons to bring the tab into view, and then click the tab.

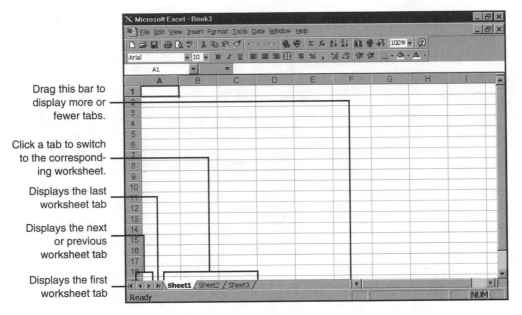

Drag this bar to display more or fewer tabs.

Click a tab to switch to the corresponding worksheet.

Displays the last worksheet tab

Displays the next or previous worksheet tab

Displays the first worksheet tab

Figure 2.2 You can move from worksheet to worksheet with tabs.

Moving Within a Worksheet

After the worksheet you want to work on is displayed, you'll need some way of moving to the various cells within the worksheet. Keep in mind that the part of the worksheet displayed on-screen is only a small part of the actual worksheet. To move around the worksheet with your keyboard, use the keys listed in Table 2.1.

Table 2.1 Moving Around a Worksheet with the Keyboard

Press This...	To Move...
↑ ↓ ← →	One cell in the direction of the arrow.
Ctrl+↑ or Ctrl+↓	To the top or bottom of a data region (the area of a worksheet that contains data), or to the first or last cell in the column if the column is empty.
Ctrl+← or Ctrl+→	To the left-most or right-most cell in a data region, or to the first or last cell in the row if the row is empty.
PgUp	Up one screen.
PgDn	Down one screen.
Home	Left-most cell in a row.
Ctrl+Home	Upper-left corner of a worksheet.
Ctrl+End	Lower-right corner of the data area.
End+↑, End+↓, End+←, End+→	If the active cell is blank, moves in the direction of the arrow to the *first* cell that contains data. If the active cell contains an entry, moves in the direction of the arrow to the *last* cell that has an entry.

If you have a mouse, you can use the scroll bars to scroll to the area of the screen that contains the cell with which you want to work. Then click the cell to make it the active cell.

Keep in mind that as you scroll, the scroll box moves within the scroll bar to tell you where you are within the file. In addition, the size of the scroll box changes to represent the amount of the total worksheet that is currently visible. If the scroll box is large, you know you're seeing most of the current worksheet in the window. If the scroll box is small, most of the worksheet is currently hidden from view.

 TIP **Fast Scrolling** If you want to scroll to a specific row within a large worksheet, press and hold the **Shift** key while you drag the scroll box. The current row is displayed as you move the scroll box.

TIP **Move to a Specific Cell** To move quickly to a specific cell on a work-sheet, type the cell's address in the **Name** box at the left end of the Formula bar and press **Enter**. (It's the box that reads "A1" in Figure 2.2.) A cell address consists of the column letter and row number that define the location of the cell (for example **C25**). To go to a cell on a specific worksheet, type the worksheet's name, an exclamation point, and the cell address (such as **sheet3!C25**) and press **Enter**.

Scrolling Through a Worksheet with the IntelliMouse

With Office 97, Microsoft introduces a new mouse called the Microsoft IntelliMouse. If you've installed the IntelliMouse, you can use it to move through a worksheet even more quickly than you can with a conventional mouse. Here's how:

To...	Do This...
Scroll a few rows	Rotate the wheel in the middle of the mouse forward or backward.
Scroll faster (pan)	Click and hold the wheel button, and then drag the mouse in the direction in which you want to pan (scroll fast). The further away from the origin mark (the four-headed arrow) you drag the mouse, the faster the panning action. To slow the pan, drag the mouse back toward the origin mark.
Pan without holding	To pan without holding the wheel button down, simply click it once and then move the mouse in the direction in which you want to pan. You'll continue to pan when you move the mouse until you turn panning off by clicking the wheel again.

Changing the View of Your Worksheet

There are many ways to change how your worksheet appears within the Excel window. Changing the view has no effect on how your worksheets will look when printed, but changing the view and getting a different perspective often helps you see your data more clearly. For example, you can enlarge or reduce the size of its text to view more or less of the worksheet at one time. You can also "freeze" row or column headings so that you won't lose your place as you scroll through a large worksheet.

Magnifying and Reducing the Worksheet View

To enlarge or reduce your view of the current worksheet, use the Zoom feature. Open the **Zoom** menu (on the Standard toolbar) and select the zoom percentage you want to use, such as **25%** or **200%**. You can enlarge a specific area of the worksheet if you'd like by selecting it first, opening the **Zoom** menu, and choosing **Selection**.

If you want, you can display your worksheet so that it takes up the full screen—eliminating toolbars, the Formula bar, the Status bar, and so on—as shown in Figure 2.3. To do so, open the **View** menu and select **Full Screen**. To return to Normal view, click **Close Full Screen**.

TIP **Fast Zoom** If you use the IntelliMouse, you can zoom in and out quickly by pressing and holding the **Ctrl** key and moving the wheel forward or backward.

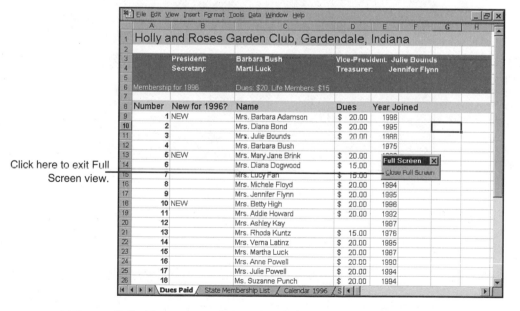

Figure 2.3 View your worksheet in a full window.

Freezing Column and Row Labels

As you scroll through a large worksheet, it's often helpful to freeze your labels so that you can view them with related data. For example, as you can see in Figure 2.4, you need to be able to view the column and row labels to understand the data in the cells.

To freeze row or column labels (or both), follow these steps:

1. Click the cell to the right of the row labels and/or below any column labels you want to freeze. This highlights the cell.

2. Open the **Window** menu and select **Freeze Panes**.

Play around a little, moving the cursor all around the document. As you do, the row and/or column labels remain locked in their positions. This enables you to view data in other parts of the worksheet without losing track of what that data represents. To unlock labels, open the **Window** menu again and select **Unfreeze Panes**.

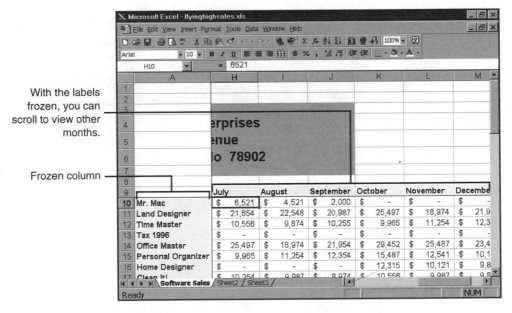

Figure 2.4 As you scroll, the frozen labels remain in place.

Splitting Worksheets

Sometimes when you're working with a large worksheet, you find yourself wanting to view two parts of it at one time to compare data. To view two parts of a worksheet, you *split* it. Figure 2.5 shows a split worksheet.

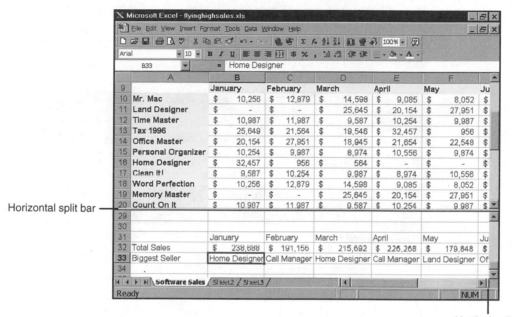

Figure 2.5 Split a worksheet to view two parts at one time.

Follow these steps to split a worksheet:

1. Click either the vertical or the horizontal split bar.

2. Drag the split bar into the worksheet window.

3. Drop the split bar, and Excel splits the window at that location. When you scroll, the two panes automatically scroll in synch.

To remove the split, drag it back to its original position on the scroll bar.

Hiding Workbooks, Worksheets, Columns, and Rows

For those times when you're working on high priority or top-secret information, you can hide workbooks, worksheets, columns, or rows from prying eyes. For example, if you have confidential data stored in one particular worksheet, you can hide that worksheet, yet still be able to view the other worksheets in that workbook. You can also hide particular columns (see Figure 2.6) or rows within a worksheet—or even an entire workbook if you want.

Columns D and E, which contain addresses and phone numbers, are hidden from view.

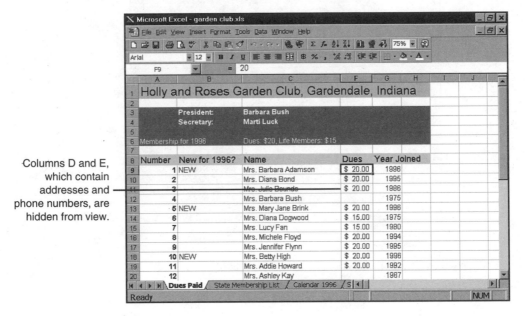

Figure 2.6 Hide data to prevent it from being viewed, printed, or changed.

So in addition to hiding data to prevent it from appearing on a report, you might hide it to prevent it from accidentally being changed. When data is hidden, it cannot be viewed, printed, or changed. This is *unlike* other changes you might make to the view (such as changing the zoom percentage), which do not affect your worksheet when printed. Hiding data *does* prevent that data from being printed.

Use these methods to hide data:

- To hide a *workbook*, open the **Window** menu and select **Hide**.
- To hide a *worksheet*, click its tab to select it. Then open the **Format** menu, select **Sheet**, and select **Hide**.
- To hide *rows* or *columns*, click a row or column heading to select it. Then open the **Format** menu, select **Row** or **Column**, and select **Hide**.

 TIP   **Hide More Than One**   To select several worksheets, press and hold **Ctrl** while you click each tab. To select several rows or columns, press and hold **Ctrl** while you click each heading.

Of course, whenever you need to, you can redisplay the hidden data easily. To redisplay hidden data, select the hidden area first. For example, select the rows, columns, or sheets adjacent to the hidden ones. Then repeat the previous steps, selecting **Unhide** from the appropriate menus.

 You Can't Hide It Completely!   It's easy to undo the command to hide data, so you can't really hide data completely as a means of security. If you give the workbook file to someone else, for example, he or she can easily **CAUTION**   unhide and view the data you hid.

In this lesson, you learned about the elements of the Excel window and how to move around within workbooks and worksheets. You also learned how to change the view of your worksheet, freeze column and row headings, and hide data. In the next lesson, you will learn how to use Excel's toolbars.

Using Excel's Toolbars

In this lesson, you learn how to use Excel's toolbars to save time when you work. You also learn how to arrange them for maximum performance.

Using the Toolbars

Unless you tell it otherwise, Excel displays the Standard and Formatting toolbars as shown in Figure 3.1. To select a tool from a toolbar, simply click the tool.

Off Duty   If a tool appears grayed, it is currently unavailable. Tools become unavailable when they are not applicable to your current activity.

Toolbar   An Excel toolbar is a collection of tools or icons displayed in a long bar that can be moved and reshaped to make it more convenient for you to use. Each icon represents a common command or task.

Here are some easy ways to learn about the available toolbar buttons:

- To view the name of a button, position the mouse pointer over it. Excel displays a ScreenTip, which displays the name of the button (as shown in Figure 3.1).

- To get help with the command associated with a particular button, press **Shift+F1**. The mouse pointer changes to a question mark. Move the question mark pointer over a button and click it.

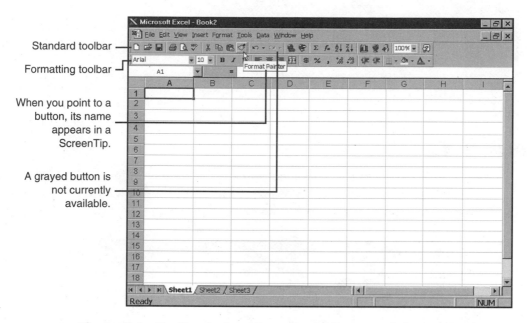

Standard toolbar —

Formatting toolbar —|

When you point to a button, its name appears in a ScreenTip.

A grayed button is not currently available.

Figure 3.1 The Standard and Formatting toolbars contain buttons for Excel's most commonly used features.

Turning Toolbars On and Off

By default, Excel initially displays the Standard and Formatting toolbars. If you find that you don't use these toolbars, you can turn one or both of them off to free up some screen space. In addition, you can turn on other toolbars (although some toolbars appear on their own when you perform a related activity).

Follow these steps to turn a toolbar on or off:

1. Open the **View** menu and choose **Toolbars**. A submenu appears.
2. A checkmark next to a toolbar's name indicates that the toolbar is currently being displayed. To turn a toolbar on or off (whichever it's not), click its name in the list to add or remove the checkmark.

 TIP **Quick View** To display a hidden toolbar quickly, right-click an existing toolbar and select the toolbar you want to display from the shortcut menu.

Excel on the Web Excel for Windows 97 allows you to open Web pages within its window. When you're working on the Web, the Web toolbar is displayed. Because the other Excel toolbars are unnecessary in such a situation, you can quickly remove them from the screen by clicking the **Show Only Web Toolbar** button.

Moving Toolbars

After you have displayed the toolbars you need, you can position them in your work area where they are most convenient. Figure 3.2 shows an Excel screen with three toolbars in various positions on the screen.

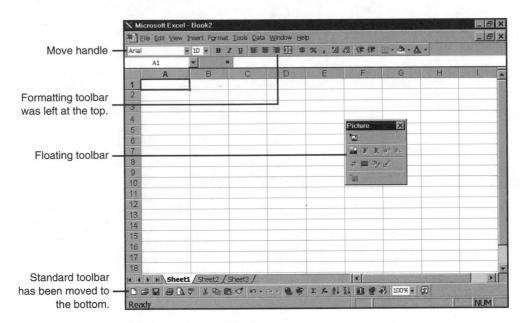

Figure 3.2 Three toolbars in various positions.

Here's what you do to move a toolbar:

1. Click a toolbar's move handle. (If the toolbar is floating in the middle of the window, click its title bar instead.)

2. Hold down the mouse button and drag the toolbar to where you want it. You can drag it to a side of the window (to a "dock") or let it "float" anywhere in the window.

294

Although you can drag a toolbar anywhere, if you drag one that contains a drop-down list (such as the Standard or Formatting toolbar) to the left or right side of the window, the drop-down list buttons disappear. If you move the toolbar back to the top or bottom of the window (or let it float) the drop-down lists reappear.

 Floating Toolbar A floating toolbar acts just like a window. You can drag its title bar to move it or drag a border to size it. If you drag a floating toolbar to the top or bottom of the screen, it turns back into a horizontal toolbar.

 Quickly Moving a Toolbar To quickly move a floating toolbar to the top of the screen, double-click its title bar. To move a docked toolbar into the middle of the window, double-click its move handle.

In Excel for Windows 97, the worksheet's menu bar is treated the same as other toolbars. This means you can move it to the side of a window, or you can float it in the middle if you want. It also means that you can customize the menu bar in a manner similar to toolbars, as discussed in the next section.

Customizing the Toolbars

If Excel's toolbars provide too few (or too many) options for you, you can create your own toolbars or customize existing toolbars. To customize a toolbar, follow these steps:

1. Right-click on any toolbar and choose **Customize** from the shortcut menu, or open the **Tools** menu and select **Customize**.

2. If the toolbar you want to customize is not currently visible, click the **Toolbars** tab and select it from the list. The toolbar appears.

3. To change the size of the toolbar icons, to turn on or off ScreenTips, or to change the animation of your menus, click the **Options** tab. On the Options tab, select the options you want to apply. For example, to make the toolbar icons larger, click the **Large Icons** option.

4. To add or remove buttons from a toolbar, click the **Commands** tab.

5. To add a button to a toolbar, select its category. (For example, to add the Clear Contents button to a toolbar, select the Edit category.) You can add menus to a toolbar as well; you'll find them listed at the bottom of the

Categories list. After you've selected the proper category, click the command you want and drag it onto the toolbar, as shown in Figure 3.3.

Drag a button to a
toolbar to add it.

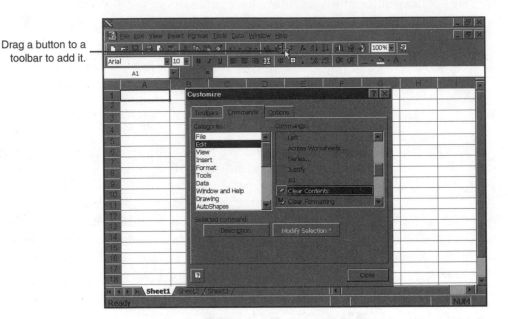

Figure 3.3 To add a button to a toolbar, drag it there.

TIP **Don't Know What an Option Is For?** Select the command and then click **Description** to learn what that command does.

6. To remove a button from a toolbar, drag it off the toolbar.

7. To rearrange the buttons on a toolbar, drag them around within the bar.

8. Click the **Close** button when you're finished.

If you decide you don't like the changes that have been made to a toolbar, you can return to its default settings (the way it was before you or someone else changed it). From within the Customize dialog box, click **Toolbars**, highlight the name of the toolbar you want to reset, and then click the **Reset** button. A confirmation box appears; click **OK**.

Creating Your Own Toolbar

Instead of changing any of the standard Excel toolbars, you can create one of your own and fill it with the tools you use most often. Follow these steps to learn how:

1. Open the **Tools** menu and select **Customize.**
2. Click the **Toolbars** tab.
3. Click the **New** button.
4. Type a name for your new toolbar (such as Jen's Favorites) and click **OK.** Excel creates a new floating toolbar.
5. Click the **Commands** tab, select the proper category for a desired button, and then drag it onto the toolbar.
6. Repeat step 5 to add more buttons to your new toolbar. When you finish, click **Close.**

If you want to delete a custom toolbar, open the **Tools** menu and select **Customize**. In the Toolbars list, click the custom toolbar you want to delete. Then click the **Delete** button in the Customize dialog box.

In this lesson, you learned how to use Excel's toolbars and to customize them for your own unique needs. In the next lesson, you'll learn how to enter different types of data.

Entering Different Kinds of Data

In this lesson, you learn how to enter different types of data in an Excel worksheet.

The Data Types

To create a worksheet that does something, you must enter data into the cells that make up the worksheet. The different types of data that you can enter, include the following:

- Text
- Numbers
- Dates
- Times
- Formulas
- Functions

In this lesson, you'll learn how to enter text, numbers, dates, and times. In Lessons 12, 13, and 14, you'll learn how to enter formulas and functions.

Entering Text

Text is any combination of letters, numbers, and spaces. By default, text is automatically left-aligned in a cell.

To enter text into a cell:

1. Click in the cell in which you want to enter text.

2. Type the text. As you type, your text appears in the cell and in the Formula bar, as shown in Figure 4.1.

3. Press **Enter**. Your text appears in the cell, left-aligned. (You can also press Tab or an arrow key to enter the text and move to another cell.) Or, if you've made a mistake and you want to abandon your entry, press **Esc** instead.

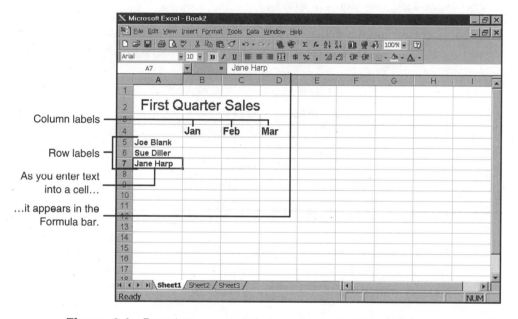

Figure 4.1 Data that you enter also appears in the Formula bar as you type it.

But It Doesn't Fit! To widen a column to display all its data, move to the column headings bar at the top of the worksheet. Then double-click the *right* border of the column you want to "autofit" to hold your data. See Lesson 18, "Changing Column Width and Row Height," for more help.

Numbers As Text You might want to enter a number that will be treated as text (such as a zip code). To do so, precede the entry with a single quotation mark ('), as in **'46220**. The single quotation mark is an alignment prefix that tells Excel to treat the following characters as text and left-align them in the cell.

Entering Column and Row Labels

Column and row labels identify your data. Column labels appear across the top of the worksheet beneath the title. Row labels are entered on the left side of the worksheet, usually in Column A.

Column labels describe what the numbers in a column represent. Typically, column labels specify time periods such as years, months, days, dates, and so on. Row labels describe what the numbers in each row represent. Typically, row labels specify data categories, such as product names, employee names, or income and expense items in a budget.

When entering column labels, press the **Tab** key to move from one cell to the next instead of pressing **Enter**. When entering row labels, use the **down-arrow** key instead.

 TIP **Entering Similar Data As Labels** When you need to enter similar data (such as a series of months or years) as column or row labels, there's a trick for entering them quickly. See the section, "Entering a Series with AutoFill," later in this lesson for help.

Adding Comments to Cells

You can use cell comments to provide detailed information about data in a worksheet. For example, you can create a comment to help remind you of the purpose behind a particular formula or data that should be updated. After you create a comment, you can display it at any time.

To add a comment to a cell, do the following:

1. Select the cell to which you want to add a comment.

 2. Open the **Insert** menu and choose **Comment** or click the **New Comment** button on the Reviewing toolbar.

3. Type your comment, as shown in Figure 4.2.

4. Click outside the cell. A red triangle appears in the upper-right corner of the cell to show that it contains a comment.

To view comments later, point to any cell that contains a red dot in its upper-right corner. Excel displays the comment.

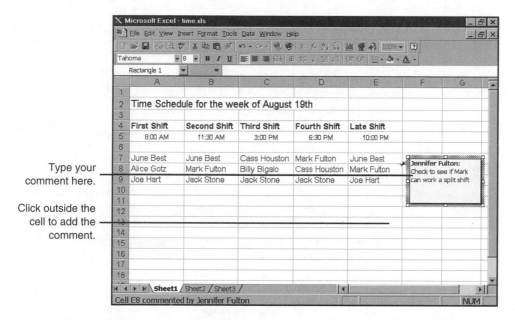

Type your comment here.

Click outside the cell to add the comment.

Figure 4.2 Adding a cell comment.

To edit a comment, select the cell that contains the note and choose **Insert**, **Edit Comment**. Make your changes, and then click outside the cell to save them. To delete a comment, click the cell, select **Edit**, **Clear**, and then select **Comments**.

Entering Numbers

Valid numbers can include the numeric characters 0–9 and any of these special characters: + – / . , ( ) $ % . This means that you can include commas, decimal points, dollar signs, percent signs, and parentheses in the values that you enter.

Although you can include punctuation when you type your entries, you may not want to. For example, instead of typing a column of dollar amounts including dollar signs, commas, and decimal points, you can type numbers such as 700 and 81295, and then format the column with currency formatting. Excel then changes your entries to $700.00 and $81,295.00 or to $700 and $81295, depending on the number of decimal points you specify. See Lesson 15, "Changing How Numbers Look," for more information.

To enter a number:

1. Click the cell into which you want to enter a number.

2. Type the number. To enter a negative number, precede it with a minus sign or surround it with parentheses. To enter a fraction, precede it with a 0, as in 0 1/2. (Otherwise Excel interprets it as a date.)

3. Press **Enter**, and the number appears in the cell, right-aligned.

CAUTION

####### If you enter a number and it appears in the cell as all pound signs (#######) or in scientific notation (such as 7.78E+06), don't worry—the number is okay. The cell just isn't wide enough to display the entire number. To fix it, move to the column headings at the top of the worksheet and double-click the right border of the column. The column expands to fit the largest entry. See Lesson 18 for more help.

Entering Dates and Times

You can enter dates and times in a variety of formats. When you enter a date using a format shown in Table 4.1, Excel converts the date into a number that reflects the number of days between January 1, 1900 and that date. Even though you won't see this number (Excel displays your entry as a normal date), the number is used whenever you use this date in a calculation. By the way, the feature that automatically formats your data based on the way you enter it is called AutoFormat.

Table 4.1   Valid Formats for Dates and Times

Format	Example
M/D	4/8
M-YY	4-58
MM/DD/YY	4/8/58 or 04/08/58
MMM-YY	Jan-92
MMMMMMMM-YY	September-93
MMMMMMMM DD, YYYY	September 3, 1993
DD-MMM-YY	28-Oct-91
DD-MMM	6-Sep

Format	Example
HH:MM	16:50
HH:MM:SS	8:22:59
HH:MM AM/PM	7:45 PM
HH:MM:SS AM/PM	11:45:16 AM
MM/DD/YY HH:MM	11/8/80 4:20

Follow these steps to learn how to enter a date or time:

1. Click the cell into which you want to enter a date or time.

2. Type the date or time in the format in which you want it displayed. You can use hyphens (-) or slashes (/) when typing dates.

3. Press **Enter**. As long as Excel recognizes the entry as a date or time, it appears right-aligned in the cell. If Excel doesn't recognize it, it's treated as text and left-aligned.

If you're entering a column of dates, you can specify the date format you want first. Then as you type your dates, Excel will automatically adapt them to fit that format. For example, suppose you like the MMMMMMMMM DD, YYYY format. Instead of typing each date in full, you could select that format for the column and then type 9/3/98, and Excel would change it to display September 3, 1998. To format a column, click the column header to select the column. Then open the **Format** menu and select **Cells**. On the **Numbers** tab, select the date format you want. (See Lesson 5, "Editing Entries," for more help.)

Not Wide Enough? If you enter a long date and it appears in the cell as all number signs (#######), Excel is trying to tell you that the column is not wide enough to display it.

CAUTION

Day or Night? Unless you type AM or PM after your time entry, Excel assumes that you are using a 24-hour military clock. Therefore, 8:20 is assumed to be AM, not PM. So if you mean PM, type the entry as 8:20 PM (or 8:20 p if you want to use a shortcut). Note that you must type a space between the time and the AM or PM notation.

CAUTION

Copying Entries Quickly

You can copy an existing entry into surrounding cells by performing the following steps:

1. Click the fill handle of the cell whose contents you want to copy.

2. Drag the fill handle down or to the right to copy the data to adjacent cells (see Figure 4.3). A bubble appears to let you know *exactly* what data is being copied to the other cells.

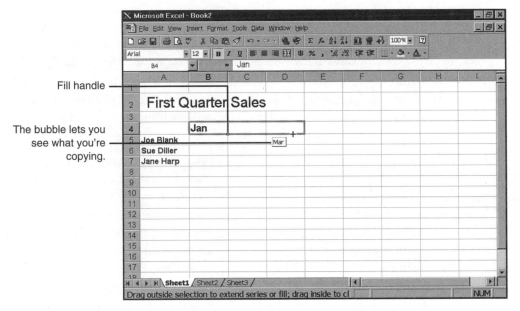

Figure 4.3 Drag the fill handle to copy the contents and formatting into neighboring cells.

If you're copying a number, a month, or other item that might be interpreted as a series (such as January, February, and so on), but you *don't* want to create a series—you just want to copy the contents of the cell exactly—press and hold the **Ctrl** key as you drag the fill handle.

TIP **Copying Across Worksheets** You can copy the contents of cells from one worksheet to one or more worksheets in the workbook. First select the worksheet(s) you want to copy to by clicking the sheet tabs while holding down the **Ctrl** key. Then select the cells you want to copy (see Lesson 5). Open the **Edit** menu, select **Fill**, and select **Across Worksheets**. Then select **All** (to copy both the cells' contents and their formatting), **Contents**, or **Formats**, and click **OK**.

Entering a Series with AutoFill

Entering a series (such as January, February, and March or 1994, 1995, 1996, and 1997) is similar to copying a cell's contents. As you drag the fill handle of the original cell, AutoFill does all the work for you, interpreting the first entry and creating a series of entries based on it. For example, if you type Monday in a cell, and then drag the cell's fill handle over some adjacent cells, you'll create the series Monday, Tuesday, Wednesday... As you drag, the bubble let's you know exactly what you're copying so that you can stop at the appropriate cell to create exactly the series you want.

Entering a Custom Series

Although AutoFill is good for a brief series of entries, you may encounter situations in which you need more control. Excel can handle several different types of series, as shown in Table 4.2.

Table 4.2 Data Series

Series	Initial Entries	Resulting Series
Linear	1,2	1, 2, 3, 4
	100,99	100, 99, 98, 97
	1,3	1, 3, 5, 7
Growth	10, 20	10, 20, 30, 40
	10, 50	10, 50, 90, 130
Date	Mon, Wed	Mon, Wed, Fri
	Feb, May	Feb, May, Aug
	Qtr1, Qtr3	Qtr1, Qtr3, Qtr1
	1992, 1995	1992, 1995, 1998

Basically, you make two sample entries for your series in adjacent cells, and Excel uses them to calculate the rest of the series. Here's what you do:

1. Enter the first value in one cell.

2. Move to the second cell and enter the next value in the series.

3. Select both cells by dragging over them. (See Lesson 6, "Creating and Saving Workbook Files," for more information.) Excel highlights the cells.

4. Drag the fill handle over as many adjacent cells as necessary. Excel computes your series and fills the selected cells with the appropriate values, as shown in Figure 4.4.

Enter the first two values of your series.

Drag the fill handle to complete the series.

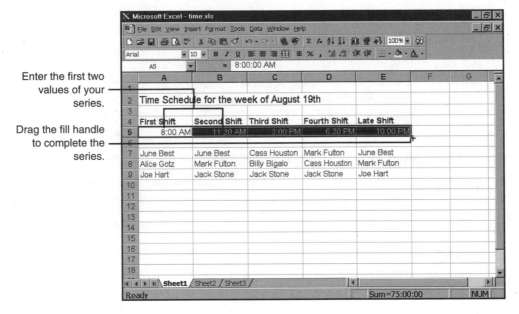

Figure 4.4 Drag to create your series.

Entering the Same Data Over and Over with AutoComplete

When you type the first few letters of an entry, AutoComplete intelligently completes the entry for you based on the entries you've already made in that particular column. AutoComplete works with data entered in columns only, not rows. For example, suppose you want to enter the countries of origin for a series of packages. You type the name of a country once, and the next time you start to type that entry, AutoComplete inserts it for you.

By default, AutoComplete is always turned on, so you don't have to worry about that. However, if it drives you crazy, you can turn it off with the **Tools, Options** command. Click the **Edit** tab and click the **Enable AutoComplete for Cell Values** option to turn it off.

Follow these steps to try out AutoFormat:

1. Type **England** into a cell and press the down-arrow key to move to the next cell down. Type **Spain** and press the down-arrow key again. Then type **Italy** and press the down-arrow key.

2. Type **e** again, and "England" appears in the cell. Press **Enter** to accept the entry. (Likewise, the next time you type **i** or **s**, "Italy" or "Spain" will appear.)

3. To see a list of AutoComplete entries, right-click the next cell and select **Pick From List** from the shortcut menu. Excel shows you a PickList of entries (in alphabetical order) that it has automatically created from the words you've typed in the column.

4. Click a word in the PickList to insert it in the selected cell.

In this lesson, you learned how to enter different types of data and how to automate data entry. In the next lesson, you will learn how to edit entries.

Editing Entries

In this lesson, you learn how to change data and how to undo those changes if necessary. You also learn how to copy, move, and delete data.

Editing Data

After you have entered data into a cell, you may edit it in either the Formula bar or in the cell itself.

To edit an entry in Excel:

1. Click the cell in which you want to edit data.

2. To begin editing, click the Formula bar, press **F2**, or double-click the cell. This puts you in Edit mode; the word **Edit** appears in the Status bar.

3. Press ← or → to move the insertion point within the entry. Press the **Backspace** key to delete characters to the left of the insertion point; press the **Delete** key to delete characters to the right. Then type any characters you want to add.

4. Click the **Enter** button on the Formula bar or press **Enter** on the keyboard to accept your changes.

Or, if you change your mind and you no longer want to edit your entry, click the **Cancel** button or press **Esc**.

Checking Your Spelling

Excel offers a spell checking feature that rapidly finds and highlights misspellings in a worksheet. To run the spelling checker, follow these steps:

1. Click the **Spelling** button on the Standard toolbar. Excel finds the first misspelled word and displays it at the top of the Spelling dialog box. A suggested correction then appears in the Change To box (see Figure 5.1).

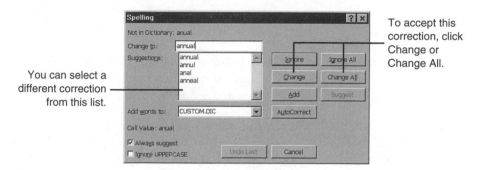

You can select a different correction from this list.

To accept this correction, click Change or Change All.

Figure 5.1 Correct spelling mistakes with the options in the Spelling dialog box.

2. To accept the suggestion and change the misspelled word, click **Change**. Or, click **Change All** to change all occurrences of the misspelled word.

3. If the suggestion in the Change To box is not correct, you can do any of the following:

- Select a different suggestion from the Suggestions box, and then click **Change** or **Change All**. (You can display additional words in the Suggestions list by clicking **Suggest**.)
- Type your own correction in the **Change To** box, and then click **Change** or **Change All**.
- Click **Ignore** to leave the word unchanged.
- Click **Ignore All** to leave all occurrences of the word unchanged.
- Click **Add** to add the word to the dictionary so that Excel won't ever flag it as misspelled again.

4. When the spelling checker can't find any more misspelled words, it displays a prompt telling you that the spelling check is complete. Click **OK** to confirm that the spell checking is finished.

Choose the Wrong Option? If you mistakenly select the wrong option, you can click the **Undo Last** button in the Spelling dialog box to undo the last selection you made.

CAUTION

Using AutoCorrect to Correct Spelling Mistakes

Excel's AutoCorrect feature automatically corrects common typing mistakes as you type. If you type a mistake (such as "teh" instead of "the") and press Enter, Excel enters the corrected text in the cell.

AutoCorrect also corrects two initial capitals. For example, if you type "MAine" and press Enter, Excel will enter "Maine" in the cell. In addition, AutoCorrect capitalizes the first letter of a sentence and the names of days.

You can teach AutoCorrect the errors you normally make, and have it correct them for you as you type. For example, if you always type "breif" instead of "brief," you can add it to the AutoCorrect list. You can also use AutoCorrect to replace an abbreviation, such as ndiv, with the words it represents: Northern Division. Here's how:

1. Open the **Tools** menu and select **AutoCorrect**. The AutoCorrect dialog box appears.
2. Type your error in the **Replace** text box.
3. Type the correction in the **With** text box.
4. Click **Add** to add the entry to the AutoCorrect list.
5. If you want to delete an entry from the AutoCorrect list, select it from the list and click the **Delete** button.

Too Quick! If you want to turn AutoCorrect off because it's "correcting" your entries before you get a chance to stop it, turn off the **Replace Text As You Type** option in the AutoCorrect dialog box.

CAUTION

Undoing an Action

You can undo almost anything you do while working in Excel, including any change you enter into a cell. To undo a change, click the **Undo** button on the Standard toolbar.

To undo an Undo (reinstate a change), click the **Redo** button in the Standard toolbar.

Undoing/Redoing More Than One Thing Normally, when you click the Undo or Redo button, Excel undoes or redoes only the most recent action. To undo (or redo) an action prior to the most recent, click the drop-down arrow on the button and select the action you want from the list. Also new in Excel 97, you can click the **Undo** button multiple times to undo multiple previous actions.

Selecting Cells

To copy, move, or delete the data in several cells at one time, you must select those cells first. Then you can perform the appropriate action.

- To select a single cell, click it.
- To select adjacent cells (a *range*), click the upper-left cell in the group and drag down to the lower-right cell to select additional cells. (If you want more help in selecting ranges of various sizes, see Lesson 9, "Working with Ranges.")
- To select nonadjacent cells, press and hold the **Ctrl** key as you click individual cells.
- To select an entire row or column of cells, click the row or column header. To select adjacent rows or columns, drag over their headers. To select nonadjacent rows or columns, press **Ctrl** and click each header that you want to select.

Range A selection of adjacent cells.

Copying Data

When you copy or move data, a copy of that data is placed in a temporary storage area called the *Clipboard*. You can copy data to other sections of your worksheet or to other worksheets or workbooks. When you copy, the original data remains in its place and a copy of it is placed where you indicate.

Clipboard The Clipboard is an area of memory that is accessible to all Windows programs. The Clipboard is used to copy or move data from place to place within a program or between programs. The techniques that you learn here are the same ones used in all Windows programs.

Follow these steps to copy data:

1. Select the cell(s) that you want to copy.

 2. Click the **Copy** button on the Standard toolbar. The contents of the selected cell(s) are copied to the Clipboard.

3. Select the first cell in the area where you would like to place the copy. (To copy the data to another worksheet or workbook, change to that worksheet or workbook first.)

 4. Click the **Paste** button. Excel inserts the contents of the Clipboard in the location of the insertion point.

Watch Out! When copying or moving data, be careful not to paste the data over existing data (unless, of course, you intend to).

CAUTION

You can copy the same data to several places by repeating the Paste command. Data copied to the Clipboard remains there until you copy or cut (move) something else.

Using Drag-and-Drop

The fastest way to copy something is to drag-and-drop it. Select the cells you want to copy, hold down the **Ctrl** key, and drag the border of the range you selected (see Figure 5.2). When you release the mouse button, the contents are copied to the new location. (If you forget to hold down the Ctrl key, Excel moves the data instead of copying it.) To insert the data *between* existing cells, press **Ctrl+Shift** as you drag.

To drag a copy to a different sheet, press **Ctrl+Alt** as you drag the selection to the sheet's tab. Excel switches you to that sheet, where you can drop your selection in the appropriate location.

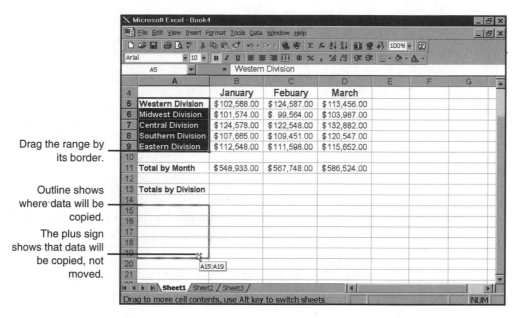

Figure 5.2 To copy data, hold down the Ctrl key while dragging the cell selector border.

Moving Data

Moving data is similar to copying except that the data is removed from its original place and placed in the new location.

To move data, follow these steps:

1. Select the cells you want to move.

2. Click the **Cut** button.

3. Select the first cell in the area where you would like to place the data. To move the data to another worksheet, change to that worksheet.

4. Click **Paste**.

To move data quickly, use the drag-and-drop feature. Select the data to be moved, and then drag the border of the selected cells to its new location. To insert the data between existing cells, press **Shift** while you drag. To move the data to a different worksheet, press the **Alt** key and drag the selection to the worksheet's tab. You're switched to that sheet, where you can drop your selection at the appropriate point.

TIP **Shortcut Menu** When cutting, copying, and pasting data, don't forget the shortcut menu. Simply select the cells you want to cut or copy, *right-click*, and choose the appropriate command from the shortcut menu that appears.

Deleting Data

To delete the data in a cell or cells, you can just select them and press **Delete**. However, Excel offers additional options for deleting cells:

- With the Edit, Clear command, you can choose to delete just the formatting of a cell (or an attached comment), instead of deleting its contents. The formatting of a cell includes the cell's color, border style, numeric format, font size, and so on. You'll learn more about this option in a moment.
- With the Edit, Delete command, you remove cells and everything in them. This command is covered in Lesson 13, "Copying Formulas and Recalculating."

To use the Clear command to remove the formatting of a cell or a note, follow these steps:

1. Select the cells you want to clear.
2. Open the **Edit** menu and select **Clear**. The Clear submenu appears.
3. Select the desired clear option: **All** (which clears the cells of its contents, formatting, and notes), **Formats**, **Contents**, or **Comments**.

Finding and Replacing Data

With Excel's Find and Replace features, you can locate certain data and replace it with new data. When you have a label, a value, or formula that is entered incorrectly throughout the worksheet, you can use the Edit, Replace command to search and replace all occurrences of the incorrect information with the correct data.

To find and replace data, follow these steps:

1. Open the **Edit** menu and select **Replace**. The Replace dialog box appears, as shown in Figure 5.3.
2. Type the text you want to find in the **Find What** text box.
3. Click in the **Replace With** text box and type the text you want to use as replacement text.

Type the data you want to find.

Type its replacement here.

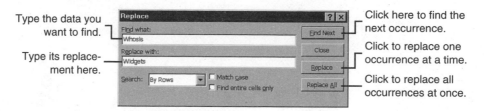

Click here to find the next occurrence.

Click to replace one occurrence at a time.

Click to replace all occurrences at once.

Figure 5.3 Finding and replacing data with the Replace dialog box.

4. In the **Search** box, choose whether you want to search for your entry by rows or by columns.

5. If you want to match the exact case of your entry, click **Match Case**. If you want to locate cells that contain exactly what you entered (and no additional data), click **Find Entire Cells Only**.

6. Click **Find Next** to find the first occurrence of your specified text. Then click **Replace** to replace only this occurrence or **Replace All** to replace all occurrences of the data you specified.

In this lesson, you learned how to edit cell data and undo changes. In addition, you learned how to copy, move, and delete data. In the next lesson, you will learn how to work with workbook files.

Creating and Saving Workbook Files

In this lesson, you learn how to create new workbooks and save workbook files.

Creating a New Workbook

You can create a new *blank* workbook, or you can use a template to create a more complete workbook. A *template* is a predesigned workbook that you can modify to suit your needs. Excel contains templates for creating invoices, expense reports, and other common worksheets.

Here's how you create a new workbook:

1. Pull down the **File** menu and select **New**. The New dialog box appears. As you can see in Figure 6.1, this dialog box contains two tabs: General and Spreadsheet Solutions.

2. To create a blank workbook, click the **General** tab and click the **Workbook** icon.

    To create a workbook from a template, click the **Spreadsheet Solutions** tab. You'll see icons for several common worksheet types. Click the icon for the type of workbook you want to create.

3. After you've made your selection, click **OK** or press **Enter**. A new workbook opens on-screen with a default name in the title bar. Excel numbers its files sequentially. For example, if you already have Book1 open, the Workbook title bar will read **Book2**.

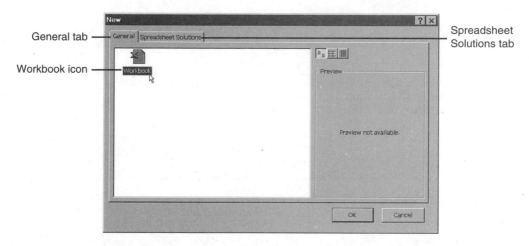

General tab

Workbook icon

Spreadsheet Solutions tab

Figure 6.1 Click the icon for the type of worksheet you want to create.

 TIP **Instant Workbook** If you want to create a blank workbook (instead of creating one from a Spreadsheet Solutions template), you can bypass the New dialog box by clicking the **New** button on the Standard toolbar. Excel opens a new workbook window without displaying the New dialog box.

 TIP **Fast Start** When you start Excel, you're normally given a blank worksheet to start. However, you can select a template instead. Just click the **Start** button on the Windows Taskbar and select **New Office Document**. Excel displays the New Office Document dialog box. Click the **Spreadsheet Solutions** tab, select the type of workbook you want to create, and then click **OK**.

Saving and Naming a Workbook

Whatever you type into a workbook is stored only in your computer's temporary memory. If you exit Excel, that data will be lost. Therefore, it is important to save your workbook files to a disk regularly.

The first time you save a workbook to a disk, you have to name it. Follow these steps to name your workbook:

 1. Open the **File** menu and select **Save**, or click the **Save** button on the Standard toolbar. The Save As dialog box appears (see Figure 6.2).

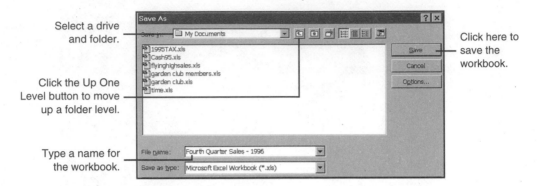

Select a drive
and folder.

Click here to
save the
workbook.

Click the Up One
Level button to move
up a folder level.

Type a name for
the workbook.

Figure 6.2 The Save As dialog box.

2. Type the name you want to give the workbook in the **File Name** text box. You can use up to 218 characters, including any combination of letters, numbers, and spaces (as in **Fourth Quarter Sales - 1996**).

3. Normally, Excel saves your workbooks in the My Documents folder. To save the file to a different folder, select it from the **Save In** list. You can move up a folder level by clicking the **Up One Level** button on the Save toolbar at the top of the dialog box. You can change to a different drive by selecting a drive in the Save In box. Here are some of the locations listed there:

- **Desktop**   Saves the file as an icon on the Windows desktop. This option is not recommended. If you want the file available from the desktop, create a shortcut to it there, as described in Part I, "Windows," of this book.

- **My Computer**   My computer is the big heading under which all your computer drives fall, such as A: and C:. You will normally save files to your C: drive, in the My Documents folder.

- **Network Neighborhood**   You would choose Network Neighborhood if you wanted to save the file to your LAN. A list of the Network Computer drives would appear from which you would choose.

4. Click the **Save** button or press **Enter**.

TIP **Default Directory** Normally, files are saved to the My Documents directory. You can change the default to your own private directory if you want. Open the **Tools** menu, select **Options**, and click the **General** tab. Click in the **Default File Location** text box and type a complete path for the drive and directory you want to use (the directory must be an existing one). Click **OK**.

 To save a file you have saved previously (and named), all you do is click the **Save** button. (Or you can press **Ctrl+S** or use the **File, Save** command.) Excel automatically saves the workbook and any changes you entered without displaying the Save As dialog box.

 Excel on the Web You can save your workbook to an FTP site on the Internet (or a local intranet), provided you have the permission to do so. First, to add the FTP site to the Save As dialog box, open the **Save In** list and select **Add/Modify FTP Locations**. In the **Name of FTP Site** text box, enter the site's address, such as **ftp://ftp.microsoft.com**. Select either **Anonymous** or **User** and enter a password if necessary. Click **Add**. After the site has been added to the Save As dialog box, you can select it from the **Internet Locations (FTP)** folder in the **Save In** list.

Saving a Workbook Under a New Name

Sometimes you might want to change a workbook but keep a copy of the original workbook, or you may want to create a new workbook by modifying an existing one. You can do this by saving the workbook under another name or in another folder. The following steps show how you do that:

1. Open the **File** menu and select **Save As**. You'll see the Save As dialog box, just as if you were saving the workbook for the first time.

2. To save the workbook under a new name, type the new filename over the existing name in the **File Name** text box.

3. To save the file on a different drive or in a different folder, select the drive letter or the folder from the **Save In** list.

4. To save the file in a different format (such as Lotus 1-2-3 or Quattro Pro), click the **Save As Type** drop-down arrow and select the desired format.

5. Click the **Save** button or press **Enter**.

TIP   **Backup Files**   You can have Excel create a backup copy of each workbook file you save. That way, if anything happens to the original file, you can use the backup copy. To turn the backup feature on, click the **Options** button in the Save As dialog box, select **Always Create Backup**, and click **OK**. To use the backup file, choose **File**, **Open** to display the Open dialog box, and then select **Backup Files** from the **Files of Type** list. Double-click the backup file in the files and folders list to open the file.

In this lesson, you learned how to create new workbooks and save workbooks. In the next lesson, you'll learn how to open and close workbook files.

Opening, Finding, and Closing Workbook Files

*In this lesson, you learn how to open and close workbook files.
You also learn how to locate misplaced files.*

Opening an Existing Workbook

If you have closed a workbook and then later you want to use it again, you must reopen it. Follow these steps to open an existing workbook:

1. Open the **File** menu and select **Open**, or click the **Open** button on the Standard toolbar. The Open dialog box shown in Figure 7.1 appears.

Select the file you want to open from the list...

...or type the name of the file here.

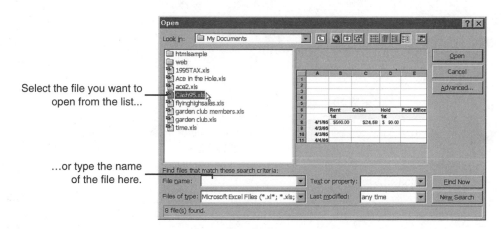

Figure 7.1   The Open dialog box.

2. If the file is not located in the current folder, open the **Look In** box and select the correct drive and folder.

Excel on the Web To open a worksheet on an FTP site to which you have access, select **Internet Locations (FTP)** from the **Look In** box and double-click the FTP site you want to search. Then click the workbook you want to open and click **Open**. To search the Web for a worksheet instead, click the **Search the Web** button at the top of the Open dialog box.

3. Click the file you want to open in the files and folders list. Or, type the name of the file in the **File Name** box. (As you type, Excel highlights the first filename in the list that matches your entry; this is a quick way to move through the list.)

TIP **Save Your Favorites** You can save the worksheets you use most often in the Favorites folder by selecting them and clicking the **Look in Favorites** button. Then, whenever you need to, you can open one of those worksheets by clicking the **Look in Favorites** button at the top of the Open dialog box.

4. To see a preview of the workbook before you open it, click the **Preview** button at the top of the dialog box. Excel displays the contents of the workbook in a window to the right of the dialog box.

5. Click **Open** or press **Enter**.

TIP **Recently Used Workbooks** If you've recently used the workbook you want to open, you'll find it listed at the bottom of the File menu. Just open the **File** menu and select it from the list.

Excel on the Web You can browse the Web for a worksheet with the Search the Web button at the top of the dialog box. But if you know the exact address of the worksheet you want to open—whether it's on the Web or on a local intranet—just type its address (such as **http://www.worldnews.com/facts.xls**) in the **File Name** text box. (You must connect to the Internet before you click Open.)

You can also open a specific workbook when you first start Excel if you want. Just click the **Start** button and select **Open Office Document**. Select the workbook you want to open and click **Open**. Excel starts, with the workbook you selected open and ready to edit.

Finding a Workbook File

If you forget where you saved a file, Excel can help you. You can use its Find Now option in the Open dialog box. Follow these steps to have Excel hunt for a file for you:

1. Open the **File** menu and select **Open**, or click the **Open** button in the Standard toolbar. The Open dialog box appears (see Figure 7.2).

Select the drive or folder to search.

Choose a time period.

Type specific text to look for.

Type the file name to look for.

Click here to search all subfolders.

Click here to begin the search.

Click here to clear all search criteria.

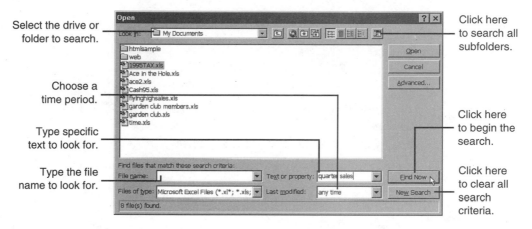

Figure 7.2   The Search options in the Open dialog box enable you to specify what you want to search for.

2. Open the **Look In** box and select the drive or folder you want to search. For example, if you select C:, Excel will search the entire C drive. If you select C: and then select the Excel folder, Excel searches only the EXCEL directory on drive C. You can select My Computer to search all the drives on your computer.

3. Narrow your search using any of the following methods:

If you want to search for a particular file, type its name in the **File Name** text box. You can use wildcard characters in place of characters you can't remember. Use an asterisk (*) in place of a group of characters; use a question mark (?) in place of a single character. (For example, if you enter **sales??**, Excel finds all files whose filenames begin with the word "sales" followed by two characters, such as SALES01, SALES02, and so on.)

You can search the contents of your workbooks for a particular phrase by typing it in the **Text Or Property** box. For example, type "**brook trout**" to find a workbook that contains the words "brook trout."

To specify a time period for the files you want to search, choose an option from the **Last Modified** box.

To have Excel search all subfolders of the drive you specify, click the **Commands and Settings** button and choose **Search Subfolders** from the pop-up menu that appears.

TIP **Do Over**   You can clear your search selections by clicking the **New Search** button.

4. When you finish entering your search criteria, click the **Find Now** button. Excel finds the files that match the search instructions you entered and displays them in the files and folders list.

5. Look through the list, highlight the file you want, and click the **Open** button.

CAUTION

File Not Found?   If the file you want is not listed in the files and folders list, you can specify more detailed search criteria by using the Advanced Find feature. Click the **Advanced** button in the Open dialog box. Enter search criteria such as property, condition, or value, and then click the **Find Now** button to search for the file using these additional criteria.

Moving Among Open Workbooks

Sometimes you may have more than one workbook open at a time. If so, you can switch back and forth as necessary to view or edit their contents. The following are several ways to move among open workbooks:

- If part of the desired workbook window is visible, click it.
- Open the **Window** menu and select the name of the workbook to which you want to switch.
- Press **Ctrl+F6** to move from one workbook window to another.

The Active Window If you have more than one workbook open, only the one where the cell selector is located is considered active. The title bar of the active workbook will be darker than the title bars of other open workbooks.

Closing Workbooks

When you close a workbook, Excel removes its workbook window from the screen. You should close workbooks when you finish working on them to free up your computer's resources so that it can respond to your commands more quickly. To close a workbook, follow these steps:

1. If the window you want to close isn't currently active, make it active by selecting the workbook from the list of workbooks at the bottom of the **Window** menu.

2. Click the **Close** (X) button in the upper-right corner of the workbook.

Close All In Excel 97, if you have more than one workbook open, you can close all workbooks at once by holding down the **Shift** key, opening the **File** menu, and selecting **Close All**.

In this lesson, you learned how to open and close workbooks, as well as how to find misplaced workbook files. The next lesson teaches you how to work with the worksheets in a workbook.

Working with Worksheets

In this lesson, you learn how to add and delete worksheets with workbooks. You also learn how to copy, move, and rename worksheets.

Selecting Worksheets

By default, each workbook consists of three worksheet pages whose names appear on tabs near the bottom of the screen. You can insert new worksheet pages or delete worksheet pages as desired. One advantage to having multiple worksheet pages is to organize your data into logical chunks. Another advantage to having separate worksheets for your data is that you can reorganize the worksheets in a workbook easily.

Before we get into the details of inserting, deleting, and copying worksheets, you should know how to select one or more worksheets. Here's what you need to know:

- To select a single worksheet, click its tab. The tab becomes highlighted to show that the worksheet is selected.
- To select several neighboring worksheets, click the tab of the first worksheet in the group, and then hold down the **Shift** key and click the tab of the last worksheet in the group.
- To select several non-neighboring worksheets, hold down the **Ctrl** key and click each worksheet's tab.

If you select two or more worksheets, they remain selected until you ungroup them. To ungroup worksheets, do one of the following:

- Right-click one of the selected worksheets and choose **Ungroup Sheets**.

- Hold down the **Shift** key and click the active tab.
- Click any tab outside the group.

Inserting Worksheets

When you create a new workbook, it contains three worksheets. You can easily add additional worksheets to a workbook.

 TIP **Start with More** You can change the number of worksheets Excel places in a new workbook by opening the **Tools** menu, selecting **Options**, clicking the **General** tab, and then changing the number under the **Sheets in New Workbook** option. Click **OK** to save your changes.

Follow these steps to add a worksheet to a workbook:

1. Select the worksheet *before* which you want the new worksheet inserted. For example, if you select Sheet2, the new worksheet (which will be called Sheet4 because the workbook already contains three worksheets) will be inserted before Sheet2.
2. Open the **Insert** menu.
3. Select **Worksheet**. Excel inserts the new worksheet, as shown in Figure 8.1.

 TIP **Shortcut Menu** A faster way to work with worksheets is to right-click the worksheet tab. This brings up a shortcut menu that lets you insert, delete, rename, move, copy, or select all worksheets. When you choose **Insert** from the shortcut menu, Excel displays the Insert dialog box. Click the **Worksheet** icon on the General tab and click **OK** to insert a new worksheet.

Deleting Worksheets

If you plan to use only one worksheet, you can remove the two other worksheets to free up memory. Here's how you remove a worksheet:

1. Select the worksheet(s) you want to delete.
2. Open the **Edit** menu.
3. Click **Delete Sheet**. A dialog box appears, asking you to confirm the deletion.
4. Click the **OK** button. The worksheets are deleted.

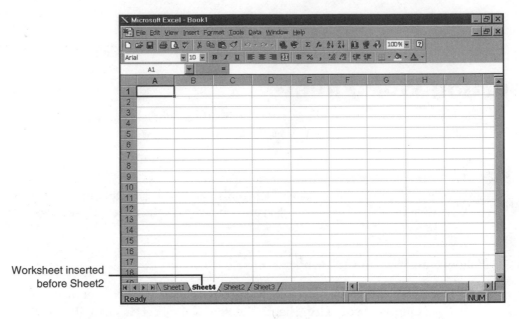

Worksheet inserted
before Sheet2

Figure 8.1 Excel inserts the new worksheet before the worksheet you selected.

Moving and Copying Worksheets

You can move or copy worksheets within a workbook or from one workbook to another. Here's how:

1. Select the worksheet(s) you want to move or copy. If you want to move or copy worksheets from one workbook to another, be sure to open the target workbook.

2. Open the **Edit** menu and choose **Move or Copy Sheet**. The Move or Copy dialog box appears, as shown in Figure 8.2.

3. To move the worksheet(s) to a different workbook, select that workbook's name from the **To Book** drop-down list. If you want to move or copy the worksheet(s) to a new workbook, select **(new book)** in the **To Book** drop-down list. Excel creates a new workbook and then copies or moves the worksheet(s) to it.

4. In the **Before Sheet** list box, choose the worksheet *before* which you want the selected worksheet(s) to be moved.

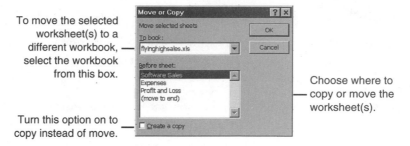

To move the selected worksheet(s) to a different workbook, select the workbook from this box.

Choose where to copy or move the worksheet(s).

Turn this option on to copy instead of move.

Figure 8.2 The Move or Copy dialog box asks you where you want to copy or move a worksheet.

5. To copy the selected worksheet(s) instead of moving them, select **Create a Copy** to put a checkmark in the check box.

6. Select **OK**. The selected worksheet(s) are copied or moved as specified.

Moving a Worksheet Within a Workbook by Dragging and Dropping

An easier way to copy or move worksheets within a workbook is to use the drag-and-drop feature. First, select the tab of the worksheet(s) you want to copy or move. Move the mouse pointer over one of the selected tabs, click and hold the mouse button, and drag the tab where you want it moved. To copy the worksheet, hold down the **Ctrl** key while dragging. When you release the mouse button, the worksheet is copied or moved.

Moving a Worksheet Between Workbooks by Dragging and Dropping

You can also use the drag-and-drop feature to quickly copy or move worksheets between workbooks. First, open the workbooks you want to use for the copy or move. Choose **Window**, **Arrange** and select the **Tiled** option. Click **OK** to arrange the windows so that a small portion of each one appears on-screen. Select the tab of the worksheet(s) you want to copy or move. Move the mouse pointer over one of the selected tabs, click and hold the mouse button, and drag the tab where you want it moved. To copy the worksheet, hold down the **Ctrl** key while dragging. When you release the mouse button, the worksheet is copied or moved.

Changing Worksheet Tab Names

By default, all worksheets are named "SheetX," where X is a number starting with the number 1. So that you'll have a better idea of the information each sheet contains, you can change the names that appear on the tabs. Here's how you do it:

1. Double-click the tab of the worksheet you want to rename. The current name is highlighted.

2. Type a new name for the worksheet and press **Enter**. Excel replaces the default name with the name you typed.

In this lesson, you learned how to insert, delete, move, copy, and rename worksheets. In the next lesson, you'll learn how to work with cell ranges.

Working with Ranges

In this lesson, you learn how to select and name cell ranges.

What Is a Range?

A *range* is a rectangular group of connected cells. The cells in a range may all be in one column, or one row, or any combination of columns and rows, as long as the range forms a rectangle, as shown in Figure 9.1.

Figure 9.1   A range is any combination of cells that forms a rectangle.

Learning how to use ranges can save you time. For example, you can select a range and use it to format a group of cells with one step. You can use a range to print only a selected group of cells. You can also use ranges in formulas.

Ranges are referred to by their anchor points (the upper-left corner and the lower-right corner). For example, the ranges shown in Figure 9.1 are B4:G8, A10:G10, and G12.

Selecting a Range

To select a range using the mouse, follow these steps:

1. To select the same range of cells on more than one worksheet, select the worksheets (see Lesson 8, "Working with Worksheets").

2. Move the mouse pointer to the upper-left corner of a range.

3. Click and hold the left mouse button.

4. Drag the mouse to the lower-right corner of the range and release the mouse button. The selected range is highlighted.

Table 9.1 lists some techniques that you can use to quickly select a row, a column, an entire worksheet, or several ranges.

Table 9.1 Selection Techniques

To Select This...	Do This...
Several ranges	Select the first range, hold down the **Ctrl** key, and select the next range. Do this for each range you want to select.
Row	Click the row heading number at the left edge of the worksheet. You also can press **Shift+Spacebar**.
Column	Click the column heading letter at the top edge of the worksheet. You also can press **Ctrl+Spacebar**.
Entire worksheet	Click the **Select All** button (the blank rectangle in the upper-left corner of the worksheet, above row 1 and left of column A). You also can press **Ctrl+A**.
Range that is out of view	Press **Ctrl+G** (Goto) or click in the **Name** box on the Formula bar, and then type the address of the range you want to select. For example, to select the range R100 to T250, type **R100:T250** and press **Enter**.

Deselecting a Selection To remove the range selection, click any cell in the worksheet.

CAUTION

Naming Cells and Cell Ranges

Up to this point, you have used cell addresses to refer to cells. Although that works, it is often more convenient to name cells with more recognizable names. For example, say you want to determine your net income by subtracting expenses from income (see Lesson 12, "Performing Calculations with Formulas"). You can name the cell that contains your total income **INCOME**, and name the cell that contains your total expenses **EXPENSES**. You can then determine your net income by using the formula:

= INCOME – EXPENSES

Giving the cells memorable names will make the formula more logical and easier to manage. Naming cells and ranges also makes it easier to cut, copy, and move blocks of cells, as explained in Lesson 5, "Editing Entries."

Follow these steps to name a cell range:

1. Select the range of cells you want to name. Make sure all the cells are on the same worksheet. (You cannot name cells and cell ranges that are located on more than one sheet.)

2. Click in the **Name** box on the left side of the Formula bar (see Figure 9.2).

3. Type a range name using up to 255 characters. Valid names can include letters, numbers, periods, and underlines, but *no* spaces. In addition, a number cannot be used as the first character in the range name.

4. Press **Enter**.

5. To see the list of range names, click the **Name** box's drop-down arrow (on the Formula bar).

Another way to name a range is to select it, open the **Insert** menu, select **Name**, and choose **Define**. This displays the Define Name dialog box shown in Figure 9.3. Type a name in the **Names in Workbook** text box and click **OK**.

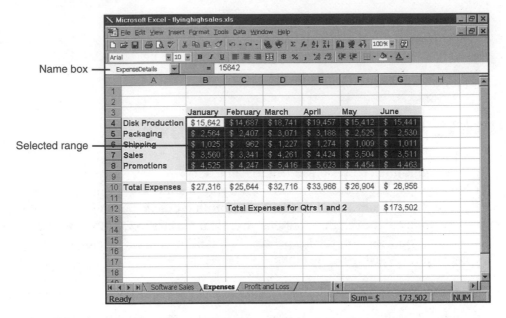

Figure 9.2 Type a name in the Name box.

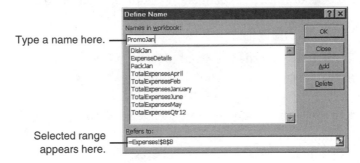

Figure 9.3 The Define Name dialog box.

The Define Name dialog box enables you to see what range a range name contains. Click a range name in the Names in Workbook list, and you'll see the cell address(es) assigned to the range name in the Refers To text box. You can edit the range or type a new one.

The dollar signs in the cell addresses indicate absolute cell references, which always refer to the same cell. An absolute cell reference will not be adjusted if changes are made to those cells in the worksheet (see Lesson 13, "Copying Formulas and Recalculating"). You don't have to type the dollar signs in the cell address. When you select cells with the mouse, Excel inserts the dollar signs automatically.

This dialog box also lets you delete names. To delete a range name, click a name in the **Names in Workbook** list and click the **Delete** button.

In this lesson, you learned how to select and name ranges. In the next lesson, you will learn how to print your workbook.

Printing Your Workbook

In this lesson, you learn how to print a workbook or a portion of one, and how to enhance your printout with headers and footers.

Changing the Page Setup

A workbook is a collection of many worksheets, which are like pages in a notebook. You can print the whole notebook at once, or just one or more pages at a time.

Before you print a worksheet, you should make sure that the page is set up correctly for printing. To do this, open the **File** menu and choose **Page Setup**. You'll see the Page Setup dialog box shown in Figure 10.1.

TIP   **Right-Click the Workbook's Title Bar**   For quick access to commands that affect a workbook, right-click the workbook's title bar. If the workbook is maximized to a full screen (and the title bar is therefore not visible), right-click the Control-menu box to access the shortcut menu. For example, to check the page setup, right-click the title bar or the **Control-menu** box and choose **Page Setup**.

The following list outlines the page setup settings, grouped according to the tab on which they appear.

Page tab

> **Orientation**   Select **Portrait** to print across the short edge of a page; select **Landscape** to print across the long edge of a page. (Landscape makes the page wider than it is tall.)

The Page tab ————

The Margins tab ————

The Header/Footer tab ————

The Sheet tab ————

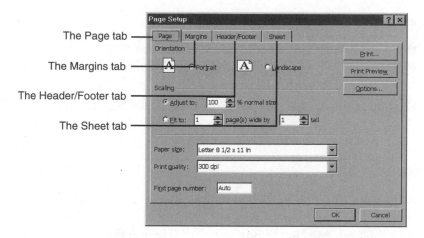

Figure 10.1 The Page Setup dialog box.

Scaling   You can reduce and enlarge your workbook or force it to fit within a specific page size.

Paper Size   This is 8 1/2 by 11 inches by default, but you can choose a different size from the list.

Print Quality   You can print your spreadsheet in draft quality to print quickly and save wear and tear on your printer, or you can print in high quality for a final copy. Print quality is measured in dpi (dots per inch); the higher the number, the better the print.

First Page Number   You can set the starting page number to something other than 1. The Auto option (default) tells Excel to set the starting page number to 1 if it is the first page in the print job, or to set the first page number at the next sequential number if it is not the first page in the print job.

Margins tab

Top, Bottom, Left, Right   You can adjust the size of the top, bottom, left, and right margins.

Header, Footer   You can specify how far you want a Header or Footer printed from the edge of the page. (You use the Header/Footer tab to add a header or footer to your workbook.)

Center on Page   You can center your workbook data between the left and right margins (**Horizontally**) and between the top and bottom margins (**Vertically**).

Header/Footer tab

> **Header, Footer**   You can add a header (such as a title) that repeats at the top of each page, or a footer (such as page numbers) that repeats at the bottom of each page.
>
> **Custom Header, Custom Footer**   You can use the Custom Header or Custom Footer button to create headers and footers that insert the time, date, worksheet tab name, and workbook filename.

Sheet tab

> **Print Area**   You can print a portion of a workbook or worksheet by entering the range of cells you want to print. You can type the range, or click the **Collapse Dialog Box** icon at the right of the text box to move the Page Setup dialog box out of the way and drag the mouse pointer over the desired cells. If you do not select a print area, Excel will print either the sheet or the workbook, depending on the options set in the Page tab.

 TIP **Don't Print That!**   Ordinarily, if there's a portion of your worksheet that you don't want to print, you can avoid it by selecting the area you want to print and printing only that selection. However, if the data you want to hide is located *within* the area you want to print, what do you do? In that case, you can hide the columns, rows, or cells to prevent them from being printed. (See Lesson 2, "Examining the Excel Window," for help.)

> **Print Titles**   If you have a row or column of entries that you want repeated as titles on every page, type the range for this row or column, or drag over the cells with the mouse pointer (see Lesson 9, "Working with Ranges").
>
> **Print**   You can tell Excel exactly how to print some aspects of the workbook. For example, you can have the gridlines (the lines that define the cells) printed. You can also have a color spreadsheet printed in black-and-white.
>
> **Page Order**   You can indicate how data in the worksheet should be read and printed: in sections from top to bottom or in sections from left to right. This is the way Excel handles printing the areas outside of the printable area. For example, if some columns to the right don't fit on the first page and some rows don't fit at the bottom of the first page, you can specify which area will print next.

When you finish entering your settings, click the **OK** button.

Previewing a Print Job

After you've determined your page setup and print area, you should preview what the printed page will look like before you print. To preview a print job, open the **File** menu and select **Print Preview** or click the **Print Preview** button in the Standard toolbar. Your workbook appears as it will when printed, as shown in Figure 10.2.

TIP **Page Setup Print Preview** You can also preview a print job when you are setting up a page or while you are in the Print dialog box. When the Page Setup dialog box is displayed, click the **Print Preview** button. In the Print dialog box, click the **Preview** button.

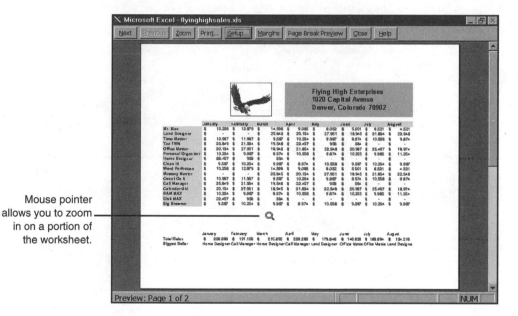

Mouse pointer allows you to zoom in on a portion of the worksheet.

Figure 10.2 You can preview your workbook before printing it.

TIP **A Close-Up View** Zoom in on any area of the preview by clicking it with the mouse pointer (which looks like a magnifying glass). You can also use the **Zoom** button at the top of the Print Preview screen.

Printing Your Workbook

After setting the page setup and previewing your data, it is time to print. You can print selected data, selected sheets, or the entire workbook.

To print your workbook, follow these steps:

1. If you want to print a portion of the worksheet, select the range you want to print (see Lesson 9, "Working with Ranges," for help). If you want to print one or more sheets within the workbook, select the sheet tabs (see Lesson 8, "Working with Worksheets"). To print the entire workbook, skip this step.

2. Open the **File** menu and select **Print** (or press **Ctrl+P**). The Print dialog box appears, as shown in Figure 10.3.

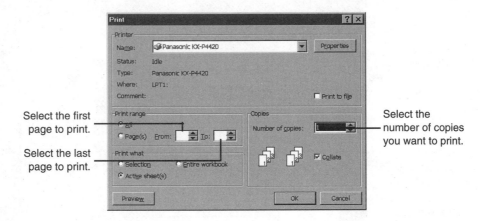

Select the first page to print.

Select the last page to print.

Select the number of copies you want to print.

Figure 10.3 The Print dialog box.

Too Quick to Print If you click the **Print** button instead of using the **File**, **Print** command, Excel prints your current worksheet without letting you make any selections.

CAUTION

3. Select the options you would like to use:

Page Range lets you print one or more pages. For example, if the selected print area will take up 15 pages and you want to print only pages 5–10, select **Page(s)**, and then type the numbers of the first and last page you want to print in the **From** and **To** boxes.

Print What enables you to print the currently selected cells, the selected worksheets, or the entire workbook.

Copies enables you to print more than one copy of the selection, worksheet, or workbook.

Collate enables you to print a complete copy of the selection, worksheet, or workbook before the first page of the next copy is printed. This option is available when you print multiple copies.

4. Click **OK** or press **Enter**.

While your job is printing, you can continue working in Excel. If the printer is working on another job that you (or someone else, in the case of a network printer) sent, Windows holds the job until the printer is ready for it.

Sometimes you might want to delete a job while it is printing or before it prints. For example, suppose you think of other numbers to add to the worksheet or realize you forgot to format some text; you'll want to fix these things before you print the file. In such a case, deleting the print job is easy. To display the print queue and delete a print job, follow these steps:

1. Double-click the **Printer** icon on the Windows taskbar, and the print queue appears, as shown in Figure 10.4.

2. Click the job you want to delete.

3. Open the **Document** menu and select **Cancel Printing**.

TIP **Clear the Queue!** To delete all the files from the print queue, open the **Printer** menu and select **Purge Print Documents**. This cancels the print jobs, but doesn't delete the files from your computer.

Upgrade Tip With Excel 97, you get a newly expanded ability to send your worksheet directly to the people who need it, instead of printing it. Open the **File** menu, select **Send To**, and then select the appropriate option: **Mail Recipient** (to send a workbook via an e-mail message), **Routing Recipient** (to route a workbook over a local network by Microsoft Mail or cc:Mail to several people), or **Exchange Folder** (to post—copy—your workbook to a Microsoft Exchange server).

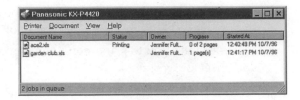

Figure 10.4 To stop a document from printing, use the print queue.

Selecting a Print Area

You can tell Excel what part of the worksheet you want to print using the Print Area option. This option lets you single out an area as a separate page and then print that page. If the area is too large to fit on one page, Excel breaks it into multiple pages. If you do not select a print area, Excel prints either the entire worksheet or the entire workbook, depending on the options set in the Print dialog box.

CAUTION

To Include or Not to Include? When deciding which cells to select for your print area, make sure you do *not* include the title, the subtitle, and the column and row headings in the print area. If you do, Excel may print the labels twice. Instead, print your titles and headings on each page of your printout by following the steps in the upcoming section, "Printing Column and Row Headings."

To select a print area and print your worksheet at the same time, follow these steps:

1. Open the **File** menu and choose **Page Setup**. The Page Setup dialog box appears.

2. Click the **Sheet** tab to display the Sheet options.

3. Click the **Collapse Dialog** icon to the right of the Print Area text box. Excel reduces the Page Setup dialog box in size.

4. Drag over the cells you want to print (see Lesson 9). As you can see in Figure 10.5, a dashed line border surrounds the selected area, and the absolute cell references for those cells appear with dollar signs ($) in the Print Area text box. (If you want to type the range, you don't have to include the $ in the cell references. See Lesson 13, "Copying Formulas and Recalculating," for more information about absolute cell references.)

5. Click the **Collapse Dialog** icon to return to the Page Setup dialog box.

6. Click **Print** in the Page Setup dialog box to display the Print dialog box. Then click **OK** to print your worksheet.

The addresses of
the selected cells
appear here.

Drag over the
desired cells.

Click the Collapse
Dialog icon to
return to the Page
Setup dialog box.

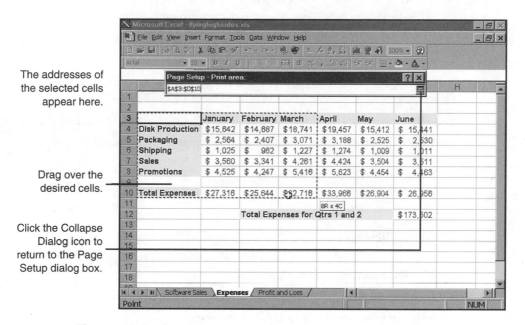

Figure 10.5 Selecting a print area.

TIP   **Set Your Area**   To set the print area without printing, select the cells you want to print later, open the **File** menu, select **Print Area**, and select **Set Print Area**.

Remove the Print Area   To remove the print area, open the **File** menu, select **Print Area**, and select **Clear Print Area**.

CAUTION

Adjusting Page Breaks

When you print a workbook, Excel determines the page breaks based on the paper size and margins and the selected print area. To make the pages look better and break things in logical places, you may want to override the automatic page breaks with your own breaks. However, before you add page breaks, try these options:

- Adjust the widths of individual columns to make the best use of space (see Lesson 18, "Changing Column Width and Row Height").
- Consider printing the workbook sideways (using Landscape orientation).
- Change the left, right, top, and bottom margins to smaller values.

If after trying these options you still want to insert page breaks, Excel 97 offers you an option of previewing exactly where the page breaks appear and then adjusting them. Follow these steps:

1. Open the **View** menu and select **Page Break Preview**.

2. If a message appears, click **OK**. Your worksheet is displayed with page breaks, as shown in Figure 10.6.

3. To move a page break, drag the dashed line to the desired location.

   To delete a page break, drag it off the screen.

   To insert a page break, move to the first cell in the column to the *right* of where you want the page break inserted, or move to the row *below* where you want the break inserted. For example, to insert a page break between columns G and H, move to cell H1. To insert a page break between rows 24 and 25, move to cell A25. Then open the **Insert** menu and select **Page Break**. A dashed line appears to the left of the selected column or above the selected row.

4. To exit Page Break Preview and return to your normal worksheet view, open the **View** menu and select **Normal**.

Drag a page
break to move it.

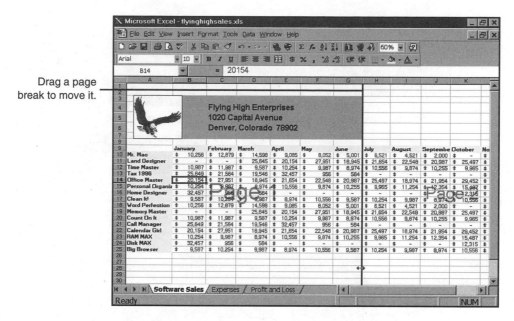

Figure 10.6 Check your page breaks before printing.

Printing Column and Row Headings

Excel provides a way for you to select labels and titles that are located on the top edge and left side of a large worksheet, and print them on every page of the printout. This option is useful when a worksheet is too wide to print on a single page. If you don't use this option, the extra columns or rows will be printed on subsequent pages without any descriptive labels.

Follow these steps to print column and/or row headings on every page:

1. Open the **File** menu and choose **Page Setup**. The Page Setup dialog box appears.

2. Click the **Sheet** tab to display the Sheet options.

3. To repeat column labels and a worksheet title, click the **Collapse Dialog** icon to the right of the Rows to Repeat at Top text box. Excel reduces the Page Setup dialog box in size.

4. Drag over the rows you want to print on every page, as shown in Figure 10.7. A dashed line border surrounds the selected area, and absolute cell references with dollar signs ($) appear in the Rows to Repeat at Top text box.

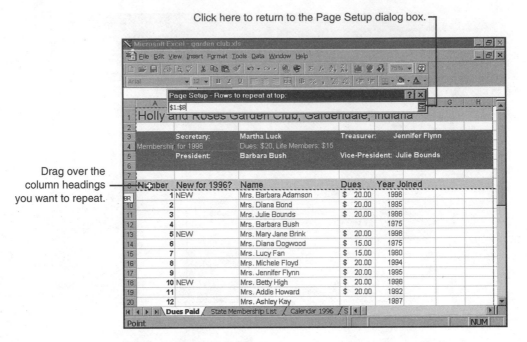

Figure 10.7 Specifying headings you want to print on every page.

5. Click the **Collapse Dialog** icon to return to the Page Setup dialog box.

6. To repeat row labels that appear on the left of the worksheet, click the **Collapse Dialog** icon to the right of the Columns to Repeat at Left text box. Again, Excel reduces the Page Setup dialog box.

7. Select the row labels you want to repeat.

8. Click the **Collapse Dialog** icon to return once again to the Page Setup dialog box.

9. To print your worksheet, click **Print** to display the Print dialog box. Then click **OK**.

CAUTION

Select Your Print Area Carefully If you select rows or columns to repeat, and those rows or columns are part of your print area, the selected rows or columns will print twice. To fix this, select your print area again, leaving out the rows or columns you're repeating. See "Selecting a Print Area" earlier in this lesson for help.

Adding Headers and Footers

Excel lets you add headers and footers to print information at the top and bottom of every page of the printout. The information can include any text, as well as page numbers, the current date and time, the workbook filename, and the worksheet tab name.

You can choose the headers and footers suggested by Excel, or you can include any other text you want. You can also use special commands to control the appearance of the header or footer. For example, you can apply bold, italic, or underline to the header or footer text. You can also left-align, center, or right-align the text (see Lesson 18).

To add headers and footers, follow these steps:

1. Open the **View** menu and choose **Header and Footer**, or click the **Header and Footer** tab in the Page Setup dialog box. The Page Setup dialog box appears (see Figure 10.8).

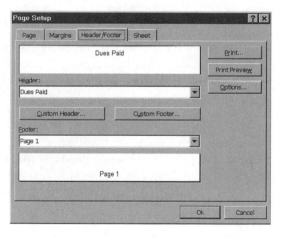

Figure 10.8 Adding headers and footers with Header/Footer options.

2. To select a header, click the **Header** drop-down arrow. Excel displays a list of suggested header information. Scroll through the list and click a header you want. The sample header appears at the top of the Header/Footer tab.

TIP **Don't See One You Like?** If none of the suggested headers or footers suits you, click the **Custom Header** or **Custom Footer** button and enter your exact specifications.

3. To select a footer, click the **Footer** drop-down arrow. Excel displays a list of suggested footer information. Scroll through the list and click a footer you want. The sample footer appears at the bottom of the Header/Footer tab.

4. Click **OK** to close the Page Setup dialog box and return to your worksheet. Or click the **Print** button to display the Print dialog box, and click **OK** to print your worksheet.

Don't Want Any Headers or Footers? To remove the header and/or footer, choose **None** in the Header and/or Footer suggestions lists.

CAUTION

Scaling a Worksheet to Fit on a Page

If your worksheet is too large to print on one page even after you change the orientation and margins, you might consider using the Fit To option. This option shrinks the worksheet to make it fit on the specified number of pages. You can specify the document's width and height.

Follow these steps to scale a worksheet to fit on a page:

1. Open the **File** menu and choose **Page Setup**. The Page Setup dialog box appears.

2. Click the **Page** tab to display the Page options.

3. In the **Fit to XX Page(s) Wide By** and the **XX Tall** text boxes, enter the number of pages in which you want Excel to fit your data.

4. Click **OK** to close the Page Setup dialog box and return to your worksheet. Or click the **Print** button in the Page Setup dialog box to display the Print dialog box, and then click **OK** to print your worksheet.

In this lesson, you learned how to print a worksheet. In the next lesson, you will learn how to add and remove cells, rows, and columns.

Inserting and Removing Cells, Rows, and Columns

11

In this lesson, you learn how to rearrange your worksheet by adding and removing cells, rows, and columns.

Inserting Cells

Sometimes, you will need to insert information into a worksheet, right in the middle of existing data. With the Insert command, you can insert one or more cells, or entire rows or columns.

Shifting Cells   Inserting cells in the middle of existing data will cause the data in existing cells to shift down a row or over a column. If your worksheet contains formulas that rely on the contents of the shifting cells, this could throw off the calculations. Be sure to check all formulas that might be affected.

CAUTION

To insert a single cell or a group of cells, follow these steps:

1. Select the cell(s) where you want the new cell(s) inserted. Excel will insert the same number of cells as you select.

2. Open the **Insert** menu and choose **Cells**. The Insert dialog box shown in Figure 11.1 appears.

3. Select **Shift Cells Right** or **Shift Cells Down**.

Figure 11.1 The Insert dialog box.

4. Click **OK**. Excel inserts the cell(s) and shifts the data in the other cells in the specified direction.

 TIP **Drag Insert** A quick way to insert cells is to hold down the Shift key and then drag the fill handle (the little box in the lower-right corner of the selected cell or cells—see Figure 11.2). Drag the fill handle up, down, left, or right to set the position of the new cells.

Merging Cells

In Excel 97, you can merge the data in one cell with other cells to form a big cell that is easier to use. Merging cells is especially handy when creating a decorative title for the top of your worksheet (see Figure 11.2 for an example). Within a single merged cell, you can quickly change the font, point size, color, and border style of your title.

To create a title with merged cells, follow these steps:

1. Type your title in the upper-left cell of the range you want to use for your heading. If you have a multiline title, like the one in Figure 11.2, press **Alt+Enter** to insert each new line.

2. Select the range in which you want to place your title.

3. Open the **Format** menu and select **Cells**. The Format Cells dialog box appears.

4. Click the **Alignment** tab.

5. Click **Merge Cells**. You may also want to make adjustments to the text within the merged cells. For example, you may want to select **Center** in the **Vertical** drop-down list to center the text vertically within the cell.

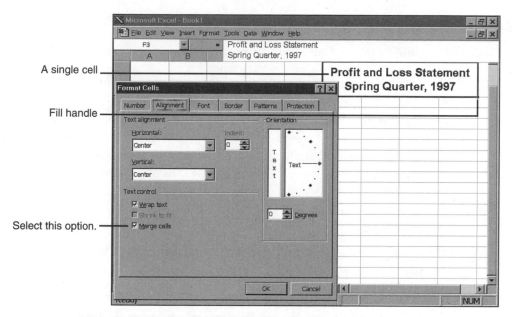

Figure 11.2 Merge cells to form a single cell.

6. Click **OK** when you're done. The selected cells are merged into a single cell, which you can format as needed.

 You can merge selected cells and center the data in the left-most cell by clicking the **Merge and Center** button on the Formatting toolbar.

Removing Cells

In Lesson 5, "Editing Entries," you learned how to clear the contents and formatting of selected cells. That merely removed what was inside the cells. But sometimes you will want to eliminate the cells completely. When you do, Excel removes the cells and adjusts the data in surrounding cells to fill the gap.

If you want to remove the cells completely, perform the following steps:

1. Select the range of cells you want to remove.

2. Open the **Edit** menu and choose **Delete**. The Delete dialog box appears.

3. Select the desired Delete option: **Shift Cells Left** or **Shift Cells Up**.

4. Click **OK**.

Inserting Rows and Columns

Inserting entire rows and columns in your worksheet is easy. Here's what you do:

1. **To insert a single row or column,** select the cell to the *left* of which you want to insert a column, or *above* where you want to insert a row.

   To insert multiple columns or rows, select the number of columns or rows you want to insert. To insert columns, drag over the column letters at the top of the worksheet. To insert rows, drag over the row numbers. For example, select three column letters or row numbers to insert three rows or columns.

2. Open the **Insert** menu.

3. Select **Rows** or **Columns**. Excel inserts the row(s) or column(s) and shifts the adjacent rows down or the adjacent columns right. The inserted rows or columns contain the same formatting as the cells you selected in step 1. Figure 11.3 simulates a worksheet before and after two rows were inserted.

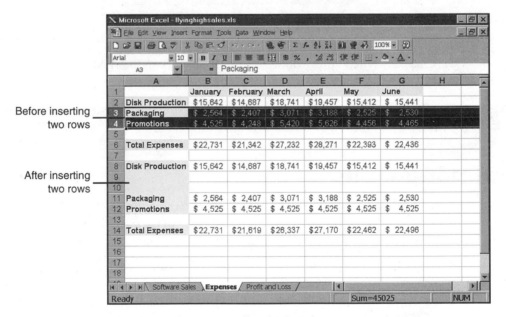

Figure 11.3   Inserting two rows in a worksheet.

TIP   **Shortcut Insert**   To quickly insert rows or columns, select one or more rows or columns. Then right-click one of them and choose **Insert** from the shortcut menu.

Removing Rows and Columns

Deleting rows and columns is similar to deleting cells. When you delete a row, the rows below the deleted row move up to fill the space. When you delete a column, the columns to the right shift left.

Follow these steps to delete a row or column:

1. Click the row number or column letter of the row or column you want to delete. You can select more than one row or column by dragging over the row numbers or column letters.

2. Open the **Edit** menu and choose **Delete**. Excel deletes the row(s) or column(s) and renumbers the remaining rows and columns sequentially. All cell references in formulas and names in formulas are updated appropriately, unless they are absolute ($) values (see Lesson 13, "Copying Formulas and Recalculating").

In this lesson, you learned how to insert and delete cells, rows, and columns. In the next lesson, you will learn how to use formulas.

Performing Calculations with Formulas

In this lesson, you learn how to use formulas to calculate results in your worksheets.

What Is a Formula?

Worksheets use formulas to perform calculations on the data you enter. With formulas, you can perform addition, subtraction, multiplication, and division by using the values contained in various cells.

Formulas typically consist of one or more cell addresses or values and a mathematical operator, such as + (addition), – (subtraction), * (multiplication), or / (division). For example, if you want to determine the average of the three values contained in cells A1, B1, and C1, type the following formula in the cell where you want the result to appear:

$$=(A1+B1+C1)/3$$

Start Right   Every formula must begin with an equal sign (=).

CAUTION

Figure 12.1 shows several formulas in action. Study the formulas and their results. Table 12.1 lists the mathematical operators you can use to create formulas.

=C19+D19+E19 determines total profit.

=E6+E7+E8 gives total income for March.

=E13+E14+E15 gives total expenses for March.

=E10-E17 subtracts expenses from income to determine profit.

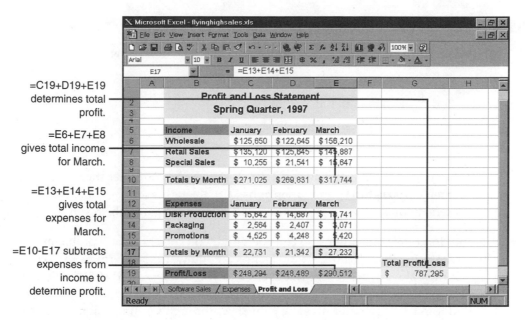

Figure 12.1 Type a formula in the cell where you want the resulting value to appear.

Table 12.1 Excel's Mathematical Operators

Operator	Performs	Sample Formula	Result
^	Exponentiation	=A1^3	Enters the result of raising the value in cell A1 to the third power.
+	Addition	=A1+A2	Enters the total of the values in cells A1 and A2.
–	Subtraction	=A1–A2	Subtracts the value in cell A2 from the value in cell A1.
*	Multiplication	=A2*3	Multiplies the value in cell A2 by 3.
/	Division	=A1/50	Divides the value in cell A1 by 50.
	Combination	=(A1+A2+A3)/3	Determines the average of the values in cells A1 through A3.

Order of Operations

Excel performs the operations within a formula in the following order:

1st	Equations within parentheses
2nd	Exponentiation
3rd	Multiplication and division
4th	Addition and subtraction

For example, given the formula =C2+B8*4+D10, Excel computes the value of B8*4, then adds that to C2, and then adds D10. Keep this order of operations in mind when you are creating equations because it determines the result.

If you don't take this order into consideration, you could run into problems when entering your formulas. For example, if you want to determine the average of the values in cells A1, B1, and C1, and you enter =A1+B1+C1/3, you'll get the wrong answer. The value in C1 will be divided by 3, and that result will be added to A1+B1. To determine the total of A1 through C1 first, you must enclose that group of values in parentheses, as in =(A1+B1+C1)/3.

Entering Formulas

You can enter formulas in either of two ways: by typing the formula or by selecting cell references. To type a formula, perform the following steps:

1. Select the cell in which you want the formula's calculation to appear.
2. Type the equal sign (=).
3. Type the formula. The formula appears in the Formula bar.

4. Press **Enter** or click the **Enter** button (the check mark), and Excel calculates the result.

 TIP ✗ **Unwanted Formula** If you start to enter a formula and then decide you don't want to use it, you can skip entering the formula by pressing **Esc** or by clicking the **Cancel** button.

 TIP **Name That Cell** If you plan to use a particular cell in several formulas, you can give it a name, such as "Income." Then you can use the name in the formula, as in =Income+$12.50. To name a cell, use the **Insert**, **Name**, **Define** command.

To enter a formula by selecting cell references, take the following steps:

1. Select the cell in which you want the formula's result to appear.
2. Type the equal sign (=).
3. Click the cell with the address you want to appear first in the formula. The cell address appears in the Formula bar.

Upgrade Tip   You can refer to a cell in a different worksheet by switching to that sheet and clicking the cell. To refer to a cell in a different workbook, open the workbook and click the cell. In Excel 97, you can even refer to a workbook located on the Internet or an intranet, if you want.

4. Type a mathematical operator after the value to indicate the next operation you want to perform. The operator appears in the Formula bar.
5. Continue clicking cells and typing operators until the formula is complete.
6. Press **Enter** to accept the formula or **Esc** to cancel the operation.

CAUTION

Error!   If **ERR** appears in a cell, make sure that you did not commit one of these common errors: try to divide by zero, use a blank cell as a divisor, refer to a blank cell, delete a cell used in a formula, or include a reference to the cell in which the answer appears.

Natural Language Formulas   Excel 97 now lets you refer to row and column headings (labels) when entering a formula. For example, if you had a worksheet with the row headings "Revenues," "Expenses," and "Profit," and you had column headings for each month, you could enter a formula such as =Jan Profit+Feb Profit or =Revenues–Expenses.

Calculating Results Without Entering a Formula

You can view the sum of a range of cells simply by selecting the cells and looking at the status bar, as shown in Figure 12.2. You can also view the average, minimum, maximum, and the count of a range of cells. To do so, right-click the status bar and select the option you want from the shortcut menu that appears.

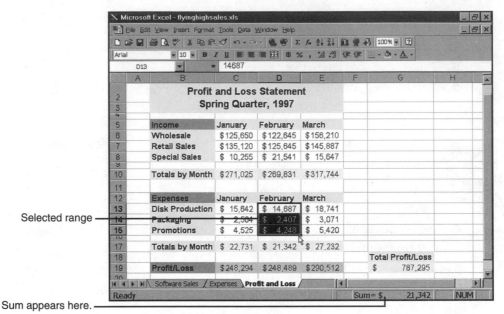

Selected range ——

Sum appears here. ——

Figure 12.2 View a sum without entering a formula.

CAUTION

Where's the Status Bar? If the status bar is not visible on your screen, you can display it by opening the **View** menu and clicking **Status Bar**.

Displaying Formulas

Normally, Excel does not display the actual formula in a cell. Instead, it displays the result of the calculation. You can view the formula by selecting the cell and looking in the Formula bar. However, if you're trying to review the formulas in a large worksheet, it might be easier if you could see them all at once (or print them). If you want to view formulas in a worksheet, follow these steps:

1. Open the **Tools** menu and choose **Options**.
2. Click the **View** tab.
3. In the Window Options area, click to select the **Formulas** check box.
4. Click **OK**.

TIP **Display Formulas Quickly** You can use a keyboard shortcut to toggle between viewing formulas and viewing values. To do so, hold down the **Ctrl** key and press ` (the accent key to the left of the 1 key; it has the tilde (~) on it). When you no longer want to view the formulas, press **Ctrl+`** again.

Editing Formulas

Editing a formula is the same as editing any entry in Excel. The following steps show you how to do it:

1. Select the cell that contains the formula you want to edit.

2. Click in the Formula bar or press **F2** to enter Edit mode.

TIP **Quick In-Cell Editing** To quickly edit the contents of a cell, double-click the cell. The insertion point appears inside the cell, and you can make any necessary changes.

3. Press the left arrow key (←) or right arrow key (→) to move the insertion point. Then use the **Backspace** key to delete characters to the left, or use the **Delete** key to delete characters to the right. Type any additional characters.

4. When you finish editing the data, click the **Enter** button on the Formula bar or press **Enter** to accept your changes.

Another way to edit a formula is to click the **Edit Formula** button on the Formula bar. When you do, the Formula bar expands to provide you with help. Make your changes to the formula and then click **OK**.

In this lesson, you learned how to enter and edit formulas. In the next lesson, you will learn how to copy formulas, when to use relative and absolute cell addresses, and how to change Excel's settings for calculating formulas in the worksheet.

Copying Formulas and Recalculating

In this lesson, you learn how to copy formulas, use relative and absolute cell references, and change calculation settings.

Copying Formulas

When you copy a formula, the formula is adjusted to fit the location of the cell to which it is copied. For example, if you copy the formula =C2+C3 from cell C4 to cell D4, the formula is adjusted for column D: it becomes =D2+D3. This enables you to copy similar formulas (such as the totals for a range of sales items) into a range of cells.

You can copy formulas by using the Copy and Paste buttons (see Lesson 5), but the following presents an even faster way.

1. Click the cell that contains the formula you want to copy.
2. Hold down the Ctrl key and drag the cell's border to the cell to which you want to copy your formula.
3. Release the mouse button, and Excel copies the formula to the new location.

If you want to copy a formula to a neighboring range of cells, follow these steps:

1. Click the cell that contains the formula you want to copy.
2. Move the mouse pointer over the fill handle.
3. Drag the fill handle across the cells into which you want to copy the formula.

TIP

Fast Copy   If you want to enter the same formula into a range of cells, select the range first. Then type the formula for the first cell in the range and press **Ctrl+Enter**.

CAUTION

Get an Error?   If you get an error after copying a formula, verify the cell references in the copied formula. See the next section, "Using Relative and Absolute Cell Addresses," for more details.

Using Relative and Absolute Cell Addresses

When you copy a formula from one place in the worksheet to another, Excel adjusts the cell references in the formulas relative to their new positions in the worksheet. For example, in Figure 13.1, cell B8 contains the formula =B2+B3+B4+B5+B6, which computes the total expenses for January. If you copy that formula to cell C8 (to determine the total expenses for February), Excel automatically changes the formula to =C2+C3+C4+C5+C6. This is how relative cell addresses work.

Cell references
are adjusted for —
column C.

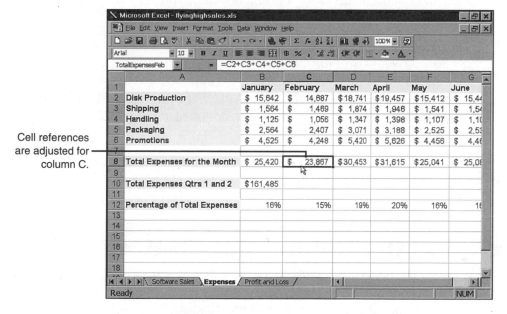

Figure 13.1   Excel adjusts cell references when you copy formulas to different cells.

Sometimes you may not want the cell references to be adjusted when you copy formulas. That's when absolute cell references become important.

 Absolute Versus Relative An *absolute reference* is a cell reference in a formula that does not change when copied to a new location. A *relative reference* is a cell reference in a formula that is adjusted when the formula is copied.

In the example shown in Figure 13.1, the formulas in cells B12, C12, D12, E12, F12, and G12 contain an absolute reference to cell B10, which holds the total expenses for quarters 1 and 2. (The formulas in B12, C12, D12, E12, F12, and G12 divide the sums from row 8 of each column by the contents of cell B10.) If you didn't use an absolute reference when you copied the formula from B10 to C10, the cell reference would be incorrect, and you would get an error message.

To make a cell reference in a formula absolute, you add a $ (dollar sign) before the letter and number that make up the cell address. For example, the formula in B12 would read as follows:

=B8/B10

You can type the dollar signs yourself, or you can press **F4** after typing the cell address.

Some formulas use mixed references. For example, the column letter might be an absolute reference, and the row number might be a relative reference, as in the formula $A2/2. If you entered this formula in cell C2 and then copied it to cell D10, the result would be the formula $A10/2. The row reference (row number) would be adjusted, but the column reference (the letter A) would not be.

 Mixed References A reference that is only partially absolute, such as A$2 or $A2. When a formula that uses a mixed reference is copied to another cell, part of the cell reference (the relative part) is adjusted.

Changing the Calculation Setting

Excel recalculates the formulas in a worksheet every time you edit a value in a cell. However, on a large worksheet, you may not want Excel to recalculate until you have entered all of your changes. For example, if you are entering a lot of changes to a worksheet that contains many formulas, you can speed up the response time by changing from automatic to manual recalculation. To change the recalculation setting, take the following steps:

1. Open the **Tools** menu and choose **Options**.

2. Click the **Calculation** tab to see the options shown in Figure 13.2.

3. Select one of the following Calculation options:

> **Automatic** This is the default setting. It recalculates the entire workbook each time you edit or enter a formula.

> **Automatic Except Tables** This automatically recalculates everything except formulas in a data table.

> **Manual** This option tells Excel to recalculate only when you say so. To recalculate, press **F9** or choose the **Tools, Options, Calculation** command and click the **Calc Now** button. When this option is selected, you can turn the **Recalculate Before Save** option off or on.

4. Click **OK**.

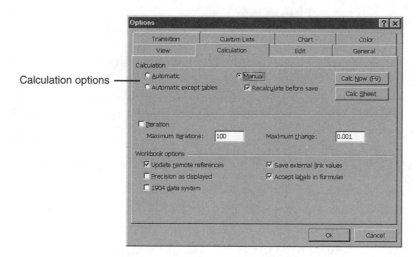

Calculation options

Figure 13.2 Change your calculation setting in the Options dialog box.

In this lesson, you learned how to copy formulas. You also learned when to use relative and absolute cell addresses and how to change calculation settings. In the next lesson, you will learn how to use Excel's Function Wizard to insert another type of formula, called a *function*.

Performing Calculations with Functions

In this lesson, you learn how to perform calculations with functions and how to use Excel's Function Wizard to quickly insert functions in cells.

What Are Functions?

Functions are complex ready-made formulas that perform a series of operations on a specified range of values. For example, to determine the sum of a series of numbers in cells A1 through H1, you can enter the function =SUM(A1:H1) instead of entering =A1+B1+C1 and so on. Functions can use range references (such as B1:B3), range names (such as SALES), or numerical values (such as 585.86).

Every function consists of the following three elements:

- The = sign indicates that what follows is a function (formula).
- The function name, such as SUM, indicates which operation will be performed.
- The argument, such as (A1:H1), indicates the cell addresses of the values on which the function will act. The argument is often a range of cells, but it can be much more complex.

You can enter functions either by typing them in cells or by using the Function Wizard, as you'll see later in this lesson.

Table 14.1 shows Excel's most common functions that you'll use in your worksheets.

Table 14.1 Excel's Most Common Functions

Function	Example	Description
AVERAGE	=AVERAGE(B4:B9)	Calculates the mean or average of a group of numbers.
COUNT	=COUNT(A3:A7)	Counts the numeric values in a range. For example, if a range contains some cells with text and other cells with numbers, you can count how many numbers are in that range.
COUNTA	=COUNTA(B4:B10)	Counts all cells in a range that are not blank. For example, if a range contains some cells with text and other cells with numbers, you can count how many cells in that range contain text.
IF	=IF(A3>=100,A3*2,A2*2)	Allows you to place a condition on a formula. In this example, if A3 is greater than or equal to 100, the formula A3*2 is used. If A3 is less than 100, the formula A2*2 is used instead.
MAX	−MAX(B4:B10)	Returns the maximum value in a range of cells.
MIN	=MIN(B4:B10)	Returns the minimum value in a range of cells.
PMT	=PMT(rate,nper,pv)	Calculates the periodic payment on a loan when you enter the interest rate, number of periods, and principal as arguments. Example: =PMT(.0825/12,360,180000) for 30-year loan at 8.25% for $180,000.
PMT	=PMT(rate,nper,,fv)	Calculates the deposit needed each period to reach some future value. Example: =PMT(.07/12,60,,10000) calculates the deposit needed to accumulate $10,000 at an annual rate of 7%, making monthly payments for 5 years (60 months).
SUM	=SUM(A1:A10)	Calculates the total in a range of cells.
SUMIF	=SUMIF(rg,criteria,sumrg)	Calculates the total of the range *rg* for each corresponding cell in *sumrg* that matches the specified criteria. For example, =SUMIF (A2:A4,>100,B2:B4) adds the cells in the range A2:A4 whose corresponding cell in column B is greater than 100.

Excel on the Web A new function, =HYPERLINK(), is used to create links to Web sites right in your worksheet. For example, =HYPERLINK(http://www.microsoft.com,"Visit Microsoft") will display the words "Visit Microsoft" in a cell. When the user clicks the cell, he is connected to the Microsoft home page. You can also use this feature to link to worksheets on your company's intranet.

Enter Text Right When entering text into a formula, be sure to surround it with quotation marks, as in "Seattle."

CAUTION

Using AutoSum

Because SUM is one of the most commonly used functions, Excel provides a fast way to enter it—you simply click the AutoSum button in the Standard toolbar. Based on the currently selected cell, AutoSum guesses which cells you want summed. If AutoSum selects an incorrect range of cells, you can edit the selection.

To use AutoSum, follow these steps:

1. Select the cell in which you want the sum inserted. Try to choose a cell at the end of a row or column of data; doing so will help AutoSum guess which cells you want added together.

Σ

2. Click the **AutoSum** button in the Standard toolbar. AutoSum inserts =SUM and the range address of the cells to the left of or above the selected cell (see Figure 14.1).

3. If the range Excel selected is incorrect, drag over the range you want to use, or click in the Formula bar and edit the formula.

4. Click the **Enter** button in the Formula bar or press **Enter**. Excel calculates the total for the selected range.

Quickie AutoSum To quickly insert the sum function, select the cell in which you want the sum inserted and double-click the **AutoSum** tool on the Standard toolbar. When you double-click the AutoSum button instead of single-clicking, you bypass the step where Excel displays the SUM formula and its arguments in the cell. Instead, you see the total in the cell and the SUM formula in the Formula bar. The problem with using this method is that you're not given a chance to "second-guess" the range of cells AutoSum decides to add.

The SUM function appears in the selected cell and in the Formula bar.

AutoSum selects a range of cells above or to the left of the selected cell.

The selected range becomes the function's argument.

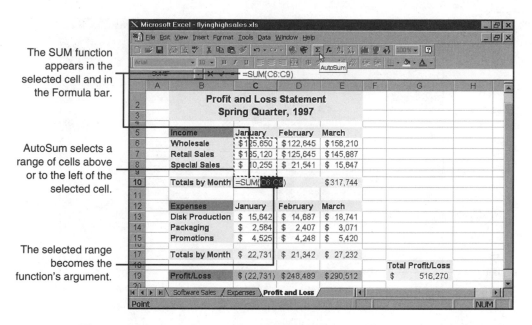

Figure 14.1 AutoSum inserts the SUM function and selects the cells it plans to total.

Using AutoCalculate

When you wanted to quickly check a total in earlier versions of Excel, did you ever use a calculator or enter temporary formulas on a worksheet? If you did, you might find Excel's AutoCalculate feature very handy. AutoCalculate lets you quickly check a total or an average, count entries or numbers, and find the maximum or minimum number in a range.

Here's how AutoCalculate works. To check a total, select the range you want to sum. Excel automatically displays the answer in the AutoCalculate area (as shown in Figure 14.2). If you want to perform a different function on a range of numbers, select the range and right-click in the AutoCalculate area to display the shortcut menu. Then choose a function from the menu. For example, choose Count to count the numeric values in the range. The answer appears in the AutoCalculate area.

Where's My Status Bar? If the status bar is not displayed, open the **View** menu and click **Status Bar** to turn it on.

CAUTION

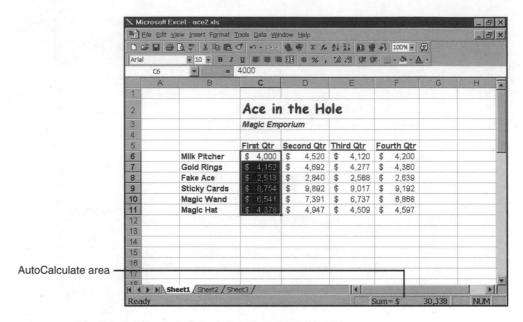

Figure 14.2 AutoCalculate lets you quickly view a sum.

AutoCalculate area

Using the Function Wizard

Although you can type a function directly into a cell just as you can type formulas, you may find it easier to use the Function Wizard. The Function Wizard leads you through the process of inserting a function. The following steps walk you through using the Function Wizard:

1. Select the cell in which you want to insert the function. (You can insert a function by itself or as part of a formula.)

2. Type = or click the **Edit Formula** button on the Formula bar. The Formula Palette appears, as shown in Figure 14.3.

3. Select the function you want to insert from the **Functions** list by clicking the **Functions** button (see Figure 14.3). If you don't see your function listed, select **More Functions** at the bottom of the list.

CAUTION

What's This Function? If you don't know a lot about a particular function and you'd like to know more, click the **Help** button in the Formula Palette. When the Office Assistant appears, click **Help with the Feature**. Then click **Help on Selected Function**.

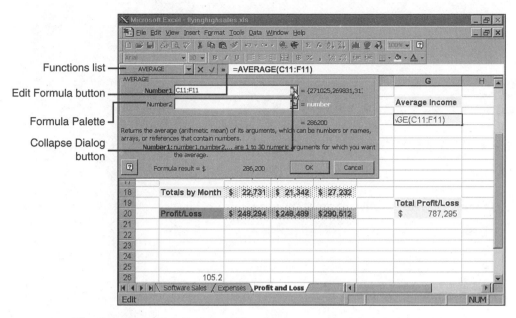

Functions list

Edit Formula button

Formula Palette

Collapse Dialog button

Figure 14.3   The Function Wizard helps you enter functions.

4. Enter the arguments for the formula. If you want to select a range of cells as an argument, click the **Collapse Dialog** button shown in Figure 14.3.

5. After selecting a range, click the **Collapse Dialog** button again to return to the Formula Palette.

6. Click **OK**. Excel inserts the function and argument in the selected cell and displays the result.

 To edit a function, click the **Edit Formula** button. The Formula Palette appears. Change the arguments as needed and click **OK**.

In this lesson, you learned the basics of dealing with functions, and you learned how to use Excel's Function Wizard to quickly enter functions. You also learned how to quickly total a series of numbers with the AutoSum tool and how to check the sum of numbers with AutoCalculate. In the next lesson, you will learn how to format values in your worksheet.

Changing How Numbers Look

In this lesson, you learn how to customize the appearance of numbers in your worksheet.

Formatting Values

Numeric values are usually more than just numbers. They represent a dollar value, a date, a percent, or some other value. Excel offers a wide range of number formats, which are listed in Table 15.1.

Table 15.1 Excel's Number Formats

Number Format	Examples	Description
General	10.6 $456,908.00	Excel displays your value as you enter it. In other words, this format displays currency or percent signs only if you enter them yourself.
Number	3400.50 (–120.39)	The default Number format has two decimal places. Negative numbers appear in red and in parentheses, preceded by a minus sign.
Currency	$3,400.50 ($3,400.50)	The default Currency format has two decimal places and a dollar sign. Negative numbers appear in red and in parentheses.
Accounting	$ 3,400.00 $ 978.21	Use this format to align dollar signs and decimal points in a column. The default Accounting format has two decimal places and a dollar sign.
Date	11/7	The default Date format is the month and day separated by a slash; however, you can select from numerous other formats.

Number Format	Examples	Description
Time	10:00	The default Time format is the hour and minutes separated by a colon; however, you can opt to display seconds, AM, or PM.
Percentage	99.50%	The default Percentage format has two decimal places. Excel multiplies the value in a cell by 100 and displays the result with a percent sign.
Fraction	1/2	The default Fraction format is up to one digit on either side of the slash. Use this format to display the number of digits you want on either side of the slash and the fraction type (such as halves, quarters, eighths, and so on).
Scientific	3.40E+03	The default Scientific format has two decimal places. Use this format to display numbers in scientific notation.
Text	135RV90	Use Text format to display both text and numbers in a cell as text. Excel displays the entry exactly as you type it.
Special	02110	This format is specifically designed to display zip codes, phone numbers, and Social Security numbers correctly, so that you don't have to enter any special characters, such as hyphens.
Custom	00.0%	Use Custom format to create your own number format. You can use any of the format codes in the Type list and then make changes to those codes. The # symbol represents a number placeholder, and 0 represents a zero placeholder.

After deciding on a suitable numeric format, follow these steps:

1. Select the cell or range that contains the values you want to format.
2. Open the **Format** menu and select **Cells**. The Format Cells dialog box appears, as shown in Figure 15.1.
3. Click the **Number** tab.
4. In the **Category** list, select the numeric format category you want to use. The sample box displays the default format for that category.
5. Make changes to the format as needed.

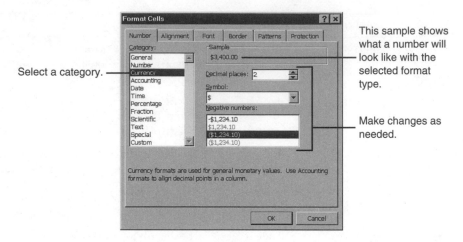

Select a category. ———

This sample shows what a number will look like with the selected format type.

Make changes as needed.

Figure 15.1 The Format Cells dialog box with the Number tab displayed.

6. Click **OK** or press **Enter**. Excel reformats the selected cells based on your selections.

CAUTION

Removing Formatting If you want to remove a number format from a cell (and return it to General format), select the cells whose formatting you want to remove, open the **Edit** menu, select **Clear**, then select **Formats**.

Using the Style Buttons to Format Numbers

The Formatting toolbar (just below the Standard toolbar) contains several buttons for selecting a number format, including the following:

Button	Name	Example/Description
$	Currency Style	$1200.90
%	Percent Style	20.90%

Button	Name	Example/Description
(not shown)	Comma Style	1,200.90
Increase Decimal	Adds one decimal place
Decrease Decimal	Deletes one decimal place

To use one of these buttons, select the cell you want to format and then click the desired button. You can also change the Number format of a cell by using the shortcut menu. Select the cell, right-click to display the shortcut menu, and choose **Format Cells**.

CAUTION

That's Not the Date I Entered!   If you enter a date in a cell that is formatted with the Number format, the date will appear as a number. With the Number format, Excel converts the date to a value that represents the number of days between January 1, 1900 and that date. For example, 01/01/1900 equals 1, and 12/31/1900 equals 366 (1900 was a leap year). To fix your problem, change the cell's formatting from Number format to Date format and select a date type.

Upgrade Tip   If you want to highlight cells that meet certain conditions, such as all values that are larger than 1,000, use conditional formatting. See Lesson 17, "Adding Cell Borders and Shading," for more information.

Creating Your Own Custom Format

If you need to enter special numbers, such as account numbers, you may want to create your own number format and use it to format your account numbers. For example, suppose your account numbers look like this:

10-20190-109

You could create a format like this:

##-#####-###

Then when you enter the number, 9089212098, for example, Excel formats it for you, adding the hyphens where needed:

90-89212-098

Mixed Metaphors Unfortunately, you can't create a format for a value that includes both text and numbers combined.

CAUTION

To create your own format, follow these steps:

1. Open the **Format** menu and select **Cells**.

2. Click the **Number** tab.

3. In the **Category** list, select **Custom**.

4. Type your custom format in the **Type** box and click **OK**.

When entering your format, use the following codes:

Displays the number (unless it's an insignificant zero)

0 Adds zeros where needed to fill out the number

? Adds spaces where needed to align decimal points

Table 15.2 shows some sample formats.

Table 15.2 Sample Custom Formats

Value Entered	Custom Format	Value Displayed in Cell
3124.789	####.##	3124.79
120.5	###.#00	120.500
.6345	0.##	0.63
21456.25	##,###.00	21,456.25
120.54	$##,###.#0	$120.54

You can enter formats for how you want positive and negative numbers displayed, along with zero values and text. Simply separate the formats with a semicolon (;) like this:

##.#0;[MAGENTA]–##.#0;[GREEN]0.00;@

In this example format, positive numbers entered into the cell are displayed with two decimal places (a zero is added to fill two decimal places if needed). Negative numbers are displayed with a preceding minus sign (–) in magenta. Zero values are displayed as 0.00 in green. Text is permitted in these cells, as indicated by the final format (@). If you do not include the text format, any text you type into the cell simply will not be displayed at all. If you want to add a particular word or words in front of all text entered into a cell, include the word(s) in double quotation marks, as in "Acct. Code:"@.

In this lesson, you learned how to format numbers and create custom formats. In the next lesson, you will learn how to format text.

Giving Your Text a New Look

In this lesson, you learn how to change the appearance of the text in the cells.

How You Can Make Text Look Different

When you type text or numbers, Excel automatically formats it in the Arial font, which doesn't look very fancy. You can change the following text attributes to improve the appearance of your text or set it apart from other text:

Font   A typeface—for example, Arial, Courier, or Times New Roman.

Font Style   For example, Bold, Italic, Underline, or Strikethrough.

CAUTION

Text Underline versus Cell Border   You can add underlining to important information in one of two ways. With the underline format explained in this lesson, a line (or lines, depending on which underline format you choose) is placed under the cell's contents. This is different from adding a line to the bottom of a cell's border, which is explained in the next lesson.

Size   For example, 10-point, 12-point, or 20-point. (The higher the point size, the bigger the text is. There are approximately 72 points in an inch.)

Color   For example, Red, Magenta, or Cyan.

Alignment   For example, centered, left aligned, or right aligned within the cell.

Font   A font is a set of characters that have the same typeface, which means they are of a single design (such as Times New Roman). When you select a font, Excel also allows you to change the font's size; add optional *attributes* to the font, such as bold or italic; underline the text; change its color; and add special effects such as strikethrough, superscript, subscript, and small caps.

Figure 16.1 shows a worksheet after some attributes have been changed for selected text.

This text is centered across columns and set in 16-point bold type.

Underline is applied to column headings.

Row headings are set in italics.

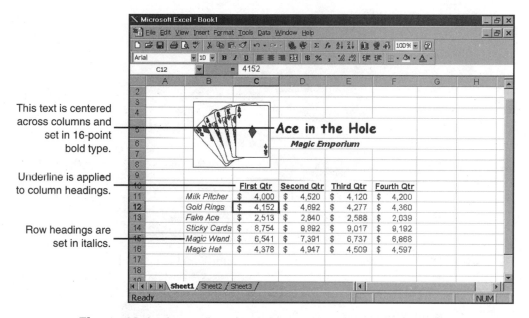

Figure 16.1   A sampling of several text attributes.

Using the Format Cells Dialog Box

You can change the look of your text by using the Format Cells dialog box. Just follow these steps:

1. Select the cell or range that contains the text you want to format.

2. Open the **Format** menu and choose **Cells**, or press **Ctrl+1**. (You can also right-click the selected cells and choose **Format Cells** from the shortcut menu.)

3. Click the **Font** tab. The Font options jump to the front, as shown in Figure 16.2.

4. Select the options you want.

5. Click **OK** or press **Enter**.

Excel uses a default font to style your text as you type it. To change the default font, enter your font preferences in the Font tab and click the **Normal Font** option. When you click the **OK** button, Excel makes your preferences the default font.

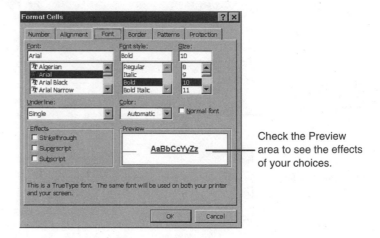

Check the Preview area to see the effects of your choices.

Figure 16.2 The Format Cells dialog box with the Font tab up front.

 TIP   **Font Shortcuts**   You can apply certain attributes quickly by using keyboard shortcuts. First select the cell(s), and then press **Ctrl+B** for bold, **Ctrl+I** for Italic, **Ctrl+U** for Single Underline (Accounting style), or **Ctrl+5** for Strikethrough.

Changing Text Attributes with Toolbar Buttons

A faster way to enter font changes is to use the Formatting toolbar shown in Figure 16.3.

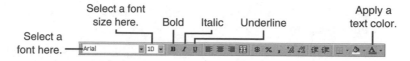

Figure 16.3 Use the Formatting toolbar to quickly make font changes.

To use a tool to change text attributes, follow these steps:

1. Select the cell or range that contains the text whose look you want to change.

2. To change the font or font size, pull down the appropriate drop-down list and click the font or size you want. You can also type the point size in the **Font Size** box.

3. To add an attribute (such as bold or underlining), click the desired button. When selected, a button looks like it has been pressed in. You can add more than one attribute to text, making it bold and italic, for example.

 TIP Change Before You Type   You can activate the attributes you want *before* you type text. For example, if you want a title in bold 12-point Desdemona type, select the cells for which you want to change the attributes, and then set the attributes before you start typing. Unlike in a word processor where you must turn attributes on and off, in Excel, selecting formats for cells in advance of typing your data has no effect on the unselected cells; data in unselected cells will be the default Arial 10-point type.

Aligning Text in Cells

When you enter data into an Excel worksheet, that data is aligned automatically. Text is aligned on the left, and numbers are aligned on the right. Both text and numbers are initially set at the bottom of the cells. However, you can change both the vertical and the horizontal alignment of data in your cells.

Follow these steps to change the alignment:

1. Select the cell or range you want to align. If you want to center a title or other text over a range of cells, select the entire range of blank cells in which you want the text centered, including the cell that contains the text you want to center.

2. Pull down the **Format** menu and select **Cells,** or press **Ctrl+1**. The Format Cells dialog box appears.

3. Click the **Alignment** tab. The alignment options appear in front (see Figure 16.4).

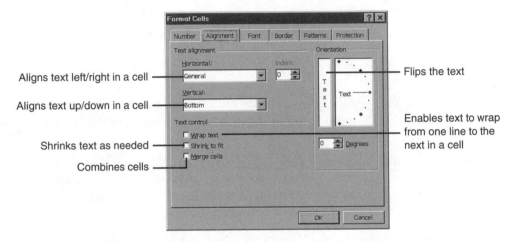

Figure 16.4 The Alignment options.

4. Choose from the following options and option groups to set the alignment:

Horizontal lets you specify a left/right alignment in the cell(s). (The Center Across selection centers a title or other text within a range of cells.)

Vertical lets you specify how you want the text aligned in relation to the top and bottom of the cell(s).

Orientation lets you flip the text sideways or print it from top to bottom (instead of left to right). This option is new to Excel 97.

Wrap Text tells Excel to wrap long lines of text within a cell without changing the width of the cell. (Normally, Excel displays all text in a cell on one line.)

Shrink to Fit shrinks the text to fit within the cell's current width. If the cell's width is adjusted, the text increases or decreases in size accordingly.

Merge Cells combines several cells into a single cell. All data is overlaid, except for the cell in the upper-left corner of the selected cells.

5. Click **OK** or press **Enter**.

 TIP **Alignment Buttons** A quick way to align text and numbers is to use the alignment buttons in the Formatting toolbar. The following buttons allow you to align the text:

 Align Left   Align Right

 Center   Merge and Center

 New to Excel 97 is the capability to indent your text within a cell. If you're typing a paragraph worth of information into a single cell, you can indent that paragraph by selecting left alignment from the **Horizontal** list box in the Format Cells dialog box (as explained earlier). After selecting left alignment, set the amount of indent you want with the **Indent** spin box.

In addition, you can add an indent quickly by clicking the following buttons on the Formatting toolbar:

 Decrease Indent   Removes an indent or creates a negative indent.

 Increase Indent   Adds an indent.

In this lesson, you learned how to customize your text formatting to achieve the look you want. In the next lesson, you will learn how to add borders and shading to your worksheet.

Adding Cell Borders and Shading

In this lesson, you learn how to add pizzazz to your worksheets by adding borders and shading.

Adding Borders to Cells

As you work with your worksheet on-screen, you'll notice that each cell is identified by gridlines that surround the cell. Normally, these gridlines do not print; and even if you choose to print them, they may appear washed out. To have more well-defined lines appear on the printout (or on-screen, for that matter), you can add borders to selected cells or entire cell ranges. A border can appear on all four sides of a cell or only on selected sides, whichever you prefer.

The Gridlines Don't Print? In Excel 97, as in Excel 95, the gridlines do not print by default. But if you want to try printing your worksheet with gridlines first just to see what it looks like, open the **File** menu, select **Page Setup**, click the **Sheet** tab, select **Gridlines**, and click **OK**.

CAUTION

To add borders to a cell or range, perform the following steps:

1. Select the cell(s) around which you want a border to appear.
2. Open the **Format** menu and choose **Cells**. The Format Cells dialog box appears.
3. Click the **Border** tab to see the Border options shown in Figure 17.1.

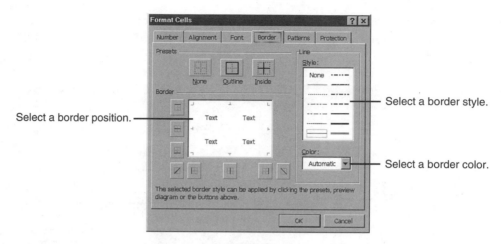

Figure 17.1 Choose border options from the Format Cells dialog box.

4. Select the desired position, style (thickness), and color for the border. You can click inside the Border box itself, or you can click a preset border pattern button to add your border.

5. Click **OK** or press **Enter**.

TIP **Hiding Gridlines** When adding borders to a worksheet, you might need to hide the gridlines to get a better idea of how the borders will look when printed. Open the **Tools** menu, select **Options**, click the **View** tab, and select **Gridlines** to remove the check mark from the check box. Of course, selecting this option has no effect on whether or not the gridlines actually print, only on whether or not they are displayed on-screen.

To add borders quickly, select the cells around which you want the border to appear, and then click the **Borders** drop-down arrow in the Formatting toolbar. Click the desired border. If you click the **Borders** button itself (instead of the arrow), Excel automatically adds the border line you last chose to the selected cells.

Adding Shading to Cells

For a simple but dramatic effect, you can add shading to your worksheets. With shading, you can add a color or gray shading to a cell. You can add colors at full strength or partial strength to create the exact effect you want. To lessen the strength of the cell color you select, you add your shading with a pattern, such as a diagonal. Figure 17.2 illustrates some of the effects you can create with shading.

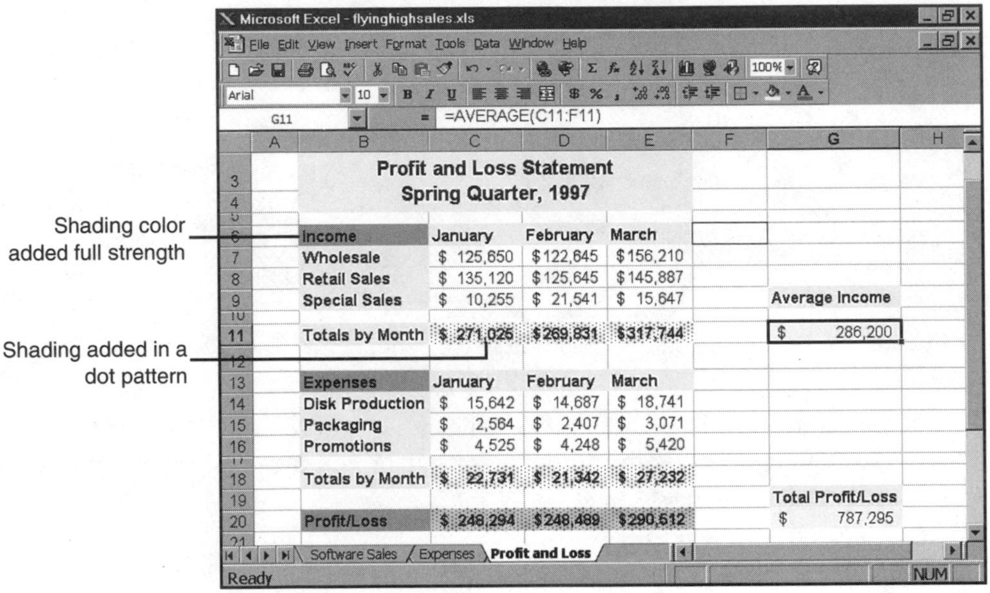

Shading color added full strength

Shading added in a dot pattern

Figure 17.2 A worksheet with added shading.

Follow these steps to add shading to a cell or range. As you make your selections, keep in mind that if you plan to print your worksheet with a black-and-white printer, your pretty colors may not be different enough to create the effect you want. Select colors that contrast well in value (intensity), and use the Print Preview command (as explained in Lesson 10, "Printing Your Workbook") to view your results in black-and- white before you print.

1. Select the cell(s) you want to shade.
2. Open the **Format** menu and choose **Cells**.
3. Click the **Patterns** tab. Excel displays the shading options (see Figure 17.3).
4. Click the **Pattern** drop-down arrow, and you will see a grid that contains all the colors from the color palette, as well as patterns. Select the shading color and pattern you want to use. The Color options let you choose a color for the overall shading. The Pattern options let you select a black-and-white or colored pattern that lies on top of the overall shading. A preview of the result appears in the Sample box.

5. When you like the results you see, click **OK** or press **Enter**.

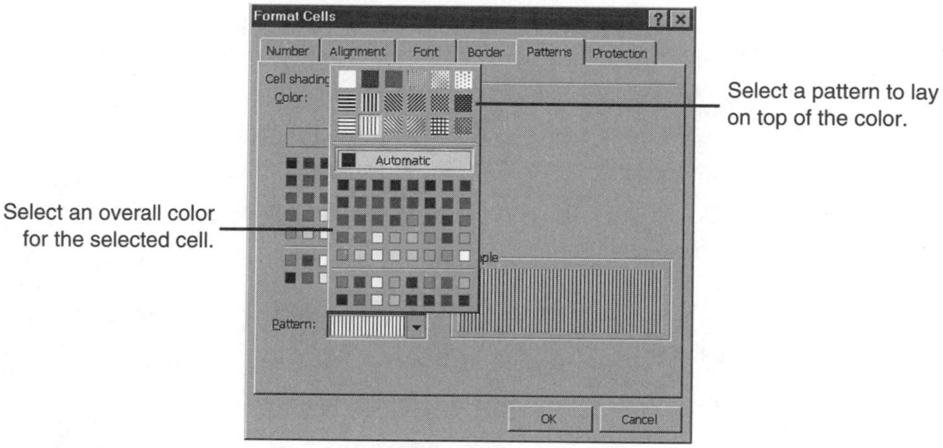

Select a pattern to lay
on top of the color.

Select an overall color
for the selected cell.

Figure 17.3 Selecting a shading and a pattern.

A quick way to add cell shading (without a pattern) is to select the cells you want to shade, click the **Fill Color** drop-down arrow, and click the color you want to use.

TIP **Quick Color** To add the color shown in the bucket of the Fill Color button, simply click the button itself—do not bother to click the arrow to the right of the button.

If the shading is too dark, consider using the Font Color button (just to the right of the Fill Color button) to select a lighter color for the text.

Using AutoFormat

Excel offers the AutoFormat feature, which takes some of the pain out of formatting. AutoFormat provides you with 16 predesigned table formats that you can apply to a worksheet.

To use predesigned formats, perform the following steps:

1. Select the worksheet(s) and cell(s) that contain the data you want to format.

2. Open the **Format** menu and choose **AutoFormat**. The AutoFormat dialog box appears, as shown in Figure 17.4.

3. In the **Table Format** list, choose the predesigned format you want to use. When you select a format, Excel shows you what it will look like in the Sample area.

4. To exclude certain elements from AutoFormat, click the **Options** button and choose the formats you want to turn off.

5. Click **OK**, and Excel formats your table to make it look like the one in the preview area.

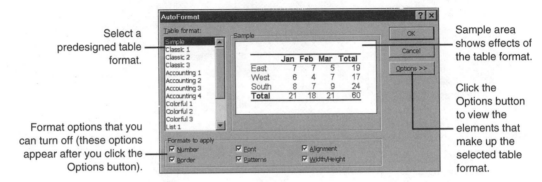

Select a predesigned table format.

Format options that you can turn off (these options appear after you click the Options button).

Sample area shows effects of the table format.

Click the Options button to view the elements that make up the selected table format.

Figure 17.4 Use the AutoFormat dialog box to select a prefab format.

Deformatting an AutoFormat If you don't like what AutoFormat did to your worksheet, select the table, open the **Format** menu, and choose **AutoFormat**. From the **Table Format** list, choose **None** to remove the AutoFormat.

CAUTION

Copying Formats with Format Painter

Excel gives you two ways to copy and paste formatting:

- You can use the Edit, Copy command and then the Edit Paste Special command and select Formats from the Paste options in the Paste Special dialog box.

- You can use the Format Painter button in the Standard toolbar.

The Format Painter lets you quickly copy and paste formats that you have already used in a workbook. Because the Format Painter button is faster, I'll give you the steps you need to paint formats.

1. Select the cell(s) that contain the formatting you want to copy and paste.
2. Click the **Format Painter** button on the Standard toolbar. Excel copies the formatting. The mouse pointer changes into a paintbrush with a plus sign next to it.
3. Click and drag over the cells to which you want to apply the copied formatting.
4. Release the mouse button, and Excel copies the formatting and applies it to the selected cells.

TIP **Faster Painter** To paint several areas at one time, double-click the **Format Painter** button. Then drag over the first section you want to paint. The cursor remains as a paintbrush, meaning that you can continue to drag over other cells to paint them too. When you're through, press **Esc** to return to a normal cursor.

Applying Conditional Formatting

If you want to highlight particular values in your worksheet, you can use conditional formatting. For example, if you want to highlight all sales figures under a particular mark, you could apply a conditional red shading.

To apply conditional formatting, follow these steps:

1. Select the cells you want to format.
2. Open the **Format** menu and select **Conditional Formatting**. The Conditional Formatting dialog box appears, as shown in Figure 17.5.

Figure 17.5 Apply formats conditionally to highlight certain values.

3. To apply a format based on the value found in a selected cell, choose **Cell Value Is** from the **Condition 1** list.

To apply a format based on the value found in a cell outside the selected range, select **Formula Is** from the **Condition 1** list.

4. Enter the value or formula you want to use as the *condition* that determines when Excel can apply the formatting you select. If you choose to use a formula, be sure to include the beginning equal (=) sign.

CAUTION

Using a Formula   If you choose Formula Is in step 3, the formula you enter must result in a true or false value (so use the IF statement). For example, if you wanted to format some cells based on whether or not a corresponding value in column A is less than 20% of projected sales (cell D12), you could use this formula:

=IF(A1<20%*D12,TRUE,FALSE)

5. Click the **Format** button and select the format you want to apply when the condition is true. Click **OK** to return to the Conditional Formatting dialog box.

6. (Optional) If you want to add more than one condition, click **Add**. Then repeat steps 3 and 4 to add the condition.

7. When you finish adding conditions, click **OK**.

 You can copy the conditional formatting from one cell to other cells using the Format Painter button. Simply click the cell whose formatting you want to copy and click the **Format Painter** button. Then drag over the cells to which you want to copy the formatting.

In this lesson, you learned some ways to enhance the appearance of your worksheets. In the next lesson, you will learn how to change the sizes of rows and columns.

Changing Column Width and Row Height

In this lesson, you learn how to adjust the column width and row height to make the best use of the worksheet space. You can set these manually or let Excel make the adjustments for you with its AutoFit feature.

Adjusting Column Width and Row Height with a Mouse

You can adjust the width of a column or the height of a row by using a dialog box or by dragging with the mouse.

CAUTION

Why Bother? You might not want to bother adjusting the row height because it's automatically adjusted as you change font size. However, if a column's width is not as large as its data, that data may not be displayed and may appear as ########. In such a case, you must adjust the width of the column in order for the data to be displayed at all.

Here's how you adjust the row height or column width with the mouse:

1. To change the row height or column width for a single row or column, skip to step 2. To change the height or width of two or more rows for columns, select them first by dragging over the row or column headings.

2. Position the mouse pointer over one of the row heading or column heading borders as shown in Figure 18.1. (Use the right border of the column heading to adjust column width; use the bottom border of the row heading to adjust the row height.)

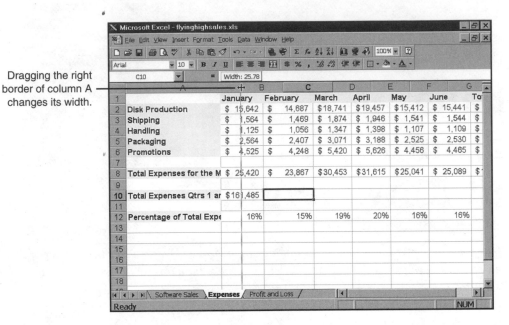

Dragging the right
border of column A
changes its width.

Figure 18.1   The mouse pointer changes to a double-headed arrow when you move it
over a border in the row or column heading.

3. Drag the border to the size you need it.

4. Release the mouse button, and Excel adjusts the row height or column width.

TIP   **AutoFit Cells**   To quickly make a column as wide as its widest entry using Excel's AutoFit feature, double-click the right border of the column heading. To make a row as tall as its tallest entry, double-click the bottom border of the row heading. To change more than one column or row at a time, drag over the desired row or column headings, and then double-click the bottommost or rightmost heading border.

Using the Format Menu for Precise Control

You can change a row or column's size by dragging the border of a row or column. However, you cannot control the size as precisely as you can by providing specific sizes with the Format, Row Height and Format, Column Width commands.

These steps show you how to use the Format menu to change the column width:

1. Select the column(s) whose width you want to change. To change the width of a single column, select any cell in that column.

2. Open the **Format** menu, select **Column**, and select **Width**. The Column Width dialog box appears (see Figure 18.2).

3. Type the number of characters you would like as the width. The default width is 8.43.

4. Click **OK** or press **Enter** to put your changes into effect.

Figure 18.2 Changing the column width.

By default, Excel makes a row a bit taller than the tallest text in the row. For example, if the tallest text is 10 points tall, Excel makes the row itself 12.75 points tall. You can use the Format menu to change the row height manually:

1. Select the row(s) whose height you want to change. (To change the height of a single row, select any cell in that row.)

2. Open the **Format** menu, select **Row**, and select **Height**. The Row Height dialog box shown in Figure 18.3 appears.

3. Type the desired height (in points).

4. Click **OK** or press **Enter** to implement the change in your worksheet.

Figure 18.3 Changing the row height.

In this lesson, you learned how to change the row height and column width. In the next lesson, you will learn how to create charts.

Creating Charts

*In this lesson, you learn to create charts to represent your
workbook data as a picture.*

Chart Types

With Excel, you can create various types of charts. Some common chart types
are shown in Figure 19.1. The chart type you choose depends on your data and
on how you want to present that data. These are the major chart types and their
purposes:

Pie Use this chart to show the relationship among parts of a whole.

Bar Use this chart to compare values at a given point in time.

Column Similar to the Bar chart; use this chart to emphasize the difference between items.

Line Use this chart to emphasize trends and the change of values over
time.

Scatter Similar to a Line chart; use this chart to emphasize the difference
between two sets of values.

Area Similar to the Line chart; use this chart to emphasize the amount of
change in values over time.

Most of these basic chart types also come in three-dimensional varieties. In
addition to looking more professional than the standard flat charts, 3-D charts
can often help your audience distinguish between different sets of data.

Embedded Charts A chart that is placed on the same worksheet that
contains the data used to create the chart. A chart can also be placed on a
chart sheet in the workbook so that the worksheet and chart are separate.
Embedded charts are useful for showing the actual data and its graphic
representation side-by-side.

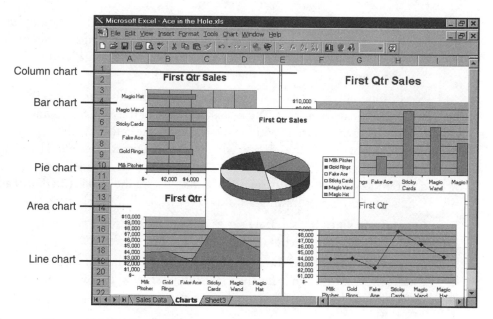

Figure 19.1 Common Excel chart types.

 Upgrade Tip Excel 97 includes many new chart types, so have fun when selecting the one you want to use.

Charting Terminology

Before you start creating charts, familiarize yourself with the following terminology:

Data Series The bars, pie wedges, lines, or other elements that represent plotted values in a chart. For example, a chart might show a set of similar bars that reflects a series of values for the same item. The bars in the series would all have the same pattern. If you have more than one pattern of bars, each pattern would represent a separate data series. For instance, charting the sales for Territory 1 versus Territory 2 would require two data series—one for each territory. Often, data series correspond to rows of data in your worksheet.

Categories Categories reflect the number of elements in a series. You might have two data series to compare the sales of two different territories

393

and four categories to compare these sales over four quarters. Some charts have only one category, and others have several. Categories normally correspond to the columns that you have in your chart data, and the category labels coming from the column headings.

Axis   One side of a chart. A two-dimensional chart has an x-axis (horizontal) and a y-axis (vertical). The x-axis contains all the data series and categories in the chart. If you have more than one category, the x-axis often contains labels that define what each category represents. The y-axis reflects the values of the bars, lines, or plot points. In a three-dimensional chart, the z-axis represents the vertical plane, and the x-axis (distance) and y-axis (width) represent the two sides on the floor of the chart.

Legend   Defines the separate series of a chart. For example, the legend for a pie chart will show what each piece of the pie represents.

Gridlines   Emphasize the y-axis or x-axis scale of the data series. For example, major gridlines for the y-axis will help you follow a point from the x- or y-axis to identify a data point's exact value.

Creating a Chart

You can create charts as part of a worksheet (an embedded chart) or as a chart on a separate worksheet. If you create an embedded chart, it will print side-by-side with your worksheet data. If you create a chart on a separate worksheet, you can print it independently. Both types of charts are linked to the worksheet data that they represent, so when you change the data, the chart is automatically updated.

The Chart Wizard button in the Standard toolbar allows you to quickly create a chart. To use the Chart Wizard, follow these steps:

1. Select the data you want to chart. If you typed names or other labels (such as Qtr 1, Qtr 2, and so on) and you want them included in the chart, make sure you select them.

2. Click the **Chart Wizard** button on the Standard toolbar.

3. The Chart Wizard Step 1 of 4 dialog box appears, as shown in Figure 19.2. Select a **Chart Type** and select a **Chart Sub-Type** (a variation on the selected chart type). Click **Next>**.

4. Next you're asked if the selected range is correct. You can correct the range by typing a new range or by clicking the **Collapse Dialog** button (located at the right end of the Data Range text box) and selecting the range you want to use.

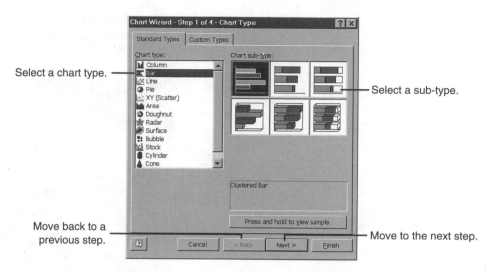

Figure 19.2 Chart Wizard asks you to choose the chart type you want.

5. By default, Excel assumes that your different data series are stored in rows. You can change this to columns if necessary by clicking the **Series in Columns** option. When you're through, click **Next>**.

6. Click the various tabs to change options for your chart (see Figure 19.3). For example, you can delete the legend by clicking the **Legend** tab and deselecting **Show Legend**. You can add a chart title on the Titles tab. Add data labels (labels which display the actual value being represented by each bar, line, and so on) by clicking the **Data Labels** tab. When you finish making changes, click **Next>**.

7. Finally, you're asked if you want to embed the chart (as an object) in the current worksheet, or if you want to create a new worksheet for it. Make your selection and click the **Finish** button. Your completed chart appears.

 TIP **Moving and Resizing a Chart** To move an embedded chart, click anywhere in the chart area and drag it to the new location. To change the size of a chart, select the chart, and then drag one of its *handles* (the black squares that border the chart). Drag a corner handle to change the height and width, or drag a side handle to change only the width. (Note that you can't really resize a chart that is on a sheet by itself.)

 TIP **Create a Chart Fast!** To create a chart quickly, select the data you want to use and press **F11**. Excel creates a column chart (the default chart type) on its own sheet. You can switch to that sheet, select the chart, and customize it.

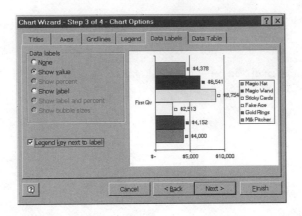

Figure 19.3 Select from various chart appearance options.

Customizing Your Chart with the Chart Toolbar

You can use the Chart toolbar to change how your chart looks. If the Chart toolbar is not displayed, you can turn it on by opening the **View** menu, selecting **Toolbars**, and then selecting **Chart**.

Table 19.1 shows each button on the Chart toolbar and explains its purpose.

Table 19.1 Buttons on the Chart Toolbar

Button	Name	Use
	Chart Objects	Click here to select the part of the chart you want to change. Optionally, you can simply click the part you want to select it.
	Format Object	Click here to change the formatting of the object whose name appears in the Chart Objects text box.
	Chart Type	Click the arrow to change the chart type, from bar to line, for example. If you click the button itself, the displayed chart type will be applied.

Button	Name	Use
	Legend	Click this to display or hide the legend.
	Data Table	Click here to add a data table, a grid which displays the data from which the chart was created.
	By Row	Click here if your data series are stored in rows.
	By Column	Click here if your data series are stored in columns.
	Angle Text Downward	Click here to angle text in selected area downward.
	Angle Text Upward	Click here to angle text in selected area upward.

Saving Charts

The charts you create are part of the current workbook. To save a chart, simply save the workbook that contains the chart. For more details, refer to Lesson 6, "Creating and Saving Workbook Files."

Printing a Chart

If a chart is an embedded chart, it will print when you print the worksheet that contains the chart. If you want to print just the embedded chart, click it to select it, and then open the **File** menu and select **Print**. Make sure that the **Selected Chart** option button is selected. Then click **OK** to print the chart.

If you created a chart on a separate worksheet, you can print the chart separately by printing only that worksheet. For more information about printing, refer to Lesson 10, "Printing Your Workbook."

In this lesson, you learned about the different chart types and how to create them. You also learned how to save and print charts. Learn how to create Web content with Excel.

Creating Web Content with Excel

In this lesson, you learn how to prepare worksheets for use on the Internet.

Saving a Worksheet in HTML Format

You can publish your Excel data on a Web site (or on your company's intranet) by converting your workbook to HTML format. HTML is short for Hypertext Markup Language and is the language in which data is presented on the World Wide Web. To display your Excel data on the Web so that others can view it with a Web browser, you must convert it to HTML.

CAUTION

Edit Your Files First Although the resulting HTML format worksheet will look the same as your original, it might not be a functional copy that you can continue to edit. The formulas may not work properly in the HTML version, for example, and PivotTables, AutoFilters, and number formats may also not transfer. It is best to convert a file to HTML format after you have made all your edits.

After you've prepared your data, follow these steps to save it in HTML format:

1. Select the first range of data you want to convert to HTML.
2. Open the **File** menu and select **Save As HTML**. The Internet Assistant Wizard—Step 1 of 4 dialog box appears, with the data range you selected in the **Ranges and Charts to Convert** list box (see Figure 20.1).

TIP **Office Assistant?** The first time you save as HTML, the Office Assistant appears asking if you need help. Click **No, Don't Provide Help Now** to make him go away.

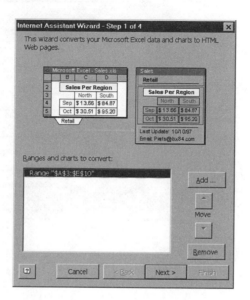

Figure 20.1 In this first dialog box, you confirm the range of data.

3. If you want to add more ranges from the workbook, click **Add**, select the next range, and click **OK**. (You can remove a range you have added in error by clicking it and clicking **Remove**.) When you're through adding ranges, click **Next**.

4. Select either **Create an Independent, Ready-to-View HTML Document** or **Insert the Converted Data into an Existing HTML File**. Choose the former if you have not already started a Web page that you want to put the data into, or the latter if you have. Then click **Next**.

5. If you're creating a new HTML document, make selections for the header and footer information, as shown in Figure 20.2, and click **Next**. If you're inserting data into an existing HTML file, you see a different screen, and you need to skip to step 8.

6. Choose whether to **Save the Result As an HTML File** or **Add the Result to My FrontPage Web**.

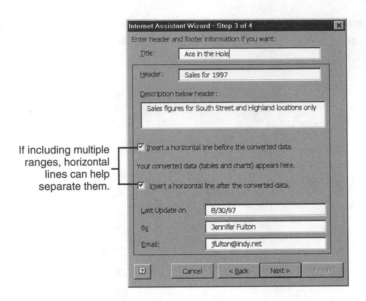

Figure 20.2 Select your header and footer information.

If including multiple ranges, horizontal lines can help separate them.

> **TIP** **What's FrontPage?** *FrontPage* is a Microsoft program that helps you create Web sites. Excel can link directly to sites created with that program. If you don't have a Web site created with that program, choose **Save the Result As an HTML File** in step 6.

7. Click **Finish**, and the selected data is converted to HTML format.

8. If you selected Insert the Converted Data into an Existing HTML File in step 4, the resulting screen looks like the one shown in Figure 20.3. Open the HTML file in which you want your Excel data placed (using an HTML editor) and add the following text, which acts as a marker, telling Excel where to place the table in the file.

```
<!--##Table##-->
```

> **TIP** **Editing an HTML File?** Inserting the converted data into an existing HTML file requires a certain familiarity with HTML codes. You must be able to open the HTML file in an HTML editing program or a regular text editor (such as Notepad) and locate the spot in the code where you want the converted data to be placed.

Then save the file in the HTML editor. Type the path to your HTML file in the **Path of the Existing File** text box in Excel, or click **Browse** and locate it manually. When you're done, click **Next**.

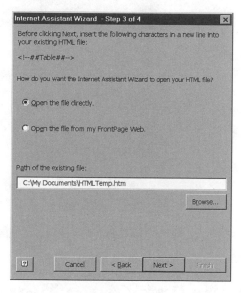

Figure 20.3   Choose your existing HTML file.

TIP **Let FrontPage Do It for You**   If you use FrontPage, select the **Open the File from My FrontPage Web** option, and the Internet Assistant Wizard opens FrontPage for you so that you can add the ##Table## marker.

9. Select a new code page if necessary, and then choose how you want the Internet Assistant Wizard to save your file (see Figure 20.4). If you want to save the result as a new file, type the name in the File Path text box. If you want the IAW to replace your existing HTML file, type its name instead or click **Browse** to select it.

10. When you're done, click **Finish**, and the selected data is added to the specified HTML file. To open the table in your favorite browser, select **File**, **Open**.

Now that you have your data in HTML format, you want to transfer it to a Web server so that people can access it. See Appendix D, "Publishing Your Work to the Internet," to learn how to transfer the HTML file to a Web-accessible file server.

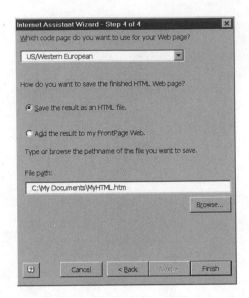

Figure 20.4   Choose how you want to save your data.

Adding Hyperlinks to a Worksheet

A hyperlink is a bit of text or a graphic that, when clicked, takes the user to a Web page, to a file on your hard disk, or to a file on a local network. To add a hyperlink to a worksheet, follow these steps:

1. Select the cell(s) that contain the text you want to use for the link. The cell, for example, might contain the text "Click here to view supporting statistics." If you do not enter any text, Excel inserts the address of the hyperlink (the file you select in step 4). If you want to use a graphic or a drawing as a link, select that instead.

2. Click the **Insert Hyperlink** button on the Standard toolbar.

3. If asked, make sure you save your workbook. The Insert Hyperlink dialog box appears, as shown in Figure 20.5.

Insert the document
path here.

Insert the destination
file location or HTML
anchor here.

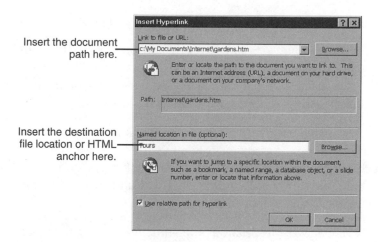

Figure 20.5 Use this dialog box to insert a hyperlink in a workbook.

4. Type the address of the Web page or file to which you want to link in the **Link to File or URL** text box, or click **Browse** to select it from a dialog box.

5. If you want to jump to a particular location within your file, enter that location in the **Named Location in File** text box. If the destination file is an Excel file, you can enter a named range, a sheet name, or a cell address. In an HTML file, you can enter the name of an anchor.

6. Click **Use Relative Path for Hyperlink** if you want Excel to use the destination file's relative address, rather than its actual address. A relative address can be easily changed if you think that the file to which the link refers will be moved to a different directory or drive.

 Relative and Absolute Addresses An absolute address is a full Internet address that includes the server address, such as: **www.mysite.com/info.htm**. A relative address assumes that the page you are jumping from is on the same server, so it references only the part of the address that might have changed, such as: info.htm.

TIP **Changing a Relative Address** To change a relative address, change the base address to which the address refers. Suppose, for example, the link points to an Excel file on your hard disk and you always saved your workbooks in the directory My Documents. Now, however, you've moved them to the F:\Public\Excel folder. You would need to open the **File** menu, select **Properties**, enter the new base address in the **Hyperlink Base** text box, and click **OK**.

7. Click **OK**. The text in the cell you selected becomes blue and underlined.

When you move the mouse pointer over this link, it changes to a hand. Next to the hand, you can see the address of the destination file. Click the link, and the destination file opens. Of course, if the link points to a file on the Internet, you need to connect to the Internet first and then click the link.

If you need to change the text that appears as the link later on, click a cell next to the link, and then use the arrow keys to move the pointer to the link cell. You can then change the text for the link by changing it in the Formula bar. To select a graphic link, press and hold down the **Ctrl** key and click the graphic. Then use the Drawing or Picture toolbar to change it.

 You can also change the destination of the link by selecting the link and then clicking the **Insert Hyperlink** button.

If you need to delete the link, select it and press **Delete**. To move the link, select it and use the **Edit, Cut** and **Edit, Paste** commands to move it to a new cell.

In this lesson, you learned how to use Excel with the Internet.

PowerPoint

Starting and Exiting PowerPoint

In this lesson, you learn how to start and exit PowerPoint.

Starting PowerPoint

Before you start PowerPoint, you must have PowerPoint installed on your computer (see Appendix A), and you should have a basic understanding of the Windows 98 or Windows NT operating system. If you need a refresher course in these Windows systems, read Part 1 of this book. Throughout this book, references are made to Windows 98, but keep in mind that in most cases, if you're using Windows NT, the information applies to you, too.

To start PowerPoint, follow these steps:

1. Click the **Start** button.
2. Move your mouse pointer to **Programs**. A menu of programs appears.
3. Move your mouse to **Microsoft PowerPoint** and click (see Figure 1.1). PowerPoint starts and displays the introductory screen shown in Figure 1.2.

The first thing you see when you start PowerPoint is a dialog box in which you choose whether you want to start a new presentation or open an existing one. You'll learn about this dialog box in Lesson 2, "Creating a New Presentation." For now, click **Cancel** to exit this dialog box.

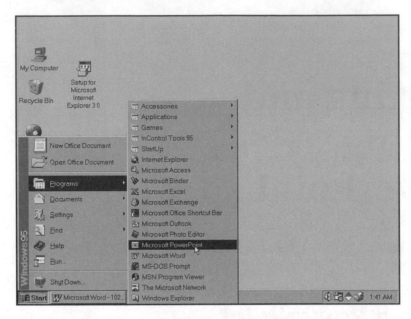

Figure 1.1   To start PowerPoint, move through the Start button's menu system to Microsoft PowerPoint.

PowerPoint's Not on the Menu?   You may have specified a different menu when you installed PowerPoint, or you may not have installed PowerPoint yet.

Help! There's a Paper Clip Talking to Me!   No, you haven't lost your mind. That paper clip is one of Microsoft Office's Assistants. Occasionally the little guy gives you a suggestion, and you have to click the appropriate button below his words to move on. The first time you start PowerPoint, he may say something. Clicking the Close (X) button for his window or pressing Esc will enable you to continue with your work. We'll look at the Office Assistants more in Appendix B.

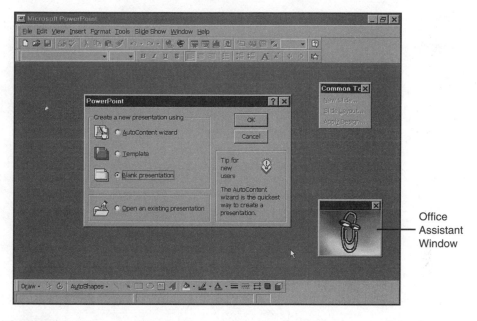

Office
Assistant
Window

Figure 1.2 When you first start PowerPoint, you see an introductory dialog box. (You'll learn about it in Lesson 2.)

Exiting PowerPoint

When you finish using PowerPoint, you should exit the application. Don't just turn off your computer! To exit PowerPoint, follow these steps:

1. If the PowerPoint dialog box is still on-screen, click the **Cancel** button to close it.

2. If the PowerPoint dialog box is not on-screen, do one of the following (see Figure 1.3):

   - Click the PowerPoint window's **Close** (X) button.
   - Double-click the **Control-menu** icon at the left end of the title bar, or click it once to open the Control menu and then select **Close**.
   - Open the **File** menu and select **Exit**.
   - Press **Alt+F4**.

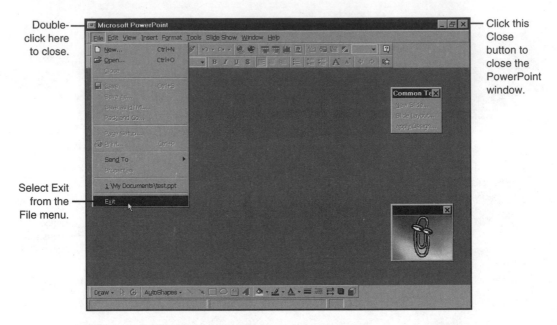

Double-click here to close.

Click this Close button to close the PowerPoint window.

Select Exit from the File menu.

Figure 1.3 You can exit PowerPoint in several ways.

3. If you're asked if you want to save your changes, select **Yes** if you want to save your changes. (If you choose Yes, see Lesson 5, "Saving, Closing, and Opening Presentations," to learn how to complete the Save As dialog box that appears.) Select **No** if you haven't created anything you want to save yet.

In this lesson, you learned to start and exit PowerPoint. In the next lesson, you'll learn how to create a new presentation.

Creating a New Presentation

In this lesson, you learn how to create a presentation in several ways.

Three Choices for Starting a New Presentation

PowerPoint offers you several ways to create a new presentation. Before you begin, decide on the method that's right for you:

- AutoContent Wizard offers the highest degree of help. It walks you through each step of creating the new presentation.

- A template offers a standardized group of slides, all with a similar look and feel, for a particular situation. Each template slide includes dummy text which you can replace with your own text.

- You can choose to start from scratch and create a completely blank presentation. With this method you can customize a presentation with your own design touches. (Building the presentation from the ground up is not recommended for beginners.)

Wizards   Wizards are a special feature that most Microsoft products offer. A wizard displays a series of dialog boxes that ask you design and content questions. You select options and type text. When you are done, the wizard creates something (in this case, a presentation) according to your instructions.

Template   A template is a predesigned slide that comes with PowerPoint. When you select a template, PowerPoint applies the color scheme and general layout of the slide to each slide in the presentation.

A Word About the PowerPoint Dialog Box

If you have just started PowerPoint and the PowerPoint dialog box is displayed, you are ready to start a new presentation (see Figure 2.1). From here, you can choose to create a new presentation by using the AutoContent Wizard, a template, or a blank presentation. Just click your choice and click **OK**, and then follow along with the steps in the remainder of this lesson to complete the presentation.

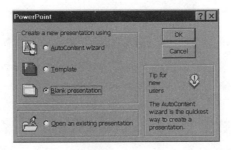

Figure 2.1 When you first start PowerPoint, this dialog box greets you. It's one method by which you can create a new presentation.

Unfortunately, the PowerPoint dialog box is available only when you first start the program. After you close the dialog box, you won't see it again until the next time you start the program. That's why the steps in the remainder of this lesson don't rely on it; instead they show alternative methods for starting a presentation if this dialog box is not available.

Creating a New Presentation with the AutoContent Wizard

With the AutoContent Wizard, you select the type of presentation you want to create (strategy, sales, training, reporting, conveying bad news, or general), and PowerPoint creates an outline for it.

TIP **Quick Start** If you click the **AutoContent Wizard** button in the PowerPoint dialog box (shown in Figure 2.1) and then click **OK**, you can skip the first three steps in the following procedure.

Here's how you use the AutoContent Wizard:

1. Open the **File** menu and click **New**. The New Presentation dialog box appears.

2. Click the **Presentations** tab if it's not already on top (see Figure 2.2).

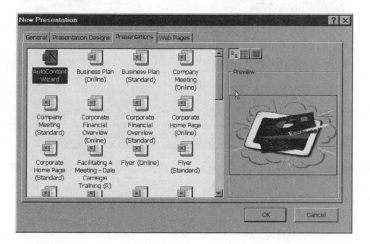

Figure 2.2 You can start a new presentation from here.

3. Double-click the **AutoContent Wizard** icon. The AutoContent Wizard starts.

Macro Warning At step 3, you might get a warning message about macros possibly carrying viruses. Click **Enable Macros** to continue.

CAUTION

4. Click the **Next** button to begin.

5. In the dialog box that appears (see Figure 2.3), click the button that best represents the type of presentation you want to create (for example, **Sales/Marketing**).

6. From the list box, select a presentation type to further narrow your presentation's purpose (for example, choose **Marketing Plan**). Then click **Next**.

7. Choose the method that best describes how you will give the presentation:

- **Presentations, Informal Meetings, Handouts** Choose this if you are planning to present the presentation with a live narrator controlling the action.

413

- **Internet, Kiosk** Choose this if you are planning a self-running presentation that does not require a live narrator.

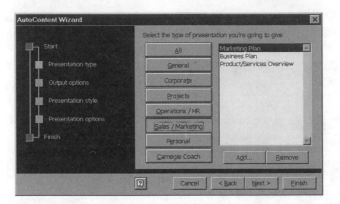

Figure 2.3 Answer the AutoContent Wizard's questions and click Next.

8. Click **Next** to continue.

9. Choose the type of output you need (such as **On-Screen Presentation**) and whether or not you need handouts (click **Yes** or **No**). Then click **Next**.

10. Enter the presentation title and your name in the blanks provided. Then click **Next**.

11. Click **Finish**. The beginnings of your presentation—with dummy text in place—appear on-screen in Outline view. (You'll learn about Outline view, as well as other views, in Lesson 4, "Working with Slides in Different Views.")

TIP **Replacing Dummy Text** You can start personalizing your presentation right away by replacing the dummy text with your own text. Just select the existing text and type right over it. See Lesson 10, "Adding Text to a Slide," for more information about editing text.

Creating a New Presentation with a Template

A template is the middle ground between maximum hand-holding (the AutoContent Wizard) and no help at all (Blank Presentation). Templates can be divided into two types: Presentation Templates and Presentation Design Templates.

- **Presentation Templates**   These templates offer much of the same help as the AutoContent Wizard—in fact, the AutoContent Wizard bases its presentation types on these. The templates provide a color scheme for slides and a basic outline for slide text. Their names reflect the purpose of the presentation; for example, "Communicating Bad News."

- **Presentation Design Templates**   These templates offer only a color scheme and a "look" for slides; you're on your own to provide the content for each slide.

To start a new presentation using a template, follow these steps:

1. Open the **File** menu and select **New**. PowerPoint opens the New dialog box.

2. If you want to use a presentation template, click the **Presentations** tab. If you want to use a presentation design, click the **Presentation Designs** tab.

3. Click the template you want to use, and a preview of the template appears in the Preview area.

4. After you select the template you want to use, click **OK**. PowerPoint creates the new presentation based on that template.

5. If you have selected a presentation template, you are ready to start editing the slides, just like you did with the AutoContent Wizard. If you have selected a Presentation Design Template, you see the New Slide dialog box (see Figure 2.4). Click the AutoLayout you want to use and click **OK**.

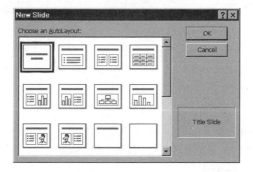

Figure 2.4   In the New Slide dialog box, you can choose a predesigned slide layout, or you can choose to design your own.

TIP **The Next Step?** To start customizing a Presentation Template, just click on the dummy text and then type new text to replace it. You can work through the whole presentation that way; the upcoming lessons, especially Lesson 10, can help.

To customize a Presentation Design Template, add more slides by clicking the **New Slide** button on the toolbar, and then create your presentation one slide at a time. See Lesson 8, "Inserting, Deleting, and Copying Slides," for help.

Creating a Blank Presentation

Are you sure you want to attempt a blank presentation on your first time out? A blank presentation has no preset color scheme or design, and no dummy text to help you know what to write. To create a blank presentation, follow these steps:

1. Open the **File** menu and select **New**.

2. Click the **General** tab.

3. Double-click the **Blank Presentation** icon. The New Slide dialog box appears (refer to Figure 2.4).

4. Click the **AutoLayout** you want to use and click **OK**.

What Next?

Now that you have the basic shell of your presentation, you need to modify and customize it. If you're not in a hurry, read the lessons in this part in order so that you can learn PowerPoint fully. However, if you are in a hurry, refer to the following lessons:

- To change the view of the presentation so that you can work with it more easily, see Lesson 4, "Working with Slides in Different Views."

- To apply a different design template or slide layout, see Lesson 7, "Changing a Presentation's Look."

- To add new slides, see Lesson 8, "Inserting, Deleting, and Copying Slides."

- To rearrange slides, see Lesson 9, "Rearranging Slides in a Presentation."

- To add and edit text, see Lesson 10, "Adding Text to a Slide."

In this lesson, you learned how to create a new presentation. In the next lesson, you'll learn how to control the PowerPoint program with menus and toolbars.

Getting Around
in PowerPoint

*In this lesson, you learn how to get around in PowerPoint and
enter commands.*

A Look at PowerPoint's Application
Window

If you created a new presentation by using the AutoContent Wizard or a template, your screen looks something like the screen shown in Figure 3.1. This screen contains many of the same elements you find in any Windows 98 or Windows NT program: a title bar, window control buttons (Minimize, Maximize, and Close), and a menu bar. For an explanation of these elements, refer to Part 1 of this book.

In addition, you see three toolbars and several windows that are unique to PowerPoint. The following sections explain how to work with these unique items.

 Toolbar A toolbar is a collection of buttons that enables you to bypass the menu system. For example, instead of selecting File, Save (opening the File menu and selecting Save), you can click the Save toolbar button to save your work. (You'll learn more about saving in Lesson 5, "Saving, Closing, and Opening Presentations.")

 Turning Off the Office Assistant The Office Assistant provides help as you work. If you don't want the Office Assistant on-screen all the time, you can easily make it disappear by clicking the **Close** (X) button in its window. To make it reappear, select **Help, Microsoft PowerPoint Help** or press F1. You'll learn more about getting help in Appendix B, "Using the Office 97 Help System."

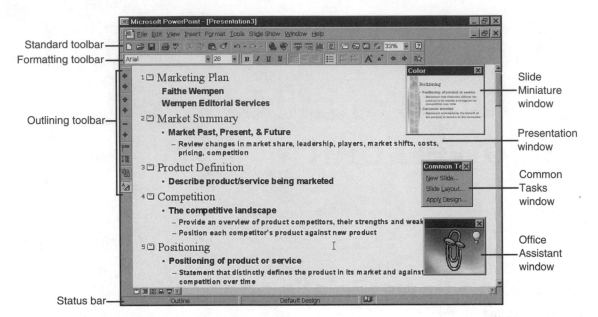

Standard toolbar

Formatting toolbar

Outlining toolbar

Status bar

Slide Miniature window

Presentation window

Common Tasks window

Office Assistant window

Figure 3.1 PowerPoint provides many tools for quickly entering commands.

New to PowerPoint 97 is the Common Tasks window shown in Figure 3.1. This is actually a floating toolbar. (You'll learn about floating toolbars later in this lesson.) You can drag it around on the screen, or you can get rid of it completely by clicking its Close (X) button. You can get it back later by right-clicking any toolbar and selecting **Common Tasks** from the shortcut menu.

The Presentation Window

In the center of the PowerPoint window is a presentation window. (It's probably maximized, in which case it flows seamlessly into the larger PowerPoint window.) You use this window to create your slides and arrange them into a presentation. At the bottom of the presentation window are several buttons that enable you to change views. Figure 3.1 shows a presentation in Outline view, whereas Figure 3.2 shows the same presentation in Slide view. For details about changing views, see Lesson 4, "Working with Slides in Different Views."

Slide Miniature Window? Slide Miniature is a new feature in PowerPoint 97. It enables you to view a small version of a slide even in nongraphical views like the one shown in Figure 3.1. You'll learn more about it in Lesson 4.

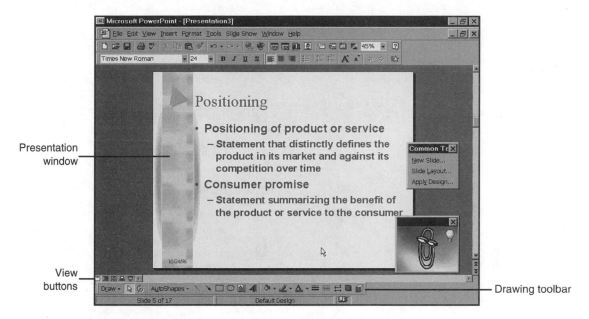

Presentation window

View buttons

Drawing toolbar

Figure 3.2 You can change views by clicking a View button.

Using Shortcut Menus

Although you can enter all commands in PowerPoint by using menus, PowerPoint offers a quicker way: context-sensitive shortcut menus like the ones in Windows 95 and Windows NT. To use a shortcut menu, right-click the object on which you want the command to act. A shortcut menu pops up (see Figure 3.3), offering commands that pertain to the selected object. Click the desired command.

Working with Toolbars

PowerPoint displays three toolbars by default: the Standard and Formatting toolbars below the menu bar (see Figure 3.1) and either the Outlining toolbar (on the left) or the Drawing toolbar (on the bottom), depending on the view. To select a button from the toolbar, click the button.

TIP **PowerPoint on the Web** A Web toolbar also exists that enables you to browse the World Wide Web through PowerPoint. It isn't turned on by default, but you can activate it by right-clicking on any toolbar and selecting **Web**, as you'll learn later in this lesson.

419

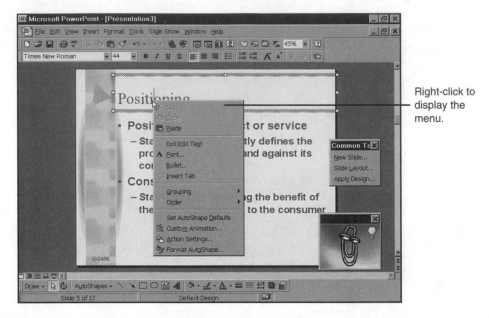

Right-click to display the menu.

Figure 3.3 Display a shortcut menu by right-clicking the object.

Learning More About Toolbar Buttons

Although I could list and explain all the tools in the Standard toolbar and in all the other toolbars, you can also learn about buttons in the following two ways:

- *To see the name of a button,* move the mouse pointer over the button. PowerPoint displays a ScreenTip that provides the name of the button.

- *To learn more about a button,* press **Shift+F1** or select **Help**, **What's This?** and then click the button for which you want more information.

Turning Toolbars On or Off

If you never use a particular toolbar, you can turn it off to free up some screen space. In addition, you can turn on other toolbars that come with PowerPoint but don't appear automatically. To turn a toolbar on or off, follow these steps:

1. Right-click any toolbar, and a shortcut menu appears (see Figure 3.4). A check mark appears beside each toolbar that is turned on.

2. Click to deselect the displayed toolbar you want to hide, or click to select a hidden toolbar that you want to display. (Remember that check marks appear beside displayed toolbars.)

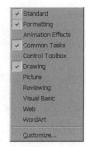

Figure 3.4 The shortcut menu for toolbars displays the names of all the toolbars.

When you click a toolbar name on the menu, the menu disappears and that toolbar appears (if it was hidden) or the toolbar disappears (if it was displayed).

Moving Toolbars

After you have displayed the toolbars you need, you can position them in your work area wherever they are most convenient. To move a toolbar, do the following:

1. Position the mouse pointer at the far left edge of the toolbar.

2. Hold down the left mouse button, and drag the toolbar where you want it according to these guidelines:

   • Drag the toolbar to a toolbar dock. Four docks exist: just below the menu bar, on the left and right sides of the application window, and just above the status bar.

   • Drag the toolbar anywhere else inside the application window to create a floating toolbar (see Figure 3.5).

 Toolbar Dock A toolbar dock is a location on the screen where a toolbar can "blend in" and meld with the PowerPoint window, instead of floating in its own separate box. By default, the Standard and Formatting toolbars are docked at the top and the Drawing toolbar is docked at the bottom.

3. Release the mouse button.

 What About Drop-Down Lists? If a toolbar contains a drop-down list, you cannot drag it to the left or right toolbar dock.

Toolbar's title bar

Floating toolbar

Toolbar's Close button

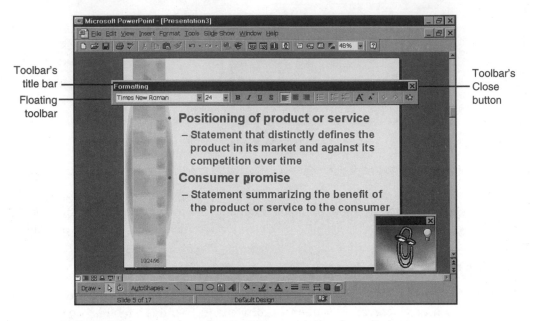

Figure 3.5 A floating toolbar.

A floating toolbar acts just like a window. You can drag its title bar to move it or drag a border to size it. If you drag a floating toolbar to a toolbar dock, the toolbar turns back into a normal (nonfloating) toolbar.

TIP **Customizing a Toolbar** To customize a toolbar, right-click it and choose **Customize**. You can then drag a toolbar button from one toolbar to another or drag a button off a toolbar (to remove it). To add a button, click the **Commands** tab in the Customize dialog box, and select a feature category from the **Categories** list in the dialog box. Then drag the desired command to any of the toolbars to create a button for it.

In this lesson, you learned about the PowerPoint application and presentation windows, and you learned how to enter commands with shortcut menus and toolbars. In the next lesson, you learn how to work with slides in different views.

Working with Slides in Different Views

In this lesson, you learn how to display a presentation in different views, and to edit slides in Outline and Slide views.

Changing Views

PowerPoint can display your presentation in different views. Having the option of selecting a view makes it easier to perform certain tasks. For example, Outline view shows the overall organization of the presentation, whereas Slide Sorter view enables you to rearrange the slides. Figure 4.1 shows the available views.

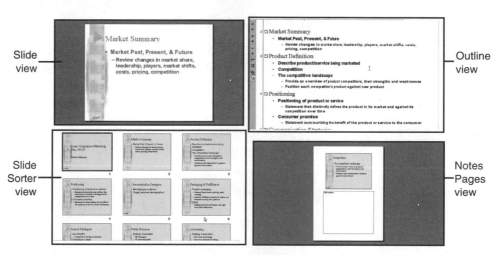

Figure 4.1 You can change views to make a task easier.

To change views, open the **View** menu and choose the desired view: **Slide**, **Outline**, **Slide Sorter**, or **Notes Pages**. A quicker way to switch views is to click the button for the desired view at the bottom of the presentation window, as shown in Figure 4.2.

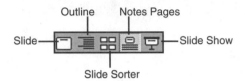

Figure 4.2 Use these buttons to change views.

 TIP **Outline to Slide View**   If you're using Outline view, you can quickly display a slide in Slide view by double-clicking the desired slide icon in the outline.

 What About the Slide Show Button?   The Slide Show button enables you to view your presentation as a timed slide show. For details, see Lesson 16, "Creating Slide Shows for Internet Use."

CAUTION

Moving from Slide to Slide

When you have more than one slide in your presentation, you will need to move from one slide to the next to work with a specific slide. The procedure for selecting a slide depends on the view you are currently using:

- In Outline view, use the scroll bar to display the slide with which you want to work. Click the **Slide** icon (the icon to the left of the slide's title) to select the slide, or click anywhere inside the text to edit it.

- In Slide view or Notes Pages view, click the **Previous Slide** or **Next Slide** button just below the vertical scroll bar (as shown in Figure 4.3), or drag the box inside the scroll bar until the desired slide number is displayed, or press **Page Up** or **Page Down**.

- In Slide Sorter view, click the desired slide. A thick border appears around the selected slide.

Drag this box until you reach the desired slide number.

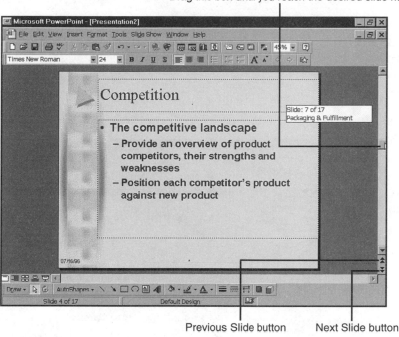

Previous Slide button   Next Slide button

Figure 4.3 Use the Previous Slide and Next Slide buttons to move between slides in Slide view or Notes Pages view.

The Slide Miniature Window

The Slide Miniature window is a new feature in PowerPoint 97 (see Figure 4.4). When the feature is active, it displays the currently selected slide in a small window on top of whatever view you're using. To turn Slide Miniature on or off, select **View**, **Slide Miniature**. You can also close the Slide Miniature window by clicking its Close button. To move the window around on-screen, drag its title bar to a new location.

In Outline view, the Slide Miniature shows a color version of the selected slide. In all other views, it shows an alternate version of the slide. For example, if you are currently displaying the slides on-screen in color, the Slide Miniature window shows them in black-and-white. Conversely, if the slides are displayed in black-and-white, the Slide Miniature window shows them in color.

The Slide Miniature window is especially useful if you are developing a presentation for two different media—for example, an on-screen presentation and a black-and-white set of printouts. Slide Miniature helps you keep an eye on the look of the slides so you do not inadvertently make a change to a color slide, for example, that would make it look unattractive or illegible when printed in black-and-white.

Slide Miniature window

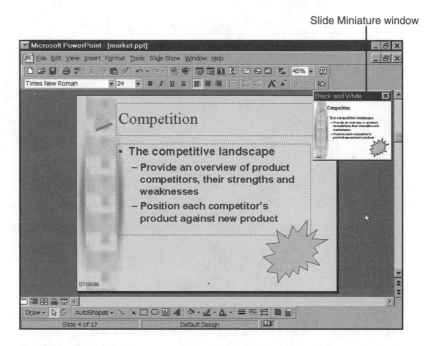

Figure 4.4 The Slide Miniature provides a thumbnail sketch of the current slide.

 TIP **Color or Black-and-White?** To toggle between black-and-white and color views on-screen, open the **View** menu and select **Black and White** (if you're currently viewing color) or **Color** (if you're currently viewing black-and-white).

Editing Slides

If you created a presentation in Lesson 2, "Creating a New Presentation," by using the AutoContent Wizard or a template, you already have several slides, but they may not contain the text you want to use. If you created a blank presentation, you have one slide on the screen that you can edit.

In the following sections, you will learn how to edit text in Outline and Slide views. In later lessons, you will learn how to add and edit text objects, pictures, graphs, organizational charts, and other items.

 Object An object is any item on a slide, including text, graphics, and charts.

Editing Text in Outline View

Outline view provides the easiest way to edit text (see Figure 4.5). Click to move the insertion point where you want it, and then type your text. Press the **Del** key to delete characters to the right of the insertion point, or press the **Backspace** key to delete characters to the left.

Position the I-beam pointer where you want the insertion point, and then click.

Microsoft PowerPoint - [Presentation2]

File Edit View Insert Format Tools Slide Show Window Help

Arial 32 **B** *I* U S

1 Acme Corporation Marketing Plan, FY-97
    Faithe Wempen

2 Market Summary
    • **Market Past, Present, & Future**
        – Review changes in market share, leadership, players, market shifts, costs, pricing, competition
3 Product Definition
    • **Describe product/service being marketed**
4 Competition
    • **The competitive landscape**
        – Provide an overview of product competitors, their strengths and weaknesses
        – Position each competitor's product against new product
5 Positioning
    • **Positioning of product or service**
        – Statement that distinctly defines the product in its market and against its competition over time

Outline   Default Design

Figure 4.5 Switch to Outline view to edit text.

To select text, hold down the left mouse button and drag the mouse over the desired text. You can then press **Del** or **Backspace** to delete the text, or you can drag the text where you want to move it.

TIP **Auto Word Select** When you select text, PowerPoint selects entire words. If you want to select individual characters, open the **Tools** menu, select **Options**, click the **Edit** tab, and select **Automatic Word Selection** to turn it off. Click the **OK** button.

Changing the Text's Outline Level

As you can see from Figure 4.5, your presentation is organized in a multilevel outline format. The slides are at the top level of the outline, and each slide's contents are subordinate under that slide. Some slides have multiple levels of subordination (for example, a bulleted list within a bulleted list).

You can easily change an object's level in Outline view with the Tab key:

- Click the text, and then press the **Tab** key or click the **Demote** button on the Outlining toolbar to demote it one level in the outline.
- Click the text, and then press **Shift+Tab** or click the **Promote** button on the Outlining toolbar to promote it one level in the outline.

In most cases, subordinate items on a slide appear as items in a bulleted list. In Lessons 11, "Creating Columns and Lists," and 12, "Changing the Look of Your Text," you will learn how to change the appearance of the bullet, how to change the size and formatting of text for each entry, and how to change the text indent for each level.

Moving a Line in Outline View

As you work in Outline view, you may find that some paragraphs need to be rearranged. One easy way to rearrange text is with the Move Up and Move Down buttons on the Outlining toolbar.

- To move a paragraph up in the outline, select it and click the **Move Up** button.
- To move a paragraph down in the outline, select it and click the **Move Down** button.

TIP **Dragging Paragraphs** You can quickly change the position or level of a paragraph by dragging it up, down, left, or right. To drag a paragraph, move the mouse pointer to the left side of the paragraph until the pointer turns into a four-headed arrow. Then hold down the left mouse button and drag the paragraph to the desired position.

Editing in Slide View

Slide view provides an easy way to edit all objects on a slide, including text and graphics. As shown in Figure 4.6, you can edit an object by clicking or double-clicking it. For text, click the object to select it, and then click where you want the insertion point moved. For graphics, double-click the object to bring up a set of tools that will help you edit it.

Most text appears on the slide in text boxes. (The only other place text can appear is within graphics.) In Lesson 10, "Adding Text to a Slide," you'll learn more about adding text to a slide, including creating your own text boxes on a slide. Then in Lessons 11 and 12 you'll learn how to fine-tune the look of your text for maximum impact.

Editing graphics is a more tricky than editing text. Future lessons discuss placing graphics on slides, and manipulating graphics.

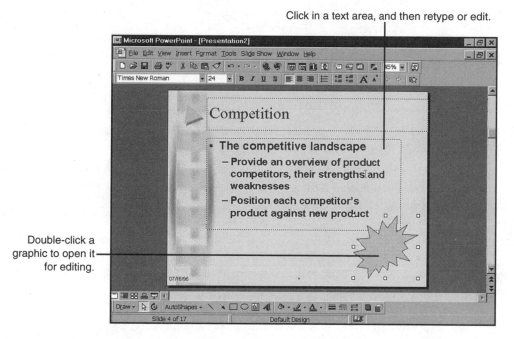

Figure 4.6   Slide view enables you to edit both text and graphics.

In this lesson, you learned how to change views for a presentation, move from slide to slide, and edit text. In the next lesson, you'll learn how to save, close, and open a presentation.

Saving, Closing, and Opening Presentations

In this lesson, you learn how to save a presentation to disk, close a presentation, and open an existing presentation.

Saving a Presentation

Soon after creating a presentation, you should save it to protect the work you have already done. To save a presentation for the first time, follow these steps:

1. Select **File**, **Save**, or press **Ctrl+S**, or click the **Save** button on the Standard toolbar. The Save As dialog box appears.

2. In the **File Name** text box, type the name you want to assign to the presentation. Do not type a file extension; PowerPoint automatically adds the extension .PPT (see Figure 5.1).

Upgrade Tip Because PowerPoint 97 is a 32-bit application, you are not limited to the old 8-character filenames as you were with PowerPoint versions designed for Windows 3.x. Your filenames can be as long as you want (within reason—the limit is 255 characters), and they can include spaces.

3. The Save In box shows the folder where the file will be saved. The default is My Documents. If you want to save to a different drive or folder, see the next section. Otherwise, continue to step 4.

4. Click **Save**.

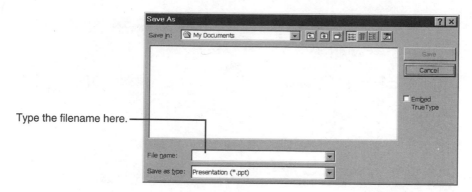

Type the filename here.

Figure 5.1 The Save As dialog box.

After you have named the file and saved it to a floppy disk or your computer's hard disk drive, you can save any changes you make simply by pressing **Ctrl+S** or clicking the **Save** button on the Standard toolbar. Your data is saved under the filename you already assigned.

To create a copy of a presentation under a different name, select **File, Save As**. The Save As dialog box appears, and you can use it in the same way you did when you originally saved the file.

Changing the Drive or Folder

The dialog boxes for opening and saving files in Windows 95 and 98 are different from the ones in Windows 3.1. The Save As and Open dialog boxes take a bit of getting used to.

To change to a different drive, you must open the Save In or Look In list. (The name changes depending on whether you're saving or opening a file.) Figure 5.2 shows this list in the Save As dialog box. From it, choose the drive on which you want to save the file.

Next, you must select the folder where you want to save the file (or open it from). When you select the drive, a list of the folders on that drive appears. Double-click the folder you want to select.

Table 5.1 explains the buttons and other controls you see in the Save As and Open dialog boxes, as well as in other Windows dialog boxes you may encounter.

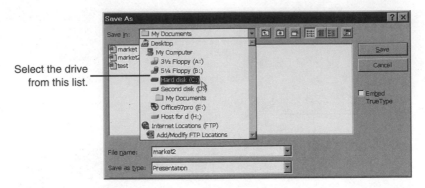

Select the drive
from this list.

Figure 5.2   Use this list box to choose a different drive.

Table 5.1   Buttons for Changing Drives and Folders in Dialog Boxes

Control	Description
	Moves to the folder "above" the one shown in the Save In box (that is, the folder in which the current one resides).
	Shows the C:\WINDOWS\FAVORITES folder, no matter which folder was displayed before.
	Creates a new folder.
	Shows the folders and files in the currently displayed folder in a list.
	Shows details about each file and folder.
	Shows the properties of each file and folder.
	Opens a dialog box of settings you can change that affect the dialog box.
	(Appears in Open dialog box only.) Switches to Preview view, in which you can see the first slide of a presentation before you open it.
	(Appears in Open dialog box only.) Adds a shortcut for the currently displayed folder to the Favorites list.

Closing a Presentation

You can close a presentation at any time. If you are working on multiple presentations, it's all right to keep them all open at once, but the more presentations you have open, the slower PowerPoint's response time to your commands will be. So you should close any presentations that you are not working on. (Although this closes the presentation window, it does not exit PowerPoint.) To close a presentation, follow these steps:

1. If more than one presentation is open, open the **Window** menu and select the presentation you want to close.

2. Choose **File, Close**, or press **Ctrl+F4**, or click the presentation window's **Close** (X) button. If you have not saved the presentation, or if you haven't saved since you made changes, a dialog box appears asking if you want to save.

3. To save your changes, click **Yes**. If this is a new presentation, refer to the steps earlier in this lesson for saving a presentation. If you have saved the file previously, the presentation window closes.

Opening a Presentation

After you save a presentation to a disk, you can open the presentation and continue working on it at any time. Follow these steps:

1. Choose **File, Open**, or press **Ctrl+O**, or click the **Open** button on the Standard toolbar. The Open dialog box appears (see Figure 5.3).

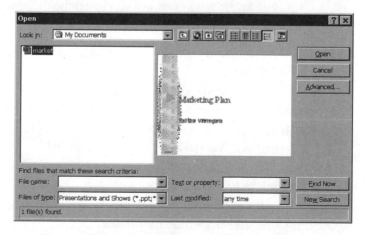

Figure 5.3   Select the presentation you want to open.

2. If the file isn't in the currently displayed folder, change drives or folders (as explained in the section "Changing the Drive or Folder," earlier in this lesson).

3. Double-click the file to open it.

Finding a Presentation File

If you're having trouble locating your file, PowerPoint can help you look. Follow these steps to find a file:

1. Choose **File**, **Open** if the Open dialog box is not already open.

2. In the **File Name** box at the bottom of the dialog box, type the name of the file for which you're looking (refer to Figure 5.3).

 Wild Cards   You can use wild cards if you don't know the entire name of a file. The asterisk (*) wild card character stands in for any character or set of characters, and the question mark (?) wild card character stands in for any single character. For example, if you know the file begins with P, you could type **P*.ppt** to find all PowerPoint files that begin with P.

3. (Optional) Enter other search criteria according to these guidelines:
   - If you're looking for a different file type, choose it from the **Files of Type** drop-down list.
   - If you're looking for a file containing certain text, type that text in the **Text or Property** box.
   - If you know when you last modified the file, choose the time interval from the **Last Modified** drop-down list.

4. Click the **Advanced** button. The Advanced Find dialog box appears (see Figure 5.4).

5. In the Look In section at the bottom of the Advanced Find dialog box, narrow the search area as much as possible by using these techniques:
   - If you are sure the file is in a certain folder, type that folder's path (such as **C:\WINDOWS**) in the **Look In** box.
   - If you are sure the file is on a certain drive, select that drive from the **Look In** list.
   - If you don't know the drive that contains the file, select **My Computer** from the **Look In** list.

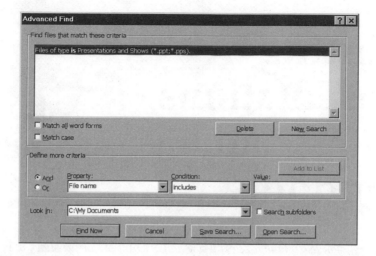

Figure 5.4   Use the Advanced Find dialog box to select the folders and drives you want to search.

6. Make sure the **Search Subfolders** check box is marked. If it isn't, click it.

7. Click the **Find Now** button. The File Open dialog box reappears, displaying the files that match your search criteria.

8. Double-click the file you want to open.

TIP   **More Search Options**   As you may have noticed in Figure 5.4, many more complex search options are available—too many to cover here. See your PowerPoint documentation for more details.

In this lesson, you learned how to save, close, open, and find presentations. In the next lesson, you will learn how to print a presentation.

Printing Presentations, Notes, and Handouts

In this lesson, you learn how to select a size and orientation for the slides in your presentation and how to print the slides, notes, and handouts you create.

Quick Printing—No Options

The quickest way to print is to use all the default settings. You don't get to make any decisions about your output, but you do get your printout without delay. To print a quick copy, use one of these methods:

- Click the **Print** button on the Standard toolbar.
- Choose **File**, **Print** and click **OK**.
- Press **Ctrl+P** and click **OK**.

When you use either of these methods for printing, you get a printout of your entire presentation in whatever view is on-screen. The following list describes the type of printout you can expect from each view.

- **Slide view**   The entire presentation prints in Landscape orientation with one slide per page. Each slide fills an entire page.
- **Outline view**   The entire outline prints in Portrait orientation.
- **Slide Sorter view**   The entire presentation prints in Portrait orientation with six slides per page.
- **Notes Pages view**   The entire presentation prints in Portrait orientation with one slide per page. Each slide prints with its notes beneath it.

Orientation The orientation setting tells the printer which edge of the paper should be at the "top" of the printout. If the top is across the wide edge, it's Landscape; if the top is across the narrow edge, it's Portrait.

Changing the Slide Setup

If you didn't get the printouts you expected from the previous procedure, you can change the output, size, and orientation of the selected presentation in the Slide Setup dialog box. To customize your printouts, follow these steps:

1. Choose **File**, **Page Setup**. The Page Setup dialog box appears on-screen, as shown in Figure 6.1.

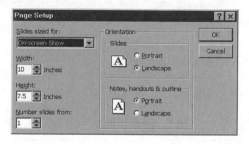

Figure 6.1 You can set the position and size of the slides on the page when you print them in Slide view.

2. Perform one of the following procedures to set the slide size:

   - To use a standard size, select a size from the **Slides Sized For** drop-down list. For example, you can have slides sized for regular 8.5 × 11 paper, 35mm slides, or an on-screen slide show.

   - To create a custom size, enter the dimensions in the **Width** and **Height** text boxes.

 Spin Boxes The arrows to the right of the Width and Height text boxes enable you to adjust the settings in those boxes. Click the up arrow to increase the setting by .1 inch, or click the down arrow to decrease it by .1 inch.

437

3. In the **Number Slides From** text box, type the number with which you want to start numbering slides. (This is usually 1, but you may want to start with a different number if the presentation is a continuation of another.)

4. Under the Slides heading, choose **Portrait** or **Landscape** orientation for your slides.

5. In the Notes, Handouts & Outline section, choose **Portrait** or **Landscape** for those items.

 TIP **Can I Print Notes and Handouts Differently?** If you want your notes printed in Portrait orientation and your handouts printed in Landscape orientation, choose **Portrait** from the Notes, Handouts & Outline section of the Slide Setup dialog box and print the notes. Then, before you print the handouts, go back to the dialog box and choose **Landscape** from the Notes, Handouts & Outline section.

6. Click **OK**. If you changed the orientation of your slides, you may have to wait a moment while PowerPoint repositions the slides.

Choosing What and How to Print

If the default print options don't suit you, you can change them. Do you have more than one printer? If so, you can choose which printer to use. For example, you may want to use a color printer for overhead transparencies and a black-and-white printer for handouts. You can also select options for printing multiple copies and for printing specific slides only.

To set your print options, follow these steps, and then print.

1. Choose **File, Print**. The Print dialog box appears, with the name of the currently selected printer in the Name box (see Figure 6.2).

2. If you want to use a printer other than the one that appears, open the **Name** drop-down list and select a different printer.

 TIP **Printer Properties** To make adjustments to your printer's settings, click the **Properties** button in the Print dialog box. The adjustments you can make vary from printer to printer, but you should be able to adjust graphics quality, select paper size, and choose which paper tray to use—among other things.

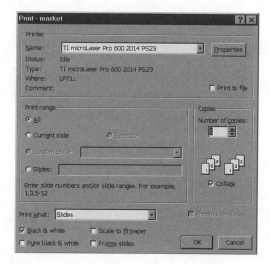

Figure 6.2 Choose your printing options in the Print dialog box.

3. In the Print Range section, choose what to print:
- Choose **All** to print all the slides in the presentation.
- Choose **Current Slide** to print only the currently displayed slide.
- In the **Slides** text box, enter a range of slide numbers—for example, **2–4**—to print multiple consecutive slides.

4. Open the **Print What** drop-down list and choose what you want to print. You can print slides, handouts, notes, or outlines.

5. If you want more than one copy, enter the number of copies you want in the **Number of Copies** box.

6. Select or deselect any of these check boxes in the dialog box as desired:

Print to File   Select this option to send the output to a file instead of to your printer.

Collate   If you are printing more than one copy, select this check box to collate each printed copy (print in the order 1, 2, 3, 1, 2, 3) instead of printing all the copies of each page at once (in the order 1, 1, 2, 2, 3, 3).

Black & White   If you have a black-and-white printer, select this check box to make the color slides print more crisply. You also can select this check box to force a color printer to produce black-and-white output.

Pure Black & White   This check box is like the preceding one except everything prints in solid black and plain white, with no gray shading. This makes all slides look like line drawings.

Scale to Fit Paper   If the slide (or whatever you're printing) is too large to fit on the page, select this check box to decrease the size of the slide to make it fit on the page. Now you won't have to paste two pieces of paper together to see the entire slide.

Frame Slides   Select this check box if you want to print a border around each slide.

Print Hidden Slides   If you have any hidden slides, you can choose whether or not to print them. If you don't have any hidden slides, this check box will be unavailable. You'll learn about hidden slides in Lesson 9.

TIP **Why Would I Print to File?**   If you don't have the printer that you want to use hooked up to your computer, you can print to a file and then take that file to the computer where the printer is. PowerPoint does not have to be installed on the other computer for that computer to print PowerPoint documents.

7. Click **OK** to print.

In this lesson, you learned how to print slides, outlines, and notes, and how to set options for your printouts. In the next lesson, you will learn how to change the overall appearance of the slides in a presentation.

Changing a Presentation's Look

In this lesson, you learn various ways to give your presentation a professional and consistent look.

Giving Your Slides a Professional Look

PowerPoint comes with dozens of professionally designed slides you can use as templates for your own presentations. That is, you can apply one of these predesigned slides to an already existing presentation to give the slides in your presentation a consistent look.

 Template A template is a predesigned slide that comes with PowerPoint. When you select a template, PowerPoint applies the color scheme and general layout of the slide to each slide in your presentation.

You can also make global changes to the entire presentation in another way: You can alter the Slide Master. The Slide Master is not really a slide, but it looks like one. It's a design grid on which you make changes, and these changes affect every slide in the presentation. For example, if you want a graphic to appear on every slide, you can place it on the Slide Master instead of pasting it onto each slide individually. When you apply a template, you are actually applying that template to the Slide Master, which in turn applies the template's formatting to each slide.

TIP **Changing the Colors on a Single Slide** If you want to make some slides in the presentation look different from the others, you're in the wrong lesson.

Applying a Presentation Design Template

You can apply a different template to your presentation at any time, no matter how you originally create your presentation. To change the template, follow these steps:

  1. Click the **Apply Design** button on the Standard toolbar, or choose **Format**, **Apply Design**. The Apply Design dialog box appears (see Figure 7.1).

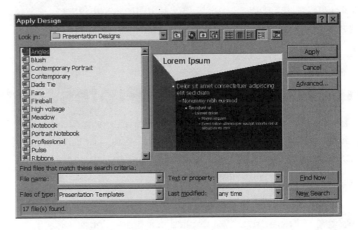

Figure 7.1 Choose a different template from the Apply Design dialog box.

2. Click a template name in the list. A sample of the template appears to the right of the list.

3. When you find a template you want to use, click **Apply**.

Using AutoLayouts

Whereas templates enable you to change the color and design of a presentation, AutoLayouts enable you to set the structure of a single slide in a presentation. For example, if you want a graph and a picture on a slide, you can choose an AutoLayout that positions the two items for you.

TIP   **Individual Slides?**   PowerPoint applies AutoLayouts to individual slides, but the template you choose and the Master Layout modifications you make affect the AutoLayouts. This becomes more evident later in this lesson.

To use an AutoLayout, do the following:

1. In Slide view, display the slide you want to change.

2. Choose **Format, Slide Layout** or click the Slide layout button on the Standard toolbar. The Slide Layout dialog box appears (see Figure 7.2).

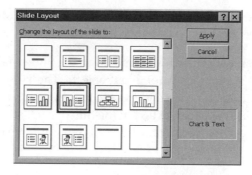

Figure 7.2   You can change an individual slide's layout with this dialog box.

TIP   **Right-Click**   A quick way to display the Slide Layout dialog box is to right-click on the slide in Slide view and select **Slide Layout**.

3. Click the desired layout, or use the arrow keys to move the selection border to it.

4. Click the **Apply** button, and PowerPoint applies the selected layout to the current slide.

Editing the Slide Master

Every presentation has a Slide Master that controls the overall appearance and layout of each slide. The Slide Master contains all the formatting information that the template brings to the presentation, such as colors and background patterns, and it also marks where the elements you use from the AutoLayout feature will appear on the slide.

To make changes to the Slide Master for your presentation, follow these steps:

1. Select **View**, **Master**, **Slide Master**. Your Slide Master appears, as in Figure 7.3.

2. Make any changes to the Slide Master, as you'll learn in upcoming lessons in this book. (Anything you can do to a regular slide, you can also do to a Slide Master.)

3. When you're done working with the Slide Master, click the **Close** button (see Figure 7.3) to return to normal view.

The two most important elements on the Slide Master are the Title Area and Object Area for the AutoLayout objects. The Title Area contains the formatting specifications for each slide's title; that is, it tells PowerPoint the type size, style, and color to use for the text in the title of each slide. The Object Area contains the formatting specifications for all remaining text on the slide.

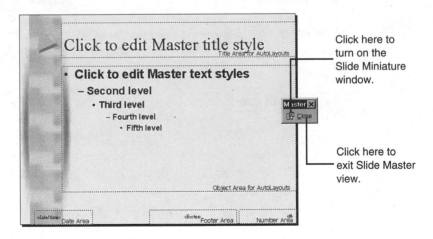

Figure 7.3 The Slide Master ensures that all slides in a presentation have a consistent look.

Slide Miniature   As you learned in Lesson 4, "Working with Slides in Different Views," Slide Miniature is a new viewing tool in PowerPoint 97. It enables you to see what the slide will look like in another format (for example, in black-and-white if the slide is currently shown in color). Turn back to Lesson 4 for more information.

For most of PowerPoint's templates, the Object Area sets up specifications for a bulleted list, including the type of bullet, as well as the type styles, sizes, and indents for each item in the list.

In addition to the Title and Object Areas, the Slide Master can contain information about background colors, borders, page numbers, company logos, clip art objects, and any other elements you want to appear on every slide in the presentation.

The Slide Master is like any slide. In the following lessons, when you learn how to add text, graphics, borders, and other objects to a slide, keep in mind that you can add these objects on individual slides or on the Slide Master. When you add the objects to the Slide Master, they appear on every slide in the presentation.

In this lesson, you learned how to give your presentation a consistent look with templates and AutoLayouts. You also learned how to use the Slide Master to make global changes to your slides. In the next lesson, you will learn how to insert, delete, and copy slides.

Inserting, Deleting, and Copying Slides

In this lesson, you learn how to insert new slides, delete slides, and copy slides in a presentation.

Inserting a Slide

You can insert a slide into a presentation at any time and at any position in the presentation. To insert a slide, follow these steps:

1. Select the slide that appears just before the place where you want to insert the new slide. (You can select the slide in any view: Outline, Slides, Slide Sorter, or Notes Pages.)

2. Choose **Insert**, **New Slide**, or click the **New Slide** button, or press **Ctrl+M**. In Outline view, PowerPoint inserts a blank slide into which you can type a title and bulleted list. In all other views, the New Slide dialog box appears (see Figure 8.1).

3. In the **Choose an AutoLayout** list, click a slide layout or use the arrow keys to highlight it. (Note that you can scroll this list for more choices.)

4. Click **OK**, and PowerPoint inserts a slide with the specified layout (see Figure 8.2).

5. Follow the directions indicated on the slide layout to add text or other objects. In most cases, you click an object to select it and then type your text.

 TIP **Cloning a Slide**   To create an exact replica of a slide (in any view), select the slide you want to duplicate. Then select **Insert**, **Duplicate Slide**. PowerPoint inserts the new slide after the original slide. You can then move the slide anywhere you want (which you'll learn to do in Lesson 9, "Rearranging Slides in a Presentation").

New Feature!   The Insert, Duplicate Slide command is new for PowerPoint 97. In previous versions of PowerPoint, you could duplicate a slide only from Outline or Slide Sorter view, and you had to use the Edit, Duplicate command. That command is still available in those views in PowerPoint 97, so you can continue to use it if you are familiar with it.

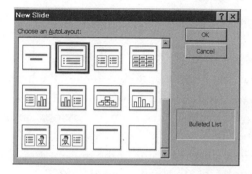

Figure 8.1   In the New Slide dialog box, choose a layout for the slide you're inserting.

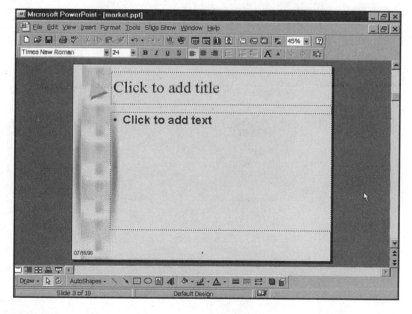

Figure 8.2   The new slide contains the blank structure you selected; you supply the content.

Adding Slides from Another Presentation

If you want to insert some or all of the slides from another presentation into the current presentation, perform these steps:

1. Open the presentation into which you want to insert the slides.

2. Select the slide located before the position where you want to insert the slides.

3. Choose **Insert, Slides from Files**. The Slide Finder dialog box appears.

4. Click the **Browse** button to display the Insert Slides from Files dialog box.

5. Change the drive or folder if needed. (Refer to the section "Changing the Drive or Folder" in Lesson 5, "Saving, Closing, and Opening Presentations.")

6. Double-click the name of the presentation that contains the slides you want to insert into the open presentation.

7. Click the **Display** button, and the slides from the presentation appear in the Slide Finder window (see Figure 8.3).

> **TIP** **View the Slides in a Different Way** Click this button if you prefer to see a list of the slide titles instead of three slides at a time. When you click the button, the display changes to a list of titles on the left and a preview window on the right that displays the selected slide.

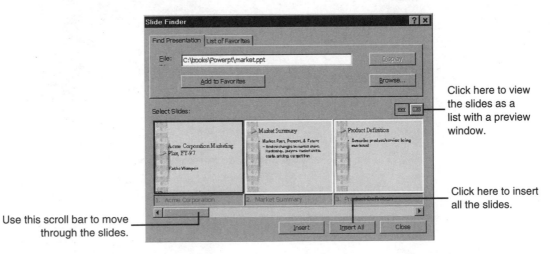

Figure 8.3 You can select any or all of the slides from the selected presentation to add to the open presentation.

8. Click the slides you want to insert and then click the **Insert** button. If you want to insert all the slides, click the **Insert All** button.

9. When you are finished inserting slides, click the **Close** button. The inserted slides appear right after the slide that you selected in step 2.

 TIP   **Make a Favorites List**   If you regularly use a certain presentation from which to insert slides, you can add it to your Favorites List by clicking the **Add to Favorites** button in the Find Slides dialog box. Then the next time you want to insert slides from that presentation, you can click the **List of Favorites** tab in the Find Slides dialog box and select the presentation from the list. You might, for example, have a presentation that contains some standard slides that you include in every presentation for a certain audience.

Creating Slides from a Document Outline

If you have a word-processing document with outline-style headings in it, PowerPoint can pull the headings from the document and use the headings to create slides with bulleted lists. Follow these steps to create slides from a document outline:

1. Choose **Insert, Slides from Outline**. The Insert Outline dialog box appears.

2. Use the Insert Outline dialog box to locate the document file you want to use. (Refer to "Changing the Drive or Folder" in Lesson 5 if you need help locating the file.)

3. Double-click the name of the document file.

Selecting Slides

In the following sections, you learn to delete, copy, and move slides. However, before you can do anything with a slide, you have to select the slide. You can select one or more slides, as explained here:

- To select a single slide, click it. (In Slide and Notes Pages views, the currently displayed slide is selected; you don't have to click it.)

- To select two or more neighboring slides in Outline view, click the first slide, press and hold the **Shift** key, and click the last slide in the group.

- To select a rectangular block of neighboring slides in Slide Sorter view, click and drag a "box" around the slides you want to include. All slides that fall into the box you drag become selected (see Figure 8.4).

- To select two or more non-neighboring slides (in Slide Sorter view only), press and hold the **Ctrl** and **Shift** keys and click each slide. You cannot select non-neighboring slides in Outline view.

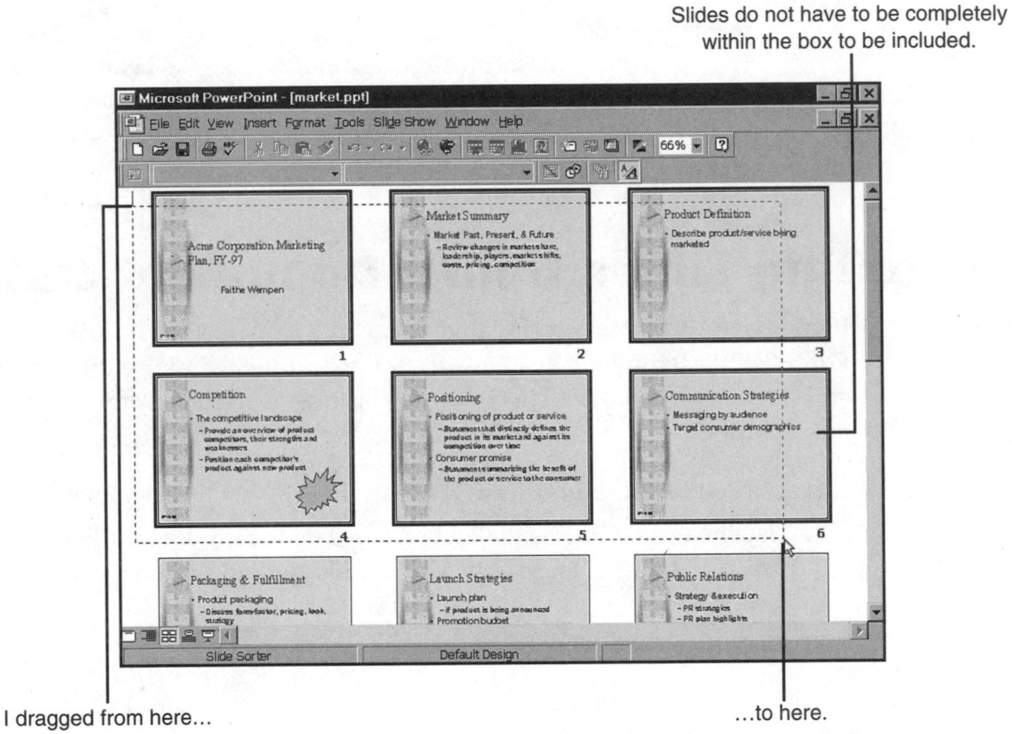

Slides do not have to be completely within the box to be included.

I dragged from here...   ...to here.

Figure 8.4 You can select a block of slides in Slide Sorter view by dragging a box around them.

Deleting Slides

You can delete a slide from any view. To delete a slide, perform the following steps:

1. Display the slide you want to delete (in Slide or Notes Pages view) or select the slide (in Outline or Slide Sorter view). You can delete multiple slides by displaying or selecting more than one.

2. Choose **Edit**, **Delete Slide**, and the slide disappears.

 TIP   **Quicker Deleting**   In Outline or Slide Sorter view, you can select the slides you want to delete and press the **Delete** key on the keyboard.

  Oops!   If you deleted a slide by mistake, you can get it back by selecting **Edit**, **Undo**, or by pressing **Ctrl+Z**, or by clicking the **Undo** button on the Standard toolbar.

CAUTION

Cutting, Copying, and Pasting Slides

In Lesson 9, you will learn how to rearrange slides in Slide Sorter and Outline views. However, you also can use the cut, copy, and paste features to copy and move slides within the same presentation or into other presentations. To cut (or copy) a slide and paste it into a presentation, perform the following steps:

1. Change to Slide Sorter or Outline view.

2. Select the slide(s) you want to copy or cut.

3. Open the **Edit** menu and select **Cut** or **Copy** to either move or copy the slide(s) to the Windows Clipboard.

TERM   **Windows Clipboard**   The Windows Clipboard is a temporary holding area for cut or copied items. You can cut or copy items to the Clipboard and then paste them on a slide, or you can cut or copy an entire slide or group of slides.

 TIP   **Quick Cut or Copy**   To bypass the Edit menu, press **Ctrl+C** to copy or **Ctrl+X** to cut, or click the **Cut** or **Copy** button on the Standard toolbar.

4. If you want to paste the slide(s) into a different presentation, open that presentation.

5. In Slide Sorter view, select the slide after which you want to place the cut or copied slide(s). In Outline view, move the insertion point to the end of the text in the slide after which you want to insert the cut or copied slide(s).

6. Choose **Edit**, **Paste** or press **Ctrl+V**. (You can also click the **Paste** button on the Standard toolbar.) PowerPoint inserts the cut or copied slides.

TIP   **Drag-and-Drop**   Although it's primarily used for moving slides, drag-and-drop also can be used for copying them in Slide Sorter view. Just press and hold **Ctrl** and drag a slide where you want the copy to go. See Lesson 9 for details.

In this lesson, you learned how to insert, delete, cut, copy, and paste slides. In the next lesson, you will learn how to rearrange the slides in your presentation.

Rearranging Slides in a Presentation

In this lesson, you learn how to rearrange your slides.

Sometimes you might need to change the sequence of slides in a presentation. PowerPoint has the capability to reorder slides in either Slide Sorter view or Outline view.

Rearranging Slides in Slide Sorter View

Slide Sorter view shows miniature versions of the slides in your presentation. This enables you to view many of your slides at one time. To rearrange slides in Slide Sorter view, perform the following steps:

1. Switch to Slide Sorter view by selecting **View**, **Slide Sorter** or by clicking the **Slide Sorter** button on the status bar.
2. Move the mouse pointer over the slide you want to move.
3. Press and hold the left mouse button, and drag to the location in which you want to insert the slide. As you drag, a line appears (as shown in Figure 9.1), showing where you are moving the slide.

CAUTION

Destination Not in View? If you have more than six slides in your presentation, you may not be able to see the slide's destination on-screen. Don't worry. Just drag the slide in the direction of the destination, and the display will scroll in that direction.

TIP **Copying a Slide** You can copy a slide in Slide Sorter view as easily as you can move a slide. Simply hold down the **Ctrl** key when you drag the slide.

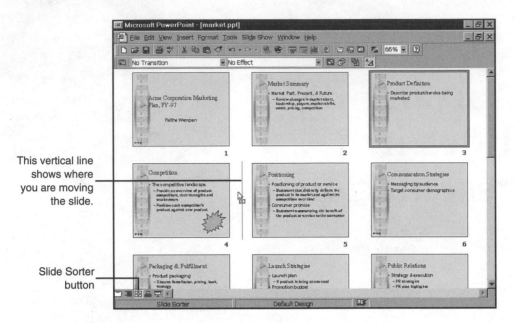

This vertical line shows where you are moving the slide.

Slide Sorter button

Figure 9.1 Switch to Slide Sorter view.

4. When the vertical line is in the location where you want the slide, release the mouse button. PowerPoint places the slide in its new position and shifts the surrounding slides to make room for the new slide.

TIP **Dragging and Dropping Between Presentations** You can even drag-and-drop slides to copy from one presentation to another. To do so, open both presentations (see Lesson 5, "Saving, Closing, and Opening Presentations," for instructions on how to open presentations). Then choose **Window**, **Arrange All**. The two windows appear side-by-side. Change to Slide Sorter view in each window, and then follow the steps to drag-and-drop slides from one presentation window to the other.

Rearranging Slides in Outline View

In Outline view, you see the titles and text that appear on each slide. This view gives you a clearer picture of the content and organization of your presentation than the other views, so you may prefer to rearrange your slides in Outline view. The following steps show you how to do it:

1. Switch to Outline view by choosing **View**, **Outline** or by clicking the **Outline** button.

2. Click the slide number or the slide icon to the left of the slide you want to move. PowerPoint highlights the contents of the entire slide.

TIP **Moving the Contents of a Slide** If you just want to insert some of the information from a slide into your presentation, you don't have to move the entire slide. You can move only the slide's data—text and graphics—from one slide to another by selecting only what you want to move and dragging it to its new location.

3. Move the mouse pointer over the selected slide icon, press and hold the mouse button, and drag the slide up or down in the outline. Or, select the slide and click the **Move Up** or **Move Down** button on the Outlining toolbar (see Figure 9.2).

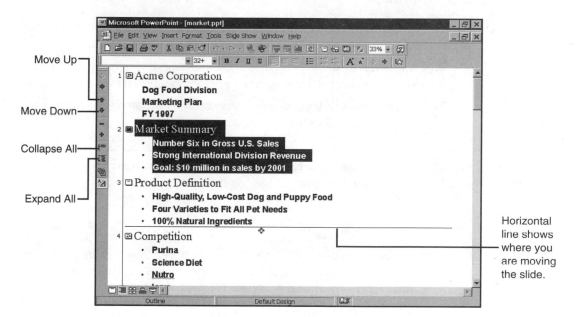

Figure 9.2 Drag the selected icon, or click the Move Up or Move Down button.

4. When the slide is at the desired new position, release the mouse button. (Be careful not to drop the slide in the middle of another slide. If you do, choose **Edit**, **Undo** and try again.)

TIP **Collapsing the Outline** You can collapse the outline to show only the slide titles. This enables you to view more slides at one time and rearrange the slides more easily. To collapse the outline, click the **Collapse All** button on the Outlining toolbar (refer to Figure 9.2). To restore the outline, click the **Expand All** button.

Hiding Slides

Before you give a presentation, you should try to anticipate any questions your audience may have and be prepared to answer those questions. You may even want to create slides to support your answers to these questions but keep the slides hidden until you need them. To hide one or more slides, perform the following steps:

1. Display or select the slide(s) you want to hide. (You can hide slides in Slide, Outline, or Slide Sorter view.)

2. Choose the **Slide Show**, **Hide Slide** command. If you are in Slide Sorter view, the hidden slide's number appears in a box with a line through it.

3. To unhide the slide(s), display or select the hidden slide(s) and choose **Slide Show**, **Hide Slide** again.

TIP **Right-Click Shortcut** To quickly hide a slide, you can right-click the slide and select **Hide** from the shortcut menu that appears.

TIP **Printing Hidden Slides?** In Lesson 6, " Printing Presentations, Notes, and Handouts," you learned about the Print Hidden Slides check box in the Print dialog box. When printing, select this check box to print the hidden slides.

In this lesson, you learned how to rearrange the slides in a presentation in either Slide Sorter or Outline view, and how to hide slides. In the next lesson, you will learn how to add text to a slide.

Adding Text to a Slide

In this lesson, you learn how to add text to a slide and how to change the text alignment and line spacing.

Creating a Text Box

As you have learned in previous lessons, you can put text on a slide by typing text in Outline view or by filling in the blanks on an AutoLayout (see Lesson 8, "Inserting, Deleting, and Copying Slides"). However, both these methods provide fairly generic results. If you want to type additional text on a slide, you must first create a text box.

 Text Box   A text box acts as a receptacle for the text. Text boxes often contain bulleted lists, notes, or labels used to point to important parts of illustrations.

To create a text box, perform the following steps:

1. Switch to Slide view or Slide Sorter view. (Refer to Lesson 4, "Working with Slides in Different Views," for help with views.) Slide view may give you a clearer view of your work area.

2. If you want the text box to appear on a new slide, insert a slide into the presentation. (Choose **Insert**, **Slide**, as you learned in Lesson 8.)

 3. Click the **Text Box** button on the Drawing toolbar.

4. Position the mouse pointer where you want the upper-left corner of the box to appear.

5. Press and hold the left mouse button and drag to the right until the box is the desired width. (It doesn't matter how far you drag down vertically: the box created will always be the same height—one line.)

6. Release the mouse button, and a one-line text box appears (see Figure 10.1).

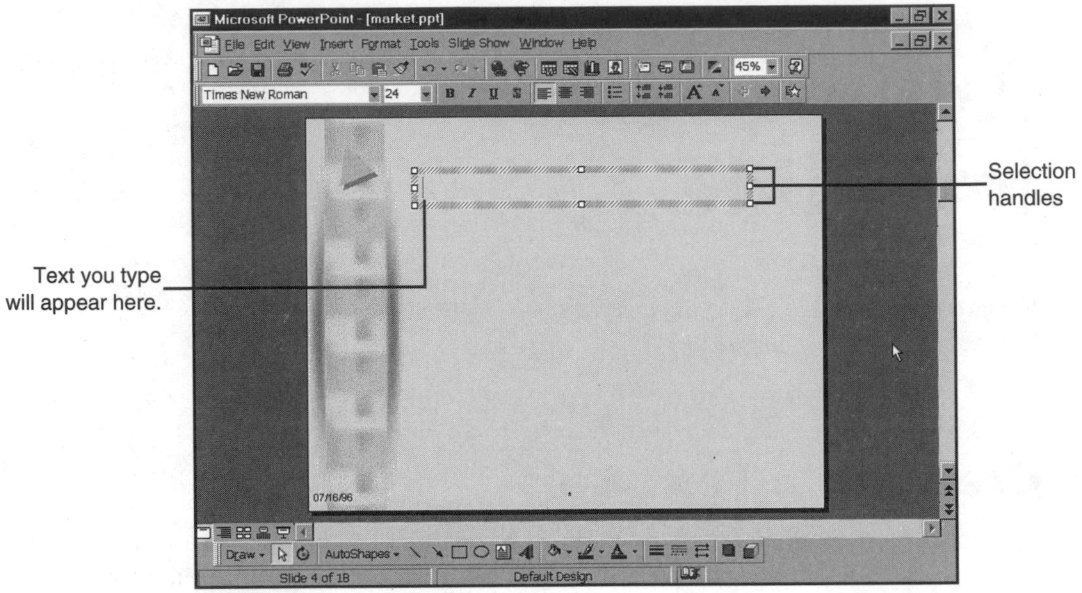

Selection handles

Text you type will appear here.

Figure 10.1 You can enter text in the text box.

7. Type the text that you want to appear in the text box. When you reach the right side of the box, PowerPoint wraps the text to the next line and makes the box one line deeper. To start a new paragraph, press **Enter**.

8. When you are done, click anywhere outside the text box to see how the text will appear on the finished slide.

TIP **Framing a Text Box** The border that appears around a text box when you create or select it does not appear on the printed slide.

Selecting, Deleting, and Moving a Text Box

If you go back and click anywhere inside the text box, a selection box appears around it. If you click the selection box border, handles appear around the text box, as shown in Figure 10.1. You can drag the box's border to move the box, or you can drag a handle to resize it. PowerPoint automatically wraps the text as needed to fit inside the box.

To delete a text box, select it (so handles appear around it), and then press the **Delete** key.

Editing Text in a Text Box

To edit text in a text box, first click anywhere inside the text box to select it. Then perform any of the following procedures:

- To select text, drag over the text you want to select. (To select a single word, double-click it. To select an entire paragraph, triple-click.)

 TIP **Auto Word Select**   When you drag over text, PowerPoint selects entire words. If you want to select individual characters, select the **Tools**, **Options** command, click the **Edit** tab, and deselect the **Automatic Word Selection** check box.

- To delete text, select the text and press the **Delete** key. You can also use the Delete or Backspace keys to delete single characters to the right or left of the insertion point, respectively.

- To insert text, click where you want to insert the text, and then type the text.

- To replace text, select the text you want to replace, and then type the new text. When you start typing, PowerPoint deletes the selected text.

- To copy and paste text, select the text you want to copy and choose the **Edit**, **Copy** command, or click the **Copy** button on the Standard toolbar, or press **Ctrl+C**. Then move the insertion point to where you want the text pasted (it can even be in a different text box) and choose the **Edit**, **Paste** command, or click the **Paste** button, or press **Ctrl+V**.

- To cut and paste (move) text, select the text you want to cut and choose the **Edit**, **Cut** command, or click the **Cut** button on the Standard toolbar, or press **Ctrl+X**. Move the insertion point to where you want the text pasted (it can even be in a different text box), and choose the **Edit**, **Paste** command, or click the **Paste** button, or press **Ctrl+V**.

Changing the Text Alignment and Line Spacing

When you first type text, PowerPoint automatically places it against the left edge of the text box. To change the paragraph alignment, perform the following steps:

1. Click anywhere inside the paragraph you want to realign.
2. Select **Format**, **Alignment**. The Alignment submenu appears.
3. Select **Left**, **Center**, **Right**, or **Justify** to align the paragraph as desired. (See Figure 10.2 for examples.)

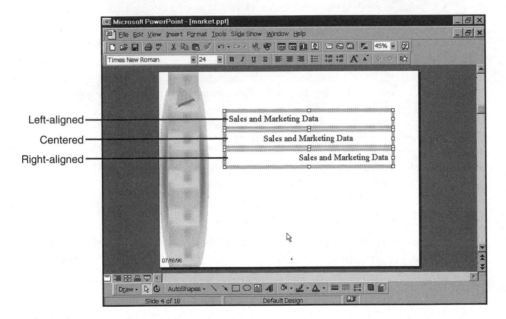

Figure 10.2 You can align each paragraph in a text box.

Some Alignment Shortcuts To quickly set left alignment, press **Ctrl+L** or click the **Left Alignment** button on the Formatting toolbar. To quickly apply centered alignment, press **Ctrl+C** or click the **Center Alignment** button. To quickly apply right alignment, press **Ctrl+R** or click the **Right Alignment** button.

The default setting for line spacing is single-space. To change the line spacing in a paragraph, perform these steps:

1. Click inside the paragraph you want to change, or select all the paragraphs you want to change.

2. Select **Format**, **Line Spacing**. The Line Spacing dialog box appears, as shown in Figure 10.3.

Figure 10.3   The Line Spacing dialog box.

3. Click the arrow buttons to the right of any of the following text boxes to change the line spacing:

> **Line Spacing**   This setting controls the space between the lines in a paragraph.

> **Before Paragraph**   This setting controls the space between this paragraph and the paragraph that comes before it.

> **After Paragraph**   This setting controls the space between this paragraph and the paragraph that comes after it.

TIP   **Lines or Points?**   The drop-down list box that appears to the right of each setting enables you to set the line spacing in lines or points. A line is the current line height (based on text size). A point is a unit commonly used to measure text. A point is approximately 1/72 of an inch.

4. Click **OK**.

Adding a WordArt Object

PowerPoint comes with an auxiliary program called WordArt that can help you create graphics text effects. To insert a WordArt object into a slide, perform the following steps:

1. In Slide view, display the slide on which you want to place the WordArt object.

2. Click the **WordArt** button on the Drawing toolbar (at the bottom of the screen). The WordArt Gallery dialog box appears, showing many samples of WordArt types.

3. Click the sample that best represents the WordArt type you want, and then click **OK**. The Edit WordArt Text dialog box appears (see Figure 10.4).

4. Choose a font and font size from the respective drop-down lists.

5. Type the text you want to use in the **Text** box (see Figure 10.4).

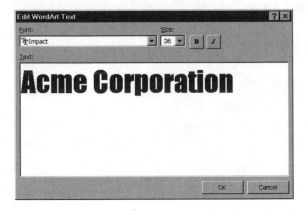

Figure 10.4 Enter the text, size, and font to be used.

6. Click **OK**, and PowerPoint creates the WordArt text on your slide, as shown in Figure 10.5.

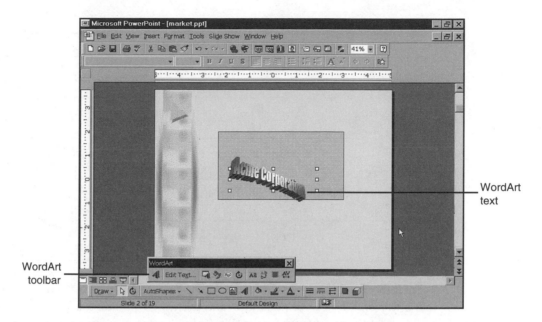

Figure 10.5   Finished WordArt on a slide, with the WordArt toolbar below it.

After you have created some WordArt, you have access to the WordArt toolbar, also shown in Figure 10.5. You can use it to modify your WordArt. Table 11.1 summarizes the buttons on that toolbar.

Table 10.1   Buttons on the WordArt Toolbar

Button	Description
	Creates a new WordArt object
Edit Text...	Edits the text, size, and font of the selected WordArt object
	Changes the type of the current WordArt object
	Changes the Line and Fill color
	Changes the WordArt shape

continues

463

Table 10.1   Continued

Button	Description
	Rotates the WordArt object
	Makes all the letters the same height
	Changes between vertical and horizontal text orientation
	Changes the text alignment
	Changes the spacing between letters

To edit the WordArt object, double-click it to display the WordArt toolbar and text entry box. Enter your changes, and then click outside the WordArt object. You can move the object by dragging its border, or you can resize it by dragging a handle.

In this lesson, you learned how to add text to a slide, change the text alignment and spacing, and add WordArt objects. In the next lesson, you will learn how to use tables, tabs, and indents to create columns and lists.

Creating Columns and Lists

In this lesson, you learn how to use tabs to create columns of text and how to use indents to create bulleted lists, numbered lists, and other types of lists.

Using Tabs to Create Columns

A presentation often uses tabbed columns to display information. For example, you may use tabs to create a three-column list like the one shown in Figure 11.1.

In addition to hardware products, we carry a varied line of software:

Business	Home	Education
WordPerfect	Quicken	Reader Rabbit 2
Microsoft Word	The New Print Shop	Oregon Trail
PowerPoint	Microsoft Works	BodyWorks
Excel	TurboTax	Where in the World is Carmen Sandiego?

Figure 11.1 You can use tabs to create a multi-column list.

In PowerPoint, you create multiple columns by using tab stops. To set the tabs for a multi-column list, perform the following steps:

1. Open the presentation and view the slide with which you want to work in Slide View.
2. Create a text box for the text as you learned in Lesson 10, "Adding Text to a Slide."
3. Click anywhere inside the text box for which you want to set the tabs.
4. If you already typed text inside the text box, select the text.

5. Select **View**, **Ruler** to display the ruler. By default, the ruler is not displayed.

6. Click the tab icon in the upper-left corner of the presentation window until it represents the type of tab you want to set:

Aligns the left end of the line against the tab stop.

Centers the text on the tab stop.

Aligns the right end of the line against the tab stop.

Aligns the tab stop on a period. This is called a decimal tab, and it's useful for aligning a column of numbers that uses decimal points.

7. Click in each place on the ruler where you want to set the selected type of tab stop (see Figure 11.2).

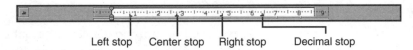

Left stop   Center stop   Right stop   Decimal stop

Figure 11.2 The ruler lets you enter and change tab stop settings.

8. Repeat steps 5 and 6 to set different types of tab stops in other positions.

9. To change the position of an existing tab stop, drag it on the ruler to the desired position. To delete an existing tab stop setting, drag it off the ruler.

10. (Optional) To turn off the ruler, select **View**, **Ruler**.

TIP **Don't Forget the Slide Master** Throughout this lesson, keep in mind that you can enter your changes on the Slide Master or on individual slides. If you change the Slide Master, the change affects all slides in the presentation. For details on displaying the Slide Master, see Lesson 7, "Changing a Presentation's Look."

Making a Bulleted List

When you enter new slides in Outline view, the default layout is a simple bulleted list. If you've done this (see Lesson 8, "Inserting, Deleting, and Copying Slides"), you've already created a bulleted list. However, you can also create a bulleted list yourself in a text box that you add to a slide, without relying on an AutoLayout. Follow these steps to change some regular text in a text box to a bulleted list:

1. Click inside the paragraph you want to transform into a bulleted list, or select one or more paragraphs.

2. Select **Format**, **Bullet**. The Bullet dialog box appears.

 TIP **Quick Bullets** To bypass the Format menu and Bullet dialog box, simply click the **Bullets** button on the Formatting toolbar to insert a bullet, or right-click and select **Bullet** from the shortcut menu. You can click the Bullet button again to remove the bullet.

3. Select the **Use a Bullet** check box to enable bullet use.

4. Click **OK**. PowerPoint transforms the selected text into a bulleted list. (If you press **Enter** at the end of a bulleted paragraph, the next paragraph starts with a bullet.)

 TIP **Moving a Bulleted Item** You can move an item in a bulleted list by clicking the item's bullet and then dragging the bullet up or down in the list.

Changing the Bullet Character

By default, whenever you click the Bullet button on the Formatting toolbar to insert a bullet, PowerPoint inserts a large dot for the bullet. However, you can change the appearance of the bullet at any time. These steps show you how:

1. Select the paragraph(s) in which you want to change the bullet character.

2. Select **Format**, **Bullet**. The Bullet dialog box appears (see Figure 11.3).

3. Click the **Bullets From** drop-down arrow and select the character set from which you want to choose a bullet. The dialog box displays the characters in the selected set.

 CAUTION **Which Character Set?** Each character set is nothing more than a font that is installed on your computer. Some fonts are better suited for bullets than others; open several and examine the characters each one contains. Wingdings is a good choice.

4. Click the character you want to use for the bullet, and PowerPoint shows it enlarged so that you can see it clearly (as shown in Figure 11.3).

467

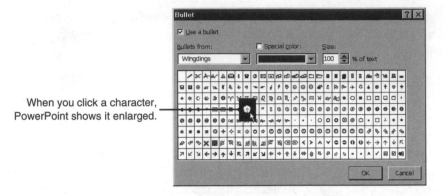

When you click a character,
PowerPoint shows it enlarged.

Figure 11.3   Choose a different bullet character.

5. To set the size of the bullet, use the up and down arrows to the right of the **Size** text box. Notice that the size of the bullet is not a fixed value—it is relative to the text around it.

6. To select a color for the bullet, click the **Special Color** drop-down arrow and select the color you want.

7. Click **OK**. PowerPoint changes the bullet for all selected paragraphs.

Using Indents to Create Lists

Indents enable you to move one or more lines of a paragraph in from the left margin, helping you draw attention to text, such as a quote. PowerPoint uses indents to create the bulleted lists you encountered in previous sections. You can use indents in any text object to create a similar list or your own custom list. To indent text, perform the following steps:

1. Select the text box that contains the text you want to indent.

2. If you've already typed text, select the text you want to indent.

3. If the ruler is not visible, select **View, Ruler**.

4. Drag one of the following indent markers to set the indents for the para-graph. (These indent markers appear on the ruler, as shown in Figure 11.4.)

Drag the top marker to indent the first line.

Drag the bottom marker to indent all subsequent lines.

Drag the box below the bottom marker to indent all the text.

Indent markers ——

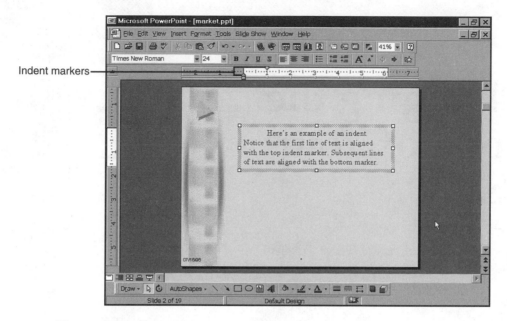

Figure 11.4   Drag the indent markers to indent your text.

5. (Optional) To turn off the ruler, select **View**, **Ruler**.

 You can create up to five levels of indents within a single text box. To add an indent level, click the **Demote** button on the Formatting toolbar or press **Tab** when the insertion point is at the beginning of the paragraph. A new set of indent markers appears on the ruler, showing the next level of indents. You can change these new indent settings as explained previously.

After you set your indents, you can create a numbered or bulleted list by performing the following steps:

1. Type a number and a period, or type the character you want to use for the bullet.

2. Press the **Tab** key to move to the second indent mark.

3. Type the text you want to use for this item. As you type, PowerPoint wraps the text to the second indent mark.

4. Repeat steps 1 through 3 for each additional item you add to the list.

In this lesson, you learned how to create columns with tabs, create lists with indents, and change the bullet character for bulleted lists. In the next lesson, you will learn how to change the style, size, and color of text.

469

Changing the Look of Your Text

In this lesson, you learn how to change the appearance of text by changing its font, style, size, and color.

Enhancing Your Text with the Font Dialog Box

You can enhance your text by using the Font dialog box or by using various tools on the Formatting toolbar. Use the Font dialog box if you want to add several enhancements to your text at one time. Use the Formatting toolbar to add one enhancement at a time.

 Fonts, Styles, and Effects In PowerPoint, a *font* is a family of text that has the same design or typeface (for example, Arial or Courier). A *style* is a standard enhancement, such as bold or italic. An *effect* is a special enhancement, such as shadow or underline.

You can change the font of existing text or of text you are about to type by performing the following steps:

1. To change the font of existing text, select the text first.
2. Choose **Format**, **Font**. The Font dialog box appears, as shown in Figure 12.1.

 Right-Click Quickly You can right-click the text and select **Font** from the shortcut menu instead of performing steps 1 and 2.

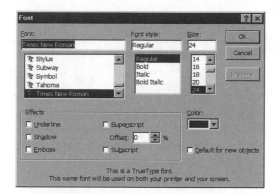

Figure 12.1 You can select a font from the Font dialog box.

3. In the **Font** list, select the font you want to use.

TrueType Fonts The "TT" next to some font names identifies those fonts as TrueType fonts. TrueType fonts are *scalable*, which means you can set them at any point size. When you save a presentation, you can choose to embed TrueType fonts so that you can display or print the font on any computer, whether or not the computer has that font installed.

4. From the **Font Style** list, select any style you want to apply to the text. (To remove styles from text, select **Regular**.)

5. From the **Size** list, select any size in the list, or type a size directly into the box. (With TrueType fonts, you can type any point size, even sizes that do not appear on the list.)

6. In the Effects group, select any special effects you want to add to the text, such as **Underline**, **Shadow**, or **Emboss**. You can also choose **Superscript** or **Subscript**, although they are less common.

7. To change the color of your text, click the **Color** drop-down arrow and click the desired color. (For more colors, click the **Other Color** option at the bottom of the list and select a color from the dialog box that appears.)

TIP **Changing the Background Color** Each presentation has its own color scheme, which includes background and text colors.

8. Click **OK** to apply the new look to your text. (If you selected text before styling it, the text appears in the new style. If you did not select text, any text you type appears in the new style.)

Title and Object Area Text If you change a font on an individual slide, the font change applies to that slide only. To change the font for all slides in the presentation, you need to change the font on the Slide Master. To change the Slide Master, select **View**, **Master**, **Slide Master**. Select a text area, and then perform the previous steps to change the look of the text on all slides.

Styling Text with the Formatting Toolbar

As shown in Figure 12.2, the Formatting toolbar contains several tools for changing the font, size, style, and color of text.

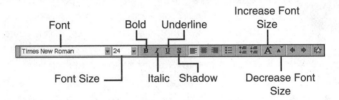

Figure 12.2 The Formatting toolbar contains several tools for styling text.

To use the tools, follow these steps:

1. To change the look of existing text, select the text.

2. To change fonts, open the **Font** drop-down list (refer to Figure 12.2) and click the desired font.

3. To change font size, open the **Font Size** drop-down list (shown in Figure 12.2) and click the desired size, or type a size directly into the box.

Incrementing the Type Size To quickly increase or decrease the text size to the next size up or down, click the **Increase Font Size** or **Decrease Font Size** button on the Formatting toolbar.

4. To add a style or effect to the text (bold, italic, underline, and / or shadow), click the appropriate button(s):

B Bold   **U** Underline

I Italic   **S** Shadow

Changing Font Color with the Drawing Toolbar

New Location for Font Color Button In earlier versions of PowerPoint, the Font Color button was on the Formatting toolbar instead of the Drawing toolbar.

The Font Color button on the Drawing toolbar (at the bottom of the screen) enables you to change the color of the selected text. The following steps show you how to use the Font Color button:

1. Select the text for which you want to change the color.

2. Click the **Font Color** drop-down arrow on the Drawing toolbar. A menu of options appears (see Figure 12.3).

3. Do one of the following:

- Click one of the colored blocks to change the font to one of the prechosen colors for the presentation design you're using.
- Click the **More Font Colors** button to display a Colors dialog box. Then click a color in that box and click **OK**.

TIP The drawing toolbar is not visible in Outline view.

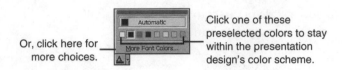

Or, click here for more choices.

Click one of these preselected colors to stay within the presentation design's color scheme.

Figure 12.3 When you click the arrow next to the Font Colors button, this menu of options appears.

Copying Text Formats

If your presentation contains text with a format you want to use, you can pick up the format from the existing text and apply it to other text. To copy text formats, perform the following steps:

1. Highlight the text with the format you want to use.

2. Click the **Format Painter** button on the toolbar. PowerPoint copies the formatting characteristics.

3. Drag across the text to which you want to apply the format. When you release the mouse button, PowerPoint applies the formats.

In this lesson, you learned how to change the appearance of text by changing its font, size, style, and color. You also learned how to copy text formats. In the next lesson, you will learn how to draw objects on a slide.

Adding Pictures, Sounds, and Video Clips

In this lesson, you learn how to add PowerPoint clip art, pictures from other graphics programs, sounds, and video clips to a slide.

Introducing the Clip Gallery

Microsoft has taken a bold new step in the Office 97 products (of which PowerPoint is one) in handling multiple media such as sounds, videos, and artwork. It's called the Clip Gallery (see Figure 13.1).

Figure 13.1 The Clip Gallery manages pictures, clip art, videos, and sounds, all in one convenient place.

Clip Art Clip art is a collection of previously created images or pictures that you can place on a slide.

You can open the Clip Gallery in any of these ways:

- Click the **Clip Art** button on the Standard toolbar.
- Select **Insert, Picture, Clip Art**.
- Select **Insert, Movies and Sounds, Sound from Gallery**.
- Select **Insert, Movies and Sounds, Movie from Gallery**.

All these methods open the Clip Gallery, but a different tab appears on top depending on which method you used. For example, if you use the Insert, Picture, Clip Art command, the Clip Art tab appears on top (as in Figure 13.1).

TIP **PowerPoint on the Web** Click the **Internet** icon in the corner of the Clip Gallery 3.0 dialog box to connect to Microsoft's Web site and download additional clip art.

Inserting a Clip on a Slide

Using the Clip Gallery, you can place any of the four types of objects on a slide: clip art, picture, sound, or movie. In the case of the latter two, you then click the object to activate it as necessary during the presentation. For example, you click the sound's icon to make it play. You also can set up sounds and movies to play automatically when a slide displays (which you'll learn to do later in this lesson).

To insert a clip onto a slide, follow these steps:

1. Open the Clip Gallery as described in the previous section.
2. Click the tab for the type of clip you want to insert.
3. Click the category that represents the type of clip you want.
4. Click the clip you want to use.
5. Click the **Insert** button.

The Clip I Want Isn't on the List! If you don't see the clip for which you're looking, click the **Import Clips** button. Then use the dialog box that appears to locate the clip and import it into the Clip Gallery. From then on, that image will be available on the Clip Gallery tab for its file type.

CAUTION

TIP **PowerPoint on the Web** Artwork, movies, and sounds can really add a lot to a PowerPoint presentation on the Web, but they also add to the size of the file—and consequently, to the time it will take a reader to download it. For this reason, try to be judicious in your use of media on presentations designed for Web use.

Inserting a Clip from a File

If you have a clip such as a bitmap image, sound file, or movie file stored on disk, you can quickly place it on a slide without using with the Clip Gallery. Just follow these steps:

1. Select the slide on which the image should be placed.

2. Select **Insert, Picture, From File**. The Insert Picture dialog box appears (see Figure 13.2).

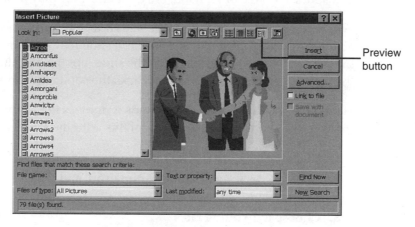

Figure 13.2 Use the Insert Picture dialog box to place any graphics image on a slide.

3. Select the picture you want to use. You can see a preview of the pictures in the Preview pane to the left of the file list. If the preview does not appear, click the **Preview** button (shown in Figure 13.2) to turn on the preview feature.

4. Click **Insert** to place the image on the slide.

If the picture is too big or too small, you can drag the selection handles (the small squares) around the edge of the image to resize it. (Hold down **Shift** to proportionally resize.) Refer to Lesson 14, "Positioning and Sizing Objects," for more details about resizing and cropping.

 TIP   **Movies and Sounds from Files**   You also can insert movies and sounds from files. Just select **Insert**, **Movies and Sounds** and then choose either **Movie from File** or **Sound from File**.

Choosing When Movies and Sounds Should Play

Slides are static for the most part: they appear, and then they sit there. Movies and sounds, on the other hand, are dynamic: they play at specific times.

When you place a movie or sound on a slide, by default the object does not activate until you click it. For example, a slide may contain a recorded narration that explains a particular graph on the slide, but the narration will not play until the person giving the presentation clicks the sound icon to activate it.

However, you may want some sounds or movies to play automatically at certain times in the presentation. You control this with the following procedure:

1. Click the object (the sound icon or movie image) on the slide.

2. Select **Slide Show**, **Custom Animation**, and the Custom Animation dialog box appears (see Figure 13.3).

3. Choose the **Timing** tab.

4. Click the **Animate** button to indicate that you want the sound or movie to play on the slide.

5. Click the **Automatically** button to indicate you want it to play without user intervention.

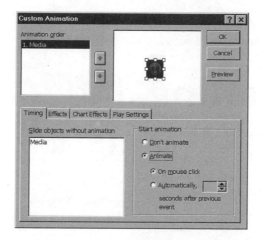

Figure 13.3   Use this dialog box to set when and how a sound or movie plays.

6. In the text box next to the **Automatically** control, enter the number of seconds that PowerPoint should pause after the previous event before playing the object.

 Previous Event?   If this is the only media clip on this slide, the previous event is the slide itself being displayed. If more than one media clip is on the slide, you can control the order in which they activate by switching their order in the Animation Order list in the Custom Animation dialog box (refer to Figure 13.3).

7. When you finish setting up your preferences, click **OK**.

 8. Switch to Slide Show view to test the slide, making sure you have set up the sound or animation to play when you want it to.

 TIP   **Continuous Play**   You can set a sound or animation to loop continuously by clicking the **Play Settings** tab and selecting the **More Options** button. Select both the **Loop Until Stopped** and **Rewind Movie When Done Playing** check boxes.

In this lesson, you learned how to add clip art images, pictures, sounds, and movies to your slides, and how to control when a movie or sound plays. In the next lesson, you will learn how to reposition and resize objects on a slide.

Positioning and Sizing Objects

In this lesson, you will learn how to select, copy, move, rotate, and resize objects on a slide.

As you may have already discovered, objects are the building blocks you use to create slides in PowerPoint. Objects include the shapes you draw, the graphs you create, the pictures you import, and the text you type. In this lesson and the next one, you will learn how to manipulate objects on your slides to create impressive presentations.

Selecting Objects

Before you can copy, move, rotate, or resize an object, you must first select the object. Change to Slide view, and use one of these methods to select one or more objects:

- To select a single object, click it. (If you click text, a frame appears around the text; click the frame to select the text object.)
- To select more than one object, hold down the **Shift** key and click each object. Handles appear around the selected objects, as shown in Figure 14.1.
- To deselect selected objects, click anywhere outside the selected objects.

TIP **Using the Selection Tool** The Selection tool on the Drawing toolbar enables you to quickly select a group of objects. Click the **Selection** tool and use the mouse pointer to drag a selection box around the objects you want to select. When you release the mouse button, PowerPoint selects the objects inside the box.

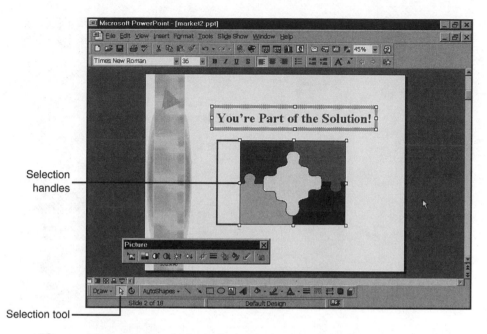

Figure 14.1   Handles indicate that objects are selected.

Working with Layers of Objects

As you place objects on-screen, they may start to overlap or stack up, making it difficult or impossible to select the objects in the lower layers. To move objects in layers, perform the following steps:

1. Click the object you want to move up or down in the stack.

2. Click the **Draw** button on the Drawing toolbar to open the Draw menu, and select **Order** (see Figure 14.2).

3. Select one of the following options:

> **Bring to Front** brings the object to the top of the stack.
>
> **Send to Back** sends the object to the bottom of the stack.
>
> **Bring Forward** brings the object up one layer.
>
> **Send Backward** sends the object back one layer.

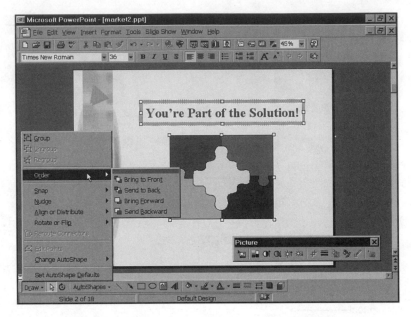

Figure 14.2 Use the Draw menu on the Drawing toolbar to change the layer on which a graphic appears on your slide.

Grouping and Ungrouping Objects

Each object you draw acts as an individual object. However, sometimes you might want two or more objects to act as a group. For example, you may want to make the lines of several objects the same thickness, or you may want to move several objects together.

If you want to treat two or more objects as a group, perform the following steps:

1. Select the objects you want to group. Remember, to select more than one object, hold down the **Ctrl** key and click each one.

2. Click the **Draw** button on the Drawing toolbar to open the Draw menu. Then select **Group**.

3. To ungroup the objects later, select any object in the group and select **Draw**, **Ungroup**.

Cutting, Copying, and Pasting Objects

You can cut, copy, and paste objects on a slide to rearrange the objects or to use the objects to create a picture. When you cut an object, PowerPoint removes the object from the slide and places it in a temporary holding area called the Windows Clipboard. When you copy an object, the original object remains on the slide, and PowerPoint places a copy of it on the Clipboard. In either case, you can then paste the object from the Clipboard onto the current slide or another slide.

To cut or copy an object, perform the following steps:

1. Switch to Slide view and select the object(s) you want to cut (move) or copy.

2. Right-click the selected object and choose **Cut** or **Copy** from the shortcut menu. (Or, select the **Edit**, **Cut** or **Edit**, **Copy** command, or click the **Cut** or **Copy** button on the Standard toolbar.)

3. Display the slide on which you want to place the cut or copied object(s). You can open a different Windows program, to paste it into, if you prefer.

4. Select **Edit**, **Paste** or click the **Paste** button on the Standard toolbar. PowerPoint pastes the object(s) on the slide.

 TIP **Keyboard Shortcuts** You can press **Ctrl+X** to cut, **Ctrl+C** to copy, and **Ctrl+V** to paste instead of using the toolbar buttons or the menu.

5. Move the mouse pointer over any of the pasted objects, hold down the mouse button, and drag the objects to the location you want them.

6. Release the mouse button.

 TIP **Deleting an Object** To remove an object without placing it on the Clipboard, select the object, and then press the **Delete** key or select **Edit**, **Clear**.

 TIP **Dragging and Dropping Objects** The quickest way to copy or move objects is to drag-and-drop them. Select the objects you want to move, position the mouse pointer over any of the selected objects, press and hold the mouse button, and drag the objects to the location you want them. To copy the objects, hold down the **Ctrl** key while dragging.

Rotating an Object

The Rotate tools enable you to revolve an object around a center point. To rotate an object to your own specifications, using Free Rotate, do the following:

1. Switch to Slide view and click the object you want to rotate.

2. Click the **Free Rotate** tool on the Drawing toolbar. The selection handles on the centering line change to circles.

3. Press and hold the mouse button and drag the circular handle until the object is in the position you want (see Figure 14.3).

4. Release the mouse button.

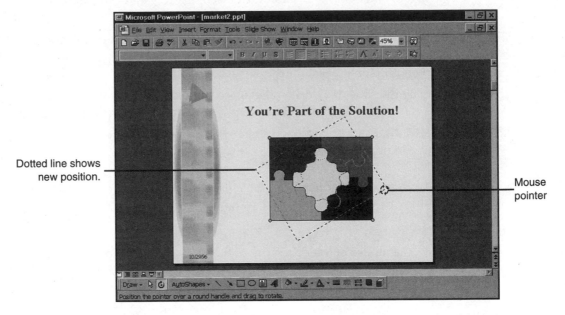

Dotted line shows new position.

Mouse pointer

Figure 14.3 You can drag the circular selection handle to rotate the object.

TIP **Other Rotate Options** The Draw menu (on the Drawing toolbar, shown in Figure 14.2) contains a Rotate/Flip submenu that provides additional options for rotating objects. You can flip an object 90 degrees left or right, or flip the object over on the centering line to create a mirrored image of it.

Resizing Objects

Sometimes an object you create or import is not the right size for your slide presentation. You can resize the object by performing these steps:

1. Select the object to resize. Selection handles appear.

2. Drag one of the handles (the squares that surround the object) until the object is the desired size:

- Drag a corner handle to change both the height and width of an object. PowerPoint retains the object's relative dimensions.

- Drag a side, top, or bottom handle to change the height or width alone.

- Hold down the **Ctrl** key while dragging to resize from the center of the picture.

3. Release the mouse button, and PowerPoint resizes the object (see Figure 14.4).

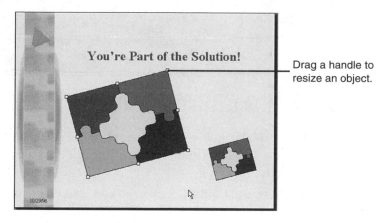

Drag a handle to resize an object.

Figure 14.4 Before and after resizing an object.

Cropping a Picture

Besides resizing a picture, you can crop it. That is, you can trim a side or corner of the picture to remove an element from it or to cut off some white space. To crop a picture, perform the following steps:

1. Click the picture you want to crop.

2. If the Picture toolbar isn't shown, right-click the picture and select **Show Picture Toolbar** from the menu.

3. Click the **Crop** button on the Picture toolbar. The mouse pointer turns into a cropping tool (see Figure 14.5).

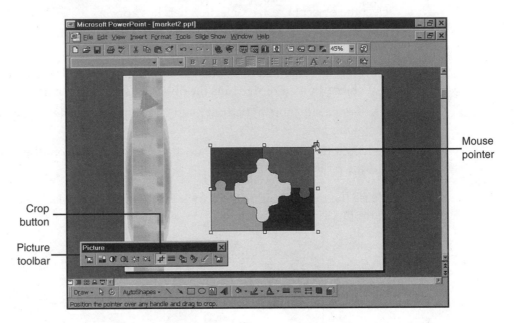

Figure 14.5 Use the cropping tool to chop off a section of the picture.

4. Move the mouse pointer over one of the handles. (Use a corner handle to crop two sides at once. Use a side, top, or bottom handle to crop only one side.)

5. Press and hold the mouse button, and drag the pointer until the crop lines are where you want them.

6. Release the mouse button, and the cropped section disappears.

 TIP **Uncropping** You can uncrop a picture immediately after cropping it by selecting **Edit**, **Undo** or by clicking the **Undo** button on the toolbar. You can also uncrop at any time by performing the previous steps and dragging the selected handle in the opposite direction you dragged it for cropping.

In this lesson, you learned how to select, copy, move, rotate, and resize an object on a slide. In the next lesson, you will learn how to change the lines and colors of an object.

Viewing and Enhancing a Slide Show

In this lesson, you learn how to view a slide show on-screen, make basic movements within a presentation, and create action buttons that enable you (or another user) to control the action.

Before you take your presentation "on the road" to show to your intended audience, you should run through it several times on your own computer, checking that all the slides are in the right order.

Viewing an On-Screen Slide Show

You can preview a slide show at any time to see how the show looks in real life. To view a slide show, perform the following steps:

1. Open the presentation you want to view.

2. Click the **Slide Show** button at the bottom of the presentation window. The first slide in the presentation appears full-screen.

3. To display the next or previous slide, do one of the following:

   - To display the next slide, click the left mouse button, or press the **Page Down** key, or press the right arrow or down arrow key.

   - To display the previous slide, click the right mouse button, or press the **Page Up** key, or press the left arrow or up arrow key.

   - To quit the slide show, press the **Esc** key.

 TIP **Start the Show!** Clicking the **Slide Show** button is the fastest way to start a slide show. However, you can also start a slide show by selecting **View**, **Slide Show** or by selecting **Slide Show**, **View Show**.

Controlling the Slide Show

While you view a slide show, you can do more than just move from slide to slide. When you move your mouse, notice the triangle in a box at the bottom left corner of the slide show (see Figure 15.1). Click that button, and PowerPoint displays a pop-up menu that contains commands you can use as you actually give the presentation. Those commands are outlined in the following list:

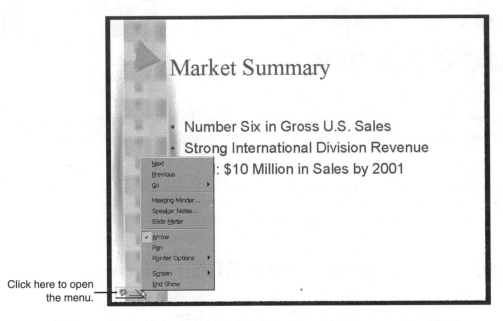

Figure 15.1 You can control the slide show while you present it with this menu.

- The **Next** and **Previous** commands enable you to move from slide to slide. (It's easier to change slides if you use other methods, though.)
- Choose **Go**, **Slide Navigator** to bring up a dialog box listing every slide in the presentation. You can jump quickly to any slide with it. You can also jump to a slide with a specific title (if you know it) by selecting **Go**, **Title** and choosing the title from the list.
- Click **Meeting Minder** to bring up a window where you can take notes as the meeting associated with your presentation progresses.
- Choose **Speaker Notes** to view your notes for the slide.
- Choose **Slide Meter** to open a dialog box that enables you to control the timing between slides. (More about timing will be presented shortly.)

- **Arrow** and **Pen** are mouse options; Arrow is the default. Your mouse can serve as an arrow to point out parts of the slide, or it can serve as a pen to write comments on the slide or circle key areas as you give your presentation. Keep in mind, however, that it is very difficult to write legibly if you use an ordinary mouse or trackball.

- **Pointer Options** enables you to choose a color for the pen and indicate whether to display or hide the pointer.

- **Screen** opens a submenu that enables you to pause the show, blank the screen, and erase any pen marks you made on the slide.

- **End Show** takes you back to PowerPoint's slide editing window.

Setting Slide Show Options

Depending on the type of show you're presenting, you may find it useful to make some fine adjustments to the way the show runs, such as making it run in a window (the default is full-screen) or showing only certain slides. You'll find these controls and more in the Set Up Show dialog box (shown in Figure 15.2). To open it, choose **Slide Show, Set Up Show.**

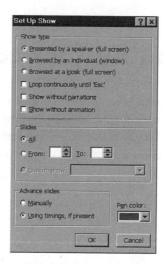

Figure 15.2 Use the Set Up Show dialog box to give PowerPoint instructions about how to present your slide show.

In the Set Up Show dialog box, you can do the following:

- Choose in which medium the presentation is going to be shown. Your choices are Presented by a Speaker (Full Screen), Browsed by an Individual (Window), and Browsed at a Kiosk (Full Screen).

- Choose whether to loop the slide show continuously or just show it once. You might want to loop it continuously if it were running unaided at a kiosk at a trade show, for instance.

- Show without narration, if you have created any. (You'll learn about narration later in this lesson.)

- Show without animation, if you have added any.

- Show all the slides or a range of them (which you enter in the From and To boxes).

- Choose a custom show if you have created one. (To create a custom show, such as one that contains a subset of the main show's slides, select **Slide Show**, **Custom Show**.)

- Choose whether to advance slides manually or by using timings you set up.

- Choose a pen color.

Adding Action Buttons to Slides

In the preceding section, you saw how the Set Up Show dialog box enables you to choose between automatic and manual advance. In most cases, you will want to have the slides advance manually because different people read at different speeds. Even if you are creating a presentation for a speaker to give, you will usually want manual advancing because you can't anticipate when the speaker may need extra time to answer a question.

As you saw at the beginning of this lesson, one way to advance or go back in a slide show is to press the **Page Down** key or **Page Up** key on the keyboard. This simple method works fine, except for two things:

- In a kiosk-type setting, you may not want the audience to have access to the computer's keyboard.

- This method simply plods from slide to slide, with no opportunity to jump to special slides or quickly jump to the beginning or end.

A new feature that solves this problem in PowerPoint 97 is the capability of adding action buttons to slides. Action buttons are like controls on an audio CD player: They let you jump to any slide quickly, go back, go forward, or even stop the presentation.

 TIP **Same Controls on All Slides?** If you want to add the same action buttons to all slides in the presentation, add the action buttons to the Slide Master. To display the Slide Master, select **View**, **Master**, **Slide Master**.

To add an action button to a slide, follow these steps:

1. Display the slide in Slide view.
2. Select **Slide Show**, **Action Buttons**, and then pick a button from the palette that appears next to the command (see Figure 15.3). For instance, if you want to create a button that advances to the next slide, you might choose the button with the arrow pointing to the right.

 CAUTION **Which Button Should I Choose?** Choose any button you like; at this point you are only choosing a picture to show on the button, not any particular function for it. However, you might consider the action that you want the button to perform, and then pick a button picture that matches it well.

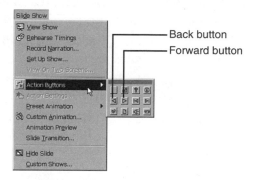

Figure 15.3 Choose the button you think your reader will most strongly identify with the action you're going to assign to it.

3. Your mouse pointer turns into a crosshair. Drag to draw a box on the slide where you want the button to appear. (You can resize it later if you want, just as you resized graphics in Lesson 14, "Positioning and Sizing Objects.") PowerPoint draws the button on the slide and opens the Action Settings dialog box (see Figure 15.4).

491

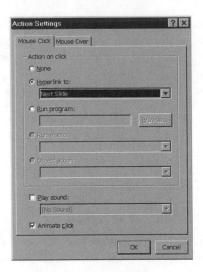

Figure 15.4 You can control the way one slide transitions to the next.

4. Choose the type of action you want to happen when the user clicks the button. Most of the time you will choose **Hyperlink To**. Your complete list of choices includes the following:

- **None**
- **Hyperlink To** This can be a slide, an Internet hyperlink, a document on your computer—just about anything.
- **Run Program** You can choose to have a program start when the user clicks the button.
- **Run Macro** If you have recorded a macro, you can have the user run it from this button.
- **Object Action** If you have embedded (OLE) objects in the presentation, you can have PowerPoint activate one when this button is clicked.

5. Open the drop-down list for the type of action you chose and select the exact action (such as **Next Slide**). Or, if you chose **Run Program**, click the **Browse** button and locate the program you want to run.

6. (Optional) If you want a sound to play when the user clicks the button, select the **Play Sound** check box and choose a sound from its drop-down list.

7. (Optional) If you want the button to look animated when the user clicks it (a nice little extra), leave the **Animate Click** check box marked.

8. Click **OK**, and your button appears on the slide.

9. View the presentation (as you learned at the beginning of this lesson) to try out the button.

Figure 15.5 shows three buttons added to a slide. Actually, they were added to the Slide Master, so the same buttons appear on each slide in the presentation. This kind of consistency gives the reader a feeling of comfort and control.

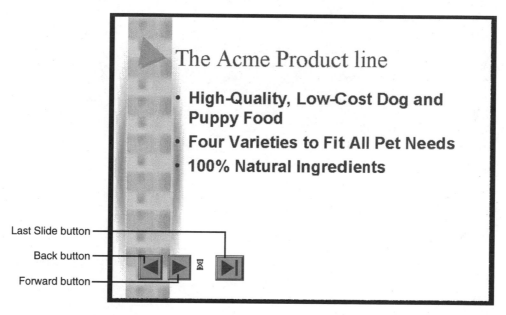

Figure 15.5 labels, top to bottom: Last Slide button, Back button, Forward button

The Acme Product line

- **High-Quality, Low-Cost Dog and Puppy Food**
- **Four Varieties to Fit All Pet Needs**
- **100% Natural Ingredients**

Figure 15.5 These control buttons display various slides in the presentation.

No Controls on Slide 1 When you add action buttons to the Slide Master, they appear on every slide except the first one in the presentation. If you want action buttons on the first slide, you must specifically add them to that slide.

CAUTION

Don't Group Each action button must be an independent object on the slide. If you group them together, they won't work properly.

CAUTION

In this lesson, you learned how to display a slide presentation on-screen, move between slides, and create buttons on the slides to control the movement. In the next lesson, you'll learn how PowerPoint makes it easy to publish your presentations on the World Wide Web or on your corporate intranet.

Creating Slide Shows for Internet Use

In this lesson, you learn how PowerPoint makes it easy to publish your presentations on the World Wide Web or your corporate intranet.

The World Wide Web is the most popular and graphical component of the Internet. Many businesses maintain Web sites containing information about their products and services for public reading. Still other businesses maintain an internal version of the Web that's strictly for employee use, and they use the company's local area network to make it available to its staff. These are called *intranets*.

Sooner or later, you may be asked to prepare a PowerPoint presentation for use on a Web site or an intranet. Don't panic! It's easier than it sounds.

Web Presentation Designs

You may have noticed in Lesson 2, "Creating a New Presentation," that when you created a new presentation, some of the presentation design templates had Online in their names. Those templates are made especially for creating presentations that will be displayed online (on the Web or an intranet) and contain special controls. The presentation shown in Figure 16.1, for example, came ready-made with navigation buttons at the bottom of each slide—you don't have to create these buttons manually. PowerPoint includes an online version of almost every template.

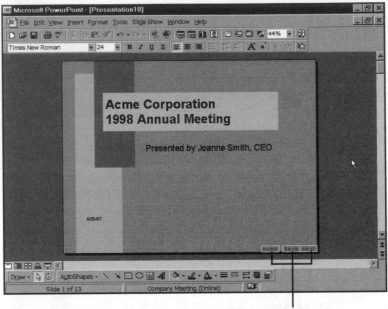

Web navigation buttons are
part of this template.

Figure 16.1 Basing your presentation on one of the online presentation design templates can give you a big head start.

Adding URL Hyperlinks

Remember in Lesson 15 when you added action buttons to a slide? The action buttons moved the presentation from slide to slide. Well, you can also assign links to Web addresses (URLs) to a button. For instance, you might have a button that takes you to your company's home page (the top page in your company's Internet site) at the bottom of every slide.

Say you've started a new presentation based on a design template for online use. It already has buttons for Previous and Next. You want to set the Home button to jump to your Web site's home page when clicked (**http://www.mysite.com**). Perform the following steps:

1. Choose **View**, **Master**, **Slide Master**. (The navigation buttons are on the Slide Master.)
2. Click the **Home** button so that selection handles appear around it.

3. Choose **Slide Show, Action Settings**. The Action Settings dialog box appears.

4. Click the **Hyperlink To** button.

5. Open the **Hyperlink To** drop-down list and select **URL** (see Figure 16.2).

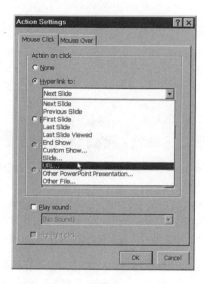

Figure 16.2 Choose URL from the Hyperlink To drop-down list.

6. In the dialog box that appears, type the URL you want to link to (for example, **http://www.mysite.com**) (see Figure 16.3).

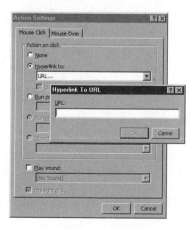

Figure 16.3 Enter the URL that you want to hyperlink to when the user clicks the button.

7. Click **OK** twice to close both dialog boxes.

Now it's time to test your hyperlink. View the slide in **Slide Show** view, and click the button with your mouse. Your Web browser should start and the selected URL should load in it, provided your Internet connection is active.

 TIP **Make Your Own Buttons** You don't have to rely on the template creating the buttons for you; you can create your own action buttons, as you learned in Lesson 15. To create a custom button and type text on it, select the blank button and then type in the button after you create it.

Saving a Presentation in HTML Format

A new feature in PowerPoint 97 is the capability to save files in HTML format. This comes in handy because it turns your presentations into documents that can be displayed in any Web browser program, without any help from the PowerPoint application. Because all World Wide Web users have Web browser programs, no one need miss out on your presentation.

The downside, of course, is that the translation is not perfect. Your presentation may not look exactly the same in HTML format as it did in PowerPoint itself. But all the text will be there, and some of the formatting.

To save a file in HTML format, follow these steps:

1. Choose **File, Save As HTML**. The **Save As HTML Wizard** opens to walk you through the process. Click **Next** to begin.

2. Choose an existing layout from the **Load Existing Layout** list, or leave the **New Layout** button selected. (You don't have any choice if you haven't created any layouts yet.) Then click **Next**.

3. Choose a page style: **Standard** or **Browser frames** (see Figure 16.4), and then click **Next**.

   Standard is a simple, one-pane view that will display correctly in almost all browsers.

   Browser frames is fancier but might not display correctly unless the user viewing the presentation has a browser that supports frames. (The last few versions of both Netscape Navigator and Microsoft Internet Explorer both accept frames.)

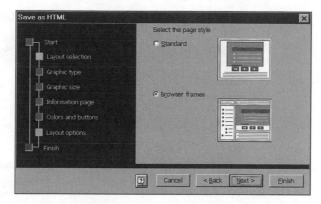

Figure 16.4 Choose between Standard and Browser frames layouts.

4. Choose a graphic type for your graphics to be exported to, and then click **Next** to continue.

   GIF and JPEG are equally acceptable standard formats for graphics. GIF is more common, but JPEG is smaller. These formats do not support animation, so any animation you have assigned will be lost.

   PowerPoint Animation format requires users to download a special PowerPoint viewer, but it ensures that your animations and effects will remain true to your original planning.

5. Choose a screen size for which your presentation should be optimized. Choosing 640×480 has long been the standard in personal computers, but lately many people have been switching to 800×600 resolution. Then click **Next**.

6. Where prompted, enter your e-mail address or your Web page address. These will be available to your users as they view your presentation. Then click **Next**.

7. Click **User Browser Colors** to go with the users' defaults, or click **Custom Colors** and choose your own. Then click **Next** to continue.

8. Click the option button next to the button style you want (see Figure 16.5) and then click **Next**.

9. Choose the additional options for the layout you chose.

   If you are using Standard layout, a screen appears for you to choose the button placement (see Figure 16.6). Click the button you want and then click **Next**.

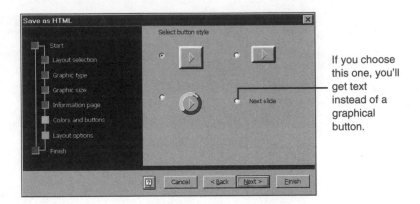

Figure 16.5 Choose the button style you want.

If you are using a Browser frames layout, click the Include Slide Notes in Pages check box if you want the slide notes to be available to the audience. Then click Next.

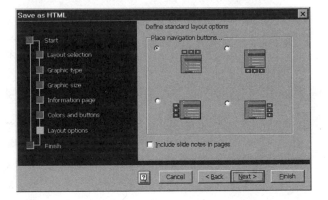

Figure 16.6 With a Standard layout, you can choose where to put the navigation buttons.

10. In the **Folder** text box, enter the folder in which you want to store your converted HTML documents. The default is \My Documents. Then click **Next**.

11. Click the **Finish** button to complete the process. A dialog box appears asking for a name for these settings, in case you want to reuse them in the future. Enter a name and click **Save**. From now on, that name will be

available at step 2 in the list of layouts. If you don't want to save the settings, click **Don't Save**.

12. Wait for PowerPoint to save your presentation. When you see a message **"The presentation was successfully saved as HTML,"** click **OK**.

After you have saved a presentation in HTML format, you must copy it to the server on which you want to make it available. If you use a modem to connect to an Internet service provider, establish your modem connection and then use the Web Publishing Wizard to upload the files to the appropriate directory on the server. If you use a LAN or intranet, consult your system administrator to find out where to put the files.

PowerPoint Viewers

PowerPoint content can be provided to Web users in two ways. One way is to save the presentation in pure HTML format. (That's what you did in the preceding steps, unless you chose PowerPoint Animation in step 4.) The PowerPoint file becomes a set of generic HTML files that are viewable in almost any Web browser, and the user's computer does not require PowerPoint to display them. With this method, you lose your animations and transitions, however, so a presentation that relies heavily on them will not be effective when presented this way.

The other way is to copy the PowerPoint presentation in its native format to the Web server and let the readers access it as a PowerPoint presentation. This is good because it preserves all your animations and transitions, but it requires that all your readers have a copy of PowerPoint installed.

A partial solution for this situation is to provide your audience with a PowerPoint viewer program. This program is a *runtime* version of PowerPoint, containing just enough of the right stuff to view your presentation on-screen. The reader can't make any changes to the presentation; it's like being permanently in Slide Show view.

TIP   **Get the PowerPoint Viewer**   You can get the PowerPoint viewer directly from Microsoft's Web site. Just visit **http://www.microsoft.com/mspowerpoint/Internet/Viewer**.

The PowerPoint Viewer is free and freely distributed, so you can provide a copy to all your users on your intranet, or you can provide a link to the viewer on your company's Web site.

TIP   **PowerPoint Plug-Ins**   If you use Netscape as your primary Web browser, you can download a variety of plug-ins for it that enable you to view PowerPoint presentations without leaving the Netscape window.

In this lesson, you learned about PowerPoint's capabilities for helping you present your slides on the Web.

Outlook

Starting and
Exiting Outlook

In this lesson, you learn to start and exit Outlook.

What Is Outlook?

Outlook is a *personal information manager (PIM)*. It lets you send and receive
e-mail, both over a local area network and over the Internet, and it helps you
maintain a calendar of appointments. Outlook also organizes your to-do list,
keeps a database of names and addresses, and keeps track of all the files you
open and work with in other Office 97 programs. It's like having a great personal secretary!

TIP **Outlook Express** Outlook is different from Outlook Express, a program that
comes with Internet Explorer 4.0. Outlook Express is a pared-down version of
Outlook that only manages e-mail and reads Internet newsgroups.

This section of the book covers the full version of Outlook 97, which comes with
Microsoft Office 97 or can be purchased as a standalone product.

Installing the Outlook Patches

Microsoft provides several free updates for Outlook 97 through its Web site that adds several new features—including a Message Preview pane (which you will see later in this lesson). The figures in this section of the book show Outlook with these patches installed.

If you have Internet access, you may want to download and install these patches now, before you begin working with Outlook. That way you will not get confused by having a different version of the program than is shown in this book. Follow these steps to download and install the patches.

1. Start your Internet connection (if needed) and start Internet Explorer. Refer to Lesson 16, "Using Internet Explorer," in Part 1, "Windows," of this book if you need help.

2. Using Internet Explorer, go to this address: **http://www.microsoft.com/ OfficeFreeStuff/Outlook/**.

3. Click the **Outlook 3-Pane Extension** hyperlink. A box appears asking what you want to do with the file.

4. Click **Run This Program From Its Current Location** and then click **OK**.

5. Wait for the patch to be downloaded.

6. If you see a Security Warning, click **Yes** to allow the installation.

7. When you see a message that the program will install the patch, asking whether you want to continue, click **Yes**.

8. Read the license agreement, and click **Yes**.

9. When the patch installation is complete (it takes only a moment), a dialog box appears telling you that the patch is installed. Click **OK**.

10. In Internet Explorer, click the **Internet Mail Enhancement Patch Final Release** hyperlink. A box appears asking what you want to do with the file.

11. Repeat steps 4 through 9 to install this patch.

12. In Internet Explorer, scroll through the list of available Outlook patches, and download and install any that you think you may need. (You need only the two patches you just installed for your screen to match the figures in this book.)

13. When you are finished, exit Internet Explorer and disconnect your Internet connection if needed.

Starting Outlook

You start Outlook from the Windows desktop. After starting the program, you can leave it open on your screen, or you can minimize it (which keeps the program running, but out of your way). Either way, you can access it at any time during your workday.

To start Microsoft Outlook, follow these steps:

1. From the Windows desktop, click the **Start** button and choose **Programs**, **Microsoft Outlook**. (If you have customized your Start menu, Outlook may appear within a folder, such as a Microsoft Office folder on the Programs menu.) Or if you have one, you can double-click the shortcut icon on the desktop.

2. If the Choose Profile dialog box appears, click **OK** to accept the default profile and open Microsoft Outlook, or choose the profile you want from the drop-down list. Figure 1.1 shows the Outlook screen that appears. (In Windows NT, Outlook cannot detect an existing e-mail provider. The user is prompted to set up the profile. If you need help, see your system administrator.)

Profile   Information about you and your communications services is created automatically when you install Outlook. The profile includes your name, user ID, post office, and some other information. If there is more than one person who uses this computer, there may be more than one profile on the list.

3. If the Office Assistant Welcome to Microsoft Outlook box appears, click **OK**. (See Appendix B, "Using the Office 97 Help System," for more information about the Office Assistant.)

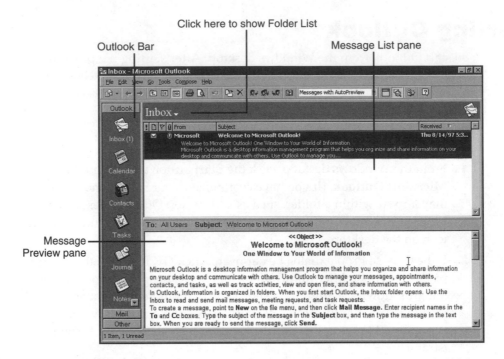

Figure 1.1   The Outlook screen is divided into several panes, each with its own function.

Understanding the Screen

You learn about Outlook's controls that you see on-screen in Lesson 2, "Using Outlook's Tools," but here is a quick preview of the screen you see in Figure 1.1.

When viewing the Inbox, which you see by default when you start Outlook, the screen is divided into two main panes. The top half is the message list. A list of all messages you have received appears here. Below the Message List pane is the Message Preview pane. The selected message from the message list appears here. You can read the entire message from the Preview pane by scrolling through (using the scroll bar), or you can open the message in its own window and read it that way, as you learn in Lesson 3, "Working with Incoming Mail."

TIP   **Controlling the Preview Area** If you have the 3-Pane Message Preview patch installed, you have a button on the toolbar that toggles on/off the message preview area.

Along the left side of the Outlook window is the Outlook Bar. It contains icons for the various views you can display. The Inbox is only one view of many, as you'll see in Lesson 2, "Using Outlook's Tools," where the program's components are explained.

TIP **Message Preview?** You will not have this unless you have downloaded the 3-Pane Message Preview patch from the Microsoft Web site, as explained earlier in this lesson.

In addition to the special Outlook controls shown in Figure 1.1, Outlook has all the standard features found in other Office 97 programs: a Status bar, drop-down menus, window controls, and so on. You can learn more about these generic Windows controls in Part 1, "Windows" of this book.

Outlook, like other Office programs, also has a toolbar of buttons across the top of the screen. You can see it in Figure 1.1. The buttons available on this toolbar change depending on what you're doing; they're different, for example, when you're composing an e-mail message than when you're scheduling appointments on your calendar. Wherever one of these buttons comes in handy, you'll see it alongside the text , as you did with the Preview button earlier in this lesson.

 TIP **Finding a Toolbar Button's Purpose** As you may already know from working with other Office 97 programs, you can hold the mouse pointer over any toolbar button to view a description of the tool's function.

Exiting Outlook

When you're finished with Outlook, you can close the program in a couple of different ways. To close Outlook, do one of the following:

- Choose **File**, **Exit** (to remain connected to the mail program)
- Choose **File**, **Exit and Log Off** (to disconnect from the mail program)
- Double-click the application's **Control-menu** button
- Click the application's **Control-menu** button and choose **Close**
- Press **Alt+F4**
- Click the **Close (x)** button at the right end of Outlook's title bar

If you receive lots of e-mail throughout the day and want to respond to it promptly, you may not want to exit Outlook; instead you may want to minimize its window and keep it running. That way you can check your e-mail without having to restart Outlook each time.

In this lesson, you learned to start and exit Outlook. In the next lesson, you learn about Outlook's tools and controls.

Using Outlook's Tools

In this lesson, you learn to change views in Outlook, use the Outlook Bar, and use the Folder List.

Using the Outlook Bar

Outlook's components are organized by folders, and each folder appears as an icon on the Outlook Bar, as well as in the Folder List. There is a folder for your incoming e-mail (Inbox), a folder for the calendar, and so on. The icons in the Outlook Bar represent all the folders available to you and provide shortcuts to the contents of those folders. You can click a folder on the Outlook Bar to quickly display that folder's contents in the right pane. Figure 2.1 shows the Outlook Bar.

Three groups are within the Outlook Bar: Outlook, Mail, and Other. Each group contains related folders in which you can work. The Outlook group contains folders for working with different features in Outlook, such as the Inbox, Calendar, and Tasks. The Mail group contains folders for organizing and managing your e-mail and the Other group contains folders on your computer for working outside of Outlook. To switch from one group to another, click the **Outlook**, **Mail**, or **Other** button in the Outlook Bar. The Outlook group is displayed by default.

Selected folder   Contents of a selected folder (Inbox)

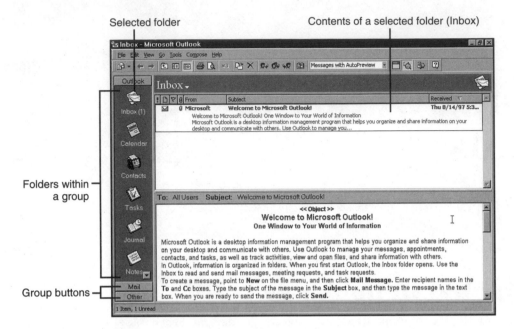

Folders within
a group

Group buttons

Figure 2.1 Use the Outlook Bar to view various items in your work.

The Outlook Group Folders

Outlook's group folders on the Outlook Bar enable you to access your work in Outlook, including your e-mail messages, appointments, and address list. Table 2.1 describes each of the folders within the Outlook group.

Table 2.1 Outlook Group Folders

Folder	Description
Inbox	Includes messages you send and receive via e-mail
Calendar	Contains your appointments, events, and scheduled meetings
Contacts	Lists names and addresses of the people with whom you communicate
Tasks	Includes any tasks you have on your to-do list
Journal	Contains all journal entries, such as telephone logs and meeting notes
Notes	Lists notes you write to yourself or to others
Deleted Items	Includes any items you delete from other folders

The Mail Group Folders

The Mail group folders provide a method of organizing your incoming and outgoing e-mail messages. Table 2.2 describes each folder in the Mail group.

Table 2.2 Mail Group Folders

Folder	Description
Inbox	Contains all received messages
Sent Items	Stores all messages you've sent
Outbox	Contains messages to be sent
Deleted Items	Holds any deleted mail messages

The Other Group Folders

The Other group contains folders that are on your computer but not within Outlook—My Computer, My Documents, and Favorites. This enables you to access a document or information in any of those areas so that you can attach it to a message, add notes to it, or otherwise use it in Outlook.

With My Computer, for example, you can view the contents of both hard and floppy disks, CD-ROM drives, and so on (see Figure 2.2). Double-click a drive in the window to view its folders and files. Double-click a folder to view its contents as well, then you can attach files to messages or otherwise use the files on your hard drive with the Outlook features.

 TIP **Moving On Up** Use the Up One Level toolbar button to return to a folder or drive after you've double-clicked to expand it and view its contents.

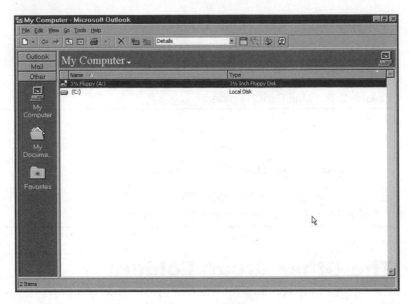

Figure 2.2   View your entire system through the My Computer folder in Outlook.

Using the Folder List

Outlook provides another method of viewing the folders within Outlook and your system besides the Outlook Bar—the Folder List. The Folder List displays the folders within any of the three groups (Outlook, Mail, or Other). From the list, you can select the folder you want to view.

To use the Folder List, first select the group you want to view from the Outlook Bar (click the Group button). Then click the **Folder List** button to display the list (see Figure 2.3).

Choose any folder from the list, and its contents appear in the list on the right. If you display another folder in the list on the right, double-click it to display its contents.

Click here to
display the
Folder List

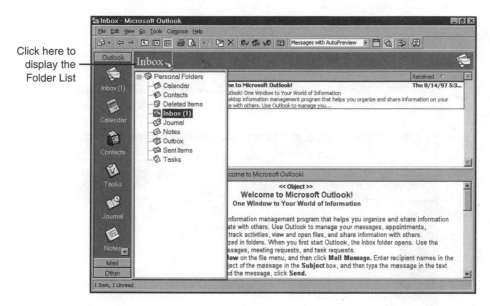

Figure 2.3 The Folder List shows all folders in the group you selected.

Changing Views

In Outlook, views give you different ways to look at the same information in a folder. Each view presents the information in a different format and organization so that you can get the most from the program.

Each folder has its own view types available; for example, the Inbox has the choices Messages, Messages with AutoPreview, By Message Flag, and Last Seven Days. The Calendar has the choices Day/Week/Month, Active Appointments, and Events. You will see examples of each folder's view types throughout Part 5.

To change a view, open the **Current View** drop-down list on the toolbar, as shown in Figure 2.4, and choose the view you want.

> **TIP** **Looking at the Inbox** The default view for your Inbox is called Messages
> with AutoPreview. In it, you see the first few lines of the message directly
> underneath the message information on the message list, as shown in Figure
> 2.4. AutoPreview is especially handy if you do not have the updates to Outlook
> 97 that enable you to see a message preview pane. (See the first lesson in this
> section to learn how you can get free updates for your copy of Outlook 97.)

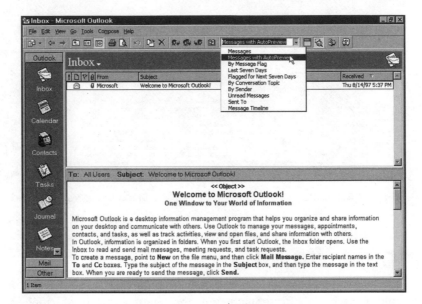

Figure 2.4 Select a view to change the format of the information.

In this lesson, you learned to change views in Outlook, use the Outlook Bar, and
use the Folder List. In the next lesson, you learn to work with incoming mail.

Working with Incoming Mail

In this lesson, you learn to read your mail, save an attachment, answer mail, and close a message.

Reading Mail

Each time you open Outlook, your Inbox folder appears (by default), and any new messages you've received are waiting for you (see Figure 3.1). As you can see in this figure, the Inbox provides important information about each message. For example, two of the messages have attachments, and some have Low or High priority flags. You learn about priorities and attachments in Lesson 7, "Setting Mail Options." In addition, the Status bar at the bottom of the Inbox window indicates how many items the Inbox folder contains and how many of those items are unread.

CAUTION

Not Getting Any Mail?   You must be connected to a workgroup, a network, or an Internet or online service to receive your incoming e-mail.

TIP   **Welcome!**   The first time you log on, you may find a welcome message from Microsoft in your Inbox. After you read the message, you can delete it by selecting it and pressing the **Delete** key.

Attachment

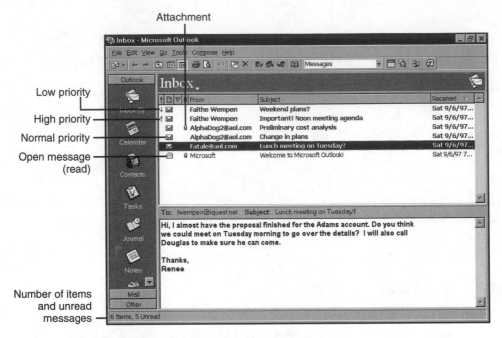

Low priority

High priority

Normal priority

Open message
(read)

Number of items
and unread
messages

Figure 3.1 Review the sender and subject before opening your mail.

To open and read your messages, follow these steps:

1. Double-click a mail message to open it. Figure 3.2 shows an open message.

2. To read the next or previous mail message in the Inbox, click the **Previous Item** or the **Next Item** button on the toolbar. Or you can open the **View** menu, choose **Previous** or **Next**, and choose **Item**.

TERM **Item** Outlook uses the word "item" to describe a mail message, an attached file, an appointment or meeting, a task, or some other Outlook data element. "Item" is a generic term in Outlook that describes the currently selected element.

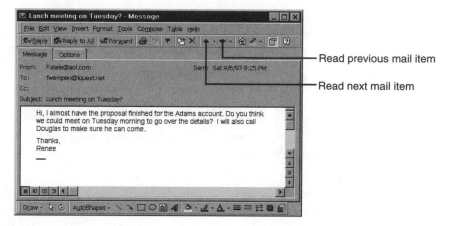

Read previous mail item

Read next mail item

Figure 3.2 The Message window displays the message and some tools for handling this message or moving on to another.

You can mark messages as read or unread by choosing **Edit**, **Mark As Read** or **Edit**, **Mark As Unread**. Outlook automatically marks messages as read when you open them. You might, however, want to mark messages yourself once in a while (as a reminder, for example). You might want to mark mail messages as read so that you don't read them again, or you might want to mark important mail as unread so that you'll be sure to open it and read it again. Additionally, you can mark all the messages in the Inbox as read at one time by choosing **Edit**, **Mark All As Read**.

CAUTION

No Mail? If you don't see any new mail in your Inbox, choose **Tools**, **Check for New Mail**, and Outlook will update your mail for you. You can choose **Tools**, **Check for New Mail On** to specify a service other than the default.

Saving an Attachment

You will often receive messages that have files or other items attached. A paper clip icon beside the message represents an attachment. You'll want to save any attachments sent to you so that you can open, modify, print, or otherwise use the document. Messages can contain multiple attachments.

To save an attachment, follow these steps:

1. Open the message containing an attachment by double-clicking the message. The attachment appears as an icon in the message text (see Figure 3.3).

2. (Optional) You can open the attachment from within the message by double-clicking the icon. The application in which the document was created (Word or Excel, for example) opens and displays the document in the window, ready for you to read. Close the application by choosing **File**, **Exit**.

3. In the message, select the attachment you want to save and choose **File**, **Save Attachments**. The Save Attachment dialog box appears (see Figure 3.4).

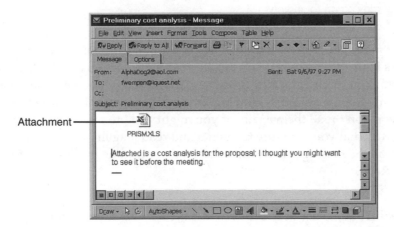

Figure 3.3 An icon represents the attached file.

4. Choose the folder in which you want to save the attachment and click **Save**. (You can change the name of the file if you want.) The dialog box closes, and you're returned to the Message window. You can open the attachment at any time from the application in which it was created.

CAUTION

Save Attachment Versus Save As You also can save the attachment by choosing **File**, **Save Attachment**. However, do not confuse this command with File, Save As. The latter command saves the e-mail message itself, rather than the attachment.

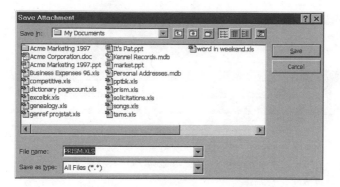

Figure 3.4 Save the attachment to a convenient folder.

Answering Mail

You may want to reply to a message after you read it. The Message window enables you to answer a message immediately, or at a later time if you prefer. To reply to any given message, open the message and follow these steps:

1. Click the **Reply** button or choose **Compose**, **Reply**. The Reply Message window appears, with the original message in the message text area and the sender of the message already filled in for you (see Figure 3.5).

   Reply to All If you receive a message that has also been sent to others besides yourself—as either a message or a carbon copy (cc)—you can click the **Reply to All** button (instead of the Reply button) to send your reply to each person who received the original message.

2. The insertion point is in the message text area, ready for you to enter your reply. Enter the text.

3. When you finish your reply, click the **Send** button or choose **File**, **Send**. Outlook sends the message.

You also can send a reply from the Inbox, without opening the message. Suppose, for example, you've already read the message and closed it, but now you've decided you want to reply. Select the message in the Inbox list and click the **Reply** button. The Reply Message window appears with the original message in the text area and the sender's name in the To area. Enter your text and send the message as you learned in the preceding steps.

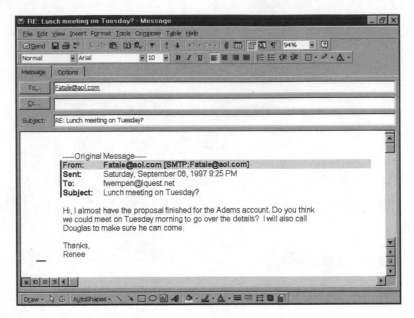

Figure 3.5   Reply to a message quickly and easily.

 TIP   **Reminder**   The next time you open a message to which you've replied, you'll see a reminder at the top of the Message tab that tells the date and time you sent your reply.

When you reply to a message, by default the reply quotes the original message. Each line has a > sign in front of it, to distinguish it from new text you add. You can type your reply at the top of the message, above the quoted text, or you can intersperse your reply lines between the quoted lines so that you are replying to specific statements. You can even delete some of the original message so you are only quoting the lines to which you want to reply.

Printing Mail

You can print e-mail messages, whether they're open or not. To print an un-opened message, select the message in the message list of the Inbox or other folder and choose **File**, **Print**. If the message is already open, you can follow these steps:

1. Open the message in Outlook.

2. Use one of the following methods to tell Outlook to print:

- Click the **Print** button on the toolbar to print using defaults.
- Choose the **File, Print** command to view the Print dialog box.
- Press **Ctrl+P**.

3. In the Print dialog box, click **OK** to print one copy of the entire message using the printer's default settings.

 TIP **More Print Info** See Lesson 14, "Printing in Outlook," for detailed information about configuring pages, or setting up the printer.

Closing a Message

When you finish with a message, you can close it in any of the following ways:

- Choose **File, Close**.
- Click the **Control-menu** button and click **Close**.
- Press **Alt+F4**.
- Click the **Close (x)** button in the title bar of the Message window.

In this lesson, you learned to read your mail, save an attachment, answer mail, and close a message. In the next lesson, you learn to manage your mail messages.

Managing Mail

In this lesson, you learn to delete and undelete messages, forward messages, and organize messages by saving them to folders.

Deleting Mail

You may want to store some important messages, but you definitely want to delete much of the mail you receive. After you answer a question or responded to a request, you probably don't have need for a reminder of that transaction. You can easily delete messages in Outlook when you finish with them.

To delete an e-mail message that is open, do one of the following:

- Choose **Edit**, **Delete**
- Press **Ctrl+D**
- Click the **Delete** button on the toolbar

If you have modified the message in any way, a confirmation message appears from the Office Assistant or as a message dialog box. Otherwise, the message is moved to the Deleted Items folder without warning.

If you're in the Inbox and you want to delete one or more messages from the message list, select a message to delete. (You can select multiple messages to delete at once by holding down **Ctrl** and clicking each message or by clicking the first message in a block and then holding down **Shift** while clicking the last message in the block). Then do one of the following:

- Press the **Delete** key
- Click the **Delete** button on the toolbar

Undeleting Items

If you change your mind and want to get back items you've deleted, you can usually retrieve them from the Deleted Items folder. By default, when you delete an item, it doesn't disappear from your system; it merely moves to the Deleted Items folder.

Deleted Items   Items stay in the Deleted Items folder until you delete them from that folder—at which point they are unrecoverable.

CAUTION

To retrieve a deleted item from the Deleted Items folder, follow these steps:

1. Click the **Deleted Items** icon in the Outlook Bar to open the folder.

2. Select the items you want to retrieve and drag them to the folder containing the same type of items on the Outlook Bar. When retrieving a deleted message from a friend or colleague, for example, you probably would want to drag it back to the Inbox. Alternatively, you can choose **Edit**, **Move to Folder**, choose the folder to which you want to move the selected items, and click **OK**.

Emptying the Deleted Items Folder

If you're really sure you want to delete the items in the Deleted Items folder, you can erase them from your system. To delete items in the Deleted Items folder, follow these steps:

1. In the Outlook Bar, choose the **Outlook** group and select the **Deleted Items** folder. All deleted items in that folder appear in the message list, as shown in Figure 4.1.

2. To permanently delete an item, select it in the Deleted Items folder, and then click the **Delete** tool button or choose **Edit**, **Delete**. You can choose more than one item to delete by holding down the **Shift** or **Ctrl** key and clicking each item.

3. Outlook displays a confirmation dialog box asking whether you're sure you want to permanently delete the message. Choose **Yes** to delete the selected item.

4. To switch back to the Inbox or another folder, select the folder from either the Outlook Bar or the Folder List.

TIP **Automatic Permanent Delete** You can set Outlook to permanently delete the contents of the Deleted Items folder every time you exit the program. To do so, choose **Tools, Options** and click the **General** tab. In the General Settings area, select **Empty the Deleted Items Folder Upon Exiting** and click **OK**.

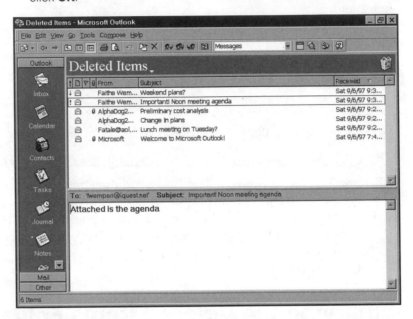

Figure 4.1 Deleted messages remain in the Deleted Items folder until you permanently delete them.

Forwarding Mail

Suppose you want to forward e-mail that you receive from a coworker to another person who has an interest in the message. You can forward any message that you receive, and you can even add comments to the message if you want. (Forwarding is different than replying because you are sending an e-mail to someone who wasn't originally a recipient.)

TERM **Forward Mail** When you forward mail, you send a message you have received to another person on the network. You can add your own comments to the forwarded mail, if you want.

You forward an open message or a selected message from the Inbox message list in the same way. To forward mail, follow these steps:

1. Select or open the message you want to forward. Then click the **Forward** button or choose **Compose, Forward**. The FW Message dialog box appears (see Figure 4.2).

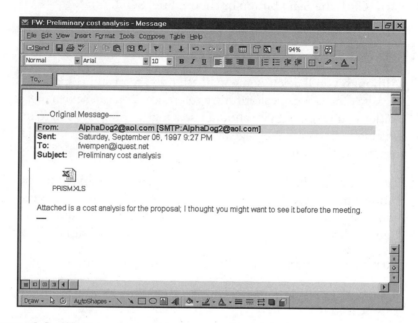

Figure 4.2 When you forward a message, the original message appears at the bottom of the message window.

2. In the **To** text box, enter the names of the people to whom you want to forward the mail. (If you want to choose a person's name from a list, click the **To** button to display the Select Names dialog box, and then select the person's name. Lesson 5 "Using the Address Book,"explains more about using the Address Book.) If you enter multiple names in the To box, separate the names with a semicolon and a space.

3. (Optional) In the **Cc** text box, enter the names of anyone to whom you want to forward copies of the message (or click the **Cc** button and choose the name from the list that appears).

4. In the message area of the window, enter any message you want to send with the forwarded text. The text you type will be a different color.

5. Click the **Send** button or choose **File**, **Send**.

Saving Mail to a Folder

Although you'll delete some mail after you read and respond to it, you'll want to save other messages for future reference. You can save a message to any folder you want, but you should use a logical filing system to ensure that you'll be able to find each message again later. Outlook offers several methods for organizing your mail.

The easiest method of saving mail to a folder is to move it to one of Outlook's built-in mail folders. You can use any of the folders to store your mail, or you can create new folders. (Lesson 15, "Saving, Opening, and Finding Outlook Items," describes how to create your own folders within Outlook.)

To move messages to an existing folder, follow these steps:

1. Select one message (by clicking it) or select multiple messages (by Ctrl+clicking).

 TIP **Making Backup Copies** You can also copy a message to another folder as a backup. To do so, choose **Edit**, **Copy to Folder**.

2. Choose **Edit**, **Move to Folder** or click the **Move to Folder** tool button on the toolbar. The Move Items dialog box appears (see Figure 4.3).

3. Select the folder you want to move the item to and click **OK**. Outlook moves the item to the folder for you.

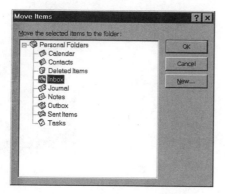

Figure 4.3   Choose the folder to which you want to move the selected message(s).

To view the message(s) you've moved, choose the folder from the Outlook Bar or the Folder List. Then click the item you want to view.

In this lesson, you learned to forward messages, delete messages, and organize messages by saving them to folders. In the next lesson, you learn to work with address books.

Using the Address Book

In this lesson, you learn to use Outlook's Address Book with your e-mail.

Opening the Address Book

The Address Book stores contact information for the people you need to communicate with so that you don't have to remember e-mail addresses and other contact information.

 To open the Postoffice Address List, choose **Tools**, **Address Book** or click the **Address Book** tool button on the toolbar. The Address Book dialog box appears, as shown in Figure 5.1.

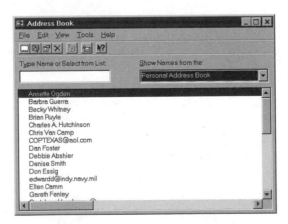

Figure 5.1 The Address Book dialog box.

Depending on your setup, you may see Postoffice Address List, Personal Address Book, or Outlook Address List in the Show Names drop-down list. It all depends on what is available on your PC and what is set as the default. You can easily switch among the available address lists by choosing the one you want from the Show Names drop-down list. The Postoffice Address List is the address list on your company's network; if you are using Outlook on a standalone computer, you will not have this.

Using a Postoffice Address List

If you are using Outlook in a business and your PC is connected to the company network, all the names within your organization usually appear on a Postoffice Address List created by your system's mail administrator. Anytime you want to send or forward an e-mail, you can select the recipients from that list instead of typing in their names manually. If you're using Windows NT on a network, you may or may not have access to the Postoffice Address List, depending on your permissions and rights. If you have questions, see your network administrator.

Post Office   A directory, usually located on the network server, that contains a mailbox for each e-mail user. When someone sends a message, that message is filed in the recipient's mailbox until the recipient receives the mail and copies, moves, or deletes it.

Postoffice Address List   A list of everyone who has a mailbox in the post office. The Postoffice Address List is controlled by the mail administrator.

Mail Administrator   The person who manages the e-mail post office. This person might also be the network administrator, but it doesn't necessarily have to be the same person.

Using the Personal Address Book

Everyone has a Personal Address Book in Outlook, even those who use Outlook at home and are not connected to a network. In the Personal Address Book, you store the names and e-mail addresses of people you contact frequently.

If you also have a Postoffice Address Book, you can copy addresses from it to your Personal Address Book. You may want to include coworkers from your department, or even people from outside of your office (whom you contact via Internet addresses). Non-networked Outlook users store all their addresses in the Personal Address Book.

 TIP **What Is This?** You may notice the Outlook Address Book in the list of address books; the Outlook Address Book contains entries you create in your Contacts list. (For more information about the Contacts list, see Lesson 12, "Creating a Contacts List.")

 CAUTION **No Personal Address Book Is Listed?** If you do not see a Personal Address Book in the Address Book dialog box, you can easily add it to your resources. Close the Address Book dialog box and choose **Tools**, **Services**. In the Services tab of the dialog box, click the **Add** button, choose **Personal Address Book** from the list, and click **OK**. In the Personal Address Book dialog box, select your preference (such as where the file is stored) and click **OK**. Close the Services dialog box and open the Address Book dialog box again; you'll now see the Personal Address Book in the list. You may have to exit and restart Outlook first.

Copying Names to the Personal Address Book

To add names to the Personal Address Book from the Postoffice Address List (or another address list), follow these steps:

 1. Choose **Tools**, **Address Book** or click the **Address Book** tool button on the toolbar. The Address Book dialog box appears (refer to Figure 5.1).

2. Select the list from the Show names drop-down list that contains the names from which you want to copy (for example, Postoffice Address List).

 3. Select the name(s) from the list box, and then click the **Add to Personal Address Book** button on the toolbar or choose **File**, **Add to Personal Address Book**. The name(s) remain on the original list, but Outlook copies them to your Personal Address Book as well.

4. To view your Personal Address Book, Choose **Personal Address Book** from the Show Names drop-down list. The list changes to display those names you've added to your Personal Address List, but the dialog box looks the same (see Figure 5.1).

Adding New Entries to the Personal Address Book

To add a completely new address to your Personal Address Book, follow these steps:

1. Choose **Tools, Address Book** or click the **Address Book** tool button on the toolbar. The Address Book dialog box appears (refer to Figure 5.1).

2. Click the **New Entry** button or choose **File, New Entry**. The New Entry dialog box appears (see Figure 5.2).

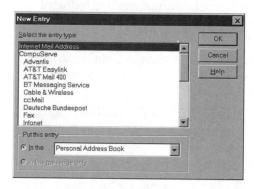

Figure 5.2   Choose a source for your new entry.

3. In the **Select the Entry Type** list, choose from the available options, and then click **OK**. For example, to add an Internet e-mail address, choose **Internet Mail Address**.

   The options you see will depend on the information systems installed on your network; for example, Microsoft Mail, Internet Mail, or some other service may be available. You can add an address entry that corresponds with one of the available information systems.

Additionally, you can choose to add one of the following two items:

- **Personal Distribution List** Use this to create one address entry for a group of recipients. When you send mail to the list name, everyone on the list receives the message. You might use this option for grouping department heads, for example.

- **Other Address** Choose this option to add one new recipient at a time. You can enter a name, e-mail address, and e-mail type for each entry. In addition, you can enter business addresses and phone numbers, and you can add notes and comments to the entry. Use this entry for Internet addresses, for example.

4. A dialog box appears in which you fill in the information about the person. The dialog box tabs depend on what type you chose in step 3, but in general, the tab where you put the required information appears on top (for example, SMTP—Internet in Figure 5.3) and optional tabs appear behind it. Enter the required information, and extra information if desired, and then click **OK**.

 SMTP Stands for *Simple Mail Transport Protocol*. A communication protocol standard for exchanging e-mail between Internet hosts.

5. When you're done working in your Personal Address Book, close the Address Book window. You're returned to the Outlook Inbox.

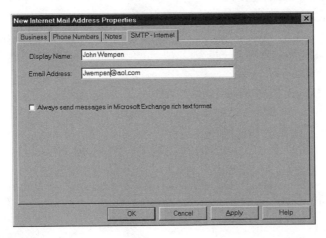

Figure 5.3 Outlook displays the tab containing the required information first. You can choose the other tabs if you want.

Viewing the List of Addresses

The following points outline some of the ways in which you might use the Address List:

- To view more details about any entry in the Address Book dialog box, double-click the person's name or click the **Properties** button on the toolbar. The person's Properties dialog box appears, with her name, address type, postoffice name, and network type listed on the Address (1) tab. Click **OK** to close this dialog box and return to the Address Book dialog box.

- Click the **Properties** toolbar button and choose the **Address (2)** tab in the person's Properties dialog box to view her phone number, office, or department, and any notes or comments that have been added to the description. Click **OK** to close this dialog box and return to the Address Book dialog box.

- If you cannot find a particular name in the list, you can search for it. Choose **Tools**, **Find** or click the **Find** button, and then enter the name for which you're searching in the **Find Name Beginning With** text box. Click **OK** to start the search.

Sending a Message to Someone in the Address Book

You can use either of the address books to choose the names of recipients to whom you want to send new messages, forward messages, or send a reply. Using the address books also makes sending carbon copies and blind carbon copies easy.

Blind Carbon Copy A blind carbon copy (Bcc) of a message is a copy that's sent to someone in secret; the other recipients have no way of knowing that you're sending the message to someone via a blind carbon copy. By the same token, you have no way of knowing whether the e-mail you receive was sent to another person.

To address a message, follow these steps:

1. Choose **Compose**, **New Mail Message** from the Outlook Inbox window, or click the **New Mail Message** toolbar button.

2. In the Message window, click the **To** button to display the Select Names dialog box.

3. Open **Show Names** from the drop-down list box and choose either the **Postoffice Address List** or the **Personal Address Book**.

4. From the list that appears on the left, choose the name of the intended recipient and select the **To** button. Outlook copies the name to the Message Recipients list. You can add multiple names if you want.

5. (Optional) Select the names of anyone to whom you want to send a carbon copy and click the **Cc** button to transfer those names to the Message Recipients list.

6. (Optional) Select the names of anyone to whom you want to send a blind carbon copy and click the **Bcc** button. Figure 5.4 shows two recipients for a message plus two more people to receive blind carbon copies.

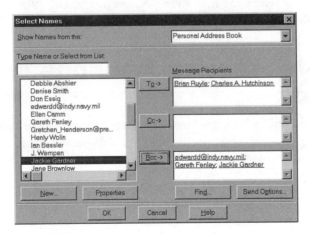

Figure 5.4 Choose the recipients from this listing.

7. Click **OK** to return to the Message window and complete your message. (For more information about writing messages, see Lesson 6, "Creating Mail.")

In this lesson, you learned to use the Address Book with your e-mail. In the next lesson, you learn to compose a message and format it.

Creating Mail

In this lesson, you learn to compose a message, format text, check your spelling, and send mail.

Composing a Message

You can send a message to anyone for whom you have an address, regardless of whether he or she is in your address book. In addition to sending a message to one or more recipients, you can send copies of a message to others on your address list. (See Lesson 5, "Using the Address Book," for more information about addressing a message and sending carbon copies.)

To compose a message, follow these steps:

1. In the Outlook Inbox, click the **New Mail Message** button or choose **Compose, New Mail Message**. The Untitled—Message window appears (see Figure 6.1).

2. Enter the name of the recipient in the **To** text box, or click the **To** button and select the name of the recipient from your Address Book.

3. Enter the name of anyone to whom you want to send a copy of the message in the **Cc** text box, or click the **Cc** button and select a name or names from the Address Book.

 TIP **One Stop at the Address Book** When you open the Address Book in step 2 by clicking the **To** button, you can also select the Cc recipients while you're there, as you learned to do in Lesson 5. You don't have to close the Address Book and then reopen it in step 3 for the Cc recipients.

4. In the **Subject** text box, enter the subject of the message.

5. Click in the text area, and then enter the text of the message. You do not have to press the Enter key at the end of a line; Outlook automatically wraps the text at the end of a line for you. You can use the Delete and Backspace keys to edit the text you enter. You also may use the Cut, Copy, and Paste functions just as you would when using most application.

6. When you finish typing the message, you can send the message immediately (see "Sending Mail" later in this lesson), or you can check the spelling and formatting, as described in the following sections.

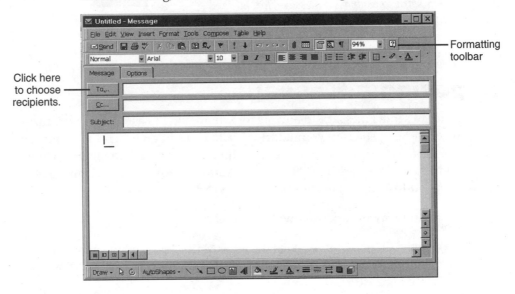

Click here to choose recipients.

Formatting toolbar

Figure 6.1 Compose a new message in the Untitled—Message window.

CAUTION

No Address! If you try to compose a message to someone without entering an address, Outlook displays the Check Names dialog box, in which it asks you to create an address. You can search for the name among the existing addresses, or you can create a new address for the name in much the same way you would create a new entry in the Address Book (see Lesson 5).

By the way, you can show or hide the message header area as you are composing your message by clicking the **Message Header** button on the toolbar. When the message header is showing, you have access to the Cc button for addressing and also the Options tab, which you learn about in Lesson 7, "Setting Mail Options." Without it, you have more room on the screen to see what you're typing.

Formatting Text

You can change the format of the text—fonts, bold, italic, and so on—in your message to make it more attractive, to make it easier to read, or to add emphasis. Any formatting that you add transfers with the message to the recipient, if the recipient is using Outlook as her e-mail client. However, if the recipient is using an e-mail client other than ' Outlook, your formatting may not transfer.

 TERM **E-mail Client** A term describing the software you use to send and receive e-mail. One of Outlook's functions is to serve as an e-mail client.

Text can be formatted in two ways. You can format the text after you type it by selecting it and then choosing a font, size, or other attribute; or you can select the font, size, or other attribute and then enter the text.

 TIP **Word in Outlook** By default, if you have Word installed, Outlook asks you the first time you start it whether you want to use it for message composition. Figure 6.1 shows e-mail composition with this feature enabled; that's why the tools in Figure 6.1 may seem familiar to Word users. (For more information about Word formatting, refer to Part II "Word," of this book.) If you don't want to use Word, open the **Tools** menu and deselect **Use Word as E-Mail Editor**. Then your message composition screen will display an abbreviated set of formatting tools, rather than Word's complete set.

To format the text in your message, follow these steps:

1. If the Formatting toolbar is not showing, choose **View**, **Toolbars**, **Formatting**. (Figure 6.1 points out the Formatting toolbar.)

Arial

2. To apply a font to either selected text or text that you are about to enter, click the **Font** drop-down arrow on the Formatting toolbar. (The default font is Arial.) Scroll through the font list, if necessary, to view all fonts on the system, and then click the font you want to apply to the text.

TIP **Quick Format** You also can format text by choosing **Format**, **Font** and selecting a font, size, and style from the Font dialog box. You also can assign bullets and alignment to text by choosing **Format**, **Paragraph**.

 3. Assign a size by clicking the Font Size drop-down arrow and choosing the size, or enter a size in the **Font Size** text box. The default is 10 point.

 4. To choose a color, click the **Font Color** tool button and select a color from the palette box that appears.

 5. Choose a type style to apply to text by clicking the **Bold, Italic,** or **Underline** buttons on the Formatting toolbar.

6. Choose an alignment by selecting the **Align Left, Center, Align Right,** or **Justify** button from the Formatting toolbar. (Justify is available only if you are using Word as your e-mail editor.)

 7. Add bullets to a list by clicking the **Bullets** button on the Formatting toolbar.

 8. Create text indents or remove indents in half-inch increments by clicking the **Increase Indent** or **Decrease Indent** buttons. (Each time you click the Indent button, the indent changes by half an inch.)

Spell Checking Your E-Mail

To make a good impression and to maintain your professional image, you should check the spelling in your mail messages before you send them. Outlook includes a spell checker you can use for that purpose. If you're using Word as your e-mail editor, you'll notice that your grammar is automatically checked.

To check the spelling in a message, follow these steps:

1. In the open message, choose **Tools, Spelling and Grammar,** click the **Spelling and Grammar** button on the toolbar (if you are using Word as your editor), or press **F7.** If the spell checker finds a word whose spelling it questions, it displays the Spelling dialog box (shown in Figure 6.2). If it does not find any misspelled words, a dialog box appears with a message that the spelling and grammar check is complete. Click **OK** to close the dialog box.

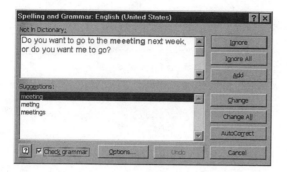

Figure 6.2 Check your spelling before sending a message.

2. The following are options available to you when Outlook flags a word that appears to be misspelled:

- **Not in Dictionary** Enter the correct spelling in this text box.
- **Suggestions** Select the correct spelling in this text box, and it automatically appears in the Change To text box.
- **Ignore** Click this button to continue the spelling check without changing this occurrence of the selected word.
- **Ignore All** Click this button to continue the spelling check without changing any occurrence of the word in question throughout this message.
- **Change** Click this button to change this particular occurrence of the word in question to the spelling in the Change To text box.
- **Change All** Click this button to change the word in question to the spelling listed in the Change To text box every time the spelling checker finds the word in this message.
- **Add** Click this button to add the current spelling of the word in question to the dictionary so that Outlook will not question future occurrences of this spelling.
- **Undo** Click this button to reverse the last spelling change you made, returning the word to its original spelling.
- **Cancel** Click this button to quit the spelling check.

3. When the spelling check is complete, Outlook displays a message box telling you that it's done. Click **OK** to close the dialog box.

TIP **Set Your Spelling Options** Click the **Options** button in the Spelling dialog box to set options that tell Outlook to do such things as ignore words with numbers, ignore original message text in forwarded messages or replies, and always check spelling before sending.

Sending Mail

When you're ready to send your e-mail message, do one of the following:

- Click the **Send** button.
- Choose **File**, **Send**.
- Press **Ctrl+Enter**.
- Press Alt+S.

 TIP **AutoSignature** Choose **Tools**, **AutoSignature** to have Outlook automatically add a message, quotation, or other text at the end of every message you send. Additionally, after you create an autosignature, you can quickly add it to any message by choosing **Insert**, **AutoSignature**.

 TIP **Using Windows NT 4.0?** You need to check your rights and permissions in relation to sending e-mail within your network. Ask your system administrator for more information.

In this lesson, you learned to compose a message, format text, check your spelling, and send e-mail. In the next lesson, you learn to set e-mail options and how to tell if the recipient has received your message.

Setting Mail Options

In this lesson, you learn to set options for messages and their delivery and tracking.

Customizing Options

Outlook provides options that enable you to mark any message with priority status so that the recipient knows you need a quick response, or with a sensitivity rating so that your words cannot be changed by anyone after the message is sent. With other available options, you can enable the recipients of your message to vote on an issue by including voting buttons in your message and having the replies sent to a specific location.

You also can set delivery options. You can, for example, schedule the delivery of a message for a specified delivery time or date if you don't want to send it right now.

To set message options, open the Untitled—Message window and click the **Options** tab. As you can see in Figure 7.1, the options on this tab are separated into four areas. The next four sections discuss each of the groups of options in detail.

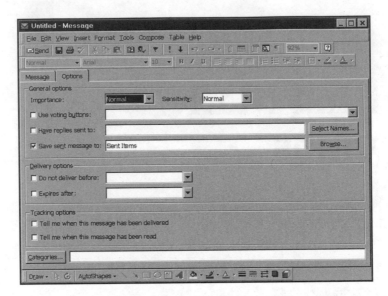

Figure 7.1 Use the Options tab to govern how your message is sent.

General Options

In the General Options area, set any of the following options for your message:

- Click the **Importance** drop-down arrow and choose a priority level of **Low**, **Normal**, or **High** from the list. (Alternatively, you could click the **Importance High** or **Importance Low** tool button on the toolbar.) When importance isn't specified, the message is given Normal Importance.

- Click the **Sensitivity** drop-down arrow and choose one of the following options:

    Normal   Use this option to indicate that the message's contents are standard or customary.

    Personal   Use this option to suggest that the message's contents are of a personal nature.

    Private   Use this option to prevent the message from being modified after you send it.

    Confidential   Use this option to denote the message's contents as restricted or private.

TIP **You Can Mark All Messages as Private** So that no one can tamper with your words, you can mark all your messages by choosing **Tools**, **Options** and clicking the **Sending** tab. In the **Set Sensitivity** box, choose the level you want.

- Select the **Use Voting Buttons** check box to add the default choices (Approve and Reject) to your message. You can also add Yes and No choices or Yes, No, and Maybe choices. If you want to provide other choices, enter your own text in the text box.

- Choose the **Have Replies Sent To** check box and specify in the text box the person to whom you want the replies sent. You can use the **Select Names** button to view the Address Book and choose a name if you want.

- Select the **Save Sent Message To** check box to save your message to the Sent Items folder by default. Or specify another folder to save the message in, using the Browse button and the resulting dialog box, if necessary, to locate the folder.

CAUTION **Outlook Recipients Only** The Sensitivity, Importance, and Voting features work only if your recipient is an Outlook user. If the message goes to someone with a different e-mail program, those features are ignored.

Delivery Options

In addition to message options, you can set certain delivery options, such as scheduling the time of the delivery. In the Delivery Options area of the Options tab (Message window), choose one or both of the following check boxes:

Do Not Deliver Before Check this option to specify a delivery date. Click the down arrow in the text box beside the option to display a calendar on which you can select the delivery day.

Expires After Select this check box to include a day, date, and time of expiration. You can click the down arrow in the text box to display a calendar from which you can choose a date, or you can enter the date and time yourself.

Tracking Options

You might want to set tracking options so that you know when the message has been delivered or read. Tracking options are like receipts: They notify you that the message arrived safely. You set tracking options from the Options tab of the Untitled—Message window.

Choose one or both of the following Tracking Options: **Tell Me When This Message Has Been Delivered** and **Tell Me When This Message Has Been Read**. If you choose these, you receive a confirmation message when the specified event happens (delivery or reading).

Categories

Outlook enables you to assign messages to certain categories such as Business, Goals, Hot Contacts, and Phone Calls. You set the category for a message in the Categories dialog box.

 Categories Categories offer a way of organizing messages to make them easier to find, sort, print, and manage. For example, to find all the items in one category, choose **Tools**, **Find Items**. Click the **More Choices** tab, choose **Categories**, and check the category for which you're searching.

To assign a category, follow these steps:

1. In the Options tab of the Message window, click the **Categories** button. The Categories dialog box appears (see Figure 7.2).

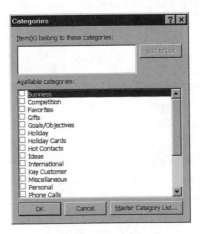

Figure 7.2 Organize your messages with categories.

2. To assign an existing category, select the category or categories that best suit your message from the Available Categories list. To assign a new category, enter a new category name in the **Item(s) Belong to These Categories** text box, and then click the **Add to List** button.

3. Click **OK** to close the Categories dialog box and return to the Message window.

Using Message Flags

A message flag enables you to mark a message as important, either as a reminder for yourself or as a signal to the message's recipient. When you send a message flag, a red flag icon appears in the recipient's message list, and Outlook adds text at the top of the message telling which type of flag you are sending. In addition, you can add a due date to the flag, and that date appears at the top of the message.

The following list outlines the types of flags you can send in Outlook:

Call	No Response Necessary
Do Not Forward	Read
Follow Up	Reply
For Your Information	Reply to All
Forward	Review

To use a message flag, follow these steps:

1. In the Message window, click the **Message Flag** tool or choose **Edit**, **Message Flag**. The Flag Message dialog box appears (see Figure 7.3).

Figure 7.3 Flag a message to show its importance.

2. Click the **Flag** drop-down arrow and choose the flag text you want to add to the message.

3. Click the **By** drop-down arrow and select a date from the calendar, or enter a date manually in the text box.

4. Click **OK** to return to the Message window.

To clear a flag, open the Flag dialog box (step 1) and then click the **Clear Flag** button.

 TIP **View the Message Header** You can view just the header of a message to allow you more message text room, by hiding the Cc, Bcc, and Subject lines. Choose **View**, **Message Header** to show only the To text box and any flag text; select **View**, **Message Header** again to redisplay the Cc, Bcc, and Subject fields.

In this lesson, you learned to set options for messages and delivery, and for tracking messages. In the next lesson, you learn to attach items to messages.

Attaching Items to a Message

In this lesson, you learn to attach a file, an object (such as an embedded file), and other items (such as an appointment or task) to a message.

Attaching a File

You can attach any type of file to an Outlook message, which makes for a convenient way of sending your files over the network to your coworkers. You might send Word documents, Excel spreadsheets, PowerPoint presentations, or any other documents you create with your Windows applications.

When you send an attached file, it appears as an icon in the message. When the recipient gets the file, he or she can open it within the message or save it for later use. However, the recipient must have the source program that you used to create the file on his or her computer. For instance, if you send a colleague a Microsoft Word file, he must have Microsoft Word to view the file he receives.

Internet Attachments If you are sending Internet e-mail (that is, to someone outside your company) and you want to attach a file, you must have downloaded and installed the e-mail enhancement patch for Outlook 97 from Microsoft's Web site. Choose **Help, Microsoft on the Web, Free Stuff** to open your Web browser to the page where you can download the patch.

To attach a file to a message, follow these steps:

 1. In the Message window, position the insertion point in the message text, and then choose **Insert**, **File** or click the **Insert File** toolbar button. The Insert File dialog box appears (see Figure 8.1).

2. From the **Look In** drop-down list, choose the drive and folder that contains the file you want to attach.

3. Using the **Files of Type** drop-down list, choose the file type—such as Excel or Word.

4. From the List box, select the file you want to attach.

5. Click **OK** to insert the file into the message. (Figure 8.2 shows a file inserted as an attachment.)

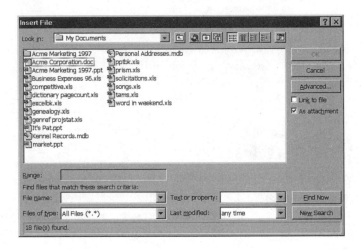

Figure 8.1   Select the file you want to attach to a message.

Attaching Outlook Items

In addition to attaching files from other programs, you also can attach an Outlook item to a message. An Outlook item can be any document saved in one of your personal folders, including a calendar, contacts, journal, notes, and tasks. You can attach an Outlook item in the same manner you attach a file.

Follow these steps to attach an Outlook item:

1. In the Message window, choose **Insert**, **Item**. The Insert Item dialog box appears.

2. From the **Look In** list box, choose the folder containing the item you want to include in the message.

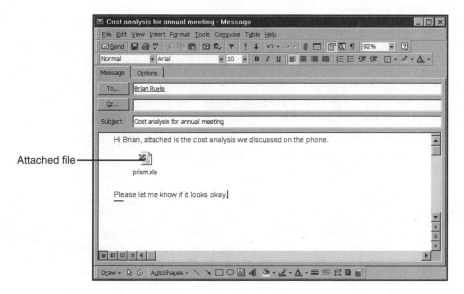

Attached file ———

Figure 8.2 The recipient can double-click the icon to open the file.

3. Select from the items that appear in the **Items** list (see Figure 8.3). To select multiple adjacent items, hold the **Shift** key and click the first and last desired items. To select multiple nonadjacent items, hold the **Ctrl** key and click the items.

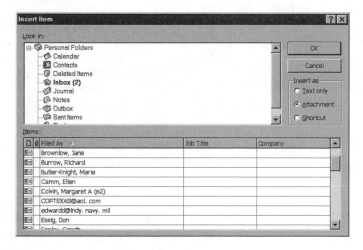

Figure 8.3 Select items from any folder in Outlook.

4. In the Insert As area, choose from the following option buttons:

• **Text Only**   Inserts the file into the message as text; however, if your file is not saved as an ASCII or other text-only file, do not use this option.

• **Attachment**   Inserts an icon representing the document. The actual file follows the message to the recipient, who then saves it as a copy.

• **Shortcut**   Inserts a Windows shortcut icon into the text. This option is best used only if the file is stored on a network drive from which the recipient can easily access it through a shortcut.

Text Only Is Only for Text!   If you try to insert a file from Word, Excel, or another application as Text Only, you end up with a lot of garbage characters in the text. That's because these program files contain special formatting codes. The only time you use Text Only is when you export the data from its native program into a text-only file first.

5. Click **OK**, and Outlook inserts the selected items in your message.

It Doesn't Work Without Outlook   Recipients who don't have Outlook are not able to view attached Outlook items. If you know the recipient doesn't have Outlook, you need to cut and paste the Outlook data into the message or retype it.

Inserting an Object

Just as you can insert an object—a spreadsheet, chart, drawing, presentation, media clip, clip art, and WordArt—in any Windows application that supports OLE, you also can insert an object into an Outlook e-mail message.

OLE (Object Linking and Embedding)   A method of exchanging and sharing data between applications; OLE is supported by most Windows applications and all Microsoft programs.

You can insert an existing object into a message, or you can create an object within a message using the source application. For example, you can create an Excel chart within your message using Excel's features through OLE.

When you send a message with an attached object, the object travels with the message to the recipient. The recipient is able to view the attachment if he or she has the appropriate software to open it. (For more information about OLE, see Appendix C, "Object Linking and Embedding.")

To attach an existing object to a message, follow these steps:

1. In the Message window, position the insertion point in the message text and choose **Insert**, **Object**. The Object dialog box appears.

2. Click the **Create from File** tab (see Figure 8.4).

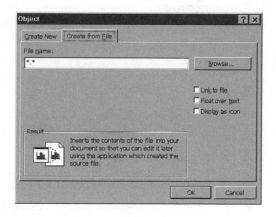

Figure 8.4 Insert an object to send with a message.

3. In the **File Name** text box, enter the path and the name of the file you want to insert. You can use the **Browse** button and the resulting dialog box to find the file if you want.

4. Click **OK**. Outlook inserts the object into the message.

After you save and open an object you've received in a message, you can resize the object to suit your needs. First select it, and a frame appears with eight small black boxes (called *handles*) on the corners and along the sides. To resize the object, position the mouse pointer over one of the black handles; the mouse pointer becomes a two-headed arrow. Click and drag the handle to resize the object.

To edit an object, double-click within the frame, and the source application opens from within Outlook. Note that you still see your Outlook message and

Outlook toolbars. However, you also see some tools from the object's native program that you can use to edit the object. Figure 8.5 shows an Excel chart object within a message. Notice the Chart toolbar and several chart icons added through OLE for use in editing.

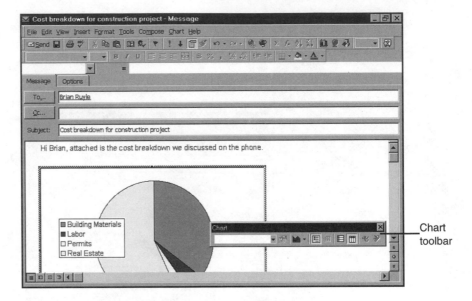

Chart toolbar

Figure 8.5 Edit the object from within your Outlook message.

In this lesson, you learned to attach a file, an object, and other items to a message. In the next lesson, you learn to organize messages.

Organizing Messages

In this lesson, you learn to view sent items, create folders, and move items to a new folder.

Viewing Sent Items and Changing Defaults

By default, Outlook saves a copy of all e-mail messages you send. It keeps these copies in the Sent Items folder, which is part of the Mail group of the Outlook Bar. You can view a list of sent items at any time, and you can open any message in that list to review its contents.

Viewing Sent Items

To view sent items, follow these steps:

1. In the Outlook Bar, choose the **Mail** group.

 TIP **Save Time** You can select the Sent Items folder from the Folders List instead of following steps 1 through 3.

2. If necessary, scroll to the Sent Items folder.

3. Click the **Sent Items** icon, and Outlook displays a list of the contents of that folder. Figure 9.1 shows the Sent Items list. All messages you send remain in the Sent Items folder until you delete or move them.

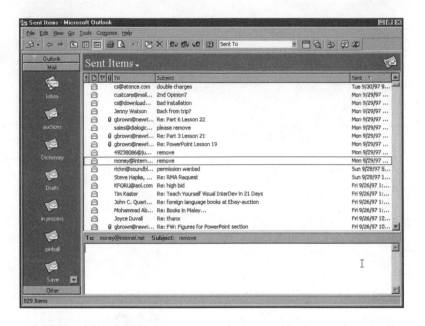

Figure 9.1 You can open any sent message by double-clicking it.

4. (Optional) To view a sent item (if you don't have the Message Preview pane showing), double-click it to open it. When you finish with it, click the **Close** (X) button.

Changing Sent Items Defaults

You can control how Outlook saves copies of your sent messages. To change the default settings for the Sent Items folder, follow these steps:

1. Choose **Tools**, **Options**, and the Options dialog box appears.

2. Click the **Sending** tab.

3. Choose one or all the following options (located near the bottom of the dialog box):

- **Save Copies of Messages in the "Sent Items" Folder**   When this is checked, Outlook saves copies of all sent messages to the specified folder. When the check box is empty, no copies of messages are saved automatically.

- **In Folders Other than the Inbox, Save Replies with Original Messages**   When this is checked, Outlook saves replies to messages in the same folder in which you store the original message. When the check box is empty, it saves replies to the Sent Items folder as long as you've checked the previous check box.

- **Save Forwarded Messages** When this is checked, Outlook saves a copy of each forwarded message you send.

4. Click **OK** to close the dialog box.

CAUTION

Too Much Mail! If you save all the e-mail you receive and send, you may accumulate so much mail that you run the risk of running out of disk space. You can and should periodically delete mail from the Sent Items folder by selecting the mail and pressing the **Delete** key; you also need to remove the deleted mail from the Deleted Items folder. (See Lesson 4, "Managing Mail," for more information.) Alternatively, you can create an archive file of the messages you've sent. The archive enables you to save items on disk or elsewhere on the system.

Creating Folders

You'll likely want to organize your e-mail in various folders to make storing items and finding them more efficient. You can create folders within Outlook that make it easier to manage your e-mail and other items in Outlook.

To create a folder, follow these steps:

1. Choose **File**, **Folder**, **Create Subfolder**. The Create New Folder dialog box appears (see Figure 9.2).

2. In the **Name** text box, enter a name for the folder.

3. Click the **Folder Contains** drop-down arrow, and choose the type of items the folder will store: Mail, Appointments, Contact, Journal, Note, or Task.

4. In the **Make This Folder a Subfolder Of** list, choose the folder in which you want to create the new folder. You can, for example, make the new folder a subfolder of Personal Folders so that it appears in lists with all the Outlook folders. Or you might want to make it a subfolder of Sent Mail.

5. (Optional) In the **Description** text box, add a comment or brief description of the folder.

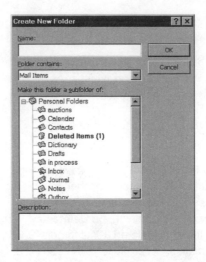

Figure 9.2 Create folders to organize your e-mail and other items.

6. If you do not have the Outlook patch installed, and you want a shortcut to that folder to appear on the Outlook Bar, click the check box at the bottom of the dialog box. (With the patch installed, you won't have such a check box.)

7. Click **OK**.

8. If the Outlook patch is installed, you next see a dialog box asking whether you want to create a shortcut on the Outlook Bar for the folder. Click **Yes** or **No**.

The new folder appears on Folders list, and on the Outlook Bar, too, if you chose that.

 TIP **Add Folder** Even if you choose not to add the folder to the Outlook Bar when you create the folder, you can add it later. Choose **File**, **Add to Outlook Bar**. In the dialog box that appears, you can select any folder name in Outlook or on the system and add it to the Outlook Bar by selecting it and clicking **OK**.

 TIP **I Want to Delete a Folder!** If you added a folder by accident or you change your mind about a folder you've added, you can delete it from Outlook. To delete a folder, select it and then choose **File**, **Folder**, **Delete** *foldername*. You also can rename, move, or copy the folder by using the commands in the secondary menu that appears when you choose File, Folder.

Moving Items to Another Folder

You can move items from one folder in Outlook to another; for example, you might create a folder to store all messages pertaining to a specific account or report. You can easily move those messages to the new folder and open them later for reference purposes. You also can forward, reply, copy, delete, and archive any items you move from one folder to another.

To move an item to another folder, follow these steps:

1. From the Inbox or any Outlook folder, open the item you want to move.
2. Choose **Edit**, **Move to Folder** or press **Ctrl+Shift+V**. The Move Items dialog box appears (see Figure 9.3).

Figure 9.3 Choose the folder in which you want to store the item.

3. In the list of folders, select the folder to which you want to move the message.
4. Click **OK**. When you close the item, Outlook stores it in the designated folder.

 You can quickly move an unopened message by dragging it from the open folder in which it resides to any folder icon in the Outlook Bar. Or, you can display the Folder List (click the **Folder List** button on the toolbar) and drag the message to the desired folder there.

You also can open the message at any time by opening the folder from the Outlook Bar and double-clicking the message. After opening it, you can forward, send, print, or otherwise manipulate the message as you would any other.

In this lesson, you learned to view sent items, create folders, and move items to a folder. In the next lesson, you learn to use the Calendar.

Using the Calendar

10

In this lesson, you learn to navigate the Calendar, create appointments, and save appointments.

Navigating the Calendar

You can use Outlook's Calendar to schedule appointments and create a to-do list to remind you of daily or weekly tasks. You can schedule appointments months in advance, move appointments, and cancel appointments. The Calendar also makes it easy to identify the days on which you have appointments.

To open the Outlook Calendar, click the **Calendar** icon in the Outlook Bar or select the **Calendar** folder from the Folder List. (Figure 10.1 shows the Calendar in Outlook.)

Outlook provides multiple ways for you to move around in the Calendar and view specific dates:

- Scroll through the schedule pane to view the time of the appointment.
- In the monthly calendar pane, click the left and right arrows next to the names of the months to go backward and forward one month at a time.
- In the monthly calendar pane, click a date to display that date in the schedule pane.
- To view a full month in the schedule pane, select the name of the month in the monthly calendar pane.
- To view a week or selected days in the schedule pane, select the days in the monthly calendar pane.

- To add a task to the task list, click **Click Here to Add a New Task**, enter a new task, and press **Enter**.
- Use the scroll bars for the task list pane to view appointments.

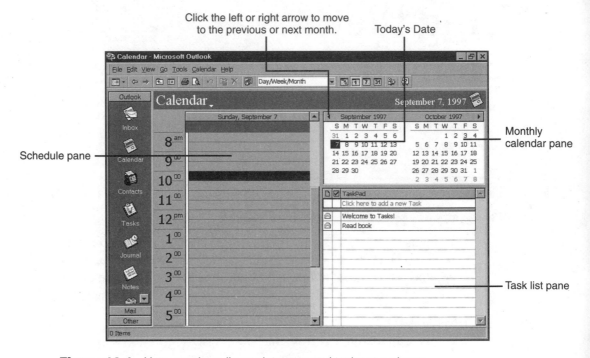

Figure 10.1 You can view all appointments and tasks at a glance.

 TIP **Change the Date Quickly** To quickly go to today's date or to a specific date without searching through the monthly calendar pane, right-click in the schedule pane and choose either **Go To Today** or **Go To Date**. If you choose **Go To Date,** a dialog box appears allowing you to specify the date and calendar in which it should appear.

Creating an Appointment

An *appointment* is an event that blocks time on your calendar. (In contrast, an *event* does not reserve calendar space.) When you create an appointment, you can add the subject, location, starting time, category, and even an alarm to remind you ahead of time.

TIP **Create Distant Appointments** You can create an appointment on any day well past the year 2000 using the Outlook Calendar.

Follow these steps to create an appointment:

1. In the monthly calendar pane, select the month and the date for which you want to create an appointment.

2. In the schedule pane, double-click next to the time at which the appointment is scheduled to begin. The Untitled—Appointment dialog box appears, with the Appointment tab displayed (see Figure 10.2).

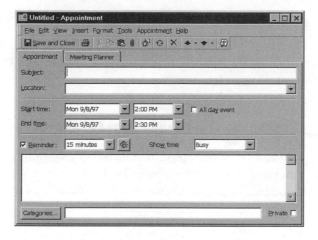

Figure 10.2 Enter all the details you need when scheduling an appointment.

3. Enter the subject of the appointment in the **Subject** text box (you can use a person's name, a topic, or other information).

4. In the **Location** text box, enter the meeting place or other text that will help you identify the meeting when you see it in your Calendar.

5. Enter dates and times in the **Start Time** and **End Time** text boxes (or click the drop-down arrows and select the dates and times).

TIP **Autodate It!** You can use Outlook's Autodate feature: Enter a text phrase such as "next Friday" or "noon" in the date and time text boxes, and Outlook figures out the date for you.

6. Select the **Reminder** check box and enter the amount of time before the appointment that you want to be notified. If you want to set an audio alarm, click the alarm bell button and select a specific sound for Outlook to play as your reminder.

7. From the **Show Time** drop-down list, choose how you want to display the scheduled time on your Calendar.

8. In the large text box near the bottom of the Appointment tab, enter any text that you want to include, such as text to identify the appointment or reminders for materials to take.

9. Click the **Categories** button and assign a category to the appointment.

10. Click the **Save and Close** button to return to the Calendar.

The Meeting Planner tab enables you to schedule a meeting with coworkers and enter the meeting on your Calendar. (See Lesson 11, "Planning a Meeting," for more information.)

Scheduling a Recurring Appointment

Suppose you have an appointment that comes around every week or month, or that otherwise occurs on a regular basis. Instead of scheduling every individual occurrence of the appointment, you can schedule that appointment in your calendar as a recurring appointment.

To schedule a recurring appointment, follow these steps:

1. Choose **Calendar**, **New Recurring Appointment**. The Appointment dialog box appears, and then the Appointment Recurrence dialog box appears (as shown in Figure 10.3).

2. In the Appointment Time area, enter the **Start**, **End**, and **Duration** times for the appointment.

3. In the Recurrence Pattern area, indicate the frequency of the appointment: **Daily**, **Weekly**, **Monthly**, or **Yearly**. After you select one of these options, the rest of the Recurrence Pattern area changes.

4. Enter the day and month, as well as any other option in the Recurrence Pattern area that is specific to your selection in step 3.

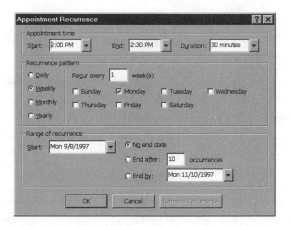

Figure 10.3 Schedule a recurring appointment once, and Outlook fills in the appointment for you throughout the Calendar.

5. In the Range of Recurrence area, enter appropriate time limits according to these guidelines:
   - **Start** Choose the date on which the recurring appointments begin.
   - **No End Date** Choose this option if the recurring appointments are not on a limited schedule.
   - **End After** Choose this option and enter the number of appointments if there is a specific limit to the recurring appointments.
   - **End By** Choose this option and enter an ending date to limit the number of recurring appointments.

6. Click **OK** to close the Appointment Recurrence dialog box. The Appointment dialog box appears.

7. Fill in the Appointment dialog box as described previously in this lesson. When you finish, click the **Save and Close** button to return to the Calendar. The recurring appointment appears in your calendar on the specified date and time. A recurring appointment contains a double arrow icon to indicate that it is recurring.

Planning Events

In the Outlook Calendar, an event is any activity that lasts at least 24 hours, such as a trade show or a conference. You can plan an event in the Calendar program to block off larger time slots than you would for normal appointments. In addition, you can schedule recurring events.

To schedule an event, choose **Calendar**, **New Event**. The Event dialog box appears; it looks very much like the New Appointment dialog box. Fill in the **Subject**, **Location**, **Start Time**, and **End Time** text boxes. Make sure the All Day Event check box is checked (that's the only difference between an Event and an Appointment). Click the **Save and Close** button to return to the Outlook Calendar. The appointment appears in gray at the beginning of the day for which you scheduled the event.

To schedule a recurring event, choose **Calendar**, **New Recurring Event**. Fill in the Appointment Recurrence dialog box as you learned to in the previous section. When you close the Appointment Recurrence dialog box, the Recurring Event dialog box appears. Fill it in as you would the Event dialog box. Then click the **Save and Close** button.

To edit an event or a recurring event, double-click the event in your calendar. As with an e-mail message or appointment, Outlook opens the event window so that you can change times, dates, or other details of the event.

In this lesson, you learned to navigate the Calendar, and create and save appointments. In the next lesson, you learn to plan a meeting.

Planning a Meeting

In this lesson, you learn to schedule a meeting, enter attendees for a planned meeting, set the meeting date and time, and invite others to the meeting.

Scheduling a Meeting

Outlook provides a method by which you can plan the time and date of a meeting, identify the subject and location of the meeting, specify what resources are needed, and invite others to attend the meeting. You use the Calendar folder to plan and schedule meetings. This feature is best employed in a network environment; if you are working on a standalone PC, you will not get the full benefit of the Calendar's capabilities.

Meeting   In Outlook, a meeting is an appointment to which you invite people and use resources.

Attendees   The people who will be attending your meeting.

Resources   Any equipment you use in your meeting, such as a computer, slide projector, or even the room itself.

To plan a meeting, follow these steps:

1. Click the icon for the Calendar folder, and then choose **Calendar**, **Plan a Meeting**. The Plan a Meeting dialog box appears (see Figure 11.1).

2. To enter the names of the attendees, click **Type Attendee Name Here** in the All Attendees list. Type in the name and press Enter. Continue adding new names as necessary.

TIP **Invite More People** You can click the **Invite Others** button to choose names from your Personal Address Book or the Outlook Address Book.

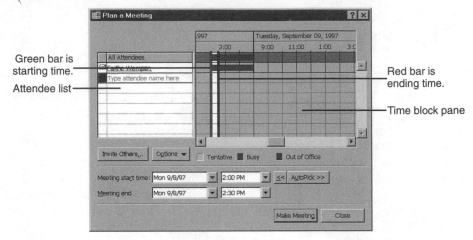

Green bar is starting time.

Attendee list

Red bar is ending time.

Time block pane

Figure 11.1 Choose the date and time of your meeting as well as the attendees.

3. To set a date for the meeting, open the left-most **Meeting Start Time** drop-down list and select the date from the calendar, or just type the date in the text box. The ending date, in the Meeting End Time drop-down list, automatically shows the same date you set in the Meeting Start Time date box. You can change the End Time date if you want.

4. To set a start time for the meeting, do one of the following:

- Open the right-most **Meeting Start Time** drop-down list and select the time.

- Type a time in the text box.

- Drag the green bar in the time block pane of the dialog box to set the start time.

5. To set an end time for the meeting, do one of the following:

- Open the right-most **Meeting End Time** drop-down list and select the end time.

- Type a time in the text box.

- Drag the red bar in the time block pane of the dialog box to change the ending time of the meeting.

6. When you finish planning the meeting, click the **Make Meeting** button. The Meeting window appears (see Figure 11.2), from which you can refine the meeting details, as described in the next section.

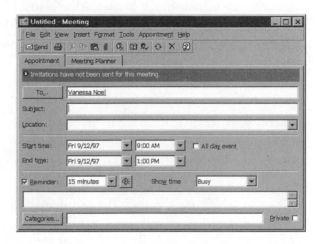

Figure 11.2 Specify the details about the meeting in the Appointment tab of the Meeting dialog box.

Working Out Meeting Details

After you plan a meeting, Outlook enables you to send invitations, identify the subject of the meeting, and specify the meeting's location. You enter these details in the Meeting dialog box.

When you schedule a meeting (as described in the previous section) you finish by clicking the **Make Meeting** button in the Plan a Meeting dialog box. When you do that, Outlook displays the Meeting dialog box with the Appointment tab in front (see Figure 11.2).

Follow these steps to specify meeting details for a meeting you've already scheduled.

1. If you did not list the attendees in the Plan a Meeting dialog box, either click in the **To** text box and enter the names of the people you want to attend the meeting, or click the **To** button to select the attendees from an address book.

2. In the **Subject** text box, enter a subject for the meeting.

3. In the **Location** text box, enter a location for the meeting.

4. (Optional) You can change the starting and ending dates or times in the Appointment tab. You also can choose the Meeting Planner tab to view the meeting in a format similar to that of the Plan a Meeting dialog box. Make any changes to attendees, time, or dates in the Meeting Planner tab.

5. (Optional) Select the **Reminder** check box and enter a time for Outlook to sound an alarm to remind you of the meeting.

6. (Optional) Enter any special text you want to send the attendees in the text box provided.

7. When you're ready to send the invitations to the meeting, click the **Send** button. Close the Meeting window by choosing **File**, **Close**, or click the window's **Close** button.

When you send an invitation, you're sending an e-mail that requests the presence of the recipient at the meeting. The recipient can reply to, save, forward, or delete your message, just as with any e-mail message. If you want the recipient to reply, choose **Appointment**, **Request Responses**, and the recipients will be prompted to reply to your invitation.

An Invitation Mistake   To cancel an invitation after you've sent it, choose **Appointment, Cancel Invitation**.

CAUTION

Inviting Others to the Meeting

If you need to add names to your attendees list—either while you're planning the meeting or at some later date—you can use your Personal Address Book or the Outlook Address Book to find the names of the people you want to invite. Additionally, you can choose whether to make the meeting required or optional for each person you invite.

To invite others to the meeting, follow these steps:

1. In either the Plan a Meeting dialog box or the Meeting Planner tab of the Meeting dialog box, click the **Invite Others** button. The Select Attendees and Resources dialog box appears, as shown in Figure 11.3.

2. Open the **Show Names From The** drop-down list and choose either **Personal Address Book** or **Outlook Address Book**.

3. To add a new name to a list, click the **New** button, and then enter the name, e-mail address, phone numbers, and other pertinent information about the name you're adding to the list.

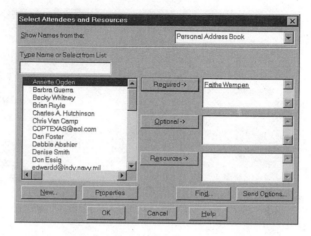

Figure 11.3 Use the address books to specify attendees to your meeting.

4. Select any name in the list on the left side of the dialog box and click the **Required** or **Optional** button to specify attendance requirements.

 TIP **Reserve Resources** If you need certain resources for your meeting, make sure that you later notify the person who is in charge of those resources so that they will be available.

5. Click **OK** to close the dialog box and add any attendees to your list.

Editing a Meeting

You can edit the details about a meeting, invite additional people, or change the date and time of the meeting at any time by opening the Meeting dialog box.

To open the Meeting dialog box and edit the meeting, follow these steps:

1. In the Calendar folder, choose the meeting date in the monthly calendar pane. The date appears in the schedule pane, and the meeting is blocked out for the time period you specified, as shown in Figure 11.4.
2. Double-click the meeting block to display the Meeting dialog box. You can edit anything in the Appointment or Meeting Planner tabs.

TIP **Any Responses?** Choose the **Show Attendee Status** option in the Meeting
Planner tab of the Meeting dialog box to see if the people you invited to the
meeting have responded to your invitation.

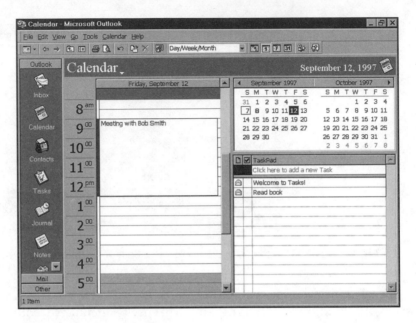

Figure 11.4 Select the meeting you want to edit from within the Calendar.

3. When you're done, choose **File**, **Close** to close the Meeting dialog box. If
you've made changes to the meeting specifics, you should also send a
message to your attendees to notify them of the change.

In this lesson, you learned to schedule a meeting, enter attendees for a planned
meeting, set the meeting time, and invite others to the meeting. In the next
lesson, you learn to create a contacts list.

Creating a
Contacts List

*In this lesson, you learn to create and view a Contacts list and
to send mail to someone on the list.*

Creating a New Contact

You use the Contacts folder to create, store, and utilize your Contacts list. (Refer
to Figure 12.1 to see the type of information you can store about each of your
contacts.)

Contact   In Outlook, a *contact* is any person or company for which you've
entered a name, address, phone number, or other information. You can
communicate with a contact in Outlook by sending an e-mail message,
scheduling a meeting, or sending a letter.

You also can edit the information at any time, add new contacts, or delete
contacts from the list. To create a new contact, follow these steps:

1. Click the **Contacts** folder or open the Folder List and choose **Contacts**. If
   you haven't used the list before, the folder is empty.

2. Choose **Contacts**, **New Contact**, or click the **New Contact** button on the
   Toolbar. The Contact dialog box appears, with the General tab displayed
   (see Figure 12.1).

3. Click the **Full Name** button to display the Check Full Name dialog box,
   and then enter the contact's title and full name (including first, middle, and
   last names) and any suffix you want to include. Alternatively, you can type
   the name directly in the text box.

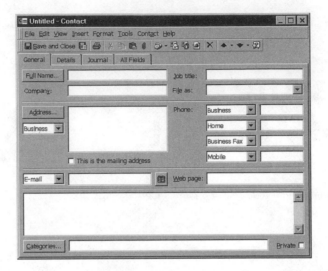

Figure 12.1   You can enter as much or as little information about each contact as you need.

   4. (Optional) Enter the client's company name and job title.

   5. In the **File As** drop-down box, enter or select the method by which you
      want to file your contact's names. You can choose last name first or first
      name first, or you can enter your own filing system, such as by company or
      state.

   TIP   Keep It Simple   The default filing method for contacts is last name first,
   which makes it easy to quickly find the contact when you need it.

   6. (Optional) Enter the address in the Address box and choose whether the
      address is **Business**, **Home**, or **Other**. Alternatively, you can click the
      Address button to enter the street, city, state, ZIP code, and country in
      specified areas instead of all within the text block. You can add a second
      address (say, the Home address) if you want.

   7. In the Phone drop-down lists, choose the type of phone number—Business,
      Callback, Car, Home Fax, ISDN, or Pager—and then enter the number.
      You can enter up to 19 numbers in each of the four drop-down boxes in the
      Phone area of the dialog box.

8. (Optional) Enter up to three e-mail addresses in the **E-mail** text box. In the **Web Page** text box, enter the address for the company or contact's Web page on the Internet.

9. (Optional) In the comment text box, enter any descriptions, comments, or other pertinent information you want. Then select or enter a category to classify the contact. You may choose from a variety of categories. Simply check the box next to the desired category.

10. Open the **File** menu and choose one of the following commands:

   - **Save** Saves the record and closes the Contact dialog box.
   - **Save and New** Saves the record and clears the Contact dialog box so that you can enter a new contact.
   - **Save and New in Company** Saves the record and clears the Name, Job Title, File As, E-Mail, and comment text boxes so that you can enter a new contact within the same company.

You can edit the information about a contact at any time by double-clicking the contact's name in the Contacts list; this displays the contact's information window. Alternatively, you can click within the information listed below a contact's name (such as the phone number or address) to position the insertion point in the text, and then delete or enter text. Press **Enter** to complete the modifications you've made and move to the next contact in the list.

Viewing the Contacts List

By default, you see the contacts in an Address Cards view. The information you see is the contact's name and other data such as addresses and phone numbers. The contact's company name, job title, and comments, however, are not displayed by default. Figure 12.2 shows the Contacts list in the default Address Cards view.

You can use the horizontal scroll bar to view more contacts, or you can click a letter in the index to display contacts beginning with that letter in the first column of the list.

View drop-down list

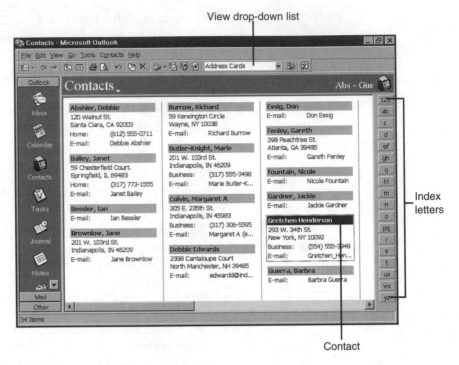

Figure 12.2 View your contacts in Address Cards view.

Do I Save View Settings? Depending on the changes you make to a view, Outlook might display the Save View Settings dialog box to ask if you want to save the view settings before you switch to a different view. If you **CAUTION** choose to save the current settings, Outlook lets you name the view and adds that view to the Current View list. If you choose to discard the current settings, your modifications to the view will be lost. If you choose to update the view, your modifications are saved with that view.

You can change how you view the contacts in the list by choosing one of these options from the Current View drop-down list on the standard toolbar:

- **Address Cards** Displays File As names (last name first and first name last), addresses, and phone numbers of the contacts, depending on the amount of information you've entered in a card format.

- **Detailed Address Cards** Displays File As name, full name, job title, company, addresses, phone numbers, e-mail addresses, categories, and comments in a card format.

- **Phone List**   Displays full name, job title, company, File As name, department, phone numbers, and categories in a table, organizing each entry horizontally in rows and columns.

- **By Category**   Displays contacts in rows by categories. The information displayed is the same as what's displayed in a phone list.

- **By Company**   Displays contacts in rows, grouped by their company. The information displayed is the same as what's displayed in a phone list.

- **By Location**   Displays contacts grouped by country. The information displayed is the same as what's displayed in a phone list.

Communicating with a Contact

You can send messages to any of your contacts, arrange meetings, assign tasks, or even send a letter to a contact from within Outlook. To communicate with a contact, make sure you're in the Contacts folder. You do not need to open the specific contact's information window to perform any of the following procedures.

Sending Messages

To send a message from the Contacts folder, select the contact and choose **Contacts**, **New Message** to Contact or click the New Message to Contact button. In the Untitled—Message dialog box, enter the subject and message and set any options you want. When you're ready to send the message, click the **Send** button. (For more information about sending mail, see Lesson 6, "Creating Mail.")

To send a message to a contact, you must make sure you've entered an e-mail address in the General tab of the Contact dialog box for that particular contact. If Outlook cannot locate the mailing address, it displays the message dialog box shown in Figure 12.3.

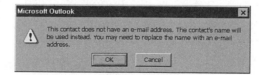

Figure 12.3   Outlook cannot send the message until you complete the address in the New Message dialog box.

Scheduling a Meeting with a Contact

To schedule a meeting with a contact, the contact must have a valid e-mail address. If no address is listed for the contact, Outlook notifies you with a message box and enables you to enter an address within the Message dialog box. If the listed address is not found, Outlook responds with the Check Names dialog box.

 To schedule a meeting with a contact, select the contact and choose **Contacts**, **New Meeting with Contact** or click the New Meeting with Contact button The Untitled—Meeting dialog box appears. Enter the subject, location, time and date, and other information you need to schedule the meeting, and then notify the contact by sending an invitation. (For more information about scheduling meetings, see Lesson 11, "Planning a Meeting.")

Assigning a Task to a Contact

Tasks are assigned through e-mail. Therefore, you must enter a valid e-mail address for the contact before you can assign him or her a task.

To assign a task to a contact, select the contact and choose **Contacts**, **New Task for Contact**. The Task dialog box appears. Enter the subject, due date, status, and other information, and then send the task to the contact. (For detailed information about assigning tasks, see Lesson 13, "Creating a Task List.")

Sending a Letter to a Contact

Outlook uses the Microsoft Word Letter Wizard to help you create a letter to send to a contact. Within the Word Wizard, follow the directions as they appear on-screen to complete the text of the letter.

To send a letter to the contact, select the contact in the Contact folder and choose **Contacts**, **New Letter to Contact**. Word opens the Letter Wizard on-screen. The Letter Wizard helps you format and complete the letter (see Figure 12.4). You can click the Office Assistant button if you need additional help. Then all you have to do is follow the directions and make your choices.

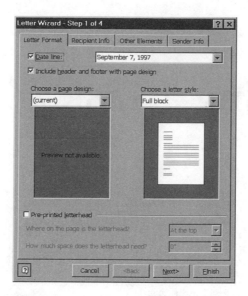

Figure 12.4   Use Word's Letter Wizard to create a letter to a contact.

In this lesson, you learned to create a Contacts list, view the list, and send e-mail to someone on your Contacts list. In the next lesson, you learn to create a task list.

Creating a Task List

In this lesson, you learn to enter a task and record statistics about it.

Entering a Task

You can use the Task folder to create and manage your task list. You can list due dates, status, priorities, and even set reminder alarms so that you don't forget to perform certain tasks.

 Task List   A *task list* is a list of things you must do to complete your work, plan for a meeting, arrange an event, and so on. Various tasks might include making a phone call, writing a letter, printing a spreadsheet, or making airline reservations.

To enter a task, follow these steps:

1. If the Tasks folder is not already open, open it from the Outlook Bar or the Folder List.

2. In the Tasks folder, choose **Tasks**, **New Task** or click the **New Task** button on the Toolbar. The Untitled—Task dialog box appears (see Figure 13.1).

3. With the Task tab displayed, enter the subject of the task in the **Subject** text box.

4. (Optional) Enter a date on which the task should be complete, or click the down arrow to open the **Due** drop-down calendar and then choose a due date.

5. (Optional) Enter a start date, or click the down arrow to open the **Start** drop-down calendar and then choose a starting date.

6. From the **Status** drop-down list, choose the current status of the project: Not Started, In Progress, Completed, Waiting on Someone Else, or Deferred.

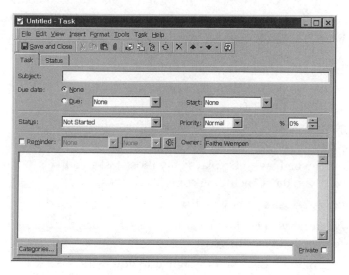

Figure 13.1 Enter data such as due dates, priority, and the subject of the task.

7. In the **Priority** drop-down list, choose Normal, Low, or High priority.

8. In the % text box, type a percentage of completeness or use the spinner arrows to enter one.

9. (Optional) To set an alarm to remind you to start the task or complete the task, select the **Reminder** check box and enter a date and a time in the associated text boxes.

10. Enter any comments, descriptions, or other information related to the task in the comments text box.

11. Click the **Categories** button and choose a category, or enter your own category in the text box.

TIP **Access Denied** Select the **Private** check box if you don't want others to see information about your task.

12. Click the **Save and Close** button when you're done.

Viewing Tasks

As in any Outlook folder, you can change how you view tasks in the list by using the Current View drop-down list in the Standard Toolbar. By default, the Tasks folder displays tasks in a Simple List view. The following is a description of the views you can use to display the Tasks folder:

- **Simple List**   Lists the tasks, completed check box, subject, and due date.
- **Detailed List**   Displays the tasks, priority, subject, status, percent complete, and categories.
- **Active Tasks**   Displays the same information as the detailed list but doesn't show any completed tasks.
- **Next Seven Days**   Displays only those tasks you've scheduled for the next seven days, including completed tasks.
- **Overdue Tasks**   Shows a list of tasks that are past due.
- **By Category**   Displays tasks by category; click the button representing the category you want to view.
- **Assignment**   Lists tasks assigned to you by others.
- **By Person Responsible**   Lists tasks grouped by the person who assigned the tasks.
- **Completed Tasks**   Lists only those tasks completed, along with their due dates and completion dates.
- **Task Timeline**   Uses the Timeline view to display tasks by day, week, or month. (Figure 13.2 shows the tasks assigned within one week.)

 TIP   **Save What Settings?**   Depending on the changes you make to a view, Outlook might display the **Save View Settings** dialog box asking if you want to save the view settings before you switch to a different view. Generally, you want to discard the current view settings and leave everything the way you found it.

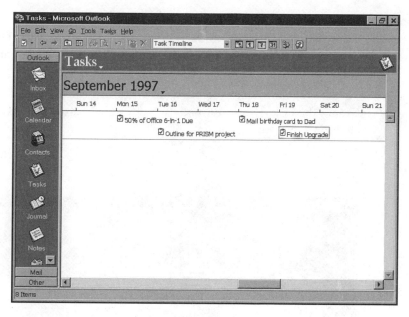

Figure 13.2   Double-click a task in Timeline view to edit it.

Managing Tasks

When working with a task list, you can add and delete tasks, mark tasks as completed, and arrange the tasks within the list. (You also can perform any of these procedures in most of the task views described in the previous section. For information about printing a task list, see Lesson 14, "Printing in Outlook.") Figure 13.3 shows the Task folder.

The following list describes how to manage certain tasks in the list:

- To quickly add a task, click the top row of the task list where it says "Click Here to Add a New Task" and enter the subject and date.

- To edit a task, double-click the task in the list. The Task dialog box appears (refer to Figure 13.1).

- To mark a task as completed, click the check box in the second column from the left, or right-click the task and choose **Mark Complete** from the shortcut menu. Outlook places a line through the task.

- To delete a task, right-click the task and choose **Delete** from the shortcut menu.

- To assign a task to someone else, right-click the task and choose **Assign Task** from the shortcut menu. Fill in the name of the person to whom you want to assign the task and click the **Send** button to e-mail him the task request.

- To assign a new task to someone else, choose **Tasks, New Task Request**. Create the task as you normally would, but send the task as an e-mail by clicking the **Send** button.

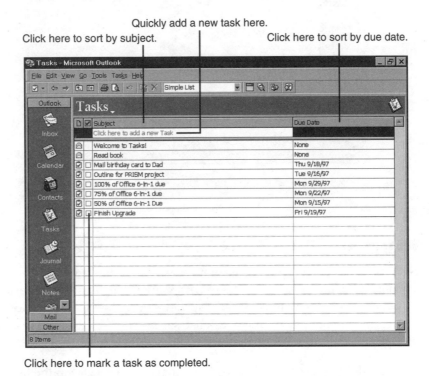

Quickly add a new task here.

Click here to sort by subject.

Click here to sort by due date.

Click here to mark a task as completed.

Figure 13.3   Add, delete, and sort the tasks in your list.

TIP   Get Rid of the Default Task   If you don't want to leave the Welcome to Tasks! task on your list, you can right-click the task and choose **Delete**.

Recording Statistics About a Task

You can record statistics about a task—such as time spent completing the task, billable time, and contacts—for your own records or for reference when sharing tasks with your coworkers. This feature is particularly helpful when you assign tasks to others because it allows you to keep track of assigned tasks and find out when they are completed.

To enter statistics about a task, open any task in the task list and click the **Status** tab. (Figure 13.4 shows a completed Status tab for a sample task.)

The following list describes the text boxes in the Status tab and the types of information you can enter:

- **Date Completed** Enter the date the task was completed, or click the arrow to display the calendar and choose the date.
- **Total Work** Enter the amount of time you expect the task to take. When you complete the job, Outlook calculates the actual time spent and enters it in this text box.

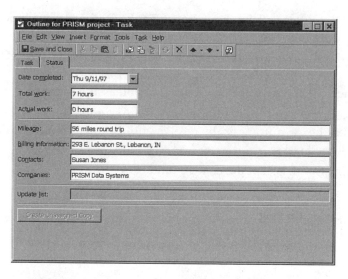

Figure 13.4 Fill in the status of the task so that you can share it with others and keep personal records.

- **Actual Work** Enter the amount of time it actually took to complete the job.
- **Mileage** Enter the number of miles you traveled to complete the task.
- **Billing Information** Enter any specific billing information, such as hours billed, resources used, or charges for equipment.
- **Contacts** Enter the names of in-house or outside contacts associated with the task. Separate multiple names with semicolons.
- **Companies** Enter the names of any companies associated with the contacts or with the project in general.
- **Update List** Automatically lists the people whose task lists are updated when you make a change to your task.
- **Create Unassigned Copy** Copies the task so that it can be reassigned. Use this button to send a task to someone other than an original recipient. If the task is not sent to someone else, the button is unavailable.

To track tasks you've assigned to others and to receive status reports, follow these steps:

1. In the Outlook dialog box, choose **Tools, Options**. The Options dialog box appears with the Tasks/Notes tab displayed.
2. In the Task Defaults area of the dialog box, check the **Keep Updated Copies of Assigned Tasks on My Task List** check box. This automatically tracks the progress of new tasks that you assign to others.
3. Check the **Send Status Reports When Assigned Tasks Are Completed** check box to automatically receive notification upon the completion of assigned tasks.
4. Click **OK** to accept the changes and close the dialog box.

 TIP **Color Coding** You also can set colors to represent tasks within the Tasks/Notes tab of the Options dialog box. Outlook offers 20 different colors from which you can choose for overdue and completed tasks.

In this lesson, you learned to enter a task and record statistics about it. In the next lesson, you learn to print in Outlook.

Printing in Outlook

In this lesson, you learn to print items in Outlook, change the page setup, preview an item before printing it, and change printer properties.

Choosing Page Setup

Before printing in Outlook, choose the print style you want to use. Each folder—Inbox, Calendar, or Contacts—offers various print styles, and each style displays the data on the page in a different way.

 Page In Outlook, this is the area of the paper on which your information prints. You might, for example, print two or four pages on a single sheet of paper.

 Print Style The combination of paper and page settings that controls printed output.

You can choose from Outlook's built-in print styles, modify the default print styles, or create your own print styles. These lists show the default print styles available for each folder.

The Inbox, Contacts, and Tasks use the following two styles:

- **Table Style** Displays data in columns and rows on an 8.5×11 sheet, portrait orientation, .5-inch margins.
- **Memo Style** Displays data with a header of information about the message and then straight text on an 8.5×11 sheet, portrait orientation with .5-inch margins.

The Calendar folder provides the Memo style, plus the following styles:

- **Daily Style** Displays one day's appointments on one page on an 8.5×11 sheet, portrait orientation with .5-inch margins.
- **Weekly Style** Displays one week's appointments per page on an 8.5×11 sheet, portrait orientation with .5-inch margins.
- **Monthly Style** Displays one month's appointments per page on an 8.5×11 sheet, landscape orientation with .5-inch margins.
- **Tri-fold Style** Displays the daily calendar, task list, and weekly calendar on an 8.5×11 sheet, landscape orientation with .5-inch margins.

The Contacts folder provides the Memo style, plus the following styles:

- **Card Style** Two columns and headings on an 8.5×11 sheet, portrait orientation with .5-inch margins.
- **Small Booklet Style** One-column page that equals 1/8 of a sheet of paper—so that eight pages are on one 8.5×11 sheet of paper with .5-inch margins. Then the portrait orientation applies to the 1/8 pages.
- **Medium Booklet Style** One column that equals 1/4 of a sheet of paper— so that four pages are on one 8.5×11 sheet of paper. Portrait orientation with .5-inch margins.
- **Phone Directory Style** One column, 8.5×11 sheet of paper, portrait orientation with .5-inch margins.

TIP **Page Setup Only Matters in Printing** No matter how you set up your pages, it will not affect your view of tasks, calendars, or other Outlook items on-screen. Page setup only applies to the appearance of a printed job.

You can view, modify, and create new page setups in Outlook. To view or edit a page setup, follow these steps:

1. Change to the folder for which you're setting the page.
2. Choose **File**, **Page Setup**. A secondary menu appears that lists the available print types.
3. Select the print type you want to view or edit. The Page Setup dialog box appears (see Figure 14.1).
4. Click the **Format** tab to view or edit the page type, to choose options (in some cases), and to change fonts.

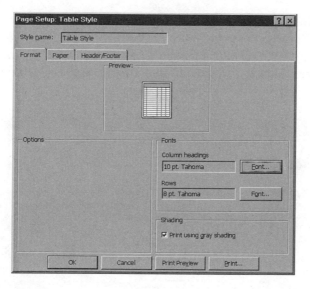

Figure 14.1 Customize the print type to suit yourself.

5. Click the **Paper** tab to view or edit paper size, page size, margins, and orientation.

6. Click the **Header/Footer** tab to view or edit headers for your pages.

7. Click **OK** to close the dialog box.

Previewing Before Printing

You can choose to preview an item before printing to be sure that it prints correctly. If you do not like the way an item looks in preview, you can change the page setup.

Before you display an item in print preview, you must navigate to the folder containing the item you want to print. Then you can choose to preview the item in any of the following ways:

- Choose **File**, **Print Preview**.
- Click the **Print Preview** button on the standard toolbar.
- Click the **Preview** button in the Print dialog box.
- Click the **Print Preview** button in the Page Setup dialog box.

Figure 14.2 shows a calendar and task list in Print Preview. You can change the page setup by clicking the **Page Setup** button and making changes in the Page Setup dialog box. Click the **Print** button on the Print Preview toolbar to send the job to the printer. Click the **Close** button on the Print Preview toolbar to exit Print Preview and return to the Outlook folder.

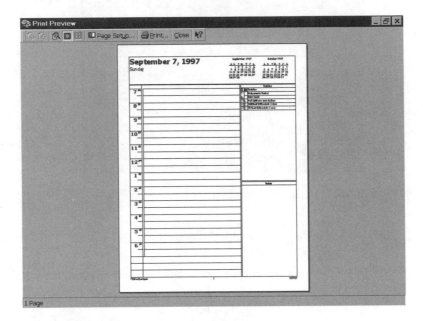

Figure 14.2   Preview the item before printing it.

 TIP   **Enlarge the View**   When the mouse pointer looks like a magnifying glass with a plus sign in it, you can click to enlarge the page. When the mouse pointer looks like a magnifying glass with a minus sign in it, you can click to reduce the view again.

Printing Items

After you choose the print style and preview an item to make sure it's what you want, you can print the item. You can indicate the number of copies you want to print, select a printer, change the print style or page setup, and set a print range.

When you're ready to print an item, follow these steps:

1. Choose **File**, **Print** or click the **Print** button on the standard toolbar. The Print dialog box appears, as shown in Figure 14.3.

2. In the Printer area of the dialog box, choose a different printer from the **Name** drop-down list if necessary.

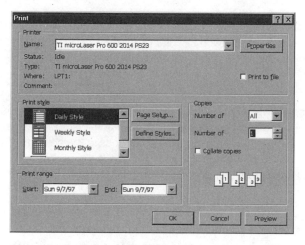

Figure 14.3 Set the printing options before printing the item.

TIP **In a Hurry?** If your computer is on a network and you notice the status of the selected printer is busy or paused, for example, choose a different printer from the drop-down list.

3. In the Print Style area, choose a print style from the list. You also can edit the page setup (with the Page Setup button), or edit or create a new style (with the Define Styles button).

4. In the Copies area of the dialog box, choose **All**, **Even**, or **Odd** from the drop-down list, and enter the number of copies you want to print. Click the **Collate Copies** check box if you want Outlook to automatically assemble multiple copies.

5. Set the print range with the options in that area. (The Print Range options vary depending on the type of item you're printing.)

6. Click **OK** to print the item.

Setting Printer Properties

Whether you're printing to a printer connected directly to your computer or to a printer on the network, you can set printer properties. The properties you set apply to all print jobs you send to the printer until you change the properties again.

 Printer Properties   Configurations specific to a printer connected to your computer or to the network. Printer properties include paper orientation, paper source, graphics settings, fonts, and print quality.

 Access Denied?   If you cannot change the printer properties to a network printer, it's probably because the network administrator has set the printer's configuration, and you're not allowed access to the settings. If you need to change printer properties and cannot access the printer's Properties dialog box, talk to your network administrator.

To set printer properties, open the Print dialog box (by choosing **File**, **Print**). In the Printer area, select a printer from the **Name** drop-down list, and then click the **Properties** button. The printers' Properties dialog boxes differ depending on the make and model of printer.

Most likely, you can set paper size, page orientation, and paper source by using options on a Paper tab in the dialog box. In addition, you may see a Graphics tab, in which you can set the resolution, intensity, and graphics mode of your printer. A Fonts tab enables you to set options on TrueType fonts, font cartridges, and so on. You might also find a Device Options tab, in which you can set print quality and other options. (For more information about your printer, read the documentation that came with it.)

In this lesson, you learned to print items in Outlook, change the page setup, preview an item before printing it, and change printer properties. In the next lesson, you learn to manage your files and Outlook items.

Saving, Opening, and Finding Outlook Items

In this lesson, you learn to save items, open items, and find items in Outlook.

Saving Items

Generally, when you finish adding a new task, appointment, meeting, contact, or other item, Outlook automatically saves that item for you or you're prompted to save the item yourself. You also can save most items in Outlook for use in other applications by using the Save As command. After you save an item by naming it, you can open that same item and edit, print, or otherwise use the saved file in Windows applications that support the file type. You might save an item—a journal entry or appointment page, for example—so that you can refer to it later, edit the original, or keep it as a record.

 Save As   When you save an item using the File, Save As command, you can designate a drive, directory, and new filename for that item, as well as a file type.

 File Type   A file type is the same thing as a file format. When you save a file, you specify a file type that identifies the file as one that can be opened in specific applications. The file extension .doc, for example, identifies a file type that you can open in Word, and the extension .txt represents a text-only format you can open in nearly any word processor or other application.

To save an item, follow these steps:

1. In the folder containing the item you want to save, choose **File**, **Save As**. The Save As dialog box appears (see Figure 15.1).

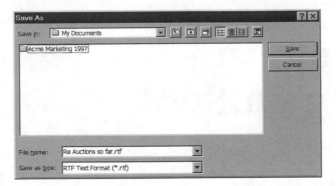

Figure 15.1 Save items as files for use in other programs, as copies of the originals, or for later use.

 TIP **Why Is Save As Dimmed?** When the Save As command is dimmed, you must first select an item—an appointment, meeting, task, or note—before you can save it.

2. From the **Save In** drop-down list, choose the drive to which you want to save the file. From the folders on that drive, select the appropriate drive.

3. In the **Save As Type** drop-down list, choose a file type. You can save the file in the following file types:

- **Text Only** Saves in an ASCII format (plain text) that you can use in other applications, such as Word, or Notepad.
- **RTF Text Format** Saves in rich text format, a format that many word processors can read. You also can use this format in Word, Outlook, or Lotus Notes, for example.
- **Outlook Template** Saves as a template (or style sheet) that you can use as a basis for other items.
- **Message Format** Saves in a format you can use in your e-mail messages.

4. Enter a name for the item in the **File Name** text box, or accept the default.

5. Click the **Save** button.

Opening and Using Saved Items

After you save items, you can open and use them in Outlook and other applications. If, for example, you saved a contact as a message file, you can insert that file into a message and send the contact's name, address, and other information to someone through an e-mail message. You can save other items—such as meeting information from your calendar—as a text file you can open in Notepad or Word to edit, format, print, or otherwise modify the file.

Opening and Using an RTF File

You can open RTF files in many word processing programs—for example, Word, Notepad, or WordPad. Unlike text-only format, RTF retains some formatting, like font choices and margins. To open an RTF file in Outlook or another Windows application, choose **File**, **Open**. In the Open dialog box, choose **Rich Text Format** (or **RTF Text Format**) from the **Files of Type** drop-down list. The saved files appear in the file list. Select the file and click the **Open** button.

CAUTION

RTF Isn't Listed? If RTF isn't listed in the application's Files of Type list box, see whether Text Only is listed. You can also save Outlook items as Text Only.

Figure 15.2 shows an e-mail message saved as an RTF file and opened in Word. After opening a file, you can format it, cut or copy items to it, insert objects, print, edit, and otherwise manipulate the file. In addition, you can open and read the attachment from within the saved RTF file.

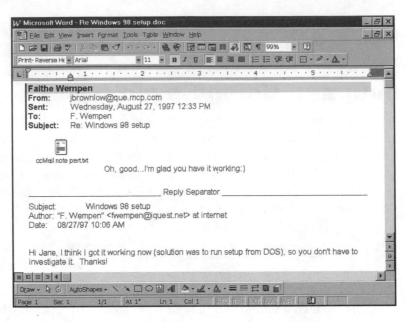

Figure 15.2   Exchanging data between applications makes your work quicker and easier.

Opening and Using a Text-Only File

You open a text-only file in much the same way you open an RTF file. In Notepad, for example, choose **File**, **Open** and choose **Text Documents** as the file type in the Open dialog box. Files saved as text-only do not retain any formatting; however, you can select the text and format it in the destination application.

Using a Message Text File

After you save an item as a message text file, you can insert the item into an e-mail message to send. Suppose you saved a contact's information or an especially long note that you want to share with someone else; you can insert the file as an object into a message and send the e-mail as you normally would. Then the recipient can open the message and the message file.

TIP **Files As Objects** As described in Lesson 10, "Using the Calendar," you can insert any existing file as an object; therefore, you can insert an RTF, text-only, or message file into any Windows document that supports OLE (Object Linking and Embedding). For more information about OLE see Appendix C, "Object Linking and Embedding."

To insert a message file into a message, open the message and choose **Insert**, **Object**. In the Insert Object dialog box, choose **Create from File**. Enter the path and filename (or click Browse to browse for it) and click **OK**. (Figure 15.3 shows a message file in the text of an e-mail.)

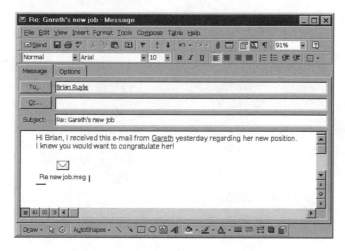

Figure 15.3 Open the MSG file by double-clicking its icon.

Finding Items

Outlook provides a method you can use to locate items on your computer. You can search for messages, files, journal entries, notes, tasks, contacts, and appointments. You can search for specific words, categories, priority, item size, and other criteria that you stipulate. Outlook's Find feature can be especially useful if your folders become full, and locating items on your own is difficult.

Criteria Guidelines you set in the Find dialog box that Outlook uses to find items, such as messages, contacts, or appointments. Included in the criteria you set may be the date an item was created, the title or subject of the item, or specific text within the item.

To find an item in Outlook, follow these steps:

 1. Choose **Tools**, **Find Items** or click the **Find Items** button on the Standard toolbar. The Find dialog box appears, as shown in Figure 15.4.

 My Dialog Box Is Different The Find dialog box in Figure 15.4 was opened from the Inbox. If you open the Find dialog box from Calendar, Tasks, or any other folder, the options in the dialog box relate to the item for which you're searching.

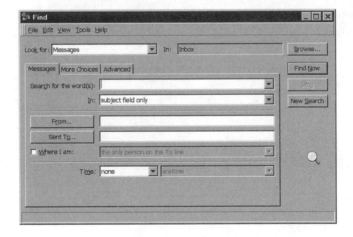

Figure 15.4 Use the Find dialog box to search for messages, appointments, and other items.

2. In any Find dialog box, choose the item for which you want to search in the **Look For** drop-down list. You can choose Tasks, Notes, Messages, Journal Entries, Files, Contacts, Appointments and Meetings, or Any Type of Outlook Item.

3. Click the **Browse** button to display the Select Folder(s) dialog box, from which you can choose the folder to search.

4. On the first tab, which is named for the item you select in the Look For list, you can enter specific words to search for, fields you want to search, dates, contact names, or file types. The second tab, More Choices, offers additional options to add to the search, such as item size and category. Set the options you want on both tabs.

TIP Narrow the Search   The more options you select and specify in the Find dialog box, the more you narrow the search, meaning that fewer items will match the search criteria. However, when you select more options, the search could take longer.

5. When you're ready to find the item(s), click the **Find Now** button. The Find dialog box extends to display a list of items that match the search criteria. In addition to the name of the item, the search results also show the folder in which you'll find the item, along with other item details.

You can perform a new search by clicking the New Search button, which clears the text boxes and previously selected options, and entering new criteria. If you want to pause or stop a search that's taking too long, click the **Stop** button.

TIP Fast Find   When you're in the Inbox, an extra Find command appears on the Tools menu: Find All. With the Find All command, you can choose to find all messages related to the selected message or all messages from the sender of the selected message. The Find dialog box appears, displaying a list of the matching messages.

Using the Advanced Search

The Find dialog box includes an Advanced tab that contains options you can use to perform more detailed searches than you can with the other options in the dialog box. On the Advanced tab, you can set multiple search criteria such as a category, author, and subject or a message flag and priority setting.

To use the Advanced tab in the Find dialog box, follow these steps:

1. Open the Find dialog box by choosing **Tools**, **Find Items** or clicking the Find Items button on the toolbar

2. (Optional) Set any criteria you want on the Item tab and More Choices tab.

3. Click the **Advanced** tab.

4. On the Advanced tab, choose the **Field** drop-down list to define more criteria. You can choose from multiple commands, each of which displays a secondary menu. The commands and secondary menus depend on the item for which you're searching. The following are a few of the fields for the Message item:

   - **Frequently-Used Fields**   Includes fields such as Categories, Created, Duration, Location, Recurrence, and Subject.

   - **Date/Time Fields**   Includes Created, Duration, and Start.

   - **All Appointment Fields**   Includes such fields as Importance, Meeting Status, Notes, Recurring, Reminder, and Resources.

   - **All Mail Fields**   Includes Categories, Created, Expires, and Subject.

   - **All Tasks Fields**   Includes % Complete, Conversation, Due Date, Mileage, Notes, Owner, and Priority.

   - **All Journal Fields**   Includes Billing Information, Company, Entry Type, Sensitivity, and Start.

5. After you choose a field, select the condition from the **Condition** drop-down list. Conditions include such constraints as whether the field is empty and exactly what values or word the field contains. For example, you might choose the field Category and the condition Contains.

6. If you choose a condition that specifies the contents of the field, next you fill in the **Value**. A value might be a name, word, note color, priority, or other text found in the item.

7. Click the **Add to List** button. Any criteria you set is listed in the Find Items That Match These Criteria list box. More items are added as you select them in the Advanced tab.

8. When you've finished setting your criteria, click the **Find Now** button.

Figure 15.5 shows the Advanced tab before adding the final criterion for which to search. The results of this search shows any messages that do not contain the words "Bender Printing" in the Message text.

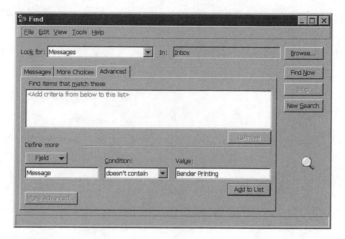

Figure 15.5 Set advanced criteria to find specific items.

In this lesson, you learned to save items, open items, and find items in Outlook.

Access

What Is a Database?

In this lesson, you learn some basic database concepts and find out how Microsoft Access handles them.

What Are Databases Good For?

Strictly speaking, a database is any collection of information. Your local telephone book, for example, is a database, as is your Rolodex file and the card catalog at your local library. With a computerized database in Microsoft Access, you can store information as these three examples do, but you can also do much more. For instance, if you keep a list of all your business customers in an Access database, you can:

- Print out a list of all customers who haven't bought anything in the last 60 days, along with their phone numbers, so you can call each one.
- Sort the customers by ZIP code and print out mailing labels in that order. (Some bulk-mailing services require you to presort by ZIP code to get the cheaper mailing rate.)
- Create a simple on-screen order entry form that even your most technically unskilled employee can use successfully.

These examples only scratch the surface of what you can do. With Access, you can manipulate your data in almost any way you can dream.

How Access Stores Your Data

In Access, the first thing you do is create a database file. That file holds everything you create for that database—not only all the data, but also the customized forms, reports, and indexes. If you have two or more businesses, you may want to create two or more separate databases (one for each business).

Tables

The heart of each database is its tables. A table is a lot like a spreadsheet. Figure 1.1 shows a data table (or just *table* for short).

Each column is a field.

Each row is a record.

The intersection of a row and column is a cell.

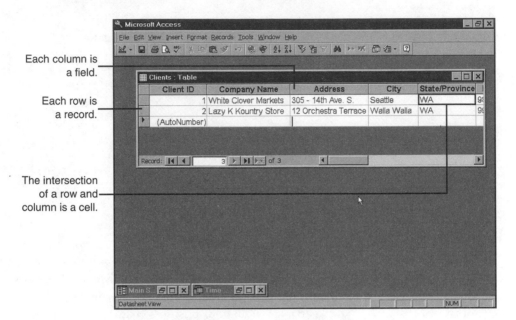

Figure 1.1 A typical table in Access.

Access stores each database entry (such as each client or each inventory item) in its own row; this is a *record*. For example, all the information about White Clover Markets, including the Address, City, State, and ZIP code, forms a single record (see Figure 1.1).

Each type of detail is kept in its own column: a *field*. For example, Client ID is one field, and Company Name is another. All the company names in the entire table are collectively known as the Company Name field.

At the intersection of a field and a row is the individual bit of data for that particular record; this area is a *cell*. For example, in the cell where the City column and the White Clover Markets record intersect, you find Seattle.

You learn how to create tables in Lesson 6, "Creating a Table with the Table Wizard," and Lesson 7, "Creating a Table Without a Wizard." Each database file can have many tables. For instance, you might have one table that lists all your customers and another table that lists information about the products you sell. A third table might keep track of your salespeople and their performance.

Forms

All the data you enter into your database ends up in a table for storage. You can enter information directly into a table, but it's a little awkward to do so. Most people find it easier to create a special on-screen form in which to enter the data. A form resembles any fill-in-the-blanks sheet that you might complete by hand, such as a job application. You learn how to create a form in Lesson 12, "Creating a Simple Form."

Access links the form to the table and stores the information you put into the form in the table. For instance, take a look at Figure 1.2. Access stores the client data entered on this form in the table shown in Figure 1.1.

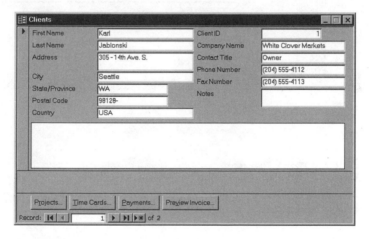

Figure 1.2 Forms make data entry more convenient.

 TIP **Multitable Forms** You can use a single form to enter data into several tables at once, as you will learn in later lessons.

Reports

While forms are designed to be used on-screen, reports are designed to be printed. Reports are specially formatted collections of data, organized according to your specifications. For instance, you might want to create a report of all your clients like the one shown in Figure 1.3.

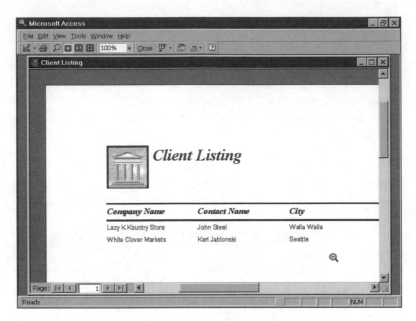

Figure 1.3   You might print this report to distribute to other employees.

   TIP   **Print Preview**   Although you create reports so that you can print them, you can also display them on-screen in Print Preview (as in Figure 1.3). You learn how to view and print reports in Lesson 18, "Creating a Simple Report."

Queries

A *query* provides you with a way of weeding out the information you don't want to see, so that you can more clearly see the information you do need. You can think of it as a sieve into which you dump your data: the data you don't want falls through the holes in the sieve, leaving only the data in which you're interested.

Many people are afraid of queries because of the technical terms associated with them (such as values, criteria, and masks). But there's no need to be wary. In Lesson 16, "Creating a Query," you learn to create and use a simple query.

How the Parts Fit Together

Even though you create tables, reports, forms, and queries in separate steps, they're all related. As I mentioned earlier, tables are the central focus of all activities—all the other objects do something to or with the table data. Reports summarize and organize the table data; forms help you enter information into the table; queries help you find information you want to use in the table. In future lessons, you will learn how each part relates to the whole database.

Access Wizards Make Databases Easy

Throughout this book, you will use the Access wizards. What's a wizard? It's a mini program that *interviews* you, asking you questions about what you want to accomplish. Then it takes your answers and creates the table, report, query, or whatever, according to your specifications. Figure 1.4 shows a sample wizard screen.

Each time you create a new object, such as a table or a form, you have the choice of creating it *from scratch* in a Design view or with a wizard to help you.

I recommend that beginners use wizards as much as possible. I use them because they're so convenient. Leave the tough stuff—the Design view creations—to those with lots of leisure time.

In this lesson, you learned some basic facts about databases and Access. In the next lesson, you will learn some strategies for planning your database. Don't skip Lesson 2, "Planning Your Database." Ten minutes worth of up-front planning can save you hours of backtracking later.

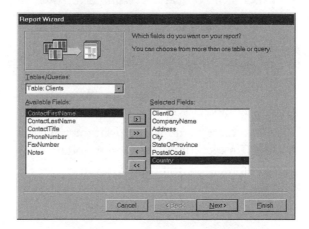

Figure 1.4   Wizards make it easy to create all kinds of database objects.

Planning Your Database

In this lesson, you learn some principles of good database design to help you plan your course of action.

Planning Is Important!

How many times have you dived enthusiastically into a new craft or skill without really knowing what you were doing? Your first attempt was probably pretty poor, whether the pursuit was pottery or computer programming. But as you worked, you probably made notes to yourself of what you would do differently next time, and the next time you did better.

With something as important as your database, however, you can't afford to learn by experimentation and trial and error. So in this lesson, I give you a crash course in the database planning that most people learn the hard way.

Before you create your database, you should ask yourself the following questions:

- What data do I want to store, and what is the best way to organize it? This determines what tables you need.
- What data entry actions do I perform in the course of my business or hobby? This determines the forms you need.
- What information do I want to know about the status of the business or hobby? This answer tells you what reports you want.

Determining What Tables You Need

How many tables will you need? Technically, you will need only one. That's the minimum with which a database can function. However, the biggest mistake most people make with Access is to put too much information in one table. Access is a relational database program; unlike more simple database programs, it's meant to handle lots of tables and create relationships among them. Figure 2.1 shows a list of tables in a database that keeps track of the employee hours spent on various projects.

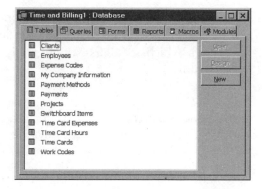

Figure 2.1 Access really shines when you take advantage of its capability to store many tables.

 TIP **Plan Tables Now!** You should plan your tables before you create your database because changing a table's structure once it has been filled with data is difficult.

Another big mistake people make is to try to make each table look like a stand-alone report. For instance, they might repeat a customer's name and address in all eight tables because they want that information readily available when it's required. This is a waste! You can easily create a report or form that includes this information whenever you need it. You really need the information only in one table.

Normalizing Your Database

When a database suffers from poor table organization, experts say it's not *normalized*. There are rules that govern how a relational database should store its tables. Those rules are called the rules of Data Normalization.

Data Normalization The process of making tables as efficient and compact as possible to eliminate the possibility for confusion and error.

There are five normalization rules, but the latter ones are fairly complicated and are used mostly by database professionals. In this lesson, I explain the first two normalization rules, which are all a beginner really needs to understand in order to avoid major mistakes.

Normalized Wizards Luckily, database professionals had a hand in creating Access's Database Wizard, so any tables you create using this feature (see Lesson 4, "Creating a New Database") will be normalized.

Rule #1: Avoid Repeated Information

You might want to keep contact information on your customers along with a record of each transaction they make. If you kept it all in one table (like the one shown below), you would have to repeat the customer's full name, address, and phone number each time you entered a new transaction! It would also be a nightmare if the customer's address changed; you would have to make the change to every transaction.

Customer Name	Customer Address	Customer Phone	Order Date	Order Total
ABC Plumbing	201 W. 44th St.	(317) 555-2394	2/5/96	$155.90
ABC Plumbing	201 W. 44th St.	(317) 555-2394	5/14/96	$90.24
ABC Plumbing	201 W. 44th St.	(317) 555-2394	7/9/96	$224.50
Jack's Emporium	1155 Conner Ave.	(317) 555-4501	6/6/95	$1,592.99
Jack's Emporium	1155 Conner Ave.	(317) 555-4501	7/26/96	$990.41
Millie's Pizza	108 Ponting St.	(317) 554-2349	8/29/96	$39.95

A better way is to assign each customer an ID number. Include that ID number in a table that contains names and addresses (see the Customers Table, below). Then you can include the same ID number as a link in a separate table that contains transactions (see the Orders Table).

Customers Table

Customer ID	Customer Name	Customer Address	Customer Phone
1	ABC Plumbing	201 W. 44th St.	(317) 555-2394
2	Jack's Emporium	1155 Conner Ave.	(317) 555-4501
3	Millie's Pizza	108 Ponting St.	(317) 554-2349

Orders Table

Customer ID	Order Date	Order Total
1	2/5/96	$155.90
1	5/14/96	$90.24
1	7/9/96	$224.50
2	6/6/95	$1,592.99
2	7/26/96	$990.41
3	8/29/96	$39.95

Rule #2: Avoid Redundant Data

You might want to keep track of which employees have attended certain training classes. There are lots of employees and lots of classes. One way to do this would be to keep it all in a single Personnel table, as follows:

Employee Name	Employee Address	Employee Phone	Training Date	Class Taken	Credit Hours	Passed?
Phil Sharp	211 W. 16th St.	(317) 555-4321	5/5/96	Leadership Skills	3	Yes
Becky Rowan	40 Westfield Ct.	(317) 555-3905	5/5/96	Customer Service	2	Yes
Nick Gianti	559 Ponting St.	(317) 555-7683	6/15/96	Public Speaking	9	Yes
Martha Donato	720 E. Warren	(317) 555-2930	5/5/96	Public Speaking	9	No
Cynthia Hedges	108 Carroll St.	(317) 555-5990	6/15/96	Customer Service	2	Yes
Andrea Mayfair	3904 110th St.	(317) 555-0293	6/15/96	Leadership Skills	3	Yes

But what if an employee takes more than one class? You would have to add a duplicate line in the table to list it, and then you would have the problem described in the previous section—multiple records with virtually identical field entries. And what if the only employee who has taken a certain class leaves the company? When you delete that employee's record, you delete the information about the credit hours, too.

A better way would be to create separate tables for Employees, Classes, and Training. Here are some examples of what such tables might look like.

Employee Table

Employee ID	Employee Name	Employee Address	Employee Phone
1	Phil Sharp	211 W. 16th St.	(317) 555-4321
2	Becky Rowan	40 Westfield Ct.	(317) 555-3905
3	Nick Gianti	559 Ponting St.	(317) 555-7683
4	Martha Donato	720 E. Warren	(317) 555-2930
5	Cynthia Hedges	108 Carroll St.	(317) 555-5990
6	Andrea Mayfair	3904 110th St.	(317) 555-0293

Class Table

Class ID	Class	Credits
C1	Leadership Skills	3
C2	Customer Service	2
C3	Public Speaking	9

Training Table

Employee ID	Date	Class	Passed?
1	5/5/96	C1	Yes
2	5/5/96	C2	Yes
3	6/16/96	C3	Yes
4	5/5/96	C3	No
5	6/15/96	C2	Yes
6	6/15/96	C1	Yes

Summary: Designing Your Tables

Don't be overwhelmed by all this information about database normalization. Good table organization boils down to a few simple principles:

- Each table should have a theme, such as Employee Contact Information or Customer Transactions. Try to restrict yourself to only one theme per table.

- If you see that you might end up repeating data in a table in the future, plan now to separate the information that will be repeated into its own table.

- If there is a list of reference information you want to preserve (such as the names and credit hours for classes), put it in its own table.
- Wherever possible, use ID numbers, as they help you link tables together later and help you avoid typing errors that come from entering long text strings (such as names) over and over.

What Forms Will You Use?

As explained in Lesson 1, "What Is a Database?" forms are data entry tools. You can arrange fields from several tables on a form, and you can easily enter data into those fields on a single screen. For instance, a timesheet form for an employee might contain fields from the Employees, Projects, and Work Codes tables. Figure 2.2 shows such a form.

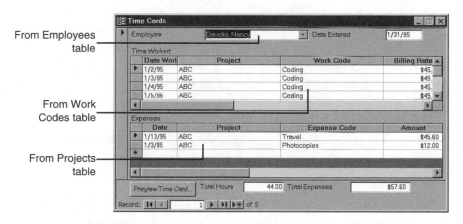

Figure 2.2 A form can link several tables.

When thinking about what forms you will need, the question is really "what actions will I perform?" The following list describes some actions that might require a form:

- Hiring employees (and entering their information in the database)
- Selling goods or services
- Making purchases
- Collecting the names and contact information for volunteers
- Keeping track of inventory

615

CAUTION

I Can't Predict What Forms I Will Need!   Although it's important to have effective forms, you can make changes to forms at any time fairly easily (unlike tables), so you don't have to know exactly what forms you want before you start. You learn to create forms in Lesson 12, "Creating a Simple Form."

What Reports Will You Want to Produce?

A report satisfies your need for information about your data. It's usually printed (unlike tables and forms, which are usually used on-screen only). For instance, you may want a report of all people who have not paid their membership dues or all accounts with a balance owed of more than $1,000.00. (You can find this information with a query, too, as you learn in Lesson 16, "Creating a Query.")

A report is usually created for the benefit of other people who aren't sitting with you at your computer. For instance, you might print a report to hand out to your board of directors to encourage them to keep you as CEO! A report can pull data from many tables at once, perform calculations on the data (such as summing or averaging), and present you with neatly formatted results.

Here are some things you can do with reports:

- Print a list of all your personal possessions with a replacement value of more than $50, for insurance purposes.
- Show a list of all club members who have not paid their dues.
- Calculate and show the current depreciated value of all capital equipment.
- List the commissions paid to each of your top 50 salespeople in the last quarter, compared to the company-wide average.

You can create new reports at any time; you do not have to plan them before you create your database. However, if you know you will want a certain report, you might design your tables in the format that will be most effective for that report's use.

In this lesson, you planned your database tables, forms, and reports. In the next lessons, you learn to start and exit Access.

Starting and Exiting Access

In this lesson, you learn to start and exit Microsoft Access.

Starting Access

There may be several ways you can start Access, depending on how you have installed it. The most straightforward way is to use the Start menu. Follow these steps:

1. Click the **Start** button and the Start menu appears.
2. Highlight or point to **Programs**. A list of your program groups appears.
3. Click **Microsoft Access** and Access starts.

 TIP **Moving Programs Around on the Start Menu** If you would prefer to have Access in a different program group, right-click the **Start** button and select **Explore** from the shortcut menu. Then use the Explorer to find and move the Microsoft Access shortcut to a different program group.

Other Ways to Start Access

Here are some other ways to start Access. Some of these require more knowledge of Windows 98 or Windows NT Workstation and Microsoft Office; if you're confused by them, stick with the primary method explained in the preceding steps.

- You can create a shortcut icon for Access and place it on your desktop. You can then start Access by double-clicking the icon.

- When you're browsing files in the Windows Explorer program, you can double-click any Access data file to start Access and open that file. Access data files have an .MDB extension and a little icon next to them that resembles the icon that's next to Microsoft Access on the Programs menu.

- If you can't find Access, you can search for it. Click the **Start** button, select **Find**, and select **Files**. In the **Named** box, type **msaccess.exe**; then open the **Look In** list, select **My Computer**, and click **Find Now**. When the file appears in the list below, double-click it to start Access.

When you start Access, the first thing you see is a dialog box prompting you to create a new database or open an existing one (see Figure 3.1). For now, click **Cancel**. (You will not be working with any particular database in this lesson.)

Figure 3.1 This Microsoft Access dialog box appears each time you start Access.

Parts of the Screen

Access is much like any other Windows program—it contains menus, toolbars, a status bar, and so on. Figure 3.2 points out these landmarks. Notice that in Figure 3.2, many of the toolbar buttons are grayed out (which means you can't use them right now). There's also nothing in the work area. That's because no database file is open. As you will see, the Access screen becomes a much busier place in later lessons when you begin working with a database. The buttons will become available, and your database will appear in the work area.

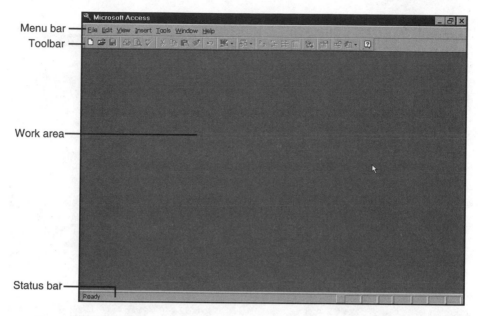

Menu bar
Toolbar
Work area
Status bar

Figure 3.2 Access has the same interface landmarks as any Windows program.

Understanding Access Toolbars

If you have used Windows programs before, you are probably familiar with *toolbars*, rows of buttons that represent common commands you can issue. Toolbar buttons are often shortcuts for menu commands.

The toolbar changes depending on what type of object you're currently working with (a table, a form, and so on) and what you're doing to it. More toolbars sometimes appear when you're doing special activities, such as drawing. To find out what a toolbar button does, point at it with your mouse pointer. Its name appears next to the pointer in a ScreenTip (see Figure 3.3). You can use ScreenTips even when a button is unavailable (grayed out).

TIP **Customizing Toolbars** You can choose which toolbars are displayed at any time, and you can even add buttons to and remove buttons from any toolbar. Right-click any toolbar and a shortcut menu appears. Use that list to choose which toolbars are displayed, or click **Customize** to open a dialog box in which you can customize a toolbar's buttons.

Close button

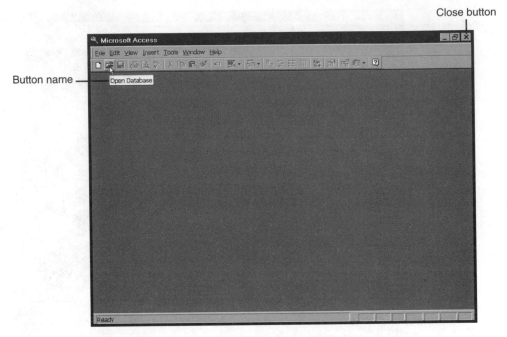

Button name — Open Database

Figure 3.3 To find out what a toolbar button does, point at it.

Exiting Access

When you finish working with Access, you should exit to free up your computer's memory for other tasks. Here are several ways to exit Access:

- Press **Alt+F4**.
- Select **File**, **Exit**.
- Click the Access window's **Close** (X) button (see Figure 3.3).

TIP **Alt+F4? File, Exit?** In this book, I use a kind of shorthand to tell you which keys to press and which menu commands to select. When you see "press **Alt+F4**," it means "hold down the Alt key on the keyboard and press the F4 key." When you see "select **File**, **Exit**," it means "click the word File on the menu bar, and then click the Exit command on the menu that appears."

In this lesson, you learned to start and exit Access, and you learned about the main parts of the screen, including the toolbar buttons. In the next lesson, you learn how to create a new database.

Creating a
New Database

*In this lesson, you learn how to create a blank database. You
also learn how to create a database with pre-made tables,
reports, and forms using the Database Wizard.*

Choosing the Right Way to Create Your Database

Before you create your database, you have an important decision to make.
Should you create a blank database from scratch, and then manually create
all the tables, reports, and forms you'll need? Or should you use a Database
Wizard, which does all that for you?

 Database Wizard   Access comes with several Database Wizards. These
are mini-programs that question you about your needs and then create a
database structure that matches them. (You will enter the actual data yourself.)

The answer depends on how well the available wizards match your needs. If
there is a Database Wizard that is close to what you want, it's quickest to use it
to create your database, and then modify it as needed. (Of course, you won't
know which wizards are available until you open the list of them, later in this
lesson.) If you're in a hurry, using a wizard can save you lots of time.

On the other hand, if you want a special-purpose database that isn't similar to any of the wizards, or if you're creating the database primarily as a training exercise for yourself, you should create the blank database.

Creating a Blank Database

Creating a blank database is simple because you're just creating an outer shell at this point, without any tables, forms, and so on. This section outlines two ways to do that.

If you just started Access, and the Microsoft Access dialog box is still displayed (see Figure 4.1), follow these steps:

1. Click **Blank Database**.
2. Click the **OK** button.

Figure 4.1   When you first start Access, you can start a new database quickly from the Microsoft Access dialog box.

If the dialog box is gone, you can't get it back until you exit from Access and restart it. But you don't need that dialog box to start a new database. At any time you can follow these steps:

1. Select **File**, **New** or click the **New** button on the toolbar. The New dialog box appears (see Figure 4.2).
2. Click the **General** tab, if necessary, to bring it to the top. Then double-click the **Blank Database** icon, and the File New Database dialog box appears.

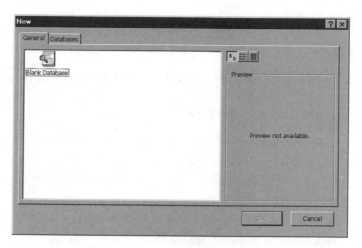

Figure 4.2 The New dialog box's different tabs give you options to create different kinds of databases.

3. Type a name for your new database (preferably something descriptive) in the **File Name** box. For example, I typed "Kennel Records." Then click **Create**. Access creates the new database, as shown in Figure 4.3.

Your database is completely blank at this point. You can click any of the tabs in the database window (see Figure 4.3), but you won't find anything listed on any of them. Later, you'll learn to create tables (Lesson 6, "Creating a Table with the Table Wizard," and Lesson 7, "Creating a Table Without a Wizard,"), forms (Lesson 12, "Creating a Simple Form"), queries (Lesson 16, "Creating a Query"), and reports (Lesson 18, "Creating a Simple Report") to fill these tabbed windows.

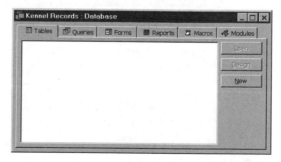

Figure 4.3 A new, blank database window.

Creating a Database with Database Wizard

A Database Wizard can create almost all the tables, forms, and reports you will ever need, automatically. The trick is choosing the right wizard to suit your purpose. Follow these steps:

1. If you just started Access, and the Microsoft Access dialog box is still on-screen, click **Database Wizard** and click **OK**. Or, if you've already closed the dialog box, select **File, New Database**. Either way, the New dialog box appears.

2. Click the **Databases** tab to display the list of wizards.

3. Click one of the Database Wizards (they're the icons with the magic wands across them). For this example, choose **Contact Management**. A preview appears in the Preview area.

4. When you've found the wizard you want, click **OK**. The File New Database dialog box appears.

5. Type a name for the database and click **Create** to continue. The wizard starts, and some information appears explaining what the wizard will do.

6. Click **Next** to continue. A list of the tables to be created appears (see Figure 4.4). The tables appear on the left, and the selected table's fields on the right.

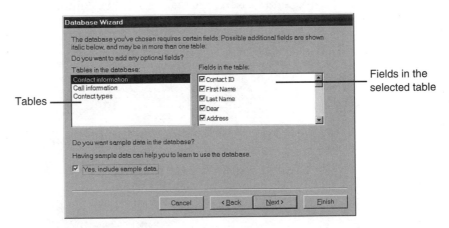

Figure 4.4 These are the tables and fields that this wizard creates automatically for you.

7. Click a table and examine its list of fields. Optional fields are in italic. To include an optional field, click it to place a check mark next to it.

I Don't Want These Tables and Fields! Sorry, that's the price you pay for going with a prefabricated wizard. You can't deselect any fields except the optional (italicized) ones. But you can delete the tables and fields you don't want later. See Lesson 8, "Modifying a Table," to learn how to delete individual fields or an entire table. If the tables and fields seem to be totally inappropriate, perhaps you are using the wrong wizard for your needs. If so, click **Cancel** and try another.

CAUTION

8. (Optional) If you are creating this database for a learning experience only, click the **Yes, Include Sample Data** check box. This tells Access to enter some dummy records into the database so you can see how they will work in the database.

9. Click **Next** to continue. The wizard asks you what kind of screen display style you want.

10. Click a display style in the list and examine the preview of that style that appears. When you have decided on a style, click it and click **Next**. The wizard asks you for a style for printed reports.

11. Click a report style and examine the preview of it. When you have decided on a style, click it and click **Next**.

12. The wizard asks what title you want for the database. The title will appear on reports, and it can be different from the filename. Enter a title (see Figure 4.5).

13. (Optional) If you want to include a picture (such as your company logo) on your forms and reports, click the **Yes, I'd Like to Include a Picture** check box. Then click the **Picture** button, choose a graphics file (change the drive and/or folder if needed), and click **Open** to return to the wizard.

14. Click **Next** to continue. When you get to the Finish screen, click **Finish**. The wizard goes to work creating your database. (It may take several minutes.)

When the database is finished, the Main Switchboard window appears (see Figure 4.6). The Switchboard opens automatically whenever you open the database.

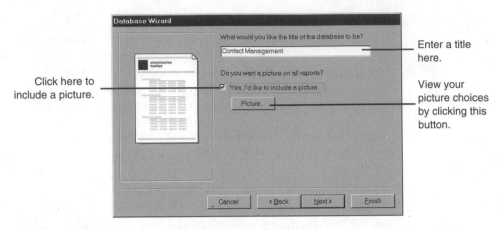

Click here to
include a picture.

Enter a title
here.

View your
picture choices
by clicking this
button.

Figure 4.5 Enter a title for the database and choose a graphic to use for a logo
(if you want).

All the databases created by a Database Wizard include the Main Switchboard.
The Main Switchboard is nothing more than a fancy form with some programming built in. It lets you perform common tasks with the database by clicking a
button. We won't be working with the Main Switchboard, so click the Main
Switchboard window's **Close** (X) button to get rid of it.

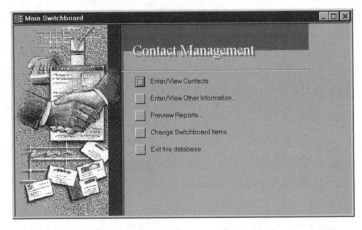

Figure 4.6 The Switchboard window is a bonus provided by the Database Wizards.

CAUTION

I Hate That Switchboard! To prevent the Switchboard from opening when you open the database, select **Tools**, **Startup**. Open the **Display Form** drop-down list, select **[None]**, and click **OK**.

Once you close the Switchboard window, you'll see the database window. If it's minimized, double-click its title bar (bottom left corner of the screen) to open it again. Click the **Tables** tab, and you see that several tables have been created for you. Click the other tabs to see the other objects created as well.

Even though you may have all the tables, reports, and forms you need, you may still want to go through the lessons in this part in sequential order to learn about creating and modifying these objects. If you're in a hurry to enter data, though, skip to either Lesson 9, "Entering Data Not in a Table," (where you learn to enter data in a table) or the end of Lesson 12, "Creating a Simple Form" (where you learn to enter data using a form).

In this lesson, you learned to create a database from scratch and using a Database Wizard. In the next lesson, you learn how to save, close, and open a database.

Saving, Closing, and Opening a Database

In this lesson, you learn to save your database, close it, and reopen it. You also learn how to find a misplaced database file.

Saving a Database

You need to save your work so that you don't lose anything you've typed after you turn off the computer. When you created the database, you saved it by naming it. When you enter each record, Access automatically saves your work. (You learn to enter records in Lesson 9, "Entering Data Not in a Table.") In Access, you really don't need to save your work until you're ready to close your database.

When you change the structure of a table, form, or other object, however, Access will not let you close that object or close the database without confirming whether or not you want to save your changes. You'll see a dialog box like the one in Figure 5.1; just click **Yes** to save your changes.

Figure 5.1 When you make changes to an object's structure, Access asks whether it should save your changes.

Notice that the Save and Save As commands on the File menu aren't even available most of the time; they're grayed out. When you have a particular object (such as a table) highlighted in the Database window, the Save As/Export command is available. You can use this command to save your table in a different format that another program (such as Excel) can read.

TIP **Using Tables in Other Programs** Another way to copy a table to another application or another database is with the Copy and Paste commands. Highlight the table in the Database window and select **Edit, Copy**. Then open a different database or application and select **Edit, Paste**. A dialog box opens, giving you the options of pasting the table structure only or the structure and the data. You can also choose to append the data to an existing tables, if the fields match up.

Closing a Database

When you finish working with a database, you should close it. When you finish using Access, exit the program (see Lesson 3, "Starting and Exiting Access"), and the database closes along with the program. But what if you're not ready to close Access? If you want to close one database and then open another, close the database using one of these methods:

- Double-click the **Control-menu** icon in the upper-left corner of the database window (see Figure 5.2).
- Click the database window's **Close** (X) button in the upper-right corner.
- Select **File, Close**.
- Press **Ctrl+F4**.
- Press **Ctrl+W**.

CAUTION **Can't I Have More Than One Database Open?** Sure you can. In fact, you might want several open so that you can transfer data between them. However, if your computer is short on memory (less than 16 megabytes), you'll want to close all files you're not using so Access will run faster.

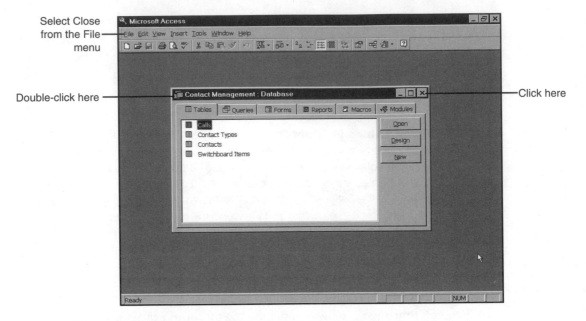

Select Close from the File menu

Double-click here

Click here

Figure 5.2 There are several ways to close a database.

Opening a Database

When you start Access the next time you want to use your database, you won't create a new datatbase from scratch as you did in Lesson 4, "Creating a New Database." You'll open your existing one.

The easiest way to open a database you've recently used is to select it from the File menu. Follow these steps:

1. Open the **File** menu. At the bottom of the menu, Access lists up to four databases you've recently used.

2. Click the database you want to open.

If the database you want to open isn't listed, you'll need to use the following procedure instead:

1. Select **File**, **Open** or click the **Open** button on the Standard toolbar. The Open dialog box appears (see Figure 5.3).

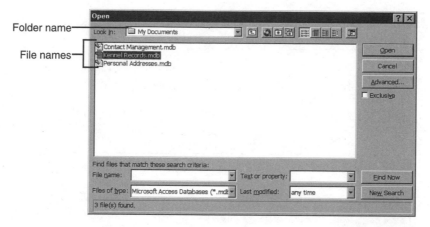

Folder name

File names

Figure 5.3 Open a different database file with this dialog box.

2. If the file isn't in the currently displayed folder, change drives and folders as necessary. (Refer to the next section, "Changing the Drive or Folder" for details.)

3. Double-click the file to open it.

Changing the Drive or Folder

Windows 95 and 98 and Windows NT Workstation applications provide a different dialog box for opening files than you may be used to with Windows 3.1 applications. It takes a bit of getting used to. Figure 5.3 shows the dialog box; Table 5.1 explains the buttons you see in it.

Table 5.1 Buttons for Changing Drives and Folders in Dialog Boxes

Button	Purpose
My Documents	Shows every drive that your computer has access to, plus your Network Neighborhood and Briefcase. Use this to choose a different drive.
	Moves to the folder "above" the one shown in the Look In box (that is, the folder that the current one is inside of).

continues

Table 5.1 Continued

Button	Purpose
	Shows the C:\WINDOWS\FAVORITES folder, no matter which folder was displayed before.
	Adds a shortcut for the currently displayed folder to the C:\WINDOWS\FAVORITES folder.
	Shows the folders and files in the currently displayed folder in a list.
	Shows details about each file and folder.
	Shows the properties of the selected file.
	Shows a preview (if available) of the selected file.
	Opens a shortcut menu of settings that affects the way the dialog box shows the files or that affects the selected file.

Network Neighborhood and Briefcase These are two special locations that you may have available on the list of folders. Network Neighborhood gives you access to computers on your local area network, and Briefcase manages files between your laptop and your main computer.

Finding a Database File

If you're having trouble locating your file, Access can help you look. Follow these steps:

1. Select **File**, **Open Database** if the File Open dialog box is not on-screen.

2. In the **File Name** box at the bottom of the dialog box, type the name of the file you're looking for (refer to Figure 5.3).

Wild Cards You can use wild cards if you don't know the entire name of the file you're looking for. An ***** wild card stands in for "any unkown characters," and a **?** wild card stands in for "any single unknown character." For instance, if you know the file begins with P, you could use **P*.mdb** to find all Access files that begin with P.

3. (Optional) If desired, enter any of these other search criteria:

- If you're looking for a different file type, choose it from the **Files of Type** drop-down list.

- If you're looking for a file containing certain text, type it in the **Text or Property** box.

- If you know when you last modified the file, choose the time interval from the **Last Modified** drop-down list.

4. Click the **Advanced** button, and the Advanced Find dialog box appears (see Figure 5.4).

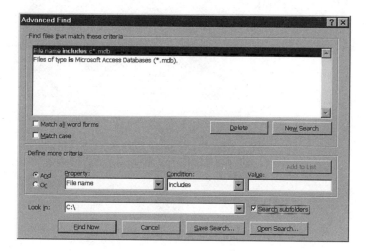

Figure 5.4 Use the Advanced Find dialog box to select which folders and drives to look in.

5. In the **Look In** section at the bottom of the Advanced Find dialog box, narrow down the search area as much as possible:

- If you are sure the file is in a certain folder, type that folder's path in the **Look In** box (for example, C:\WINDOWS).

633

- If you are sure the file is on a certain drive, select that drive from the **Look In** list.
- If you don't know which drive contains the file, select **My Computer** from the **Look In** list.

6. Click to select the **Search Subfolders** check box if necessary.

7. Click the **Find Now** button. The Open dialog box reappears, listing all files that were found that matched your criteria.

8. Double-click the desired file to open it.

In this lesson, you learned how to save, close, and open a database. In the next lesson, you learn how to create a table using Table Wizard.

Creating a Table with the Table Wizard

In this lesson, you learn to create a table using the Table Wizard. (To learn how to create a table from scratch, see Lesson 7, "Creating a Table Without a Wizard").

Why Create a Table?

Tables are the basis for the whole database. Tables hold your data. Everything else is just dress-up. If you created an empty database in Lesson 4, "Creating a New Databae," you'll need to create tables now following the plan you developed in Lesson 2, "Planning Your Database." If you used the Database Wizard to create your tables, you can create new tables here to augment them, or you can skip to Lesson 8, "Modifying a Table," where you'll learn to modify and customize the tables.

When you create a table, you can create it "from scratch," or you can use the Table Wizard. This lesson covers the Table Wizard; Lesson 7, "Creating a Table Without a Wizard," covers the less-automated method.

The Table Wizard can save you lots of time by creating and formatting all the right fields for a certain purpose. Access comes with dozens of pre-made business and personal tables from which to choose. You can pick and choose among all the fields in all the pre-made tables, constructing a table that's right for your needs. Even if you can't find all the fields you need in pre-made tables, you may want to use the Table Wizard to save time and then add the missing fields later (see Lesson 8).

Table Wizards   There are three Table Wizards—the standard one, the Import Table Wizard, and the Link Table Wizard. In this lesson, you'll be working with only the standard Table Wizard.

How Can I Know Beforehand?   You won't know exactly what pre-made fields Access offers until you start the Table Wizard and review the listings; if you find that none of the available tables meets your needs, you can click **Cancel** at any time and start creating your own table (see Lesson 7, "Creating a Table Without a Wizard").

Creating a Table Using the Table Wizard

If the fields you want to create are similar to any of Access's dozens of pre-made ones, the Table Wizard can save you a lot of time and effort. With the Table Wizard, you can copy fields from any of the dozens of sample tables. To create a table using the Table Wizard, follow these steps:

1. Select **Insert**, **Table** from the menu bar along the top of the screen. Or in the Database window, click the **Tables** tab and click **New**. The New Table dialog box appears (see Figure 6.1).

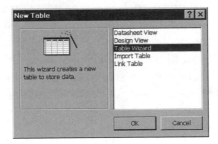

Figure 6.1   Indicate how you want to create the new table.

TIP   **Use the Toolbar**   Instead of following step 1, you can click the **New Object** drop-down arrow on the toolbar. A drop-down list of the available object types appears. Select **New Table** from that list.

2. Click **Table Wizard** and click **OK**. The Table Wizard window appears (see Figure 6.2).

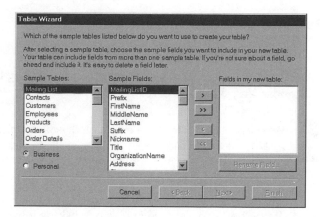

Figure 6.2 Choose your table's fields from those that come with any of the pre-made tables.

3. Click a table in the **Sample Tables** list. Access then displays its fields in the Sample Fields list.

TIP **Business or Pleasure?** There are two separate lists of tables. By default, you see the Business list. To see the Personal list, click the **Personal** option button below the Sample Tables list (see Figure 6.2).

4. If you see a field that you want to include in your new table, select it in the **Sample Fields** list; then click the **>** button to move it to the Fields in My New Table list. To move the entire contents of the selected Sample Table to your list, click the **>>** button.

TIP **Name Change!** If you see a field that is close to what you want, but you prefer a different name for it, first add it to your list (as described in steps 3 and 4). Then click the field name to select it, click the **Rename Field** button, type a new name, and click **OK**. This renames the field on your list only—not on the original.

5. Repeat steps 3 and 4 to select other fields from other sample tables until the list of fields in your new table is complete. (You can remove a field from the list by clicking the **<** button, and you can remove all the fields and start over by clicking the **<<** button.) When you're finished adding fields, click **Next** to continue.

6. Next the wizard asks for a name for the table. Type a more descriptive name to replace the default one.

7. Click **Yes, Set a Primary Key for Me** to have the wizard choose your primary key field, or **No, I'll Set the Primary Key** to do it yourself. If you choose Yes, skip to step 10.

 Primary Key Field   The designated field for which every record must have a unique entry. This is usually an ID number, because most other fields could conceivably be the same for more than one record (for instance, two people might have the same first name).

8. A dialog box appears (see Figure 6.3) asking which field will be the primary key. Open the drop-down list and select the field.

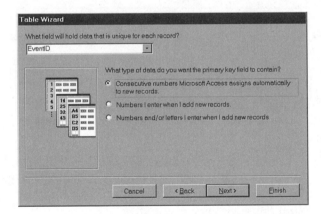

Figure 6.3   You can set your own primary key for the table.

9. Choose a data type for the primary key field:

- **Consecutive numbers Microsoft Access assigns automatically to new records.** Choose this if your primary key field is a simple record number. (That is, if you're numbering the records you enter consecutively as you enter them.)

- **Numbers I enter when I add new records.** Choose this if you want to enter your own numbers. Access will not allow you to enter any letters. This choice works well for unique ID numbers such as driver's license numbers.

- **Numbers and/or letters I enter when I add new records.** Choose this if you want to include both numbers and letters in the field. For instance, if your primary key field will contain vehicle identification numbers for the cars in your fleet, you will need to enter both numbers and letters.

10. Click **Next** to continue.

11. If you already have at least one table in this database, a screen appears asking about the relationship between tables. Just click **Next** to move past it for now.

12. At the Finish screen, click one of the following options:

- **Modify the table design.** This takes you into Table Design view, the same as if you had created all those fields yourself. Choose this if you have some changes you want to make to the table before you use it.

- **Enter data directly into the table.** This takes you to Table Datasheet view, where you can enter records into the rows of the table. Choose this if the table's design seems perfect to you as-is.

- **Enter data into the table using a form the wizard creates for me.** This jumps you ahead a bit in this part of the book; it leads you right into the Form Wizard covered in Lesson 12, "Creating a Simple Form."

13. Click **Finish**, and you're taken to the area of Access that you indicated you wanted to go (in step 12).

If you decide you don't want to work with this table anymore for now (no matter what you selected in step 12), click the **Close** (X) button for the window that appears.

Now you have a table. In the Database window, when you click the **Tables** tab, you can see your table in the list (see Figure 6.4).

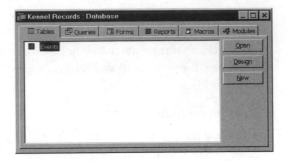

Figure 6.4 Now you have a table on your Tables tab.

Now What?

From here, there are a number of places you can go:

- To learn how to create a table from scratch, go on to Lesson 7, "Creating a Table Without a Wizard."
- To modify the table you just created, jump to Lesson 8, "Modifying a Table."
- To enter data into your table, skip to Lesson 9, "Entering Data in a Table."
- To create a data entry form for easier data entry, check out Lesson 12, "Creating a Simple Form." (Don't do this yet if you still want to modify your table.)

In this lesson, you learned to create a new table using the Table Wizard. In the next lesson, you learn how to create a table without the wizard.

Creating a Table Without a Wizard

In this lesson, you learn to create a table in Table Design view.

Why Not Use a Wizard?

Access's wizards are very useful, but they do not offer the flexibility you have when performing the equivalent tasks "from scratch." For instance, if you want to create a table that contains special fields not available in a wizard, you are better off creating that table in Table Design view. You'll learn to do that in this lesson.

Creating a Table in Table Design View

To create a table in Table Design view, follow these steps:

1. Select **Insert**, **Table** or, from the Database window, click the **Table** tab and click the **New** button. The New Table dialog box appears (see Figure 7.1).

Figure 7.1   Start your new table in Design View.

TIP **Quick! A New Object!** Instead of step 1, you can click the **New Object** drop-down arrow on the toolbar. A drop-down list appears, showing the available object types. Select **New Table** from that list.

2. Click **Design View** and click **OK**. Table Design view opens (see Figure 7.2).

Start typing the first field name here.

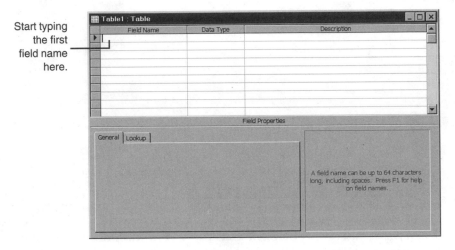

Figure 7.2 From Table Design view, you can control the entire table creation process.

3. Type a field name on the first empty line in the **Field Name** column; then press **Tab** to move to the Data Type column.

TERM **Field Naming Rules** Field names—and all other objects in Access for that matter—can contain up to 64 characters and can include spaces and any symbols except periods (.), exclamation marks (!), accent grave symbols (`), or square brackets ([]). However, you may want to stick with short, easy-to-remember names.

4. When you move to the Data Type column, an arrow appears there for a drop-down list. Open the **Data Type** drop-down list and select a field type. (See the section "Understanding Data Types and Formats" later in this lesson if you need help deciding which field type to use.)

5. (Optional) Press **Tab** to move to the Description column, and then type a description of the field. (The table will work fine even without a description.)

6. In the bottom half of the dialog box, you see Field Properties for the field type you selected (see Figure 7.3). Make any changes desired to them. (See "Understanding Data Types and Formats" later in this lesson for help.)

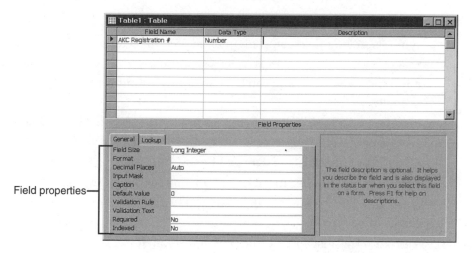

Field properties—

Figure 7.3 The Field Properties change depending on the field type.

TIP **Switching Between Views** At any time after you've entered the first field, you can switch to Datasheet view to see how your table is going to look. Just select **View**, **Datasheet**. You may be asked to save your work before you enter Datasheet view. If so, click **Yes**, enter a name, and click **OK**.

7. If you have more fields to enter, repeat steps 3 through 6.

8. Click the Table Design window's **Close** (X) button.

9. When you are asked if you want to save your changes to the table, click **Yes**. The Save As dialog box appears.

10. Type a name for the table in the **Table Name** text box and click **OK**.

CAUTION

No Primary Key! When you close Table Design view, you may get a message that no primary key has been assigned. See the section "Setting the Primary Key" later in this lesson to learn what to do.

Understanding Data Types and Formats

Each field must have a type so that Access will know how to handle its contents. Here are the types you can choose from:

Text Plain, ordinary typed text, which can include numbers, letters, and symbols. A Text field can contain up to 255 characters.

Memo More plain, ordinary text, except this one doesn't have a maximum field length. So you can type an almost infinite amount of text (64,000 characters).

Number A plain, ordinary number (not a currency value or a date). Access won't allow any text in a Number field.

Date/Time Just that—a date or a time.

Currency A number formatted as an amount of money.

AutoNumber A number that Access automatically fills in for each consecutive record.

Yes/No The answer to a true/false question. It can contain either of two values, which might be Yes or No, True or False, On or Off.

OLE Object A link to another database or file. This is an advanced feature that I don't cover in this book.

Hyperlink A link to a location on the World Wide Web.

Lookup Wizard Lets you create a list to choose a value from another table or list of values in a combo box for each record. It is another advanced feature that I won't cover here.

In addition to a field type, each field has formatting options you can set. They appear in the bottom half of the dialog box in the Field Properties area. The formatting options change depending on the field type, and there are too many to list here. But these are some of the most important ones you'll encounter:

Field Size The maximum number of characters a user can input in that field.

Format A drop-down list of the available formats for that field type. You can also create custom formats.

Default Value If a field is usually going to contain a certain value (for instance, a certain ZIP code for almost everyone), you can enter it here to save time. It will always appear in a new record, and you can type over it in the rare instances when it doesn't apply.

Decimal Places   For number fields, you can set the default number of decimal places so a number will show.

Required   Choose **Yes** or **No** to tell Access whether a user should be allowed to leave this field blank when entering a new record.

Setting the Primary Key

Every table must have at least one field that has a unique value for each record. For instance, in a table of the dogs your kennel owns, you might assign an ID number to each dog, and have an ID # field in your table. Or you might choose to use each dog's AKC (American Kennel Club) registration number. This unique identifier field is known as the Primary Key field.

You must tell Access which field you are going to use as the Primary Key so that it can prevent you from accidentally entering the same value for more than one record in that field. To set a primary key, follow these steps:

1. In Table Design view, select the field that you want to use for the primary key.

2. Select **Edit**, **Primary Key** or click the **Primary Key** button on the toolbar. A key symbol appears to the left of the field name, as shown in Figure 7.4.

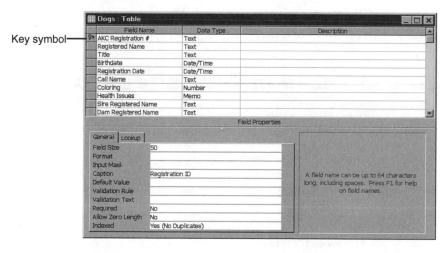

Figure 7.4   The primary key field is marked by a key symbol.

Primary Key Field The designated field for which every record must have a unique entry. This is usually an ID number, because most other fields could conceivably be the same for more than one record (for instance, two people might have the same first name).

Switching Between Design and Datasheet Views

When working with tables, you can use one of two available views—Design view or Datasheet view.

One easy way to switch between the views is to click the **View** drop-down arrow on the toolbar (it's the leftmost button); then select the view you want from the drop-down list that appears.

The following steps teach you another way to switch between views:

1. Open the **View** menu.
2. Select **Table Design** or **Datasheet**, depending on which view you are currently in.
3. If you're moving from Table Design view to Datasheet view, you may be asked to save your work. If so, click **Yes**.
4. If you're asked for a name for the table, type one and click **OK**.

Creating a Table in Datasheet View

Some people prefer to create a table in Datasheet view. However, Access designed Datasheet view for data entry and viewing, not for table structure changes. I do not recommend creating the table this way, because you do not have access to as many controls as you do with Table Design view.

To create a table in Datasheet view, follow these steps:

1. Select **Insert**, **Table**.
2. Click **Datasheet View** and click **OK**. A blank table opens, as shown in Figure 7.5.

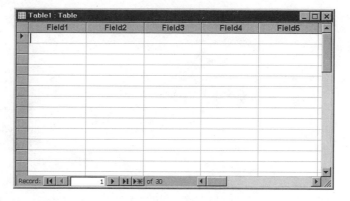

Figure 7.5 Creating a new table in Datasheet view gives you a quick, generic table.

CAUTION

How Do I Set the Field Names? When you create a table in Datasheet view, the fields have generic names such as Field1. To change a field name, click the present name to select the column. Then select **Format**, **Rename Column**, type the new name, and press **Enter**.

3. Make any necessary changes to the design of the table (as explained in Lesson 8, "Modifying a Table").

4. When you finish making changes, click the table's **Close** (X) button. Access asks if you want to save the design changes.

5. Click **Yes**. When Access asks for a name for the table, type one and click **OK**.

In this lesson, you learned to create a table without the help of a wizard. Before you enter data into your table, you should make sure it's exactly the way you want it. In the next lesson, you learn how to make any needed changes to your table.

Modifying a Table

In this lesson, you learn how to change your table by adding and removing fields and hiding columns.

Now that you've created a table, you may be eager to begin entering records into it. You learn to do that in Lesson 9, "Entering Data Not in a Table." Before you begin, you should make certain that your table is structured exactly as you want it, so you won't have to backtrack later.

Editing Fields and Their Properties

No matter how you create your table (whether with or without the Table Wizard), you can modify it using Table Design view. If you create the table without Table Wizard, Table Design view will look very familiar to you.

To enter Table Design view, do one of the following:

- From the Database window, click the **Table** tab, select the table you want to work with, and click the **Design** button.
- If the table appears in Datasheet view, select **View**, **Table Design.**

 Don't forget, you can quickly change views with the View button at the far left end of the Standard toolbar. Click the **View** drop-down arrow and select a view from the list that appears.

Once you're in Table Design view (see Figure 8.1), you can edit any field, as you learned in Lesson 7, "Creating a Table Without a Wizard." Here is the general procedure:

1. Click any field name in the **Field Name** list.

2. If desired, click the field's Data Type area and select a new data type from the drop-down list.

3. In the Field Properties area (the bottom half of the Table Design screen), click any text box in order to change its value. Some text boxes have drop-down lists, which you can activate by clicking in the box.

4. Repeat steps 1–3 for each field you want to change.

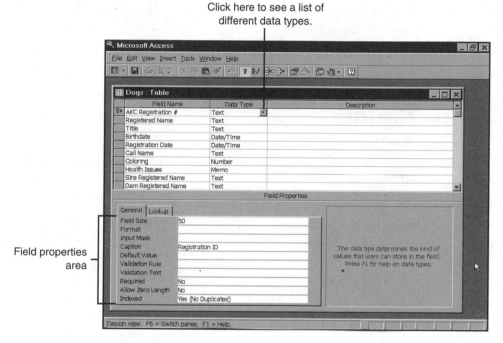

Click here to see a list of different data types.

Field properties area

Figure 8.1 In Table Design view, you can modify the attributes of any field.

CAUTION

I Need More Help! For those who created their table without a wizard, the above steps will be self-explanatory. However, if you used Table Wizard, you may be lost right now. Review Lesson 7, "Creating a Table Without a Wizard," to get up-to-speed.

Adding Fields

Before you enter data into your table (see Lesson 9, "Entering Data Not in a Table"), you should make very sure that you have included all the fields you'll need. Why? Because if you add a field later, you'll have to go back and enter a value in that field for each record that you've already entered. In addition, if you change the field length, you risk truncating or invalidating data that's already been entered.

You can add a field in either Table Design view or Datasheet view. Try it in Table Design view first, since you're already there:

1. Select the field before which you want the new field to appear.

2. Click the **Insert Rows** button on the toolbar or select **Insert**, **Row**. A blank row appears in the Field Name list.

3. Enter a name, type, description, and so on for the new field. (Refer to Lesson 7, "Creating a Table Without a Wizard," if necessary.)

Deleting Fields

If you realize that you don't need one or more fields that you've created, now is the time to get rid of them. Otherwise, you'll needlessly enter information into each record that you will never use.

Don't Remove Important Fields! Be very careful about deleting fields once you start entering records in your table. When you delete a field, the information for each record stored in that field is deleted, too. The best time to experiment with deleting fields is *now*, before you enter any records.

You can erase fields in either Table Design view or Datasheet view. To delete a field in Table Design view, follow these steps:

1. Switch to Table Design view if you're not already there.

2. Select a field.

3. Do one of the following:

   - Press the **Delete** key on your keyboard.
   - Click the **Delete Rows** button on the toolbar.
   - Select **Edit**, **Delete Row**.

If you prefer, you can delete the field in Datasheet view. Whereas there's an advantage to using Table Design view to add fields, there's no significant difference when you delete fields. You can accomplish a field deletion easily in either view. Follow these steps to delete a field in Datasheet view:

1. Switch to Datasheet view if you're not already there.

2. Select the entire column for the field you want to delete.

3. Select **Edit, Delete Column**.

Hiding a Field

If your table includes a field that you don't want to use at the moment but that you will want later, you may want to hide it instead of deleting it. There are two advantages to hiding a field:

- If you have entered any records, you can preserve the data you've entered into that field.

- The Field Properties you set when you created the field will remain intact, so you don't have to re-enter them later.

You must hide a field using Datasheet view; you cannot hide it using Table Design view. Follow these steps:

1. Switch to Datasheet view, if you aren't there already.

2. Select the field(s) you want to hide.

3. Select **Format, Hide Columns**. The columns disappear.

To unhide the column(s) later, follow these steps:

1. Select **Format, Unhide Columns**. The Unhide Columns dialog box appears (see Figure 8.2). Fields with a check mark beside them are displayed; fields without a check mark are hidden.

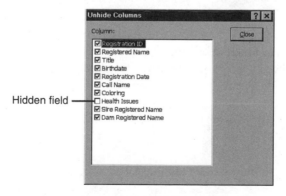

Figure 8.2 You can either unhide or hide fields from the Unhide Columns dialog box.

2. Click the check box of any field that you want to change. Clicking the box switches between hidden and unhidden status.

3. When you're finished, click the **Close** button.

Hidden fields are still very much a part of your database. To verify that, switch to Table Design view. You'll still see them in Table Design view, along with all the other fields.

Deleting a Table

Now that you've created a table and worked with it a bit, you may discover that you made so many mistakes creating it that it would be easier to start over. (Don't feel bad; that's what happened to me the first time.) Or you may have several tables by now, and you might decide that you don't need all of them. Whatever the reason, it's easy to delete a table. Follow these steps:

1. From the Database window, click the **Tables** tab.

2. Select the table you want to delete.

3. Select **Edit**, **Delete** or press the **Delete** key on your keyboard.

4. A message appears asking if you are sure you want to do this. Click **Yes**.

 TIP **Cut versus Delete** You can also cut a table. Cutting is different from deleting, because the table isn't gone forever; rather, Access moves it to the Clipboard. From there, you can paste it into a different database or into some other application. However, because the Clipboard holds only one item at a time, you will lose the table when you cut or copy something else to the Clipboard.

In this lesson, you learned how to modify your table by adding and removing fields, hiding fields, and editing the information about each field. In the next lesson, you begin entering data into a table.

Entering Data into a Table

In this lesson, you learn how to add records to a table, how to print the table, and how to close it

At this point, you have created your table structure and you've fine-tuned it with the settings you want. It's finally time to enter records. Open the table and start.

TIP **Other Ways to Enter Records** Entering records directly into a table, which you learn to do in this lesson, is not always the best way to enter records. If you have many records to enter, it's often more efficient in the long run to take the time to create a form with which to do your data entry. You learn to create a form in Lesson 12, "Creating a Simple Form."

Entering a Record

If you read Lessons 1, "What is a Database?" and 2, "Planning Your Database," (and I hope you did!), you know that a record is a row in your table. It contains information about a specific person, place, event, or whatever. You enter a value for each record into each field (column) in your table.

First you must open the table. Remember that to open a table, you can double-click it in the Database window, or click it once and then click **Open**. Then follow these steps to enter a record:

There's a Number in the First Column! If you've set up the first field to be automatically entered (for instance, a sequentially numbered field with Autonumber), start with the second field instead.

CAUTION

1. Click in the first empty cell in the first empty column.

 Cell   The intersection of a row and a column. It's where you enter the data for a particular field for a particular record. Sometimes, the word field is used to mean the entry in a field for an individual record, but "field" actually refers to the entire column. Cell is the proper name for an individual block.

2. Type the value for that field.
3. Press **Tab** to move to the next field, and then type its value.
4. Continue pressing **Tab** until you get to the last field. When you press Tab in the last field, the insertion point moves to the first field in the next line, where you can start a new record.

 Insertion Point   When you click a field, you see a blinking vertical line, called an *insertion point*, which tells you that is the place where anything you type will appear.

5. Continue entering records until you've filled them all.

Some Data Entry Tricks

Sure, you *can* enter all your data with nothing more than the Tab key and some typing. But here are a few keyboard tricks that will make the job easier:

- To insert the current date, press **Ctrl+;** (semicolon). To insert the current time, press **Ctrl+:** (colon).
- If you have defined a default value for a field (in Table Design view), you can insert it by pressing **Ctrl+Alt+Spacebar**.
- To repeat the value from the same field in the previous record, press **Ctrl+'** (apostrophe).

Moving Around in a Table

In the preceding steps, you pressed Tab to move from field to field in the table. There are other ways to move around, and you might actually find them to be more convenient. For instance, you can click in any field at any time to place the insertion point there. Table 9.1 summarizes the many keyboard shortcuts for moving around in a table.

Table 9.1 Table Movement Keys

To Move To	Press
Next field	Tab
Previous field	Shift+Tab
Last field in the record	End
First field in the record	Home
Same field in the next record	Down arrow
Same field in the previous record	Up arrow
Same field in the last record	Ctrl+Down arrow
Same field in the first record	Ctrl+Up arrow
Last field in the last record	Ctrl+End
First field in the first record	Ctrl+Home

Printing a Table

Normally, you will not want to print a table—it won't look very pretty. A table is just a plain grid of rows and columns. Instead, you'll want to create and print a report that contains exactly the data you want (see Lesson 18, "Creating a Simple Report").

However, sometimes you may want a quick printout of the raw data in the table. In that case, follow these steps:

1. Open the table.

2. Click the **Print** button on the Standard toolbar. Access prints the table.

> **TIP** **More Printing Control** You can set some printing options before you print if you want. Instead of clicking the Print toolbar button, select **File**, **Print.** Then choose your printing options from the Print dialog box and click **OK.** Access prints the table according to your specifications.

Closing a Table

By now you have probably discovered that a table is just another window; to close it you simply click its **Close** (X) button or double-click its **Control-menu** icon (see Figure 9.1).

Control-menu icon   Close button

Figure 9.1   Close a table the same way you would close any window.

In this lesson, you learned to enter records into a table, to print the table, and to close it. In the next lesson, you learn to edit your table data.

Editing Data in a Table

10

In this lesson, you learn how to change information in a field, select records, and insert and delete records.

Very few things are done perfectly the first time around. As you're entering records into your table, you may find you need to make some changes. This lesson shows you how.

Changing a Cell's Content

Editing a cell's content is easy. You can either replace the old content completely or edit it. Which is better? It depends on how much you need to change; you make the call.

Replacing a Cell's Content

If the old content is completely wrong, it's best to enter new data from scratch. To replace the old content in a field, follow these steps:

1. Select the cell whose contents you want to replace. Do this by clicking it or by moving to it with the keyboard (see Table 9.1 in Lesson 9, "Entering Data Not in a Table").

If you are going to select the cell by clicking it, position the mouse pointer at the left edge of the field so the mouse pointer becomes a plus sign (see Figure 10.1). Then click once to select the entire content.

2. Type the new data. The new data replaces the old data.

Figure 10.1 To select a field's entire content, make sure the mouse pointer is a plus sign when you click.

Editing a Cell's Content

If you need to make a small change to a cell's content, there's no reason to completely retype it. Instead, edit the content. Follow these steps to learn how:

1. Position the mouse pointer in the cell so the mouse pointer looks like an I-beam (see Figure 10.2).

2. Click once, and an insertion point appears in the cell.

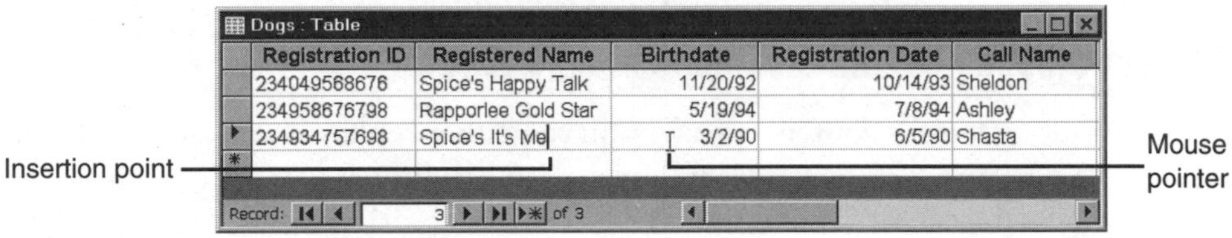

Figure 10.2 Click in a cell to place the insertion point in it.

3. Use the arrow keys to move the insertion point to the location in the cell where you want to start editing. Table 10.1 lists a number of key combinations you can use to move within the cell.

4. Press **Backspace** to remove the character to the left of the insertion point, or press **Delete** to remove the character to the right of it. Then type your change.

Table 10.1 Moving Around Within a Cell

To Move...	Press...
One character to the right	$\rightarrow$
One character to the left	$\leftarrow$

To Move...	Press...
One word to the right	Ctrl+→
One word to the left	Ctrl+←
To the end of the line	End
To the end of the field	Ctrl+End
To the beginning of the line	Home
To the beginning of the field	Ctrl+Home

Selecting Records

In addition to editing individual cells in a record, you may want to work with an entire record. To do this, click in the gray square to the left of the record (the record selection area). Access highlights the entire record—displaying white letters on black—as shown in Figure 10.3.

Record selection area ──

A triangle marks the
selected record.

Registration ID	Registered Name	Birthdate	Registration Date	Call Name
234049568676	Spice's Happy Talk	11/20/92	10/14/93	Sheldon
234958676798	Rapporlee Gold Star	5/19/94	7/8/94	Ashley
234934757698	Spice's It's Me	3/2/90	6/5/90	Shasta

Figure 10.3   The selected record.

You might want to select several records as a group to perform an action on all of them at once. To do so, select the first record, press and hold down **Shift**, and select the other records. You can select only adjacent groups of records; you can't pick them from all over the list.

TIP   **Selecting All Records**   There are several quick ways to select all records at once. You can click the blank box at the intersection of the row and column headings; you can press **Ctrl+A**; or you can choose the **Edit**, **Select All Records** command.

Understanding Record Selection Symbols

When you select a record, a triangle appears in the record selection area (see Figure 10.3). In addition to the triangle, you might see either of these icons in that area:

 Being entered or edited

 New Record

Only One Triangle If you select several records, only the first one you click will have the triangle symbol beside it. That doesn't matter, though; they're all equally selected.

CAUTION

Inserting New Records

Access inserts new records automatically. When you start to type a record, a new line appears below it, waiting for another record (as you see in Figure 10.3). You can't insert new records between existing ones. You must always insert new records at the end of the table.

What If I Want the Records in a Different Order? It's easy to sort your records to put them in any order you want. You learn how to sort in Lesson 15, "Sorting and Filtering Data."

CAUTION

Deleting Records

If you find that one or more records is outdated or doesn't belong in the table, you can easily delete it. You can even delete several records at a time. Here's how:

1. Select the record(s) you want to delete.

2. Do any of the following:

- Click the **Delete Records** button on the toolbar.
- Press the **Delete** key on the keyboard.
- Select the **Edit**, **Delete** command.
- Select the **Edit**, **Delete Record** command.

 Delete versus Delete Record If you select the entire record, there's no difference between these two commands. However, if you select only a portion of the record there is a difference: Delete removes only the selected text, while Delete Record removes the entire record. You cannot undo a deletion, so be careful what you delete.

Moving and Copying Data

As with any Windows program, you can use the Cut, Copy, and Paste commands to copy and move data. Follow these steps:

1. Select the field(s), record(s), cell(s), or text that you want to move or copy.

 2. Open the **Edit** menu and select **Cut** (to move) or **Copy** (to copy). Or, click the **Cut** or **Copy** button on the Standard toolbar.

3. Position the insertion point where you want to insert the cut or copied material.

 4. Select **Edit**, **Paste** or click the **Paste** button on the Standard toolbar. Access places the cut or copied material in that location.

 Moving and Copying Entire Tables You can move and copy entire objects—not just individual fields and records. From the Database window, select the table, report, query, and so on, that you want to move or copy. Then execute the **Cut** or **Copy** command, move to where you want the object to go (for example, in a different database), and execute the **Paste** command.

In this lesson, you learned to edit data in a field, to insert and delete fields, and to copy and move data from place to place. In the next lesson, you learn about table formatting.

Formatting a Table

In this lesson, you learn to improve the look of a table by adjusting the row and column sizes, changing the font, and choosing a different alignment.

Why Format a Table?

Most people don't spend a lot of time formatting Access tables simply because they don't have to look at or print their tables. They use data entry forms (Lesson 12, "Creating a Simple Form") to see the records on-screen and reports (Lesson 18, "Creating a Simple Report") to print their records. The tables are merely holding tanks for raw data.

However, creating forms and reports may be more work than you want to tackle right now. For instance, if your database is very simple, consisting of one small table, you may want to add enough formatting to your table to make it look fairly attractive. Then you can use it for all your viewing and printing—foregoing the fancier forms and reports.

Even if you decide later to use a form or report, you might still want to add a bit of formatting to your table so it will be readable if you ever need to look at it.

Changing Column Width and Row Height

One of the most common problems with a table is that you can't see the complete contents of the fields. Fields often hold more data than will fit across a column's width, so the data in your table appears to be truncated, or cut off.

There are two ways to fix this problem—make the column wider so it can display more data, or make the row taller so it can display more than one line of data.

Changing Column Width

Access offers many different ways to adjust column width in a table; you can choose the method you like best.

One of the easiest ways to adjust column width is to simply drag the column headings. Follow these steps:

1. Position the mouse pointer between two field names (column headings). The mouse pointer turns into a vertical line with left- and right-pointing arrows (see Figure 11.1). You'll be adjusting the column on the left; the column on the right will move to accommodate it.

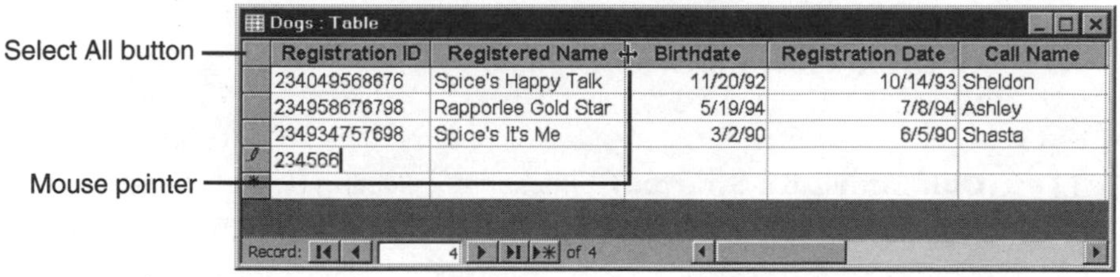

Figure 11.1 Position the mouse pointer between two column headings.

2. Press and hold the mouse button and drag the column to the right or left to increase or decrease the width.

3. Release the mouse button when the column is the desired width.

Another more precise way to adjust column width is to use the Column Width dialog box. Follow these steps:

1. Select the column(s) whose width you want to adjust. If you want to adjust all columns, select them all by clicking the Select All button (see Figure 11.1).

2. Select **Format**, **Column Width**. The Column Width dialog box (shown in Figure 11.2) appears.

3. Do one of the following to set the column width:
   - Adjust the column to exactly the width needed for the longest entry in it by clicking **Best Fit**.

- Set the width to a precise number of field characters by typing a value in the **Column Width** text box.

- Reset the column width to its default value by selecting the **Standard Width** check box.

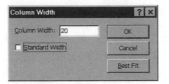

Figure 11.2 Adjust column width precisely here.

4. Click **OK** to apply the changes.

TIP **Column Width Shortcut**   Instead of selecting Format, Column Width, you can right-click the column and select **Column Width** from the shortcut menu that appears.

Changing Row Height

If you don't want to make a column wider but still want to see more of its contents, you can make the rows taller.

Which Rows Should I Adjust?   It doesn't matter which row you've selected; the height you set applies to all rows. You can't adjust the height of individual rows.

CAUTION

One way to make rows taller is to drag one of their dividers, just as you dragged a column in the preceding section. Position the mouse pointer between two rows in the row selection area; then drag up or down.

Another way is with the Row Height dialog box. It works the same as the Column Width dialog box except there's no Best Fit option. In this dialog box you have two choices. Right-click the column, select **Row Height**, and enter a new height. Or, select **Format**, **Row Height**, enter the new height, and click **OK**.

Changing the Font

Unlike in other Access views (like Report and Form), you can't format individual fields or entries differently from the rest. You can choose a different font, but it automatically applies to all the text in the table, including the column headings.

Font changes you make in Datasheet view will not appear in your reports, queries, or forms; they're for Datasheet view only.

Why Would I Change the Table Font?   You might want to make the font smaller so you can see more of the field contents on-screen without having to adjust column width. Or you might make the font larger so you can see the table more clearly.

CAUTION

To choose a different font, follow these steps:

1. Select **Format, Font**. The Font dialog box appears (see Figure 11.3).

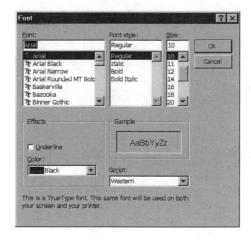

Figure 11.3   The Font dialog box lets you set one font for the entire table.

2. Choose a font from the **Font** list box.
3. Choose a style from the **Font Style** list box.
4. Choose a size from the **Size** list box.

5. Choose a color from the **Color** drop-down list.

6. (Optional) Click the **Underline** check box if you want underlined text.

7. You can see a sample of your changes in the Sample area. When you're happy with the look of the sample text, click **OK**.

TIP   More Cell Appearance Changes   Another way you can change the look of your table is with the Cells Effects dialog box. Select **Format**, **Cells** to see it. You can change the background color, the color of the gridlines between each row and column, and whether or not the lines show.

In this lesson, you learned how to format a table. In the next lesson, you learn how to create a simple data entry form.

Creating a Simple Form

In this lesson, you learn to create a form, both with and without the Form Wizard.

Why Create Forms?

As you saw in Lessons 9, "Entering Data Not in a Table," and 10, "Editing Data in a Table," you can do all your data entry and editing in a table, but that may not be the best way. For one thing, unless you set your field widths very wide (see Lesson 11, "Formatting a Table"), you probably won't be able to see everything you type in the field. Also, if you have data you want to enter into several tables, you have to open each table individually.

A better data entry method is to create a form. With a form, you can allot as much space as needed for each field, and you can enter information into several tables at once. You can also avoid the headaches that occur when you try to figure out which record you're working with on a table; each form shows only one record at a time.

There are three ways to create a form:

- AutoForm is great when you want an extremely quick, generic form that contains all the fields in a single table.
- Form Wizard provides a compromise between speed and control; you can create a form by following a series of dialog boxes and choosing which fields the form will contain.

- Creating a form from scratch is the most difficult way, but it's the method that provides the most control.

Each of these is explained in this lesson.

Creating a Form with AutoForm

The easiest way to create a form is with AutoForm. AutoForm simply plunks the fields from a single table into a form; it's the least flexible form, but it's very convenient. Follow these steps:

1. From the Database window, click the **Forms** tab.

2. Click the **New** button. The New Form dialog box appears (see Figure 12.1).

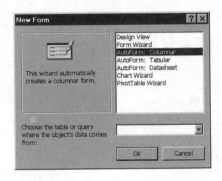

Figure 12.1 Choose how you want to create your form.

3. Click **AutoForm: Columnar** to create a columnar form (the most popular kind). This creates a form that contains your fields in a single column. Alternatively, you can click **AutoForm: Tabular** for a form that looks like a table or **AutoForm: Datasheet** for a form that looks like a datasheet.

4. Open the drop-down list at the bottom of the dialog box and choose the table this form will be associated with.

5. Click **OK**, and the form appears, ready for data entry.

If the form created by AutoForm is not what you want, delete it and try again with the Form Wizard (as explained in the next section). To delete the form, simply close it and answer **No** when asked if you want to save your changes.

Creating a Form with Form Wizard

The Form Wizard offers a good compromise between the automation of AutoForm and the control of creating a form from scratch. Follow these steps to use the Form Wizard:

1. From the Database window, click the **Forms** tab.

2. Click the **New** button. The New Form dialog box appears (see Figure 12.1).

3. Click **Form Wizard**.

Don't I Have to Pick a Table? When using the Form Wizard, you don't have to choose a table from the drop-down list in the New Form dialog box; you'll choose it in step 5.

CAUTION

4. Click **OK** to start the Form Wizard (see Figure 12.2).

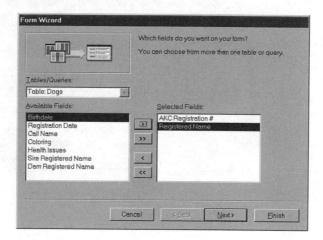

Figure 12.2 The Form Wizard lets you choose which fields you want to include from as many different tables as you like.

5. Open the **Tables/Queries** drop-down list and choose a table or query from which to select fields.

6. In the **Available Fields** list, click a field that you want to include on the form, and then click the > button to move it to the Selected Fields list.

7. Repeat step 6 until you've selected all the fields you want to include from that table. If you want to include fields from another table or query, repeat steps 5 and 6 to choose another table and other fields.

TIP **Selecting All Fields** You can quickly move all the fields from the Available Fields list to the Selected Fields list by clicking the **>>** button. If you make a mistake, you can remove a field from the Selected Fields list by clicking it and clicking the **<** button.

8. Click **Next** to continue. You'll be asked to choose a layout—**Columnar** (the most common), **Tabular**, **Datasheet**, or **Justified**. Click each of the buttons to see a preview of that type. When you've made a decision, click the one you want and click **Next**.

9. The wizard asks to choose a style. Click each of the styles listed to see a preview of it; click **Next** when you've chosen the one you want.

10. Enter a title for the form in the text box at the top of the dialog box.

11. Click the **Finish** button, and the form appears, ready for data entry, as shown in Figure 12.3. The first record in the table appears in it.

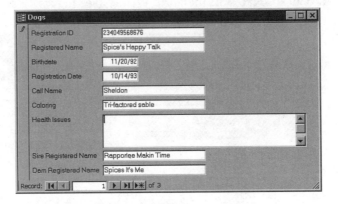

Figure 12.3 The Form Wizard's simple but usable form.

Creating a Form from Scratch

The most powerful and most difficult way to create a form is with Form Design. In Form Design view, you decide exactly where to place each field and how to format it. The following steps initiate your use of Form Design view; you learn more about this view in Lesson 13, "Modifying Your Form."

1. From the Database window, click the **Forms** tab.

2. Click the **New** button, and the New Form dialog box appears.

3. Click **Design View**.

4. Select a table or query from the drop-down list at the bottom of the dialog box. This is important. You won't have the opportunity to change your selection later.

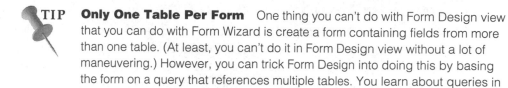

TIP **Only One Table Per Form** One thing you can't do with Form Design view that you can do with Form Wizard is create a form containing fields from more than one table. (At least, you can't do it in Form Design view without a lot of maneuvering.) However, you can trick Form Design into doing this by basing the form on a query that references multiple tables. You learn about queries in Lesson 16, "Creating a Query."

5. Click **OK**. A Form Design screen appears, as shown in Figure 12.4. You're ready to create your form.

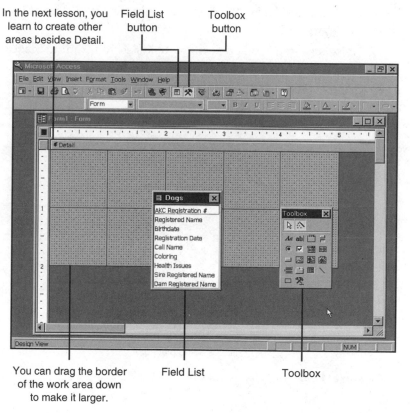

In the next lesson, you learn to create other areas besides Detail.

Field List button

Toolbox button

You can drag the border of the work area down to make it larger.

Field List

Toolbox

Figure 12.4 Form Design view: a blank canvas on which you design your form.

TIP **Toolbox and Field List** You'll want to use the Form Design toolbox and the Field List shown in Figure 12.4. If they're not visible, click the **Toolbox** button and/or the **Field List** button in the toolbar.

Adding Fields to a Form

The basic idea of the Form Design screen is simple—it's like a light table or pasteup board where you place the elements of your form. The fields you add to a form will appear in the Detail area of the form. The Detail area is the only area visible at first; you'll learn to add other areas later in the next lesson.

To add a field to the form, follow these steps:

1. Display the Field List if it's not showing by clicking the **Field List** button or selecting **View, Field List**.

2. Drag a field from the Field List onto the Detail area of the form (see Figure 12.5).

3. Repeat step 2 to add as many fields as you want to the form.

Don't worry about crowded labels; you fix that in the next lesson.

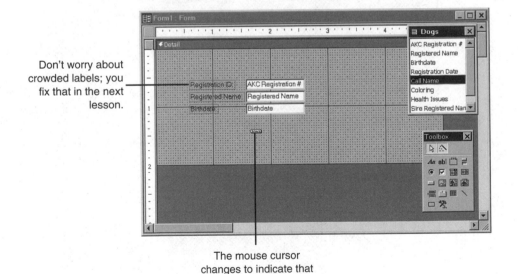

The mouse cursor changes to indicate that a field is being placed.

Figure 12.5 Drag fields from the Field List to the grid.

You can drag more than one field to the form at once. In step 2, instead of clicking a single field and then dragging it, do one of the following before you drag:

- To select a block of fields, click the first one you want, press and hold **Shift**, and click the last one.

- To select non-adjacent fields, hold down **Ctrl** and click on each one you want.

- To select all the fields on the list, double-click the **Field List** title bar.

You can move objects around on a form after you've initially placed them; you learn how to do this in Lesson 13, "Modifying Your Form." Don't worry if your form doesn't look very professional at this point. In the next several lessons, you'll learn how to modify and improve your form.

TIP **Using Snap to Grid** If you find it hard to align the fields neatly, select **Format**, **Snap to Grid** to place a check mark next to that command. If you want to align the fields on your own, select it again to turn it off.

If you are satisfied with your form, close it by clicking its **Close** (X) button. When asked if you want to save your changes, choose **Yes**. Type a name for the form in the text box provided and click **OK**. If, on the other hand, you want to make more modifications to your form, leave it open and skip to Lesson 13 now.

Entering Data in a Form

The whole point of creating a form is so you can enter data into your tables more easily. The form acts as an attractive "mask" that shields you from the plainness of your table. Once you create a form, follow these steps to enter data into it:

1. Open the form, and then do one of the following:

- If your form appears in Form Design view, select the **View**, **Form** command or click the **View** drop-down arrow and select **Form View** to enter Form view.

- If the form isn't open at all, click the **Form** tab in the Database window and double-click the form's name or click the **Open** button.

2. Click the field you want to begin with and type your data.

3. Press **Tab** to move to the next field. If you need to go back, you can press **Shift+Tab** to move to the previous field. When you reach the last field, pressing Tab moves you to the first field in a new, blank record.

   To move to the next record before you reach the bottom field, or to move back to previous records, click the right and left arrow buttons on the left end of the status bar.

4. Repeat steps 2 and 3 to enter all the records you want. Each record is saved automatically as you enter it.

 TIP **Data Entry Shortcuts** See the section "Some Data Entry Tricks" in Lesson 9, "Entering Data Not in a Table," for some shortcut ideas. They work equally well in forms and tables.

In this lesson, you created a simple form and added data to it. In the next lesson, you learn how to make changes to your form to better suit your needs.

Modifying Your Form

In this lesson, you learn to modify a form. You can use any form, created in any of the ways you learned in Lesson 12, "Creating a Simple Form."

This lesson is about making changes to forms. At this point, you might have a very rough form that you created from scratch, or you might have a polished, good-looking form that the Form Wizard created for you. The steps are the same no matter with what you're starting. (The examples in this lesson use a form created with Form Wizard.)

Moving Fields

The most common change to a form is moving fields around. You might want to move several fields down so you can insert a new field, or you might want to just rearrange the order in which the fields appear. From Form Design view, follow these steps:

1. Click a field's name to select it. Selection handles appear around it (see Figure 13.1). You can select several fields by holding down **Shift** and clicking each one.

2. Position the mouse pointer so that it becomes a hand (see Figure 13.1). If you're moving more than one field, you can position the mouse pointer on any of the selected fields.

3. Press and hold down the left mouse button and drag the field to a different location.

4. When the field is at the desired new location, release the mouse button.

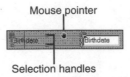

Figure 13.1 To move a field, select it and drag it with the open hand mouse pointer.

CAUTION

The Label Moved Without the Field Attached! Be careful when you position your mouse pointer over the field you want to move. Make sure the pointer changes to an *open* hand. If you position the mouse pointer over the top left selection handle for either the label or the field, the mouse pointer changes to a hand with a pointing finger, and when you drag, the label (or the field box) moves independently. This can be handy for special situations, but it's probably not what you want right now.

Adding Text

The next most common change is adding text to the form. You might add titles, subtitles, or explanatory text, for example. To do so, follow these steps:

1. If the Toolbox is not displayed, select **View**, **Toolbox** or click the **Toolbox** button on the toolbar.

2. Click the **Label** tool in the toolbox (the one with the italicized letters *Aa* on it). The mouse pointer changes to a capital A with a plus sign next to it (see Figure 13.2).

3. Click anywhere on the form where you want to create the new text. A tiny box appears. (The box will expand to hold the text as you type.)

4. Type the text.

5. Press **Enter** or click anywhere outside the text area to finish.

CAUTION

Text Dragging Don't worry about positioning the text as you create it. You can move text in the same way that you move fields. Just click it, position the mouse pointer so that the open hand appears, and then drag it to where you want it.

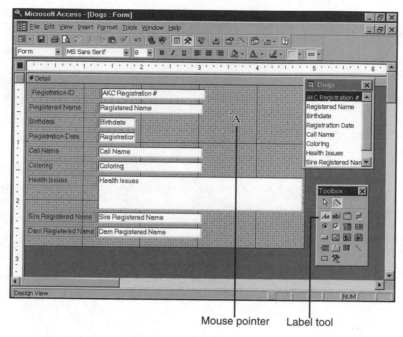

Mouse pointer   Label tool

Figure 13.2 Select the Label tool in the toolbox.

Viewing Headers and Footers

You have been working with the Detail area so far, but there are other areas you can use, as shown in Figure 13.3. To display these areas, follow these steps:

1. To view the Page Header/Footer, select **View**, **Page Header/Footer**.

2. To view the Form Header/Footer, select **View**, **Form Header/Footer**.

3. To turn off either area, repeat step 1 or 2 as appropriate.

After you display any of these headers and footers, you can add text to them the same way that you learned to add text in the preceding section. For instance, you might add a title for the form in the Form Header area.

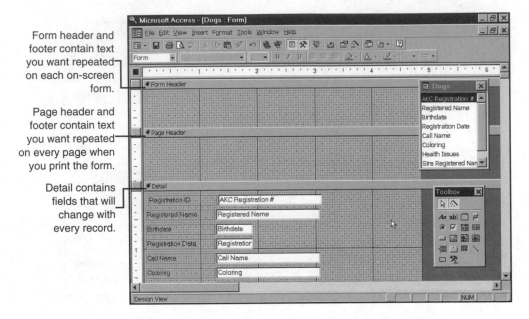

Form header and footer contain text you want repeated on each on-screen form.

Page header and footer contain text you want repeated on every page when you print the form.

Detail contains fields that will change with every record.

Figure 13.3 Each form can have several areas.

Changing Field Lengths

Suppose you want the Registration ID field area to be capable of displaying more characters. You just drag the field entry area to make it longer so more characters will show. Follow these steps to see how it works:

1. Click the field entry area to select it. Selection handles appear around it.

2. Position the mouse pointer at the right edge of the field entry area so the mouse pointer turns into a double-headed arrow (see Figure 13.4).

3. Drag the field to its new length and release the mouse button.

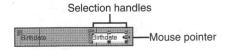

Selection handles

Mouse pointer

Figure 13.4 You can change the size of the field entry area by dragging it.

You can resize the labels for each field in the same way: position the mouse pointer at the left end of one of them and drag until the box containing the label is the desired length.

Formatting Text on a Form

After you place all your information on the form (that is, the fields you want to include and any titles or explanatory text), the next step is to make the form look more appealing.

All the formatting tools you need are on the Formatting toolbar (the second toolbar from the top in Form Design view). Table 13.1 shows the controls and describes each one. To use a control, select the element you want to format, and then click the appropriate toolbar button.

Some controls, like the font and size, display drop-down lists. You click the down arrow next to the button, and then select from the list. Other controls are simple buttons, such as Bold and Italic. Still other controls—the coloring and border buttons, for example—are a combination of a button and a drop-down list. You click the button to apply the current value, or you click the down arrow next to the button to change the value.

Table 13.1 Controls on the Formatting Toolbar

Button	Function
CustomerID	Lists the fields in the table you are using
Arial	Lists the available fonts
10	Lists the available sizes for the selected font
B	Toggles Bold on/off
I	Toggles Italics on/off
U	Toggles Underline on/off

continues

679

Table 13.1 Continued

Button	Function
	Left-aligns text
	Centers text
	Right-aligns text
	Fills the selected box with the selected color
	Colors the text in the selected box
	Colors the outline of the selected box
	Adds a border to the selected box
	Adds a special effect to the selected box

 TIP **Changing the Background Color** You can change the color of the background on which the form sits, too. Just click the header for the section you want to change (for instance, **Detail**) to select the entire section. Then use the **Fill/Back color** control to change the color.

 TIP **AutoFormat** Here's a shortcut for formatting your form. If you created the form with Form Wizard, you already saw AutoFormat at work. To see it again, select **Format**, **AutoFormat**. You will be asked to choose from among several predesigned color and formatting schemes.

Changing Tab Order

When you enter data on a form, you press **Tab** to move from one field to the next, in the order they're shown in the form. This progression from field to field is the tab order. When you first create a form, the tab order runs from top to bottom.

When you move and rearrange fields, the tab order doesn't change automatically. For instance, if you had 10 fields arranged in a column, and you rearranged them so that the 10th field was at the beginning, the tab order would still show that field in 10th position even though it would be at the top of the form. This makes it more difficult to fill in the form, so you will want to adjust the tab order to reflect the new structure of the form.

TIP **Tab Order Improvements** To make data entry easier, you might want to change the tab order to be different from the obvious top-to-bottom structure. For instance, if 90 percent of the records you enter skip several fields, you might want to put those fields you don't use last in the tab order, so you can skip over them easily.

Follow these steps to adjust the tab order:

1. Select **View**, **Tab Order**. The Tab Order dialog box appears (see Figure 13.5).

Figure 13.5 Use the Tab Order dialog box to control the tab order in your form.

2. The fields appear in their tab order. To change the order, click a field and then drag it up or down on the list.

3. To quickly set the tab order based on the fields' current positions in the form (top-to-bottom), click the **Auto Order** button.

4. Click **OK**.

In this lesson, you learned to improve a form by moving fields, adding text, adding formatting, and adjusting the tab order. In the next lesson, you will learn to search your database to find specific information.

Searching for Data

In this lesson, you learn the most basic ways to search for data in a database using the Find and Replace features.

Using the Find Feature

The Find feature is useful for locating a particular record that you have previously entered. For instance, if you keep a database of customers, you might want to find a particular customer's record quickly when he is ready to make a purchase, so you can verify his address. Or, to continue the dog kennel example we have been using, you could quickly find the record for the dog with the call name of Sheldon so you can look up his birth date.

 TIP **Finding More Than One Record** If you need to find several records at once, Find is not the best tool. It finds only one record at a time. A better tool for finding multiple records is a filter, which you will learn about in Lesson 15, "Sorting and Filtering Data."

To find a particular record, follow these steps:

1. Switch to either Datasheet view or Form view. Either one supports the Find feature.

2. Click in the field that contains the data you want to find, if you know which field it is. For instance, if you're going to look for a customer based on his last name, click in the **Name** field.

 3. Click the **Find** tool in the toolbar, or select **Edit**, **Find**, or press **Ctrl+F**. The Find dialog box appears (see Figure 14.1).

Figure 14.1 Use the Find dialog box to find data in a record.

4. Type the text or numbers that you want to find in the **Find What** text box.

5. Open the **Match** drop-down list and select one of the following:

> **Whole Field** finds fields where the specified text is the only text in that field. For instance, the search text "Smith" would not match "Smithsonian."

> **Start of Field** finds fields that begin with the specified text. For instance, the search text "Smith" would match "Smith" and "Smithsonian," but not "Joe Smith."

> **Any Part of Field** finds fields that contain the specified text in any way. So the search text "Smith" would match "Smith," "Smithsonian," and "Joe Smith."

6. If you want to search only forward from the current record, open the **Search** drop-down list and select **Down**. If you want to search only backward, select **Up**. (The default is All, which searches all records.)

7. To limit the match to only entries that are the same case (upper and/or lower), select the **Match Case** check box. As a result, the search text "Smith" would not match "SMITH" or "smith."

8. To find only fields with the same formatting as the text you type, select **Search Fields As Formatted**. With this option on, "12/12/98" would not find "12-12-98," even though they represent the same date, because they're formatted differently. The Search Fields as Formatted option is available only if you select **Search Only Current Field** (see step 9).

TIP **Don't Slow Down** Don't use the Search Fields as Formatted option unless you specifically need it, because it makes your search go more slowly.

9. To limit the search to the field where you clicked when you started this procedure, select the **Search Only Current Field** check box. (Do this whenever possible because it makes the search faster.) However, if you don't know what field the data is in, you shouldn't check this.

10. Click **Find First** to find the first match for your search.

11. If necessary, move the Find dialog box out of the way by dragging its title bar so you can see the record it found. Access highlights the field entry containing the found text (see Figure 14.2).

When the Search Only Current Field option is on, the title bar shows which field is being searched.

Access highlights the found text.

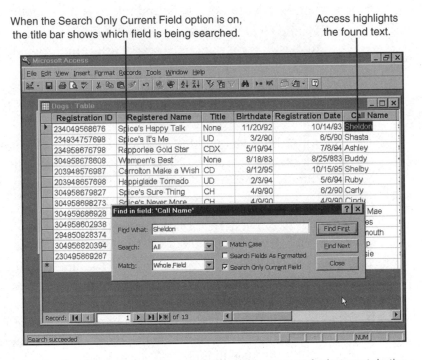

Figure 14.2 One instance at a time, Access displays records that contain the selected text.

12. To find the next occurrence, click **Find Next**. If Access cannot find any more occurrences, it tells you **The search item was not found**. Click **OK** to clear that message.

13. When you finish finding your data, click **Close** to close the Find dialog box.

Using the Replace Feature

Replacing is a lot like finding; it finds the specified text, too. But as an extra bonus, it replaces the found text with text that you specify. For instance, if you found that you misspelled a brand name in your inventory, you could replace the word with the correct spelling. Or, in our dog kennel example, you could find the dog named Sheldon and change his name to Sherman, if his new owners changed his name.

To find and replace data, follow these steps:

1. Select **Edit, Replace** or press **Ctrl+H**. The Replace dialog box appears (see Figure 14.3).

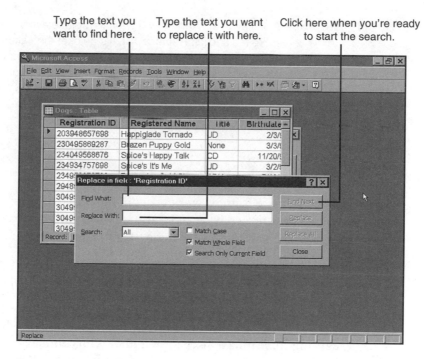

Figure 14.3 You can find specific text and replace it with different text.

2. Type the text you want to find in the **Find What** text box.

3. Type the text you want to replace it with in the **Replace With** text box.

4. Select any options you want, as you learned to do with the Find dialog box in the previous section.

685

There's No Match Compared to the Find dialog box, the one thing that the Replace dialog box lacks is the Match drop-down list. The Replace feature always uses the Any Part of Field option for matching.

CAUTION

5. Click **Find Next**, and Access finds the first occurrence of the text.

6. If necessary, drag the title bar of the Replace dialog box to move the box, so you can see the text that Access found.

7. Click the **Replace** button to replace the text.

8. Click **Find Next** to find other occurrences if desired, and replace them by clicking the **Replace** button.

TIP **Replace All** If you are certain you want to replace every occurrence of the text in the entire table, click **Replace All**. It's quicker than alternating repeatedly between Find Next and Replace. Be careful, however! You may not realize all the words that might be changed. After all, you wouldn't want to change "will" to "would" and later find that "willfully" had been changed to "wouldfully."

9. When you finish replacing, click **Close**.

Other Ways to Find Data

The Find and Replace features work well on individual records, but there are several more sophisticated ways of locating data in your database, as you will learn in upcoming lessons. They include the following:

- **Sorting** Rearranging the data on-screen so it's easier to skim through the list to find what you want. See Lesson 15, "Sorting and Filtering Data."

- **Filtering** Narrowing down the list to eliminate the data you know you don't want to see. See Lesson 15, "Sorting and Filtering Data."

- **Querying** Creating a more formal filter with complex criteria that you can save and apply again and again. See Lessons 16, "Creating a Query," and 17, "Modifying a Query."

- **Reporting** Creating a printed report containing only the records and fields that you're interested in. See Lessons 18, "Creating a Simple Report," and 19, "Customizing a Report."

In this lesson, you learned to find and replace data in a database. In the next lesson, you will learn about two other ways of locating data: sorting and filtering.

Sorting and Filtering Data

In this lesson, you learn how to find data by sorting and filtering.

Access has many ways of finding and organizing data, and each is good for a certain situation. As you learned in Lesson 14 "Searching for Data," Find and Replace are great features when you're working with individual instances of a particular value (finding Mr. Smith's record quickly, for example). This chapter explains two other ways of finding what you need.

Sorting Data

Although you enter your records into the database in some sort of logical order, at some point, you will want them in a different order. For instance, we might enter the dogs in our kennel according to registration number, but later we might want to look at the list in order of the dogs' birth dates, from oldest to youngest.

The Sort command is the perfect solution to this problem. With Sort, you can rearrange the records according to any field you like. You can sort in either ascending order (A to Z and 1 to 10) or descending order (Z to A and 10 to 1).

TIP   **Which View?**   You can sort in either Form view or Datasheet view. I prefer Datasheet view because it shows many records at once.

Follow these steps to sort records:

1. Click anywhere in the field by which you want to sort.

2. Click the **Sort Ascending** button or the **Sort Descending** button on the toolbar. Or if you prefer, select **Records, Sort,** and then choose **Ascending** or **Descending** from the submenu. Figure 15.1 shows our table of dogs sorted in Ascending order by birth date.

Access sorted the table by this column.

Registration ID	Registered Name	Title	Birthdate	Registration Date	Call Name
304958678608	Wempen's Best	None	8/18/85	8/25/85	Buddy
234934757698	Spice's It's Me	UD	3/2/90	6/5/90	Shasta
304959686928	Spice's Krazy 4 U	UDX	4/9/90	4/9/90	Betsy Mae
304958698273	Spice's Never More	CH	4/9/90	4/9/90	Cindy
304958679827	Spice's Sure Thing	CH	4/9/90	6/2/90	Carly
304958602938	Princess of the Ring	None	8/12/91	8/15/91	Bubbles
294850928374	Princess Bride	None	11/20/92	10/14/93	Loudmouth
234049568676	Spice's Happy Talk	None	11/20/92	10/14/93	Sheldon
304956820394	King of the Hill	CD	2/3/94	5/6/94	Champ
203948657698	Happiglade Tornado	UD	2/3/94	5/6/94	Ruby
234958676798	Rapporlee Gold Star	CDX	5/19/94	7/8/94	Ashley
203948576987	Carrolton Make a Wish	CD	9/12/95	10/15/95	Shelby
230495869287	Brazen Puppy Gold	None	3/3/96	5/6/96	Boopsie

Record: ◄◄ ◄ 4 ► ►◄ ►* of 13

Figure 15.1 Access sorted this table in Ascending order by the Birthdate column.

3. If you want to restore the records to their presorted order, select **Records, Remove Filter/Sort.**

What Is Presorted Order? If you defined a Primary Key field when you created your database (see Lesson 4, "Creating a New Database"), the records appear sorted in ascending order according to that field by default. This is the order they revert to when you remove a sort (as in step 3). If you save the datasheet or form without removing the sort, the sort order becomes part of that object.

Filtering Data

Filtering is for those times when you want to get many of the records out of the way so that you can see the few that you're interested in. Filtering temporarily narrows down the number of records that appear, according to criteria you select.

Filters Versus Queries Queries also narrow down the records displayed, as you will learn in Lesson 16, "Creating a Query." Using a filter is easier and quicker than using a query, but you can't save a filter as a separate object for later use. (However, you can save a filter as a query, as you learn later in this lesson.)

There are three ways to apply a filter: Filter By Selection, Filter by Form, and Advanced Filter/Sort. The first two are the most common for casual users, as you will discover in the following sections. The third method is only for advanced users.

 TIP **Sorting and Filtering** Neither of the filtering methods you learn in this lesson enable you to sort at the same time that you filter. However, it's easy enough to sort the filtered records using the same sorting process you learned earlier in this lesson.

Filter by Selection

Filtering by selection is the easiest method of filtering. But before you can use it, you have to locate an instance of the value you want the filtered records to contain. For example, if you want to find all the dogs in your table that have earned the title of "CD" (Companion Dog), you must first locate a record that meets that criteria. You then base the rest of the filter on that record.

To filter by selection, follow these steps:

1. In a field, find one instance of the value you want all filtered records to contain.

2. Select the value using one of these methods:
   - To find all records in which the field value is identical to the selected value, select the entire field entry.
   - To find all records in which the field begins with the selected value, select part of the field entry beginning with the first character.
   - To find all records in which the field contains the selected value at any point, select part of the field entry beginning after the first character.

 3. Click the **Filter by Selection** button on the toolbar or select **Records, Filter, Filter by Selection**. Access displays the records that match the criterion you selected.

Figure 15.2 shows the Dogs table filtered to show only dogs that have earned the "CD" title.

Access filtered the table by this column.

Figure 15.2 The result of a filter is a list of records that match the criterion.

TIP Filtering by More Than One Criterion With Filter by Selection, you can filter by only one criterion at a time. However, you can apply successive filters after the first one to further narrow the list of matching records.

You can also filter for records that don't contain the selected value. After selecting the value, right-click it and select **Filter Excluding Selection**.

You can cancel a filter by clicking the **Remove Filter** button (which is the same as the Apply Filter button) or by selecting **Records**, **Remove Filter/Sort**.

Filter by Form

Filtering by form is a more powerful filtering method than filtering by selection. With filter by form, you can filter by more than one criterion at a time. You can also set up "or" filters, which find records that match any one of several criteria. You can even enter logical expressions (such as "greater than a certain value").

To filter by form, follow these steps:

1. In Datasheet or Form view, click the **Filter by Form** button on the toolbar or select **Records**, **Filter**, **Filter by Form**. A blank form appears, resembling an empty datasheet with a single record line.

2. Click the field for which you want to set a criterion, and a drop-down arrow appears. Click the arrow and select the value you want from the list. Or, you can type the value directly into the field if you prefer.

3. Enter as many criteria as you like in various fields. Figure 15.3 shows two criteria, including a criterion that uses a less-than sign (a mathematical operator explained in Lesson 16, "Creating a Query").

4. If you want to set up an "or" condition, click the **Or** tab at the bottom of the Filter by Form window and enter the alternate criteria into that form. Notice that another Or tab appears when you fill this one, so you can add multiple "or" conditions.

5. After you enter your criteria, click the **Apply Filter** button on the toolbar. Your filtered data appears.

As with Filter by Selection, you can undo a filter by clicking the **Filter** button again or by selecting **Records**, **Remove Filter/Sort**.

Click here to create an "or" criterion.

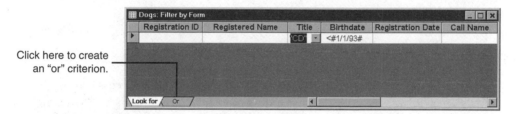

Figure 15.3 This query finds all dogs that were born before 1/1/93 and have a "CD" (Companion Dog) title.

Saving Your Filtered Data As a Query

Using filters is a convenient alternative to creating a simple query from scratch. You can save a filter as a query and use it as you would use a query; it even appears on your Queries list in the Database window. (You learn more about working with queries in Lesson 16, "Creating a Query.") To save a filter as a query, follow these steps:

1. Display the filter in Query by Form view.

2. Select **File**, **Save As Query** or click the **Save** button on the toolbar. Access asks for a name for the new query.

3. Type a name and click **OK**. Access saves the filter.

In this lesson, you learned how to sort and filter your database. In the next lesson, you begin learning about queries, which provide a more sophisticated way of isolating and organizing information.

Creating a Query

In this lesson, you learn how a query can help you find the information you need, and you learn to create a simple query using the Simple Query Wizard. You also learn how to save and print any query's results, and you learn about other Query Wizards that Access provides for special situations.

What Is a Query?

As you learned in Lesson 15, "Sorting and Filtering Data," Access offers many ways to help you narrow down the information you're looking at, including sorting and filtering. A query is simply a more formal way to sort and filter. Queries enable you to specify the following:

- Which fields you want to see
- The order in which the fields should appear
- Filter criteria for each field (see Lesson 15)
- The order in which you want each field sorted (see Lesson 15)

 TIP **Saving a Filter** When the primary purpose of the query is to filter, you might find it easier to create a filter and save it as a query. See Lesson 15, "Sorting and Filtering Data," for details.

In this lesson, you create a very simple query, which may not do everything you want it to do. But in the next lesson (Lesson 17, "Modifying a Query"), you learn how to modify it to make it more powerful.

Creating a Simple Query Using Query Wizard

The easiest way to create a query is with a Query Wizard, and the easiest Query Wizard is the Simple Query Wizard. (The other Query Wizards are *special-use* ones that you will probably never need; they're described later in this lesson.)

The Simple Query Wizard enables you to select the fields you want to display—that's all. You don't get to set criteria for including individual records, and you don't get to specify a sort order. (You learn to do those things in Lesson 17, "Modifying a Query.") This kind of simple query is useful when you want to weed out extraneous fields, but you still want to see every record.

 TERM   **Select Query**   The query that the Simple Query Wizard creates is a very basic version of a Select query. The Select query is the most common query type. With a Select query, you can select records, sort them, filter them, and perform simple calculations (such as counting and averaging) on the results.

To create a simple Select query with the Simple Query Wizard, follow these steps:

1. Open the database you want to work with and click the **Queries** tab.
2. Click the **New** button. The New Query dialog box appears.
3. Click **Simple Query Wizard** and click **OK**. The first box of the Simple Query Wizard appears (see Figure 16.1). This screen may look familiar; it's similar to the first screen of the Form Wizard you worked with in Lesson 12, "Creating a Simple Form."
4. In the **Tables/Queries** drop-down list, choose the table from which you want to select fields. For example, I'm going to use the Dogs field.
5. Click a field name in the **Available Fields** list and click the > button to move it to the Selected Fields list. Do the same for any other fields you want to move, or move them all at once with the >> button.
6. Select another table or query from the **Tables/Queries** list and add some of its fields to the Selected Fields list if you want. When you finish adding fields, click **Next**.
7. Next you're asked whether you want a Detail or a Summary query. Choose whichever you want; if you're not sure, stick with **Detail**, the default. If you choose **Summary**, the Summary Options button becomes available,

which you can click to open a dialog box of summary options. When you're finished, click **Next**. The next dialog box appears (see Figure 16.2).

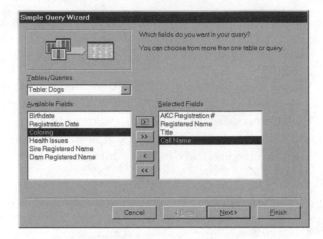

Figure 16.1 The Simple Query Wizard first asks which fields you want to include.

Figure 16.2 Enter a title for your query.

Relationships Required If you are going to use two or more tables in your query, they must be joined with a relationship. See Lesson 21 to learn how to create relationships between tables.

CAUTION

8. Enter a title for the query in the **What Title Do You Want for Your Query?** text box. I'm going to call mine Dog Names.

9. Click **Finish** to view the query results. Figure 16.3 shows my results.

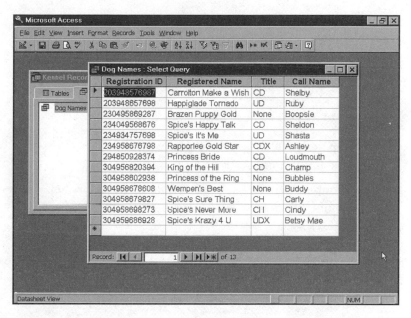

Figure 16.3 The results of my Select query.

This simple query is actually too simple; it has limited usefulness and doesn't show off any of Access's powerful query features. You could get the same results by hiding certain columns in Datasheet view! Luckily, the Select query is much more powerful than the Simple Query Wizard makes it appear, as you see in the next lesson. But before you go there, take a look at a few basics that apply to any query.

Saving a Query

When you create a query, Access saves it automatically. You don't need to do anything special to save it. Just close the query window and look on the Queries tab of the Database window. You see the query on the list.

TIP **Close the Query?** You close a query window the same way you close any window—by clicking its **Close** button (the X in the upper-right corner).

Rerunning a Query

At any time, you can re-run your query. If the data has changed since the last time you ran the query, those changes will be represented.

To re-run a query, follow these steps:

1. Open the database containing the query.

2. Click the **Queries** tab in the Database window.

3. Double-click the query you want to re-run, or click it once and click the **Open** button (see Figure 16.4).

Double-click here to open the Dog Names query.

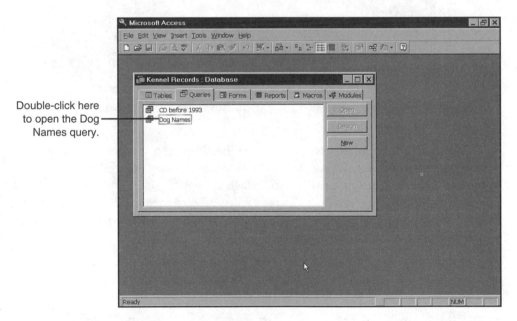

Figure 16.4 You can redisplay any query by opening it from the Queries tab.

Working with Query Results

Query results appear in Datasheet view, as shown in Figure 16.3. You can do anything to the records that you can do in a normal Datasheet view (see Lesson 10, "Editing Data in a Table"), including copy and delete records and change field entries.

For example, you may want to update a sales database to change the Last Contacted field (a date) to today for every record. From your query results window, you could make that change. Or perhaps you want to delete all records for customers who haven't made a purchase in the last two years. You could delete the records from the query results window, and they would disappear from the table too.

Of course, with the latter example, it would be easier if the records were sorted according to the field in question—and the Simple Query Wizard you learned about in this lesson won't enable you to sort. However, in Lesson 17, "Modifying a Query," you learn about some other, more powerful Query Wizards that enable you to choose more options.

Printing Query Results

The query results window not only edits like a datasheet, but the window also prints like one. To print the query results, do the following:

1. Make sure the query results window is active.

2. Select **File**, **Print** or press **Ctrl+P**. The Print dialog box appears.

3. Select whatever print options you want, and then click **OK**.

 If you don't want to set any print options, you can simply click the **Print** button on the toolbar to print, bypassing the Print dialog box.

Other Query Wizards

Access's query features are very powerful; they can do amazingly complicated calculations and comparisons on many tables at once. You can create queries with their own dialog boxes for custom entry of special criteria, link a query to external databases (databases in other programs), and much more.

Unfortunately, the process for creating a lot of these powerful queries is quite complicated. It's enough to give casual users a major headache. That's why in this book, I stick to the basic Select type of query, which does almost everything an average user needs to do.

Some intermediate Access Query Wizards can help you experiment with more complex query types without causing too much stress. These Query Wizards appear on the list when you click the New button on the Queries tab. I don't cover any of that in this book, but you may want to try them out yourself:

- **Crosstab Query Wizard**   Displays summarized values (such as sums, counts, and averages from one field) and groups them by one set of facts listed down the left side of the datasheet as row headings and another set of facts listed across the top of the datasheet as column headings.

- **Find Unmatched Query Wizard**   Compares two tables and finds all records that do not appear in both tables (based on a comparison of certain fields).

- **Find Duplicates Query Wizard**   The opposite of Find Unmatched. It compares two tables and finds all records that appear in both.

In this lesson, you learned to create a simple query and to save, edit, and print query results. In the next lesson, you learn how to modify the query you created.

Modifying a Query

In this lesson, you learn how to modify the query you created in Lesson 16, "Creating a Query," using Query Design view.

Introducing Query Design View

In Lesson 16, "Creating a Query," you created a very simple query using the Simple Query Wizard. That query selected and displayed fields from a table. There's a lot more you can do with your query when you enter Query Design view.

Query Design view is much like Table Design view and Form Design view, both of which you encountered earlier in this part. In Query Design view, you can change the rules that govern your query results.

Opening a Query in Query Design View

To open an existing query in Query Design view, follow these steps:

1. Open the database that contains the query you want to edit.
2. Click the **Queries** tab.
3. Click the query you want to edit, and then click the **Design** button.

Figure 17.1 shows the query from Lesson 16, "Creating a Query," as it looks in Query Design view. You learn how to edit it in this lesson. (This query has only one table. If it had more than one, each table would be displayed in a separate box listing its fields.)

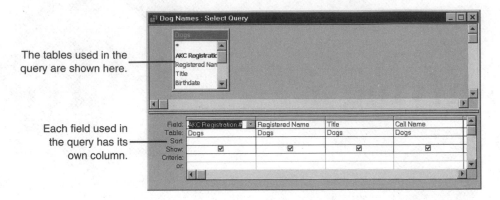

The tables used in the query are shown here.

Each field used in the query has its own column.

Figure 17.1 In Query Design view, you can edit a query you have created.

Starting a New Query in Query Design View

Instead of using the Simple Query Wizard to begin your query (as you did in Lesson 16, "Creating a Query"), you can begin a query from scratch in Query Design view. As you become more familiar with Access queries, you might find that this is faster and easier than using a wizard.

To begin a new query in Query Design view, follow these steps:

1. Open the database in which you want the query.
2. Click the **Queries** tab in the Database window.
3. Click the **New** button.
4. Click **Design View** and click **OK**. The Show Table dialog box appears, listing all the tables in the database.
5. Select the table you want to work with and click the **Add** button.
6. Repeat step 5 for each table you want to add. Don't forget that if you use more than one table, a relationship must already be established between the tables (see Lesson 20, "Creating Relationships Between Tables").
7. Click **Close** after you finish adding tables. The Query Design view window opens, as in Figure 17.1, but no fields are selected yet.

Adding Fields to a Query

If you created your query from scratch (as in the preceding set of steps), the first task you need to do is add the fields with which you want to work. You can also use this same procedure to add additional fields to an existing query.

 TIP **Adding More Tables** You can add additional tables to your query at any time. Just click the **Show Table** button on the toolbar or select **Query**, **Show Table**. Then select the table(s) you want and click **Add**. Click **Close** to return to your query design.

There are three ways to add a field to a query. All methods are easy; try all of them to see which you prefer.

Here's the first method:

 TIP **Only One Table?** If you are using only one table in the query, you can skip the first two steps in this procedure.

1. Click in the Table row of the first blank column. A down arrow button appears, indicating a drop-down list is available.
2. Open the drop-down list and select a table. The tables available on the list are the same as the table windows that appear at the top of the query design window.
3. Click the Field row directly above the table name you just chose. A down-arrow button appears, indicating a drop-down list is available.
4. Open the drop-down list and select a field. The fields listed come from the tables you chose for the query. The field's name appears in the Field row, in the column where you selected it.

Here's the second method of adding a field:

1. Scroll through the list of fields in the desired table window at the top of the Query Design box, until you find the field you want to add.
2. Click the field name and drag it into the Field row of the first empty column. The field's name appears in that location.

The third method is to simply double-click the field name in the field list. It moves to the first available slot in the query grid.

Deleting a Field

There are two ways to delete a field from your query:

- Click anywhere in the column and select **Edit, Delete Column**.

- Position the mouse pointer directly above the column so the pointer turns into a down-pointing black arrow. Click to select the entire column, and then press the **Delete** key or click the **Cut** button on the toolbar.

 Cut versus Delete If you cut the column instead of deleting it, you can paste it back into the query. Just select the column where you want it, and then click the **Paste** button or choose **Edit, Paste**. Be careful, however, because the pasted column will replace the selected one; the selected column doesn't move over to make room for it. Select an empty column if you don't want to replace an existing one.

Adding Criteria

Criteria will be familiar to you if you read Lesson 15, "Sorting and Filtering Data," which dealt with filters. You use criteria to choose which records will appear in your query results. For example, I could limit my list of dogs to those whose birth dates were before 8/5/94.

 TIP **Filters versus Queries** If the primary reason for creating the query is to filter, you may want to create the filter part first using one of the procedures described in Lesson 15, "Sorting and Filtering Data," and then save the filter as a query. You can open that query in Query Design view and fine-tune it as needed.

To set criteria for a field that you have added to your query, follow these steps:

1. In Query Design view, click the Criteria row in the desired field's column.
2. Type the criterion you want to use, as shown in Figure 17.2. Table 17.1 provides some examples you could have entered in Figure 17.2, as well as the subsequent results.

In Figure 17.2, Access added # symbols because you are working with a date. For other types of criteria, Access adds other symbols, such as quotation marks around a text or number string.

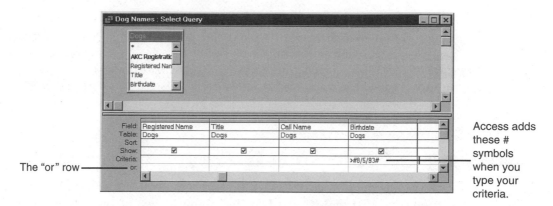

The "or" row ——

Access adds
these #
symbols
when you
type your
criteria.

Figure 17.2   Enter criteria into the Criteria row in the appropriate field's column.

Table 17.1   Sample Criteria for Queries

Enter This	To Get Records Where This Value Is...
8/5/93	Exactly 8/5/93
<8/5/93	Before 8/5/93
>8/5/93	After 8/5/93
>=8/5/93	On or after 8/5/93
<=8/5/93	On or before 8/5/93
Not <8/5/93	Not before 8/5/93
Not >8/5/93	Not after 8/5/93

TIP   **Text, Too**   You can also enter text as a criterion. The **<** and **>** (before and after) operators apply to alphabetical order with text. For instance, **<C** finds text that begins with A or B.

Did you notice the "or" row under the Criteria row in Figure 17.2? You can enter more criteria using that line. The query will find records where any of the criteria is true. When you enter criteria into the "or" row, another "or" row appears, so you can enter more.

What About "And"? When you have two criteria that must both be true, you can put them both together in a single Criteria row with the word "And." For instance, you might want birth dates that were between 12/1/93 and 12/1/95. You could put all that in a single Criteria row, like this: >12/1/93 And <12/1/95.

CAUTION

Sorting a Field in a Query

After all this complicated criteria discussion, you will be happy to know that sorting is fairly straightforward. To sort any field, just follow these steps from the query results window:

1. Click in the Sort row for the field you want to sort. A drop-down arrow appears.

2. Open the drop-down list and select **Ascending** or **Descending**.

Later, if you want to cancel sorting for this field, repeat these steps, but select **(not sorted)**. Refer to Lesson 15, "Sorting and Filtering Data," for more information about sorting.

Showing or Hiding a Field

Some fields are included in your query only so you can filter or sort based on them. You may not necessarily be interested in seeing that field in the query results. For instance, you may want to limit your query to all dogs born before 8/5/93, but you don't want each dog's birth date to appear in the query.

To exclude a field from appearing in the query results, just deselect its check box in the Show row. To include it again, select the check box again.

Viewing Query Results

When you're ready to see the results of your query, click the **Run** button on the Query Design toolbar or select **Query**, **Run**. Your results appear in a window that resembles a datasheet (see Figure 17.3).

Figure 17.3 The results of a kennel query based on birth dates.

In this lesson, you learned to modify and strengthen your queries. In the next lesson, you learn how to create a simple, attractive report suitable for printing and distributing to others.

Creating a Simple Report

In this lesson, you learn how to create reports in Access using AutoReport and Report Wizard.

Why Create Reports?

You have learned many ways to organize and view your data, but until now each method has focused on on-screen use. Forms help with data entry on-screen, and queries help you find information and display the results on-screen.

You can print any table, form, or query, but the results will be less than professional-looking because those tools are not designed to be printed. Reports, on the other hand, are specifically designed to be printed and shared with other people. With a report, you can generate professional results of which you can be proud, whether you're distributing them on paper or publishing them on the Internet.

There are several ways to create a report, ranging from easy-but-limited (AutoReport) to difficult-but-very-flexible (Report Design view). The intermediate choice is Report Wizard, which offers some flexibility along with a fairly easy procedure.

Using AutoReport to Create a Report

If you want a plain, no-frills report based on a single table or query, AutoReport is for you. You can go back and improve its appearance later, when you learn about customizing reports in Lesson 19, "Customizing a Report."

You can create either a Tabular or a Columnar report. A tabular report resembles a datasheet, and a columnar report resembles a form. They are
equally easy to create.

To create a report with AutoReport, follow these steps:

1. Open the database containing the table or query on which you want to
   report.

2. Click the **Reports** tab in the Database window, and then click the **New**
   button. The New Report dialog box appears (see Figure 18.1).

3. Click **AutoReport: Columnar** or **AutoReport: Tabular**.

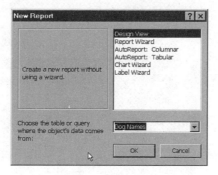

Figure 18.1   Choose one of the AutoReports from this window.

4. In the drop-down list at the bottom of the dialog box, select the table or
   query on which you want to base the report.

Multiple Tables?   AutoReports can use only one table or query. If you want
to create an AutoReport that uses several tables, first create a query based on
those tables, and then base the AutoReport on the query.

CAUTION

5. Click **OK**. The report appears in Print Preview. See the section "Viewing
   and Printing Reports in Print Preview" later in this lesson to learn what to
   do next.

As you can see in Print Preview, the AutoReports' output is not much better
than a raw printout from a table or form. If you want a better-looking report,
try Report Wizard, which is explained in the following section.

Creating a Report with Report Wizard

The Report Wizard offers a good compromise between ease of use and flexibility. With Report Wizard, you can use multiple tables and queries and choose a layout and format for your report.

Follow these steps to create a report with Report Wizard:

1. Open the database containing the table or query on which you want to report.
2. Click the **Reports** tab in the Database window, and then click the **New** button. The New Report dialog box appears (refer to Figure 18.1).
3. Click **Report Wizard** and click **OK**. The Report Wizard starts (see Figure 18.2).

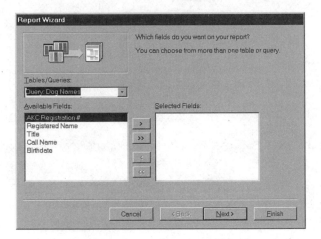

Figure 18.2 The first Report Wizard screen.

 TIP **Multiple Tables/Queries Allowed** You don't need to select a table or query from the drop-down list in the New Report dialog box in step 3 because you will be selecting tables and queries in step 4 as part of the wizard.

4. Open the **Tables/Queries** drop-down list and select one of the tables or queries from which you want to include fields.

5. Click a field in the **Available Fields** list, and then click the > button to move it to the Selected Fields list. Repeat this step to select all the fields you want, or click >> to move over at once all the fields .

6. If necessary, select another table or query from the **Tables/Queries** list and repeat step 5. When you finish selecting fields, click **Next**. The next screen of the wizard appears (see Figure 18.3).

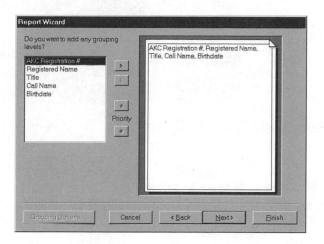

Figure 18.3 Set your report's grouping.

7. If you want the records grouped by any of the fields you selected, click the field and click the > button. If you want to select more than one group- ing levels, select them in the order you want them. Then click **Next** to move on.

 TERM   **Grouping?** The instructions on the screen are a bit cryptic. By default, there are no groups. You have to select a field and click the > button to create a grouping. For instance, if I had several dogs with the same birthday, I could identify them by grouping my dogs using the Birthdate field. Grouping sets off each group on the report. If you select a field to group by, the Grouping Options button becomes active, and you can click it to specify precise group- ing settings.

8. Next you're asked what sort order you want to use (see Figure 18.4). If you want sorted records, open the top drop-down list and select a field by which to sort. You can select up to four sorts from the drop-down lists. Then click **Next**.

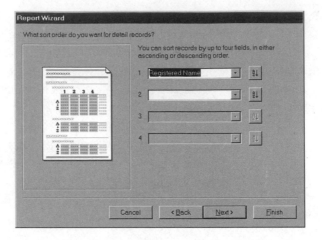

Figure 18.4 Set the sort order.

 TERM
Ascending or Descending? By default, Access sorts in ascending order (A–Z). Click the **AZ** button next to the box to change the sort order to descending (Z–A) if you want. See Lesson 15, "Sorting and Filtering Data," for more information about sorting.

9. In the next dialog box (shown in Figure 18.5), choose a layout option from the Layout area. When you click an option button, the sample in the box changes to show you what you selected.

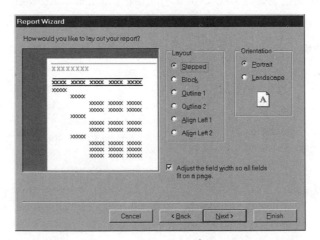

Figure 18.5 Choose the layout of your report.

CAUTION

Where Are All the Layouts? If you didn't choose any groupings in your report, your layout choices will be limited to three: Columnar, Tabular, and Justified. The layouts shown in Figure 18.5 are unique to grouped reports.

10. Choose the orientation for your printed report: **Portrait** (across the narrow edge of the paper) or **Landscape** (across the wide edge of the paper). Then click **Next** to continue.

11. In the next wizard dialog box, you're asked to choose a report style. Several are listed; click one to see a sample of it. When you're satisfied with your choice, click **Next**.

12. Finally, you're asked for a report title. Enter one in the **Report** text box and click **Finish** to see your report in Print Preview (see Figure 18.6).

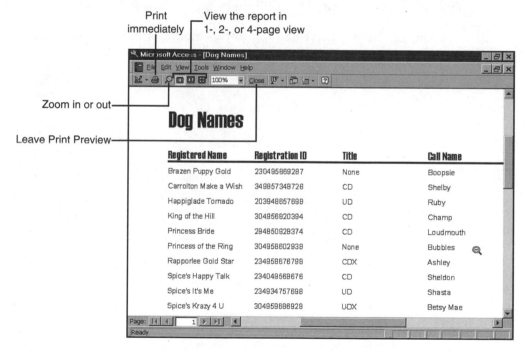

Figure 18.6 Here's a very simple report with no grouping.

Viewing and Printing Reports in Print Preview

When you finish a report with either Report Wizard or AutoReport, the report appears in Print Preview (as shown in Figure 18.6). From here, you can print the report if you're happy with it, or you can go to Report Design view to make changes if you aren't. (You learn more about the latter in Lesson 19, "Customizing a Report").

If you want to print the report and specify any print options (such as number of copies), open the **File** menu and select **Print**. If you want a quick hard copy, click the **Print** button on the toolbar. Click the button appropriate to what you want to do. Figure 18.6 points out some of the other useful buttons available in Print Preview. To go to Report Design view, click **Close**. (Report Design view is actually open, it's just obscured by the Print Preview window.)

In this lesson, you learned to create and print a simple report. In the next lesson, you learn how to work in Report Design view to customize your report.

Customizing a Report

In this lesson, you learn to use Report Design view to make your report more attractive.

Entering Report Design View

When you finish previewing a report you have created, close Print Preview and you're automatically in Report Design view. If you want to come back to Report Design view later from the Database window, perform these steps:

1. Click the **Reports** tab.
2. Click the report you want to modify.
3. Click the **Design** button. The report appears in Design view, as shown in Figure 19.1.

Report Design view might seem familiar to you; it looks a lot like Form Design view. Almost everything you learned about editing forms in Lesson 13, "Modifying You Form," applies also to reports. As in Form Design view, there is a toolbox of common editing tools.

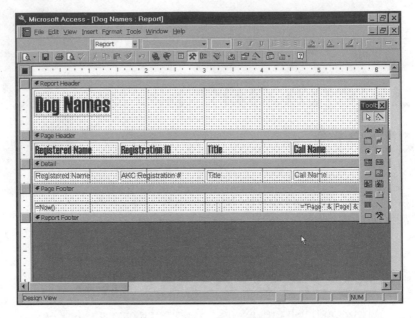

Figure 19.1 The report created in the previous lesson, as it looks in Design view.

Working with Objects on Your Report

Working with report objects in Report Design view is exactly the same as working with objects in Form Design view. An object is any control, such as a field name or a title. Turn back to Lesson 13, "Modifying Your Form," for the full story, or follow the brief review here:

Selecting objects Just like in Form Design view, you select an object on your report by clicking it. Selection handles (little squares in the corners) appear around it. See Lesson 14, "Searching for Data," for more details.

Moving objects To move an object, first select it. Position the mouse pointer over a border so the pointer turns into an open black hand. Then click and drag the object to a new location.

Resizing objects First, select the object. Then position the mouse pointer over one of the selection handles and drag the handle to resize the object.

Formatting text objects Use the Font and Font Size drop-down lists on the toolbar to choose fonts; then use the Bold, Italic, and Underline toolbar buttons to set special attributes.

You can also add graphic lines and objects to reports, just as you do forms.

 TIP **Access on the Web** You can assign hyperlinks to objects on your forms and reports. They aren't *hot* (that is, they don't actually link) on the printouts, but if you save a report in Microsoft Word format, the hyperlinks can be activated when you open the document in Word.

Adding and Removing Fields

You can add more fields to your report at any time. Follow these steps to add a field to your report:

1. If you don't see the Field List, select **View, Field List** or click the **Field List** button on the toolbar. A floating box appears listing all the fields in the table you're using.

2. Drag any field from the Field List into the report. Place it anywhere you want in the Detail area.

Don't worry if the field isn't in the right place or if it overlaps another field; you learn to fix that in the next section. To delete a field, click it and press the **Delete** key. This deletes the reference to the field from the report, but it remains in the table from which it came.

Arranging Your New Fields

When you add a field to your report, you're actually adding two things: a label and a text box. These two elements are bound together: the label describes the text box, and the text box represents the actual field that will be used (see Figure 19.2). You can change the label without affecting the text box; for instance, you could change the label on the Coloring field to Dog Color without affecting the contents. To change a label, just click it and retype it.

Text Box   Label

Position the mouse pointer
over the larger handle to
move the object separately.

| Coloring: | Coloring |

Figure 19.2 The text box and its label.

By default, when you move the text box, the label follows. When you position the mouse pointer over the border of the text box, and the pointer changes to an open hand, that's your signal that the label will follow the text box when you drag it.

However, you can also move the text box and the label separately. Notice that in the upper-left corner of each, there is a selection handle (square) that's bigger than the others. When you position the mouse pointer over that handle, the cursor becomes a pointing hand. That's your signal that you can click-and-drag the object separately from the other.

Moving the label separately can come in handy when you don't want the label to appear in its default position (to the left of the text box). For instance, you might want the label to appear above the text box.

Adding Labels

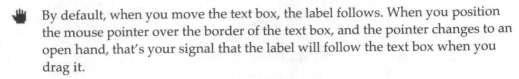

In the preceding section, you saw how to add a field (a text box and a label bound together). But you can also add labels by themselves, with extra text in them that is not necessarily associated with a particular field. For instance, you might add an informational note about the report in general. To do so, click the **Label** button in the toolbox, and then click anywhere on the report and start typing. When you finish, click anywhere outside the label.

Adding a Calculated Text Box

The most common thing that text boxes hold is references to fields, as you have seen in this lesson. However, text boxes have another purpose: they can also hold calculations based on values in different fields.

Creating a calculated text box is a bit complicated. First you have to create an unbound text box (that is, one that's not associated with any particular field). Then you have to enter the calculation into the text box. Follow these steps:

1. Click the **Text Box** tool in the toolbox, and then click-and-drag on the report to create a text box.

2. Change the label to reflect what's going to go in that box. For instance, if it's going to be Sales Tax, change it to that. Position the label where you want it.

3. Click in the text box and type the formula you want calculated. (See the following section, "Rules for Creating Calculations," for guidance.)

4. Click anywhere outside the text box after you finish.

Rules for Creating Calculations

The formulas you enter into your calculated text box use standard mathematical controls:

+	Add
–	Subtract
*	Multiply
/	Divide

All formulas begin with an equals sign (=), and all field names appear in parentheses. Here are some examples:

To calculate a total price by multiplying the value in the Quantity field by the value in the Price field, enter **=(Quantity)*(Price)**.

To calculate a 25% discount off the value in the Cost field, enter **=(Cost)*.075**.

To add the total of the values in three fields, enter **(Field1)+(Field2)+(Field3)**.

TIP   **More Room**   If you run out of room in the text box when typing your formula, press **Shift+F2** to open a Zoom box, where there's more room.

In this lesson, you learned to customize your report by adding and removing objects, moving them around, and creating calculations. In the next lesson, you learn how to create relationships between tables.

Creating Relationships Between Tables

In this lesson, you learn how to link two or more tables together so you can work with them as you would a single table.

Why Create Relationships?

In Lesson 2, "Planning Your Database," you were encouraged to make separate tables for information that was not directly related. As you have learned along the way, when you create forms, queries, and reports, you easily can pull information from more than one table. But this works best when there is a well-defined relationship between the tables.

For instance, I might have two tables containing information about my customers. One table, called Customers, contains their names and addresses; the other, called Orders, contains their orders. The two tables would have a common field: Customer ID#. All records in the Orders table would correspond to a record in the Customers table. (This is called a *many-to-one* relationship because there could be many orders for one customer.)

As another example, in my dog kennel database, I have several tables describing my dogs and their activities. I have a table listing all the different colorings a dog can have. I could create a relationship between the Dogs table and the Coloring table, matching up each dog's coloring field with one of the accepted colors listed in the Coloring table. This would ensure that I didn't record any dog's coloring as a type that's not allowed.

More Complicated   Relationships can be extremely complicated and thorny. I'm showing you only simple examples in this lesson because that's probably all you need as a casual user. For more information on relationships, see your Access documentation or the book *Using Access 97, Special Edition*, also published by Que Corporation.

Creating a Relationship Between Tables

To create a relationship between tables, you open the Relationships window and add relationships from there. Follow these steps:

1. From anywhere in the database select **Tools, Relationships**.

2. If you have not selected any tables yet, the Show Table dialog box (shown in Figure 20.1) appears automatically. If it doesn't, open the **Relationships** menu and select **Show Table** or click the **Show Table** toolbar button.

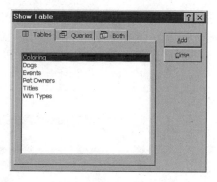

Figure 20.1   Add tables to your Relationships window.

3. Click a table that you want to use for a relationship, and then click the **Add** button.

4. Repeat step 3 until you have selected all the tables with which you want to work. When you're finished, click **Close**. Each table appears in its own box in the Relationships window, as shown in Figure 20.2.

TIP   **Make It Bigger**   If you can't clearly see all the fields in a table's list, drag the border of its box to make it large enough to see everything. I have done that in Figure 20.2 to make the Dogs table completely visible.

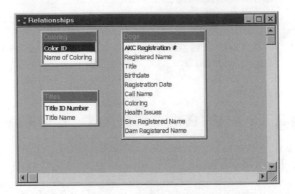

Figure 20.2 I added three tables to my Relationships window.

5. Click a field in one table that you want to link to another table. For instance, I'm going to link the Coloring field in my Dogs table to the Color ID field in my Coloring table, so I click the Coloring field in the Dogs table.

6. Hold down the mouse button and drag away from the selected field. Your mouse pointer will turn into a little rectangle. Drop the little rectangle onto the destination field. For instance, I'm dragging to the Color ID field in the Coloring table. The Relationships dialog box appears (see Figure 20.3).

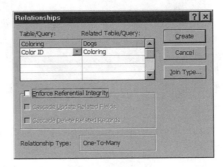

Figure 20.3 The Relationships dialog box asks you to define the relationship you're creating.

7. Choose any Referential Integrity options you want (see the following section "What Is Referential Integrity"), and then click **Create**. If all goes well, a relationship is created, and you see a line between the two fields in the Relationships window (see Figure 20.4).

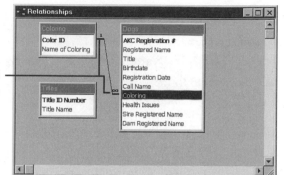

You won't get the Infinity and 1 symbols on this line if you didn't choose Enforce Referential Integrity.

Figure 20.4 The line represents a relationship between the two fields.

Relationship Symbols Notice in Figure 20.4 that next to the Dogs table there's an infinity sign (looks like a sideways 8), and next to the Coloring table there's a 1. These symbols appear in relationships where Enforce Referential Integrity is turned on. The infinity sign means *many*—that means many records in this table can match a single record (hence the 1 sign) in the related Coloring table.

What Is Referential Integrity?

Referential Integrity keeps you from making data entry mistakes. It says, essentially, that all the information in the two fields should match. If there is an entry in one table in the linked field that doesn't exist in the other, it's a problem that Referential Integrity corrects.

An example will make this clearer. In the Coloring field in my Dogs database, I have a number that matches up with the Color ID field in the Coloring table. The Coloring table lists all the allowable colors for the breed of dog. I don't want my clerks to be able to accidentally enter a number in the Dogs table that doesn't match up with one of the colors in the Coloring table, so I chose to Enforce Referential Integrity. Now Access won't let anyone enter anything in the Coloring field of the Dogs table (the *many* or infinity side) except one of the numbers contained in the Color ID field in the Coloring table (the one side).

What happens if someone tries? It depends on which of the other two check boxes shown in Figure 20.3 were marked.

Here is a summary of the check boxes and their functions:

- **Neither Marked**   Access gives an error message that you need a related record in the "[Table Name]" and will not allow you to make the entry.
- **Cascade Update Related Fields**   If this check box is marked and you make a change to the related table (in our example, the Coloring table), the change will be made in the other table (the Dogs table) as well. For instance, if I decided to change a certain coloring number from 7 to 8, and I made the change in the Coloring table (the one side), all the 7s in the Dogs table (the many side) would change to 8s.
- **Cascade Delete Related Fields**   If this check box is marked and you make a change to the *one* table (for instance, Coloring) so that the entries in the related table aren't valid anymore, Access deletes the entries in the related table. For instance, if I deleted the record in the Coloring table for Coloring ID number 3, all the dogs from my Dogs table that had coloring number 3 would also be deleted.

The first time you try to use Referential Integrity, you will likely get an error message because there is usually some condition that prevents it from working (as Murphy's Law goes). For instance, when I first created the relationship shown in Figure 20.4 with Enforce Referential Integrity marked, Access would not allow it because the field type for the Coloring field in the Dogs table was set to Text while the Color ID field in the Coloring table was a number. (It didn't matter that I had entered only numbers in the Coloring field in the Dogs table.)

Editing a Relationship

After a relationship is created, you can edit it by redisplaying the Relationships dialog box (refer to Figure 20.3). To do so, double-click the relationship's line. From there, you can edit the relationship using the same controls you did when you created it.

Removing a Relationship

To delete a relationship, just click it in the Relationships window and press the **Delete** key. Access will ask for confirmation. Click **Yes**, and the relationship disappears.

In this lesson, you learned how to create, edit, and delete relationships between tables. In the next lesson you will learn how to use Access to link your work to the Internet.

Setting Up a Database for Internet Use

In this lesson, you learn how to take advantage of Access 97's Internet capabilities to link your work to the Internet.

Some Internet Basics

The Internet is a vast collection of connected computer networks, with the most popular component being the World Wide Web. With a Web browser program, you can display any of millions of specially-formatted pages by entering the appropriate address. Most of these Web pages are stored in a format known as *Hypertext Markup Language (HTML)*.

Access provides two ways to interact with the Internet—incoming and outgoing. In other words, you can provide Access information to people who use the Internet, or you can provide Internet information to people who use your Access database.

To provide information to incoming users (that is, visitors to your Web site), you can make parts of your database available by saving tables in HTML format and copying the files to an *Internet host*—a computer that's directly connected to the Internet. If your company provides an Internet connection through its LAN (local area network), your HTML files most likely will be stored on a host computer within the LAN. If you use a modem to connect to the Internet, the local host that provides your dial-up access might also provide space on its server for your HTML files.

You can also set up hyperlinks to other URLs within a database so that your database users may access Web sites, either on a company intranet or on the global Internet. A separate window is displayed when the user clicks a hyperlink from within an Access database.

Uniform Resource Locator (URL) A URL is a Web address. Most URLs begin with http:// followed by the site's name—for instance, **http://www.mcp.com**. Some URLs also contain specific directory and filenames, like this: **http://www.mcp.com/Pub/index.htm**. Pub/ is a directory, and INDEX.HTM is a file.

Hyperlink A hyperlink is a bit of text or a picture that serves as a clickable link to a Web site. When you click a hyperlink, your Web browser program opens and displays the Web page.

Saving Access Objects in HTML Format

Access provides a quick way to save multiple files in HTML format simultaneously. You can save these files either to your local hard disk or directly to the server. If your server is using Microsoft software (Microsoft Web Server or Personal Web Server), you can even set up dynamic links to your Access database so that the person accessing it always sees the most recent data.

Follow these steps to save Access objects in HTML format:

1. Open the database containing the objects you want to publish.

2. Select **File**, **Save As HTML**. The Publish to the Web Wizard opens.

3. Read the introductory information and then click **Next** to continue.

4. Select the objects you want to publish (see Figure 21.1). Each object type has a separate tab. Then click **Next** to continue.

5. Next you're asked about templates. If there is another HTML file that you want to use as a template for those you are now creating, type its path in the text box, or click the **Browse** button to locate it. To use different templates for different pages, click the check box below the options. Then click **Next**.

6. If you clicked the check box in step 5, an extra screen appears asking you to specify what templates go with which documents. Select specific objects from the list, and then click the **Browse** button to find the HTML file to use as a template for them. When you're finished choosing templates, click **Next** to continue.

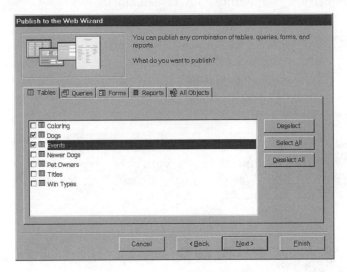

Figure 21.1 Place a checkmark beside each object you want to save in HTML format.

7. Next you're asked whether you want static (HTML) or dynamic (HTX/ IDC or ASP) pages. Dynamic pages are updated automatically when your Access database is updated, but require your server to be running Microsoft server software. Static pages are ordinary exported HTML files. Choose static or dynamic, or click the check box below the options to indicate that you want some of each type.

8. If you selected the check box in step 7, an extra screen appears (see Figure 21.2) in which you must specify which pages should be static and which should be dynamic. Click an object on the list, and then click the **HTML**, **HTX/IDC**, or **ASP** option buttons to choose the object's status. HTML is static; the other two options are dynamic formats. Ask the system administrator which format you should use. Repeat this selection process for all objects on the list, and then click **Next** to continue.

CAUTION

Use Dynamic Pages Sparingly Dynamic pages take longer for a user to access than static ones, because the server has to check your Access database each time a user visits the page. If you do not anticipate the information for a particular object changing frequently, it's better to save it as a static page.

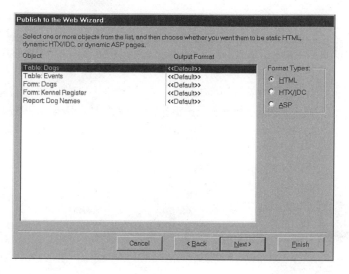

Figure 21.2   You can specify which pages should be static and which should be dynamic in this dialog box.

9. If you chose dynamic for any of your pages, a screen appears asking you for information about the server—the server's Data Source Name and, optionally, the username and password you use to connect to the server. You also enter ActiveX Server Output information in this screen. (ActiveX is a means of dynamically linking data; if you don't understand what it is, you probably don't need to use it.) Enter the information, and then click **Next**.

Server Info?   If you are not sure about your server information, ask your system administrator or service provider. Don't try to guess about this information.

CAUTION

10. Next you're asked about storage. By default, all HTML files are saved on your hard disk. Specify the drive and the folder in the text box labeled **I Want to Put My Web Documents in This Folder**.

11. If you want the HTML files saved on a server too (in addition to the copy kept on your hard drive), click one of the **Yes** buttons at the bottom of the dialog box. (They are not available if you are not currently connected to your server.) The options are as follows:

Yes, I Want to Run the Web Publishing Wizard to Set Up a New Web Publishing Specification. Use this one the first time, to set up the information for your server. If you choose this, the Web Publishing Wizard starts, and you must work through its series of dialog boxes and supply the needed information.

Yes, I Want to Use an Existing Web Publishing Server Whose *'Friendly Name'* **Has Been Set Up Previously**. Use this option after you have already set up your server's information to use the same server that you used the last time. Select your server's *Friendly Name* from the drop-down list.

Friendly Name When you use the Web Publishing Wizard to set up your server's information, you're prompted to enter a *Friendly Name* for it. This is a plain-English name that you can readily identify with the server. For example, I might call the Macmillan Publishing server *Macmillan*.

12. Click **Next** when you're finished specifying the storage locations.

13. Next you're asked whether you want to create a home page. If you select the **Yes, I Want to Create a Home Page** check box, a home page HTML file is added to the storage location(s) you specified in step 10. This is like a table of contents that organizes links to the other files.

14. If you marked the check box in step 13, enter a title for the page in the **What File Name** text box. This is the name the file will be saved as (for example, Default).

15. Next, you're asked whether you want to save your Wizard answers in a Web Publication file. Click **Yes** and enter a profile name.

16. Click **Finish**. Access generates the HTML files you specified and posts them to the location(s) you specified.

Inserting Hyperlinks into an Access Object

A hyperlink can be added to an Access database in two ways. The first is to create a field in a table and set the field's Data Type to Hyperlink. Then, any text that you enter into that field becomes a hyperlink that you can click to open a specified Web page. In Figure 21.3, for example, a Breeder's Home Page field is being set up in the Dogs table to hold URLs for the home pages of the breeders from which dogs were brought. Then, as you can see in Figure 21.4, URLs can be entered into that field, which immediately become underlined hyperlinks.

Hyperlink data type

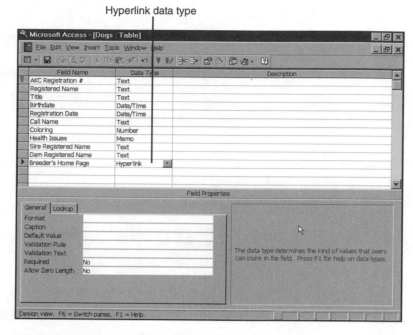

Figure 21.3 By setting the Data Type to Hyperlink, you are telling Access that any data entered in this field is a URL.

TIP **Not for Web Use Only** You can hyperlink to a document on your hard disk or on your LAN instead of a Web address. If, for instance, you have a supporting document for a record, such as a contract in Word, you can enter the path to the document in a hyperlink field (for example, c:\My Documents\contract1.doc).

The other way to set up a hyperlink is to add it to a form or report. This way, it's not associated with any particular record, but rather with the entire form or table. For example, perhaps on a form for accessing your company's phone book, you might put a hyperlink to the company's home page.

Follow these steps:

1. Open the form or report in **Design** view.

2. Click the **Insert Hyperlink** button on the toolbar. The Insert Hyperlink dialog box appears (see Figure 21.5).

729

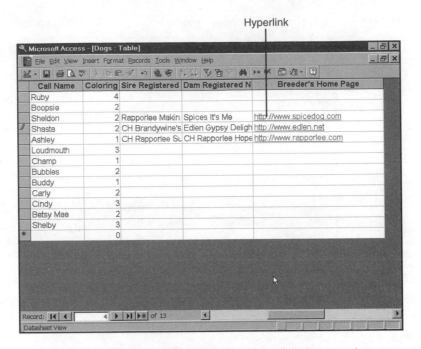

Figure 21.4 Any data entered into a field with a Hyperlink data type becomes a hyperlink.

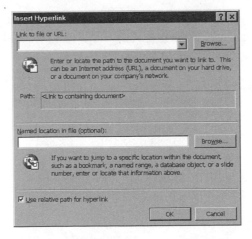

Figure 21.5 Specify the URL for the hyperlink in the Insert Hyperlink dialog box.

3. Enter the file or URL to hyperlink to in the **Link to File** or **URL** text box. (You can click the **Browse** button to browse for it if you don't know the exact name and location.)

4. Click **OK**. Access inserts the hyperlink in the active section. You can drag it to move it to any position on the form you like, just as you can move any object on a form (see Lesson 13, "Modifying Your Form").

The preceding method inserts a simple text hyperlink that lists the URL. If you want something fancier, you can create a picture and assign the hyperlink to the picture. Follow these steps to use a picture for your hyperlink:

1. Insert a picture into the report or form (**Insert**, **Picture**).

2. Right-click the picture and select properties from the shortcut menu that appears.

3. In the Properties dialog box, click the **Format** tab.

4. Type the URL in the **Hyperlink Address** text box (see Figure 21.6).

5. Close the **Properties** dialog box. Now when you click the picture, it activates the hyperlink.

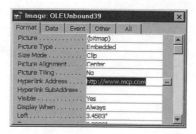

Figure 21.6 Specify a URL in the Hyperlink Address text box and the picture becomes a hyperlinked object.

TIP **No Hyperlink Address on the Format Tab** If you don't see Hyperlink Address on the Format tab in step 4, Access does not recognize the object as an image. Close the **Properties** dialog box. Then right-click the image again and choose **Change To**, and **Image**. Then try the above steps again.

In this lesson, you learned how to connect your Access data to the Internet.

Appendixes

Installing
Microsoft
Office 97

In this lesson, you learn how to install Microsoft Office 97 on your computer so that you can begin using it.

What Is Installing?

When you get a new application like Microsoft Office, it comes in a compressed format on a CD or a set of disks. You must run a Setup program to copy the needed files to your hard disk and decompress the compressed data.

 TIP   **Run from CD**   Office 97 does provide an option to run the Office applications directly from the CD, saving disk space on your PC. However, to set this up, you must still run the Setup program, as you learn to do later in this lesson.

Installing Microsoft Office

To install Office on your PC, follow these steps:

1. Close all open applications.
2. Insert the Microsoft Office 97 CD in your CD-ROM drive. A dialog box opens automatically.

CAUTION

No Dialog Box Opened! If no dialog box opened when you inserted the CD, your computer may not be set up to Autorun CDs. Just open the **My Computer** window and click (or double-click) the CD drive's icon. Then locate and click (or double-click) the **Setup** icon.

3. Click the **Install Microsoft Office** button.

4. At the Welcome dialog box, click **Continue**.

5. In the Name and Organization Information dialog box, enter your name and organization. Then click **OK**.

6. If asked to confirm your name and organization, click **OK** again.

7. If you're asked for the 11-digit CD key, find it on the sticker on the back of the jewel case and enter it. Then click **OK**.

8. Next, you see your product ID number. Write it down on your registration card, and then click **OK**.

9. Choose the drive and folder into which Microsoft Office is installed. The default is the Program Files folder on the same drive that Windows is installed on (see Figure A.1). Click **OK** to accept, or click **Change Folder** and select a new location.

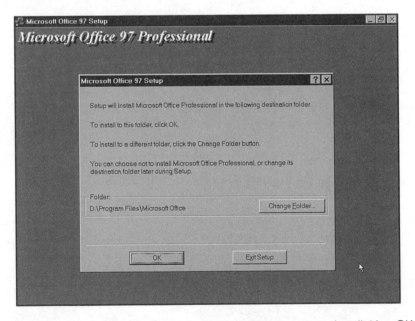

Figure A.1 Accept the folder chosen by the installation program by clicking OK, or click Change Folder and choose your own.

10. Choose the type of installation you want:

- **Typical** Installs the most common components. This is the easiest method, and most users are happy with the options installed.

- **Custom** Enables you to choose exactly which components you want. This is for experienced users and those who don't use certain Office products at all.

- **Run from CD-ROM** Sets up Office to run mostly from the CD. Because it copies very few files to your hard disk, it's ideal for users who are short on disk space; however, it requires that the CD be in the drive whenever an Office component is running.

If you chose Typical or Run from CD-ROM, skip to step 14. If you chose Custom, the Microsoft Office 97 Custom dialog box appears (see Figure A.2).

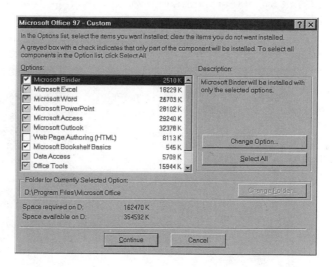

Figure A.2 Click the check boxes to select or deselect categories and options.

11. In Setup's Custom dialog box, you see a series of components with check boxes. A check in a white-background box means all options for that component will be installed. A check in a gray-background box means that only some of the component's options will be installed. Use these methods to choose which components and options you want:

- To select all Office components, click the **Select All** button.
- To deselect an entire component, click its check box to remove the checkmark.
- To choose which options of a component are installed, click the component, and then click **Change Option**. A dialog box appears, showing the options for that component, each with its own check box you can use to activate or deactivate it. Click **OK** to return to the main screen. Refer to Table A.1 (in the next section) for some ideas about what to select.

12. When you finish selecting options, click **Continue**.

13. If the installation program finds old Office components, it asks whether you want to remove them. Click **Yes**.

14. Wait for the Setup program to copy the files (see Figure A.3). When you see the message **Microsoft Office 97 Setup Was Completed Successfully**, click **OK**. You are now ready to use Microsoft Office.

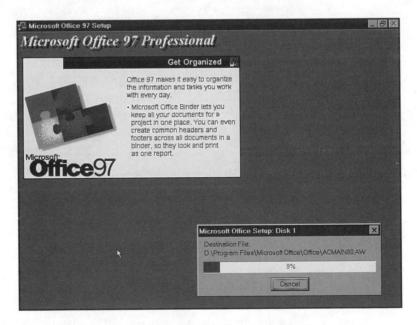

Figure A.3 It takes several minutes for the Setup program to copy its files; a progress bar at the bottom of the screen shows how far it has progressed.

TIP   **Uninstalling?**   To uninstall one or more of the Office 97 components, open the Control Panel and double-click **Add/Remove Programs**. Then on the Install/Uninstall tab, double-click Microsoft Office 97 on the list of installed programs. The Setup program opens and you can choose which components to add or remove.

Custom Installation: Some Advice

It's hard to know exactly which options to choose in a Custom installation if you're a beginner. Table A.1 provides some ideas of some components you might want that are not installed by default.

Table A.1   Options Not Installed by Default that You Might Want

Component	Option	Comments
Word	Wizards and Templates	If you like using templates, select all these. Only some are installed by default.
Word	Help	If you are a WordPerfect user, install Help for WordPerfect Users.
PowerPoint	Content Templates	Three extra templates are available (Business Plan, Corporate Home Page, and Progress Presentation) when you select Additional Content Templates.
PowerPoint	Animation Effects	If you use sounds in your presentations, you may find these sound files useful.
PowerPoint	Presentation Translators	If you need to convert presentations from Harvard Graphics for DOS or Lotus Freelance 1.0 through 2.1, install this.
Outlook	Lotus Organizer Converters	Install this if you have Organizer files you want to use in Outlook.
Excel	Spreadsheet Templates	This installs the Expense Report Template and Purchase Order Template.
Excel	Add-Ins	Install the File Conversion Wizard if you have a group of files you will be converting to Excel format.
Excel	Spreadsheet Converters	The Quattro Pro 1.0/5.0 (Win) converter is not installed by default.

continues

Table A.1 Continued

Component	Option	Comments
Access	Sample Databases	If you want to follow along with the examples in the Access section of this book, or if you want some samples to examine, select these.
Web Page Authoring (HTML)	(No options)	If you plan to create Web pages, you definitely need these tools.
Office Tools	Microsoft Office Shortcut Bar	This is not installed by default, although it was in previous releases of Microsoft Office. If you're accustomed to using it, install it.
Office Tools	Microsoft Photo Editor	This is a new utility program that scans, edits, and converts images.
Converters	Text and Filters	It is recommended that you install all these. You never know what file formats you may encounter.
Converters	Graphics and Filters	You should install all these.

Installing Internet Explorer

If you use the Internet or if you want to learn how, you want to install Microsoft's Web browser, Internet Explorer (IE).

 TERM   **Web Browser**   A Web browser enables you to view graphical content on the Internet. To use it, you must have an Internet connection. If you don't have one, run the Internet Connection Wizard that comes with IE 4. (Choose **Start**, **Programs**, **Internet Explorer**, **Connection Wizard**.)

After you run the Microsoft Office installation program, an icon appears on your desktop called Setup for Microsoft Internet Explorer 3.0. If you are in a hurry to get online, you can install this version (IE 3) by double-clicking that icon and following the prompts.

However, the newest version of Internet Explorer, version 4.0, offers many extra features. It is recommended that you upgrade to that version. There is no charge to do so.

If you do not have any Web browser installed at all, you need to install IE 3.0 and then use it to navigate to the Microsoft Web page where IE 4.0 can be downloaded.

Installing Internet Explorer 3.0

If you don't have a Web browser at all, you should install IE 3.0. After you've finished installing IE 3.0, you can either continue to use it or connect to Microsoft's Web site to download version 4.0.

Follow these steps to install Internet Explorer 3.0:

1. Double-click the **Setup for Microsoft Internet Explorer 3.0** desktop icon.
2. A dialog box asks if you want to install the program. Click **Yes**.
3. Read the licensing agreement, and then click **I Agree**.
4. Wait for the Setup program to install the files you need. If the Version Conflict dialog box appears, asking you if you want to keep an existing file, click **Yes**.
5. At the message **Do You Want To Restart Your Computer Now?**, click **Yes**.

After your computer restarts, you are ready to use Internet Explorer. You can use it through your Microsoft Network account or with any other Internet connection.

Downloading Internet Explorer 4.0

To get the most recent version of IE, you need to use a Web browser to visit the Microsoft Web site. Follow these steps:

1. Start your Internet connection and your Web browser.
2. On the Address (or URL) line, type the following and press Enter to open a Web page from which you may download Internet Explorer 4.0.

   http://www.microsoft.com/ie/ie40/download

3. Click **Download Internet Explorer 4.0**. A page appears with a drop-down list, from which you can choose your version.
4. Ensure that **Windows 95 and NT** is selected on the list, and then click **Next**.
5. A drop-down list appears listing the available languages. Choose **US English**, and click **Next**.

6. Next, a page appears with a series of links. They all point to different locations, but they all download the same file. Click any of them (preferably one located close to your town).

TIP **File Size?** If the file size listed seems small, it is. You are downloading only an installation program, not IE itself at this point. The installation program, in turn, downloads the appropriate IE components.

7. A dialog box appears asking whether you want to save the program to disk or run it directly from the Internet. Click **Save This Program to Disk** and click **OK**.

8. A box appears prompting you to choose a location for the file. If you have a Temp folder, that would be a good place. If not, just store it in any handy spot (like in My Documents). Then click **Save**.

9. Wait for the download to finish. It should not take very long.

10. When you see Download Complete, click **OK**.

11. Close your Web browser and use Windows Explorer to navigate to the folder where you downloaded the file.

Installing Internet Explorer 4.0 from a Download

Now that you have downloaded the IE 4.0 installation program, let's run it.

CAUTION

Long Download This takes a long time (up to several hours), so don't start it when you are in a hurry to get something else done. You can minimize the download window and work on other things on your computer, but it may make the download take even longer and your other programs may run more slowly.

1. Using My Computer or Windows Explorer, navigate to and double-click the file **IE4SETUP.EXE**. The Setup program starts. When the licensing agreement appears, click **Yes** to accept it.

2. On the Download Options screen, choose **Download Only**. (This is a precaution in case you ever need to reinstall IE 4.0.) Then click **Next**.

3. Open the Download Option dialog box and choose the installation you want (**Standard** or **Full** are your best choices unless you are short on hard disk space). Then click **Next**.

4. On the Desktop Update screen, choose **Yes** to get the desktop update. Then click **Next**.

5. On the Active Channel Selection screen, click your country on the list, and then click **Next**.

6. On the Destination Folder screen, enter the temporary folder into which to copy the installation files and then click **Next**, or just click **Next** to accept the default entered.

7. Wait for the Setup program to download site information. It may take a few minutes.

8. Choose a download site from the list provided (any one that's close to you will do) and click **Next**.

9. Wait for the download to complete. It may take several hours.

10. When you see a message that installation is finished, click **OK**. You're done!

11. Disconnect your Internet connection if needed.

12. Run the **Setup** program in the folder that you downloaded the software into, and follow the on-screen prompts to complete the installation.

Now you are ready to use Internet Explorer 4.0, as described in Part 1, Lesson 16, "Using Internet Explorer."

In this lesson, you learned how to install Microsoft Office 97 and Internet Explorer. In the next lesson, you learn about the Office 97 Help system.

Using the Office 97 Help System

In this lesson, you learn about the various types of help available to you in Microsoft Office programs.

Help: What's Available

Because every person is different, the programs in the MS Office suite offer many different ways to get help with the program. You can:

- Ask the Office Assistant for help.
- Get help on a particular element you see on-screen with the What's This? tool.
- Choose what you're interested in learning about from a series of Help Topics.
- Access the Microsoft On the Web feature to view Web pages containing help information (if you are connected to the Internet).

Asking the Office Assistant

You have probably already met the Office Assistant; it's the paper clip character (or other character, if someone else has used your computer and chosen a different character) that pops up to give you advice. It appears the first time you start each of the Office programs to ask if you need help getting started, and again when you are attempting certain new tasks. Don't let its whimsical appearance fool you, though; behind the Office Assistant is a powerful Help system.

TIP   **No More Answer Wizard**   The Office Assistant replaces the Answer Wizard feature from Microsoft Office for Windows 95.

Turning the Office Assistant On and Off

By default, the Office Assistant is activated, and it sits in a little box on top of whatever you're working on, as shown in Figure B.1. You can turn it off by clicking the **Close** (x) button in its top-right corner.

Figure B.1   The Office Assistant appears in its own window, on top of the program window.

To turn the Office Assistant on again, click the **Help** button in the Standard toolbar or select **Help, Microsoft Word Help** (or Access, or PowerPoint, or Outlook—whatever program you're using at the moment).

Kinds of Help Office Assistant Provides

When you first activate the Office Assistant, a bubble appears next to (or above) its box asking you what kind of help you want (see Figure B.2). You can do any of the following:

- Type a question in the text box provided to tell the Office Assistant what kind of help you need.
- Select one of the Office Assistant's guesses about what you need help with.
- Click the **Tips** button to get any tips that the Office Assistant can provide for the task you're performing.
- Click the **Options** button to customize the way the Office Assistant works.
- Click **Close** to close the bubble (but leave the Office Assistant on-screen).

If you close the help bubble, you can reopen it at any time by clicking the **Help** button on the Standard toolbar, by pressing **F1**, by selecting **Help, Microsoft Word Help** (or whatever program you're in), or by clicking the Office Assistant window.

Figure B.2 Office Assistant at your service, asking what you need help with.

 TIP **Extra Tips Along the Way** Sometimes you see a light bulb next to the Office Assistant in its window as in Figure B.1. This means that the Office Assistant has a suggestion for you regarding the task you're currently performing. To get the suggestion, just click the light bulb. Then click the **Close** button when you finish reading the suggestion.

Asking the Office Assistant a Question

If you need help on a particular topic, you can type a question into the text box shown in Figure B.2. Follow these steps to see how it works:

1. If the Office Assistant's help bubble doesn't appear, click the **Help** button on the Standard toolbar.

2. Type a question into the text box. For instance, you might type **How Do I Print?** to get help on printing your work.

3. Click the **Search** button. The Office Assistant provides some topics that might match what you're looking for. (Figure B.3 shows the Office Assistant's answer to the question How Do I Print? in Word.) The options may be a little different in the other Office applications.

4. Click the option that best describes what you're trying to do. If you were to choose Print a Document from Figure B.3, a Help window would appear with instructions for the specified task.

   If none of the options describes what you want, click the **See More** arrow to view more options, or type a different question into the text box.

The Help window that appears (containing the task instructions) is part of the same Help system you can access with the Help, Contents and Index command. (See "Managing Help Topics You've Located" later in this lesson for information about navigating this window.)

Figure B.3 The Office Assistant asks you to narrow down exactly what you are trying to accomplish so that it can provide the best help possible.

Using the Help Topics

A more conventional way to get help is through the Contents and Index command on the Help menu. When you open the Help system, you move through the topics listed to find the topic in which you're interested.

Several tabs are in the Help system, so you can use Help the way you want. To access the Help system, select **Help**, **Contents and Index** to produce the Help Topics screen. The following sections explain how to use the tabs and topics contained in Microsoft Help.

Contents

The Contents tab of the Help system is a series of books you can open. Each book has one or more Help topics in it, and some books contain other subbooks! (Figure B.4 shows a Contents screen.)

To select a Help topic from the Contents tab, follow these steps:

1. Select **Help**, **Contents and Index**.

2. Click the **Contents** tab.

3. Find the book that describes in broad terms the subject for which you're looking for help.

Closed book

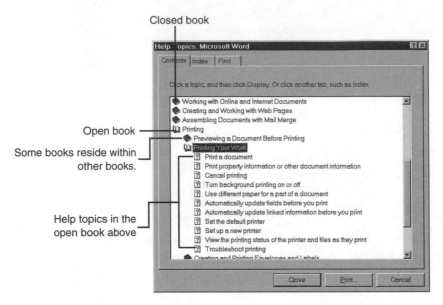

Open book

Some books reside within other books.

Help topics in the open book above

Figure B.4 The Help Contents screen is a group of books that contain help information.

4. Double-click the book, and a list of Help topics appears below the book, as shown in Figure B.4.

5. Double-click a Help topic to display it.

6. When you finish reading a topic, click **Contents** to go back to the main Help screen or click the window's **Close** (X) button to exit Help.

Index

The Index is an alphabetical listing of every Help topic available. It's like an index in a book.

Follow these steps to use the index:

1. Select **Help, Contents and Index**.

2. Click the **Index** tab.

3. Type the first few letters of the topic for which you are looking. The index list jumps quickly to that spot (see Figure B.5).

4. Double-click the topic you want to see.

Type what you're looking for here.

The list jumps to
match what you
typed as closely
as possible.

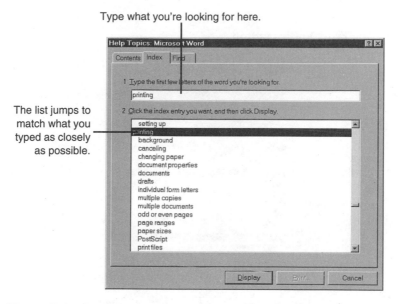

Figure B.5   Browse topics alphabetically with the Index.

Find

The Index is great if you know the name of the Help topic you're looking for—
but what if you're not sure? That's where Find comes in handy. Find searches
not only the titles of Help topics, but their contents, and it retrieves all the topics
in which the word(s) you typed appear.

To use Find, follow these steps:

1. Select **Help**, **Contents and Index**.
2. Click the **Find** tab. The first time you use Find, you are asked to build the
   Find index. Click **Next**, and then click **Finish** to do it.
3. Type the topic you're looking for in the top box (1).
4. If more than one line appears in the middle box (2), click the one that most
   closely matches your interest.
5. Browse the topics that appear at the bottom (3), and click the one that
   matches the help you need (see Figure B.6).
6. Click the **Display** button or press **Enter**.

When you're finished reading a topic, you can return to the Find screen by clicking the **Help Topics** button.

Type the topic you want to find here.

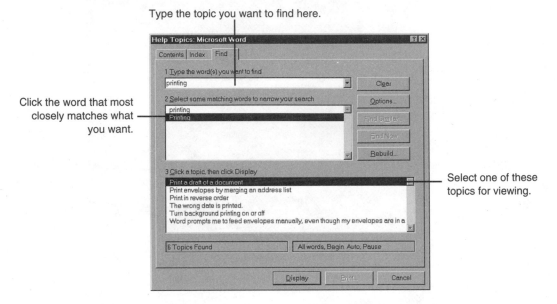

Click the word that most closely matches what you want.

Select one of these topics for viewing.

Figure B.6   Use Find to locate all the Help topics that deal with a certain subject.

Managing Help Topics You've Located

No matter which of the four avenues you choose for finding a Help topic (the Office Assistant, Contents, Index, or Find), you eventually end up at a Help screen of instructions like the one shown in Figure B.7. From there, you can read the information on-screen or do any of the following things:

- Click an underlined word to see a definition of it (for instance, see **main document** in Figure B.7).

- Click a button to jump to another Help screen. For instance, in Figure B.7, there is a >> button and a button with a curved arrow on it. You can click these to jump to other screens of related information.

- Print a hard copy of the information by clicking the **Options** button and selecting **Print Topic**.

- Copy the text to the Clipboard (for pasting into a program such as Microsoft Word or Windows Notepad) by clicking the **Options** button and selecting **Copy**.
- Return to the previous Help topic you viewed by clicking the **Back** button.
- Return to the main Help topics screen by clicking the **Help Topics** button.
- Close the Help window by clicking the **Close** (x) button.

Click an underlined word
to see a definition of it.

Close the Help window
by clicking here.

Click a button to jump to
another Help screen.

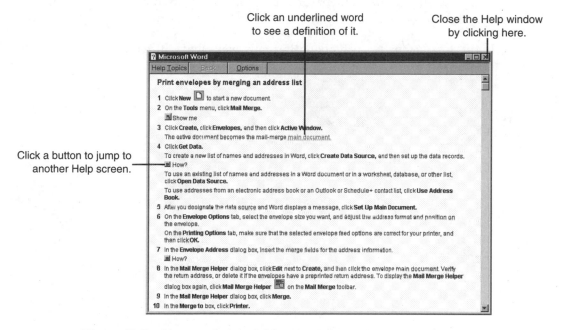

Figure B.7   After you find the information you need, you can read it on-screen, print it, or move to another Help topic.

TIP   **Microsoft on the Web**   New for Office 97 is built-in access to Microsoft's Web site, where you can find additional Help information. Establish your Internet connection, and then select **Help**, **Microsoft On The Web** and choose from the Web pages listed on the submenu to jump directly to one of them.

Getting Help with Screen Elements

If you wonder about the function of a particular button or tool on the screen, wonder no more. Just follow these steps to learn about this part of Help:

1. Select **Help**, **What's This?** or press **Shift**+**F1**. The mouse pointer changes to an arrow with a question mark.

2. Click the screen element for which you want help. A box appears explaining the element.

In this lesson, you learned about the many ways that Office offers help. In the next lesson, you learn about Object Linking and Embedding.

Object Linking and Embedding

In this lesson, you learn about creating dynamic links and embedding with OLE.

What Is Object Linking and Embedding (OLE)?

OLE (pronounced "oh-LAY") stands for Object Linking and Embedding. It is a Windows feature that enables the Windows applications that employ it to transparently share information.

For example, you might create a quarterly report in Microsoft Word that contains an Excel chart. Each quarter, the Excel data in the chart changes. When it comes time to generate the next quarterly report, you could find the most up-to-date version of the Excel chart, copy, and paste it into the report; or you could use an OLE link to automatically update the report with the changes made in each supporting document.

What Is Linking?

When you link an *object* to a *container file*, any changes you make to the object in its native application are automatically made to the object in the container file. The object in the container file remains a mirror image of the object in its native application, regardless of how many times you update the original object.

Object   An *object* is any snippet of data that you want to link to another document. It can be as small as a single character or as large as a huge report with many graphics.

Container File   A *container file* is the file that's receiving the object. If, for example, you're linking an Excel chart to a Word document, the Word document is the container file.

What Is Embedding?

When you embed an object, you insert a copy of it into your document, in the same way you might with the regular Paste command. A link to the source file is not maintained. However, embedding does offer something that regular pasting does not. When you embed an object into a document, a link is maintained to the original application; you can double-click that object at any time to open the application and edit the object.

A good example of an embedded object would be a company logo, created as Microsoft WordArt, that's embedded as part of a letterhead document created in Word. As an embedded object, all the information about the logo is maintained in the letterhead document so that you do not have to worry about managing or locating a separate file for the logo. When you do need to change the logo, double-click it to open WordArt and edit the logo.

Linking and Embedding with Paste Special

The easiest way to link and embed is with the Paste Special command on the Edit menu.

When an object is pasted into a document with the regular Paste command, the object is dropped in, with no information about its origin. In contrast, when an object is pasted into a document with Paste Special, several pieces of information about the object are stored as part of the container file, including the source file's name and location, the server application, and the location of the object within the source file. This extra information is what makes it possible for the object to be updated whenever the source file is updated.

OLE needs the name of a *source file* to refer back to later in order to link, so you must save your work in the source program before you create a link with OLE. However, if you merely want to embed, and not link, you do not have to have a named source file. The only information OLE needs to edit the object later is the name of the *server application* (the application in which it was created).

Source File   The file from which the information to be pasted originated.

Server Application   The server application is the native application for the object that's being linked or embedded. For instance, if you embed an Excel worksheet into a Word document, Excel is the server application.

Container Application   The container application is the application in which the container file (the file to receive the object) is created. For instance, if the container file is a Word document, Microsoft Word is the container application.

To link or embed with Paste Special, follow these steps:

1. Copy the desired object to the Clipboard with the **Edit**, **Copy** command.

2. Open the container file (the file where you want to paste) and position the insertion point where you want it.

3. Select **Edit**, **Paste Special**, and the Paste Special dialog box appears. (The one for Word is shown in Figure C.1; they are similar in all Office applications.)

4. Choose **Paste** or **Paste Link**, depending on the type of connection you want:

    • **Paste**   Pastes the contents of the Windows Clipboard into the document at the location of the insertion point. The link is not maintained, but you can double-click the pasted material to edit it. (This is embedding.)

    • **Paste Link**   This option is available if the contents of the Clipboard can be linked back to its source file. With this option selected, a link is created between the source file and the container file. If you have not saved the source file, the Paste Link option is not available.

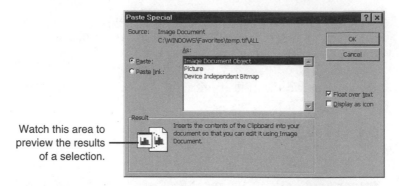

Watch this area to preview the results of a selection.

Figure C.1 The Paste Special dialog box.

5. Select the format you want to use from the As list. The formats listed change depending on the object type. Some formats you might see include

- **Object**   A type that ends with the word Object is a recognized OLE-capable format that you can either link or embed. If you want to embed, you should choose a data type that ends with the word "object." In Figure C.1, for example, you would choose Image Document Object.

- **Formatted Text (RTF)**   This data type formats text as it is formatted in the source file. If the text is formatted as bold italic, it is pasted as bold italic. This format does not support embedding.

- **Unformatted Text**   No formatting is applied to the object when this data type is selected. This format does not support embedding.

- **Picture**   This data type formats the object as a Windows metafile picture. It does not support embedding.

- **Device Independent Bitmap**   This data type formats the object as a bitmap picture, such as a Windows Paint image. It does not support embedding.

6. (Optional) If you want to display the pasted object as an icon instead of as the data itself, select the **Display As Icon** check box. This option is only available if you have selected Paste Link. This is useful for pasting Sounds and MediaClips because you can double-click one to play it later.

7. (Optional) If you want the object to appear inline with the rest of the document's text, make sure the **Float Over Text** check box is deselected. When selected, this check box forces the pasted object into the drawing layer of the document, where it can be moved freely over the top of the document.

8. Click **OK**. The object is embedded or linked into the container file, depending on the options you chose.

When deciding which options to select in the Paste Special dialog box, pay close attention to the notes that appear in the Result area. These notes tell you what happens if you choose OK with the present set of options.

Linking or Embedding an Entire File

If you want to link an entire file to your document—an entire Excel spreadsheet, for example—you can use the Object command. It appears on the Insert menu of most Windows applications.

Unlike with Edit, Paste you do not have to open the source file to retrieve the object. You can perform the entire procedure without leaving the client application. Follow these steps to learn how:

1. Start the client application (the one to receive the object), and then create or open the container file. You use Microsoft Word as the client application in this example.

2. Select **Insert**, **Object**. The Object dialog box appears.

3. Click the **Create from File** tab at the top of the dialog box. The dialog box changes to show a File Name list box (see Figure C.2).

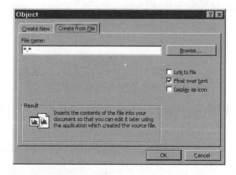

Figure C.2   Use the Object dialog box's Create from File tab to choose an existing file to link or embed.

4. Click the **Browse** button, and select the name of the file you want to insert and link or embed in the container file. For example, use an Excel worksheet. Navigate through the directories and subdirectories to locate the file if it does not appear in the current directory. When you locate the file, double-click it.

5. If you want to link, make sure the **Link to File** check box is selected. This creates an active link between the source file and the destination file. If you merely want to embed, not link, make sure it's deselected.

6. Select or deselect the **Float Over Text** and **Display As Icon** check boxes as desired. (See the descriptions of these controls earlier in this lesson.)

7. Click **OK**. The dialog box closes, and the source file is inserted into the container file.

CAUTION

Whole Files Only   Remember that using the Insert Object command links or embeds an entire file to the container file. You cannot use this command to link an individual object (such as a range of Excel cells) to the container file. Instead, use the steps in the "Linking and Embedding with Paste Special" section earlier in this lesson.

Creating a New Embedded File

The Insert Object command also can help you create a brand-new file and embed it at the same time. (You can't link with this procedure because to link you must already have a named file from which the object is coming.) Say, for example, that you want to insert an Excel spreadsheet into your Word document, but you haven't created the spreadsheet yet. You can do it all at once with the following procedure:

1. Open the container document and position the insertion point where you want the linked or embedded file to go.

2. Select **Insert**, **Object**, and the Object dialog box appears (see Figure C.3).

3. With the **Create New** tab displayed, select the type of object you want to create from the **Object Type** list box.

4. Click **OK**. The application you selected opens within Word, and you can create the object. (Notice that the toolbar buttons and menu commands change to be appropriate for that application.)

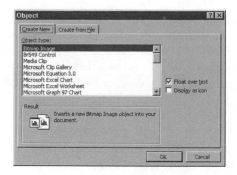

Figure C.3 Select the type of file you want to create.

5. When you're finished working with the object, select **File**, **Exit** and **Return to Application** (the exact name of the command depends on the container application). The object is now embedded in your container file.

Editing Embedded Objects

Editing an embedded object is where the greatest advantage of embedding comes into play. You do not have to remember the name and location of the source file that you used to create the embedded object. You double-click the object and the source application starts, enabling you to edit the object.

Follow these steps to edit an embedded object:

1. Open the document containing the embedded object you want to edit.
2. Double-click the object or choose **Edit**, **Object**. The native application of the embedded object starts and displays the object.
3. Edit the object using the server application's tools and commands.
4. Click a portion of the container document or select **File**, **Exit** and **Return to Application** from the object's native application. The object's native application closes, and you are returned to the container document.

CAUTION

Modified Launch Some objects perform a function or action when you double-click them, instead of opening the source file for editing. For example, Windows Sound Recorder objects play a sound when double-clicked. To edit objects like this, hold down the **Alt** key and double-click the object.

Editing Linked Objects

After you have created a linked object, you may want to edit and update the information in the object. At this stage, you realize the full benefit of an OLE link because you can edit the object one time, and it is updated in every document to which it is linked.

There are two ways to edit a linked object. The first is to start at the source file, using the server application to make changes to the object. The second is to start at the container file and let the link information lead you to the correct source file and server application. With the second method, you do not have to remember the name of the source file or even which server application created it. In the next sections, you learn how to edit objects by using these two methods.

Editing from the Source File

To edit a linked object starting from the source file, follow these steps:

1. Start the server application, and then open the source file that contains the object you want to edit.
2. Edit and make changes to the object.
3. Save the document and close the server application.
4. Switch to (or start) the client application and open the container file. The changes should automatically be reflected in the container file.

If the changes are not reflected, the document may not be set up to automatically update links. Skip to "Managing a Link's Update Settings" later in this lesson to learn how to update the links.

CAUTION

Now You See It, Now You Don't Some client applications let you edit or make changes directly to the object that is linked to the container file without starting the server application. This can cause problems because the source file is not being changed, only the image of the object. The changes you make to the image are wiped out when the object is updated via the source file. You do not have this problem with Microsoft Office products, but it may occur with other non-Microsoft applications.

Editing from the Container File

Editing from the container file is quick and easy because you do not have to find and open the server application manually. To edit a linked object from the container file, follow these steps:

1. From the container file, double-click the linked object you want to update. The server application starts and displays the source file.

2. Edit the object in the source file, making as many changes as necessary.

3. Choose **File**, **Save** in the server application.

4. Choose **File**, **Exit** in the server application. You're returned to the container file, which reflects the changes you made to the linked object.

If double-clicking the object does not start the server application, open the Links dialog box by choosing **Links** from the **Edit** menu. Select the link you want to edit and click the **Open Source** button. The server application starts and displays the source file.

Managing a Link's Update Settings

After you have created a linked object, you can control when changes to the source file are updated in the container file(s). You can update a link manually or automatically. If a link is set to be updated manually, you must remember to follow the update steps each time you change the source file that contains the linked object. With the automatic setting enabled (the default update setting), the changes you make to the source file are automatically updated each time you open the container file.

To set a linked object to be manually updated, follow these steps:

1. Open the container file that contains the object link you want to update.

2. Choose **Edit**, **Links**. The Links dialog box appears (see Figure C.4). For the linked objects in your document, the list indicates the link name, the pathname of the source file, and whether the link is set to update automatically or manually.

Figure C.4 You can control each individual link in your document.

3. Select the link you want to update.

4. Change the Update setting to **Manual**.

5. Update the link by clicking the **Update Now** button in the Links dialog box. The object is then updated with any changes that were made to the source file.

6. Click **OK** to close the dialog box.

7. Choose **File**, **Save** to save the document and the changes to the link settings.

With the link set for manual update, you must repeat step 5 of this procedure each time you want the linked object to reflect changes made in the source file.

Locking and Unlocking Links

In addition to setting link update options to manual and automatic, you can lock a link to prevent the link from being updated when the source file is changed. A locked link is not updated until it is unlocked.

To lock or unlock a link, follow these steps:

1. Open the document containing the linked object.

2. Choose **Edit**, **Links**. The Links dialog box appears (see Figure C.4).

3. Select the link you want to lock.

4. To lock the link, select the **Locked** check box. To unlock the link, make sure the check box is empty.

5. Click **OK** to close the dialog box.

Breaking Links

If at some point, you decide that you want a linked object in your document to remain fixed and no longer be updated by its source file, you can break (or cancel) the link. This does not delete or alter the object, it merely removes the background information that directly ties the object to its source file. The object becomes like any other object that was placed by Windows' copy and paste operation.

To break or cancel a linked object, follow these steps:

1. Open the container file that contains the object whose link you want to break.

2. Select **Edit, Links** (or **Link Options** in some applications). The Links dialog box appears, showing linked object information.

3. Select the link name of the object you want to break.

4. Click **Break Link** (or **Delete** in some applications). A warning box may appear cautioning that you are breaking a link. Click **OK** or **Yes** to confirm your choice.

In this lesson, you learned how to create and manage OLE links and embedding. In the next lesson, you learn how to use Microsoft Office applications on the Internet.

Publishing Your Work to the Internet

In this lesson, you use Microsoft's Web Publishing Wizard to upload your HTML-format documents to an Internet server.

Understanding HTML Documents

In each of the Office 97 component parts of this book, you learned how to save your work in HTML (Hypertext Markup Language) format, in preparation for transferring it to the server where it can be accessed by the public.

When you save your Office 97 work in HTML format, and that work contains graphics, you are actually saving several files: the HTML file itself and individual graphics files for each graphic. Suppose, for example, you have a Word file with three images. In Word, the images are embedded in the Word file so that when you save the Word file, everything is contained in a single .doc file. But when you save that same document in HTML format, you end up with four files:

- An HTML file (for example, page.html)
- Three graphics files (for example, image1.gif, image2.gif, and image3.gif)

To publish your work to the Web so that other Internet users can see it, you need to transfer not only the HTML file, but all the associated graphics files, to the server.

Server   In this lesson, "server" refers to your Internet service provider's computer or the networked file server in your company's LAN (local area network) where you can store your Web pages for public reading.

You can transfer the files to the server by using an FTP (File Transfer Protocol) program, if you have one, but Microsoft provides a wizard that does the job quickly and easily, so most beginners will want to use it.

Acquiring the Web Publishing Wizard

You probably need to install the Web Publishing Wizard. A version of it is on the Office 97 CD, in the ValuPack/WebPost folder. You can install it from there, or you can download a more recent (better) version from Microsoft's Web site. Downloading the new version is recommended, because it's better and easier to use and because if you use it, you will be able to follow along with the steps later in this lesson.

To download and install the new version, do this:

1. Start your Internet connection if it is not already running, and open Internet Explorer (either version 3.0 or 4.0 will work fine).

2. Go to the following site:

   http://www.microsoft.com/windows/software/webpost/

3. Click the links to find the version appropriate for you (for example, the version for Windows 95/NT) and the download site nearest you (for example, one in North America).

4. When the box appears asking you what you want to do with the file, click **Save the File to Disk** and choose a temporary folder on your computer in which to download it. C:\Windows\Temp is suggested.

5. Wait for the download to complete.

6. Navigate to the new file on your hard disk using Windows Explorer and double-click it to install the program. The downloaded file was called wpie15-x86.exe, but your file may be named slightly differently depending on your choices of links in step 3.

7. Follow the on-screen prompts to install.

8. Restart your computer before you attempt to use the Web Publishing Wizard.

Preparing Your Files for Uploading

You will be uploading either a single file or a single folder at a time. That means that you have to run the wizard many times if you have many files to upload. The shortcut, of course, is to create a separate folder on your hard disk and put all the files into it that you want to upload. Then just run the wizard once and upload that one folder. (Refer to Part 1 of this book for Windows file management help.)

Running the Web Publishing Wizard

The Web Publishing Wizard takes information that you provide about the Web address and the FTP server and transfers files for you. Before you run this, you need two important bits of information from your service provider:

- The URL or Web Address that your potential readers use to connect to your pages. This begins with http://, such as http://www.mcp.com/mypages.
- The physical location on the server where you should save your Web pages. This probably begins with ftp://, such as ftp://ftp.mcp.com/mypages.

Actually both addresses point to the same location, but when you transfer the pages to the server, you use a method called FTP (file transfer protocol) that enables you to upload content. In contrast, when viewers read your pages, they use a method called HTTP (Hypertext Transfer Protocol) that lets them read your pages but not change anything on them.

After you have both of the needed addresses, follow these steps to publish a file or folder to the server:

1. Connect to your server (for example, dial your service provider with your modem) if you are not already connected.
2. Select **Start, Programs, Microsoft Web Publishing, Web Publishing Wizard**. The Web Publishing Wizard opens.
3. Click **Next** to begin.
4. First, you're asked to locate the file or folder on your system that you want to publish, as shown in Figure D.1. Do any of the following:
   - If you know the exact name and path, type it in the text box.

- To browse for a file, click **Browse Files** and use the Browse dialog box that appears to locate the file you want to upload.
- To browse for a folder, click the **Browse Folders** button and use the Browse for Folder dialog box to locate the folder you want. Select or deselect the **Include Subfolders** check box as needed for your situation.

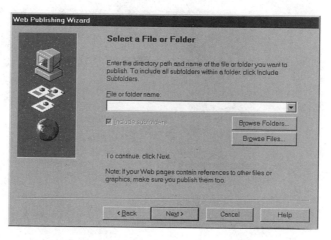

Figure D.1 First, you tell the wizard what file or folder to publish.

5. Click **Next** to continue.

6. In the Descriptive Name text box, type a name for the Web server to which you're publishing. This can be any name that helps you remember the server—for example, Acme Corporation Server. Click **Next**.

7. In the Service Provider field, choose **FTP** (for most service providers). Then click **Next**.

CAUTION

Not FTP? The drop-down list in step 7 provides for other transfer methods besides FTP, but FTP is by far the most commonly used method. If you've been through these steps once and the wizard dumps you back here after step 10 saying it's the wrong type, contact your service provider and find out what to choose here instead of FTP. If you choose something other than FTP, the rest of the steps here may not match what you see on-screen, but just follow the prompts and you should be fine.

8. Next you're asked to enter the URL that visitors to your page will use (as shown in Figure D.2). Enter it in the **URL or Internet Address** text box. (If you don't know what it is, ask your service provider's technical support representatives or your system administrator on your network.) A Web address might look something like **http://www.iquest.net/~fwempen**, for example.

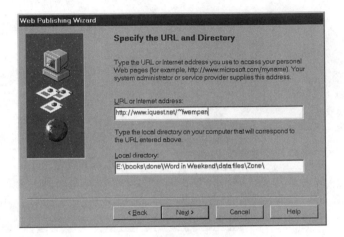

Figure D.2 Next, tell the wizard where your visitors are to point their browsers to visit your pages.

9. In the Local Directory text box, the path to the file or folder you chose earlier should already be entered; just confirm it and click **Next**.

10. Next you're asked about the FTP site—the physical address of the server where you've been instructed to save the files. Enter the server's address in the FTP Server Name text box, as shown in Figure D.3. (For example, mine is ftp.iquest.net.)

11. In the Subfolder text box, enter the path on the server to the folder where you are supposed to save your files. Then click **Next**.

12. Click **Finish**. You're prompted for your network user ID and password to log onto the server.

13. Enter the user ID and password in the fields provided and click **OK**. The Wizard publishes your files to the server.

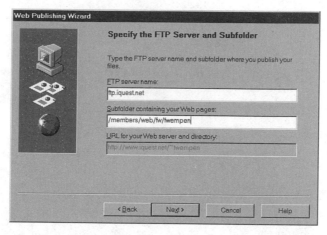

Figure D.3   Enter the FTP information here.

CAUTION

FTP ID   In step 13, you enter the FTP user ID and password. Usually, this is your regular user ID and password for your service provider's system, but some systems may require different ones for FTP. Contact your service provider if your normal user ID and password don't work.

14. When a message appears that the pages have been published, click **OK**.

You also can use an FTP program to transfer your files to the server. An FTP program can transfer all the files, not just the HTML files. One popular FTP program is WS_FTP, which is shareware and available for download at many Internet file archive sites. To find this or other FTP programs, point your browser to **http://www.shareware.com**. However, unless you already have an FTP program that you know how to use, you will probably find it easier to use the Web Publishing Wizard.

Saving Files Directly to the Server

You also can save HTML files to the Internet directly from most of the Office 97 programs, through the Save As HTML command. (You learned about this command in the respective earlier parts of this book for each program.)

While you are saving in HTML format, you can save directly to the Web location. The disadvantage to this method is that no associated graphics files are saved to the server—only the raw HTML files. That means if you use graphics on your page, you will have to upload them separately to the server.

For example, the following steps show how to do it for Word:

1. Make sure your Internet connection is active.
2. Open the HTML file to transfer, and choose **Save As HTML**. The Save As HTML dialog box opens.
3. Open the **Save In** drop-down list and choose **Add/Modify FTP Locations**. An Add/Modify FTP Locations dialog box appears.
4. Enter the address of the site in the Name of FTP Site text box. For example, **ftp://ftp.iquest.net** can be used. Notice that the path entered to the folder is not where the files are stored; that can be completed after connecting.
5. Click **User** and type your username in the text box.
6. Type your password in the Password text box.
7. Click **Add** to add that FTP site to the list that Word maintains, and then click **OK** to close the dialog box.
8. Back in the Save As HTML dialog box, the new address you just created appears. Double-click it.
9. If you entered the address, user ID, and password correctly, the Save As HTML dialog box shows all the folders on the server to which you have access. Double-click the folder you want, and keep double-clicking folders until you have made your way to the exact folder where you are supposed to save your files.
10. Make sure that the filename in the File Name text box is correct, and then click **Save**. Your file is saved directly to the server.

In this lesson, you learned how to publish your work from Office 97 programs to a server connected to the Internet.

Index

Exit command (File menu)
exiting
Access, 620
databases, 629-630
queries, 696
tables, 656
Excel, 281
workbooks, 325
Outlook, 510
PowerPoint, 409
presentations, 433
toolbars, 420-421
Windows applications,
49-50
Windows Explorer, 72
Word, 130
columns, 251
documents, 266
Explorer (Windows), 60-72
customizing display,
61-65, 69-72
file list, 70
sizing windows, 69
status bar, 72
toolbar text labels, 72
with Internet Explorer
4.0 installed, 62-64
without Internet
Explorer 4.0, 64-65
disks
copying, 92
formatting, 89-91
free space,
determining, 88
labeling, 91
drives, 68
files/folders, 66-68
copying/moving, 76-79
creating, 81-82
deleting, 82-83
finding, 75
opening/closing, 68
renaming, 84-85
selecting, 67-68, 73-76
undeleting, 83
icons, 70
starting, 66
toolbar, 71

F

Favorites
Excel Favorites folders,
322
PowerPoint, creating
Favorites Lists, 449
faxing documents (Word),
167-168
Fax Wizard, 134
fields (Access)
automatically inserting,
653
deleting, 650-651
from queries, 702
displaying, 704
editing, 648-652
length, 678-679
hiding, 651-652, 704
inserting, 649-650
forms, 672-674
queries, 701, 704
reports, 715
naming, 637, 642
navigating, 675-676
primary keys, 638, 645-646
reports, 715-716
tables, 719
see also columns
File menu commands
Access
Close, 629
New, 622
New Database, 624
Open, 630
Open Database, 632
Print, 655
Save, 629
Save As, 629
Save As HTML, 725
Save As Query, 691
Excel
Close All, 325
Exit, 281
New, 316
Open, 321
Page Setup, 342

Print, 340
Print Area, 343
Save, 317
Save As HTML, 398
Send To, 341
My Computer, New, 82
Outlook, 575
Add to Outlook Bar,
558
Add to Personal
Address Book, 532
Close, 523
Exit, 510
Folder, Create
Subfolder, 557
Folder, Delete, 558
New Entry, 533
Open, 595-596
Page Setup, 588
Print, 522-523, 591
Save As, 594
Save Attachments, 520
Send, 521, 528
PowerPoint
Close, 433
Cut, 451
Exit, 409
New, 413
Open, 433
Page Setup, 437
Print, 436
Save, 430
Save As HTML, 498
Windows
Close, 49
Exit, 50
New, 47
Open, 49
Save, 47
Save As, 47
Windows Explorer
Delete, 83
New, 82
Rename, 84

Complete and Return this Card
for a *FREE* Computer Book Catalog

Thank you for purchasing this book! You have purchased a superior computer book written expressly for your needs. To continue to provide the kind of up-to-date, pertinent coverage you've come to expect from us, we need to hear from you. Please take a minute to complete and return this self-addressed, postage-paid form. In return, we'll send you a free catalog of all our computer books on topics ranging from word processing to programming and the internet.

Mr. ☐   Mrs. ☐   Ms. ☐   Dr. ☐

Name (first) ☐☐☐☐☐☐☐☐☐☐ (M.I.) ☐ (last) ☐☐☐☐☐☐☐☐☐☐☐☐☐☐

Address ☐☐☐☐☐☐☐☐☐☐☐☐☐☐☐☐☐☐☐☐☐☐☐☐☐☐

City ☐☐☐☐☐☐☐☐☐☐☐☐☐ State ☐☐ Zip ☐☐☐☐☐ ☐☐☐☐

Phone ☐☐☐ ☐☐☐ ☐☐☐☐ Fax ☐☐☐ ☐☐☐ ☐☐☐☐

Company Name ☐☐☐☐☐☐☐☐☐☐☐☐☐☐☐☐☐☐☐☐☐☐☐☐

E-mail address ☐☐☐☐☐☐☐☐☐☐☐☐☐☐☐☐☐☐☐☐☐☐☐☐

Please check at least (3) influencing factors for purchasing this book.

Front or back cover information on book .... ☐
Special approach to the content .... ☐
Completeness of content .... ☐
Author's reputation .... ☐
Publisher's reputation .... ☐
Book cover design or layout .... ☐
Index or table of contents of book .... ☐
Price of book .... ☐
Special effects, graphics, illustrations .... ☐
Other (Please specify): _____ ☐

How did you first learn about this book?

Saw in Macmillan Computer Publishing catalog .... ☐
Recommended by store personnel .... ☐
Saw the book on bookshelf at store .... ☐
Recommended by a friend .... ☐
Received advertisement in the mail .... ☐
Saw an advertisement in: _____ ☐
Read book review in: _____ ☐
Other (Please specify): _____ ☐

How many computer books have you purchased in the last six months?

This book only .... ☐   3 to 5 books .... ☐
books .... ☐   More than 5 .... ☐

4. Where did you purchase this book?

Bookstore .... ☐
Computer Store .... ☐
Consumer Electronics Store .... ☐
Department Store .... ☐
Office Club .... ☐
Warehouse Club .... ☐
Mail Order .... ☐
Direct from Publisher .... ☐
Internet site .... ☐
Other (Please specify): _____ ☐

5. How long have you been using a computer?

☐ Less than 6 months   ☐ 6 months to a year
☐ 1 to 3 years   ☐ More than 3 years

6. What is your level of experience with personal computers and with the subject of this book?

	With PCs	With subject of book
New	☐	☐
Casual	☐	☐
Accomplished	☐	☐
Expert	☐	☐

Source Code ISBN: 0-7897-1515-5

7. Which of the following best describes your job title?

Administrative Assistant .... ☐
Coordinator .... ☐
Manager/Supervisor .... ☐
Director .... ☐
Vice President .... ☐
President/CEO/COO .... ☐
Lawyer/Doctor/Medical Professional .... ☐
Teacher/Educator/Trainer .... ☐
Engineer/Technician .... ☐
Consultant .... ☐
Not employed/Student/Retired .... ☐
Other (Please specify): _____ ☐

8. Which of the following best describes the area of the company your job title falls under?

Accounting .... ☐
Engineering .... ☐
Manufacturing .... ☐
Operations .... ☐
Marketing .... ☐
Sales .... ☐
Other (Please specify): _____ ☐

9. What is your age?

Under 20 .... ☐
21-29 .... ☐
30-39 .... ☐
40-49 .... ☐
50-59 .... ☐
60-over .... ☐

10. Are you:

Male .... ☐
Female .... ☐

11. Which computer publications do you read regularly? (Please list)

_____
_____
_____
_____
_____
_____
_____
_____
_____

Comments: _____
_____
_____

Fold here and scotch-tape to mail

Check out Que® Books on the World Wide Web
http://www.mcp.com/que

As the biggest software release in computer history, Windows 95 continues to redefine the computer industry. Click here for the latest info on our Windows 95 books

Make computing quick and easy with these products designed exclusively for new and casual users

Examine the latest releases in word processing, spreadsheets, operating systems, and suites

The Internet, The World Wide Web, CompuServe®, America Online®, Prodigy® —it's a world of ever-changing information. Don't get left behind!

Find out about new additions to our site, new bestsellers and hot topics

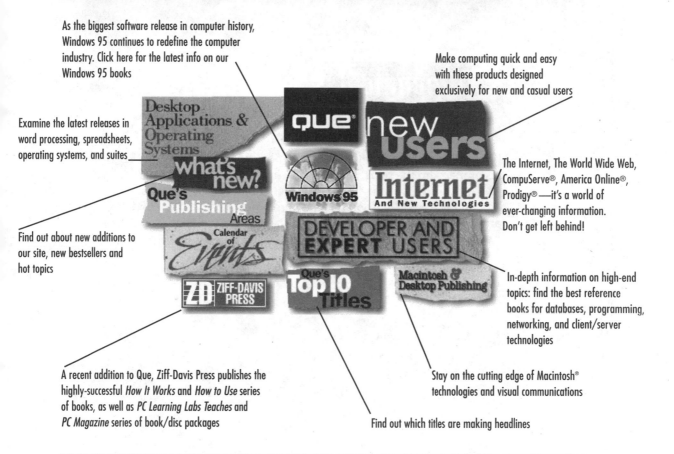

In-depth information on high-end topics: find the best reference books for databases, programming, networking, and client/server technologies

A recent addition to Que, Ziff-Davis Press publishes the highly-successful *How It Works* and *How to Use* series of books, as well as *PC Learning Labs Teaches* and *PC Magazine* series of book/disc packages

Stay on the cutting edge of Macintosh® technologies and visual communications

Find out which titles are making headlines

With 6 separate publishing groups, Que develops products for many specific market segments and areas of computer technology. Explore our Web Site and you'll find information on best-selling titles, newly published titles, upcoming products, authors, and much more.

- Stay informed on the latest industry trends and products available
- Visit our online bookstore for the latest information and editions
- Download software from Que's library of the best shareware and freeware

MACMILLAN COMPUTER PUBLISHING USA

A VIACOM COMPANY

Technical ---- Support:

If you need assistance with the information in this book or with a CD/Disk accompanying the book, please access the Knowledge Base on our Web site at **http://www.superlibrary.com/general/support**. Our most Frequently Asked Questions are answered there. If you do not find the answer to your questions on our Web site, you may contact Macmillan Technical Support **(317) 581-3833** or e-mail us at **support@mcp.com**.